GOVERNING DYNAMICS:

HOW TO UPLIFT

SCHOOL PERFORMANCES,

RAISE EMPLOYEES' PRODUCTIVITY &

ATTRACT PROSPERITY

VOL 2

By

Festo Michael Kambarangwe

KAMBARANGWE INSTITUTE OF LEADERSHIP & INNOVATION

Dar es Salaam, Tanzania, EA

Governing Dynamics: How to Uplift School Performances, Raise Employees' Productivity & Attract Prosperity Vol 2

By
Festo Michael Kambarangwe

All Rights Reserved
Copyright © 2016 by Festo Michael Kambarangwe

Printed in the United States of America

No part of this publication may be reproduced, stored in a retrieval system, or transmitted in any form or by any means, electronic, mechanical, photocopying, recording, scanning, or otherwise, except for a few short quotations, without either the prior written permission of the Publisher, or authorization of the Copyright holder.

While the publisher and author have used their best efforts in preparing this book, they make no warranties with respect to the accuracy or comprehensiveness of the contents of this book. Besides, they also understand that the advices contained herein may not be suitable for every person's or organization's situation.

Other books by Festo Michael Kambarangwe

How Universities Under Develop You!
What Business Leaders Should Know but They Don't.
What Makes People Rich and Nations Powerful
Governing Dynamics: How to Uplift School Performances, Raise Employees' Productivity and Attract Prosperity.
A Sick Nation and How to Heal It.

Festo Michael Kambarangwe

Wonders of Serengeti:
The Fall of Man & the Return of the Beast (also published as :)
I kissed a Snake
Mohammedans: Victims or Villains? (Also as)
The Audacity of love: I married a Muslim & Discovered True Mohammedans

"O philosophy, life's guide! O explorer of virtue and expeller of vices! What could we and every generation of men have been without thee? Thou hast produced cities; thou hast called men scattered about into the bond of fine social life; thou hast united humans first of all amongst themselves in houses, next in the communion of marriage, then by mutual literature and speech; thou hast discovered law, thou hast been the teacher of morality and order; to thee I fly for refuge; thee do I ask for aid; to thee I entrust myself, as formerly for a large part, so now completely and entirely..."

— Marcus Tullius Cicero

"It is a functional fact that the under developed nations of the world have much to contribute on the social, cultural and spiritual basis to modern thinking!"

—Tom Sharpe in Vintage Stuff

Festo Michael Kambarangwe

A REFLECTION FROM THE BOOK: A SICK NATION AND HOW TO HEAL IT

"Welcome, or unwelcome, agreeable, or disagreeable; whether this shall be an entire slave nation, is the issue before us." —A. Lincoln

After eyeing the title of this book—A SICK NATION AND HOW TO HEAL IT—you probably exclaimed: "A sick nation? Ridiculous! This is a ridiculous title!" It is not. Nations really get sick! Well, what is a nation? "There is no such a thing as society," rightly observed Margaret Thatcher, "There are individual men, and women, and families." If therefore there are no societies or nations for that matter, but individual men and women, if in total the majority of these individual men and women are sick on permanent basis, certainly that nation is sick. No? This is nothing new. The wealth of a nation is quantified as a sum of the incomes of each individual household—ask any economist. By analyzing the individual person's health, thereupon establishing the health status of their nation—and solutions—we can heal and restore the whole nation.

Consider a nation with enviable natural resources: gold, diamond, wildlife and bursting rich bowels of oil and gas slumbering under the feet of its youth—the youth who loathe classrooms, professions and industry; in their place preferring quick fix, drugs, black-market, and environment-endangering activities etc! Is it important to heal such a nation? What is the fate awaiting such a nation—and her neighbors? The recent Ebola virus, impoverishment, insecurity, and therefore terrorism elsewhere and mass emigration to the EU help to put that question into perspective.

Can a nation break away from quick fix, and responsibly take charge of her affairs once again? How do we address fading loyalty to the nation, unity and harmony when sectarian sentiments, indolence and corruption choke the nation; when thousands of her youth drown in the Mediterranean fleeing seeking to reach Lampedusa or Malta? The chief task of a nation craving to progress, is to explore and develop its natural resources, which is impossible without first developing, yes, the Human Resource, i.e. work-skills; but indeed to address the mindset or character of its youth and the leadership especially, and restoration of a nation's ethos and ideals.

Truly, "Under these circumstances, to spend four or five years in learning dead (subjects), is to turn our backs upon the goldmine in order to amuse ourselves catching butterflies," and therefore, development "beyond rudiments was wishful thinking." In retrospect, I can see why Noah Webster called passionately upon Americans "to unshackle (their) minds and act like independent beings," shouting out: "You have been children long enough; subject to control and subservient to the interests of a haughty parent…You have an empire to rise…and a national character to establish and extend…" In the end, "Unquestionably educational aims and especially school reform must be relevant or meaningful to our times. If the schools are not adaptable to changing conditions and social forces, how can we expect them to produce people who are (Ornstein & Hunkins in Curriculum Principles, Foundations and Issues)?"

TRIBUTES TO THE AUTHOR

"You know what! You never stop encouraging, inspiring, and motivating me! Thank you for the insights. Can't explain the way this helps me multiply and grow bigger and bigger! You give me the pressure—you encourage me to move forward!" —Maria Mwakasege; university graduate and one time author's coworker

"Finally, now I've stumbled upon a book that bespeaks what I consider as right solutions to our problems as a society." —Michael Ogwari John; HR director and (at the time) acting principal secretary for the Ministry of health

"I congratulate you for a book with so much useful insights." — Dr. Alawi Shaban Swabury, Member of the UN Business Sector Steering Committee on Finance for the Development-New York; CEO of ESSB Berlin

"I'm deeply pleased and inspired to read your work. Well done. This is an incredible achievement. I truly appreciate your efforts for coming up with such a work to benefit all. I assure you of my support. I'm currently out of the country when I return I'll definitely contact you! Indeed to say I'm proud of you, will be understatement!!" —Helen Michael; former author's co-worker who has served in different capacities among several world-class international organizations

"By the way I've always been an admirer of your writing skills and style! It's like watching Mikel Arteta playing football! You just sit back and enjoy it to the last drop! It's incredible!" —Emmanuel Kanagisa; marketing professional and of course a great fan of Arsenal Football Club

"Congratutions, Festo. This is a great work! Surely, Africans should enumerate on what you have accomplished...this is a tremendous achievement." —Alex Modest; communication specialist

"Quite appealing!" —Dr. Alphoncina Nanai

"You truly are contributing to The Making of a Nation!" —Leonard C. Kitoka; prominent entrepreneur, consultant and managing partner with Innovex Development Consulting Limited

"Inspirational indeed!" —Benedict Emmanuel; thinker, economist and one time author's classmate

"Oh, yeah, he is an inspiration indeed!" —Cyrus Gabone; top finance professional, with education and work skills from both in Tanzania and the UK

"Felicitations!" —Chelaus Rutta; a University of Dar es Salaam and Makerere learned economist serving with IMF in Dar es Salaam.
"Happy is the person who will put you to use!" —Julius Mitinje; a finance professional

"I'm sure people will benefit a lot from you. Festo is a blessing and an inspiration to us! I've said this several time. I repeat..." —Francis Nanai; CEO, Mwananchi Communication Nation Media Group)

"You have proved the old adage as Arthur Gordon put it: 'The real measure of commitment is action'. You have set yourself on a greatness journey in which you are soon achieving. You inspire people by unveiling unto them their own riches; that being the greatest good you can do for another person which is not just sharing your riches but to reveal to them their own... Indeed you are headed for greatness. Bravo!! —James Tapela; a Zimbabwean consultant and one time author's coworker

"I'm proud of your accomplishment after you decided to quit a very lucrative job at Celtel in Dar es Salaam choosing to write books. Once again, congratulations.., you have made us all proud. Hope you will manage to get these books in the East and Southern African bookstores. It's a great work and I feel especially like I am part of it. Your works is truly very relevant to our people. Salutes..." —Laurean Rugambwa Bwanakunu; MD MSD

"Hats off! Congratulations are in order even though it has not come to me as a surprise! I remember you during secondary school debating sessions; you were simply superb. This is just a continuation of what you could do...I advise you again to really think of what more you can do in the future (considering that the vengeance of the economic crisis is still ongoing and social and economic disorders at their peaks). Yes; indeed; Festo did make us all proud." —Edward (John) Munyangabe

"I'm proud of your achievement. And thank you for this gift. Given the response I see, I suggest that the priority now should be to make these books available in the local market."—Respicius Didace; prominent Lawyer based in Dar es Salaam, Tanzania

"I like your emphasis on common sense—a commodity which is often short in supply!"—Phillip Parham (referring to the original idea of this work at the time when he was British High Commissioner to Tanzania)

"Congratulations Mr. Kambarangwe. I must say we share a lot regarding education and how to advance this country." —An undisclosed billionaire, lawyer, businessman and politician

"You know what, you are very gifted my brother. I am impressed. Congratulations! I must say you are in another league. You have exceeded my expectations. Now I believe that for a nation to break from underdevelopment and move towards prosperity, it needs a group of few individual thinkers, local as well as international, as its growth Think Tank, and it is in this RARE CLASS that you, the author, belong. — Kiteja Ntobela Mayunga; graphics designer and designing entrepreneur

"Being your brother, I may possibly take your accomplishment so lightly, you know! Quite frankly, if I didn't know you I would say, "Wow! This guy is a genius! Truly this is something out of ordinary. Congratulations." —The author's elder sibling

"This is a great piece of work!" —John Ernest Kitoka; intellectual columnist and consultant based in Dar es Salaam, Tanzania

"You have made a very big difference. Your work is an answer to those who doubt that ordinary individuals like you and I can make a big difference. Knowing that you were quietly accomplishing a splendid work for humanity, I have waited endlessly for this book. Now that your work has finally brought out its face, I am sure people will give it the pledge of allegiance." —Vitalis Michael, graduate of Mass Communication

"You are a very carefully selected talent yourself. You refused to take droplets of dollars coupled with tiny favors from without yourself and decided to harness many facets of riches from within your own self and discovered a YOU—a wonderful approach indeed! You refused to accept small principles of money—making from working for which you were not born to do and entered a red hot tunnel which delivered you the other side as a new and pure person! You are an example to all who still labor in the process of self-discovery. Congratulations comrade!" —Zephrine Galeba; intellectual, attorney, entrepreneur and Managing Partner GRK Advocates

"This is not just a book. It is the philosophy of life." —Albert M.M; Principal Editor in Dar es Salaam

"Very powerful indeed! Like a religious sermon."—Doctor Solomon Auclace Mlau

"Praise the Lord! I believe no ordinary human means can accomplish this magnitude of feat without the intercession of the Higher Powers." —Alex William Rwabitara Bwanakunu, the author's nephew

"People say you cannot judge whether a person shall go to heaven before he dies, until the judgment day, but I can suggest that if from such a noble commitment like yours cannot help us judge the soul of person, what else can?"—Jack G, an intellectual academician, student of PHD at the time

"With the accomplishment of this magnitude, now you can die!" —Daudi Michael Kambarangwe; author's sibling

Festo Michael Kambarangwe

For the Glory of God and my Country

ABOUT THE AUTHOR

Festo Michael Kambarangwe is the third born to Pudensiana Kambarangwe (also known as Mama Julius, (daughter to Mathias and Theresa alias Mkaka). The author is thirteenth to Michael Kambarangwe who left behind 50 minus four children and 70 grand and great grandchildren when he was laid to eternal rest in 2009 in Biharamulo not very far from Bukililo, in Bushubi, a small village where he was born during the then Tanganyika. An only son to Augustine Kambarangwe, one of the first prominent converts to Christianity and a teacher during the Germans back in the colonial Biharamulo district; which prompted Michael Kambarangwe, the author's father to pursue education at the junior seminaries of Rutabo and Katoke before he studied at Rubya seminary but later preferred family life to priesthood. Brother to Kigenza and Rwaburundi, Augustine was the son of Ndabikunze, one of many sons and daughters of Rwabigimba who reigned in the place of his father Kibogora, king of Bushubi, which was a Hinda state, thus closely linked with Karagwe and Biharamulo—from which it split (journals.cambridge.org/production/)—kingdoms founded after the split of Bunyoro-Kitara. The great Bunyoro-Kitara was the Chwezi kingdom about which the Encyclopedia Britannica (http://www.britannica.com/place/eastern-Africa#ref418922?), indicates that its rulers, the Chwezi, first settled in Bigo in western Uganda from the mid-14th century and later—with evidence of radioactive carbon dating—around the turn of the 15th century the Chwezi moved to, and ruled the south under rulers of the Hinda clan founded by Ruhinda the First, beginning with Nkore in Uganda and later in Karagwe, Buhaya, Biharamulo and Busubi (viz., Bushubi), to the southeast of Lake Victoria in modern day Tanzania, long before the white men set their boots on the mainland soil; time when even names like Tanganyika or Tanzania, Kenya or Uganda existed.

Bushubi made its mark in the recorded history when she was under Kibogora, the king that the American explorer Henry Morton Stanley writes about meeting seeking permission to cross the kingdom on his way to Ujiji before that famous greeting: "Dr. Livingstone, I presume," on meeting Dr. Livingstone at the bank of one of the deepest rivers in the whole world, River Tanganyika in 1840s in his book The Sources of the Nile (www.amazon.com). The kingdom fell under German East African colony in 1890s following the German notorious liar, Karl Peters, tricking Chief Mangungo of Msovero into blindly signing the documents handing over the rest of Tanzania to the Germans. According to E. K. Lumley, the first British district officer in the kingdom in his book Forgotten Mandate (www.amazon.com), Bushubi remained fairly independent because both Germans and British were stationed in Biharamulo until during the reign of King Nkundabagore—Augustine Kambarangwe's cousin brother—when the British first started ruling directly from within the kingdom. Bushubi was ruled by Theogenes Nsoro, the official last king of Bushubi, when, on independence in 1961, the kingdom was unified with other pre-colonial states to form the independent Tanganyika which later in 1964, united with Zanzibar to form the modern day Tanzania before kingdoms were abolished under Tanzania's first president, Julius Kambarage Nyerere. (N/B: Mark the foregoing piece of history, for you will need it a little later).

Based in Dar es Salaam, Tanzania, East Africa, the author resides in Mbezi Louis, a few miles from the coastline of the Sea of Dar es Salaam (also curiously known as Indian Ocean). He is happily married to Nafro daughter of Mzee Miki Magetta (RIP) and Mwalimu Moshi Miki Magetta daughter of Mzee Njahite and Mwana Mhawila. The author and his wife, God graciously blessed with precious children Princess Felista, Priscilla Sasha, Michael Junior (RIP), Patricia Cleopatra and Prince Kennedy Ruhinda.

In memory of—and with gratitude to—the true Ideal Scholar, and right role model to all true scholars, leaders of men, and all worthy men and women now living, and billions more yet unborn: Mwalimu Julius Kambarage Nyerere, the first President of Tanzania

ACKNOWLEDGEMENTS

First of all, I am grateful to my father (RIP) and mother, my auntie Mama Regina, my sister Candida, and John Rubin for the part they played in receiving, building and presenting the thesis I present in this book. I am profoundly thankful to you my wife Nafro for your unremitting support—morally and materially—the support without which not only this book wouldn't be out, but I too, the author wouldn't count much! I can't find words to thank you, really. I am indebted to you. Thank you.

I would also like to thank Leonard Kitoka and Kaiza Patrick Batenga for their financial support—the support that helped to bring my writing career back on track. I also acknowledge the support you accorded me as brothers and sisters and friends. Among you are: Joshua and Domina, Zephrine Galeba, Kanagisa, Gosebert, James Kabakama, Projestus Rwehumbiza, Mo Kamilagwa, Rugambwa Bwanakunu, Amos Benjamin, Benedict Emmanuel, Francis Nanai, Michael John, Veran Matunda, Dr. Dani. Werema Chacha, Msisi, Baguma, Fredrick Nshekanabo, Charles Karugendo, Loigwana and Victoria, Sophia Gunda, Martin, Lukumay, Philon Fabian, and my brothers Clement, Julius Best, Fortunatus and Vitalis, for your various invaluable inputs and your support in purchasing every single copy of my book titles; and yes to Fr. Valentine Rwelengera, Sister Sleeva Metu, Hellen Michael, Jackson Gahima, Dr. Aclaus Mlau, Joachim Shirima, Renatus Theobard, Eliza Renatus, Emma Alex, Dr. Swabury Alawi, Maria Mwakasege, Johaness Rwazo, Amani Mworia, Alex Modest, Emanuel Kajura, Chelaus Rutta, Edward Muyangabe, Martin Ngoga, Julius Mitinje, James Tapela, Cyrus Gabone, Respicius Didace, Jackson Sebeza, Alex William, John Ernest, Daudi Michael, Sosthenes, Barnabas, Richard Cement, and all of you who have supported and encouraged me in various other ways toward the publication of this book.

I cannot forget my teachers at Kaigara and Katera Primary Schools, Kahororo Secondary School, Ihungo High School and at the University of Dar es Salaam for the part of initiation they played into the making of me: Mwl. Julian, Mwl. Calist, Mwl Semu Kahatano, Mwl. Muhammad, Tr. Katerengabo, Mwl. Fidel, Mwl. Pulkelia, Tr. Agricola a.k.a Galileo, Tr. Malimbu, Tr. Ishengoma, Mwl. Kaluka, Mwl. Buberwa, Tr. Rugemalira, Tr. Bengesi, Tr. Bakuza, Pancrace Binamungu, B. Bakura, Tr. Ntamakulilo, Mwl. Bayona, Tr. Byarugaba, Dr. Likwelire, Dr. Mpango, Prof. Msambichanka, Dr. Limbu, Prof. Assad, Prof. Amani, Dr. Rutasitara, among others.

Also, I cannot forget my employers, coworkers and friends among different organizations I worked with—the people who helped me one way or the other—and in various ways, inspiring me to learn what I have presented in this book. I thank among them: Mahendra Patel, Salum Chama, Mgwasa Masululi, Gideon Mkama, Zerubabel Nzowa, Peter Louis, Malcolm Butlin, Brian Fenton, Gordon Cook, Andrew Mbwambo, Malaki Sitaki, Paschal Bikomagu, Justo Bituro, Khadija Madawili, Gopi Mundkur, Frank Stermose, Thomas Jacobsen, Lars Rask, Leah Nkhulu, Kippi Warioba, Robert Kayanda, Pendo Butenge, Rutta kakoki, Hilda Kinyunyu, Erica Namwene, Norah Kassala, Ibrahim Mchumo, Mihayo Wilmore, Mike Dabally, Godfrey Mugambi, Margaret Kossitany, Yesse Oenga, Zuhura Muro, Abdiel Mengi, Zoeb Hasuj, Anupam Pundit, Rama Krishna, and Maral Kanan—among others.

To my brothers Benjamin and Edward, for regularly sending me beverages that have helped to see me through the sleepless days and nights putting together the ideas that are now finally in one piece. Finally, but not least, I thank my wonderful children: Princess, Priscilla, Patricia and Prince for putting up with me during those grim times—times when I couldn't fully be there for you, absorbed in writing the manuscript for this book. It is because of your understanding and patience that the work of writing this book became easy, without which it would be utterly painful. To all of you: Princess, Priscilla, Patricia and Prince, let me say it one more time, I love you and I am proud of you!

To all of you, and all those whose names have, for no clear reasons, skipped my memory, let me say: You all have been a blessing to me and I cannot thank you enough!
To all of you let me state: "It was kind of you to share my troubles. And you…sent me help now and again (Philippians 4.14-23)!" And indeed because of what you have been to me, to date, "I've loved you with an everlasting love (Jer. 31:3)!" May God bless you and adddddd unto you—abundantly!

Lastly, but not least, I want to go on record to call attention to the fact that I am also, and in large measure, indebted to the authors now living, and many long departed to the next world—yes authors, writers and publishers of different works in their different genres for the transgenerational wisdom through time and space, wisdom wrapped up in their magnificent works—works that are products of a unswerving obligation—wisdom passed down from generation to generation—and for their dedication to make the world a better place for those of us now living, and billions yet unborn. On behalf of every other worthy man and woman now living, I thank them, for really what else is there that can guide mankind better—something that sets man far apart from other organisms—while as well, timelessly reserving the same precious priceless wisdom for the future generations? Along with my gratitude to all worthy authors, writers and publishers, let me say that you, yes, you my reader, are just a wonderful partner!

Finally, but not in the order of importance, the author is humbled before God, recognizing that He is the Principal Author of ideas, Primary Author of everything we ever think of, do, have, and hope to become. I thank Thee Lord, recognizing that truly such an endeavor of drop out of employment and of finally writing, and eventually publishing a book of this nature, demands making very hard sacrifices aside from the magnitude of peace of mind, an incredible recollection—and yes A Beautiful Mind required, all of which are ordinarily scarce in supply—in the human domain. Indeed, an accomplishment of this magnitude cannot be an exclusive work of man—and man alone! Without doubt I have accomplished this work with the benefaction of the Supreme Power—or, in words of Napoleon Hill, The Supreme Intelligence. It is for this reason that I whisper: "Dear Lord," I whisper, "Our Father in heaven, I thank Thee, I thank Thee, I thank Thee!"

—Author

PREFACE: OUR NATION IS AT RISK

"Therefore he who thinks he stand let him take heed lest he fall."
— *Apostle Paul (1 Cor.10-12)*

"He is my dearest friend who points out my drawbacks to me;
And gives me gift by doing so!"
—*The Holy Prophet (Mohammed-PBUH)*

On the 9th of February 2012, I received an e-mail with which I am going to begin this discussion. It was addressed to what its author chose to call "Stakeholders of education in the country." Though I am not certain if it was also carbon copied to the minister for education, Dr. Shukuru Kawambwa, one thing I know for sure though. The scope of that memo was far reaching that I believe it addressed stakeholders of education across the globe. That's why, considering how education is key to the advancement of humanity, I chose to interpret it and reprint it in here before the manuscript went to the publisher. Here's that memo!

"My dear comrades," he began,"I'm writing this note seeking your support—the support from you personally as individual citizens, parents and institutions—in addressing the problem our education system is facing here in Tanzania.

"That our children are complaining about the quality and scope of education," Benny continued, "is no longer a secret. This episode came to its climax in 2011, marked by the actions of a number of students who seated for the National Secondary School Examinations (that year)," he asserted. Then he reviewed how the executive secretary of the National Examination Council, Dr. Joyce Ndalichako, left everyone in the country in total shock when she read the papers of some of these students! Briefly, here is the story. Among these graduating students, instead of filling right answers in the answer sheets, he, deliberately, filled in false answers. How do we know? We know it was deliberate because some of these candidates filled names such as 50 Cent, Beyonce, etc. In general, these students didn't care to do, let alone to pass the exams. In some other answer spaces, they filled in their ambitions among which hip-hop or rap music, modeling and several other quick fix approaches to wealth stood at the top of the list. Did this happen two hundred years ago? Did it happen a million miles away from civilization? Nah! Were these students nuts or insane? No. They were not insane or sick in the head. They simply knew what they were doing. They wanted to defy and show how they loathe the conventional education. We know it was creative boycott! How do we know this is true? We know it was deliberate because one of these candidates was later that same year said so in an interview with Clouds FM Radio, one of the most celebrated radio stations in Dar es Salaam, Tanzania, on launching his newest music single.

Did we say it was deliberate? We are certain of their deliberate and premeditated because: One, some of these candidates didn't fear the consequences of their actions. That's why some of them made their identities public. A student like this one meant what he said. Number two; we are certain of this fact because on air with Clouds FM Radio in Dar es Salaam Tanzania, this candidate went on record explaining how he hated the traditional education in Tanzania. Why? It didn't address immediate or even long term needs of the students. It didn't address the needs of the society. It didn't address unemployment. It didn't address individual student's calling or vocation.

Did I say they knew what they did do and say? It is a point worth of analysis. During the same interview one of these students introduced his new rap single. Benny's email was long and somber. But suffice to say here that he predicted the downfall of the nation unless education system in the country was fixed. What has defied human imagination until as I write, is that this trend has become a fashion year after year! Would you then be shocked if I told you that the level of education among schools, productivity at workplaces, fidelity and a sense of duty in the family, and civilization or humanity as a whole has hit the rocks? Not me! Not even the Association of Tanzania Employers, no?

The editorial of the Guardian of June 5, 2008, titled "Education System Overhaul Overdue," evidenced that ATE, the Association of Tanzania Employers, had declared that most graduates perform poorly at work. That wouldn't amount to much if it was a question of motivation. What is shocking is that our graduates from our schools, colleges and universities are under qualified.

A Kiswahili newspaper in Tanzania, recently released an article with a title that says it all: Tunaajili Vyeti; viz. we only hire certificates (not ability or credibility). Surprisingly, many don't realize that this observation doesn't only reflect the collapse of education and malfunction of the education sector in the country alone; that it transcends into other fields of social life and throughout the nation as a whole.

Going back to Benny's email, I suspect that he wrote it as an anti-thesis to the above event. Pondering a little more about what Benny posed as a question to the nation as a whole, we would probably be led to the core of the problems we are facing generally as a nation and specifically deficiencies in our education system. He questioned asking thus: Is there any lessons? What do we learn from such boldness from such a young person? Well, besides reflecting a person who knew what he or she was doing, it more than anything reflects the mindset of the youth today. And that's why it isn't fun anyhow—anymore.

It can never be so! It's a tragedy to the education system, households, the country and humanity as a whole! And this is not fiction albeit how tantalizingly sinister it may seem. And this dilemma is not unique only to Tanzania. On April 26, 1983, pointing to the literacy crisis and to the collapse in the standards at the secondary and the college levels, the National Commission on Excellence in Education (in the United States, of all countries) warned: 'Our Nation is at risk, (Ornstein and Hunkins, 1998 3rd Ed).' Think about it! If the United States is at risk, what about the low income dependent countries like ours?

Though I have no way of knowing whether it was consciously or reflexively, but referring to the actions of these boys and gals, I can only say my experience with humanity has proved that in the long run people tend to pull away from anything that is not only harmful but also useless. Mark my words! That's how naturally people show dissatisfaction. That's how people embrace any changes that have commitment to their problems at heart. And mind you, this isn't simply my own creation? It is rather a credible verity. The IMF, the International Monetary Fund magazine for February-March 2006 revealed that following a study of the same nature that the Association of Tanzania Employers revealed in 2008, India's industry has begun reeducating its graduates immediately after they are hired. It is why we see robust growth in the industry sector in a country we traditionally classed as a cricket and Bollywood nation. Malaysia's economic triumph has also to do with this insight. While many find our graduates deficient in scholarly or technical qualifications, on the contrary, we at KI find graduate employees overqualified for day-to-day mainstream employment at workplaces—which is what a flock of employees are hired for! This is to say, they are not only under or over qualified but they are indeed ill-qualified—which is to say they are not only irrelevant but rather far-removed from the actual needs of employers or life on the ground. Thomas Merton once identified this trend as the "mass production of people literally unfit for anything except to take part in an elaborate and completely artificial charade." This book—together with her twins in the series—has been written to respond to the immediate as well as long term challenges our society is facing today.

Is this problem only typical or chronic to Tanzania alone? Nay! We have already highlighted that yes, India was facing the same problem, but indeed the trend of incompetency or wrong choices is pervading the whole world little by little. What rather surprises me more is that, the problem remains far from receiving due attention. This is happening mainly because of ignorance, indifference because of what can be termed as local as well global contemporary tradition.

Take Nigeria for instance. Nigeria was a country that one time produced the cream of minds—exemplary scholars and productive and innovative workforce. Nigeria was home to excellent minds including economists, scientists and authors in the fiber of the Nobel class Professor Chinua Achebe and Wole Soyinka. Where is it now? What has happened to Nigeria can be summed up thus: Nigeria has now drowned in the unfathomable mayhem—the mayhem that began with academic collapse. But that didn't end there. The academic collapse brought forth political and economic collapse, in whose footsteps followed rampant financial corruption and further moral corruption.

Going back to the collapse, the circle went on and on until today when the beautiful country that was once the Africa's pride and superpower intellectually, economically and footballically—if I may coin that word! Who didn't take pride in the Super Eagles? Mind you the author is Tanzania! Yet, he and his colleagues watched Nigeria play world cup and the Olympics dripping with pride and joy to be Africans. Who didn't fall in love with such dazzling Nigerian footballers as J.J Okocha, Talibo West, Tijan Babangida, Nwanko Kanu, Sunday Olisey, Emannuel Amunike, Rashid Yekini, etc? Who wouldn't admire Nigerian actors like Pete Edochi, Kanayo Kanayo—among others? Which African soul didn't leap up in joy watching Agbani Darego being crowned the world maiden with the most inner beauty? But where is that Nigeria now? She is now home to low levels of productivity at work and low morale not only on the football pitch but also on the war fronts with Islamists and low morale even in fighting personal battles. Do I have to say that Nigeria today is home to economic, social, political and sectarian friction? Do I truly have to substantiate my assertions concerning the foregoing statements? That a great nation is on its downfall unless someone, new leadership, does something really big is no more speculation. (And as for the reader, don't dwell so much on Nigeria as you read. What about you, your country?)

Now the one BIG question is this: is there remedy? Truly, you cannot address eradication of poverty, and enhance wealth creation, without first addressing backsliding education: moral and intellectual. On discussing the legacy of Mwalimu Nyerere a couple years ago, a re-known scholar and senior lecturer at the University of Dar es Salaam Dr. Ayub Rioba said in an a television panel discussion in Tanzania that, yes we have identified three enemies of, or challenges facing, our nation's development namely: poverty, disease and ignorance, but he stated that because of our scarcity of resources, we cannot adequately fight these three enemies—we cannot adequately address these three challenges—if we fight them from all fronts. In order therefore to triumph over the enemy, we must focus our scarce resources and efforts primarily on fighting ignorance! His point is this: if we fight and defeat ignorance, we will naturally have defeated the other two enemies—poverty and diseases. Besides, by fighting ignorance, by addressing weaknesses in our education system, we will also have addressed the weakening political inactivity, family institution, quick fix i.e., corruption, low spirit toward self-reliance and youth unemployment, the other critical factors that together conspire to stifle the beautiful nation we all love.

With quick fix pervading our classrooms and academia, households, workplaces and the politburo in our society, one cannot but foresee doom in the near future unless something really big and comprehensive is done. Let me emphasize: It is to this effect that this book has been written.

ILLITERATE GRADUATES—WITH SIMILE TO NIGERIA
On October 15 2012 Abdul Rasak Umoru posted on the Facebook an article that may shock you. Not me! Not anymore! The title of the post? NYSC (National Youth Service Corps) Rejects Illiterate Graduates! Then the story followed: Three "graduates" of Enugu State University of Science and Technology mobilized to participate in the National Youth Service Corps scheme have shown lack of competence and intelligence level expected of genuine degree holders, Blueprint learnt last night. In

education circles, questions are being asked over the competence of the university and indeed other institutions of learning. (The three corps members' names and matriculation numbers are not included here for anonymity). According to documents obtained by Blueprint, the three "graduates," "who are serving in Niger, Lagos and Adamawa states respectively, were rejected, with formal letters sent to the state coordinators by their areas of primary assignment and forwarded to the NYSC headquarters in Abuja.

The national headquarters, in a (letter dated) August 29, 2012 letter signed by the Director General of NYSC, N.T. Okore-Affia, had informed the NUC of the presence of corps members who displayed "glaring lack of academic ability and intelligence level expected of genuine Nigerian graduates, which were consistently exhibited by the three students from the Enugu State University of Science and Technology."Attaching copies of letters from NYSC secretariats in Niger, Adamawa and Lagos, Okore-Affia noted: "As contained in the reports, the corps members exhibited signs of incompetence and low intelligence level which range from inability to complete registration formats correctly to not being able to teach pupils at nursery school level. These inadequacies led to their rejections by their employers in their various states of deployment."The case, according to an insider's account, has baffled the National Universities Commission (NUC) and prompted the setting up of a committee to "verify the integrity of the degrees," and find out if there was collaboration by the university. Federal education authorities are suspecting a wide-ranging scam that might have been going on for years.

Does the author have to substantiate on the above with his own words? Here comes an alarming substantiation on what we have presented above, which describes the situation spot-on.

In an article that the editor posted on the website http://www.nigeriaintel.com on August 28, 2013, Salisu Suleiman, wrote beginning with administrative slipups before he launched into core problem of our education: "It would be difficult," he wrote; "It would be difficult for the uninitiated to appreciate the level of decay and fallen standards without a reflective look at what Nigerian universities (or Tanzanian universities for that matter) used to be like. Personally," Mr. Suleiman continued, "I have received a number of shockers: As a primary school pupil, taking dictations in class was routine; teachers didn't have to repeat themselves too many times and only spelt out words pupils were not familiar with. Some 20 years later as a doctoral student in one of Nigeria's 'top' universities, I was dumfounded to find professors dictating notes to the class—and being told they were dictating too fast!" I wish it was fiction, but it really happened. And because not much has changed since then, I suspect those professors are still there, dictating worthless notes to aspiring PhDs. Perhaps I should not have been so alarmed; a few years earlier while pursuing a master's degree, all but one lecturer dictated notes to the class or gave us antiquated notes to photocopy.

"Although this happened a while ago, it would not be surprising to find the same lecturers dictating the same old notes to new students. Or that some students in my class with whom I took those tedious notes are now themselves lecturers and professors repeating watered down versions of the same notes to students who, not surprisingly, would rather be anywhere else but in class. Trying to appreciate the collapse of our educational system, I look back at the schools I attended and the fine, well-trained and dedicated teachers we had. Not only was education free, all books were also provided free. Reading was a worthy and admirable pastime and I remember buying my very first book by myself at just seven. Today, asking university students to buy or read any kind of book would be seen as punitive. In retrospect, the quality and variety of teachers in our secondary schools was astonishing… Nigerian teachers loved their jobs because they chose to be teachers. As preparation for GCE, candidates were taught how to write and answer questions in examination conditions and sitting for WAEC at fourteen or fifteen was not unusual —even in public schools.

"While waiting to secure admission to a university, I recall spending time reading a wide variety of works and authors. There were no computer games, Internet, or cable TV, so I discovered writers like James A. Michener when I read The Source. The interregnum enabled me to find John Steinbeck, Leon Uris, Irwin Shaw and James Clavell. Devouring William L. Shirer's 1,600 page book The Rise and Fall of the Third Reich was routine. University offered another opportunity to interact with, and learn from, lecturers from every part of the world…in addition to some excellent Nigerian teachers. To enable students adapt to university life, there were special instructors who taught Study Skills—specifically how to order classes, tutorials, presentations and how to use the library. Again, this was in Nigeria, and yes, in a government owned university. Even students in technical fields participated in liberal studies and learned things as abstract as numismatics, carbon 14 and lexicostatistics. They read the works of Lombroso, Chaucer, Gramsci, Tocqueville, Bentham, Mills, Nietzsche, Marcuse, Ibn Khaldun, Hitti and Pareto. They consumed

Ousmane Sembene's prose and memorized poetry from Soyinka's edition of Poems of Black Africa.

"It was with a sense of pride that students studied African resistance from Menelik II, the Maji-Maji Rebellion to the Mau-Mau Movement. Heated discussions in class saw Europe built and Africa dismembered. Students learned about oral African literature and European poetry. Bismarck, Stalin, Roosevelt, Hitler, Churchill, Haile Selassie, Omar Mukhtar, Nyerere and Nkrumah came alive in class. Undoubtedly, students from Nigerian (or for that matter Tanzanian) universities were highly regarded.

"With this history, it is clear that even if all of (Academic Staff Union of Universities of Nigeria) ASUU's demands are met; it would be a long while before Nigerian (or for that matter Tanzanian) universities return to their glory days. In the meantime," concludes Salisu Suleiman, "our public universities will continue to churn what, to be frank, amounts to little more than illiterate graduates."

Table of Contents

A Reflection From the Book: A Sick Nation and How to Heal It..v

Preface: Our Nation Is At Risk...xvii

PART I: INTRODUCTION-WHY THIS BOOK WAS WRITTEN.....1

1. WEAKNESSES IN OUR EDUCATION SYSTEM—THE MOTIVATION WHY THIS BOOK WAS WRITTEN......................3
2. THE IDEAL SCHOLAR CONCEPT—AND HOW IT WAS HATCHED UP...55
3. THE IDEAL SCHOLAR CONCEPT, EDUCATIONAL STANDARD AND NATIONAL PHILOSOPHY...........................76
4. HOW BADLY DO WE NEED TRANSFORMATION?...................85
5. WE NEED IDEALS AS TRAVELERS NEED COMPASS.........112
6. BENEFITS OF THE PROGRAM TO STUDENTS, PARENTS, TEACHERS, SCHOOLS, THE GOVERNMEMNT AND THE COMMUNITY..129

PART II: THE IDEAL SCHOLAR..157

7. VOILA! BEHOLD THE IDEAL SCHOLAR: KNOW THYSELF—AND THE EDUCATED SLAVE...158
8. SELF-ESTEEM: LOVING ONESELF AND THE QUEST FOR PERSONAL LIBERTIES..168

9. EDUCATION: A CONCEPT UNKNOWN EVEN TO THE MEN OF EDUCATION AND WHY OUR SCHOOLS PRODUCE ILLITERATE GRADUATES AND EDUCATED SLAVES...........199

10. SELF-ADVANCEMENT AND THE ILLITERATE GRADUATE...211

11. THE IDEAL SCHOLAR READS (AND WRITES)................217

12. THE IDEAL SCHOLAR DOES NOT ONLY HAVE A DEFINITE NOBLE PURPOSE OR GOAL IN LIFE, BUT HE ALSO AIMS HIGHER...236

13. THE IDEAL SCHOLAR PURSUES SPECIALIZED TRAINING AND IS SELF-TRAINED..250

14. THE IDEAL SCHOLAR IS FUTURISTIC AND FOCUSSES MORE ON THE FUTURE RATHER THAN THE IMMEDIATE CAUSE..262

15. PERSISTENCE AND DETERMINATION..........................269

16. THE IDEAL SCHOLAR IS A HARDWORKING RESULTS FOCUSED PERSON..285

17. THE IDEAL SCHOLAR TAKES RESPONSIBILITY OF HIS LIFE AND THE LIVES OF THE OTHERS............................301

18. GRATITUDE..309

19. THE IDEAL SCHOLAR IS TIME CONSCIOUS..................317

20. SELF-RELIANCE AND PURSUIT FOR PERSONAL LIBERTIES...320

21. THE IDEAL SCHOLAR IS MONEY CONSCIOUS................337

22. ORDER..345

23. THE IDEAL SCHOLAR IS WISE AND SENSIBLE—AND THEREFORE HAS PLANS AND A SET OF PRIORITIES..........348

24. THE IDEAL SCHOLAR IS A SOCIABLE AND MORAL PERSON..358

25. IDEAL SCHOLAR IS A GOOD COMMUNICATOR.............365

26. EXCELLENCE AND QUALITY OF WORK..........................376

27. ATTENTION TO THE CUSTOMER: A DARK SCAR IN OUR SOCIETY, AND A BARRIER AGAINST BUSINESS GROWTH AND FOREIGN INVESTMENTS...388

28. THE IDEAL SCHOLAR IS A THINKING MAN—AN INNOVATIVE AND IMAGINATIVE PERSON.........................396

29. THE IDEAL SCHOLAR HAS A BEAUTIFUL MIND: HE IS A CRITICALLY THINKING OPEN MINDED PERSON................402

30. THE IDEAL SCHOLAR IS A JUST PERSON AND MINDFUL OF OTHERS...413

31. OTHER QUALITIES: LOYALTY, PATRIOTISM, FORGIVING AND EMPATHY..426

32. THE IDEAL SCHOLAR IS KEEN TO OPPORTUNITIES, CONSCIOUS TO FAULT AND A RISK TAKER........................431

33. THE IDEAL SCHOLAR HAS THE THIRD EYE AND THE SIXTH SENSE...447

34. THE IDEAL SCHOLAR IS A FAMILY MAN........................452

35. SELF CONTROL: THE IDEAL SCHOLAR IS RATIONAL, TOLERANT AND SELF-RESTRAINED...................................463

36. JUSTICE TO GENDER DIFFERENCES.............................473

37. THE IDEAL SCHOLAR AND ECOSYSTEM........................481

38. DOES THE IDEAL SCHOLAR BELIEVE IN GOD?..................484

39. THE IDEAL SCHOLAR LEADS OTHERS—AND LEADS BY EXAMPLE..493

40. THE IDEAL SCHOLAR IS IMPACTFUL; A REAL "HE-MAN" WHO TOUCHES THE LIVES OF THE PEOPLE AND ENVIRONMENT AROUND HIM..503

41. CAN WE IDENTIFY THE IDEAL SCHOLAR: A REAL HE-MAN?...512

PART III: FINALE: THE WISE AND FOOLISH BUILDERS..533

42. SELF-CRITICISM: BEING HONEST TO ONESELF..534

43. PERSONAL SELF-CENSORSHIP AND LASTING PROSPERITY..550

EPILOGUE 576

   CONTACT US: CALL US NOW..590

BIBLIOGRAPHY AND RECOMMENDED READING..592

PART I

INTRODUCTION: WHY THIS BOOK WAS WRITTEN

"I must walk toward Oregon, and not toward Europe. And that way the nation is moving, and I may say that mankind progress from east to west... We go eastward to realize history and study the works of art and literature, retracing the steps of the race; we go westward as into the future, with a spirit of enterprise and adventure."

—Henry David Thoreau, "Walking," *Excursions*, p. 267 (1894)

1. WEAKNESSES IN OUR EDUCATION SYSTEM—THE MOTIVATION WHY THIS BOOK WAS WRITTEN

"It is our choices, Harry, that show what we truly are, far more than our abilities." —J.K Rowling, Harry Potter and the Chamber of Secrets Harry Potter #2

One afternoon few years ago, someone knocked on my door. As I opened the door, two men ferried in a couple of goods: a bunch of banana, a whole leg of a goat, beverages and yes, a case of beer! It was my sister. Having myself grown up surrounded by banana plantations back in the village, she knew how banana mixed with goat's meat was my favorite *staple*. She also knew, I suppose, that I had an enormous respect for beer, having served in a brewery with Tanzania Breweries and later with Carlsberg. Why all these gifts? Well, she had come home for the first time after she began working a couple of months back after her graduation from the University of Dar es Salaam. I also suppose she brought home the gifts out of the sense of gratitude because she had been raised under my watch. But that's just a part of my point. Then, recalling one Kabentenge, one of her greatest friends at the kindergarten back in time, I asked her if she had heard from her, or if they were in touch. Well, she had not heard about her for a very long time. To be fair with my sister, she couldn't know if her friend continued with education or not, having moved from the village when I first brought her under my tent in Bukoba after which she advanced from Tumaini Primary School down-town Bukoba and then to the secondary school in Kigoma and Shinyanga, before she went to high school in Morogoro after which she joined the university. That's how their paths parted forever!

What's my point? There are many Kabenteges out there, as there're very very few Vickys. The reason why these two friends had their ways parted forever, an explanation why probably Kabetenge dropped out of school, or rather why she didn't advance to secondary school let alone high school or university, is yes the difference in facilities available to each student, but indeed there is more to it. This can be explained by a hypothetical situation where the same Vicky, my sister, had been brought up in two different circumstances, under the watch of two different persons with different education as far as raising children is concerned.

Given that the two persons managing her education had the same commitment to see her through to the university, and had resources available to them, both persons in Vicky would most certainly advance to the university–and probably at the same time. The point is this: yes the two persons would graduate, but to what extent? What potential contribution would these two persons have upon themselves, their respective families, employers, and the nation as a whole? If students are to succeed in their academic journey, we have got to prepare them, to give them guidance. We have to teach them how they should sail through their schooling journey. They should learn how to conduct themselves, how to relate with the other people around them; they must be taught how to educate themselves; how to choose appropriate vocation; and to learn, from the onset, that having a major goal in life and working hard toward that goal during and after school is necessary if they have to not only realize their dreams, but make a difference.

Indeed, in order to be able to repair the situation, the situation where we have so many Kabentenges in the country today, and be able to prepare our students powerfully, we must endeavor to openly identify and establish the weaknesses within the education system. Both the students and educators should appreciate these weaknesses in order to address them, and to meet them head-on. If we don't do so, we run the risk of disappointing the youth, and ultimately dissuade them out of school, failing them altogether, whether they drop out or graduate without purpose in life. Following the lessons from an article: *What Is Education For? Six Myths about the Foundations of Modern Education and Six New Principles to Replace Them* by David Orr, also adapted in his commencement address to the graduating class of 1990 at Arkansas' College many were prompted to wonder why such speeches are made at the end, rather than the beginning, of the collegiate experience.[1]

---

[1]*Adapted from:* http://www.davidworr.com/files/What_is_Education_For.pdf

The major challenge that Kabentenge faced, the disadvantage majority faces is purely of the tangible nature: Classrooms, laboratories, availability of books or teachers, etc. That's why this chapter is dedicated to this purpose. That's in part why this book was written. But there is more to the school failures or generally the failure of education and overall social-economic dysfunction in a country like Tanzania. This is, in the main, what this book was written. Notice that in highlighting such weaknesses we are not pointing fingers. No! We are all to blame. Yes, we are not going to close our eyes on good intentions, or even some good efforts our academics, educators, policy makers and the administration have shown, or done, as we write. But in the wake of continued downward spiral of our education, morals and economy, we are forced to ask ourselves what significant efforts have we produced over this past? Where were we when the education we have in place, policies and culture—the culture of indifference and anarchy—have robbed us of the prosperity and dignity we anticipated now that we see imminent broken education system, corrupt social principles, and generally an impending broken society? Is this exaggerated? Well, let the skeptic look at as many indicators as possible in order to arrive at an informed conclusion. Let the skeptic consider the social, economic and moral indicators as possible to make a good judgment.

To make things easy for the reader, the author submits to worthy men and women wherever they may be to read a book "A Sick Nation and How to Heal it," for fresh insights that may lead him to the danger signals alerting us that all is not okay—if we don't wake up and stand on our toes determined to transform ourselves, the education system as a whole and the society in general. And having not stepped aside, passing the buck, playing blame games, myself accepting his responsibility to all this mess at least at household, workplace and community level, let me go on record to emphasize that this message is not something the author writes exclusively for our immediate society. No sir! That's why all of us are forced to retrace a question that Jesus asked his disciples over 2000 ago: "What have you done more than the others?" If we are to change and see meaningful change, this is the right attitude. This is the right attitude if we have to correct the recurring weaknesses in our education system, and the society as a whole. This is the right approach should the society rise from its knees and stand on its feet once again. That is why we chose to review, in this very book, the weaknesses that conspire to choke our education system, and ultimately choke the society as a whole.

What you are going to read therefore is a set of these weaknesses summed up in order to alert the reader, and indeed highlight the challenges ahead among the students of any academic level if they should triumph—along with their families, businesses, communities and the society as a whole—over these weaknesses and reap abundantly from their education. We, as well, highlight these weaknesses for the educators, the policy makers—and implementers—in order to allow them to catch a glimpse of what is happening without their traditional domain. To learn effectively, to lead efficiently, we must be broad minded. This book was written to offer suggestions that would effectively help you, the reader, make decisions pertaining to education, career, family and the people around you. That's why here now you are going to be taken through some of the major weaknesses in our education system, weaknesses that will lead you to solutions thereof.

WEAKNESSES INHERENT IN OUR EDUCATION SYSTEM

Weaknesses in any young education system like ours aren't few or any trivial. They are on the contrary vast and far reaching that we cannot go into details much as we would have liked to do so. That's why we will highlight these weaknesses knowing that we have such numerous and vast researches into such areas, books and academic papers that can be used to furnish what we sum up here. Such detailed academic research works include The Promise, a book by the illustrious Professor Maliyamkono (and Mason). That's why we submit to the reader to find and read such books and papers—books and policy papers that aren't any short in supply. With this in mind, here we are now going to enumerate some of the most apparent weaknesses in our education system—weaknesses that annihilate the education in the country in general and stifle social economic as well as moral growth of our society.

Firstly, there's a great failure to comprehend what is the real meaning, and the major goals and roles of education. Failure to be in sync with the foregoing question on the part of the student, the educator, the policy maker—and implementer—and the society as a whole, logically leads to the failure in striving to seek or pursue real education. What do we seek in school? Did we know this when we were in school? Did our teachers know? Do they? Did they, the teachers, even know what they were seeking in teaching us? Do they know? Does the policy maker, or implementer, know? Do we care, anyway?

Again, greater attention in our classrooms today is cast upon such disciplines as biology, marketing, economics or mathematics, etc. instead of guiding students to find who they really are, and thus how connected each one of them is with the disciplines in question—disciplines they pursue. Students should be guided to identify and recognize who they are and thus each one's calling and therefore the vocations they ought to pursue. When students choose combinations or vocations blindly, can we expect anything worthwhile from such students—and teachers? And what about that society? Addressing this weakness will help to solve the old problem of spending too much time in classrooms only to come out to spend another long part of one's life in a vocation he didn't anticipate or like; or even a vocation or job he can't perform well. Today we see many graduates quitting their current professions after they have wasted very long time and too many resources; after they have sacrificed a lot before discovering who one real is or what he or she wants to do, have and be.

When teaching biology or mathematics for instance, the educator, by the nature of our education system or tradition, tends to innocently treat—and I repeat: they innocently treat the learner as a machine, because most educators believe that that's the best, if not the only way, to teach. They do so because they believe the individual learner is like a machine whose being can only be expressed in his physical form. Humans aren't machines. They are neither robots nor soulless beings. They have a soul—another half that is real—aside from the intellect. No matter how much the other half is imponderable, and yes intangible, this other half, the soul, is real. What's more, this intangible *person* in us is the one that indeed controls the body. And, sadly, that is what totally and often sorrowfully forgotten—or generally unthought-of!

This assertion suggests that the combination of the mind with the soul is indeed supreme than the body itself—the body we so highly regard and provide for—at the expense of the most important part of our persons. They, I mean the body, mind or intellect, and soul, are interdependent nonetheless. Wallace D. Wattles wasn't wrong when he suggested that; "None of these is better, or holier, than the other and vice versa;[2]" a statement we offer to improve by asserting that indeed the body is a servant of the other selves, i.e., the mind, or intellect and the soul, something that our education system or curriculum doesn't concern itself with.

---

[2] *This statement has been paraphrased from the book Science of Getting Rich by Wallace D. Wattles*

And this isn't a strange idea—an idea that is without support. No! In his program *Just for Today*, Frank Crane, the fourth tenet for a daily program for a victorious life reads thus: Just for today I will take care of my body. I will exercise it, care for it, nourish it, not abuse it nor neglect it; so that it will be a perfect machine for my will!" A perfect machine? Mistaken word? Misspelled? No sir! A perfect machine! That's what the body is!

Based on the above argument, and judging from the majority of our youth graduating from our schools today's, we can fairly say that our curriculum has failed to build purpose and responsibility in a child's life. We therefore need to put emphasis on the choice of vocation or career during lower levels. We need to encourage every student to seek and pursue his or her own calling during early levels of schooling. A positive, potentially successful education should not only teach someone to do something, but also why.

Have you not observed that today many learned people whine and lament in deep sorrow even after they have become successful scholarly? What happens is that they failed to make the ends meet despite acquiring the college education. So unhappy and uncertain of the their bearing in life, they choose to go for the second or the third degree hoping that the master's degree or the PHD will come to their rescue or answer to their financial, personal or social problems. They forget that though education has life of its own, degree papers don't. They are what they are—papers at large! What they get therefore instead is frustration and some more problems. These problems emanate from having themselves further distanced from their own persons in the process of acquiring the today's education. If you don't believe me, count and see. The most frustrated men and women in our society today are men and women of education!

Before this book went to the publisher, I met a couple of my old acquaintances who more than demonstrate the foregoing assertion. One had successfully graduated from a college at the time when we first met. He then chose to work as an independent promotion and advertising agent. He was now a second year student in law! Another fellow working as an auditor with the Revenue Authority opted for an MBA. That didn't shock me much. What I didn't understand is why he was doing a first degree in law only a couple of years after he had graduated with an MBA on top of a bachelor's degree! Why? I would like to suggest that there is another person within us whose needs have not been addressed through their previous disciplines. That's the other half that is dissatisfied, lamenting, weeping from being butchered, calling out for the attention of its needs and life.

What is the source of this problem? It is inherent within the curriculum and the system as a whole. A human being therefore is a set of his whole, i.e. his body, his intellect and soul or spirit. Sadly most guardians and schools and institutions tend to focus on the body as are most medical institutions, while others like the church tend to focus on the soul. Many writers address the intellect or mind alone as are many schools but addressing the human form in its components singularly than its entirety will unfortunately never work and therefore we have no option but to change the strategy.

Our curriculum has failed to institute or establish national standards or ideal. Without going deep into it, let's pose a question here: But do we really need these ideals? I believe by imparting such ideals to our people, we can help bring the gaps and the imperfection we are born with. It is also important because born imperfect; we grow up disorderly, lacking coherence all over our own persons. If we are not healed during these formative years, we become and remain broken and loose, missing some of the ingredients—ingredients that so far exist within us which only need to be rekindled, remodeled or rearranged to meet the challenges of the ever changing world. This can only be done by filling the gaps or rearranging the body, intellect (a term about which in this book we may use interchangeably with the term *mind*) and soul together. We can best do it by letting loose what is wrong displaying where we are wrong and who we ought to be only if we change. But transformation demands commitment and passion because it always is a slow process. It is never quick fix or a mere event. Education—or reeducation—and the making of a man, or society, therefore are what we can call *Work In Progress*. It must be allowed to grow organically.

One of the greatest failure of our education system, worldwide—within which lie the solution—is to fail to establish, and thereupon, failing to produce ideal scholars—real or genuine scholars. As a result of the sad foregoing mishap, we fail to produce ideal scholars. This is centrally due to a complete absence of KPI's, or indicators, in establishing, and therefore establishing who really is the ideal scholar, or model graduate. The ideal scholar or model graduate evolves out of, and with, the superior character one exhibits at the time when he graduates. That is to say a graduating student's technical skill on graduation is almost kaput if he cannot exhibit superior character and strong moral fiber in as far as his attitude or impact is concerned. That's why it is hard, or rightly impossible, to identify a credible or rather the ideal scholar, or job candidate today. We see many of our youth with degree papers colorfully sparkling with alphas and betas but individuals who can do or create nothing really tangible in real life or on the ground.

Part of the foregoing weakness, is the failure to produce ideal role models among our youth. By undermining the men of education on the part of the government and corporations—whether deliberately or unawares—while instead putting money or social capital, or both, on the uneducated through promotion of art, sports and movies, aside from cunning racketeer *gold diggers*. Despite good intentions of generating employment for the least privileged in terms of access to education, the net result is the sad promotion of quick fix as means to wealth and fame, and as a result, low motivation for education. If we ascertained that we produced all-rounded scholars, individuals who are fully qualified to get or create advantageous jobs or positions and a certain station in the society, we would help scale back the rate of school dropouts—and vice and crime in the society—vice and crime that escalates through different forms of less tainted quick fix aside from corruption, armed robbery, prostitution, drugs, black market, terrorism, emigration to SA or Europe—vices that choke the health of the society.

If we had the ideals or virtues in place, if we implemented the same, and if we so produced role models from amongst our scholars, young men and women with admirable character and positions in the society, we would help create ideal citizens from even amongst those who didn't go to the university, people with a glimpse of what life should be like, people who are eager and able to pursue a new way of life—a certain way of living—now accessible through the educated members of the society—members of the society they today look at with contempt. This is a pledge we made through the book How Universities Under Develop You—to impart education to the rest of the members of the society, members who didn't have the privilege of the acquiring the university education. This is one of the major inspirations why this book was written. And by all standards, this is a noble endeavor, is it not?

Our schools and instructors today tend to concentrate with core subjects like biology of mathematics or even professions and work skills without connecting them with actual individual's day to day life. And as a result they tend to impose on students what one should read or do in schools.

This is the source of the stagnation we see in our education as a nation today. We teach students to emulate what we do or teach and students who for innate reasons cannot follow through are reprimanded, penalized, failed and as a result put off in as far as education is concerned! We should rather help each one to seek his or her calling. We also don't see due attention on building self-reliance and industriousness, risk taking and punctuality in our education or curricula today. These values are badly lacking in our society today. These are otherwise the entrepreneurial values which can help to build a larger middle class crucial for trickledown effect to the masses of local people in terms of technical knowhow and the GDP.

If we cannot help the students to have a grip over their own persons, to have control over their thoughts through mindset change, self control, self respect and patriotism, we curtail growth of our children whether they graduate from the Kindergarten or the University. And if education cannot help the graduates to acquire this ideal—to have the ability to have a grip on themselves, to have the control over their persons in their own possession—what then is education for? Plato was more than right when he said: "The first and best victory is to conquer self. To be conquered by self is, of all things, the most shameful and vile!" This is the major source of failure in education system. And an initiated reader will recognize that this problem doesn't only end there—I mean in the education system only. It then slowly but steadily crawls toward workplaces where it ruins productivity and therefore the health of the individual and his household—before it escalates into the whole organization and the society as a whole.

There's also a failure of establishing what we want in training students coupled with how we establish abilities of our students relative to the training or education so acquired. What do we want for instance when we set questions? Let us rationalize together.

I have learned that not one school but almost in the whole district, no one got the answer for one specific question in mathematics in one national examination. Why? Were they all dumb? Nope! Language! Vocabulary used. Here's the question in Kiswahili. *Kokotoa namba mraba ya 36.* While otherwise the students knew the essence of the question, which was the square root of 36, but they failed to get the meaning because the term *Kokotoa* was an incomprehensible vocabulary to both the students and their teachers. For most of these poor Tanzanian boys and girls, it was a vocabulary they had never heard of. It was like being asked one's name in ancient Chinese. Indeed instead of examining the abilities of the students in mathematics, the exam tested their Kiswahili language proficiency. Instead we should use that language that is understood by candidates and leave language proficiency to examinations in the languages papers. Often students fail even though they know the answer. Why? They couldn't determine what the examiner expected from the candidates!

Part of the problem is the instructor himself—and the instruction itself—in as far as how one is conditioned. Schools, and therefore teachers, should instead teach and then test if the learner understands the concept so taught. The purpose of exams was originally not meant to fail the students or candidates. Instead it was primarily meant to show both the students and their teachers where they still lag behind and hence the areas where they ought to put more concentration. Educators must help students to understand the meaning of questions. Students learn better under the teacher who can inspire them to find within themselves the reason to study and the reason to advance their lives. This is a teacher with the faith and purpose of advancing his own life and those of the others around him. And any teacher who has this faith and purpose can pass on the same hope and purpose to his students. He cannot help giving hope and courage to his students. And if he cannot, then teaching is not part of his calling or practice.

Through the proceeding chapters we will discuss how we see our youth diverging from education itself, professional vocations and industry with mania for quick money and hence quick fix. This is a handicap which our education curriculum or system doesn't concern itself with. Indeed the teachers themselves and the system contribute to the problem when they don't know or fail to give their all to the students. At workplaces, we have seen people getting employed, or promoted because they speak the best English, forgetting that English language is not a mark of intelligence or talent only to be shocked to find that that some of such individuals are complete nincompoops when it comes to performance and actual delivery of results, or how one relates with the others, how he contributes to profitability and business sustainability through his own work or by leading or influencing others to do, have and become better as persons and environment around them etc. Too often our graduates today hide in weak departments which don't have appetite to develop right KPI's. The Marketing Department is a case in point. Please read What Business Leaders Should Know But they Don't, and How Universities Under Develop You! Others in the category work as receptionists or advertisers on one hand, or politicians—on the other. What does this say?

There are other weaknesses in our education system worth to mention whether graduates are locally produced or procured from abroad—from without the local domain. Our education system has not helped us to establish who really is the ideal graduate or scholar. Yes, we understand that to graduate successfully, one must meet a certain bottom line, .yet we have proved that because of the problems inherent in our education system—problems such as that of having many subjects one has to contend with, the teaching methodology and how examinations are set, students don't read in depth. They lack concentration. Did I say they lack? No! That's not it. They don't need it. I mean they don't have to concentrate. Truly they are induced to be so by how we teach and assess performance. Others cannot endure the experience of reading books in the library. They hate it—and that 'it' is the actual reading whereas on the other hand it is the book or the library if not the education itself. The ubiquitous books in the library make them feel drowsy. They like to hang out in a bar or pub somewhere in the vicinity of their campus, and prefer to peruse through their school notes amidst flashy half-naked waitresses serving the best affordable liquor brands in the campus outfits.

There's an increasing tendency that libraries are being vacated whereas the popularity of group discussions is on the sharp rise. Why bother? Afterall overcrowding has forced lecturers to encourage students to provide very short answers, preferably mere outlines. Imagine! I'm not saying outlines are worthless academically. They work better during junior classes. The author realizes, in retrospect, that answering a question at high school required more preparation and it was more strenuous than the energy we needed at the university! It shames me to have to say I believe I learned more during my high school and secondary school than at the university! Outlines could be meaningful without anything in harm's way, only if students first had read widely and in depth. But that's not what's happening. It shouldn't therefore astonish you to realize that best performers at the university are therefore likely to be not the best students—students who have read extensively and acquired in depth knowledge! There is no motivation to do so. Why should they if they can pass even without straining themselves? Would you then be surprised if I told you the best employees we hire or promote at work aren't the very best candidates? To get to the bottom of this problem, we suggest that the senior lecturers, the corporate executives, administrators and policy makers examine themselves first, and report their findings to themselves—not to the author!

Laziness or quick fix is on the rise and it is like weeds. It is always there. Hard work or even extensive reading must be sown and watered to thrive. What students do today is to pick up lecture notes and compare them with past papers and then they prepare answers for all topics and cram them. Why can't they score at the top of the classes when in fact teachers actually use the same old watered down papers to procure the examination questions? The semester mode of examining capabilities of the students has helped to worsen the situation. Students don't have any more any incentive to seek in-depth comprehension. Why should they when they can simply cram a few topics and answer the questions and then forget everything thereafter? After all they don't need this knowledge at work where they do completely different things.

I have seen students of economics or finance working as salesmen or advertisers whose job description is to help beautify a bar with banners of the beer brands, liquor or cigarettes they sell. And they are happy. For them the salary is what matters most. Indeed you don't need Harold Dommar Model or econometrics to be able to drive a beer branded single cabin pickup car and deliver cases of beer, do you? The problem is that the good crammers are more likely to be eligible for advanced degrees. They will be credible for better jobs. And what about the omnivorous reading students, those who read in depth? They will score lower marks for they will seem to confuse the time-conscious lecturer with winding arguments. Then the end of 3rd or 4th year soon comes. They, the serious students, fail or scrape with a C.

Because of the problem we have mentioned already—quick fix and scarcity of resources which resonate in—overcrowding in our classrooms, there's also a tendency among the *smart* candidates to share the answers amongst themselves. Why not! Afterall it is a less painful experience to both students who work together to get the answers. Besides, students who are friends to one another tend to sit quite close to one another for whatever reasons. And the overcrowded classes accelerate cheating facilitating students to copy from one another, a habit that whereas it may not necessarily be encouraged by the school authorities, but it is seldom discouraged for the good name—or business—of the school and the teachers. Lie? Oh no! I am certain that as witnesses, many of the purveyors of this habit or syndicate will read the foregoing statement with the palms of their hands cradled on their faces—like the Adili's two elder wicked brothers in Shaban Robert's great book, Adili na Nduguze, Kiswahili for Adili and his brothers!

During my three years at the university, I discovered that sadly, most of our youth, the students don't prefer to sit in the front rows. They prefer the dark corners and shady spots—a sad habit common among them cockroaches—not among upright men or women. What I am trying to say is that our education system—or structure—doesn't prepare our students to graduate as ideal scholars. Therefore judging a student's capability by the answers he puts on the papers remains not only deficient, mind you? it is also misleading. We are convinced that, under these circumstances, written examinations should be merged with direct interviews—if we have to evaluate a candidate's ability. The analyses are favored by the observations we made concerning students who read extensively and learn in depth. Yes the outline answer system may not suit them but such students tend to perform better at work and in the long run they outsmart the high grade racketeers who score top marks in classes. We need to spot this setback and encourage the reading students lest they fall for quick fix. To get the right answers we mustn't overshadow the real problem. Otherwise we will be discussing wrong problems and hence we should expect nothing but wrong answers.

The foregoing weakness relates closely with our curriculum having excessive load of subjects one has to take which exerts mounting pressure to teaching staff, administration, students and parents. With such a massive load, the students tend to find a means to pass whether they understand the subjects or not.

There's another problem that works against morale, or motivation, to work hard whether in a classroom or workplace. Work hard as you may, but you can't make it to the top—for whatever reason—nepotism or high level of unemployment. Just recently a panel of experts revealed through a discussion on ITV in Dar es Salaam that one director could be paid 15 million a month while a local staff from majority poor families scrapes with five even two hundred thousand shillings. This is to say we cannot expect morale and productivity under such an environment where the manager is paid a 100 fold the average employees. I doubt if the payroll reflects what one produces!

With educational infrastructure or opportunities skewed to the rich thus many vendors or hawkers popularly known as *Marching Guys* or simply Machinga in Dar es Salaam, Tanzania, and school dropouts are then packed in the already clogged informal sector. My biggest worry about our informal sector is that it is hard to distinguish it from black market. It is a dark sector. It is in here where vices become credible industry and human flesh—whether it is the flesh, or skin of the albino or of a whore—as good as any other economic goods or traded products. Whore houses provide good examples of such dark sectors where human flesh is displayed sold and bought as any other material goods—something immoral at least in this continent—the continent that at least still upholds a certain level of purity as a social ideal. Recently a Kenyan man was caught ready-handed with an illegal merchandize he was trying to smuggle into the country. The merchandize was walking on its two feet. The albino man was then released and walked free. Made from human skin knuckles, or even his genitals such dark marketers sell human body as potion for quick wealth. It may surprise you to learn who the customers are. Most are high ranking executives, business executives and politicians who have had top *education;* so our sources—the witchdoctors themselves—say.

Again, education and teaching methodologies don't seem to fully engage all students. It seems that today only capable students are given the attention. We must find means to give slow learners a chance to try. This is related to another failure which is greed and selfishness. In this set, there's a corrupt mind and the greatest evil or enemy of the nation: corruption! The foregoing assertion is behind a great lack of empowerment and building the capacity of the others! Indeed, according to Lafarge, "We believe that entrusting people with responsibilities and not merely tasks is the best way to leverage their skills, initiatives and innovations."

Besides, we face other challenges such as quality itself. What is the quality of the education we receive or give? What is the quality of the environment for schooling? As such, there is under utilization of the academic infrastructures, such as the libraries or laboratories. Less work is done there for either lack of facilities or complete collapse of inspiration to do so by both the examiners and the students as we shall discuss further. There is yes, low but also misuse of the budgets so allocated.

There is also the psychological part of the problem. For maximum results a kid must feel safe and not afraid or threatened by or in the classrooms. He must feel kindness and secure if he has to develop belief in himself. The teacher must show great willingness to inspire a sense of pride in oneself and self-reliance. This spirit then goes on to build good character, positive attitude and strong desire to excel. Educators must encourage students to look more at their strength than weaknesses.

Teachers and methodologies must encourage and build a sense of pride, freedom of choice and taking responsibility. They must help the student to stand on his own feet and think with his head articulating with his mind.

This thus promotes eagerness to learn and achieve. Building him to muster self-confidence that he can do, have and be anything he dream of, without necessary scoring an alpha, and at the same time pressing him to always seek only the best and to strive toward thinking, doing, having and becoming more and better every day is the most important attribute of the ideal or model education, teacher and methodology.

We have talked about patriotism. How does it fit in the mix? We have seen backsliding patriotism on the part of the learned citizens than on the part of the unlearned. We have recently seen how local people sponsor or support the foreign football clubs than their local clubs. While indeed the foreign clubs do better than our local teams, but how do you grow them when you undermine them? Recently a big event happened in the country and the nation was rocked in series of national competition here in Dar es Salaam not in Spain or England! Barcelona played against Real Madrid, Liverpool played against Manchester United, and Chelsea played against Milan etc. The whole city was rocked in a frenzy of festivity, fans paying huge sums of money in support of their dear clubs. Then surprise, well—shock rocked the author when he attended one of these matches. He was shocked to find no Rooney or Messi or Drogba on the pitch. Were these clubs the real Real-Madrid's or Chelseas? No sir! The teams playing in Dar es Salaam, Tanzania, were not the real Reals, Milans, Mancheters or Chelseas. No! It was the local fans who competed wearing the shirts of the foreign club wear, not those of Yanga, Azam or even Simba.

Why not organize the competitions in the names of the local football clubs as it was in the past? In the past, under Mwalimu Nyerere' watch, through schools and media, we used to honor Yanga, Simba, Pan, Pamba, Maji-Maji, CDA, African Sports, Coastal Union, as well as the local music—among other products or services. I am ashamed, aren't you? Yes there may be mismanagement among our local clubs and the society as a whole, but that appreciation on its own doesn't save us from shame. What have we done about it? What has been the response from the politicians and academicians so far? In fact nobody cares or watches what is going on, for most are busy chasing the dollar—or fun!

The form of education we get has made us stoop so low so that in our inferior mentality we cannot see any good in ourselves. We cannot praise anything homemade. Anything homegrown is local and hence or synonymously, a poor product. What has our curriculum done to emancipate the mind at home? The current education is so quiet about freeing our people from mental slavery. Low self-esteem or mental slavery is the worst form of sickness the colonial education and slavery helped to sow in our people's minds. And without freeing our minds, an act which is itself the beginning—and the end—of learning, can we say our graduates are educated or learned? Can we say we truly have ideal scholars? If we go through schools and graduate without having our minds freed—which is indeed the essence of education—can we say then that our education is healthy or sound? You cannot innovate anything or even concentrate and accomplish a praiseworthy feat when you are a victim of very low self-esteem. This is the major source of failure in education system, in the workplace as well as in sports today.

Any performances: academic, financial or productivity at work can rarely be attained without self-confidence and self-love. The foregoing tragedy emanates from the lack of self concept or self awareness among our people. If our education was such a healthy endeavor it would help us answer all these questions. Let us face it. We have failed as nations and individuals to do self-searching fifty years now down the line. Failure to know who one is or what he ought to be and to be ready to pay the price has plunged many into persistent self-pity and inferiority complex. Many folks with low self concept, accept whatever is thrown at them. They feel no more pity to purchase and own the overused goods and services as a culture or norm, or even to accept grants and gifts in form of pocket change or food leftovers. Albeit, economic problems, Zimbabwe under Robert Mugabe, has often lived this spirit, rejecting to stoop that low!

It is because of persistent mental slavery and thereupon low self-esteem that it is a norm in such societies we termed a Sick Nations, to proudly buy, and wear, the secondhand brassieres or underpants we see all over the roadsides sold at throw away prices along the streets—and what surprises me is that nobody cares! You realize that this is indeed one example of low self- esteem. Without education or attention on self-concept, our education doesn't help each of our children to establish, identify and pursue his or her innate calling, and indeed to reclaim his or her humanity and dignity. Such students, who don't know or love who they are then go through their years in school without passion because they study what they didn't love or choose. Then they will get a job they didn't love or choose. They have no motivation or enthusiasm as a result. How can they? Enthusiasm, as we shall see, is derived from the Greek word *En Theos*, viz. *In God*. Our medium of contact with God is through ourselves, the inner self. If you cannot talk to your inner self you cannot find a calling that is in God, by God and from God, or *En Theos*. The lack of enthusiasm passion, motivation and determination is then passed on to the workplaces. Can you then wonder at why the multitudes of our graduates do nothing, or so little at work? Not me!

With our focus on the theory, also there's no or there is low level of practice among schools today. The worst part is that the theory or material in use is habitually of the long dead past! Having life of its own, education should—and always does—evolve to meet the fast changing world trends effectively and efficiently. Today there are more opportunities to learn from the streets today and in the corners of the city opposite the universities than is available in classrooms.

For instance take the business sector as an exemplar. Today we experience an unprecedented wave of the unlearned local entrepreneurs thriving more than the learned folks. It follows therefore that in turn, the self made street entrepreneurs have become better lecturers of business management in areas of their specialization than our scholars. No wonder many people today turn to them for business professional advice or scholarly solutions regarding business than their opposite number—the educated scholars. While we don't bless any attempt to belittle importance of education albeit its handicaps, we don't discourage any noble attempts to correct the structure or system of our education; or even the curriculum as a whole. We truly find that any attempt to offer any useful insights into our education or society in general as something that is no more less than a noble and dignified endeavor, and the effort urgent and holier like any life threatening emergency.

"THE CUNNING INTELLECTUAL DISCIPLINE OF SCHOOLMEN"
Our graduates today seem only to possess surface education—an education that is indeed "free of knowledge," in words of the shining Kenyan scholar, Professor P.L.O. Lumumba. Ellen G. White called it "The cunning discipline of schoolmen." Education is bigger than that. Life is better than that. With the present state of affairs, it is only the schools through innovative curriculum that should come to the rescue of our society.

What then is the intellectual cunning discipline of the schoolmen? It is tact, business language and poise, the face value of our scholars today. Most of our scholars today simply have tact, business language, polished speech and poise——paying lip service to their expectations. Whereas we encourage language proficiency, we care less about jargons, a tool that our schoolmen use as ploy to cover their insecurity. With jargons and tact, our men of education have become accomplished skillful manipulators, exercising manipulations of various sorts to get jobs and win promotions without actually having something tangible to contribute to the organizational goals of profitability, continuity and lasting impact and goodwill—among others. It doesn't represent the actual work done or delivery of results which is the distinguishing factor for true men of education. That's how thus far today this growing tradition among our men of education has become the liability to themselves and the society as a whole.

Indeed education should prepare and distinguish men and women of education from the herd by what—and how—they bring positive change and impact to any work and environment they are in. Indeed, Lafarge was brilliant: "While we value efforts and good will," quotes www.lafarge.com, "but we are convinced accountability is ultimately about delivering results"—feasible, accomplishable, applicable results." Notice that the foregoing statement is important because however impactful and probably cool this or any other lesson can be, but if there is no follow-up plan, the anticipated change tends to disappear in the daily routine of life. In his book *How Students Fail,* John Holt suggests that the so called successful students become cunning strategists in a game of beating the system—figuring out how to outsmart the teacher, how to get the answer out of the teacher, or how to fake the answer. To be sure, schools should be more humane places where students can fulfill their human potentials. With this in mind, schools should be more humane and learning itself human centered (Ornstein and Hunkins, 1998).

Again our education today tends to put more emphasis on competition amongst students, and as a result they end up competing with one another rather focusing on their own persons and goals. No wonder seldom do our scholar innovate anything. Few actually possess their own lives as a result. They tend to focus on what others have done better than what they personally can do better. This trend ruins creativity or innovativeness which is one of the pivotal abilities we expect from our graduates. The ideal graduate or scholar will have a certain distinguished character and attitude. He or she is a creative person who will enhance new ways of doing things. He will generate more and better products and services in terms of quantity and quality.

There's also a failure to inspire students and employees to desire the best and how to seek prosperity. Success or prosperity doesn't come as accident or by sheer luck. It often comes as a result of "no-return-no surrender!" attitude. Schools ought to place adequate attention on self-esteem and self-confidence and attention on patriotism or the love for oneself and one's country. and the current trend of rampant illegal emigration of our youth abroad, low family values, collapse of marriage as an institution, excessive drinking and cohabiting or single mothers' families and a growing nation of street children etc. alongside rampant poverty all manifest weaknesses in our education system.

There is also a complete lack of, or little attention on self-reliance, self-employment and entrepreneurship, and as a result we mould students to be employed—by others, and in incompatible and loathsome vocations and positions—for life. And as a result, they are never productive, prosperous or any happy, a curse they endure for the rest of their lives! This is the greatest tragedy for a truly learned person. No educated person should allow himself to be fixed in a box of thought pattern and income group. In retrospect, I can see how our education has also failed to address the weakness of our youth to conform and disgracefully giving in accepting to work only as second or third in charge leaving the top position to the foreigners. This has successfully helped to butcher the local folk's self-worth and therefore escalation of low self-esteem. And one more time, let me emphasize the question of self-esteem because nothing greater was ever accomplished by a person with low self-esteem. The foregoing weakness is a dark scar in our education system.

It is no accident therefore that schools today tend to produce people who put more emphasis on position than service they offer, focus on personal benefits than positive change they bring, and authority instead of duty they render. This then distorts the mindset of our graduates who assume the position of the boss or executive whose duty is to order others around. Our scholar assumes he deserves nothing but to rule others. He is not a front line member of staff. They are managers and directors. They are not people who actually mould pots from clay. They have reversed the order of things. Today the unlearned have actually become the potters and the factory owners as a few educated folks become buyers of the pots or serve as employees in the potter's factory. Surprisingly, the herd of the educated folk is happy to be hired in areas of managing others or even auditing and keeping books of accounts for the semi literate potter. Why? The enlightened illiterate has burning desire to succeed. He has a goal in life and has attitude of a winner on top of the fact that they are actually on the ground, in action, working, doing, not imagining things, building castles in the air, as most academic theorists, men of education do. And I write these lines without any sense of happiness, mind you! In fact I do so so tearfully.

We also see schools today putting more emphasis on technical skills, if any, than thinking, conceptualizing and articulating ideas into more defined thoughts or concepts and plans which then are interpreted into feasible tangible results. Our education system and curriculum have failed to promote or enhance both imaginative, innovative, hard working scholars who exhibit the spirit of working as a team—for themselves and the team. And they do not only lack ability to think about the problem and its solution, but also when they do so they are afraid to pass on their experiences, suggestions or thoughts. This is, in the main, due to inferiority complex springing from both slavery and colonial machinery viz., colonial education.

With rampant prejudice in the hiring and promotion at work, a mark in school or credibility is no longer the deciding factor. This has helped to further butcher the bewailing national self-esteem as it multiplies wrong prioritization, nepotism, gossip and backbiting in the society, turning our society into a people with low or complete lack of openness and therefore secrecy in all levels. We tend to say one thing in front of the camera and another behind closed doors. These are the weaknesses that our education must address.

Our people exhibit very low level in interpersonal skills. This failure to address the same interpersonal skills through curriculum in schools is not our best ally. We see also the weakness of considering "communication," as only a study for the specific degree courses such as management or marketing. Instead it should be a necessary course for every student in the country. Thus *Communication* as a term has been wrongly interpreted to be synonymous with information and not a study in "human relationships." Communication isn't a specialized training for special courses but rather a compulsory study for every vocation—and every student, employee and every profession in the land. With globalization we cannot live in isolation. Rather we are a diverse human society that demands everyone to come out and communicate with other people. Most of our people seem to prefer hiding their heads in the sand fearing to speak out before new introduces especially the foreigners. This is a handicap our curriculum has got to address.

Globalization doesn't really seem to favor people who can't communicate effectively, efficiently and freely. In our homes, the couple that communicates effectively, efficiently and freely tends to grow in love and wealth. An organization that has one of the best communication skills, wins loyalty from the customers. It is not the quality of the products or services or even the lower prices that attract and retain customers. The secret of the winning brand is in the people and how they communicate and relate first with one another and then with their suppliers and especially the customers.

Recently in one of the parliamentary sessions, a prominent academician and Member of Parliament and at the time Deputy Minister, Dr. Harrison Mwakyembe suggested that we have got to elect candidates who can speak up in the conferences. Among the culprits he specified, such as members of East African parliament, he indicated that very few Tanzanian representatives had actually spoken during the parliamentary sessions over the past decade. Let's face it. This is due, in the main, to the fright of speaking out in the public aside from low English language proficiency. It could also be due to lack of knowledge—or education—the education of a certain kind! As a result? We shut up. We zip our mouths and become great listeners. All said, one problem still emerges. And it emanates from the foregoing weakness. We are going to be selecting a candidate provided he or she can speak fluent English. The worst end-result is that of tilting all the top posts or positions to the children from the wealthy families—individuals who can afford English medium schools for their children. The most privileged are the Cambridge model scholars, though language proficiency is not necessarily a good indicator of one's academic excellence especially in a country like ours where English is a second or third language.

Mastering English language isn't synonymous to being educated nonetheless. Besides, not every fluent English speaker is a good communicator. Language isn't synonymous to communication as we are about to see. This is a great handicap for the cohesion of the nation as these criteria make such stations *No-Go-Areas* for the majority of students from what is popularly known as *Saint Kayumba* or the self-help community schools.

This is nothing but the survival of the fittest. It is the law of the jungle. If this trend goes on, it is likely to breed another big problem. It will guarantee the passing on of the spicy positions and power to a few on one hand, and ruination or damnation of the masses on the other. Are we prepared for such outcomes? Are we aware by doing so we are pulling down democracy building a sultanate? In the present condition, without heeding the foregoing admonition, we are not building a democracy but a monarchy which in the medium term will cause social strife and political disorder. These consequences are undesirable. They are unwelcome.

Our curriculum concentrates or concerns itself with the general knowledge as we least pay attention to specialized practical education. Indeed specialized knowledge is now weeping from being butchered.

Another failure, a failure that almost a sin of biblical proportions, is the tendency of forcing students to spend longer time more than necessary in schools and classrooms in particular. Schools have got to find a way to train up students in as short time as possible thus allowing them to be able to join the workforce as early as possible and at the time when they are active and daring unlike today when graduates join the workforce only old and slack and fearful to cross the lines—fretful of pushing the boundaries—incapable of initiatives or innovation and thus playing the game in order to remain in the payroll. The foregoing is also the offshoot of another problem we also identify as one of major weaknesses, i.e. having not only too many, but less relevant and unrelated incompatible studies. It is no wonder our workforce is too slow and less effective productively.

There is, in short, lack of coordination in the society. Whereas the adults place the blame on their children's indifference to education, the youth feel, as writes Maliyamkono, that education doesn't automatically produce result of direct practical benefits.[3] And they have justification as we are going to learn hereafter. We should start having in place, the specialized package or education that addresses personal vocational aside from the needs amongst the specific disadvantaged communities. The foregoing statement describes the weakness of overriding slow learners and almost a complete absence of a friendly environment for the mentally and physically handicapped. Because we cannot predict what the children will be in the future; we have got to give them equal chances knowing too well that some students develop during primary school and others during high school or college. But as well, we must not ignore special talents. Some children are simply out of ordinary. Treating them in the same way as the ordinary average students is not right, and it is to deny the nation the talents we badly need in areas of innovation or leadership.

Innovation, creativity and flexibility are also another weeping set of values emanating from the structure and system of our education. We have as a

---

[3] *The Promise p.442 by Professor Maliyamkono and Masson.*

result successfully failed to produce an innovative and creative or inventive people who can think out of the box, people who can consider other options in addressing the challenges we face. As a result our people tend to compete with one another or submit to the past, fearing to challenge the status quo: the systems, structures and circumstances we face in schools or at workplaces, private or public.

Educators should reinvent and embody various best practices in terms of teaching methodology and in various areas of the pedagogy. Teachers must as well be extensively trained in vast areas aside from their areas of specialization in order to be entrusted to sandwich the methodology with their best suited examples or styles through personalization of the content and methodologies—if students have to see beyond their present domain or vicinity.

What does the forgoing assertion mean? It means that, yes we have got to have the curriculum in place, but for a greater teaching or learning experience, teachers should be free therefore to supplement teaching with personal life's experience and the material of their own. Football stars like Ronaldo de Lima, Thierry Henry, Cluivert, Zidane, Messi, Ronaldinho etc all tended to play well when allowed to sandwich the game with their own natural talents. If we fail to recognize this secret we are working to ruin many talents and it isn't healthy for anyone. Sadly often individual teacher's experiences and knowledge are undermined and teachers are turned into parrots as a result students fail to learn from their instructors' valuable experiences—talents and experiences—we should be nurturing among the teachers. This is another advantage of informal instruction such as the one we are advocating for through this very book—and its twin sisters in this series. We believe that private instructors and practitioners have to be incorporated in the education system. This has an advantage of bridging the gaps in our compartmentalized knowledge typical in our schools today, and shortening learning process.

Right in this very book—alongside its twin sister books in this series—we are offering an addition to few existing sources of learning—and to specialized knowledge. Through this book and subsequent programs, we are offer specialized schooling, coaching and self-training intended to encourage more resources in such areas of innovative curriculum. Notice however that we aren't naïve or big headed to suggest that the existing education, its system or curriculum should be completely discarded, plucked out and dumped into the recycle bin. Yet we encourage guts. We advocate audacity to rethink about everything that needs changes. But while we encourage students to do recollection and summon their own experiences, we believe that "man must be told what to do by higher powers because man is incapable of thinking for himself—before he learns truth and be able to think for himself.[4]"

Therefore we encourage students to learn from their own experiences as well as experiences of the others, acquire knowledge through public and private libraries, colleges, schools, internet worldwide webs, etc but as well and probably most importantly learn to draw out, to develop from within themselves. Through this book, its series and subsequent training programs we give a helping hand. We don't simply write this book as a theory book. We endeavor to practically help students and youth to muster, and therefore master desire for prosperity and personal engagement. Desire for prosperity is a key component on the road to promotion of innovation, self learning and the spirit of hard work. We must help students and workforce to learn how to succeed. We know that everyone is a winner in his or her area—even those who are presently considered as downright-failures.

Schools and educators must instill in the students the desire to learn, and help them identify their potential, and eventually develop their faculties in order to be able to successfully generate wealth or whatever end they may choose. And they can only do so by conducting themselves in a certain way. Recognizing the fate of our graduates or scholars today, a group of brainwashed youth and adults who imagine classroom education alone can warrant their path to power, fame, recognition and wealth, we have got to emphasize the fact that education by itself is not enough. Indeed a learned person is not necessarily one who has an abundance of general knowledge—or number of degrees—for that matter but one who is manifested through his work.

It is neither the abundance of talent, nor availability of capital in any of its limitless forms, be that classroom education of financial capital, that one can succeed. We must help students to recognize and be able to exude from the fact that success is based upon deeper internal factors. We have got not only to make them see this fact but learn how to master it and benefit from it. Again that is where our conventional education goes wrong today. They profess attainment of knowledge and that they have a lot in abundance. What they lack is the ability to help their students to specialize

---

[4] *Source: The Da Vinci Code by Dan Brown p.268*

or organize that knowledge into some specific ways and forms to make it practically beneficial to themselves, people and environment surrounding them.

Let's take an example from the study of economics. It is not enough for a student of economics to possess knowledge for instance that money is medium of exchange. It isn't enough. The author studied economics to know what he is talking about. We need to organize the ideas into how money works and how it is attained; how it works and why must it be circulated to generate more money. To get to using money efficiently we need to bring an intangible part of why we need money or any other goal so badly enough as to be an obsession. We need to help the students mix emotional part of an equation in attaining the state of mind that is ripe and fitting to attract money, wealth or health and happiness or any end one may choose. Emotion is something that touches a person himself but rather a big failure on the part of modern day education which treats education itself on one hand, and students on the other, as inert soulless things—and the lecturers and teachers as stone saints. Yes it is intangible but education has life of its own. It has to be given food, nurtured and clothed to survive and thrive in a certain brand of life. This can best be done by a serious commitment to engage the students and the youth in revisiting what we need as a society—and how to get there. The students and educators as well ought to know that the greater the emotional attachment one has to a project, the lower the possibility that that person will stop pursuing it, and therefore the lower the possibility of failure.

A major student of economics himself, the author failed to find any tangible lesson on how to attract money or wealth and happiness or prosperity in any career or vocation one may choose in traditional theory of economics. It is no wonder many professional economists or graduates of finance are themselves poor, disoriented altogether, or both. The foregoing statement is correct even though it may turn out to be shocking news and astounding to both the reader and the economists themselves! And what about the university dons? After graduation, the author observed that we needed a faculty in economics that touched people's own lives directly. A faculty that would teach how households can learn to think and to practice, plan, make, retain and regenerate money—and of course having attained the money, acquire ability to use it sustainably (and) advantageously. With introduction of the concept of Michael Economics or Michonomics in the author's previous book, namely: What Makes People Rich and Nation powerful, we do hope some distinguished universities will pursue this idea and develop a separate faculty which shall take Michonomics to another level.

Yet, as for disadvantaged communities, and because I strongly believe in what I am going to say, let me go on record emphasizing that it is not facilities and facilities alone that determine success of a person or community in one area or another. discussing the factors behind wealth and prosperity, Wallace D. Wattles said in his great book *Science of Getting Rich* that: "Talented people get rich, and blockheads get rich; intellectually brilliant people get rich, and very stupid people get rich; physically strong people get rich, and weak and sickly people get rich..." So what's that thing that is not education or genius yet it governs growth and dynamics that govern prosperity? So education isn't enough, is it? Here is that thing: It is character. It is the moral strength as we will demonstrate through the proceeding chapters. Indeed, nothing else takes the place of character. That's why this book was written. It was written to put emphasis on the child upbringing—it was written to put emphasis on character and attitude—you realize, don't you? The proverbs rightly recommend thus: "Train up a child in the way he should go: and when he is old, he will not depart from it!"

Our education must therefore address the culture or traditions and ethos of a society as a plus or impediment to growth. Successes, or failures of another, of one group of people or one community in our society, whether tribal, religious, racial or regional, is not mainly because of the facilities or inert faculties available to it. There is a lot to do with culture and traditions of that society that are deep rooted and at heart in that society's ethos and mindset which are passed down from one generation to another. To transform any society, those in the decision making as individuals on one hand, and the policy makers cadre on the other, must go back to the basics. That's why we went to great trouble to prepare, in this series, a chapter on the principled universe—and submit to you that you go back and read it in the previous books such as A SICK NATION AND HOW TO HEAL IT. Provision of facilities to such a society today will not instantly generate the desired results unless we learn both from the internal factors for such underdevelopment as well as learn from more academically or financially advanced groups, communities or regions.

Talking about the Principled Universe and going back to the basics, we have tabled the accomplishment of the northern region in Tanzania, regions like Kilimanjaro and Arusha, regions whose successes when compared with the coastal or central regions as no accident—at all. Go to Kenya or

Nigeria and make analysis of why one region develops while another retrogresses. If we want to advance such least developed and disadvantaged communities let us watch closely what they do that those from other regions don't do and vice versa. Watch the ethos of such communities as compared to their opposite number. Why do some regions get prosperous and own almost all major businesses in the land; or even why the children from such communities perform at the top in classes as it is in politics and professions while others remain mediocre? Are they from a different species, race or society? Nay! We cannot go on learning from another hemisphere when lessons are tremendously abundant right here at home. All races, all regions, all religions, all tribes, all nations are the same except for their traditions and ethos. This is another area the education system on its own or with its arm in the arm of the government and policy makers, must look into and exercise its role as big brother in enhancing the overall mindset change or paradigm shift.

Our education is being stifled by another key foe—resource mobilization and distribution. In most non-developing nation, resources are skewed toward administration. Little is directed in research and education. We see as a result many among these elites running into politics. Why? Politicians are like the gods. Some people believe our leadership commits very little finances into our local education and hospitals because they send their children and patients abroad. Yes it could be an offshoot of the problems of our education here at home, but we have experienced a sustained escalation of fake degree certificates not only in the country but also from most of these degrees are from outside the country.

You recognize we are engaged in the analysis of the weaknesses in our education system—weaknesses that conspire to under develop our society in general—and specifically to devastate the hopes of the majority in our society. Let's face it. Yes, we have problems with financing our education; yes our economy is still young; yes we inherited problems of slavery and colonialism, yet the question is this: what have we done about it? What about our priorities as individuals or as a nation? That is why we need a kind of education that is conceived within our very needs, environment and weaknesses. That's why we need homegrown initiatives—initiatives that will change the thought pattern of the students as well as their teachers and the leadership as a whole. By leadership, I mean leadership at the household, business sector, educational and religious institutions and the society as a whole. We need an education or academic innovation that allows us to get more relevant material that promotes ability to work hard but above all getting more with less.

At the head of all our weaknesses in education sector, is the curriculum itself. Our curriculum is out-of-date and greatly dependent on foreign teaching materials. The curriculum itself and the books are seldom homegrown and therefore less relevant. What I am attempting to say is that we need to tap from our people's intellectual wealth, something we have in abundance but which we have allowed to rust out of lack of use. We pride ourselves of being rich in natural resources such gold and diamond and gas, much as we talk about Mt. Kilimanjaro, the wild animals, the islands of Zanzibar, but we forget the most important resource we have in Tanzania; and that is the brains, the and intellect mind of our people. This is where we have to invest heavily. This is where we must tap wealth from. And that's not all. The worst part of it, is when the alien materials are imported into the country whether free or not but intending to promote foreign interests through cultural and psychological means; to indoctrinate and domesticate another nation into a perpetual stooge that remains as a gold mine, punching bag or guinea pig and a dumping hole, and source of cheap labor and markets.

Is this, I mean the foregoing sad endings, realities or mere insinuation on the part of the author? Well, look at Haiti! Also analyze closely the natural wealth of countries like Tanzania or Congo D.R, in comparison to the situation on the ground. Please make reference to a book: *A Sick Nation and How to Heal it,* and give yourself a favor by taking time to listen to President Magufuli's speeches during his first 100 days in office!

I recently visited Mwananchi Communication offices, and I fell in love with their mission. Mwananchi is a leading media house in the country. Their vision reads thus: "To enrich lives of people and empower them to promote positive change in the society through superior media content." that's beautiful. That's why I am going to repeat it paraphrase: "To enrich the lives of the people by enhancing positive mindset and empowering them through the content that sets their minds free." That's what we should be doing as leaders of men, academics, educators, writers and authors: injecting positive ideas that set free the minds of our people and weeding out the opposite. Both the government and academics must see to it that we innovate, develop and promote internally homegrown more relevant educational materials that more adequately address our problems. Despite the need to learn from others we must come to terms with the fact that the teaching materials, methodology that are rarely home grown; the reading and teaching materials, the methodologies or in general the education system that is founded on the model or needs of another country will never solve problems of another country—or meet her needs.

As such, we have in place less relevant materials—and methodologies. It is due to our teaching methodologies that we see low inspiration to read and write books or practice things we learn in schools testing validity of how we can personally put them to use here at home. And this is no speculation from a clueless author. You can read more about the same in the great work by two distinguished men: Professor Maliyamkono and Mason.[5] Because of this need, Renaissance named the voluminous subject-matter of scholarship, Litterae Humaniores or, "the more human literature", the literature that humanizes. Connected with the low self-esteem and less meaningful priorities, we put more money in arts or music and sports than we put in education or specifically writing and reading books. It is the mindset that pervades the society in this country that we put more money in beauty or liquor drinking competition instead of developing skills or character or other more developmental agenda. This culture ought to change for otherwise we are about to turn the country into an *Entertainment Dance Hall* instead of a *Workshop*. Karl Marx was right warning us that; *"A society will collapse if it ceases to produce material wealth."*

But recognize that when we talk of our problems or weaknesses, the agenda at our hands doesn't end with knowledge of these weaknesses. It ends, or has its ends in addressing weaknesses in our society such as wrong priorities in the leadership, inaction and indifference amongst our people, mass laziness and business as usual, mass emigration from workplaces and classrooms by the youth, silent teachers' boycott on one hand and helplessness on the part of the students; it ends in taking off from abject poverty that pervade our society and ultimately forging forward to growth and prosperity. These changes we dream of—the changes we crave, deserve and demand—cannot be realized without having home grown impetus in place. We see therefore a need for new teaching approach and especially infusing superior character and secondly creativity first in schools but also among homes and workplaces. We see great need to teach practical things far from general knowledge. Education must focus on making life better, longer and meaningful for—well, the majority!

---

[5] *Source: The Promise page 439*

There is also the problem of double standards following the double syllabi curriculum. Use of, or duality in, the medium of instructions viz. Kiswahili and English; a sudden shift from Kiswahili to English at the secondary level for the Tanzanian public schools plus regional educational infrastructural imbalance has steadily helped to hand over the control of education, professions and politics into the hands of the few. These are few regions and families that have access to quality education as far as pupil to teacher or pupil to facility ratio is concerned. If not well addressed, this imbalance is likely to, if it has not yet perfected, a modern day monarchy, as the masses are turned into subjects or slaves in their own countries. In the long run social discontentment will cause unrest and hatred between the privileged and the deprived, a contention whose repercussion I cannot dare evaluate out of fear of making them real! Subject to the foregoing arguments—arguments we have laid down justifying that education is only accessible by the few—as a society we end up with no option but placing towering interest on the students who are learned from foreign colleges abroad. This ends up in the same mess of serving the fatty jobs on the silver platter to only those educated overseas. Such syllabi as Cambridge tend to alienate citizens and carve up people between potential senior executives and mainstream employees; or even between the leaders and the led, the lords and the squatters.

The foregoing weakness creates another problem. It clusters the powers to influence education and who gets educated or hired or appointed how and where, how much one is paid etc, in the hands of the few, their families and cronies. And that's not all. One of the major goals of education is to free the society. With the foregoing worrisome looming consequence, we foresee the enslavement of the masses by the few. And this is not any healthy. Yet, whereas the academicians may seem to be pointing fingers to the politicians concerning political racketeering and nepotism, I want to go on record blowing a whistle about something that is often in the shadow— and therefore least discussed. We sniff a growing tendency of academicians passing on the academic opportunities into the hands of a very very narrow group of close relations or protégés. Close observations show that just as politicians, some academicians just tend to exercise discrimination in education thereby determining where one gets in the field of education. Now because these few privileged too themselves gain opportunities both in politics and workplaces, indeed with academic clout and political maneuver, these few academicians and politicians have helped to alienate the masses from the two most important systems or structures that decide the nature of their livelihood.

Not only that we have a very low access to books, but also our education system doesn't promote reading and writing culture. Failure to seek self-development, self training and self-advancement after one graduates and especially when one gets employed is connected quite closely with the foregoing weaknesses. Upon graduation very few, of the few, of our graduating youth strive for self-advancement. Reading or writing isn't their concern anymore. We need to promote reading and writing. Reading and writing must be given a place in the final credibility. We must make reading and writing part of culture not only among our meager elites but essentially the society as a whole.

Here again is another weakness that stands tall in the throat of our education pipe that it is already choking the future of education and the nation as a whole. And this is the confusion of the meaning of school. What is a school? Do we know? Schools today are a business venture like any other: a restaurant, a hotel, or even an alternative to a shop. Any wealth-hungry man opens a school—which is not a bad thing—except for what purpose. Defining school plainly as a training institution, college or university as http://dictionary.reference.com/browse/school does, a mistake many do, is unhealthy to a society like ours. A school is best defined as "a learning center for larger community; it reflects the norms and values of the community, and the community sees the school as an extension of the community (Ornstein and Hunkins (1998, p. 160)."Education has become an exorbitant service cutting off the majority from access it—and hence blocked from such an invaluable transformational social service. Private schools have become champions in discriminating students from a certain income group, and thus the school fees are higher and impossible for an average Tanzanian.

And this isn't my imagination, or insinuation. It was made public just recently (2013-2014) when President Kikwete addressed the school administration at Feza School. We have mentioned that education is skewed towards the few. We have, as well, experienced thereupon how the structure of our education has helped to serve the top positions on the silver platter to the few, positions amongst the corporations, public services, as well as in politics. It is also almost sinister to assume that these few privileged run into politics either because that's where the major piece of our national pie is skewed, or even to protect their ill-gotten loot, thus we see such a handful of the people amongst us who tend to professionally trek into politics. This is not, and should not be, unexpected under these circumstances.

A well learned graduate, nonetheless, is the one who having established his calling and thus having chosen his vocation, would not waste his many years of studying, say, the human body, or making or running a business, medicine, laws, or rocket science, and then waste his time seated in the big airy building doing nothing whether that building is a parliament or hotel, if not, once again, for financial benefits accruing to it. I write this because it is part of the mix. But the former is a strong reason when put on the beam balance. A well learned person wouldn't put money first when it comes to matters of vocation or humanity, or especially he wouldn't fail to make money through his own imaginative capability elsewhere in one's line of chosen vocation instead of opting for a do-or-die battle over the contents therein the ballot box. We have seen learned men and women who incite people to fight and kill and die only to gain, or retain power! Such a person is not the ideal scholar.

The foregoing argument isn't intended to undermine the differences in, or freedom on the part of our people's callings or choices of vocations such as politics; or even discouraging majority from attempting their luck from the pot of gold elsewhere though? No! I actually advocate professional fluidity or mobility. Yet there's something I do not understand—something that is almost sinister—when a person spends years seeking a PhD and then comes back to contest for a political position that is far detached from his line of vocation. We see two things here. This gentleman is either ill-educated, or there is a serious malady in our education system and society in general.

The source of all these weaknesses can be traced, in the main, from human ego and personal interests. But it is also due to the mindset that is slowly thriving amongst some individuals amongst these institutions. It is assumed that some of our academicians and politicians believe no one outside their established circles can contribute advantageously to the establishment. This is erroneously wrong, and to continue thinking in this line is a mistake of horrendous epidemic proportions. Our curriculum today has to put more emphasis on the society-centered interests thus taking into consideration the needs of the society and all social classes. And thus not only schools but also households and workplaces must become change agents—agents of social change and institutions for reforms. Gender imbalance is another area we must address. We have few women in some professions as are few men in others. Take professions such as nursing. We look at the male nurse with contempt. We have, for instance, fewer female engineers as we have many female front desk attendants and customer services agents.

We see art, and artists themselves, receiving generous endorsement and sponsorships from our leaders in the government and in the business sector, while the same people seem to be less enthusiastic when it comes to sponsoring, let alone recognizing local efforts or innovations in more developmental areas such as science or literature—truth be told! By innovation here I mean new ideas or usages; new ways of doing things or applying or turning ideas into tangible products or services. If we don't encourage reading and writing culture we are not helping doing away with dependence on foreign materials. To be well learned, to be genuine scholars, a country's population needs homegrown materials. this is the handicap we must address. Yes, we know even in the western societies today the present generation reveres artists and sportsmen. But we can't simply cut and paste anything they do.

We must recall that that's why the "lost generation" bug is prevalent today. Must we not remind ourselves the greatness of the last few generations in the western society? Must we not remind ourselves that it all probably emanated from the reverence the society placed on thinkers, and not entertainers? Must we not recall the reverence of Socrates, Plato, Shakespeare, Emerson, among others or even Mwalimu Nyerere here at home? And when I talk about such reverence, I am not exaggerating. This was documented by Dale Carnegie: According to The Encyclopedia Britannica, Leo Tolstoy was, during the last 20 years of his life "probably the most venerated man in the whole world." For twenty years before he died—from 1890 to1910—an unending stream of admirers made pilgrimage to his home in order to catch a glimpse of his face, to hear the sound of his voice, or even to touch the hem of his garment. Every sentence he uttered was taken down in a notebook, almost as if it were a "divine revelation."[6]

Let us consider English literature. Our dependence on Nigerian or Kenyan authors, or minds, minds such as Chinua Achebe or Ngugi wa Thion'go let alone European or American novelists doesn't much help our education. Local books bear more relevant material and context more relevant to the lives of our people notwithstanding the need to devour every book from every society. Yet we need books and material that our people easily relate to first, before they can find inspiration to read from outside the box.

---

[6] How to Stop Worrying and Start Living Rev. Ed pp. 99-100

That's why we need to promote local writers and their works notwithstanding a challenge to improve access or availability of publishing services and quality of the local works. As I write this statement I know the challenge I will face from most of my readers who are pro-modernity. Not everything more modern is equally more relevant to every society.

Furthermore, lack of training and development plus adequate salary benefits make teaching as a profession an undesirable career or vocation of last resort. Yes we have shortage of teachers for sciences, we experience students opting for business studies out of misinformation and failure to help them to identify their calling or compatible vocations aside from the deep-rooted mindset for quick fix. It is no wonder many underperform even with great abilities when it comes to paperwork, albeit itself a major weakness amongst our men of education. The performance of graduates should be judged on criteria that relate to their ability to respond flexibly, creatively and competently to work and national or development agenda with the needs of the employer and the nation's at heart.[7] Truly school graduates and candidates should be judged by skills and character they exhibit beyond the classroom examination results.

Another weakness we have got to address is the fact today most of our instructions are limited to the lectures which are themselves more theoretical. Without the engagement of the students themselves in the actual learning process, practice and in thinking and actual execution of the same planned goals, we are killing inventiveness and confidence among the people to innovate and the aspiration to be self-reliant or self-employed. This alone calls for participation of the people in the planning and executing any such growth agenda both in the curriculum and on the ground.

Astoundingly, the problem our education faces is not only quantity of education available to our students, but also the quality of the intake in terms of the material or content. This is mainly due to the teaching materials or content available being less relevant to our society's needs and the needs or challenges of now as we highlighted above. The schools ought to revolutionalize the frame of mind of the future nation. This can be done through the reorientation of the mindset of the children. Education must address the major challenge the nation is facing, challenges such as low

---

[7] *Adapted from The Promise P.426:*

patriotism and low self-esteem, and give students the ability to forecast their future—and toward some form of direction. If anyone doubts such a need, let me repeat that it is because of low love for the self and the nation that we experience brain drain mainly abroad aside from our scholars and professionals trekking into politics. It is for lack of direction that the number of school dropouts is on the rise. I recently attended a parents-teachers meeting at Barbro Johansson Model Girl's Secondary School—because Princess is instructed there—and one and major concern from parents was to address the same. Student should yes, be prepared to educated themselves well while in school, but also to get prepared for life after school.

Furthermore failure to establish individual's needs is eating in the education system and therefore the society's prospects for growth and development. Education as an entity on one hand, and the educators on the other hand; or the society as a whole, must learn to identify and meet custom-made educational needs and programs thereof. Failure to meet needs of the other stakeholders in education in the country such as the students themselves, households, the business sector, the government, development partners and the general public leads to another failure namely failing in prompting parents and governments to rally behind our schools and education as a whole or the workplace growth agenda. In conjunction with the needs of the individual, are the needs of the community such as leadership skills. Leadership as a skill must be taught to all students in our schools. It is a tool toward self regulation or self control and ability to rallying others towards a common goal, or even to push the boundaries—when it is necessary.

There's also a failure which should be near the head of the list: failing to teach family values and initiation of the youth into adulthood. Our youth must appreciate their responsibilities as they turn to adulthood. They must be prepared to begin to be responsible citizens. Such responsibilities include their civic roles as citizens: hard work and patriotism and safeguarding the national integrity against sectarian interests, the values which are pivotal for any nation's cohesion and advancement. Our curriculum must bequeath responsibilities to the youth as social individuals as well as a group. With the sense of the African extended family, and yes our level of development as a society, we must learn to appreciate and fulfill our roles as sons or daughters, brothers or sisters and parents i.e. fathers or mothers or guardians; as well as to recognize that they are someone's neighbor recognizing that we affect one another. They must exercise these roles at one point in time. Therefore they must learn to appreciate their roles in the family or community and society in general.

Indeed, "Show me a country with strong family ties or unit and I'll show you the strong and powerful nation," so aptly quotes the book What Makes People Rich and Nations Powerful. Our education, thereupon, has got to transform the thought-pattern of our people and the mindset amongst the elites so that they are willing—and able—to seek and promote new ideas, especially ideas from the local folks. New ideas work as the engine for growth. The academicians must be brought up in such a way that they will render to the nation the service of seeking and acquiring ideas from outside the traditional school or academic settings. It is important to do so in order to unravel the problems we face today and equip students and the nation as a whole to meet the future with optimism and confidence.

Other areas we must not forget include interdependence and cooperation, self respect, HIV/AIDS and gender based violence leading to single parent families, cohabiting and a nation of the street children which together deepen social disorder leading to a slaving or no state country in the likes of Somalia or Haiti. In short, education has to address family problems, leadership, skills in dealing with people, collective responsibility, punctuality, innovation, etc. It must address the immediate relevant needs of the community such as HIV/AIDS, drugs and addiction to alcohol or nicotine, migration and environmental studies and importance of ecosystem or biodiversity now that we experience disproportionate mass slaughter of wildlife such as the rhinos, elephants and fish and vegetation and rivers and the ecosystem as a whole. We have many borders and interactions in terms of cross border movements and intermarriages and therefore a need to teach the sense of diversity and unity as a nation regardless of our differences and backgrounds.

Our curriculum must as well instruct our youngsters in the sources and solutions in such areas as religious and sectarian extremism. Hence our curriculum must impart self-esteem, self-love and self-confidence to the youth notwithstanding the importance of the love for others. English language is one of such barriers in countries like Tanzania and thus needs close attention and reintroduction amongst all levels in our schools. This is an important endeavor today than before especially with globalization and EAC at hand.

Other areas we must emphasize include rejecting poverty in all its forms—spiritual, moral, and mental, cultural and material poverty. Talk about innovative curriculum, our curriculum must impart and promote the desire to excel, but as well the sense of living a balanced life as individuals and community, a life that is in harmony with oneself and the people and environment around us. Our people, our society, must hate suppression and seek to reclaim their personal as well as national dignity. They should therefore be taught how to be self-reliant and self-employed. Thus they should as well learn to acquire such attributes as being self-starters, hard working, creative and innovative. Our education must address punctuality and time management.

Education must also serve as a means to build moral fiber and enable broader freedoms in terms of thoughts, deeds and choices of station in life. By doing so, we raise the national income. So far the national income is a sum total of all households incomes. In Tanzania family problems, drugs, drinking problem, education in immigration and naturalization and training in self-esteem and self-confidence are key since such aspects exist. We have to promote patriotism and address timidity. This is one of the symptoms of low self-confidence and poor self expression. In it there is lack of self-esteem too.

Furthermore, the Tanzanian youth needs to master such other qualities as abilities in dealing with people, how to muster self-esteem or self-confidence which together work as tools to master introversion—timidity and indifference, nervousness and apprehension—signs of fear or low self-expression and very low patriotism common among our candidates today. Importantly, the Tanzanian youth must be taught to be open minded, outgoing and a little carefree in their interactions. Oftentimes, timidity comes from fear of making mistakes—and therefore there arises a need to train them to focus on the big picture and that we learn through mistakes. Failure to deal with people hampers a person's natural ability to sniff opportunities and having identified them, to make the most of whatever he pursues, much as he ought to be conscious to fault. Thus our curriculum has to teach how to acquire open mindedness, ability to interact positively and become self starters, outgoing and self confident as individuals and society as a whole.

Our people must curb shyness which comes from fear of doing mistakes. The author knows a few colleagues who have managed to be stars at one time or another in their own fields. Not necessarily that such outgoing characters, and I beg to mention a few names here, such personalities as Idd Wangea, Kibamba Deus, Charles Kimune, Diodorus Buberwa Kamala P, or Zitto Kabwe—among others—were top students in their respective classes, nor that they were genii as compared to others who now remain in obscurity. No sir! That's not what differentiates such personalities from the herd. What differentiates them was nothing but their bravery, self-confidence and a knack on dealing with people. When the uninitiated person finds such guys at the top in their respective chosen vocations wonders, believing they were genii in their respective classrooms! Such personalities are not necessarily so!

As such, from henceforth this analysis seeks to identify such a knack as genius itself! Such self confident personalities can bend the situations into their favor. They can swiftly influence others and win them, rallying them behind their way of thinking—or votes! And the author knows it is true and urgent because he went to school with a couple of such personalities. We are born endowed with every capability to have, do and be who we are born to have, do and be but we seldom think of what we have at our disposal, always thinking—instead—of what we lack as observed Schopenhauer. The catch is this: wealth and health are opportunities for everyone who knows they come with responsibilities. Indeed, when the youth have, or feel the sense of responsibility, the society shouldn't worry an inch!

Our curriculum must therefore address and promote morals, ethics, good thinking, better choices and better and broader freedoms such as freedom of thought, deed and choices of station in life. They must be trained and induced to be wealthy as individuals and households. The youth or our students and society in general must be disciplined and to be orderly. If we can induce individual students to be responsible, hard working and wealthy individuals we will have made the whole nation wealthy. Besides, as we have already seen, national income as a study is no rocket science. It is simply a sum total of all individual family incomes.

In a nut shell, here are other areas education in Tanzania and any country ought to address through schools and workplaces include: Family problems, drugs abuse, drunkenness, self neglect and faith in the future and hope for better tomorrow. We badly need orientation in patriotism and immigration. Did I say badly? How badly? With excessive emigration to SA or abroad to Europe and America; and with a great number of naturalized citizens and poverty, there is very low self- esteem in the country We know people who say they had better be born as dogs abroad than live as a human in the country. Thus they badly need training programs in self- esteem self-confidence or generally self-love.

There are also very low levels of thinking and putting imagination to work amongst our people. Most of the top organizations are branches of big corporations abroad. That's where all marketing or even production strategies are sourced. There is, for instance, the question of land use and natural resources. As compared to our neighbors such as Kenya or Rwanda, Uganda or Burundi, we in Tanzania have plenty of land. We must innovate and develop different faculties and enact policies that will ensure the land and natural resources are not only in the hands of our people but also that they are using the vast resources we have in possession to our advantage. We must develop curriculum that develops love and expertise for the agricultural sector in order to own and benefit from the land resources we have in plenty. We have forests, and in the same line we have vast water bodies and coastline, we must as well teach lumbering and attention to forests as well as fishing as part of land use.

There is also a critical culture of introversion and low resilience and being too good to foreigners in our society. Much as we must address fair play, yet to address aggressiveness or competitiveness, or call it assertiveness, is critical. Related to the above, we need to address is motivation amongst our staff. Many employers in the country lament about motivation among our people. They say so justifying why they employ Kenyans and Ugandans beside Asians. We cannot sit back and keep on watching our people graduating with first classes in engineering or economics or business or engineering but fail to deliver as top executives at work and so finding themselves placed under the *hardworking and focused industrious* Kenyan, Ugandan, Indian or Rwandan not to mention the Westerners. We see our people saying come what may. They may leave a job without fighting back or in areas such as sports let foreign team win without striving for the second try. We see order waning. We see people throwing away wastes anywhere; they attend natural calls along the highway. We cut trees like we are crazy. We cherish charcoal and find little or no force to invest in solar power or biogas and wind energy. Our environment ecosystem and the wild animals are on the brink of extinction on everyone's watch but no one cares! Our curriculum and the education system must address these social and environmental challenges should our nation rise back on her knees and stand on her feet once again, and yes once again regain dignity we had during Mwalimu Nyerere's era.

We need to set standards for our youths in terms of living standards and wealth potential. When by way of our actions and achievement, set high standards for them, we set new heights for our people. We need to emphasize ethics and morals that the good religions teach albeit the call for secular education among our schools. If you cannot prepare and set a younger generation in order when they are still young, it will be hard to repair them when they grow up, hard like attempting to mend a broken mirror. Haven't we been admonished to "Train up a child in the way he should go and when he grows up he shall not depart," says the Proverbs. Indeed discipline is akin to diligence: "sees thou a man diligent in his business? He shall stand before kings," so says proverbs 22:29. You recognize that you are engaged in identifying and analyzing the challenges the schools and employers and the society as a whole face if we have to enhance change.

Here is another key point. High national incomes help nations to foot their bills—expenditure on administration and investment in development. But economies are transformed by the people themselves. We have recently discovered gold and gas and oil. We have discovered uranium too. How are we responding to the needs of exploiting these treasures? Shall we keep sending raw gold abroad or fill the booming mineral and gas industry or uranium sites with foreign job seekers when our people are on the streets? With reference to tanzanite, a study we have analyzed through this series, we reckon that no country ever developed by surrendering its resources to the foreign businessmen who employ foreigners in top jobs while setting aside sewage and cleaning or wage labor as the only standard occupations fit for the local people. Botswana, Uganda, Rwanda, China, Brazil, India, the Tigers, even the British American colony known today as USA provide evidence of the undisputed role of people in their own state of affairs: peace, cohesion, self-advancement and prosperity, individually and nationally—one way or another.

Here now comes one of the most critical challenges our curriculum should address: religious sentimentalism, fundamentalism or radicalism, realizing that we are not immune to the ominous experiences from the recent events in the CAR or Nigeria, Somalia, Iraq, Pakistan etc... compared with the tribal or ethnic communities such as we see in Kenya, Uganda, Rwanda and Burundi, societies that as such have to educate their youth about dangers of ethnic divisions and how to mitigate such dangers, we in Tanzania face a significant element of religious divide within our society today. Presently we see escalating distrust and hatred between our major religions. Surprisingly, it is no longer exercised behind closed doors. Religious tolerance has waned so badly. The support the religious radicalism is getting from abroad and within seems to be escalating both in scale and sophistication. Such problems must be addressed by the roots

Schools are responsible for the development of young minds. They must teach students to hate violence and reproach extreme religious fanaticism by the roots. Schools must find ways to address the history of our country in the face of religions illustrating how what we have in common cunts more than our differences. We must endeavor to educate our people that God loves all of us and the fact that all our major religions are but imports. If religions don't help us live longer, better and harmoniously amongst ourselves, then we must come to the realization that like any imports, imports packaged outside the country for the benefits of their own manufacturers, then we need to repackage them here at home, filtering them to suit our realities, and bring to light the facts that are seldom brought to our attention. Such enlightenment like the fact that China and India form the majority of the earth's population on earth as an assemblage, but that the assumption that the two or three major religions here at home are the only religions on the earth is in fact simply misleading and thereof help to water down radicalism. To realize wholeness, the children and the youth must be helped to develop a sense of a balanced living as individuals and society as a whole. Our education or curriculum must sow peace and harmony not only within individuals but as well within the society and the environment in which we live. To be at peace with oneself and the others around one another, the students must be nurtured to be able to respect others and manage their own persons.

Very cautiously, we must plainly educate our children to respect one another despite diversity in terms of regional or tribal differences, races, religions etc. While we cannot enforce intermarriage among our people, yet in order to bring about harmony, peace and unity, we shouldn't discourage it. I believe probably the time is now when the government must work to prove we are a secular nation. We must address the fact that religious conflicts are more lethal than even tribal wars. And here is why. Religion is an emotional subject. And as such when people are emotional they know no limit. This is indeed the reason why we need new insights into religious education. Secondly, such conflicts, religious conflicts, are often financed by local machines with commercial or political interests and fueled by foreign powers with global neo-colonial interests. That's why it is so easy for a small scale religious dispute to befall as an international war.

We must find ways to review and educate our masses how millions of people die each year due to religious conflicts than from any other conflicts or even malaria and HIV/ AIDS put together It is worthwhile to report here that what the author has written for Tanzania, the same we have written for

Nigeria, Egypt, or even the Middle East and Ireland. And as such we need to start this task now not later, for otherwise the society will be faced with calamity of horrendous epidemic proportions— if we deter or delay. How urgent? One of my readers will ask and it is a good question. We must indeed focus our attention on the children and the youth as the previous chapters in this series indicated (please read A Sick Nation and How to Heal it). We must focus our attention upon the children for otherwise if we cannot transform them now, when they grow up it will be almost impossible to transform them then, like repairing a broken mirror!

Besides, in a generation when mediocrity is praiseworthy, and thus prevalent and on the rise, when productivity is falling, when no students or employees and our children at home cannot do anything without serious supervision, we need to instill and implant in them the moral code or ethics that will guide them along the way. And this is the meaning of education, the purpose and the role of education. As for the parents, schools, the workplaces, places of worship and the governments, if you don't buy into this idea, and so letting your children to blow their own brains off, I'll not of course be delighted by it especially when now we have placed an alternative remedy before you. But there's nothing I can do more—that's your choice. Their lives are in your own hands now. There is no other remedy to their problems. As such, we must throw a challenge to ourselves as a society by asking such questions—as we have paraphrased from Bob Proctor's—I must say—magnificent book, You Were Born Rich—:*1. How have we been conditioned? 2. Why are we getting the results we are getting? And 3. Finally; how can we change our way of thinking; or our conditioning (?)* I cannot agree more with Bob Proctor that: "That is not an easy thing to do. It takes much discipline. It takes a tremendous desire. It takes a lot of diligent effort, which is the probable reason so few people ever actually change. There's much more to yourself than meets the eye. And you must apprehend this "hidden factor of your personality,"[8] as Bob Proctor calls it.

The foregoing statements envelope one of the most critical challenges our education faces, namely, the teachers themselves. Our academicians must learn to work with—and within—the society rather than work from without. They must learn to connect with the society rather than working primarily with the books of references which sadly the masses consider to

---

[8] *Adapted from You Were Born Rich by Bob Proctor*

be a little less relevant, less meaningful. But we know that both the lecturers and policy makers have been schooled under the same system the circumstances seem to hold responsible. They cannot, therefore, swiftly be dissimilar from the mindset or shortcomings from the education system that perfected them, can they? The attitude or even the proficiency of a person can seldom be dissimilar to the shortcomings of the system or curriculum itself. As such, the quality or concentration of the teachers in the classrooms, and therefore their motivation and impact in the classrooms are not immune to faults, are they? This is question one ought to ask oneself. For instance, one cannot fail to hold responsible the system that allows professional academicians who keep trekking into politics or into petty businesses from their traditional specialization on which the nation has invested so massively.

We all know people who are schooled here at home and later receive government scholarships abroad to specialize in every other rare profession you may think of: medicine, laws, economics, engineering—you name it—yet on return, they end up opening up bars and guest houses—the quick money making machine, so they say. The author is heartened by the fact that there is also an internal will and efforts are underway to air the weaknesses in our education and to amend the syllabi. But to transform our education we need to work on our mindset incredibly hard. Success in this area is key, if positive transformation has to take place. It is therefore important to teach leadership skills amongst schools and at workplaces in order to prepare new leaders. Generally speaking, whereas yes, we can reform the old leaders, but: "The world will have to look for a new timber for its leadership (if it has to develop once again).[9]"

With reference to the foregoing, our education system or curriculum must start focusing afresh on teaching as a profession itself. Teaching has to be dignified and projected as any other professional job through better pay, social capital, and promotion into other services such as political appointments or priority into leadership and job or professional mobility unlike today when to be a teacher is considered as a professional prison cell. To mitigate this challenge, the government and private school owners and society as a whole must consider and place some sort of not only economic but also social capital on the teaching profession. We must

---

[9] *Think and Grow Rich unabridged edition Embassy Books page 118 by Napoleon Hill*

together rethink the way of improving the pay, not baselessly but based on calculation of minimum requirement by a teacher and his family and generally the upkeep and academic as well as social economic advancement of the individuals engaged in education process and sector. We all know teachers make better leaders even when compared to the military or journalists who it seems to me have won graces in the eyes of the appointing authorities, such that they get more appointed roles in the country today. Teachers must be trained and in turn they must train in areas such as self-development, in order to be able to promote professional mobility and make it possible for the teachers to constantly seek personal growth than decay in the bottom of the bottle drunk out of low self worth and helplessness. They must be made fluid so that they can relocate when they need to in order to make teaching an enthusiastic job rather than a German chamber.

One of the most important elements is that teaching as a profession should not be considered as a moral duty but instead as an exciting career. Recently in Tanzania teachers who demonstrated boycotting working conditions for teachers helped to put that question into perspective. They rallied holding banners that displayed the slogan: "Ualimu sio Wito. Ni Kazi." That is to say teaching is a vocation or career like others. It isn't work of charity or volunteer services. Teaching must be made a respected job, and not as vocation of last resort. It should be a dream career. An interest in children is a sine qua non to teaching as a profession. Teachers must be groomed to love both the children and the nation as a necessary condition for dedicated teaching career. Of profound importance we need to keep seeking and engaging teachers in innovation and delivering new ideas—ideas they too, benefit from.

Talk of innovation, there must be an innovative way of according teachers with privileges in such areas as the parliamentary special seats or several committees which are now filled by racketeer businessmen and petty political bourgeoisie. Such privileges should be made available for teaching personnel as incentives. Teachers must be given promotion on regular basis in terms of stay and longevity at work. They must be considered for several leadership positions as a priority after a certain number of years of service. To ensure this happens efficiently we must encourage self development, personal growth and continued desire for success among teachers. Indeed we must overturn the old slogan: *Ualimu Ni Wito;* which meant teaching is just a duty and moral obligation and not a profession. Today "Ualimu sio Wito; ni Kazi;" teaching is not a duty but an exciting career. Teaching as a profession must necessarily be made to be looked at and indeed made to be a respected vocation. Recently BBC announced that it has been observed that in Scandinavia, almost out of 30 people applying for jobs, one chooses teaching not as last resort but as a dream career or vocation. This is not exhaustive and the author recognizes that it is just a drop in the sea, but of profound importance is to seek new ideas.

To transform education as a whole we need qualified and dedicated teachers. We know we needed whatever teachers that would be available during independence but a herd of near failures that opt for teaching as last resort cannot take the nation forward. Here you cannot point fingers to the teachers we have in place. It is the administration that can change the situation by offering incentives to great teachers and people who have a calling for teaching and train them as the government replenishes their demands. Today we treat the needs of the teachers as the last resort when it comes to remuneration. And that's why we can have candidates of last resort opting for teaching. That's why our budget on education is not that thick, itself directed to recurrent than innovative areas. That's why we have a world of work before us if we have to develop as individuals and the society as a whole. And I speak this with true feelings because of my love for teaching as a profession, aside from what it does to the society.

Also the space or facilities, classrooms and the teachers themselves—their numbers and class in relation to the numbers and needs of students—especially among public schools all conspire to stifle the quality of education. Another inherent factor is the priority the government, the household, the business sector and the society as a whole each singularly place on education illustrated by the budget each sets aside for the same which work to stifle morale on the part of the educators and the students. Concentration or preparations on the part of the teachers and the time dedicated to teaching leaves a lot to be desired. The number of our scholars trekking into politics does more than validate the foregoing assertion. Yes addressing the budget we set aside for education and wages for teachers and scholars in the field can add social value and dignity to education as a discipline and to the educators themselves aside from working environment and monetary gains thereby attracting top performers from all fields into teaching, making it possible to regain and retain some of the academic migrants, but let the reader note that a checkbook can never solve all human challenges.

And this analysis or conclusion isn't simply the author's own good guess. I mean this isn't a petition that is designed and signed by only this author, no? Read for yourself Professor Maliyamkono's wonderful assessment of our education in his magnificent book The Promise.[10] In words of professor Maliyamkono: *"All of these short comings have served to marginalize the Tanzania student over the ten years."* The fact that we have inherited the curriculum and our elites therefore trained under the British or American curricula has helped to sow the mindset among our scholars and the administration that to succeed in education and any other thing we have to cut and paste programs from abroad. The worst part is that we have been conditioned to believe that we cannot do anything meaningful on our own unless it is sourced from abroad. The point is this: Even when they aren't necessarily discouraged, homegrown efforts aren't encouraged. The situation is so deeply rooted that even the administration and the scholars themselves proclaim that we can't do anything on our own.

And what's the role of the government in education? The government must take leadership role—not managerial tasks. It should coordinate and support such efforts as one being presented to you now. But the failure is also a result of how the government itself is structured. We find it to be a little troublingly curious to have different ministries watching over the education and youth affairs sectors. Education across all levels and administration of the labor and youth affairs should be under or coordinated by one leadership. This alone can allow coordinated efforts and harmony among the decision makers and the programs themselves. Besides, education as a whole isn't connected with the workplace agenda. In total there's lack of harmony amongst such ministries as ministry for education, for labor or employment and another one overseeing policies and needs or agenda of the youth.

Should the government impose its agenda or even the leadership on education system or be one that promotes better conditions for teaching, competitiveness and innovation? Ornstein and Hunkins identify the following roles of the government: To identify critical educational issues; synthesize the vast amount of knowledge regarding education; promote research regarding curriculum materials: support the application and dissemination of knowledge about curriculum materials; encourage the preparation of persons interested in the field of education, including curriculum. The government must also take charge of the children with

---

[10] Source: The Promise p. 417

special needs i.e. those with learning difficulties such as blindness or deafness (Ornstein and Hunkins, 1998 p.226). This shouldn't be misinterpreted as if we should close the eyes on the need of nurturing the children with special talents.[11]

ECONOMICS OF OUR SCHOOLS AND EDUCATIONAL INSTITUTIONS

Before we close this chapter, we must try to address the economics of our schools and the rest of educational institutions. This may not be an exhaustive analysis, but let it be used therefore to highlight the need to have one that is. Success of the whole educational transformation lies in enhancement and availability of better educated teaching staff and not candidates of last resort. If we must come to the rescue of the teaching profession, we should know that this endeavor transcends teaching as an abstract entity. It envelopes the teachers as individuals and their families, the nation and humanity as a whole, if we have to reclaim the dignity of the teaching profession and teachers themselves not to mention the future of the nation and humanity as a whole.

Thus, for the schools and colleges to address the financial problems they face in order to adequately address the aforementioned challenges, thinking out of the box is necessary. For this to happen, the government and private school owners have got to look at the way of improving the pay of the teaching professionals. This shouldn't be done as guess work. It shouldn't be baseless but based on calculation of the bottom line or minimum daily requirement of the individual teacher and his family such as meals for a family of two and four children, their clothing, schools fees, housing, and transport to and from work and generally the upkeep of their families.

The foregoing statement is worth further consideration and meditation now that schools are said to be overcharging their services. The question is this: how do schools charge fees? is it according to actual running costs? Many are asking: How do they know if a million or four million shillings is adequate? These aren't my own emotions. Recently president Kikwete addressing teachers and owners of Feza Schools in Dar es Salaam put that into perspective. Schools ought to table all cost— recurrent cost— including tear and wear, repair and furniture chairs and chalks and teaching materials together and divide that by the number of exact students they

---

[11] Source: The Promise Maliyamkono and Mason (1982) P. 437.

expect to enroll during the first five years for instance, alongside the overheads. In all fairness you cannot place all the cost to run your school from January to December on the weak shoulders of the first year students. If you do so, you will safely arrive at a minimum cost of running a school per child and top up your staff salaries and directors' dividends and bonuses as well as other incidentals, in order to arrive at the real accounts of profit and loss. That way we can get a fair level of fees per school commensurate the added value it delivers. School management should be able to account for the fees and breakdown the revenue and cost analysis when they ask the parents to pay more fees. Such is an instance when a government doesn't pay for such necessary but new and maiden courses such as this one—I mean Building the Ideal Scholars Program—among other initiatives. With parents' awareness, they cannot reject to pay for such a service with imponderably invaluable value to schools and students and their families and the nation as a whole thereof.

SCHOOL'S ECONOMICS

Yet school management and the government ought to look out of the box and stop making money off the backs of the miserable parents. Schools must meet the circle of success head-on if they have to manage schools and advance education successfully. Schools thus need to offer education as something enlightening but also as a quality product or service. To have quality you need better teachers. To have better teachers you need to pay higher salaries and the teachers developed not only academically, but also morally, socially and economically. To transform their mindset you have to transform their lives. This demands dough. That's why you have to think of alternatives out of the box.

The school management ought therefore to transform their mindsets in order to be able to seek, advance and embrace new ideas. They must seek ideas from outside the traditional school settings. Recently Kodak, a giant of the past century in the business of cameras, has just been declared bankrupt. Why?! Kodak didn't reinvent itself to match the fast changing world. These aren't my words. It was a BBC documentary. Search it for yourself. Schools must cut down the overheads seeking new ways of leveraging the economies of scale putting to maximum use of the premises and fixed capital by bringing new ideas or programs under one tent whether by partnership or joint ventures between schools or colleges and the innovators.

Schools and the administration ought to invent alternative means to help the teachers and the staff earn extra income through various sources. These sources should be handy and compatible to the teaching profession and environment. Presently we see teachers being engaged in activities to help them generate extra income but they undermine education and themselves as persons. Forced tuition on the part of the students, or selling various cookies to students cannot help the teachers and teaching profession itself, education system and the society itself to regain our dignity and reclaim the good teaching environment.

Handier and more compatible sources can include but not be limited to education for the adults seeking new skills, students mentoring, public speaking and communication skills courses that can be run by teachers themselves in collaboration with the external educators addressing such audiences like the adults in the informal sector and yes within the formal sector. Mwalimu Nyerere used to say: *Elimu haina mwisho!* That is to say there was no end to educating oneself—especially today in the face of rapidly changing world and therefore need for new educational needs etc.

To furnish the ever emerging demand for more revenues, here are suggestions covering areas schools can consider for instance teaching languages such as English or Chinese or French courses for the adults and businessmen at a fee—taught by the teachers themselves as internal facilitators. With growing importance of such languages as international languages in the face of globalization, the same languages can be taught even among their students as extras at an extra fee. Why not! Also areas in innovative training for adults who missed out on the formal school education or people wishing to learn new skills as well as the children or youth and dropouts who choose to return to education; or the ones who are currently employed persons wishing to muster and master new skills in business or growth related disciplines for senior personnel such as engineers or researchers who may need new skills in areas of running a business in stations such as management or top decision making positions.

Other opportunity areas include accounts and tax education for men in business; self employment: starting and running your own business or entrepreneurship: life before and after retirement; public speaking and building self-confidence to lead others; family and matrimony; working relationship and gender balance etc. There is also the workplace training such as how to re-claim capabilities and passion among staff; attention to the future prospects—such as new success factors and business drivers especially after economic crisis besides changing trends to meet the fast changing world trends in the face of the tremendous rapidity of pace of change especially with globalization and the *imponderable* ICT.

We realize that the demand for adult education as well as entrepreneurship is already booming on epidemic proportions. People want to be self-reliant—to employ themselves. They also want to stand on their feet and speak up. Indeed, public speaking and communication skills present another hotcake set that therefore can generate not only income for schools and teachers but also excitement. And we know excitement generates motivation to all involved, and therefore productivity. The nagging question is that: do the teachers have such skills or education? The answer is that they can learn them and the whole thing can be done in partnership with practitioners in such fields. Indeed these are but a drop in the sea when you attempt to explore all possibilities.

FINALE
We have, through this chapter, discussed the weaknesses in our education system and the society as a whole. We know yes that these suggestions aren't any handier. Yet these weaknesses project the weaknesses we will always paralyze our education system and the future of the society as a whole if no such as thinking out of the box. Education is the key change agent if we have to transform our society. As individuals and the society in general, we have to evaluate and thereupon transform the education system if we should see a prosperous, equitable and peaceful society. In other words, we must change or ground into chaos for indeed if we as individual persons, households, organizations and nations don't adapt to the changing world, and no matter how successful that individual person, household, organization or nation is at the moment, it will not be far too long before in words of Boyd Bode, one *"would be circumvented and left (far) behind."*[12]

As we come to the end of this chapter, we hope you noted through this chapter, how the fiber of our education has been weakened. These weaknesses, have weakened both the education and the society as a whole, and will still do so in foreseeable future, unless we act—and act now. If we don't, these weakness which others may consider as trivial matters, will bring down our economy to its knees and leave our nation a broken society. We have, through this analysis, seen that the prevailing education is failing—if it has not yet already failed. We should therefore begin now to seek options. This noble duty of reshaping the education—and society

---

[12] *Boyd H. Bode, Progressive Education At Crossroads (New York, Newson, 1938) in Ornstein and Hunkins, (1998) p.46*

thereof—shouldn't be a one man's—or even a one department's—show. We are all victims—at least in the long run.

Beginning with students—and their parents—who apart from paying high fees, have placed their future hopes on their schooling children—they are all already unhappy with the system that doesn't provide not only employment but also education that would otherwise afford them any other options after they graduate from the university—of all levels! We have seen that employers have lost confidence in our graduate students. Why? because they are ill-qualified. "All these shortcomings," concluded Professor Maliyamkono in his analytical book The Promise, "All these shortcomings have helped to marginalize the Tanzania student,"[13] We are indeed concerned because it will continue to do so until we do something and something real big and out of the box! Fortunately, with this book and its twin sisters in this series, that *'outside-of-the-box'* is no longer out of reach; not anymore!

We also hope that the reader realizes that after these weaknesses have marginalized the Tanzania student, they will marginalize, and in the end, weaken the Tanzania citizen, his family and the nation and its future as a whole. Recognize also that, with the experiences of companies like Kodak, or even recently the banking industry, not to mention the experiences of old days pinnacle nations such as Greek, Rome, Ottoman, the British Empire, USSR etc, experiences that illustrate that failing to reinvent themselves, they all found themselves either going under, or tracing themselves in the middle when they should actually be leading. That's what I write for Tanzania, I write for Uganda, Kenya, China, Japan, Australia, France, US or even the UK. Recognizing that education is probably the most important tool with which any society can transform itself, the authors needs not emphasize that we need new ideas in the domain of education and learning.

Here therefore, as we edge to the end of this foresight, we recall what in his magnificent book *Think and Grow Rich*, Napoleon Hill suggested that we must address the aspect of leadership if we have to progress. He said that if we have to transform the society, "Leadership….in education will become a necessity," he wrote. "This is especially true in the field of education. The leader in that field must in the future find ways and means of teaching people how to apply knowledge they receive in schools; he or she must

---

[13] Source: Maliyamkono and Mason page 418

deal more with practice and less theory," he concluded. We have reached where we are today because of the failure to respond to the same challenge, and as a result, our walk for prosperity has not only been lengthened? No! It seems now to be heading to nowhere! Change is necessary for otherwise we must get prepared to accept the only prospect I can only foresee which is not any inspiring. We must thereupon be prepared to ground into miseries and witness our society give its last breathe as it will soon naturally give its ghost away, dust to dust forever and ever! Amen!

Now as we come to the end of this simple analysis, an analysis on the weaknesses and setbacks in education and our society, weaknesses and setbacks that have piled up painting an inelegant picture, a picture that fearlessly, stubbornly stares at us now demanding answers, let me state this clearly: I didn't write this book to please or displease anyone. Out of honesty, honesty to myself, to my fellow citizens and mankind as a whole, a quality we are going to observe as an ideal virtue any man of education and any committed citizen ought to uphold, I wrote this book fearlessly to inspire change—lasting meaningful change. Now that I have done my part, I leave the rest into your capable hands, because in the first place it is your life and the future of your children, the nation and mankind as a whole that are at stake. Taking my liberty to borrow a word of wisdom from Mwalimu Julius Kambarage Nyerere, and what a great ending? For indeed if: "There are people who believe that…ideas…associated with my name are now dead and should be properly buried…I disagree. Great ideas don't die so easily; they continue nagging, and every human society in history ignores them at its own peril!"

2. THE IDEAL SCHOLAR CONCEPT— AND HOW IT WAS HATCHED UP

"Alice came to a fork in the road. 'which road do I take? ' she asked.
'Where do you want to go?' responded the Cheshire Cat. 'I don't know.' Alice answered. 'Then,' said the Cat, 'it doesn't matter!'"
—Alice in the Wonderland by Lewis Carroll

INTRODUCTION
Through the previous works and chapters, indeed through the book "A Sick Nation and How to Heal it;" we conversed about the crumbling education and the education system as a whole. We also indicated how we have produced a lost generation thereby helping to undress and leave g a society's ethos bare, naked, and stripped to the bone; and so putting on view the inexplicable weaknesses inherent in our society—and the world beyond—considering the invaluable significance the youth wedge if a society has to progress. We fear that our fear is fearfully imminent, looming higher and higher especially today. We fear that we are truly backsliding far back into a weaker and a more dependent society. And notice that when I say society, I mean we are backsliding into a weaker and more dependent station, yes, a weaker and more dependent station firstly as a nation, but more so as a species—the human species. We shall further this discussion going forward.

I AM NOT ON MY OWN
But a question arises: Is this dilemma, the fear that our society runs the risk of backsliding into a weaker position, my own creation, or one based on unfounded theses? Well, you are privileged to hug your present position and cherish your opinion, and it doesn't itch me one bit. No! It doesn't! But much as it doesn't itch me personally, it is important that you know the

truth concerning my predictions—predictions about your fate, that f your family and your society as a whole—if you don't change. Besides, my friend, I am not alone. I mean I am not on my own in as far as this fear is concerned. So, if you so dearly loved your position, if you loved your position so much that you intended to stubbornly cling to it—literally with your molar teeth—my friend, think again! For as Eddy Murphy observed in his immortal movie *Coming to America: "Traditions must, and do always change my friend!"*

FATHER VALLENTINE RWELENGERA OF BIHARAMULO PARISH, TANZANIA

I met Father Valentine when I visited Biharamulo town, in Tanzania, for my father's first anniversary of his exodus from the earth to the next world. Himself—Father Valentine—being the director of one of the schools in the district, I can say I was therefore privileged to cruise with him in his brand new Toyota Land Cruiser after he had officiated the holy mass for that event. I call it a privilege because I was doing the preliminary work towards writing this book—the idea he himself helped so much to inspire—and I thank him for that. As we drove through his parish, we conversed about many things. One of his concerns as a man of God and school director, and therefore responsible for spiritual upbringing, he indicated that the backsliding of the morals among the youth is a result shaky upbringing among our families yes, but as well among our secular schools in the country today. And you cannot blame the schools for you cannot teach religious faith or ethics discriminately in schools in a secular state like ours.

Yet his concern is evidenced by the huge gap we see among seminary schools and the public schools in the land today. The seminaries have always risen to the face of the national examinations every year. They have constantly produced top academic performances. They, therefore, produce top performers at work and generally therefore, the model sons and daughters any parent would be proud of. To be brief, the products of these catholic seminaries have remained at the top of the tree of success as employees and executives regardless of the profession they choose to pursue. I know a host of such individuals but here are few of such personalities you would yourself be proud to sire and raise as your own sons—or daughters. I can close my eyes and enumerate a list of names of such individuals but that would fill the book. That's not what you want. That's why I will bring only few names here.
Let me start with Fred.

FRED SILVERSTER BAYONA NSHEKANABO

To begin with, this is not work of fiction. It is real. Go on now! When Fred was in grade six, his visionary father, Mr. Bayona, serving as a local court magistrate in one of the counties in Muleba, Tanzania, a persona known personally to the author, took him to the seminary school. He left the seminary when he was in high school. I will talk about Fred later but for now let me say that though Fred is the third born in this family which lacked no school fees or academic support, yet a couple of years later he, Fred, having graduated from the secular high school and college, got hired as a junior bank staff before he began rising until as I write. He is today a director of finance for this mammoth of a bank in the country with branches worldwide. It comes to me as no surprise that he is the spine of that family of seven siblings and a model to many. What made him so special? Certainly not his birth albeit the coincidence of the KP Number we introduced on discussing The Principled Universe in a book A Sick Nation and How to Heal it. Please make reference to the book.

MICHAEL K.

Recognize that you are engaged in the discussion of ho—and why—I wrote this book, or therefore how the ideal scholar concept was hatched. So I will tell you about one more person. That person is a person I know very well. Indeed I can say with no doubt whatsoever that he has contributed to the making of this book even though at the time when it was being written, he had already ascended to the next world. This gentleman had ethics of high order. I know this was part of the upbringing he got at the Rubya Seminary during the colonial era, the same school Fred had to attend many years later. I know that yes his forefathers had a firm grip on ethics, but his unique standards were shaped and infused in him during his formative years in the seminary. What I am saying is that it is in the seminary that his character was shaped.

How do I know all this? Or how do I know it is true? I know all this is true because this gentleman is my father—Michael Kambarangwe. And that's what probably connected the both of us; I mean Father Valentine, and the author. I have given this narrative to evidence Father Valentine's concerns. Let me say something before we move on. I insist I have given this account for no other reason than to connect you with the gap we see in our education today. Indeed I am certain that the author didn't write it to brag about his own father. Far from that!

Do we need any further substantiation? Probably one more case in point will do the reader justice, a case in point that many moderate child-focused parents share! Reread the foregoing statement before you move on to this case in point!

ISMAIL MASSANGA AND FORTUNATUS MICHAEL

I know one Ismail Massanga having personally schooled with him at high school and also at the University of Dar es Salaam having also gone to the same training unit during the national military service. I also know he is not Christian. But whether his decision was based on academic research having come back from one of the most prestigious universities in Europe for his advanced degree in humanities, or whether it was based purely on human instincts, I have no way of knowing. But one thing I know about it—and that something is what is indeed my message.

Very recently I met him at a teachers-parents meeting at St. Ann's where the author's children also attend. Wondering how he could have forfeited his non Christian background to allow instead his children to pursue a school that is mainly run on Christian principles, he shocked me when he said he was not only interested in the kind of the teaching such schools offer, but that "religion was religion," he said. I reckon he meant—and I learned from him—that for him God was huger and vaster than the religions. If his children relinquished their traditional faith to follow any other that was somehow progressive according to their will, or understanding, "so be it," he told me pointblank.

He was not going to deny his children a chance in education and an opportune decent life, or even lose an opportunity to rid himself with trouble of transport and finances to send his children in more appropriate schools far away, away where he would be able to look after his children, only for fear of getting his children introduced to other religions. This is indeed a decision he shares with the author's brother when he, Fortunatus, sent Patrick to Nyanshenye Secondary School, a Muslim institution back in Bukoba.

So here are some of the things we ought to ask ourselves in relation to the conversation I held with Father Vally. One: where did we go wrong? Two: how do we reconcile these two positions viz. being a secular state yet a state that is yearning, literally weeping for the religious ethics or principles, and sound character and attitudes? Indeed I cannot overstate the gap that was caused by the abolition of ownership of schools by religious institutions or rather how it contributed to the backsliding of education as we experience today. Yes, it was a necessary step to both nationalize and *secularize* schools and education therefore for the cohesion of our young society, and that's certainly why Mwalimu Julius Nyerere being religious himself, and catholic at large, from among whom many schools were nationalized and secularized he still chose to abolish both the ownership and the teaching of religion in schools—most of which were catholic too!

Though it was itself a necessary step towards national cohesion, the decision didn't help much to build the moral fiber amongst the youth, and the nation as a whole. We instead see that it resulted in the decay of the morals following the vacuum that was never filled—until as I write—and therefore the need to reconstruct or build afresh the national ideals. It is to this end; it is for this cause that I wrote this book. I wrote this book because though the Mohammedan teaching through the *Hadith* does so well when it advocates that a person must be judged based on his or her intentions, but good intentions alone will never shield your fault anymore when you go wrong or fail to remedy the situation or repeat the same mistake time and time again.

Without developing a secular code of morals, ethics or conduct in its place, abolishing a peaceful, non violent, and kill-no-one, work-hard and give-to-others religious teaching places the move under the microscope. I am trying to say that however a great move that was in terms of building a cohesive society and averting the woes of religious contention that we see in the non secular states in the Middle East or among the states that declare themselves to be secular only on the papers but don't indeed practice secularism because of tribal or religious sectarian sentiments. We have so many of such states in Africa too. But in the main why we fail when we have no such guidelines in place is because of human nature. It is in the nature of the beast to sin as excellently quotes Romans 7:24-25: "Oh wretched man that I am! Who will set me free from this weak body?" says Paul Apostle. So then, on the one hand I myself with my mind am serving the law of God, but on the other, with my flesh the law of sin.[14]

That's why we need ideals in place—ideals which we don't only need to have on the papers, albeit a very important step, but also to see them implemented.

---

[14] *Romans 7:24-25New American Standard Bible (NASB)*

We also must say that we appreciate that, the traditional initiation ceremonies such as Jando and Unyago among such communities like the Kurya or Masai, representing models of training for the youth, had their own inherent deep problems from mutilation of young girls and its lifelong stigma, gender discrimination, enmity and instilling warlike attitudes that triggered the thievery of cattle and other properties like land heightening intertribal conflicts and endless wars. Nonetheless, at least the traditional community had something on which to fall back. Lack of such initiation programs, programs which helped to initiate the youth into adulthood and loyalty to their society, has helped to retard the society as it strayed the youth from social ethics and moral fiber, the society and the future by throwing all cautions to wind.

Take Robert Nester. Bob Nester Marley grew up on the streets. He naturally therefore had no adequate formal schooling with a disadvantaged single–mother-family in Jamaica—of all countries. But proper upbringing his mother afforded him and the little schooling and initiation into self-reliance and significance of personal initiative he acquired that helped him to conquer the world with nothing but reggae music. That's why, and how, he later admitted that: *"If my mother didn't give me education, I would be a damned fool."*

Initiations were practical programs for mental, intellectual and emotional preparation of youth to recognize their responsibilities in the society. As we delve into developing such a program that would fill the vacuum among our not only in our schools but also among our families and workplaces, let us recall also that we did blunder big time when we abolished the national service—albeit its shortcomings. This was a program that intended to prepare the youth and graduates as they were about to meet the future. The author knows the national service taught these ethics because he attended the maximum one year term at Buhemba.

Why now? Why all of a sudden we say we need change? This is a great question we have to ask ourselves. We see tremendous collapse of morals among the people and rampant irresponsibility among the youth. There is also collapse of family institution and increased rate of street children. We also see indolence at workplaces. In the face of economic crisis, and now that the EA Community has brought out its face, we experience a great challenge to reassess competence and competiveness and attention to time or punctuality on one hand, but remodeling our priorities on the other hand as our major challenge if our nation and the society and the human race as a whole have to stand tall once again. Indeed, transforming our education system has been long time in coming. You recognize, with respect to Tanzania, we needed transformation long ago. Indeed we had to implement this program immediately after independence of the flag in 1961.

We needed to shift from colonial educational agenda—an agenda—that intended to produce modest workforce to facilitate as clerks—not thinkers, experts or writers like Shaban Robert, Mwalimu Nyerere, Shafi Adam Shafi and a couple others whose writings are transformational and educative. We need an education that endeavors to empower and build capacity to rightly think—and do and be—among the local people. *"Thinking," Said Abu Bakr, "is the food of the mind."*

Fr. Valentine's concern was not anyhow remote, or in any way immaterial. Concerned about moral and spiritual crisis in education, David Purpel coined an education he named *The Liberation Theology*. Besides, according to Allan C. Ornstein and Francis P. Hunkins: *"While such theology is not taught directly in the schools, many are attending to the issues of poverty and oppression, which reflect the orientation... attention to compassion and justice to the less fortunate of the world...*(p.372). That's how the author decided it was important to create a program that sought to critically examine the cultural heritage of our society as well as the entire civilization. That's why he, the author, is not afraid to examine controversial issues. That's why he is consciously committed to bringing about social and constructive change and cultivate a culture of futuristic thinking, one that considers the realities of the world and enlists students and teachers in a definite program to enhance cultural renewal and interculturalism.[15]

Talking about the urgency f this training, indeed when we moved from Ujamaa to market-led economy, as a country, we ought to have done something about education in order to address competitiveness, entrepreneurship and time consciousness etc, the ideals badly lacking in our society today! We also needed to start addressing that success or prosperity isn't about luck or chance but burning desire, determination, planning, consistence and indeed action. The recent economic downturn does more than emphasize the need for flexibility, new business drivers

---

[15] *Adapted from Allan C. Ornstein and Francis P. Hunkins, Curriculum Foundations, Principles and Issues 3rd Edition p.51*

and success factors. Nothing can be far from truth that building character and moral fiber in our society addressing integrity hard work and family values and interdependence among is at the mantle of the prospects for success or failure in building the future nation we crave.

Astounding as it may seem, I found that there was no such a book examining our state of affairs or addressing handicaps in our education system as an antidote to our social and economic problems. Indeed I found that such a book or program was long time in coming. Because there was no such a book—a book addressing a person's or specific nations inner environment and therefore relevant inputs and self learning format, a book addressing and redressing character and mind-set, a program that would fill the gap between what they teach today and what they ought to teach, I chose to write one myself. Wattles in his magnificent book Science of Getting Rich recommended thus: "A person must not only think, but his personal action must supplement his thought..." This is a great piece of advice, a precious counsel. And he didn't end there. "Do not wait," he continued; "Do not wait for a change of environment before you act; get a change of environment by action."

ZITTO KABWE
Addressing the parliament on the pressing need for the national service recently, Hon. Zitto Kabwe, a member of parliament from one of the Lake Tanganyika constituencies of Kigoma in Tanzania, he volunteered to join the initiation. He recognized that the programs taught patriotism, self-confidence, hard work, decency, order or discipline among others. These, sir, are gaps this book or training program intends to fill. These are some of the benefits—themselves a drop in the sea—this program places at your door steps.

MICHAEL OGWARI S. JOHN
When Michael Ogwari John, the human resources director at the ministry of health, and at the time acting as principal secretary, saw the preceding works towards this book, works that set ground for this book or program, said: "Now, finally, I am confident I have set my eyes on the kind of books or programs that bespeak (and address) our educational (and social) problems!"

LEONARD MAHANDARE KITOKA
When the volume one of this very book, also rewritten as A Sick Nation and How to Heal it, got out and got on the social media, when it got into the attention of one of the most successful young self made entrepreneurs

in this part of the continent, a man who is also the senior consultant and managing partner at Innovex Development Consulting Limited, Leonard Mahandare Kitoka, he called the author congratulating him saying: "Congratulations! examining your book, I realize that it is only a handful of our scholars who have written a book like this one," he said, "—well," on the second thought, "I suppose," he continued, "I suppose that probably no one has written a book like this one before!"

ZEPHRINE GALEBA

I recently met Zephrine Galeba—a prominent lawyer and an intellectual. When i say he is one i know what I mean. I can assure you that you will cherish the experience of meeting him for the rest of your days. I know it is true because i know him at persona level having gone through the same class during high school and at the university. After he had had the opportunity to read the author's works, he stated that: *"This is the kind of education the society needs now. It is the kind of education the society needs now because it is about the problems we face, problems such as integrity and delivery of quality results, in the midst of the burgeoning mediocrity in the society."*

ELI WIESEL AND DAVID ORR

Through the preceding chapters, we stripped bare the morals of the present day's youth and the ethos of our society. We also did present to you how our education has not helped to change the grim situation we are in as a society. Didn't we also show how we were rather shocked to find that our scholars—as a group and not necessarily as individuals—present grimmer problems to the society than even the unlearned? But is it exaggerated? Fiction? Insanity? Malice? Oh! No sir. Really this position isn't my own exaggeration. And really it is no news to the truthful and initiated few. Suffice to say here that we know that all major financial scandals, scandals that have left the nation with shame and on its knees aren't the illiterate countryside humble citizens, or even junior employees whether in private or public services, but instead they are our most privileged scholars—executives and politicians—men with, and in, the powerful positions.

In his award winning article adapted from his commencement address to the graduating class of 1990 at Arkansas College "What Is Education For? Six Myths About the Foundations of Modern Education, and Six New Principles to Replace Them," David Orr discussed the grim weakness in our education—global education—today.

He indicated, in his speech, that Elie Wiesel made similar point to the Global Forum in Moscow when he said that the designers and perpetrators of the Holocaust were the heirs of Kant and Goethe (the highly and best educated persons even as we speak). In most respects, according to Wiesel, the Germans were the best educated people on Earth, but their education did not serve as an adequate barrier to barbarity.

What was wrong with their education? In Wiesel's words: "It emphasized theories instead of values, concepts rather than human beings, abstraction rather than consciousness, answers instead of questions, ideology and efficiency rather than conscience." The same could be said of the way our education has prepared us to think about the natural world. It is a matter of no (small) consequence that the only people who have lived sustainably on the planet for any length of time, couldn't read, or, like the Amish, do not make a fetish of reading. My point is simply that education is no guarantee of decency, prudence, or wisdom. More of the same kind of education will only compound our prudence, or wisdom. More of the same kind of education will only compound our problems. This is not an argument for ignorance, but rather a statement that the worth of education must now be measured against the standards of decency and human survival the issues now looming so large before us in the decade of the 1990s and beyond. It is not education that will save us, but education of a certain kind. We talk of managing growth factors. What might best be managed is indeed oneself, us: human desires." In words of David Orr, "it makes far better sense to reshape ourselves to fit a finite planet than to attempt to reshape the planet to fit our infinite wants."

BARRY LOPEZ

In the words of Barry Lopez: "(I am) forced to the realization that something strange, if not dangerous, is afoot. Year by year the number of people with firsthand experience in the land dwindles. Rural populations continue to shift to the cities.... In the wake of this loss of personal and local knowledge, the knowledge from which a real geography is derived, the knowledge on which a country must ultimately stand, has come something hard to define but I think sinister and unsettling."

RALPH WALDO EMERSON
Hey, David Orr, you are not alone. Not only Elie Wiesel or Barry Lopez thinks this way but also Emerson had seen it two centuries before he found it much the same sinister and unsettling. "The civilized man has built a coach," said Emerson, "but has lost the use of his feet. He is supported on

crutches but lacks so much support of muscle. He has a fine Geneva watch," continued Emerson, "but he has lost the skill to tell the hour by the sun. A Greenwich nautical almanac he has, and so being sure of the information when he wants it, the man in the street doesn't know a star in the sky. The solstice he doesn't observe, the equinox he knows as little; and the whole bright calendar of the year ,without a dial in his mind. His notebooks impair his memory; his libraries overload his wit..."

WYNNE, RYAN, C.S. LEWIS, ORNSTEIN AND HUNKINS, AND NAPOLEON HILL

With reference to the handicaps inherent in the society's ethos, and the youth being the major victims, the recurring question surfaces once time and time again. Is this book or training program on building the ideal scholars realistic? Is it universal or only baseless and regional or barely any more than tribal? Do we really need it? How badly?

Beginning with the last concern, Napoleon Hill wrote in Think and Grow Rich that if we have to transform the society, "Leadership .... will become a necessity," he wrote. "This is especially true in the field of education," continued Napoleon Hill emphasizing that: "The leader in that field must in the future find ways and means of teaching people how to apply knowledge they receive in schools; he or she must deal more with practice and less theory." And the author concurs with Napoleon Hill. Here is what I paraphrased from Think and Grow Rich, "The demand for leadership has greatly exceeded supply. Today we experience a great lack of leadership almost in every other field. We may teach existing leaders to learn to be better leaders but we have got to find new timber elsewhere." For true change to happen we need new ideas. We also need leadership in the whole scheme. We don't need people who will prophesy solutions and dump opinion on the table and run and hide waiting in anticipation for miracles to happen. This—inaction—is the handicap of our leaders—at household level, corporate leaders as well as religious, academic and political—leaders and policy makers.

You are about to see what Wynne and Ryan presented as a list of moral qualities, or character exhibited by a society that has to prosper and is effectively functioning. This they adapted from C.S. Lewis. And you are about to realize that *you can live with love toward others* and that this is not an *idealistic extortion*. But as suggested Ornstein and Hunkins, since conflict is bound to arise with diverse groups they will deal with... conflict in nonviolent ways...to assume selflessness, a willingness to see beyond themselves and their own needs.[16] You recognize that with escalating religious or sectarian sentiment, the foregoing statement is critical, and hold more water than before.

And here is the cream of the whole thing. In his book *The Abolition of Man*, Lewis indicated that many of his ideas reflect the thinking of many cultures through time: Babylonians, ancient Egypt, old Norse, Greeks, Romans, Chinese, Indians, Christians, Hebrew, Islamic, Anglo-Saxon, and Americans. To his list naturally are included other cultures from Europe, Asia and Africa. An effectively functioning society requires of its members human kindness; Individuals in the society owe a social love and loyalty to their parents; They owe a social love to and responsibility for themselves and their own families; Its citizens exhibit some degree of honesty; All members of society have an obligation to help the poor, sick, and less fortunate; Its citizens respect basic property rights; Its citizen's respect the personal rights of others.[17] Humans are individuals who are unique but who cannot live in isolation. The human nature is such that he is selfish and domineering. (Though truly the world changes but), Robert Hutchins was right on the whole when he noted that: *"The function of man as man is the same in every society...the aim of every educational system is the same in every age and in every society...it is to improve a man as man ...*

"(And the therefore) *the answers to all educational questions derive from the answer to one question: What is human nature* (Ornstein and Hunkins 1998 p. 38)?

"In the end, *"Unquestionably educational aims and especially school reform must be relevant or meaningful to our times. If the schools are not adaptable to changing conditions and social forces, how can we expect them to produce people who are* (Ornstein and Hunkins, 1998 p.167)?" You be the judge therefore. Aren't the foregoing points relevant to us today? Isn't this program almost a response to the above call of change? Besides, you do realize, don't you? That not only the students and teachers

---

[16] *Allan C. Ornstein and Francis P. Hunkins, Curriculum Foundations, Principles and Issues 3rd Edition p.397*

[17] *Adapted from Edward a. Wynne and Kevin Ryan Reclaiming Our Schools 2nd edition from Allan C. Ornstein and Francis P. Hunkins, Curriculum Foundations, Principles and Issues 3rd Edition p.372*

could do with such a program but also the backlog of our workforce and the society as a whole? And since parents and leadership have a role to play this program and book are also meant for them. Thu, having come this far, you realize that this author was compelled by' these considerable forces—forces that had mounting pressure—to create a program and write this book in response to the foregoing arguments.

Looking at our society today, many people recognize that wealthy men desire and acquire the best of almost everything they set out to do, have and become, but only few recognize the majority of the wealthy—and every other successful people, have obsession to work hard—much as still fewer recognize that the fewest of the wealthy people only manage to remain wealthy and age in dignity! Why? Though we shall deal with matter in full a little later, but briefly, here's the answer. Quick fix! It is get rich or die trying principle. Kill and get money; prostitution; armed robbery; and as a result, too much pressure or stress and thereof rampant drinking and drugs due to an excruciating pain of the conscience. Aside from HIV/AIDS and death, it is sad that only very few of my readers know that there's also the mortification of the soul and the intellect aside from insanity!

We need a new thought—and indeed a new thought pattern. This book is written that you may be among the few of the fewest who know the secret of the lasting, abiding wealth, peace and happiness. It is written that you may realize that you have no more options: transform *or lose ground! And this is not baseless.* At the end of the great economic slump of the last century—times very close to ours, Napoleon Hill, rightly suggested something I have paraphrased below from his book *Think and Grow Rich* which reads thus: "This changed world in which we live, is demanding new ideas, new ways of doing things, new leadership, new inventions, new methods of teaching, new methods of marketing, new books, new literature, new features for radio, new ideas for moving pictures…and (definitely), definiteness of purpose!"[18]

BENEDICT EMMANUEL BUGUFI
Now that we have highlighted concerns, and need for new education, I am indeed heartened to share a hunch I have unaware shared with one of the most notable persons among people I know at personal level, a person I

---

[18] *Adapted from Think and Grow Rich by Napoleon Hill*

have had the privilege of ever meeting. I chose to reprint a note I received from him featuring in one of the previous chapters because this very chapter and the proceeding ones represent the concept to which the note-writer referred. But because we described it fully in the book A Sick nation and How to Heal It—a book I ask you to read—I will just mention the key point, which is this: positive mind. In its abridged form, the note read thus: "My dear friends ... I've had a persistent hunch that something in our society is pervasively going wrong...I fear that there's a profound crisis on the cards... (Which) Mr. Kambarangwe has elaborately explained...in his work *Building the Ideal Graduates and Productive Workforce..."*

As you take a pause in order to meditate a little longer upon the notes above which we received, realize that the following pages are going to delve into the problem we face as a society as well as expound solutions that will not only address but redress the situation as many have spoken above. What we have to do is to respond with class and dignity thereby averting the looming crisis that Benedict Emmanuel's hunch had presented to him.

THE ORIGIN OF THE CONCEPT: THE AUTHOR'S UPBRINGING
I didn't hatch this program from out of the blue. How? Why? What researches are behind this work to make credible? Is the author's standing or authority foolproof? Can we learn from such a humble author? Well, before I tackle this question, let me first admit that yes, I may not be the most learned, or even the most experienced, person when it comes to the complexities of the pedagogy, or education as a teaching profession in general, but I am not a complete nincompoop when it comes down to an analysis of the society, child upbringing and personal and national growth! Yes I have had to furnish my knowledge with various other relevant sources or inputs, but the work is originally part of my life or rather part of me. The concept was build upon the foundation of upbringing that the author's parents, through their forefathers, had passed down to his big brothers and sisters thereof trickling down to the author—and I humbly thank my parents especially, but as well my big brothers and sisters and yes my teachers for that, and most certainly so should you, the nation and human society as a whole. Along with the above, I—and so should you—thank all good and bad role models amongst my colleagues, acquaintances and strangers from whom I have also learned quite a lot.

Concerning the credibility of what is placed before you, recall that as said Paul Valery, the great French philosopher, "Science (or research) is a collection of successful recipes," isn't this they say? Well, it is yes a collection of well-researched and tested successful techniques or ideas, but it is also an observation, mere follow up, and lessons from the analysis under microscope. Research is indeed also a collection of lessons from failed persons and ventures—in which falls all who are encased in their traditional domain and without a thought, question this assertion—educated or not—people who are aren't ready to learn. "Every man I meet," said Ralph Waldo Emerson, "Every man I meet, is my superior I some way. In that I learn of him!"

Now I want to tell you a story about a young boy I know—a person who is closer to me than anyone else—a story I want you to learn from. But before we proceed, let me insert a word of counsel to a skeptic who will still be questioning the author's standing or authority or even the flawlessness of the very training program or a form of education we present for our schools and children. To cynics and skeptics, here is their answer. Not every inventor or innovator was a person who could be said to highly classed in terms of conventional education. Read the bibliographies of Henry Ford, Thomas A. Edison, Abraham Lincoln, Prophet Mohammed, Jesus, you name it! Not all the sophistications we see in modern computers or aircrafts were available in the first computer or aircraft. Indeed all, yes, all monumental successes started in humble beginnings. Besides, "Education has no boundaries," aptly counseled Professor Maliyamkono in his great book The Promise.

Back to my little story! During his early life, the life of a young man I know, he managed situations that would make mighty adult people shrink. Like the young biblical David, he gained ways and means and confidence to think, and do a variety of things. That gave him experience that really diffused into the core of his being. He, the young boy, also had a unique but also mysterious experience of looking after his own life and lives of the others. Among the persons he looked after is a very old lady. Whether this lady was 90, or 111 at the time, the author has no way of knowing, for this old lady was from the past ancient pre-numbers generation. She knew not anything about numbers or her age let alone alphabets or geography—and it didn't itch her one bit. It is a curious experience I guarantee you. It is even more curious because this person was not only old, but also female. It is also more interesting, because this lady was not blood related to the boy. Besides, the boy was not a slave. And he wasn't paid for his services. Yet she was so old that apart from failing to spell names properly, she literally did nothing except sit there and wait for *Krizto Pasto*—as she named this young future author—to look after her and do all the chores including preparation of food and setting of the table and dish washing.

It was even more imponderable because this young boy didn't only look after her and her alone. He also looked after the two other souls who were this old woman's grand children. Strange as it is, the narrative is true. It is still more curious that when he, the young boy, looked after the old granny and her grandchildren her own daughter was still breathing living a healthy and probably wealthy life only five miles away. What's incredibly unprecedented was the faith both her daughter and her son in law must have had in this young boy. Think about it: entrusting not only your old mother, but also your first two sons—sons you love so dearly—to a mere *toddler*—if you know what I mean. And that's not all. Igabiro (part of Siina—a cattle herding country in Katera, Kyerwa, Karagwe, Tanzania—presents a sad story because all about its traditional ancient life is gone, fenced and the people, literally thrown out) was at the time infested with the predators among which lions and cheetah were ubiquitous beside hyenas and hippos and big and small pythons and rattlers. But he, the young boy, was not slaving. He was not a slave. He was not even doing all this backbreaking incredible chores for money. No sir!

Yet, besides looking after the flock and parking himself under the maternal cattle, milking fifteen heads mornings and evenings 24/7 all year round, serving also as the minister of defense, he did it for free and curiously contentedly. He did it contentedly because the flock was his father's. This old woman was my father's mother-in-law. The boys who were like the biblical Yusuf and Benjamin were my half brothers, and this boy I am talking about, you must have now realized that, I am he. The author was made to literally put on the biblical Judah's shoes. It was he whom old Jacob trusted to look after the flock and the boys. It is notably curious because the author was himself but a teenager. Quite a unique experience, huh? Dad never spoke much about it but once, and only once, he assigned the author the position of Judah. In secret? No sir! It was before his brothers and sisters. He didn't do that based on apparent blessings Judah had had over his siblings though? No madam! He only did so based on the fact that the author, like the biblical Judah, was his fourth born son.

Through the previous books, you may have been led to the fact that the author helped manage his father's farm. This is an extension of lessons thereof. I didn't notice anything then. But now I realize that dad—in his own unique way—should have had enormous trust on the future author so much. My step mother should have trusted the future author even more. The old step granny and my half brothers should have more than trusted me too. God above must have sent down this miracle that I learn from it so that one day I could put this unique experience to some worthy use like the one you are engaged in right now. That was the beginning of the making of this book and training, and a blessing I will cherish all my breathing life. To have not shared this experience, and more so, to have not written this book, availing the training to my children and the future generation, would be not only unreasonable and unfair to many, it would be—well, it would be sin—and sin of biblical proportions—and disgrace to God!

And this is not my own exaggeration. Recall the account of the three servants who were given a fortune to keep when their master journeyed to a far country. Who was blessed? One who dug a hole and hid the treasure in there genuinely wishing to keep safe what was not his? No sir! Wasn't it one who multiplied it? Read it for yourself in the holy bible. They are the words of Jesus—whom even non Christians acknowledge as a philosopher and prophet, our Lord who remains in his own league. When Winston Churchill was called to lead up the war efforts for the Great Britain, he remarked something which is my own message. He said: "All my life has prepared me for this hour.[19]" That is why I have mustered the audacity to put this account on the printable paper availing it to people near and far across time and space. And that's why I am thankful to God Almighty—and so should you!

Now back to the author; that was the first part of his initiation into the future work now wrapped up in the book in your hands—and the training program at your disposal. He, thereupon, went on to join secondary school where he was enrolled in a boarding school far away from home. He began brushing shoulders and learning from strange people he didn't even care much about—at the time—people that turned out to be priceless to him. He graduated from several secular schools and colleges undertaking religious and military lessons thereof before he began working as a manager of people. When I say people I mean managing my own superiors, peers and subordinates among them enthusiasts and troublemakers. You realize, don't you, that we are all not only managed, but also manage those who manage us, if you know what I mean? This experience helped the author to muster the very small but otherwise unmatched secrets from the deepest parts of the souls and minds of the mysterious creation—the creation ever that God Almighty had the misfortune of making—the humankind. Through this experience the author mastered and mustered the secret of life

---

[19] *Adapted from The Seven Habits of Most Successful People by Steve R. Covey*

we could reasonably call EDUCATION, for true education is in organizing yourself, the nature, and people around you toward a worthy accomplishment that benefits all involved—to their n^{th} generation. Yet the greater privilege that certainly contributed largely to the crafting of this program is the second experience or the second chance if he didn't learn from the previous ones being a teen at the time. It began, and proceeded, with the preliminary preparation to write this book.

In my preparation to write this book I resigned from any kind of employed work. I resigned because I needed time to gather facts and meditate upon the mountain of work that was ahead of me and the sea of thoughts I had to swim across. During the early part of this time I did a great deal of thinking as well as reading. During this period of time, I also recall doing intensive self censorship. Though I had graduated in economics, though I had served in different organizations as manager, I was astounded to find that I was not happy. I realized that my education, the university, and my job—being employed—all didn't help to emancipate me, my family, the nation and humanity as a whole. This enlightenment did help to bring perspective and to lay down a mountain of information I needed to make informed decisions about my future.

Then the unique event happened. The author and his wife God blessed with a wonderful daughter and her brother. Not twins though? The blessing came in series, one at a time. The author's spouse, herself a much occupied government officer, as you should expect, brought the great intensity of demands to bear even to the greatest mind like her. You do not necessarily have to be in the category mentioned in the previous statement to be forced to meet the challenge head on if you are the kids' father at the time when your wife works at the headquarters of a busy government bureau, and you have four children between yourselves—I mean you and your wife.

We had had two younger children but had two bigger girls all along. Notice that the author hadn't been forced to produce these wonderful children, no! He got them because he wanted to! So he had to take the responsibility gracefully. This is not a common experience, is it? Uncommon experiences—experiences that are especially perilously dangerous—tend to hatch uncommon, and often, very advantageous experiences. You can quote the foregoing statement, going forward. Mark my words! This one was no different. It accorded the author another opportunity to regenerate the sense of child upbringing he had neglected, considered as a woman's—his wife'—chore. As I write the statement, I would like to make it clear that I have deliberately assisted my children's nanny to look after our own children, literally babysitting them myself. I am curious why God sent down this experience at the time when I chose to write the very book.

But one thing I know though—and am grateful to God. It is why Patricia and Prince feature into this book. The opportunity helped the author to recall the experience in its fullest the privilege of having looking after my younger siblings long ago before I graduated from high school and the military national service—after which I took under my tent and began looking after several of my younger siblings, my niece and nephews. You probably realize that as I endeavored to write the book developing the program we present to you now, the experience generated with it the emotions that came in handy to perfect the work at hand. Together therefore, the experiences accorded me the privilege to be personally fully engaged—physically, intellectually, emotionally and spiritually—in nurturing of the younger minds of tomorrow.

As I look at how exemplary and resourceful they are not only to themselves, the family, the neighborhood, the employers and the nation and humanity as whole, I feel proud for the humble part I played in their preparation. As I thank Prince and Patricia, my wife, my parents and siblings, and my young brothers and sisters for the part they played, I admit that to look after the young people whom you love, preparing them to one day become truly great men and women—great persons—they are today is an engaging task. It is yes an engaging task but since it demands love and total devotion it leaves lots of blessings to the responsible person. As a proud brother, father and uncle, looking after them as any responsible person would look after his own children; I can only wish that one day my children can look upon my siblings as their role models—a family that makes me proud. Besides this wish, I truly hope for, my life, my conscience has been blessed because of this responsibility that not by my own effort, but only providentially fell upon me. If there is anything in my life that has ever brought immeasurable blessings personally to me, then this is it. And you know why? Here is why. "Part of the fragrance of the flower," so goes a Chinese saying: "remains in the hand of the giver." In the same line, J. Barrie aptly said that "Those who bring sunshine into the lives of others cannot keep it from themselves." Ralph Waldo Emerson said: "It is one of the most beautiful compensations of life that no one can sincerely try to help another without helping their self." This in itself helped the author realize how invaluable developing the program based on this experience can be.

That is, briefly, how as I grew up and saw how great people they had turned out to be, I realized it would be invaluable if I organized this concept into a more practical, accessible and handier training program for our schools, families and workplaces—or even places of worship—from the indistinct education I had received from my parents, an education I had passed on to my young brothers, sisters, nieces, nephews, Princess Felista, Priscilla, Patricia and Prince Ruhinda. We would, as a society, benefit invaluably if we reaped from the same program especially with the imminent moral and educational crisis we deem imminent especially among the youth, but also among the adults.

That's how I developed this concept into self management and personal leadership program, a program that is more practical, more accessible and handier to all worthy people. Before I end, I would like to insert one piece of testimony: That's how I began packaging and selling humans at premium price. And this isn't an act of honking one's own trumpet, on the part of the author. Indeed, a couple of my colleagues, aside from my family members, colleagues who had opted for working instead of college education resigned and decided to go the university. Some of them are lecturers now holding doctorates a others serve as senior government officials holding advanced degrees; a couple of our house maids were married or remarried officially. In fact one was engaged, and though she was a Muslim, she was remarried to a young Christian, in church! I recently met one Ngaiza. He had since completed his master's degree. He admitted publicly before his colleagues that it was through the author that he changed his mind and rearranging his priorities, chose to pursue higher education—an education of a certain kind. Super Rwamkina called the author all the way from Murongo, on the Tanzania-Uganda border, appraising the author, his family and especially his father on the role they have played in showing the way to the rest of the village and beyond.

Is it also not my wish—having helped in the transformation of my people into nobler, more practical, more productive, more resourceful and more prosperous and holier people; a more prosperous human community—that one day this program became national and international educational program? Having perfected the dream, the dream of having contributed to the refinement of humanity, I don't look forward to being rewarded let alone to be recognized for the humble part I have played in creating a program that changes the lives of our people and the human species as a whole. For after all, that's why we are scholars. That's why we were born humans—and not beasts. We were born with a purpose to fulfill—to make the world a little better—whether by the work of our hands or intellect.

Finally, in the end, I am glad for—and with—you. I am glad because I didn't labor for nothing. My search for truth—the truth behind the secret of success—has not been in vain. As you have already seen, and are about to see still more; "The search for truth is nothing less than a direct experience of life. Wrestling with moral ambiguities is where heroism is born. Contributing to the wellbeing of humanity gives us purpose and meaning. Building who we are with our own blueprint defines what character is all about. Justice purifies our vision. Humility enlightens our perspective. Love completes us like nothing else can. Courtesy draws it all together while brotherhood unites us all."[20]

---

[20] *www.chivalrynow.net/articles/life.htm*

3. THE IDEAL SCHOLAR CONCEPT, EDUCATIONAL STANDARD AND NATIONAL PHILOSOPHY

"A life without cause, is a life without effect." —*Barbarella*

Coined by the author in his first book How Universities Under Develop You! The term Ideal Graduates—the ideal scholar—and thereof Building Ideal Graduates or Scholar as a program therefore represents an attempt to respond to the discrepancy we discussed through the previous chapters. In the book, the author reports how having graduated from the university, he assumed he was learned, educated, equipped, and prepared to face the challenges ahead. He thought jobs were up for the grab, promotions, wealth, and happiness guaranteed! But alas! Securing a job was an uphill journey, and the job itself and the workplace disappointing. And this doesn't end there. Not only at work, but also in the society as a whole, there are standards or established way, or pattern of life by which a person can lead a successful career, and thereupon, meaningful life. Besides we need ideals because we have no standards as human societies. There are no KPIs for all men. Lincoln was right. Character is the root of credibility and reputation is mere its shadow. Character and attitude of a person or society form a stronger indicator of the prospects of one's future than the degree certificates or even financial capital—the money—we one may have under his belt.

With his experience as a student at the university, but more so with reflections from both the university and at work years later, the author realized that what they teach at the university—is not nearly sufficient, and in fairness, most of what they teach there is fast becoming irrelevant. Learning is never static but a deliberate, consistent, and continuous process. He learned that instead, rarely are people encouraged to keep on advancing themselves, much as the education as an entity is itself static and often rarely futuristic. Therefore, if education itself fails to continuously engage and adapt to new challenges and meet the pace of the "fast changing world" to stay abreast with what it is required to deliver, especially today in the face of ever-changing technology, consumer tastes, globalization, and now the disillusioned youth and society, in all fairness, it becomes nothing but an obsolete, naïve piece of information that is simply useless.[21]

The Ideal Scholar as a concept therefore, did spring from the disarray in our education as well as from among our scholars, or appropriately, our men of education. It was this rather sad realization that led the author to conclude that there is a significant disarray or discrepancy in our education system—and thereupon, discrepancy in the society. And the major handicap is that we find no common factors or qualities among our men of education. Our graduates lack common qualities amongst themselves and among different academic disciplines or professions. Now if one person is a graduate of economics and another of marketing as another is a scientist and an engineer and a rocket scientist and biologist and lawyer surely they cannot technically learn the same things. But they should be able to think, act and conduct themselves in a certain specific and common way—the way of the men of education they are supposed to be. This common thought pattern, conduct or character is what really can be considered to be education. If there are no such intersections, or connections, among our graduates what then is education? Or, more importantly, what is education for?

While we appreciate existence and importance of our diversity in terms of character, culturally and vocationally we recognize a great need of establishing a middle ground or bottom line for our professionals and the rest of the citizens. Let's now, together, attempt to identify some outward characteristics of a couple different professionals which in part tell us something about their instructions themselves or the mode of instruction itself and how they have been brought up.

---

[21] ***ADAPTED FROM*** *How Universities Under Develop You!*

Lawyers: though we know the dress or speech we put on doesn't say everything about us, but we find a significant break among our men of education in how they dress. We also realize how we dress says something about us. As for lawyers they dress in black suits and speak certain jargons. They crave titles and admiration. They are suspicious of any word, deed or person. And like most professionals, they are buried in their own only little world of laws and massage courtroom judgments. Most have personal pride. They tend to live in isolation—in their small groups. They tend to believe they deserve respect from everyone else while they remain on the receiving end.

Engineers: most engineers dress casually—and their language is vulgar. They have high opinion of no other profession but engineering. For them analysis is nonsensical. But on the brighter side they crave doing, action, results—concrete ones. Policemen: they are suspicious individuals seeking evidence to sentence anyone but themselves for wrong doing. They are never truthful and cannot be trusted as true friends indeed. They are egotistical and ready to fix anyone provided they can benefit financially or professionally. Rarely do they go to church. And they believe every wealthy man should give them money instead of working hard to get what they want. Rarely are they self reliant in spirit. Reading books or news is distasteful to most folks among the law enforcers. Self-advancement is not their regular cup of tea.

Marketers: most of them tend to be more talkative and lazy, doing a lot of talking than doing! For many there is a very fine line between the marketers and con men. Some typical old school markers believe that the best salesman is one whose capability to seduce girls is handy! No wonder many persons in that field land into promiscuity. You probably have noticed that marketers are rarely good family men! They hate evaluation of what they do. They tend to pass the buck on fixing their hopes on the hardworking fellows in the organization and—or— at home. Most are *lifeists* and unreliable rarely waking up early from long nights meeting customers in the bars.

Teachers tend to dress formally and modestly. They speak with dignity—when they are motivated. Discouraged, most tend to love a drink—like doctors. Politicians: most prefer to talk that do the work itself. Rarely are they productive or innovative in the true sense of producing material wealth. They crave power, to rule and reign over others. Most—I repeat, most—are people who are calculating, opportunists and manipulative, advocates of quick fix! And this is not my insinuation. A great politician said it himself. He said: "The best minds are not in the government. If they were any, business would hire them." Can you guess who made this conclusion? It was President Ronald Regan—of all Presidents—and yes of all countries. Selfish are they that they secretly worship old school monarchy for which they line up their children. They tend to assume they have all answers—and because of this inherent trait since the days of Socrates many have painted them as liars—and generally unpredictable! Few actually trust them.

And suddenly this idea about the middle ground is not irrelevant. It is neither alien nor something extraterrestrial. If we have to have a comprehensive and definite end we have to have a kind of direction or bottom line expectation from whatever we set out to do. Without the middle ground or big picture until as I write is a sign that education has lacked comprehensive purpose and direction. The ideals or core values we introduce therefore help to build the intelligent and productive middle ground among the different professions. You probably have noticed that I inserted a phrase "intelligent and productive," middle ground. If we don't address such commonness, we may end up where most societies are today: a society with corrupt lazy gossiping minds; a mediocre workforce and an academia that is resigned upon thinking but one that labors in pursuit for politics and financial personal gain at the expense of everybody else but its masters—the business minded, power infested politicians—rather than individuals or political parties striving to serve the nation. And as for the teachers, as wrote Ornstein and Hunkins, if curriculum is not followed by a maintenance plan, it tend to disappear into the daily routine of the classrooms; with teachers sometimes personalizing the programs to the point where they have little remembrance to the original curriculum (Ornstein and Hunkins 1998, p. 202). And according to Dewey the method of surrounding the students with materials but not suggesting a purpose or a plan but rather allowing students to respond according to their interests is really stupid and attempts the impossible which is always stupid (Ornstein and Hunkins 1998, p. 86).

Besides, if you thought the author is setting out to accomplish something unthought-of and therefore uncalled for, you are in for a big shock. Paraphrasing what Ornstein and Hunkins stated, let me say that: *"Diversity and cultural pluralism are hallmarks of any current society. Yet for instance there are things about those who live in the United States (or the United Republic for that matter), that define them as Americans, (or Tanzanians for that matter,) and not, say, Canadians or Mexicans or Ugandans, Kenyans, Burundians, Kenyans Congolese, Malawians,*

Mozambicans, Zambians, Rwandans or Arabs for that matter. There are certain behaviors, attitudes and outlooks that define a model personality or ideal Tanzanian graduate or citizen for that matter. Certainly, Americans, as products of American schools, are disguisable from Europeans or any other nationals as are Tanzanians disguisable from East Africans or any other nationals.

Curricularists must recognize that, despite our differences, we Tanzanians, or any other nation for that matter, do share some common dimensions: *a national social civic culture is shaping us. This national civic culture even contours how we go about forming and transforming our social scenes. A prime purpose of public school is to nurture an understanding of and participation in this macro civic culture while recognizing the diversity of the microcultures that influence civic culture. Schools ought therefore to be designed to foster the health and wellbeing of national culture. But as Conrad Arensberg and Arthur Niehoff put forth:"What is meant by American (or for that matter Tanzanian) culture?"* [22]

A related question is whether there is a model (or ideal) American (or for that matter the model Tanzanian) personality? Ruth Benedict wrote "No culture yet observed has been able to eradicate the differences in temperament of persons that compose it." Yet members of a society do have much in common...so that individuals behave in similar, but it identical, ways... The norms of society govern interpersonal relations and produce a model or for that matter ideal personality, that is, the attitudes feelings and behavior patterns that most members of a society share. Thus despite the current talk about cultural pluralism there still exists a model or ideal personality...we have a core around which we construct our social reality. Yes we have different subcultures but they are all interwoven into our macro social fabric. In other words, irrespective of religion national origin race class and sex there are points of likeness that will occur more frequently amongst us than amongst people living in other countries. The author doesn't refuse that we exhibit a great diversity in wealth, education, manners, and tastes. Despite diversities of ethnicity traditions and wealth we possess a *"surprising conformity in language, diet, hygiene, dress, basic skills, land use, community settlement, recreation, etc."* While we are indeed a diverse and varied mix of peoples, we do have some shared views

---

[22] *Allan C. Ornstein and Francis P. Hunkins, Curriculum Foundations, Principles and Issues 3rd Edition p. 138*

and beliefs (good or bad) that define us. We are closer together in our moral outlooks, political beliefs and social attitudes than one would find in other countries...we share ideals even though we frequently fall short of attaining them.[23]

It is therefore one major purpose and (or) role of education—and indeed, of our schools, and thereof households and workplaces—to build on this foundation to establish, identify and develop the ideal Tanzanian personality. Overall, the ideal scholar or a model graduate concept, or rather ideal person is, generally speaking, the ideal human personality. We have seen that, generally, there is common culture or characteristics in a certain society and generally any nation. But it is not advisable that we leave such a pillar to the invisible hand of the society to decide. In America, the educators realized that a new nation had to differentiate itself from its colonial mother England. Webster argued that the United States should have its own system of language as well as government. The language of the Great Britain, he reasoned, "should no longer be our standard; for the taste of her writers is already completed, and her language on the decline. By the act of revolution, the America people had declared their political independence from England, and now they needed to declare their cultural independence as well."[24]

However fantastic is the fact that there naturally develops similarity among people in the same locality or nation, we cannot afford to throw all cautions to the four winds. We need to set standards—high standards. We cannot afford to let everyone person or community in a nation set ones goal however too little or pathetic that goal is. The foregoing statement explains why we need to establish the middle ground or bottom line. The books; are they perfect. Well, it doesn't matter. What matters they will make you think about it. Besides, *this model personality should not be regarded as a dogma. It is rather a guiding principle or bottom-line of our expectation of personality and character of our graduates and ultimately the rest of citizens.* Besides, different colleges or campuses and workplaces tend to wedge own cultures of their own which are then passed on to

---

[23] *Allan C. Ornstein and Francis P. Hunkins, Curriculum Foundations, Principles and Issues 3rd Edition p. 138-139*

[24] *Allan C. Ornstein and Francis P. Hunkins, Curriculum Foundations, Principles and Issues 3rd Edition p. 67*

students hence every other college, campus or workplace pervade its own culture transfused with the culture of the hosting community , society or country. And this is not safer for our countries which are tribal and sectarian but also pervading with such bad habits as laziness, drinking habits, self-interest, quick fix and gambling, drugs, promiscuity etc.

Though this isn't conclusive, please recognize that as nations have bureaus of standards for the products or services sold in the country—we need a tool that can help to bring about the common ground for a graduate from any country or discipline—the standard that pertains to their self-conduct rather than pass marks. But as well we have experienced a disproportionate incompetency among our graduates. We have seen either incompetent or corrupt architects or engineers building below standards to reap the value off the top. How many politicians are allegedly convicted of signing wrong and disastrous contracts out of incompetence or personal gain? We have seen dishonest or incompetent or even negligent doctors operating the head instead of a doing a knee surgery on one patient while operating the leg of a patient supposed to undergo the surgery of the skull.

Lately we heard shocking news. An operating team of doctors and assistants finished successfully the surgery of the abdomen of a patient and hurriedly stitched up the stomach leaving a set of operating scissors in the abdomen. We have heard and experienced some of our teaching or corporate personnel drinking during class or work hours. Have we not heard of men sleeping with goats or sheep or adult males and females who rape the infants? We have been shocked by news of parents who raped their own children across all sexes. This can be due to incompetence of our men of education or inappropriate education. But more it is so due to poor character, recklessness or generally the collapse of, or absolutely absence of morals in the society.

Having graduates who only score top of their classes when they did so in different disciplines and have big discrepancies in their true persons; or when we rarely find anything in common in terms of how they are really productive or work as agents of positive change in the society but rather the most ineffectual and corrupt and perilous members of the society is out of proportions. Since they do different disciplines we all need in the society only superior character or positive change they bring to the society is what can really identify our graduates as really true scholars or men of education. Yet until as we write we are certain that when you closely look at our graduates you will not find anything that connects them. If we can trace among engineers, lawyers, accountants, rocket scientist, economists, teachers etc; if we can find and have in place something or identity that connects them, that's really what is education.

Furthermore; as we address character we provide for or nourish the other parts of human whole; viz. the intangible human element. A human being is truly bigger or rather more than the human body w can see and touch. Schools therefore should find a way to address yes, the needs of the body, but also the soul with its spiritual needs as well as the psyche or mind with its intellectual needs. I am aware that probably someone is saying this mere religious talk. It isn't. I swear. Take Libyan people for instance. Gaddafi provided them with housing, food, Medicare, education, etc. Yet they took arms and sacrificing their lives, they marched on crossing a forest of detonated bombs and smoking Kalashnikovs waving away a forest of glistering bayonets across lakes and rivers of blood to overthrow the man who actually supplied them with almost every other bodily provision. Think about it! He gave them monthly allowances bigger than the average salary range in modern economies, free, of course, on the silver platter whether they worked or not. Think about it! Why? Their other selves: *the intellect or mind and soul or spirit* wept for self expression.

Internationally we have what is called ISO—International Organization for Standards. It was established to put in place quality standards for any product or services wherever it is produced. The knowledge of branding surrounds commonness and reliability. The men of education are by themselves a brand. If we can't buy a brand that changes colors like a chameleon what about our scholars, If standardization is imperative for products or services, wouldn't you agree that developing standards or especially the bottom line of expected character and responsibilities among our scholars or graduates, making them more identifiable and reliable is far more important? If we can't identify anything in common among our men of education, especially in the ways of contributing positively not only to the individuals own lives, but indeed to the nation and humanity in general, what then is education?

The foregoing statement places responsibility upon the author to substantiate how worth education has to be. Education should make a substantial difference not only in the material wealth of the individual but as well as in his character especially. Education must really make a man of education stand out from the crowd as an exemplary and model personality—a person we call ideal scholar. His education must not only be advantageous to himself, but also to his family, the community and people around him, and the nation and humanity as a whole. His contribution to the nation must not hand to mouth or something that is time bound. His thinking and contribution should be futuristic—something that is ahead of its time —and indeed timeless. When we say timeless we know nothing stands the test of time. But we mean it must be something with great impact. That's not all. It must be something from which generations after him will may use to develop ideas commensurate with their time and needs—needs whose at heart there is the essence of enhancing and prolonging a complete living for the individual, his family and community ,his nation and humanity as a whole..

In words on Elliot Eisner:"We would like our children to be well informed—that is, to understand ideas that are important, useful, and powerful. And we also want them to have appetite for and to think analytically and critically, to be able to speculate, and imagine, to see connections among ideas, and to be able to use what they know to enhance their own lives and contribute to their culture." Then, "If education doesn't teach us these things," as aptly asked Leopold; "then what is education for?"[25] Really, otherwise what is education for?

---

[25] www.context.org/iclib/ic27/orr/

4. HOW BADLY DO WE NEED TRANSFORMATION?

> *"Our source of direction is found in our guiding philosophy. Without philosophy (we make) mindless vaults into the saddle like Stephen Leacock's character who flung himself from the room, flung himself upon the horse, and rode madly off in all directions.26*
> —William van Til

Through the previous works or preceding chapters in this series, we indicated how the youth today have resigned upon education. We discussed how the youth have turned and rebelled against the conventional approach to life; how the youth have rebelled against education; how they don't believe anymore in hard word; how they, instead, endeavor to succeed through quick fix and or surrender to whatever life throws at them. Because of low sense of dignity, and therefore low self-esteem and low or complete lack of the desire to prosper, to succeed, to excel, to be top, it is almost a proverb lately that, youth see schools as "Nightmare Hall," or a "Witch's Den," and therefore, to be asked to go into classes is like to be led toward Auschwitz. The youth have lost appetite for everything good that life can offer surrendering to mediocrity. You can see this growing tendency among our job seekers, if any! In, words of Cathy Williams in her wonderful novel Wife for Hire, they tend to "decide in favor of something slightly less stress inducing, such as copy typist!" Indeed, it is time to break away from this little charming affair!

---

[26] Allan C. Ornstein and Francis P. Hunkins, *Curriculum Foundations, Principles and Issues 3rd Edition p. P32*

Are these my own sentiments? Baseless sentimental feelings? emotions? Oh no! It is not a pack of lies as others would wish to imagine. If you are one of such individuals who believe the author is a pessimist and all is okay, think again. And as you do so, please read What Makes People Rich and Nations Powerful. A country to progress must have rational priorities. Ours seem to have long since been distracted not only by ICT and globalization, but also Dstv—or simply put entertainment.

To illustrate: During the last century, the American youth rebelled against education. They rebelled against almost every other conventional ways of life. According to THE MAKING OF A NATION, a program run by The Voice of America, during this time many young people decided they no longer needed to follow the conservative traditions of their parents and grandparents. This was THE AGE OF JAZZ. It was a period known until as I write as THE ROARING 1920s. It is the time when female folks boycotted traditional values of the time at an industrial scale and began clubbing and drinking in public; they began dressing and dancing erotically.

We have warned against the Entertainmenation of the nation and thereupon reintroduced the notion of The Principled Universe vs. growth through the previous works and chapters in the same series of this book pushing for the return to the basics.[27] To some individuals, it was considered as an intelligent way of meeting new rising challenges. And to their illusion, these youth made money and so did their communities. The nation as a whole appeared to have become wealthier. But lo! It was a bubble or an economic boom on the papers—a boom resulting not from real value from the farms or factories but resulting from trading and middlemanship. There was no actual growth in industry, or in productive science or technology. A few innovations were made in classes or in factories and indeed very few people worked in real terms. The gap between the rich and the poor escalated. And what? Though the productivity and revenue on the paper looked bigger but people were not motivated to work anymore. And the growth they realized was only a bubble. And like all bubbles, it was only to be blown up by the wind beginning with the crash of the stock market followed by loss of jobs, homes and hopes for the future. That was, in short, what was behind the great depression!

---

[27] *Make reference to a book, A Sick Nation: How To Heal It*

We who live in this generation have experienced something very close in nature and similar in fashion to the foregoing explanation, and are still struggling to see ourselves out of it. And when I say "we" I mean all of us. Not even the Unites States, Japan or Greece or the whole European Union is any safer. China too! Her economy is no longer growing at a two digit figure anymore. The US needed Franklin Roosevelt's new deal to bring the hope back. Aren't we being presented with some sort of new deal in here? Do we now still have to ask if we do really need transformation? How badly?

Considering the significance of this age group, the youth, and its roles in the society, and how they are actually backsliding, as we have discussed in the previous —especially through A SICK NATION AND HOW TO HEAL IT—or chapters in this series, I cannot overemphasize how we need transformation. But before that, let us reason together. How did we find ourselves in this mess? We simply arrived where we are because we have discounted our ways of life throwing all cautions to the four winds. The programs that helped cultivate our own civilization don't exist anymore. Our society is experiencing outrageous pursuit for "modernity." Even though modernity itself is no sin but we have wrongly defined it as *western*, and anything *western is foolproof*, and therefore persistent love for everything western. As a result? We have accepted intellectual slavery, and therefore little, if any success, has to be expected, and fewer people should be expected to prosper thereof.

Surprisingly, the author has also observed that even those who succeed today do so by sheer chance. The path they follow cannot be said to be airtight or failure-proof. Curiously, a significant number of those who succeed today do so through the Law of the Jungle, or the survival of the fittest. It is a tooth for a tooth; a nail for a nail battle! Animal eat animal—*crawl your way up, no matter what. Just climb even if it is by bringing others down.* By itself this law cannot sustain itself for long. It is also untenable. They have no sure or sustainable formula to win. It is no wonder they become rich one day and poor the next day. It is because for instance steal to be rich but again overuse the loot only to become poor again. Then they steal again and again. No wonder we have ubiquitous examples of wealthy men and women who are convicted and brought before law to answer over organized robbery or embezzlement of the public funds. We need a comprehensive and sustainable path to prosperity. That's what we present to you through this book—in this series.

Without ideals our graduates seem to have just had skills to perform some tasks, but that's all. Now if we could find that they have certain qualities in common, these qualities are what we could call education. The preceding statement can be established by the discrepancy we find among various disciplines or professions and graduates thereof. This "something" which separates two persons, is a compass, about which we need. It is a vision or a set of principles or internal guidance. "We say it is internal because it is often deep-rooted and works on its own. It even works without our deliberate actions. This is in the end the mindset or thought pattern that we have developed. It is our character.

Back to our question: Do we need transformation? How badly? Before I tackle this question, let me first admit that yes, I may not be the most learned person when it comes to pedagogy, or even sociology, but I am not a complete nincompoop in areas of the mind or human desires or aspiration and development . ! That's why I can say with confidence that to say we need transformation is an understatement. But that's one thing. We also need new kind of thought and thought pattern. That's why in my preparation to write this book, having been disillusioned with conventional rigid education, albeit itself not a complete flop, but one based on the traditional thought pattern which asserts that things should remain as they are, whereas we believe as times change, education must tag along, I read extensively the books that can be said to on the wrong side of the curriculum. That's why i didn't read biology or any such text books. I did so having determined that all we needed was a new kind of education—an education about you or me as a person and not as about an organ such as liver or a tooth, and its functionality, but about man in his wholeness.

From the foregoing scope, a learner will also find it is in his benefit to learn about the people and environment around him. That's how advantageous is going out of the box; that's why aside from the Koran and the bible, I read books that are wrongly classed as inspirational. I refuse to regard them as such. They are not inspirational per se. This is a mutant definition. They are more than that. Yes they inspire people, which is a good thing, but as well they educate—and educate us better about us in our wholeness than do such text books we used to class as scholarly, books about biology, anthropology, or even history or civics, for they address us in our wholeness, touching our hearts, intellect and souls. Whether the novel idea is nobler, or the existing education system or policy isn't completely ineffective in its wholeness is not an issue. The issue is that: "We can't solve problems," aptly counseled Albert Einstein, "by using the same kind of thinking we used when we created them."

We read the Malaysian story and find that transformation had to be done both at individual corporation or employee level but indeed for the change to be sweeping and lasting, it has to go beyond individuals—corporations or persons. It has to envelope the whole nation—to wrap all circles of social, economic, academic and religious, or moral life of the society and humanity in its entirety—especially with emergence of radical religious groups. That's why I say we need a revolution. And yet it is not revolution revolution, if you know what I mean? I don't mean political revolution or coup d'état! No! I mean intellectual or mind revolution. What we need is a social and cultural revolution. But it all begins in, and with, the mind. Such a sweeping transformation cannot be successful without the revolution, or evolution—one way or the other—in our education and the society in general. If it can come by revolution as such, or by evolution, or even through both, this is a happy ending, and it goes down well with every well wisher of his or her community, nation and humanity as a whole.

Let us together analyze this challenge: The youth form two third of this country's population. Two, the youth group in the country—the back-bone of the nation is unfortunately either unemployed or under employed. They are, thirdly, a group that has lost hope, turning to drugs, alcohol, ganja, prostitution, robbery and other vices thus making the youth a group very prone to HIV/AIDS, and as a result. Loss of national manpower in terms of deaths, uselessness or hopelessness, poverty and insecurity too many—and extinction of the nation—the nation we seek to preserve. Furthermore, this group if not looked-after—and now; it is going to be a cost to the public, the government and tax payers in terms of insecurity, medication and opportunity cost. That is why the fourth phase administration in Tanzania for instance has taken several commendable measures—to empower the youth. The government has also placed the youth in top positions in sports, arts and education. Youth empowerment is pivotal to national development because in my view, a country whose youth aren't progressing is a nation that is certainly progressing backwards. In words of John F. Kennedy: "The future promise of any nation can be directly measured by the present prospects of its youth."

THE ASPECT OF GENDER IN THE MIDST OF THE YOUTH-NATIONAL DEVELOPMENT EQUATION

What about gender relationship in regards to gender exploitation and disuse of our natural resources and especially the human resources? Regarding the significance of the gender aspect into the whole equation, an important note about gender balance and empowerment has to be made.

Recent research figures show that females are majority than males in many economies—thus they form a larger proportion of youth and population as a whole. Because women are sidelined they have turned to informal economy. The informal economy contributes a larger share of our economy—and women play major role in this area—an area that unfortunately orphaned! That is if we have to re-channel resource toward growth path, we have got to empower yes, the youth, but also we must equally empower girls and females folks in general. Youth empowerment and developing both gender groups is thus a critical antidote if we have to progress. Indeed according to Hillary Rodham Clinton: "Human rights and women rights are one and same thing!"

In explaining the pivotal role of the youth or generally the human resource, for instance in the 1990s, Australia "realized had to emphasize human resources...(Note that)The only difference between Japan, (the second economic power for forty years) and Australia is that (in Japan) they have better management of their humans (that is, human development). Japan is a country with fewer physical resources (a tiny and fragmented infertile disjointed land but this lucky nation) it only has its people. And yet, they are outperforming Australia.[28]" It is doubtless consistent with the foregoing analysis, that Malcolm Turnbull, the newly elected Australian prime minister, stated recently challenging Australian academics and policy makers that Australia should change its aims of education from educating Australians to grow their economy by digging stuff from the ground straight to the market, to one that instead should emphasize inventions, technology and innovation; an education that enables value addition and reaping off the top rather than selling crude stuff such as mineral ores, or agricultural products. We have also witnessed how the economies that depend largely on oil and gas almost crumbling to the record low.

Dutch Shell company has issued a report indicating a fall of its revenues by 80% from last year (2015) to date hand in hand with job loss of 10, 000 workers. That's the kind of education we need here at home in Tanzania, here in Africa—and the rest of LDCs. Dutch shell company has issued a report indicating a fall of its revenues by 80% from last year (2015). That's the kind of ideal we need to emphasize in our schools, as well as at workplaces. With the experience of the fall of the economies that depend

---

[28] *John O. Miller in How to Lead, How to Manage Executives by James C. Sarros, 991 p. 181*

on oil and gas such as Nigeria and Russia, or even the African countries that depend on exportation of raw agricultural products, does the author still need to illustrate any further?

Shocking revelation eh, isn't it! The contrast between the two nations above teaches us that it is not the macroeconomic policies or even the physical resources that differentiate the two or three countries economically, but the people. But since the youth form the two third of our working force, that's where we should focus our attention. The lessons from the two countries further teach us that material and financial assets cannot work for us if we don't develop intellectual capital which we have in abundance. Ultimately, I am convinced that, the difference rises from a nation's leadership and culture: priorities, innovation, hard work, patriotism and concern for the future, etc. The aggregate experiences of Japan, Switzerland, Uganda or even Botswana; or even singular individual experiences in our families and at work back to back with setbacks in countries like Congo, Kenya, Libya and Iraq etc prove the critical role of people in development rather than natural resources such as the ocean, arable land, minerals, oil and gas etc[29].

Unfortunately our curriculum doesn't place appropriate attention on students themselves but studies: chemistry, economics, biology etc. The workplaces place more attention to making money than the feelings and aspirations of the employees! As a result of this recklessness on our priorities, the youth themselves with nowhere or no one to turn to! If this trend is not checked—and I don't see it happening soon—we cannot reclaim the youth and the nation as a whole. That's why we need to connect studies we teach with individuals' day to day lives. We have got to emphasize qualities of character and personality not only to supplement but more importantly to cement the educational intake. We cannot, unfortunately, accomplish such a feat without deliberate pursuit of correct, transformational education. Surprisingly, we see only very few people pursuing true change. That's why we wrote this book.

Nationally, we see more public and corporate focus and funds being channeled behind modeling, music and art. We see the artists glorified as national heroes and role models. Fewer individuals buy or read books. Very few individuals care about self-advancement. Skewed to art, the

---

[29] *Adapted from What Makes People Rich and Nations Powerful*

administration's sentiments and corporate funding are skewed away from reading or writing books and building libraries. We see more beauty contests and music festivals and dance or beer drinking competitions, as we see fewer and fewer books or essays writing or reading competitions. Many are the people who do very little to nourish the mind or intellect let alone the soul concentrating with the leisurely pleasures of the body. That's how we reached where we are. Abu Bakr was right. *"Thinking is the food of the mind.*

What does the foregoing assertion say? Simply put, we need more attention and more light into the other parts of our own persons. Ornstein and Hunkins rightly observed thus: Specific courses in self management (i.e. management) of one's intellect, emotions, and ...inner awareness will allow us in some ways to remake ourselves regarding mind, body and spirit. The courses of the future will acknowledge that the students are more than talking heads... Wattles D. Wallace said in his book Science of Getting Rich: *We live for the body, we live for the mind, and we indeed live for the soul. No one of these is better or holier than the other..."*

Yet I am convinced that Mr. Wallace was writing in a polite way and used his humblest phraseology not wishing to offend some individuals in his audience. He knew the ego of men. That's who we are. Human nature detests criticism. Remember also that that was around the beginning of this century when he wrote his magnificent all-time book. However with recent needs in our society and education in particular I chose to be plainer! And it is to your own good! And here is the truth we want to paint in black and white. The intangible person viz. the intellect or mind or the intellect and the soul or spirit put together is holier than the tangible person—the body! Yet many have turned to the body and forgotten this other self. How humans can reverse the order of things for personal gain albeit out of ignorance is so shocking! It does more than shame me to know that I belong to the same species! Subsequently, "Do not be deceived; God cannot be mocked, for whatever a man sows, that he will also reap. For he who sows to please his own flesh will, from flesh reap destruction; but he who sows to the spirit, will from sprit reap eternal life," as wrote Paul apostle to Galatians so I do unto you now. So am I emphasizing thus, "Let us not grow weary in doing good, for in due season, we shall reap..."

Probably you do now realize now that we live in the world where every ideal person, every ideal citizen and every law abiding citizen who plays around the governing rules, enjoys freedom of thought and freedom of deed unequaled anywhere? Sadly most of us have never taken inventory of the advantage of this freedom. We have never compared our unlimited freedoms with curtailed freedom in other countries. We have freedom of thought, freedom in the choice and enjoyment of education, freedom in politics, freedom in choice of business profession or occupation, freedom to accumulate and own without molestation all the property we can accumulate, freedom to choose our place of residence, freedom in marriage, freedom through equal opportunity to all races, freedom to travel from one place to another, freedom for choice of food and freedom to aim for any station in life for which we have prepared ourselves (I will repeat this. It is a key word: Freedom to aim for any station in life, for which we have prepared ourselves and our children), even for the presidency of the United Republic. If anyone questions this last assertion revisit the biographies of former presidents namely: Mwinyi, Mkapa and Kikwete.

In the end if we don't make a decisive shift—and now, I don't see us improving. Let me emphasize the lessons from Australia. We cannot progress without progressing the youth. My nearly forty years of active life have led me to an indisputable conclusion: a country whose youth aren't progressing is a nation that is certainly progressing backwards. Truly I cannot overemphasize how significant is a shift in our priorities and particularly focusing on enlightenment of the youth on their aspirations and their roles for themselves, their families and the society as a whole if we have to turn the tables around. And I am not on my own in this fair conclusion. Aristotle said: "All who have meditated on the art of governing mankind have been convinced that the fate of empires depends on the education of youth." John F. Kennedy concluded that: *"The future promise of any nation can be directly measured by the present prospects of its youth."*

HOW THE IDEAL SCHOLAR CONCEPT IS INDISPENABILE AND WHY THE IDEAL PERSON CAN NEVER FAIL

Now is this program truly essential? Why now? To answer both questions beginning with the first: Yes it is. Our youth and society in general have lost the sense of direction—and everything that can make one great—that some being an individual person, family, educational institution, business or a nation—hangs in balance. And without the sense of direction, the individuals and nations will lead to the road that leads to nowhere—something that this training addresses. And as for the second, we don't simply need change. We need it urgently. And there is more to it than that; which is: Transform or lose ground. In the previous chapters we discussed how we see the youth back sliding into potential failures. With this realization the author concluded therefore that we needed a kind of training that would help transform the youth. Yes our schools today can teach some professional skills but that is as far as they can go. Schools don't give due knowledge and especially attention to the actual ability to meet life's challenges. It is these abilities that make people move from thinking to doing and getting results. At the moment we can't seem to think straight, we can't plan and can't do or execute anything because we have literally nothing to do. And therefore we can't get any results.

This is the essential part of education, failure of which debases education—and educators thereof—as it also dooms the students and the future of the nation. The Promise, a book by Professor Maliyamkono so aptly comments thus, "education is (and should be) perceived not only as infusing knowledge but also as equipping citizens with the ability to understand and unravel problems within the society caused by the ever changing economic, technological, and social environment in which we live."

Besides, to emphasize importance of the program we put ourselves and the program itself to test. We welcome the challenge. And here is that challenge. The ideal graduate or scholar cannot fail. Truly, nothing can come between an ambitious and focused a person. Not poor school facilities or financial constraints. I'm again a living witness. We can talk of Barack Obama or Bill Clinton. Bill Clinton was brought by what you could term as a single mother who wasn't near wealthy. Obama was a skinny boy with a funny name from a single mother's family brought up by his maternal granny. You can as well talk about Richard Williams, the Williams' Sisters' father. He knew it would be a hassle for his daughters to make it through academics and that it would be a lot easier in tennis. Yet you can find a couple of such role models around you, witnesses you can relate to.

The ideal person cannot fail. No he can't. Never! He can't fail because he is immune to failure. His character repels failure. To inherit good character is worth more than to inherit wealth. Probably we should recall King Suleiman. He chose to have wisdom—or generally to always think and decide and behave well—than ask for wealth or longer life. Then god told him that:"Because you have asked for wisdom and not your own life or wealth or life of your enemies, I'll give you wisdom and all other blessings you didn't ask for!" and so it was.

How then is it worth such a program that creates this change in your child or spouse? Prophet Isaiah says thus: "go and lighten up for your light has come (Isaiah 60: 1)." But for the reverse it is written: "For the wages of sin is death (Romans 6.22). The blessings of virtue, well, when you are virtuous, you receive blessings Jesus introduced as: *Having life and having it in full.* As we are about to take you through the virtues of the ideal scholar, it is probably decisive to comprehend that there're advantages only the ideal person gains. The ideal scholar or person, as a magnet attracts all things he wants in life. Indeed a person worthy of living, crave these qualities unless he forgoes affluence and sacrifices the greater things life offers in the spirit of prayer and giving.

Well, the ideal scholar may—by miracle of miracles—fail in biology, history or any subject for that matter as if for miracle but will still be decent and make proper living. He would still be great and at some point in time will experience a comeback. But here's the fact: an ideal man cannot fail because he is hardworking, disciplined, active listener listens to instructions actively, perseveres, and is patient and temperate. Even if he or she fails in biology or mathematics, he will still on average be the best in everything on which he puts his heart.

Talk about the comeback. Here's the fact: the ideal person cannot fail! Why? Because he is disciplined; he is hard working, an active learner or listener who has a definite noble goal to accomplish in life. He is therefore a person who perseveres toward his or her goal; he or she is patient and temperate. He or she has self-control of high order as we shall further discuss. But of major importance—he or she has a greater desire for and faith in prosperity. According to the bible(adapted from Galatians 5.22.23), *"the blessing of the spiritual transformation is love, joy, peace, longsuffering, kindness, goodness, faithfulness, gentleness and self-control. (And what's more,) against such blessings there's law."* When I say it is a law, I mean it is a set of new ideas or guidelines enhancing human development. It enhances success in schools, households and workplaces. It is a tool to elevate students and workforce desire for self learning, a tool to help students study or employees to work without or with minimum supervision—and with fewer resources. It is a tool for loyalty. A tool to that enhances employees' productivity and tool that will help double your business' profitability; shorten the breakeven point and speed up the ROI. It is a tool that will crucially enhance prosperity among individuals and naturally their whole society.

In the end, this program "conjures up" the ideal scholars—ideal scholars who become bearers of ideal responsible and productive employees, ideal leaders, and still more importantly—the ideal future mothers and fathers and indeed, ideal families and responsible citizens. Myself the author of the program, I trust if I'd gone through the program twenty years ago, I would have accomplished a greater feat many years back. Many respondents suggest the same sentiment! I'm a witness and a walking billboard of this fact! You now realize that with this program, even when one fails in biology or history, as if by miracle anyway, but still he will be decent and make proper living. He or she would still be great and at some point in time, out of the same miracle, will make a comeback. The foregoing explains why even if, by miracle, he or she fails in biology or mathematics, he will remain the best in many other areas—areas of his or her choice! How can such a person fail then? Impossible! And this is no theory and I'm a witness and a walking billboard of this fact!

Let me substantiate. Truly my many years of observation have proved that no one ideal person ever failed. Growing up in a big family, the author has even from a very close range watched over a hundred different heads belonging to his extended family; and he can without doubt say that even when overall his family being not far from what you could call good people but he can specify two or three of his brothers and sisters who are very close to the ideal person he has laid down. And I can assure you that it isn't the DNA or IQ, i.e., Intelligence Quotient that differentiates two persons, or three. Look around your neighborhood And you will notice that however humble one's growth can still be said to be when compared to that of Bill Gates or one's peers from the well-to-do families, you will realize that those who grow, have grown almost solely because of the moral values and standards they set long ago choosing them as their ideals. You will see them achieve whatever they set out to do or be when others grumble in confusion. I am often led to believe that if some people haven't achieved beyond what they have achieved, it is only because they haven't decided to do so considering someone's true potential in terms of human natural abilities and superior character.

I also know in my family, individuals who are highly classed as more capable intellect-wise who have not made relatively significant accomplishments—individuals highly classed as an intelligent minds but who still struggle to attain towering potential. Well, because I know it is never too late, I believe with this analysis, anyone can make it anytime. Analysis is the beginning of every success. Has the author made so much reference only or mainly about people around him, and therefore making the analysis a little less far reaching or realistic? Now it is your turn to digest the same. So now take a little break and look around you, your family or friends and neighbors. Don't read on for a couple of seconds. Okay? One, two, three, four…Come on! Go on…

You see! And I am not shocked that you have arrived at the same conclusion. Indeed an ideal person can accumulate wealth and live a balanced healthy life he chooses however simplistic it may seem to be—and vice versa. The assertion looks so simple. But indeed all great success stories started from the very humble beginnings. The training thereof isn't meant for only the elites or the learned. Through this training even the unlearned get educated, literally, and acquire the privilege of maintaining upper hand over their own lives and destinies. Indeed: "The fruit of the spirit is love, joy, peace, forbearance, kindness, goodness, faithfulness, gentleness and self-control. Against such things there's no law (Galatians 5:22-23)!"

In writing this piece of stuff, Paul apostle had an experience of his background. He knew what he said. I've never seen such a high level of barbarism among animals! And that's not enough. It is crude. Uncultured. Unthoughtful. To follow diligently this set of ideals as your guide to a new way of life is almost like an insurance cover against failure. Anyone who already recognizes this secret will follow the instructions almost religiously! Recognize we are engaged in analyzing why and how an ideal person can never fail.

Now you should have heard of Alexander the Great. One day he was inspecting his battalion when he found one sentry asleep. "What's your name?" he asked. Sleeping as a sentry and especially during war was a crime whose penalty was death on the guillotine. The great leader knew one had to change to be a better person. So instead of killing him or threatening him *to do so*, he chose to teach him a lesson. That's why he asked: "What's your name?" "Alexander!" the guy replied. Then Alexander the emperor admonished his subject "Change your name or change your habit," and vanished. To change your habit means to adapt and live by it, by the new rules. For Alexander the Great, the name Alexander was not just a name. It represented bigger meaning than just nomenclature. We should not forget that our choices in life are influenced by the information we have at hand. When we don't expose our children to inspiration, better guided information, they will pick up whatever information they will find and make decisions based on them. Let us not allow our children to grow up in senselessness. That's why we ought therefore to train up a child in the way he should go and when he is old he will not depart from it. Building ideals is a beginning of child upbringing.

As parents we ought to ask ourselves such questions as how much are we spending on leisure, pleasure, drinks and clothing? People don't take education and the day's works seriously. Parents are not home to look after children. Children have no right inspiration and as a result, their children are mix up with bad boys and that is the beginning: That is when they start picking up deplorable habits! Most importantly, we must ask ourselves: what is my role s a father or mother? Do we know? Crystal clear? I doubt! Read more on the role of parents in the book What makes people rich and nations powerful.

As a father myself, let me say, we shouldn't allow that to happen. What children pick up at early age forms fiber of the personality they will become? The children have got to learn to stand on one's own feet and face up to realities of life. Otherwise you are running a risk of having your daughter or son spending all his or her life standing on other people's two feet or patched on one of his or her own! Indeed a child should not be brought up like a china doll, one who does nothing or one who cannot be made to think on his own—with his own mind, for otherwise he will have half a mind to call his own![30] To expect your child to be anything less is not only impossible, but it is also unreasonable. We reap what you sow, don't we? The concept of Ideal Scholars answers to that—and compels them to follow through at will! They become messengers and patrons of the idea when they know it is for their own good—when they know there's a lot for them in it! Truly, the moral code, or one cannot succeed or prosper without such qualities—qualities wrapped in a certain ethics and integrity.

Now the question comes. Does anyone who succeeds have all these ideals? No. Not all who are successful are ideal persons. There are people who are successful in their areas of profession or are wealth who are not necessarily ideal humans. They are successful or wealthy because they used foul or inherited wealth or positions. This is not a group of people I talk about. I talk about people who work hard smartly and manage to rise from poverty to affluence or success in their vocations. Besides, without these ideals or qualities even if one succeeds, his success is seldom long term. Bigger and long term success must and should be sheltered by a certain set of

---

[30] *Vintage Stuff by Tom Sharpe p13-14!*

conditions or qualities which is a set of these ideals. We live in an era where we already know that the destiny of our lives is in our own hands. We also know that we are the ones who can make the difference. Besides, no matter how good you are, you can always be better. Astonishingly, no matter whether you are already the best, you can still be better as a person, your character or what you do. You might not be initiated in the ways of economics to know this, but be informed that in economic theory, there is a notion of The Second and First Best. Yet with our history of slavery, colonialism and Ujamaa policy all which worked to stifle self- esteem and thereof competitiveness and industriousness. We can generally call competitiveness and industriousness the desire or obsession for success or victory or prosperity.

Slavery, colonialism and Ujamaa policy together worked to stifle the desire to be top, to excel, to triumph. They together thereof created hopelessness and a tradition of placing less value on education or generally fighting back, and hence surrender to whatever life throws at them. It follows therefore that we experience a constantly growing number of school dropouts and a culture of quick fix. Besides, challenges emanating from modern-day globalization and advancement in ICT and now the recent economic downturn all place more pressure on us to depend on our own resources— intellectually and financially. That's why we need, more than ever before, to rise above our circumstances and build new foundations for our future society. Today we see the greatness of countries such as the USA and imagine it was always there and it never was under the threat from within or without. Never.

If a society has to develop and its economy to continue growing, needs to keep looking at its own foundations—the culture, structure, and principles—and rebuild or, where necessary build new ones altogether. Despite her successes as a pinnacle nation on the planet, the United States reevaluated the core of her greatness—which is education—in its famous *Cardinal Principles of Secondary Education* by the Commission on The Reorganization of Secondary Education in 1918, a highly progressive document influenced by Flexner's work *A Modern School* and Dewey *Democracy and Education*, in this document the commission stressed the whole child (not just the cognitive area of study*)*, education for all youth (not just college-bound youth*)*, diversified areas of study (not classical or traditional studies*), common culture, ideas, and ideals for the democratic society (not religious, elitist, or mental, discipline learning).*[31]

1.　　　　In other words, schools must teach subjects, and therefore education, that has value aside from mere preparation for college or more learning. It must be education of modern nature useful in preparing the youth for the changed conditions of the society. Education had therefore to prepare the children for a complete living. To illustrate that the transformation in the society and therefore in education is inescapable despite the well documented and highly praised cardinal principles, only twenty years later the educational policies commission of the NEA, which included the president of Harvard and Cornell universities, the commissioner of education and a number of progressive educators issued a report entitled *The Purpose of Education In American Democracy*. Concerned with out-of-school youth and unemployment resulting from the great depression these educators issues a comprehensive set of four goals: self realization, human relations, economic efficiency and civic responsibility... (Ornstein and Hunkins, p. 155). The commission continued to modify the document until in 1944 when the emphasis was placed on the whole child and life adjustment. Subject matter was deemphasized while social psychological vocational moral and civic responsibilities were stressed. In general the traditional concept of the curriculum as a body of subjects came under attack from progressive educators the major emphasis focused on the child centred, experience centred and activity centred curriculum(Ornstein and Hunkins:　p.85). Indeed as wrote Franklin Bobbitt in his book the Curriculum: "We need principles of curriculum making. We didn't know that we should first determine objectives from a study of social needs. We supposed education consisted only of teaching the familiar subjects. We had not come to see that it is essentially a process of unfolding the potential abilities of students...we had not learned that studies are means not ends (Ornstein and Hunkins: p.85)."

After I had published my first two book titles, a close colleague of mine, Amos Benjamin, remarked that I, the author, don't realize how great that accomplishment was. His name is Amos Benjamin. At the time I didn't realize the deeper meaning of his words in full. I came close to his sense a

---

[31] *Adapted from Allan C. Ornstein and Francis P. Hunkins, Curriculum Foundations, Principles and Issues 3rd Edition p.83*

couple of years later after I had published my third book I titled w*hat Makes People Rich and Nations Powerful.* That's when I met the executive editor for the Dar es Salaam University Press. I don't have to mention his name here. But the point is this. After he had perused through my books he remarked something that is my message. Looking in my eyes, with a twinkle in his, he said yours aren't simply books. This isn't even a mere literary work. It is a philosophy of life. These are the books that can transform individual persons and the society as a whole. Probably he was right.

2.   In their, I must say magnificent, book Curriculum Foundations, Principles and Issues 3rd Edition Allan C. Ornstein and Francis P. Hunkins wrote thus*: Philosophy is central to curriculum because the philosophy advocated…influences the goals or the aims and content …of the curriculum…philosophy not only allows us to understand schools and their curricula, but also to deal with our own personal systems of perceptions, beliefs and values—the way we perceive the world around us and how we define what is important to us. It helps to understand who we are, and, to some extent, where we are going (Ornstein and. Hunkins, p. 155).*

Then the authors go on to emphasize that*: Philosophy deals with the larger aspects of life, the problems and prospects of living, and the way we organize our thoughts and facts. It is an effort to see life in and its problems in full perspective. It requires looking beyond the immediate to causes and relationships to future developments. It involves questioning one's own point of view as well as the views of the others; it involves searching for defined and defensible values, clarifying ones beliefs and attitudes, and formulating a frame work for making decisions and acting on these decisions. Philosophical issues have always impacted and still do on schools and society*(Ornstein and Hunkins: p.31) . The role of education doesn't end there. Thus*:* The schools have to be democratic and comprehensive institutions that therefore enhance social and political reforms. In order to be an expanding industrial modern economy schools and education therefore must produce not only skilled but also innovative and productive workforce(Ornstein and Hunkins: p.76). Kerr cautions that *Education is fundamentally a human activity—not technical or economic.* Education…should nurture human beings in ways that enhance their humanness and their connectedness to others in the human family. Our intelligence… should involve our emotions, our very spirits (Ornstein and Hunkins: p.393.)

Probably this is relevant to all humanity since despite our different levels of our standards and social statuses as individuals or nations no one has reached the maximum of his or her potential. Certainly the forgoing is most relevant to the environment of the poor masses and the least developed countries or dependent economies. The following is an analysis summarized by Ornstein and Hunkins: Hailed by Paulo Freire in his book *Pedagogy of the Oppressed,* asserts that "...*the purpose of education is to enlighten the masses about their present state of being denied their rights (and that the ideal methodology has) to design situations in which they recognize their state of being and feel dissatisfied with it, and finally to gain those skills and competencies requisite for correcting the identified inequities (Ornstein and Hunkins 1998 p. 254)."* It therefore follows that individuals must learn those ways of engaging in a critique of knowledge. *Learning is reflective*; *it is not externally imposed by a person in power. Education leads to freedom and emancipation...knowledge is not a finished product that sits in a unit plan or course syllabus. Such a document... (if not critiqued) indoctrinates. Learning is something that results from interaction between and among people. It comes by challenging content as well as critiquing the purposes of the information presented in the curriculum (Ornstein and Hunkins 1998, p. 254).* According to Habermas, emancipation is the goal of education. This emancipation refers to individuals gaining those awarenesses, competencies, and attitudes to enable them to take control of their lives *(Ornstein and Hunkins 1998 p. 254).*

The analysis continues. According to Robert, young students must accept the responsibility for educating themselves, and they must garner the courage to resist indifference to freedom (*Ornstein and Hunkins 1998,* p. 254). Education must solve persistent life situations. It should also help address the contemporary social problems. Education must address question from all areas of living. It should also address the reconstruction of the society (Ornstein and Hunkins 1998, p. 257). Education must, according to Herbert Spencer, sustain life, enhance life, aid in rearing children, maintain individuals and social and political relations, and enhance leisure tasks and feelings (p. 257). Generally speaking, education must enhance acquisition and comprehension of knowledge, problem, solving skills, and ...thinking. It must enhance person to self person to person to society interactions. These...subsume the emotional and psychological aspects of individuals and their adaptive aspects with regard to home, family, church, and local community...that allow the individual to function in the home on the job and as a citizen and member of the larger society. To these dimensions Ornstein and Hunkins added Dealing with the development and maintenance of strong and healthy bodies, Dealing with values and appreciation of arts, dealing with values and behavior...and Dealing with the recognition and belief in the divine and the view of transcendence(or spirituality)—(Ornstein and Hunkins 1998, p. 270).

3.

From Spencer's essay *What Knowledge Is Most Worth For?* He concluded that for individuals to lead successful lives they needed preparation in...: "Direct self preservation indirect self preservation for example securing food, shelter, and earning a living, parenthood, citizenship and, leisure activities. In the United States, the NAE or National Education Associations Commission on the Reorganization of Secondary Education issued a report called *Cardinal of Principles of Secondary Education* speaking of the role of education in our democratic society thus: *education in a democracy both within and without the school, should* develop in each individual the knowledge ,interest ,ideas, habits ,and powers whereby *"he will find his place and use that place to shape both himself and the society toward even nobler ends."*

Ornstein and Hunkins suggest that: perhaps influenced by Spencer, the commission employed the organizational principle of important life activities to organize categories of curriculum aims, or in our context goals. These include: health; command of fundamental processes; worthy home membership; vocational education; civic education; worthy use of leisure; ethical character. The commission noted that the definition of education needed to reflect the philosophy and practice of democracy. Education must cherish and inculcate its moral values, stress knowledge and information essential to its institutions and economy, and foster a creative and sustaining spirit (leading to) self-realization, human relationships, economic efficiency and civic responsibility.

The aim of self realization was to encourage inquiry, mental capabilities, speech, reading, writing, numbers, sight and hearing, health, knowledge, health habits, public health, recreation, intellectual interests, aesthetic interests, and character formation. The aim of human relationships included humanity friendship, cooperation with others, courtesy, appreciation of the home, conservation of the home, homemaking, and democracy in the home. The aims of economic efficiency encompassed work, occupational appreciation, personal economics, consumer judgment, efficiency in buying, and consumer protection. The aims (or goals) of civic responsibility related to social justice, social activity, social understanding, critical judgment, tolerance, conservation of resources, social application of science, world citizenship, law observance, economic literacy, political citizenship, and devotion to democracy (Ornstein and Hunkins 1998, p. 270-271).

While we acknowledge existence of atheists, and of course—perplexed? No—overwhelmed by multiplicity and the diversity of the quite antagonistic Gods, we still believe education must also help address moral and spirituality without attempting to be evangelical or sectarian. I bring up this point not for religious concerns, but for the good spirituality does to people even when the Pope or I cannot explain how it works. And this is no new thing. There are so many things we enjoy—things which help to strengthen our humanity and advance our accepting of others yet whose modus operandi or source of their miracles we know not. Such things include electricity the sunlight or even how it sunlight converts itself into starch. Dale Carnegie wrote in his enlightening book *How to Stop Worrying and Start Living* that: the fact that we don't understand totally the mysteries of our bodies or electricity or a gas engine doesn't keep us from using and enjoying them. The fact that I don't understand the mysteries of prayer and religion no longer keeps me from enjoying the richer happier life that religion brings...I no longer have the faintest interest in the differences in creeds that divide the churches. But I am tremendously interested in what religion does for me..."[32]

James Moffett in his work *The Universal Schoolhouse* suggests that a curriculum that emphasizes spirituality enables students to enter *"on a personal spiritual path unique to each that nevertheless entails joining increasingly expansive membership of humanity and nature."* He cautions that if society is to foster knowledge and power without commensurate development of morality and spirituality then society is courting disaster (Ornstein and Hunkins p. 256-7). Education must also help the individual to improve self understanding to learn self concepts and basic attitudes and to guide their own behavior, leading to genuineness of behavior, empathy, and respect for self and others;[33] and thus develop into fully functioning persons. (Why? Because)...it is only when students learn and understand...and gain knowledge and power to use it that the curriculum (or education) has actual worth...*(Ornstein and Hunkins, 1998 p.100).*

---

[32] *Dale Carnegie, How to Stop Worrying and Start Living Revised Ed. P. 193*

[33] *Allan C. Ornstein and Francis P. Hunkins, Curriculum Foundations, Principles and Issues 3rd Edition p.256*

4.
5.   Indeed knowledge as knowledge per se or information on its own is almost useless. It is useless and good for nothing unless the person, who acquires it, is capable of processing it into useful and meaningful ends. The best form of knowledge therefore is the one that doesn't only bring with it useful information but one that gives you, —well, give is not the best word. Push is the word. Therefore the best form of knowledge is the one that doesn't only bring with it useful information but one that pushes you to act and thereof transforming your life and the lives of the people and environment around you. It is that knowledge that gives you upper hand and makes your lives of people and environment around you better.

In Ornstein and Hunkins (1988), Dewey considered education as the means of perpetuating and improving the society. To perpetuate and improve society therefore education had to be selective in determining and organizing the experiences of the learners. It is: *a primary responsibility of the educators...* (to) be aware of the general principles of shaping of actual experiences by environing conditions (and to understand) what surroundings are conducive to having experiences that lead to growth (p. 138). Education according to George Counts must help the society to be totally reorganized to meet the common good...a more just and equitable society (p. 261).

It is thereof Harold Rugg[34] believed that the schools engage the children in a critical analysis of the society in order to improve it. Education must also not only address or more aptly, overemphasize the affairs of the child without considering man's crucial social conditions and problems. Indeed the fast changing realities in the world today demand we reevaluate our curriculum and education as a whole but also reeducate the whole society. Reeducating the youth alone is unrealistic without reeducating the adults who still view the world in the lenses of the last generation and therefore failing to understand the youth or aptly to reconcile themselves with the needs of today. Without rallying the adults behind transformation and the growth agenda, we create a conflict between the youth who are the manpower and the adults who are both the leaders and decision makers. Besides, without reconciling the two, the conflict therein cannot support the thrust our society is demanding today.

---

[34] *(Ornstein and Hunkins, 1998 p. 261*

Education has to help condition or modify and shape behavior. It has to guide a child through his developmental stages.[35] It has to help solve problems a learner or society as a whole is facing. It has to help him meet his needs by giving him power over his feelings and attitudes or rather by allowing him to put his personality to better use..

Our schools should serve our children so that they can develop understandings, beliefs and actions that deepen their participation in their local, national, and world communities in a ways that exhibit a commitment to certain intellectual, civic, and moral understandings and behaviors.[36] However caution must be taken. *Creating educational goals is really a continuing activity...* (Ornstein and Hunkins 1998, p. 274)....in a dynamic changing chaotic world education is the only means by which individuals will gain the understandings competencies attitudes and dimensions of spirit that will allow them to be players and adapt to the evolving times and influence the very nature of times and the quality of all things, both human and natural. Society, viewed globally, depends on our rising to these challenges(Ornstein and Hunkins 1998(Ornstein and Hunkins 1998, p. 401).

The role of education—according to Ilya Prigogine and Isabell Stengers—is not only *to transmit that which is good in the society...(but) Many of us are coming to grasp that being alive is not only being but becoming.*[37]

With ICT and globalization let alone diversity and migration internal rural to urban and externally displaced people who are integrated into the economy schools and indeed education must help to take on board all the groups of people and integrate them in order to eliminate class and undue distinctions. Schools must teach subjects and therefore lead to an education: *having value aside from mere preparation for college or more*

---

[35] *Allan C. Ornstein and Francis P. Hunkins, Curriculum Foundations, Principles and Issues 3rd Edition p. 101*

[36] *Adapted from Allan C. Ornstein and Francis P. Hunkins, Curriculum Foundations, Principles and Issues 3rd Edition p. 142*

[37] *Allan C. Ornstein and Francis P. Hunkins, Curriculum Foundations, Principles and Issues 3rd Edition p. 394*

learning. It must be education of modern nature useful in preparing the youth for the changed conditions of the society.[38]

Besides: *The major purpose of education was to prepare the children and the youth for a complete living. Curriculum needed to be arranged according to this purpose. It has to be constructed in such a way that it can prioritize human activities so as to advance human survival and progress. Therefore it had to sustain life, enhance life, aid in rearing children, maintain one's social and politician associations, enhance leisure, tasks and feelings.*[39]

Talking about direction, is further admonished: Equally dangerous …is…indecision or lack of any philosophy, which can be reflected in attempts to avoid any commitment to any sets of values. A measure of positive conviction is essential to prudent action... (Allan and Francis 1998, P. 33). In short our philosophy of education influences, and to a larger extent determines, our educational decisions, choices and alternatives (Allan and Francis 1998, P. 32).

Probably you already realize how this work—the work of attempting to bring about a sense of standard and direction to education and the community in general—is so critical. You also realize it is not my creation. In a, I must add magnificent, book Curriculum Foundations, Principles and Issues 3rd Edition, philosophy is given much emphasis thus: *"Philosophy provides educators…with a framework or frameworks for organizing schools and classrooms. It helps them answer what schools are for, what subjects are of value, how students learn and what methods and materials to use. It provides them with a frame work for…determining the goals of education, the content and its organization, the forces of teaching and learning and in general what e experiences and activities they wish to stress in school and classrooms. …philosophy becomes the criterion for determining the aims, means and ends of curriculum (or education)…philosophy becomes principles for guiding actions.*[40]

---

[38] *Adapted from Allan C. Ornstein and Francis P. Hunkins, Curriculum Foundations, Principles and Issues 3rd Edition p. 76*

[39] *Allan C. Ornstein and Francis P. Hunkins, Curriculum Foundations, Principles and Issues 3rd Edition p.71*

[40] *(Ornstein and Hunkins, 1998 Page pp 32-33.*

John Dewey defined philosophy as: *the general theory of education;* and that *the business of philosophy is to provide (the framework for the) aims and method (of schools) ...an explicit formulation of the ...mental and moral habitudes in respect to difficulties of contemporary life...* Schools therefore are factories of our people, preparing them to be who the society projects them to be within limits of course. According to Dewey: *"Education is the laboratory...the educational and social philosophy ...can serve as the first screen for developing the social program...philosophy attempts to define the nature of good life and a good society* (Allan and Francis 1998, P. 33).*"*

At this juncture, you will have recognized that a few of our graduates, those who have managed to have a grip on any form of ideals, have done so only by chance. And that's not good anyway. That means most of our graduates and employees today behave in a haphazard manner and thus perform or produce far less results, results that are below their true potential. Schools, parents, the community and the government too will benefit big time and steadily if schools help to address the collapse of morals and character among our youth. If we did so, we would give the youth some of Goal in life and therefore a sense of direction in their lives. William van Til said: "Our source of direction is found in our guiding philosophy. Without philosophy (we make) mindless vaults into the saddle … flung himself from the room, flung himself upon the horse, and rode madly off in all directions (Allan and Francis 1998,P. 32).

Probably the best explanation is provided by Stephen Covey in his book The Seven Habits of Highly Successful People. He called that "sense of direction" which makes one the ideal scholar or person, a compass. It is about which he writes thus: "We are more in need of a vision or destination and a compass (a set of principles or directions) and less in need of a ("divine" dogmatic, static fixed and rigid) road map. We often don't know what the terrain ahead will be like…much will depend on our judgment at the time… (It is) an inner compass (that) will always give us direction. Effectiveness — often even survival — doesn't depend solely on how much effort we expend, but on whether or not the effort we expend is in the right jungle and the metamorphosis taking place in most every industry and profession demands leadership first." The sense is this. By building big picture we help students to form total intellectual capability not a set of narrowly defined skills. This is unrealistic in real world since we meet different problems in different environments and are therefore required to solve problems holistically as we anticipate and meet them—generally speaking.

WHY FEW PEOPLE AND NATIONS THRIVE WHILE OTHERS FAIL

Though I have said this before but because of my enormous conviction in the common sense of building the inner compass, let me repeat it here. I was meeting Sr. Sleeva to sell the idea of having this program absorbed into her school programs. Herself a great teacher, leader and servant of God, she is the coordinator of the Congregation of Catechist Sisters of St. Ann's in Tanzania. And the headmistress at St. Ann's of Mbezi Louis in Dar es Salaam Tanzania. My children go to school at St. Ann's. To emphasize the importance of this training I highlighted that humans need principles—just like Ten Commandments—to guide them! But just like the Commandments, people deliberately or unawares rebel against them because they are just commandments! People crave an engagement—and involvement. Before they adapt anything people ponder about what is in it for them. The concept of ideal graduates or scholars answers to that—and compels them to follow through not only obediently and courageously but willingly! And what's more when they know what they gain from such an engagement, knowing it is for their own good, they become messengers and patrons or matrons of the idea!

Think of a person thrown into the jungle in the middle of his sleep in the night. It is natural that when he wakes up and he has no sense of direction with a sense of the grid references. Again think of our children in the face of ICT and globalization. Think of the Television programs and liberalization. Unless we build these ideals and endeavor to teach them and impart them to our children we will otherwise be throwing all cautions to the wind. Now here is the question some of the business minds reading here are already asking: Does it apply to business! Yesssir! "The individual who wants to reach the top in business," said J. Paul Getty 1892-1976, American Oil Tycoon: "must appreciate the might of the force of habit and must understand that practices are what create habits. He must be quick to break those habits that can break him and hasten to adopt those practices that will become the habits that help him achieve the success he desires."

Truly the ideal man cannot fail. The simplicity of the idea shouldn't dissuade you. Little tricks do too big differences. We often succeed or fail not because of the big things we did do or didn't do well. The difference is often due to how we responded to bits and pieces; for better or worse. Think of a round steering wheel and small as it is, it governs an enormous set of truck and trailer. And how on earth does as simple and unlikely the two strips of leather reigns lead such an enormous animal as a horse wherever the holder wishes? St. James called this compass a rudder. And it seems to me he revered the idea so much that he didn't only preach about it. He recorded it down when he wrote thus: "If we put bits into the mouths of horses, that they may obey us, we guide their whole bodies. Look at ships also, though they are so great (but) are driven by (invisible) strong winds; (yet) they are (only) guided by a small rudder, wherever the will of the pilot directs." Did you ever think about it? "How great a forest, (yet) is set ablaze by small fire?" asks the great apostle).

A CLOSING WORD
I trust that by simply thinking about the assertions in this chapter you have begun realizing that indeed not only Benny, Fr. Vally, Zitto Kabwe, Michael John, Leonard Kitoka, Zephrine Galeba, David Orr, or even Eli Wiesel—among others—but you and I have reasons to worry about the future of our society. Besides, you realize now that this is a big moment for you; am I not right? You realize this is a must read book for the disadvantaged. It is a book to enlighten them about opportunities and the secrets behind success and prosperity!

It is no surprising therefore that this is a book for the children of the rich and the rich too! The wealthy families and successful executives aren't any safer. Apart from the fact that it is unpredictable how worthy a rich man will be in the next ten years, the fate of their children is predictable. We can safely predict the future prospects of their children because we know such children have stopped advancing themselves or working hard just because their parents are wealthy. They are the sole heirs of great fortunes. So why think or work any harder. The reason for this is that with changing social and economic environment in the society today, no one knows for sure what will happen to one's job or wealth in the medium term. We have the experiences of the Northern Rock, General Motors and City Group among others which were rescued by nationalization. They were lucky. With economic crisis, many companies closed. The running ones aren't running profitably. Startups decline in numbers when compared to when they were established and their life span has receded so much.

Building the Ideal Graduate (or Scholar) therefore is a *maiden* breed of program intending yes to uplift—but as well to make such a shift sustainable—performances academically and financially for schools and corporations as well as households and nations—through building of the fine character and superior moral fiber among the youth, the students and the workforce. It is a tool to enhance desire for prosperity, quality, excellence, productivity, profitability and sustainability in the organization and community as a whole.

In the end, this tool or program "puts together" the ideal scholars, responsible and productive employees, and ideal leaders as we shall further the discussion on the benefits from the training, and still more important—the ideal future mothers and fathers and indeed, ideal families and responsible citizens. Indeed as we now move on to review these ideals, values or virtues, let me say that here is an attempt to realize a man whom God refers to in the first book of Samuel: *Behold here's the man of whom I spoke to you! It is he who shall rule over my people (1. Samuel 9:17).* If anyone of my readers thought this was a little sport on the part of the author, let him think again. To all skeptics, Let him notice that it was probably for the importance of this analysis that the Ugandan President, Yoweri Kaguta Museveni introduced a ministry for ethics and integrity and appointed not anybody else, but a priest, Fr. Simon Lokodo to head it. Let the doubter recollect that it is probably for the same reasons, arguably inconclusive as the sole indicator, why Uganda Cranes have thrashed national team both here at home and away 3-Nil severally.

Now with the publication of the book now on your lap, and now that you can access this training program if you so desire to transform your life by not only dreaming but also turning the dreams into realities; now that we have already chalked down and placed before you the path to whatever you have always dreamt of achieving; tonight, we bequeath the future of this country into your own capable hands—ladies and gentlemen.

5. WE NEED IDEALS AS TRAVELERS NEED COMPASS

"If you don't know where you are going, you'll end up somewhere else."
—*Yogi Berra*

I was flying in charter plane from Mwanza to Arusha Kilimanjaro International Airport in 2001. As the plane set itself twenty thousand feet in the sky above the clouds I realized I had lost a sense of direction. Buddhist teaching was right. In the sky there is no east or west. I couldn't tell where was relative to the grid references—south of north, east or west. I didn't know we headed north or south. I couldn't make out of we were on the west or east of my hometown. Simply put, I couldn't tell where we were—or where we were heading for. If this then was the case with the pilot how could we be certain to land at the Kilimanjaro International Airport and not on the waters of the Indian ocean—or on the icecap of the Kilimanjaro? This thought shocked me. That's when I peered over and noticed that the pilot. He was surprisingly comfortable! This didn't do much to help my situation. In fact it disturbed me more. That's when I confronted him and asked the pilot how he knew we were in the right direction.

He told me he knew we were in the right direction. How? By use of some compass or GPS. This helps him first to know where he is going; and secondly, to register where he is relative to where he wants to go. From this knowledge, this information, he is able to establish the direction and speed. That's how he is able to know whether we have arrived or not yet even when he cannot see the ground. This is the exact analogy of our lives. If you don't have a sense of direction in the form of moral values and principles—or in this case ideals—you may not know who you are, what you are doing, or why you are doing what you are doing. What is so tragic is that you will never know why you are living—in the first place. When you reach this stage of not knowing that you need to have ideals, or why you are living, you will never find meaning in your life and therefore in anything else. You can then never amount to anything from henceforth because you won't put your effort in anything. That's why you can never learn or amount to anything worthwhile from henceforth. Therefore at personal level, be on familiar terms with who you are—and your background. What are the circumstances behind your situation? Accept reality such as where you went wrong. Then press on or change direction. After getting there, stay there. That's what William Holden didn't do.

THE LOSERS
During my ground work in writing a book you are now reading, I walked aimlessly in the streets and brushed shoulders with a cross section of people as they went about in their ways. Then, one day, suddenly a billboard bigger than the earth itself stood before me along the highway. It read: *Speed Limit 50 Kilometers per Hour*. Underneath this instruction, a solemn counsel followed: *Speed Kills!* I didn't care about it until a car crossed speeding than light itself. I sensed people were indeed imperfect. I excused him. Probably he hadn't read the billboard. Then I crossed over to Sunset Bar. That is in Mbezi Luis Dar es Salaam Tanzania EA. I ordered a beer. On the back label it was written in a motherly tone emphasizing that it was not for the under 18. And the ad made sense to me for first time. I had considered such ads as useless. Yet I have never seen a bartender asking my age before serving me with a drink. The label added *Drink Responsibly*. I didn't know what it meant. What was the limit or what we could call responsible drinking?

Then I saw a girl and boy apparently the Under-18 and they were drinking Safari Lager, one of the strongest beer brands. The boy actually made a cocktail with Konyagi a local spirit, itself a very hard liquor to make his drink even hotter i.e. more alcoholic and therefore more dangerous. I said they were probably young and naive and that they didn't know what they were doing. Then I closed my eyes and instinctively began praying. It was that the famous prayer: *Oh God! Forgive them because they don't know what they are doing*! I was wrong. A man walked up and moved toward my direction. He was staggering though. He almost fell on me. He held a key—in his hands. I held my breath! I didn't like what would happen. I was wrong to think the underage didn't know what they were doing because of age—or that probably they couldn't read the back labels. This *Over-Age* and obviously a man of education fooled me. The key in his hand wasn't a key to his house. It was a key into the car. A big billboard still read as you come and go: *"Don't drink and drive"*. This man had drunk to the brim—literally. Yet he needed more drink.

He drove past my car missing it by inches almost hitting other drunks staggering in and out. Then I decided I should leave this place. I left. I walked along the road to Mbezi Goba and parked the car at Timover Bar and Guest House. Two love birds emerged out of the blue. I recognized them. They were the two teenagers I had met some time ago. They staggered again only this time toward the guest house. They were not husband and wife. They were sex hungry teenagers. Not lovers. The big billboard again beckons them and it spoke to them as it read in capital letters "*HIV KILLS*". Then it added the ABC approach: "Abstain, Be faithful, Use a Condom." They were not married. The second option was therefore out of question. Their hope lay in the third stupid advice. Condomize.

I watched them closely as they glanced at the billboard. Under the influence of alcohol the boy's parts between the pockets were already bulging on the top of arousal. A girl was giggling. Off they crossed and the gates to their hired lovebird net otherwise gates to hell. They didn't even use the third absurd option that was for their protection. They got out an hour later a little troubled and they vanished as they had come. I asked for a stick of cigarette a king-sized Embassy filter cigarette and a lighter and lit one to sooth my nerves. I actually stopped smoking many years ago. I wanted to get over my saintly disposition. What was there in vices? Why people liked that which was not healthy or good to themselves and mankind? As I sucked it I read on the poster advertising Embassy as saying *Smoking Is Not Healthy to Your Body* right in front of me. I pulled half that stick to match with the hype and people around me at the bar counter but threw it away.

At the counter people smoked as if they didn't know how to read. I realize now how fatal we run the risk of saying this thing is bad and another is dangerous singlehandedly. I realized we needed a teaching that was comprehensive in nature, one training people to actually have a disposition of a certain kind allowing them to pursue life of a certain kind. That is why I am humbly delighted that finally here we have that kind of a comprehensive teaching in one piece of a book or training program. Once-off haphazard prohibitions such as Don't Speed Up, Don't Drink And Drive, alcohol Not Recommended for the Underage Don't Drink Irresponsibly or even Cigarette Is Harmful To Your Health or HIV /AIDS is real have proved to be ineffective therefore. Abstain, stick with single spouse or condomize as a philosophy has never been effective. Men could really be so irrational.

A person was feeling unwell. He went to see the doctor. The doctor diagnosed him and realized he had drunk too much of the hot stuff of strong alcohol and therefore he hadn't eaten well. Above that he was a chain smoker who resented his wife. He got tired of her nagging and the undue control she imposed on him. The marriage had gone over its sell-before-date. And therefore he chose to leave her. Wifeless he lived the life of his own he called *Living Large Life*. Then the doctor approached him very politely and told him that he was not sick.

The drunk was so stunned. But he was unhealthy because of too much hard alcohol and cigarettes. He, the drunk, nodded as the doctor practiced the maximum of his counseling profession. Then, concluding the doc said something like this: *I advise that you stop drinking and smoking. Why? They both kill you—only slowly.* The drunk staggered on his feet and shouted out aloud as he banged or hit the door missing the door knob asking the doc angrily: *Are you mad? I thought you were a man of education. Whoever wants to die so quickly?* As he left crossing the highway, the car outside hooted excitedly and the admirer of the slow death almost died so rapidly.

Such are people with talents or education without good character. Some are successful until as I write but in the long run, despite vast talents they end up as a result in the middle while they should actually be leading. I have indicated how some dropouts have succeeded exceedingly. Those falling in this category had a clear vision and mission to accomplish. They had a goal in life that they craved to accomplish. But on top of a goal in life they have morals and winning character. That's why when such opportunity presents itself they grab it almost instantly. Bill Gates and Steve Jobs are such great inspirers to drop outs. But they should celebrate the Gates and the Jobs inspirations with caution. No dropout succeeds without proper plans or hard work which requires good character.

Though a traditional average graduate is able to snap his finger and get what he wants as far as work is concerned, real life doesn't work like that. In real life you can't snap your finger and lo! Things fall in place and behold things are sorted out because you so decree.

What are we trying to say? Here it is. For our successes or accomplishments to be long-term and with lasting, they must be sheltered by a set of ideals or qualities. Why? Here is why. Not everything begets the same outcomes. Not every path leads to the same destination. If you don't know where to go you will go nowhere. Indeed "if you don't stand for something," as aptly said Malcolm X, "you will fall for anything." The universe is arranged in such a way that it tends to respond to people who seek excellence—and seek it constantly—in words and deeds. The Brits knew it when they said: Spare a rod and spoil a child!! In other words building ideal graduates or scholar is to develop and it is to build and finally to live by discipline. It is living in a certain way! Apostle Paul counsels thus: "M*y son, do not regard lightly the discipline of the Lord! Nor lose courage when you are punished by Him. For the Lord disciplines him whom he loves and chastises every son who he receives! It is for discipline that you have to endure....For the moment discipline seems painful rather than pleasant (though? later it yields the ...fruit...to those who have been trained by it!"* (Hebrew 12.5.11)

In summary, this kind of an individual, I mean the individual ideal person, family, organization or society has the right cause. With the right cause, backed by superior character, he or she has the right course before him. Coupled with the fact that the universe is principled, such a person cannot fail. Let us look at one of such exemplars. He is the exemplary ideal scholar. He, is the ideal person—the ideal human! And he isn't a fictitious character the author has crafted to suit his story. He was crafted by the One Above. Not me. He is real. The author bears witness that he is a breathing person living with us today. Probably you have not met him personally, but through the following notes you will find that in your vicinity there could be such a person, however few and distant apart they are. Now, voila! Behold the ideal scholar. Voila! Behold the advantages you get—and retain—only when you are the ideal person.

MALAKI SITAKI: A BREATHING EXEMPLAR OF HOW INVALUABLE IS CHARACTER

Here comes an intriguing story. It is a true story about one Malaki Sitaki. The author was privileged to meet Malaki Sitaki in the year 1998. The date was the fourth of October. His name was peculiar as was going to be his disposition. It was, I mean the name, was Malaki Sitaki. We met at Tanzania Breweries. Both had graduated from the same University (of Dar es Salaam). He only had graduated two years before the author. We had been amongst two hundred applicants who were scanned and finally shortlisted and interviewed for the two rewarding marketing officer positions. The coincidence was that just the two of us had been successfully passed the interview and hired the same fourth day of October 1998! We went through work orientation together! That's how we got ourselves into a new company that pervaded beer culture—unfortunately!

Everybody knows that in every dark cloud, there is a silver lining, but very few know that the reverse is also true. Indeed in every adversity there is an equal magnitude of equivalent opportunity.

True to his name, a man who is not a gold-digger, whereas everybody else of course excepting Mr. Sitaki indulged in pleasure or what we christened to be ambiance,, romance, fun, or even loyalty to the beer culture, but it was self-seeking and quick fix, as they indulged in excessive beer drinking and pleasure, he saw it a inanity—and insanity! He protected his sense of sanity to the full. Not that ambiance or fun is by itself sin? No! But whereas many of new employees joined the department with strict moral codes, soon they laid their old codes to rest and reinvented new ones trying hard to fit in. And I don't blame anyone. I also believed it was a way of creating bonds with the new company and coworkers. But I now know that it was due to either peer pressure or lack of strong moral codes altogether! That's not Malaki though!

If you jump to the paragraph that precedes the immediate one above, you will see that I said *unfortunately* when I referred to the beer culture. I said so because not only does beer intoxicate its drinkers?! It indeed has a tendency to intoxicate all souls in its vicinity with its culture—beer culture. What then is beer culture? It is having beer into your life. Or, it is giving up on your virtues and letting beer govern you—and your life. When a stage in your life reaches when you can't eat breakfast unless you first knock at least one beer, that's a good signal that you have graduated into the culture. When you cannot stay home, I mean when you stop feeling homesick and instead you feel bar-sick or beer-sick then you have graduated into the culture. You have graduated into the culture also when your hands shake because you have not yet had a gulp on your beer, or when your family or friends need you that have to track down from your favorite bar, or when you are famous in bars and your friends are bar friends, then you are naturally a master into the culture you so much revere. When you cannot save the money or time for any other more important matters such as reading a book or to sleep, or when you have stopped witnessing the sun rise from the east but you only see it fall into the clouds in the west because you are in a bar 24/7, then you have successfully graduated into this curious culture. Mark this statement because it gives a good beginning of an assessment of someone's virtues.

Don't play with beer. It has no mercy. It intoxicates even the saints. And I don't mince my words. If it vanquished the archangel, and God's own right-hand man at the time, then who am I or you? When it got into his head, he, Lucifer, was beguiled to imagine he was a God. The net result was the expulsion from the good heaven. That's why a mortal human, a man who can resist the powerful charm that is enveloped in a bottle when all about him celebrate its civility, that heart should be a great soul, don't you think so? (Well, for now it doesn't matter what your thoughts are. It will when we have finished with you). That's how I began noticing that Malaki was indeed unique. I indeed reckoned for first time how really by teaching or imparting our children with virtues or the ideals or core values we prepare and empower them because we trust them and their ability to make right decisions and stand of their own feet.

Like Daniel, Meshach, Shadrack and Abednego, Malaki observed certain life's principles and watched them to the letter, having grown up under the strong hand of a churchman. No wonder even after he had become independent, he did not depart! The proverbs were right: train up a child in the way he should go and when he grows up he shall not depart. Yes, as a marketing officer for the very product whose iniquities he knew very well, he had to sell the good things there are in beer industry. Stunned? No. Don't be. There is a silver lining even in a dark cloud. Beer was the top revenue earner and employer nationally at the time as it is still among top employers and tax payers as I write. Beer pays for the government so that we have the security and infrastructure such as Medicare and education we depend on for our livelihood.

What distinguished Mr. Sitaki from a herd of average souls was that he vowed that he was going to live to his word. And what was his word? It is this: beer is a good product for such reasons and only when it is not abused. So he had vowed that he was going to drink when necessary. And what distinguished him the more he didn't throw all cautions to the four winds. He set his limits. And I will tell you his limit. It was set at a maximum of two beers per day when he had to drink! Notice that he didn't set a limit because he was a spend thrift or a miser? No. We who were in the officer's and manager's ranks had the sky as our limit? —no! That's not it. Our limit of drinking was the cellar. Beer was free of course. It kept coming, flowing in like the waters of lake Kagera, the other side of Nile, proportionate to someone's gulping capability or rather the radius of that someone's esophagus. Yet Malaki managed to observe that maxim to the letter!

Unawares, his peers enjoyed his company for obvious reasons. They had good reasons to. They would top up their drinking with his share of free beers he often left untouched. But sons of Adam can be quite unpredictable. Some hated him! His unbending moral standard didn't sit well with the hard line beer loyalists—the conformists. They didn't miss the *Whys*! He didn't cope; He wouldn't work well with the beer customers; he was full of himself; he didn't fit in; he wasn't man enough etc. etc. they claimed! And the list was indeed listless. It stuns me now reckoning how a couple others had given in to the threats but not him. Malaki didn't budge. And what's more they didn't end there. They even informed in the way of complaining to his superiors about the tragedy that was imminent: "We were going to lose beer market share!" why? "It was because of poor marketing personnel!" With credit to the man I still regard so highly, and at the time with powers of almost the regional CEO, Zerubabel Nzowa. He didn't judge him based on the magnitude of propaganda that hovered around the brewery, but by actual results he delivered. They partied and spent nights in bars especially over the long weekends which as a principle began on the Fridays through Sundays! That was the lifestyle to many and curiously it was praiseworthy!

Then something happened! Peter Louis set his boots on the Tanzanian soil, and began serving as the head of Tanzania Breweries marketing department in the region. That's when the inevitable happened!

Like how King Nebuchadnezzar spotted Daniel, Meshach, Shadrack and Abednego, Louis immediately spotted Malaki! Then the next thing he did was also another inevitable thing! He promoted him as his assistant as regional manager! Notice that he had spotted him from among a herd of officers most of whom were senior to him? But that didn't stop Louis to elevate him a few levels higher, setting him literally, in charge of others! I thought, and am still convinced that Malaki wasn't one bit any superior in the ways of intelligence than the herd he had distinguished himself from. And it doesn't matter anyway! I was naive! I didn't know how superior character transcended intelligence by far. He was and I believe he still is a fair and an honest person! I still believe he is still as upright as is humanly possible. That is how things began wheeling around him. Honesty, I mean being honest to oneself, to others and to God happens to be so transparent that even bankers, sponsors and benefactors tend to respect and trust such a person. And you cannot blame or praise them! They want the best for the company and for themselves. His is such a pleasing and captivating personality such that acquaintances and likewise everyone else he comes across will love to see, hear, accompany and go all out to assist him. What's more, keen people can sniff honesty even at a distance!

No wonder whatever he stands for, finds its way to success. If he is a salesman—a salesman of any merchandize, services or ideas--his audience will love to listen to what he has to say. They will not only buy from him but they will happily pay premium price for his product or service. And mark you, and probably what astonishes me most, is that when people are happy with you, they will buy from you not because your merchandize is necessarily superior to others'? No sir! They do so in the main because of his superior character. Superior character starts first and then it goes on to makes his services or products quality products or services. Superior character reflects in whatever we touch or associate with! An ideal person will be promoted at work whereas his peers will be stunned failing to reconcile with what he does that they don't do! And when I say promotion or growth, I don't mean a once off promotion or growth! I mean sustainable growth. It is because he is of service and honest, that he wins support and fondness from his parents, spouse (who will normally be one), children, sincere work-mates etc. etc. And what is more, not only his family and acquaintances, but also the strangers will tend to find him irresistible even at first sight! The biblical Joseph had such a persona. Jude his brother falls under this category too (Refer to What Makes People Rich and Nations Powerful).

You now recognize that if you commit yourself to personal transformation, here's your moment! The moment of truth! Wealth, health friendship, freedom, happiness and peace of mind are yours from this very moment going forward. As you read here right now you realize that this concept is therefore a choice between life and death—choice between lack and abundance—to lighten up on you. Probably you already recognize that when I endeavored to write this book, and when you chose to buy and read the book you are now reading we both made a noble choice! At the end of the day we live to leave an impact! No one who is reading this book now will leave on, a hundred and ten plus one years from now! No one! Not the author, not you the reader! Anyone who can choose to read a book like this one cannot fail to see this truth. Surely anyone who chooses to read a book like this one would love to have a legacy and an impact!

Yes, it is worthwhile to accumulate any of the six precious gifts of life I've mentioned in the previous statement in as much, and as rapidly as possible. But the statement remains only valid if the speed with which you so accumulate wealth will not compromise with the sustainability of your wealth by infringing other people's wellbeing. That is to say your endeavor to be well off doesn't or shouldn't make others worse off. With reference to Malaki's distinction, that is illustration of how worth the concept of

Building Ideal Scholars addresses changes on the personal level! Now you ask what about the nation. Not only nations but also corporations are formed by people. Indeed nations are formed wherever people are. If you can make everyone of your citizens a carbon copy of the Malaki Sitaki personality I have presented, I bet you have a nation very close to the heavenly world and its population almost a crowd of earthly angels. And how badly we need that state in this country!

But did Malaki learn to be the distinction he has become at school? No sir! Fortunately the author happens to know him personally as you already know. And I count it a privilege to be one of the two souls that were selected for the same job with the giant brewery in the country at the time from a crowd of candidates in 1998. The author was also privileged to share an apartment with Malaki to grasp his background. And this is the secret that every murmured about later. He was brought up in a family led by a Christian bishop. With due respect to the atheists and pagans whom I have watched so closely, most true religious men tend to have the fear of the Lord, and as a result they tend to do and be good. So we can say Malaki was privileged to be brought up under such strict, airtight hand of clergyman who knew what superior character meant to a young man in the form of Malaki Sitaki. He knew that to look after his congregation better he had to look after his closest ones like Malaki. Didn't the Brits say charity starts at home? And I suppose he knew to do it better than he knew the back of his hand.

You recognize I am attempting to explain that Malaki's triumph didn't come from being unique intellectually, or that he had any other advantage. No! He was no genius, and he had no any benefit such education or training, or even facilities that others didn't have. No sir! Let us, now, take a little break as far as our analysis of Malaki Sitaki as we turn the page to introduce Emmanuel Okwii based on an analysis by a renowned Tanzania columnist, Edo Kumwembe!

EDO KUMWEMBE'S ANALYSIS OF SUCCESS
Writing about one of the most talented footballers of our time in East Africa, sports and social analyst Edo Kumwembe wrote under the title: "Usishangae Kumwona Okwii Uwanja wa Taifa!" That is to say, that though Emanuel Okwii, a Ugandan football ace (who has played for our major clubs in the country so successfully), a footballer who had been finally contracted by a top flight European football club we keep anonymous for now, don't be astonished to see Okwii so soon here at home playing amongst our local footballers, Edo warned. Why? Mr.

Kumwembe suggests that probably he had imitated the character that pervaded our teams and players that has made most Tanzania footballers fail to play among top clubs abroad. He said that Okwii should have long since played among the European football clubs for he has all it takes to do so if he hadn't imitated the culture generally pervading our people but especially our players and artists—the culture of indolence and leisure. Because of our indiscipline and indifference, he illustrated that when Okwii quite ordinarily made a late appearance to the training—which happened with frequent regularity—both the spectators and the leaders of the club erupted in sheer delight to catch a glimpse of his face—instead of disciplining him! Edo Kumwembe said it was different in Europe.

We would be welcoming Okwii back into our national stadia because probably he had inherited the culture of this society where people preferred quick fix; and had no dreams for bigger things. He seemed to suggest that most of our people have no obsession for big success craving cheap popularity instead, something on which our society so generously offer. Just as we cross our fingers praying that Okwii doesn't fail himself this time, we would as well pray for him as Jean Matata Christophe—probably the most illustrious Burundian Singer—thus did sing suggesting that because of her character, Sabina's marriage could only be saved by prayers! In short, success of a person or a society is not based on the extent of physical resources that one has. Character or attitude has more to do with one's success than one's—gift— talents or any other factors singularly or combined. Yet in fact to attempt to explore beyond Edo Kumwembe's analysis, we must ask ourselves why should our players go to play in Europe—and not the other way round?[41]

Back to Malaki Sitaki, by now there is one question you should have asked, shouldn't you? Here is that question—and I will most delightedly answer it. The question is this: Where is Malaki now as I write? Well, it is sixteen years since, but he is still at the same company. And what's more, when some of his peers were fired, a herd of the same peers who despised him report to him in his senior executive position he holds now. Not only that. Some of the guys he reported to also report to him as we speak. He occupies the same oval office Zerubabel Nzowa I mentioned to have had so much power like any CEO. (I have been informed that in fact he has recently been promoted to a senior national role yet one more time.) Once

---

[41] *Source: Mwanaspoti July 13, 2015*

again I have put before you the testimony that truly: "The fruit of the spirit is love, joy, peace, forbearance, kindness, goodness, faithfulness, gentleness and self-control." And I have testified to you that "Against such things there's no law!" Like a seedling fixed near the wetness of the flowing river, Malaki flourishes on in harmony with what the Psalms describe so romantically thus: "The righteous will flourish like a palm tree; they will grow like a cedar of Lebanon." Truly, character is superior to any other life's skills. Emerson was right. "Character is higher than intellect. A great soul will be strong to live as well as to think."

Enough with spirituality now! So far this book is more of a practical book than emotional fantasy. What then is an ideal? In this material we shall consider ideals as a term that represents core values or guiding principles. In this introduction it would be incomparably significant that we recognize that to succeed in any endeavor we need to have or practice a set of core values or qualities. Building Ideal Scholar therefore brings back the sense of building character and moral fiber among our people. It is a tool to enhance desire for prosperity, quality, excellence, productivity, profitability and sustainability in the organization and the nation as a whole.

Truly, no short cuts to success—i mean long term success. I have said this with open mindedness. Malaki didn't standout only because he was Christian. All true religions share a sense of responsibility: compassion and diligence. I say so because I know a person who was brought up in a typical Christian family reported to the author that he had *devoured* all but one of the twelve barmaids from a nearby night club. And I know another person who is a typical criminal, like a person who knew no God. I have written the above knowing too well that no one is immune to trials and tribulations of life. No one! The author himself is not ashamed to report that he is not any infallible. But even though a feeling of fallibility has happened to me with frequent regularity, I am delighted to report that the religiously spiritual Michael and the intellectual Kambarangwe have always waged a hard-fought battle in the containment of the bodily barbaric beastly raw Festo.

The good thing is that the dual has often triumphed. The bad news is that the lone beast is more natural and therefore more powerful amongst the three of my 'selves.' It is only the Christian God who has the *holy* Trinity. Man's trinity is any holy. Probably the worst precedent is that when this duel or combat is happening I am always there watching helplessly. Like a football coach yes who has trained his team but can't get himself in the pitch to play and has already substituted his three permissible substitutes. He has no other option. He can do nothing at his whipping. He cannot even run away or hide from the painful scenes happening before him for he is no more than a spectator. If you transform your thought pattern, nature itself comes to your service in handy and with it whatever you have ever asked for.

BOTSWANA: A CASE STUDY OF NATIONAL IDEALS AND THE WEALTH OF NATIONS

With reference to Malaki Sitaki, we have established why we need personal ideals. With personal ideals we are ready to draw a line between what is good and what is not. That's what made Malaki different, special, successful. He was different, special and successful because he knew what he wanted and knew what he should not do. To be brief Malaki had a goal in his every day's life. The same applies to households, organizations and nations. Without having established the vision, mission, values and virtues, households, organizations and nations; any of these is not any safer. Such an entity has thrown all cautions to the four winds.

When for instance a society has no values and virtues; when it has not laid down a set of ideals as its guiding philosophy, anything is permissible and therefore everybody does what is good in his own eyes. That's how we have our people throw wastes; spit or piss on every spot around the streets or highway, and—what's more—we let them go free. A manager and his subordinate leave the office at ten in the morning for a nearby hotel room for bed, beer and breakfast in the beginning of the working day, and we let them go free! Senior government officials or company executives divide the cake amongst themselves, and you let them go free. Then the habit goes on and on such that the employee in retaliation—almost instinctively—steals, or rather picks up the stationary as the medical practitioner lifts up the medical kit and sells them for personal gain, and the country let's them off the hook.

You will recognize this failure when in a country this trend goes on and on until when we legalize the supermarkets for stolen goods—products or humans. You don't have to get a passport to witness this scenario if you are in Dar es Salam or any major such cities. Just go to Gerezani Market in Kariakoo if you are in Dar es Salam. Then the trend, the curve, shifts its balance. The farmer burns down the bush for fresh pasture of his flock, and you let them go free; the employees don't work, and you let them go free; a wealthy man buys out the public land and fences it for his own use, and you let them go free; a few racketeers and their benefactors besiege a national park and mercilessly abduct and kill elephants and rhinos chopping off the horns and tusks from the innocent rhinos and elephants, and with the tusks, airlifting them along with the breathing giraffes along with a variety of other animals out of the country and you let them go free.

The children are turned into drug addicts and walking cocaine stockpiles and no one cares. The criminals aren't arrested and if there is pressure they are put behind bars only temporarily for the victim's own good; until when the atmosphere cools down on the outside, and only the next day, they are back on the streets trading in the same illegal merchandize that threw them in the custody in the first place. Indeed there an incentive to loot and steal in this godforsaken country. And you can't blame them. There is no standard or benchmark to follow. And not only that, sir! Such lifters, wealthy male and female gold-diggers whose doctrine is "the dog-eat-dog, crawl your way to the top; anything for a buck, baby" mentality, are praised as futuristic and focused role models. They are role models for in this country money is praised no matter whether it is dirty or bleeding money. There is rampant anarchy in that country and no one cares. And when I say this I am not concocting a fiction story here. Only recently, the Indian civil servant has been fired after taking leave 25 years ago and never returned to work, reported the Express (www.express.co.uk/news/world/550913). How often have we heard of ghost workers who are on the public payroll and no one is held responsible?

The trend goes on and on until when the obvious, the worst, happens. Because of anarchy and incentive to steal money and votes, these clever individuals don't stop in their tracks. They then pass on to buy votes and put on the leadership robes in the administration. The recent *election-related corruption Saga* has helped to put this assertion into perspective. Half or more of government funds then, go unaccounted for, and no one is concerned! It is not surprising when seventy five of businesses goes unlicensed; 80 percent of revenues unaccounted for, and thus over fifty percent of potential government revenues through taxes and levies untraceable—and declared lost—as the country's leadership goes out on official begging trips! Surprisingly, there is no shame among the people and their leaders in that country! And that is an understatement. A country that is rich ending up playing the role of a beggar! Indeed this is a nation divided against, and at war with itself. And such as a nation is divided against itself, there can be nothing to make it stand—not even the donor funds. Again, the recent debt cancellation for many of the highly indebted countries puts the foregoing assertion into perspective.

That's why it doesn't matter anymore whether a country is mineral wealthy or has greater tourist attractions or other natural resources potential. Its resources are siphoned and channeled outside the country benefiting the foreigners and a handful of local mercenaries or cohorts in the administrative roles and robes; and surprisingly the people vote them back in their positions, or, to be more objective, they let them rig elections. And this is easy for the masses are no longer concerned with what happens counting it as fate and their afflictions as destiny! And still no one cares! In fact one could say no leader is more concerned with democracy unless it helps to further his personal or group interests. The recent elections throughout the continent and world over have helped to put that into perspective. We have leaders who are in power doing less to encourage the masses to participate in popular democracy leaving that work to the opposition who themselves do the same once elected in power.

But we can change for better. We can learn make better decisions if we have to take a grip on our own lives. For that's what Botswana did. Uganda is following the same path. Rwanda too. We have Singapore and Malaysia to learn from. China was rural only thirty years ago. Japan was still under developed less than a century ago and devastated From American atomic bombs only less than 70 years ago. Germany too was razed and demolished only less than 60 years ago. Today? Take Botswana for instance. Only about four decades ago, she was a poor country. But on another important November day, that unforgettable year, i.e. November 14, 1968, DeBeers announced they had finally discovered diamonds in Botswana. And Seletse Khama (RIP) the then president and DeBeers signed a fifty-fifty percent share in the stake that changed life of Botswana as a country and her people almost forever until as I write right now and here in Mbezi Louis Dar es Salaam, Tanzania.

To cut the long story short, Botswana—either as a society or its leadership—had ideals and benchmarks. You cannot let the investor choose what to declare or give back as grant. That is another way of analyzing a nation with no ideals, another way to identify a sick nation. Truly, you and I can no longer question the wisdom in the words of the proverbs: "He who hath no rule over his own spirit is like a city that is broken down, and without walls.... (Proverbs 25:28)" Such a city is what we call "Shamba la Bibi" in Dar es Salaam—a no-man's-land!

THE MALAYSIAN CASE STUDY
The recently much cerebrated Malaysia economic growth didn't come out of blue. The Wikipedia en.m.wikiodis.org indicates that it began its astronomical growth in 1991 after its former Prime Minister Mahathir Mohamed outlined his ideal for Malaysia vision 2020. Also known as Wasawasa 2020 vision 2020 is a Malaysian ideal introduced by the Mahathir Mohamed during the tabling of the sixth Malaysian plan in 1991. The vision calls for the nation to achieve a self sufficient industrialized nation by 2020 by encompassing all aspects of life from economic prosperity social wellbeing educational world-class political stability as well as psychological balance. Probably this philosophy is summed up in Premier Mahathir Mohamed's speech to his nation I will copy here to, and for, all worthy people: "We know that the wealth of a country depends on the ability and skills to translate the resources into products and services that can be marketed. The very rich oil producing countries had oil throughout the centuries of their existence. But," he continued;" they only became rich when this oil was piped from the bowels of the earth and sold...Gold in the ground and wealth under our feet doesn't make us rich. But producing and selling it will. This is elementary."

The article: *How Did Malaysia Do That* by Mark Arend (www.siteselection.com) indicates that Malaysia produces about 50000 engineering graduates...each year...engineers with more than just a degree—they require critical thinking skills and leadership capability and an appreciation of ethics—of doing something right not just on time. Companies such as Strand have built an in house training program to cultivate these qualities in its engineering staff. "We worked on how they were thinking and but we also gave them an environment where that thinking can thrive. We gave them responsibility but gave them strong support," said Naguib Mohd Nor, Strand's chief Operating officer. To illustrate importance of such a training program other companies have begun sending their hires to Strand for training. What is dramatic is that the program has since been adopted by the government ... it is the *Added Value* thinking that was missing in different industries preventing their migration to a more service oriented focus from a commodity basis.

SUMMARY
Through the previous chapters we indicated that our colleges and schools—astonishingly schools of all levels from preschool to the university—produce graduates who are incongruent and themselves as persons, far removed from one another's disposition, aside from poor work

skills, that clearly put on display how uneducated they are despite their many years of being instructed. We have also indicated that most of our graduates today aren't any different from their own persons minus education. What we are trying to say is that our conventional education doesn't transform the person himself apart from certifying him as a person who has just spent a number of years in the schools classrooms at the campus learning some skills which themselves are shallow with shallowness that limit the desire and ability to pursue self-advancement.

But we must ask ourselves before we go on. Is really this assertion—the assertion that there is disarray among our graduate—a mere assumption by this author? Nay! We have support from a number of research works. We have indicated that in Tanzanian the association of Tanzania employers declared that there was a great discrepancy between what graduates study at the university and what they can actually deliver. The BBC has recently reported about the same verity among even the most advanced economies and universities. The IMF magazine of February-March 2013 indicated that in India corporations have recognized the gap and therefore have since begun putting in place the in-house schools to address the gap we are addressing through this work and program. How does such a program benefit the society? That's our next analysis.

6. BENEFITS OF THE PROGRAM TO STUDENTS, PARENTS, TEACHERS, SCHOOLS, THE GOVERNMEMNT AND THE COMMUNITY

"If you are going to be a successful duck hunter, (then) you must go where the ducks are." —Paul "Bear" Bryant

Through the previous chapters, we laid down the basis for writing this book and thereof training program we present along with this book. Here now let us sum up benefits involved in the undertaking. Highlighting benefits is important cause because we cannot choose to invest in anything unless it benefits us personally, corporately or at the society or national level. But you cannot identify benefits the customer gains from any product or service without first identifying what the term customer really means and therefore what are his or her needs. What does the term customer mean anyway?

IDENTIFYING YOUR CUSTOMERS AND WHAT THEY WANT—AND WHY

Are customers that important to you? What does the term customer mean? Who really are your customers? You cannot know who your customers are without being on familiar terms with the term itself. A customer is a person who buys goods or a service (www.cambridge.com). He is also known as buyer: a person or someone who buys something from you. When a buyer is satisfied with your goods and services, he becomes a regular customer. In business, the customer is the king. That is to say he is always right. Any potentially successful business does everything in its power to satisfy the customer. That is why businesses go to greater heights to customize their products and services to match the buyer's or user's needs hence offering each customer the custom-made products and services. In other words, a business strives to offer products and services specially made for a particular buyer. The customer becomes a client when he receives services of that same firm regularly for significantly and sustainably long time. To achieve that feat, businesses always aim at giving their clients personal attention because if you don't, customers will take their custom elsewhere.

You now realize understanding a customer is an important study because any business entity is in business yes, to do business profitably but what's more important is to keep on doing that business sustainably. In order to be able to have sustainability, a business has to make sure it retains its customers. It will do so by provision of the best products and services. Retaining its customers a business must begin by identifying or establishing customer wants and developing products and services to cater for those wants. That's not enough though. And that's the mistake many do. It's not the best products or services you offer that determine your prospects in that business. Do you display or advertise them. That is to say do you make an effort to let people know that you offer what they need? When they almost ambush and besiege your shop, are the products and services readily available. How do you obtain them?

When they taste or consume the products and services you offer do they get satisfied. That is to say are their expectations met? How do you look after their concerns after they have purchased from you in terms of defective products or flawed services? What is the spirit in which you serve them? This is how you build reliability and likeability for your products or services. This is how you woo and nurture the prospects or the prospective customers into to try your products. Having tried the products you want them to be regular customers and not once off customers or buyers. You intend to make him a client who buys regularly and in bulky from your shop. If you provide the best services, he or she will then become an ambassador, one who goes out and speaks favorably about your company and products. Often an ambassador then goes on to become a partner. A partner is one who joins hands in the business by investing in it or by the goodwill he adds to your business as an ambassador of that business. That's why even without investing in the business financially; he is naturally part of the business or partner. A partner has business interest from the gains he is making from it whether by best custom-made services or dividends.

You recognize that this analysis is essential because you cannot make a customer happy without knowing who one is and therefore his or her wants. These wants include the form of products, services or the package of products on offer, the manner in which it is offered! This is the only way you can turn a prospects into trying your products. It is how you can turn the once off customers into regular customers, and customers into clients, clients into ambassadors, ambassadors into patrons and partners. Customers today are more than ever-before demanding—demanding: solutions, services, value, attention, recognition, involvement, wider choices, change, easiness, reliability, quality, etc. That's why today students and parents are asking aggressively enthusiastically what is in schooling for them. They ask: what do we gain if we study and get back to the streets—less—as before. Remember education, is as observed Dale Carnegie: the "ability to meet life's situations."

Indeed, he couldn't be more right: "education is not knowledge, but action!" That's why parents rightly question the returns gained from the fees and opportunity cost of time and resources so invested. And that is their right. One cannot separate curriculum development (or development of any program) from the people involved in the process or from those who will experience the curriculum. One cannot decontextualize the process... (indeed the) key focus of curriculum activity is not the content, the subject matter per se, but rather the individual. Subject matter tentatively selected in the development process has importance only to the degree that a student can find meaning in it for himself or herself (Ornstein and Hunkins, 1998 p.203). Indeed teachers and students but parents must not only take positions they must be change agents to improve the society. They a right to take sides to stand up for the better reasoned partialities they can teach as a result o free meticulously examination and communication of all relevant evidence (Ornstein and Hunkins 1998, p.51).

That is why today both schools and corporations ought to demonstrate their self worth to their employees much as students and employees ought to prove their self-worth in terms of performance and productivity, innovation, leadership etc—to keep their employers in order to earn promotions, fame or recognition. Likewise, schools and businesses ought to always see the need to keep the customer happy—not once though, but through services you offer—and the manner and spirit in which these products and services are offered.

IDENTIFYING THE PRINCIPAL PLAYERS IN THE EDUCATION SECTOR—AND WHY

Considering the changes that have happened over the recent past, it is essential to get an idea on the principal players within the educational sector. This analysis is so essential because it is these players that have either driven change or restricted development in the recent past and in the same way the ones whose response will develop or doom the sector. According to the Promise: "What is clear is that education in Tanzania is a sector that can only benefit from participatory approach… (if education has to be transformational and beneficial to all, it has to encompass) public and private sectors, donors and most importantly, the people."

But what do they have to gain? In words of Professor Maliyamkono (p.423), "Accountability about performance rests first and foremost with Tanzanians (themselves)!" The foregoing statement is very crucial because of our history. We need to relook at our education as well as engage the people because colonial education served the colonial masters interests and not for the people! The government that takes the backseat—in leadership and provision of progressive education is seldom for, or people-led. This could be a strong indicator of how weak that government is.

Who are the customers of the educational subsector? As for schools your partners include, but not limited to the following stakeholders:

Firstly the students themselves
Parents who together with students are the primary customers for schools just as end-users are to a retailer business. The teaching and non teaching staff is to a school what employees are to a business.
- School administrators and owners, shareholders and directors are to schools as are the management teams are to corporations.
- Business sector and other employers are to the school as is the neighborhood or community is to corporations.
- Ministries involved apply the same way to schools as do to corporations.
- The Government, and
    - The development partners etc.
-

From the foregoing analysis you realize that should any business thrive, calls for the spirit of cooperation among all stakeholders in the sector because of interdependence there's amongst them. As a final point for schools or corporations, to keep you not only on the ball but also on the top and the money rolling in, you have got to uphold your grip on the parents or guardians of the your students. The logic is simple. They are the ones who enroll students into schools. You must also evidence the difference you make into their lives. What do they lose doing away with you? They want a clear difference through their children's performances not only academically but also in their day to day lives!

The parents expect their children to behave and to be dependable whether they are under your watchful eyes or not. They expect good manners whether their children are in public or in private schools. And the latter is an important remark since this book and training thereof is a self management and personal leadership program. Parents as are retailers and wholesalers are closely associated with immediate benefits of your business and indeed are decision Makers whether to buy from you or to take their custom to someone else next door!

Before people buy into your idea just like buying your product or services, they need to know what is in it for them. They need to know what they gain. You must make it clear and different from its substitutes. So keep these questions in mind: What is in it for my customers? What do they gain? Is it tangible or significant enough? Is it satisfying and sustainable?

THE MODERN DAY STUDENT: WITH SIMILE TO CLEOPATRA PATRICIA

We have indicated that today's youth are losing—no; that's not it—they have already lost hope in education. They have lost hope in the future—and indeed in themselves. They are wretched. And we share the blame. They have reached here because they aren't listened to or even guided to find answers pertinent to their problems. They aren't given a chance to try. I started writing this book when Patricia was but a week's old baby. As she grew up and it was in her fifth month, self expression as part of her great need to communicate was obviously her top most obsessions. Then one day she was astonishingly unnaturally quiet and cool. That's when the radio interested her. That's when she struggled to pick it up and try to see who speaks in this faceless person. Then I noticed her as she found no body in the radio.

But she didn't get answers and her urge was unbearable such that she began licking it. Her most active sensory organ at the time was the tongue. So licking anything in front of her was her way of getting to know something about anything in front of her. Unfortunately that was not possible. I couldn't let her put everything in the mouth. Indeed she was so very so sensitive that when asleep a little sound would alarm her and she would respond. Something bad happened. The light went off. I lit a torch. That diverted her attention. But touching or even watching the torch wasn't appropriate or couldn't meet her curiosity. Once again she started licking it. I couldn't let her as you would expect a responsible loving father would do. That's when trouble ensued. In rebellion she cried with vigor. She was no longer the same Patricia I know. She was an unfriendly person—a rebel. Imagine a rebel of a toddler! The time was 7.12 evening. And that was June 17, 2011. Apart from this, she has had a lot of signs of super intelligence if we can develop it, and we should. She is very alert. Any little sign of abnormality around her she would raise an eye brow. If it persisted she twisted her head.

How is this related to the subject about the youth? How is it related to the youth? That is how and where the youth have reached. They want to express themselves. Self expression and involvement are their top agenda but we don't engage them. As intelligent and consumed with curiosity as they are, they tend to lose fire and rebel against any further engagement. They will then either surrender, or lose passion, and turn to quick fix in the model of GET RICH OR DIE TRYING. In extreme form of their reaction, they surrender upon fate and throw all cautions to the wind. As for Patricia, I needed to buy her a variety of dolls and toys to help keep her curiosity or fire burning. Keeping such a trait in check turns her into a rebel. And the worst is that when she struggles unsuccessfully for long she surrenders and accepts herself as a failure. That's how exactly the youth turn to quick fix and surrender to hopelessness and drugs. Henry Ford was right. "Any man (or woman) who stops learning is old no matter whether he s 20 or 80!"

Is the foregoing analysis about the youth viable? Let's examine the facts together. With the rate of school dropouts, we ought to ask ourselves why youth turn down the classes. Well, we may call it quick fix toward success but students and parents are asking what is in schooling for them. They ask what do we gain if we spend seventeen years or twenty in school, and then get back to the streets—uneducated and jobless—as before but only older—and inactive! With the publication of this book, with this program, we are convinced that if you give us your time, we will prove to you, in words of Horace Mann that: "Education has a market value" with a yield similar to "common bullion." The "aims of Industry…and wealth of the country" would be augmented "in proportion to the diffusion of knowledge,"[42] albeit knowledge, or rather education of a certain kind!

---

[42] Ornstein and Hunkins (1998), p. 73

BENEFITS TO TRAINEES OR STUDENTS

This program is important because it provides trainees with expediency or practicality as I've mentioned before. "Education is not knowledge, but action!" This book and its twin training program provide you the reader and the trainees with the "ability to meet life's situations."

The program helps trainees to gain ability and courage to see and—most importantly—accept who they are. This is indeed the most important part of any form of sensible education. This program provides you with an education that helps trainees find out what could be wrong with themselves—than pointing fingers—and how to correct it. Trainees will get opportunity to see their shortfalls and learn from them. It helps them work toward correcting what they can but as well gain ability to accept what one cannot change and thus live at peace with oneself. Charity starts at home. Harmony cannot blossom if it doesn't siring forth from the primary beneficiary.

It helps them learn what they would otherwise learn after many years of struggle. It shortens years of learning. It teaches the trainees to set goals and be inspired to work toward those goals. This program bridges trainees' knowledge base using homegrown relevant tested experience and thus shortening their learning life. Students will accomplish whatever they wanted to, in less than half the time or still do more in same span of one's active life time. The program makes it possible to get more for less. It helps students gain a chance of avoid blunders they would fall into—if they otherwise remained uninitiated and blind. Students are taught to make right decisions pertaining to career or vocation, gain how to manage themselves better, their families and others and environment around them; manage HIV/AIDS, relationships, gender and thus live longer, balanced and happy, meaningful lives etc.

What will our new package of offer to schools do to elevate performance of school? We are confident that with this program we are going to enable students acquire the desire or the inclination of seeking success and prosperity. We do this by guiding students to recognize they are unique and special as persons—every one of them—current good as well as poor performers—and that they have some special specific talents—and that is a fact and you know it—and that they came here on earth for a purpose. Besides, we are deeply convinced that "Man was created in the image of God. (So) I (like Julius Kambarage Nyerere) refuse to imagine a God who is poor, ignorant; superstitious, fearful, oppressed, wretched; which is the lot of majority of those He created...Men are creators of themselves and their (present) conditions, (and) under the current present conditions we are creatures not of God but of our 'own selves'" appropriately said Julius Kambarage Nyerere in a speech in New York October 16, 1970.

With this good beginning, we guide our trainees toward each one's appropriate choice of vocation; profession, craft or occupation that suits each one according to his or her talents and desires. That is exactly why we don't dictate—do this or that—what we can only do is to offer useful suggestions. We help instill in them an ability to search for an inner glow—an inner calling—that is specific for everyone.

We offer service and advice that lead to new inspirations; inspirations that lead to development of new and personally developed ideas etc, all of which are advantages to schools, students, education and the nation as a whole. To do this properly, effectively efficiently, having assisted with stirring up the minds of the students to think and find their own calling—their appropriate choices and priorities—we help build confidence in decision-making and how to accomplish everything they set out to do, that is getting things done, getting dreams realized, achieving one's goals.. This is a very fundamental part of our training which is what is missing in schools today. And, mind you, when we say schools, we mean all levels of education including colleges and universities.

Recently I visited a prominent lawyer, entrepreneur and employer in the city. And this was his prime concern with our education. He said we need an education that will enable our people to think, plan and act. And that's not all. It is important to keep on keeping on! That's what makes the difference between a handful of successful and unsuccessful majority in the country. Many do one thing today and soon it turns boring and they drop it. That includes marriages too. And that's where it fits very well. So it isn't abnormal to find people with a series of employers in their history; a series of women and fiancés or fiancées.

I know the foregoing analysis may seem to be a little more of personal affair and thus you may think we are meddling into people's affairs. No! It reflects in our lives and the environment and the neighborhood we live. It reflects in a series of undone, pending works without forgetting the forgotten unfinished works and thus poverty and bigger dependence ratio with social economic and political strife that naturally follows it. Career success, winning a fair fine lady or any other accomplishment are not wooed and retained differently. You must have heard that: A fainted heart never won a fair lady. Bill FitzPatrick was right. Everyone admires the bold, courageous and daring; no one honors the fainthearted, shy and timid. If you are not bold and courageous, you will never make a big difference in your life. Confidence and courage come with education of a certain kind.

BENEFITS TO THE PARENTS
What will parents gain from such an education? Firstly we know that many parents crave schools with better education—education that helps in building the moral fiber amongst their children aside from academic excellence. That's why many parents strive to educate their children abroad in expensive schools. This training program will help parents save the moneys they would otherwise be forced to pay in such schools. Closeness of the parents to the children also helps to keep children under a constant watchful loving eye of the caring parents and teachers who are themselves invited to study and get initiated in this training program. The foregoing argument is corroborated by the fact that the students tend to follow rumor, mob-psychology, and "political correctness," wishing to conform, to please everybody else but themselves, their families and God, unaware that they lose track in the process. This situation is so rampant today heightened by internet, television, social networks and globalization. That's how the victims try drugs, immorality, promiscuity, drop out of school, choose Hip-hop and fashion as career etc. With attention on self-awareness, this program acts as rumor management tool.

Through the change in the behavior and attitudes of their children, the parents will benefit from raising responsible children. They will also realize the value of money they invested in education for their children. Responsible children will take care of family business efficiently. But probably of most importance the responsible children will take care of their parents when they retire. You also need your children to look after you when you get old. Responsible children guarantee a continued family business and name etc. The English saying has it thus; a good name is worth more than a million dollars. The parents will gain peace of mind, and be assured with security during old age. In short we pluck thorns from the children and put roses in their places. What can parents pay for such a service?

BENEFITS TO THE TEACHERS
The teachers will gain in many ways. They will start teaching effortlessly because students cooperate fully recognizing it is to their own advantage to cooperate. The teaching staff will become motivated and thus more productive when they are in their own vocations or aware that it is to their good. With cooperative students teachers will concentrate with

teaching than disciplining stubborn children and hence increased school performances. Aware of their calling and increased self awareness teachers rediscover themselves and their vocations or how best to execute their duties as teachers. Besides, they will be inspired to pursue self development and personal growth or career growth and as a result benefit the students, the school and the society in general. You realize that teachers themselves are students and parents and so they gain also as trainees and parents.

BENEFITS TO THE SCHOOL AND SHAREHOLDERS

The school owners and shareholders will benefit financially as a result of high enrollment by improved performances by inspired teachers and students. Character and academic performances will then impel parents to enroll their children at this school. The training fosters motivation among teaching and non-teaching staff and as a result they will be motivated to work hard. The staff will be inspired toward creativity and cooperation and thus become more productive. The schools will position itself at the top and gain status and recognition due to added value and high performance as a result of this training and thus it will be possible to gain premium fees. With this training you can change work and quality levels of existing teachers. Opportunities are vast than we can enumerate here as the world today is crying for expansion—Napoleon Hill was right. With vast and untapped potential or opportunities in the country, our people's talents are lamenting against their being strangled.

The school will gain in many ways. The teaching staff will teach with ease. Also; teachers will effortlessly teach and manage students since students will be cooperative. Teachers will concentrate on their job of teaching. Teachers will be motivated by new induction and work environment and the new spirit of cooperation. Teachers will access self development and personal growth. They will learn to see new sources of income and career growth.

Schools will benefit financially as the result of high enrollment. They will earn high standing or reputation due to new institutional character emanating from the value that the program adds to its curriculum, besides high performance. This will naturally earn you the right to earn premium from your services. The school owners and shareholders will benefit financially as a result of high enrollment by inspired students and parents.

How? The training program will "make you an appealing, charismatic person. Students will want to learn from you, bosses to promote you, banks to lend you money and customers to buy your products or services."[43] Thus you will also gain from motivation among teaching and non-teaching staff who will be motivated to work hard. The staff will be inspired to re-invent themselves and thus more innovation and initiatives that will lead to their becoming more dynamic and more productive. The schools will gain status and recognition due to added value. High performance will persuade parents to enroll their children in your school. Also as a result of this program, it will be possible to gain a premium on your services. With this training you can change work and quality levels of existing teachers. Opportunities are indeed vast and unprecedented as the social economic world today is crying for expansion.

NEW CHALLENGES FACING SCHOOLS AND HOW WE CAN HELP YOU

As you read recognize that this program is almost a necessity today than ever before. Today the challenges to run schools, households, businesses and nations effectively mount high.

With this challenge, schools, households, businesses and nations need to reorganize for efficiency, seek and pull in new ideas, think about specialization, putting to use the economies of scale in terms of overheads with reference to available facilities and infrastructure. If this is implemented, schools like corporations will gain immeasurably with no any additional cost—in terms of overheads. It is more than worthwhile for your students—young or adults—to refresh their skills. The endeavor is invaluable to parents and the nation as a whole. This endeavor has stunning advantages in terms of financial prospects for your school. To even think of this change you need teachers. Availing yourself with quality teachers is only possible when you fetch not only a better but constant training. Availing quality teachers alone isn't enough.

To retain them you have got to pay better salaries. A paycheck alone is never an antidote though; how is the environment and the game itself? How is the school a healthy place for teachers and staff mentally and socially? Attaining and retaining former teachers isn't enough. You need new ideas. To get new ideas you need to attract new teachers and fresh

---

[43] Source: Bill FitzPatrick, *Action Principles*

blood. However, education in the country is considered to be unaffordable. You therefore have to charge affordable school fees to be able to attract many students and provide education to many—which is your moral duty. To keep the school running profitably, efficiently and sustainably you need new ideas, ideas to make more money and instill motivation among the teachers, parents and students. Such ideas include new teaching to students which attract more enrollments.

The program also delves into new sources of revenue for schools such as adult education to adults; students mentoring; life skills and aspect in the future prospects; elf development among staff and teachers; personal growth among stakeholders and—how to build gainful partnerships; motivation and inspiration that teachers can teach with ease; education in communication skills, cooperation which can start by engaging stakeholders such as students in decision making etc; you can even introduce new training program or lessons in languages such as French or Chinese for independent individuals, the children and adults in your neighborhood. This is a viable business especially with globalization, the nature of world business and social trends today.

Other areas that can help uplift performances and persuade parents to enroll their children into your school include HIV and AIDS awareness and avoidance; aspects into gender and sexual violence education. You have got to be new and keep astride with technology and world trends. This is not enough nonetheless. You have got to be a pioneer of these trends or rather trend setters to be able to satisfy stakeholders and customers: teachers, parents, students, etc.

We advocate for these new areas of training because, firstly, we understand you run a school for both a true noble duty of educating the youth but as well you are a commercial educational enterprise. Being a commercial enterprise, you are in business to make money and stay profitable. And notice that we are concerned with your profitability because otherwise you will close down, leaving our children with no schools, or offer low quality education, and both outcomes aren't any delightful to anyone.

Finally if you can prove your impact through performance of your students academically and in life then you can attract parents to enroll their students. And what's more, with these new areas of training, you can charge a premium price and get it. Alongside this book, we at KI, are certain to help you as schools or institutions and corporations to remain sustainable and profitable, with fully fledged training program covering these areas. Based on our past vast experience from selling of products and services, marketing, branding and now as researcher, writer and published author we are confident of bettering your schools performance and of course make money for all stakeholders—together.

We are all witnesses of how students are hardly adequately prepared at the time they graduate and leave the schools. Having experienced failure, and after having passed through a long path to success, we are certain schools and students who access this training, this new approach—an inside out approach—will surprise not only schools in the neighborhood, but also their parents, themselves as individuals, and the nations beyond. Should I keep it as a secret, that I am a witness of this verity? Students who attend this course even the poor performers will dwarf students who did boast of better performances before. And this is the performance indicator, proving the invaluable significance of this training as our testimonies follow at the end of the book. Considering the practicality of this program, and the very fact that students aren't any happy with an educational program that consumes the largest part of their youthful active life chained in zoos called schools only to get out incapacitated and unable to manage themselves or their lives. They find life of the modern graduates humiliating. They don't find pride in graduating from schools to get out and depend on their least schooled siblings or parents and the government they should be leading or supporting.

With introduction of such highly demanded services and training in public speaking and entrepreneurship the school gains new sources of revenue and additional courses offered by schools in cooperation with the author and outsiders such as KI offered under your own tent. At this point one question remains. Is there a market for such training programs? Let us ponder about it a little more.

We know many people who are in wrong vocations due to the flaws in the current education system. Many want to change jobs and relocate in more compatible vocations. There're majority who still struggle to acquire some basic winning character to be able to undergo behavior change. We know people who cannot stand up and speak in front of people without actually fainting from fright.[44] We see many people who still work not because they

---

[44] *Adapted from Dale Carnegie's How To Win Friends And Influence People*

want to, but because they fear the *Unknown*. Communication and public speaking together forms another gap amongst our adults—learned or not. Indeed, "The highest-paid personnel even in engineering, observed Dale Carnegie "are frequently not those who know most about engineering. One can for example hire technical ability in engineering, architecture, accountancy, or any other professions at nominal salaries.

But the person who has technical knowledge plus ability to express ideas, to assume leadership and to arouse enthusiasm among people—that person is headed for higher earning power... aptly said Rockefeller.[45] "The ability to deal with people is as purchasable commodity as sugar or coffee and I'll pay more for that ability than for any other," said John D. Rockefeller. Such courses for adults, courses that allow them to think on their feet, imparting them with actual experience, effective speaking, the fine art of getting along with people on everyday basis in business as in interviews and self-confidence, relationships and self employment and entrepreneurship are highly demanded by adults.[46]

Furthermore, some professions like engineering are not highly trained in communication skills so they badly need such training. The same goes for a good number of adults in engineering, accounting and auditing. Businessmen need to be able to talk to the Revenue Authority, and indeed also relevant in any the corrupt society where the police force or any other technocrats with insurmountable authority and power, the skills they need to meet such powerful men and women without melting out in the fear of self expression. "Knowledge (or rather education) must prepare individuals for the world of bureaucracy. Bureaucracy is a growing social phenomenon that also characterizes modern society. The school system is one of many formal institutions that are run by complicated machinery of social organization; actually, it is the first of many bureaucratic organizations that the child will encounter in life. The individual in school, in church, in the

---

[45] *How to Win Friends and Influence People, Pocket Books by Dale Carnegie rev. ed P xiv*

[46] *Source: Adapted From How to Win Friends and Influence People By Dale Carnegie*

military, in the hospital, or on the job and in dealing with the government must learn to cope with the enormous size of bureaucracy."[47]

With this program, we add value to conventional education and thereof uplift school performances academically and thus enhance increased enrollment of students by parents—parents who are eager to pay a premium for such services. With new areas of training we can together increase income potential to schools, making it possible to pay better salaries and retain top mind teachers and thus swell financial earnings of the school, its management and directors. The foregoing opportunity then creates a possibility of advancing the scope and reach of education in the country in such areas as invention and on a bigger picture, self sustaining economy.

Indeed, "We come to life's maturity with as little preparation for the pressure of experience as a bookworm asked to do ballet," rightly said David Seabury in his book How to Worry Successfully.[48] Notice also that first and fast starters—trend setters and opinion leaders tend to reap more and in many various other ways than the followers can imagine. Starters tend to gain ownership of any idea or way of life. Remember "He that comes first to the hill may sit wherever he will!" On the contrary, the person who takes no chances (nor risks) has to take whatever is left when others are through choosing! This is not the position you desire for your school, company, family or society.

BENEFITS TO THE GENERAL PUBLIC
you realize that the rich parents and career people who tend to be absorbed in their careers and business rather with little time for the children, by imparting these qualities and ideals to the children, we will allow the parents to manage their careers and businesses better or easier and without fear of losing their children through unfathomable and deplorable manners that pervade the outside world such as drugs, drunkenness, indolence, prostitution etc. Through this training program, we instill the children to abhor such a way of behaving or thinking, often because they realize it is

---

[47] *Allan C. Ornstein and Francis P. Hunkins, Curriculum Foundations, Principles and Issues 3rd Edition p. 153*

[48] *How To Stop Worrying And Start Living Revised edition Pocket Books P. xviii*

not only immoral but also self-defeating. A good example is probably provided by the children of the rich. Notice the fact that they, the children of the rich, tend to behave differently from how their parents conducted themselves when accumulating wealth such that they start losing ambition, humility and temperance. They become pompous, showy and promiscuous. They stop chasing wealth but indulge in spending it. This program will help both the school and parents to bring them back on track. Those from poor families will get to know the secret of making money, insights into persistence and aiming high.

With this training they will gather themselves up—through self management, personal leadership and self-advancement—and stand up and fight back. Again, instead of pomp and being promiscuous or even stopping from chasing wealth indulging in spending it, they will learn to seek wealth and recognize life is in one's own hands. We will save the youth from dangers of globalization and their parents' busy career-life. Let the rich parents consider what really is the benefit of gaining the trophy of owning the whole world at the expense of losing one's own family?

This training helps to re-gain and retain both the career and family. We will help them take advantage they have of the background in and awareness of wealthy and prosperity and its good. They say, *"Seeing is believing."* The Bible says, *"Faith comes from hearing."* This idea sounds true because you cannot aim for something you don't know or imagine of already. No wonder we see the rich families becoming richer and wealthier as sons and daughters of the super rich get themselves ingrained with a wealth mentality. Through this book we will give them ability not only to retain but exceed their parent's levels of success and prosperity. Probably you need to take the break and ponder about the fact a little more before you go on.

But we see the children of the teachers become teachers as doctors become doctors, because they grow up within a family of doctors. In the same manner the children of the economists, bankers, lawyers as well as sons and daughters of the goat herders or hand hoe farmers tend to fill the shoes of their parents. Why? We also see sons of superstar film actors stepping in the shoes of their parents. We see Amitah Bachan and his son Abishek in Bollywood. We see the William Sisters dominate tennis. We have seen three George Bush administrations in the White House. The Kennedys have permeated the American politics for generations even when we should not attempt to keep our eyes and mouths shut about such ubiquity of sons and daughters of the African presidents retaining their father's positions on their fathers' retirement or departure to the next world—even when they are incompetent. We don't even have to go to West Africa or ponder about dictatorships on the few corners of the continent. We can sit here and see or hear sons and daughters of the retired politicians in their fathers or mothers positions even here at home in East Africa or just across the border. The same phenomenon is true about the son or daughter of a goat herder, a hand hoe farmer, a prostitute and a beggar. We must therefore choose rightly.

Again, yes the training while it allows the children to learn from their parents, but also it helps spread the enlightenment or pass on the preparedness of the mindset of such families to the rest of the majority in our society. The training will help to ward off the danger of creating a monarchy among democracies at the same time averting civil wars that are likely to happen when only a few families are privileged to know the secret of success and prosperity leaving the masses in deprivation and desolation unaware of what they can do to change their lives. As for the poor if they know that each of us is born unique; and each of us was ordained to fulfill an only goal or role of its kind and thus strive to bring one major difference in the world; and if they learn to find it in themselves their scope of success is unfathomable.

How do we heal this chronic epidemic? We have to start from how conditioned each group has been and that as a result they get what they get as a result of how they have been conditioned. Indeed you cannot reap what you didn't sow! To change, therefore, they have to change their mindset and lifestyle. With such knowledge the poor see the opportunities within their reach and threats they face in their present position or circumstances. This allows them to learn from their shortfalls and thereby getting inspiration to seek to be successful by setting goals and working toward them while avoiding blunders they would fall into if they remained uninitiated. They can as well be able to make right decisions pertaining to career or vocation and how to manage themselves HIV/AIDS and others around.

The parents and guardians will benefit from changed behavior and attitudes of their children—becoming more responsible persons. As for busy executives and rich parents who tend to be absorbed in their careers and business rather with little time for the children, by imparting these qualities and ideals to our children, we will allow the parents to manage their careers and businesses better and without fear of losing their children to bad manners and drugs. Children of the rich tend to behave differently from how their parents did when accumulating wealth such as losing humility and temperance, will gather themselves up and have control over their lives.

Again, instead of pomp and promiscuity or even stopping from chasing wealth but indulging in spending, they will learn to seek wealth and recognize life is in one's own hands. We will save the youth from dangers of globalization and their parents' busy career-life—the two plagues we find ourselves in unprepared. This training let us the wealthy parents and too business executives to question the benefit of gaining the trophy of owning the whole world at the expense of losing your own family? This training helps to re-gain and retain both the career and family. The training program helps bring them back on track. What can these parents pay in return?

In his great book You Were Born Rich Bob Proctor seconds the foregoing assertion by revealing that the coaching, in one form or another, has been practiced only among a small minority of enlightened individuals or families for centuries. Only recently has this enormously powerful engine for personal transformation begun to receive mainstream attention on a global scale. I believe this miraculous turn of events is the result of a spiritual shift that is taking place in the world: Individuals in great numbers are realizing that they have deep reservoirs of talent and ability —that they possess the inherent power within themselves and they can use it to shape their destinies.

It is in the same line that the children from the poor families will be exposed to the secret of prosperity and zero tolerance against poverty, insights into the desire for success, possibility, and faith in themselves, persistence, and aiming higher. We teach them to be industrious, muster and master courage, hope, tolerance enthusiasm, to be passionate, perseverance and to have determination and burning desire to acquire what they set out to get. We will teach them the secret of success: that success isn't at all about talent or our core skills but character and attitude. The program helps impart to them the winning mentality and to learn that one's life is in one's own hands. In short, we reveal that in everyone, there's a "special one."

Yet that isn't enough. For unless we initiate them into the secret and the possibilities therein one tends to remain a weakling fearing to try accepting poverty as destiny. But no one can change his circumstances without changing the way he thinks, behaves, relates and lives. We are all witnesses of how poorly most of our youth conduct themselves whether because that's how they think it should be or because they don't know what they are doing. That's why we ought to train them to recognize there's a certain way—and a specific one at that—that leads to success and prosperity, that otherwise they are heading for a tragic future.

What's more, we train them how to muster and master how to pursue this path successfully. We impart courage to start over, and over again. We make them know that vices like weeds grow naturally whereas virtues are hard to keep like nurturing a garden; that good seeds must be sown. The gardener must also put manure. A garden has also to be watered and constantly looked after by removing weeds and pests before it can generate harvests. Beside the winning attitude, the children from poor families benefit by being encouraged to appreciate the incentive there are for a poor son or daughter who will begin by scraping from the scratch. We teach them that it's not inheritance or luck that lifts someone's life.

Such possibilities like improving the house, buying a new bicycle, a goat or cow or a hand hoe; possibility to buy or grow food stuff or other provisions for his poor family tend to boost his morale and the passion to keep working harder and hence his poor circumstances as advantage rather than disadvantage. That is how the training program helps bring them back on track. It's not like the children from the wealthy families. The house is there. There's plenty of food and the family wallet is thick. The family has not only a car but several of them and there's generally nothing to inspire them for higher goals as it is for a poor family despite the fact that they have a head start.

The rich have amassed wealth but have lost their heads in the folly of their technological, financial and material achievements. Ralph Waldo Emerson was right. "The civilized man has built a coach, but has lost the use of his feet. He is supported on clutches, but lacks so much support of the muscle." has come true. With this book and training we help you perk up the coach, while we work to reclaim and advance the use of your feet. To the poor we raise role models from amongst themselves and thus creating and reinforcing possibilities for the younger generations. But that's why we created this training in order to benefit both groups. We train both groups on how to be successful and having been successful how to use their accomplishments to better and impact the quality of their own lives and of the environment and people around them—which is the handicap of most of our today's academic instructions. We need both groups. We cannot—and shouldn't—kill the poor because they are poor, or wipe-out the rich because they are rich.

Indeed, "You cannot help the poor by destroying the rich," said Abraham Lincoln, "You cannot strengthen the weak by weakening the strong. You cannot bring about prosperity by discouraging thrift. You cannot lift the wage earner up by pulling the wage payer down. You cannot further the brotherhood of man by inciting class hatred. You cannot build character and courage by taking away men's initiative and independence. You cannot help men," continued Abe Lincoln, "You cannot help men permanently by doing for them, what they could and should do for themselves." Indeed, with this training program exposing the secret of success, it acts as a code breaker working to break the deadlock behind our backwardness. Now, what can these parents or the government pay in return for such a service like ours?

BENEFITS TO THE GOVERNMENT
Before we talk of benefits of the program to the government and community in general let us take a look at Kibera slum in Nairobi Kenya or Manzese in Dar es Salaam Tanzania or even Kawempe in Uganda—among other slums. Here're facts about the slums. That's where you find the largest population density in the country or community. As if that's not enough that's where you find population of the youth outnumbering the elderly people by far as compared to general population statistics. Here's where you find people who turn out to be drug addicts. They are a group of youth who are engaged in not only idling but also crime.

They instead of helping in production of material wealth physically or creating conditions for efficiency, they stifle growth instead and increase the dependence ratio at household and national level. In summary they are a group of people in their prime time for highest innovation and productivity but otherwise useless as far as their contribution or output they produce is concerned. They are a burden to their families the community and the nation as a whole in terms of opportunity cost incurred. They are spending without earning a dime. They steal and rob. They terrify the neighborhood. They fill government prisons regularly. They are provided for by the government of course on the shoulders of few tax payers' money. They engage themselves in crimes such as killing or rape and prostitution. They constitute nothing but are indeed a burden to the productive population. They become a burden by reducing or weakening the workforce pulling down the average income per person and weakening the domestic or internal market.

Now think of an educational program that can overturn such a condition by transforming this mess into a blessing and a curse into a cause such as increased self respect, personal and collective responsibility and productivity per person in Kibera or Manzese or Kawempe. This is a kind of a training that can completely transform this larger population segment of youthful population into people who work hard in order to earn not only a living but meet the top desires of their lives such as consumption of goods and services in the country. We would turn this den of vices into a haven of workshops and markets. We would turn them into factories workers and buyers of products so produced and thus cutting down the imports and dependence ratio at household and national level and create hubs of economic and social development. In summary the government and country as a whole gain in terms of producing positive, progressive, competitive and pragmatic population—badly needed especially today with East African Community at hand.

A pragmatic conscious population tends to breed responsible citizens; pragmatic conscious population breed responsible public servants. Responsible citizens tend to be cooperative with the leadership. Responsible people breed creative and productive children. Responsible citizens breed better and responsible future leaders. Responsible citizens lead to widened tax base. Responsible citizens breed better families and finally responsible citizens enhance better neighborhood. Remember we can choose our friends but we cannot choose our neighbors.

The program acts as a bridge between the best schools and the poor ones, the bridge between the high income earners and low earners, the poor and rich etc. Again with the paradox of common schools and special schools based on income brackets, fees, apprenticeship, infrastructure and teachers availability, we need to support the program among schools and workplaces as a tool for empowerment and inner capacity building. Through this program we give a chance to all since some students develop after primary level and other later in high school, during or even long after graduation and hence we have got to give them a chance to try for you don't know who they will be. We don't know who children or students are at tender age hence with this program we give a chance to choose what they can do and be and specialize in that area. If we don't attempt to fight the stereotype about who can and who cannot succeed—who can and who cannot perform at the top of the class or in certain field of study be that racial, class or gender, "the students failure becomes a sort of self-fulfilling prophecy," as aptly wrote Carmen Jessica De Menech (An Exercise in the

Worldmaking 2007, p.27). With this training program we emphasize that everyone has to choose one's own vocation. By doing so, if we do so, we will increase everyone's performance and so reduce variation in scores and income gap.

Besides, by bridging the gaps in terms of incomes this program guarantees to increase the middle class in the country which is pivotal in developing the industry in the country. Surely this training seems to be the only remedy you need now as a country through schools and workplaces and households if you have to turn the tables around and transform a poor country into an enviable strong economy. What then is the amount of money could buy such a program.

Additional benefits include increased opportunities for everyone and possibility for a better station in life and jobs for majority. And I say "increased opportunities for everyone and possibility for a better station in life and jobs for majority," because there are no miracle of stopping some from slipping through the net. Such opportunities include: better financial and social economic benefits, better healthcare, family planning and birth control, regulation of inappropriate time of marriage and ability to pay fees and manage the family and thus a better family and strong family institution for the whole country guaranteeing powerful and successful next generation. Such a program thus creates healthy opportunities such as career growth and skilled workforce; that produce more and better products and services and thus also trickle down effects in form of financial and technical skills; the government reaps the top through widened investment opportunities and employment for everyone and thus widened tax base and strong and independent economy.

As a nation and community in general, we will all reap tremendously in terms of transformed population that is hardworking, self-reliant and more inclined to self-employment. The forgoing quality naturally lead to wealth and job creation, fame and recognition in various limitless other sorts and generally transforming the country into an industrious and prosperous nation. You must have not missed the fact that we can as well develop this proposition as a program exportable to the outside and create employment and wealth for the local people. If we did so, we would together transform our families, *schools, businesses* and the nation as a whole from beggars to givers.

We would transform the economy into one powerful force to reckon with both internally and beyond our neighborhood internationally changing from an economy or nation in the status of the horse in the today's international socio-economic model of horse and rider. And it can be done. It all begins with the mind. China, Japan, North Korea and Brazil or even Venezuela has tried to work from outside the box. We see America is the super power and pinnacle nation today. But that's where they were during the British rule. *T.D Jakes was right when he observed that, two men can be faced with same chaos. Yet one will find opportunity therein while another will ground in chaos. Where do you fall? That's upon you to judge, or choose to do, and become!* We recognize, nonetheless, that you realize your options are far limited. These are but a few benefits. You can and should add more to the list.

CONCLUDING NOTE ON BENEFITS

Did I say concluding note? No! What we have highlighted is in fact the beginning of the potential benefits this program offers you. We promise you that through the proceeding chapters in this very book and its twin titles, you will identify and learn in more details the difference these ideal can make—and how. With support of everyone in implementing this program, we are going to pluck thorns from our youth and the society as a whole and put roses in their places. We are going to assist the employed adults and those that are near retirement to learn not only to be prepared for retirement but for self employment. Those who now labor so unhappily in the jobs they don't love, or didn't choose in the first place; jobs in which they don't gain enough out of their sweat, will learn to switch to their most compatible and profitable vocations anytime they want to. I am convinced that you are finally coming to terms with Napoleon Hill that: "There's no fixed price for a sound idea." I hope before you finish this book, you will have realized that the big moment for you as an individual, your family and community, your school, business organization, the nation and humanity as a whole has just been set right at your door steps.

LAST WORD: CALL FOR ACTION

Truly if you have to prosper, indeed in order for you to realize the benefits we so confidently promise, you must change or transform your life. To do so, to change, you need to begin with transforming your own life, to see to it that you are in sync with the kind of life you need to attract. Unlike in the past, no more shall your heritage or background count anymore if you should grow. Today individual persons, households, organizations or nations that shall rise and stand out are those that choose to seek and to align themselves with the right character and attitude. In the end it will be those seeking change, it will be that person or household or society implementing change that shall reap at its right time the privilege of power, wealth, recognition, fame and all benefits emanating from internal but as well as power vested upon them by not only their own peers but as well their superiors. As such, this privileged person, family of society will reap wealth, health, freedom and happiness—and indeed the most precious gifts we can dream of while on this planet.

Am I promising that you will receive these blessings instantly? No sir! It can delay. And don't expect sympathy from the author. That's how it is. It cannot be otherwise. It must be so because change itself is a gradual process, it is an investment for the future. Let it take roots. We are however certain that you will realize in the near future that you wouldn't care to set monetary limit on implementing this program—yes you as a person, household, ministry, an institution or as a corporate organization and a nation as an entity in world civilization, politics and economics. To turn down this suggestion is doing students, employees, the parents, employers and the nation as a whole, a great deal of injustice. On the other hand, if you support the scheme, availing the program to the schools and workforce, someday—and yes soon enough—somebody will discover and reward you tremendously for you will have helped to propel the nation to another height. In supporting this program, not far too long from now when somebody will discover and reward you tremendously for the positive change you will have helped to institute. And that's not all. Very soon the world will discover and reward you for your service of high order to humanity. But the choice lies with you!

Indeed I'm truly positive that with your cooperation in your present position as school director, parent, student, teacher, corporation, development partner, education officer, minister for education, minister of youth and works, minister for East African Cooperation etc, members of parliament or even the president himself, you are doing the households, schools, corporations, education system and nation as a whole a greater good! As a nation, with your support, our schools, households, businesses and partners will gain additional value that would remain unthought-of under the conventional education. Schools and the people therefore will ward off contempt and from hence forth regain dignity.

This transformation will further bring class and dignity to our schools, teaching career, education system and our citizens as a whole. This is why we should take chances. Indeed, "There's no fixed price for a sound business or social economic idea!" I'm sure, after you extend your helping hand you will find yourself highly privileged. Besides the truth is you cannot support something as noble as this one and remain in obscurity. That's why one day not only someone but the world will discover you and reward you and your posterity. Without a doubt, the big moment for you as an individual, your school, business organization, community, families and the nation as a whole has just been set right at your door steps. Yet, for a community to progress, it needs constant transformation. Growth is a process. Any development is never a disconnected event or set of events. We count an honor to be part of the change— the change that has actually already come—whether everyone knows it or not.

Finally, as we close this chapter, let me remind you that the decision you make with regard to this program is critical. As such, this is not a kind of decision you make and move on and then life goes on like business as usual! No! Sorry! With the decision you make today, your life will never be the same again. We know how badly you need this program. But, we can't dictate or choose for you. Secondly before you choose not to cooperate but instead stick with the past, well, I've got news for you. And it's no good news. Because of the law of nature without innovation and constant pursuit of progress only intelligent and productive persons and dynasties adapting to environmental changes will not only survive but also thrive. Less intelligent and weak mediocre people would slowly disappear—sooner or later!

And this isn't my own creation once again. It is Herbert Spencer's. If a nation doesn't adapt to the changing world, no matter how top it is at the present, it will not be, shamefully, far too long before in words of Boyd Bode; *"It would be circumvented and left behind."* Is this mere dire prediction or guess work from some pessimist? No sir. Today in the Zambezi Valley a few miles away from where I am writing this book, most elephants mother mono horn or completely hornless calves because of poaching. Indeed "Like species human mind, intellect, business organizations, educational institutions, families and nations; if they don't evolve and adapt to new and changing environment, they become extinct!"

Truly, to forgo the future clinging instead with the past is self defeating. Without evaluating your virtues against your accomplishments, you are destined to fail. To do that is a right thing to do. It is itself righteous. It benefits you personally, much as it benefits your offspring and humanity as a whole. And King David taught in the Psalms: "The righteous will flourish like a palm tree; they will grow like a cedar of Lebanon." King Suleiman son of King David considered the wisest and wealthiest man and ruler of all time concluded thus: "Seest thou a man diligent in his business? He shall stand before kings," counsels the wise king.

Now what can a person pay to gain such a feat. What can a person pay to have life under his or her control? What can a school pay to have all its students acquire such a superior character and to win in classes as well as at work and home. What can a corporation pay to have its employees acquire such values? What can it pay to stand out of the crowd? What is the price of having customers queue at your doorsteps scrambling to pay top dollar for products and services you offer when next door products or services of same fiber and quality decay on the shelves amongst the adjacent shops?

Now before we close this chapter, we have got to answer to what we, at Kambarangwe Institute of Leadership and Innvation do to bring about this change. We provide an unbiased picture of faults and virtues required to make a big difference between success and failure. Based on our reserches on the gaps in education today following weaknesses inherent in the conventional education which is no longer sufficient hand in hand with close observation of the successful people and those who fail, we center on the mindset creating or consolidating a set of winning superior character of core values. These values or qualities work as antidote prescribed agaist failure. Probably you question our asertion that the convntional education is nolonger adequate. You are right. you need us to validate such a strong asertion.

To illustrate, take two persons or teams and give them same-same tools. One will exceed expectations, as another will complain of poor tools; one team will be crowned champions as another sits at bottom! Likewise, take two companies selling similar products. One will have a constant flow of customers paying top dollar for its products, while next door products decay on the shelves. Take two graduates of finance or economics; give them a million dollars each. One will make a fortune as the million dollars will, like water, filter through the fingers of another fellow. "Compared with what we ought to be," observed Professor William James: "we are only half awake...making use of only a small part of our physical and mental resources. Stating the same thing broadly, the human individual thus lives far within his limits. He possesses powers of various sorts which he habitually fails to use..." This, Sir, is the gap we fill! This, Madam, is the difference we make!

To testify, to substantiate, let me as the author of this very book and program say that, I am confident if I'd read this book or gone through this very program twenty years ago, I would be—well, I can't even tell where I would be right now. Probably in the sky! I would have accomplished so much long ago! And this is not my own conviction. Well, have you ever asked yourself where you would be if things were right, right from the beginning or if you ever knew how to tame such a situation—or yourself? I have tossed the same question placing the same position to groups of trainees—executive and corporate employees and students; and also to the teaching staff from different companies and I have almost regrettably witnessed severally adult trainees dry a tear or two only after having adequate time to ponder a little seriously about the question. I have seen many respondents so many times dry a smoke of tears from their eyes pondering about their present situation in relation to where they ought to have been that I am no longer any sentimental about their emotions anymore.

Let's talk about Saul. Up to the time that God called him to lead His people, Saul was probably among the most upright young men in the whole Israel. He was blessed with a tall and great body as well as having mentally superior character throughout all Israel. How do we know? I mean that how do we illustrate that he had superior character and first class virtues? We know this is true from that moment he was called to be crowned king. Even when he knew gains he would get for himself being anointed king such as wealth and power, as the prophet Samuel, elders and the masses gathered to witness their first King ever, on the day when he was to be crowned king over all Israel, he hid himself, literally running away abdicating the throne he hadn't even assumed already why? He was a selfless person, well—that was long before absolute power corrupted him absolutely! And he had reason to, for afterall people hadn't voted for him. How could he really be sure if it was the people's will?

Who wouldn't want such a person for a son, daughter, employee, neighbor, friend or spouse? What nation would not want such a person for its own king or leader? Probably Mwalimu Nyerere referred to King Saul when cautioning the nation about people who use all their might and clout to win elections. Such people aren't any virtuous. God Himself speaking to Prophet Samuel on the latter's first instance of setting sight on Saul, declared the blessings of the ideal person saying: "Behold, here's the person of whom I spoke to you. It is him who shall rule over my people!"[49] We can as well illustrate the benefits of the ideas we teach right now by analyzing what happened when greed and envy and impatience and injustice seized him, I mean King Saul. God stripped him of his blessings and dethroned him once and for all. Read it for yourself in the first book of Samuel chapters 15 and 16. Indeed Lincoln was right: "Character is the root of credibility. Chop off roots and the tree falls…!"

---

[49] *1 Samuel 9:17*

PART II

THE IDEAL SCHOLAR

*"Behold here's the man of whom I spoke to you!
It is he who shall rule over my people!"*
—God (1. Samuel 9:17)

7. VOILA! BEHOLD THE IDEAL SCHOLAR: KNOW THYSELF—AND THE EDUCATED SLAVE

"Where there is no vision, the people perish."—Proverbs 29:18

INTRODUCTION
It may shock you to actually learn that very few employers and managers are happy about their employees. But it should not be so. Parents, reverends and sheikhs, teachers, army commanders, kings and queens and presidents are as about unhappy about their children, congregations, students, soldiers and their citizens. It may come to you as a shock to know that many of our people—learned and unlearned alike—don't even know or love why they are doing what they are doing. If the foregoing assertion is somehow true, would you then wonder why they underperform?

Is it my own creation or imagination? Is Kambarangwe the only author with this imagination you consider to be cynicism on the author's part! I refuse to believe I am the only author now living who believes that our people fall short of our expectations. Thinking about managers or leaders of people that you and I are as parents, teachers, reverends or imams, army commanders, kings and queens, prime ministers and presidents, it reminds me of God. God is the principal author and manager or leader of men. I will not shock you to tell you that he too is a disappointed manager of men! The bible reports about God's disappointment in men in Romans 3:23. "For they have all sinned and have fallen short of the glory God."

But since that exemplar is more spiritual, biblical, and therefore less realistic to some of my readers, let us consider a more human illustration.

In his book *The Seven Characteristics of Highly Effective* people , Stephen R. Covey reports about the familiar lamentation among many managers—if not all. "I have taken a course after course of effective management training," he wrote about the typical manger's lamentation, "I expect a lot out of my employees and I work hard to be friendly toward them and to treat them right. But," he continued, "I don't feel any loyalty from them. I think if I were home sick for a day, they would spend most of their time gabbing at the water fountain. Why can't I train them to be independent and responsible—or find employees who can?" need we say more? That's the challenge facing all researchers and economists. It is a challenge facing all parents and all football managers as well as politicians who wish to turn their people from mediocrity to hard working individuals and nation states.

We are delighted to announce that here is the fulfillment of that training program—a training that began with your skills based education and the preceding chapters in this book intending to answer to this critical lamentation amongst most managers of people in our families, schools, workplaces and nation states. It is a training that shapes the character of our people imparting them with such qualities—qualities that push them to the edge of insanity with obsession to work hard in order to achieve their goals and to make a difference in their lives and lives of those around them. But here is a very fundamental secret. This secret of success is based on our belief that you were not born to fail but to thrive and excel, and because we believe the environment around you is what discourages us, we believe this program is like a garage in which we install back the inbuilt compass or guiding values transforming these individuals into persons who are immune to failure.

Notice that from the first page of this book until now, we have been preparing ourselves for this hour. You now recognize why we have got to study these ideals so closely and gain knowledge about how to make them become part of our daily lives. Did I say: "our daily lives?" Well, there are two amendments we should make. Here is the right phrasing. We have got to study these ideals so closely and gain knowledge about how to make them part of not only our own hourly lives but also the lives of the people and environment around us.

But before we proceed to the ideals, let us recap on what we have discussed so far. And the whole thing can be summed up thus: Can this training really heal a nation—a nation we identified as a sick nation? The ideal scholar never fails. The ideals we impart to our trainees are like insurance policy against failure. Take the ideal employee for instance. What is the difference does he make or bring to work? What value does he add to the department and organization as a whole? How really does the ideal scholar or person we bring into being transform the whole country? The ideal scholar naturally becomes the ideal employee. The ideal employee is productive and innovative. He adds value to a department—on one hand through innovation, productivity and profitability he helps generate for the department—and on one hand he adds value to the organization and the nation as a whole. An ideal father or mother; he breeds and imparts good character and values to his children who then help shape the future generation and therefore sustainable national prosperity.

Notice also that he adds value to the department or organization not only by work of his hands and mind alone. No. Yes, it starts from his thoughts and deeds, but most importantly through the people around him, the people he helps transform directly or indirectly through his character or leadership—or both. You recognize that if we set out to produce as many ideal scholars as possible in our families, schools and work teams, we will have transformed the whole nation. But is this—the philosophy we lay down—baseless or only regional? No sir! It is universal. Indeed the ideal scholar is a person you would like your son or daughter to be like—whether you are in Tanzania or Texas. You would like to have this personality as your son or daughter whether you are Greenland or even in Arabia. This personality we call *Ideal Scholar* or person has qualities you would crave your spouse to have in his or her possession. He or she is indeed a person you would like to marry, yes you the reader, excepting of course, if you're a Catholic pope, bishop, priest, nun or monk. If you are a Catholic pope, bishop, priest, nun or monk, the foregoing immediate gain isn't for you sorry. You will gain in having zealous upright God -fearing congregations as compensation nonetheless. Indeed the endeavor of producing ideal scholars or persons, leaves everyone gainful—one way or the other.

To describe a little more about the personality of this very ideal scholar, he or she is a kind of a person you crave to hire as your employee if you are a hiring manager, or a business owner. He is a person you would love to have as your employer or head of your department. As a businessman he is a person you would be willing to partner with. He is a person you would like to be your neighbor. He or she is a person you would not regret if he were your father, mother, president of the country you love and in which you live—a country you would like your children and their children's children to live generation after another forever—and ever amen. Now because you make sense of how inevitable these ideals are, you may choose to cram them. The ability to cram them on its own isn't enough. Indeed anyone can read this book and cram it such that he repeats it verbatim. He can repeat it verbatim to an audience without himself having understood the content. But that isn't what the author intended for you—yes you the reader—and your family. To train others, one has to be trained first. Having created the ideals and the course, we teach you how to acquire these values. To make the most of this training, you should go to a great deal of trouble to search and learn who or what you are; why you need these ideals, how to acquire them, when and how to connect them and leverage from each of these ideals.

We have through the preceding pages described how technical or work skills on their own are almost useless if the graduate or trainee lacks moral or ethic values: character and good attitude. Suffice to say here that you may have all teachers and trainers teaching or training you in all other subjects, such as biology, auditing, engineering, geography or languages, but if they don't teach you one most important aspect—an aspect of conducting yourself in certain way. Sadly, this is what is happening on the ground. We who went to school, traditional schools, were taught very little in as far as real life or the secret behind prosperity is concerned. If they don't teach you about not only how character is paramount but also benefits or importance of living in a certain way, they mislead you. Because our schools and most post school trainers don't teach you this secret, today we find many souls that are destined to live their whole lives as frustrated and unhappy failures despite their colorful degree papers. That's not what you want to happen to you. That's not what you want to happen to your children. It is not what you want for your students and employees. Let me illustrate.

Anyone who at one time was a student at Ihungo Secondary School and all Kagera in the late eighties down to early nineties can easily recall Mugaywa Magafu. Mr. Magafu was a genius—no doubt about it. If you only looked at his papers you would say: Wow, or shout Halleluiah. If you were blood related, you would place lots of your hopes in him! But he was a little unsociable. And you wouldn't love that. How do I know? I was school secretary general after joining my high school at Ihungo when Mr. Magafu was in his form four. Let us now consider another kind of genius. Take football genius like Balotelli. You watch him play and you get convinced that there is more to an ideal human, as there is more to an ideal employee, the top salesman, the top scorer in each subject in a class, or football game. That's not the nation you want to build. It is doubtless in response to this paradox that Benjamin Franklin, a famous American Diplomat, Scientist, and Writer concluded that: "Genius without an education is like silver in the mine."

BEHOLD! THE IDEAL SCHOLAR

Here now comes, finally, a set of the qualities of the ideal scholar—in a nut shell though. We present them in a nutshell because we will bring you a more detailed package in the second volume of this very work. Now, voila! Behold the ideal scholar.

The ideal scholar recognizes that he, is! Does the statement tantalize you? It shouldn't! By this we mean he recognizes that he is not work of fiction: he is not fiction itself. He is real. He himself and his life are a reality. Now because he is real, he has to identify who he really is. This is basically what Socrates summed up as Know Thyself. In his solemn pursuit to know who he is, the French philosopher Descartes began by actually doubting if he really was. That is to say, he began by attempting to establish if he really existed before he could identify who he really was. In his doubt about his own being i.e. if he himself or life itself were a reality, he then concluded that he himself on one hand and life itself on the other were a reality. In the original version of his statement about his doubt and conclusions about his study, he concluded thus: Donc, si je doute, je pense, et si je pense, je suis! That is to say: Therefore if I doubt, I think, and if I think, I am!

Now we have chatted about the need to, and the pursuit for establishing and identifying one's person, by which we mean he has to be in sync with his whole person—his body, mind and soul. Moreover, as an educated person he is aware or has educated himself about himself—his body, mind and soul, he also learns about the people and his environment around him—which therefore forms five major primary areas he will centre his learning intentions and efforts viz. his body, mind and soul, the people and environment around him. He does so knowing that his own person, the people and environment around him affect one another. Therefore for his wellbeing, his prosperity, he has to be on familiar terms with each of these aspects. The mistakes our educators do, and which they do so skillfully, is that they teach you history, they teach you about the environment and even the microbes around us, they teach you, geology and metaphysics and astronomy and about the sky and stars; they teach you even the most complex mathematics such calculus and logarithms. But what surprises me is that they don't teach you that most important subject you would like and deserve to know more than any other subject. You know what that subject is? Yes you are right. That subject is YOU—knowledge about—and skills to manage—a YOU. And this—this subject about you—is the most central subject to education, or acquisition of knowledge. That's why you are destined to live your life as a frustrated and unhappy failure despite your colorful degree papers if you don't learn about you. We teach you to seek and be you—the real you that God created and gave dominion over the whole world and all that dwell in it, above it and all in between.

Most graduates today don't know who they are. That's why they look at themselves either indifferently, or contemptibly; instead of looking at themselves with deep gratitude to the maker for having made them as such. To know yourself you must appreciate your background as well as your present and finally where you want to go. Yes it is about the outward person but more so the inner person. I've myself forced myself to fit in other people's personalities. It is self-torture. It is vandalism of the self. I've tried it, I know how it is. You can't change who you are—I mean you can't be someone else—and for goodness sake, love who you are. But for that to happen, it begins with the taking the possession of yourself. But you cannot repossess yourself without basically knowing who you are. This is the beginning. Unfortunately, most folks learn to regroup and retrace their feet when they already old and done with it. In retrospect, this author's father wasn't different. Growing up dad taught us only English and Kiswahili. Though I heard him soak in the vernacular a few times with his old acquaintances and relatives, he never spoke to us in Kishubi. Not once! But as he grew old , surprisingly he suddenly began teaching us how they greet back home and demanded that we salute him as such. That's maturity. That's education. Emerson was right. "As we grow old, wisdom steals inward."

Writing about Seven Habits of Highly Effective People, Stephen Covey wrote this a standard lamentation among business executrices. It is a typical standard lamentation among men and women who don't know who they are—basically. Here is the standard lamentation of the typical learned business executive, "I have set and met my career goals," wrote Stephen Covey, "and am having tremendous professional success. But it's cost me my personal and family life. I don't know my wife and children any more. I am not even sure I know myself and what is really important to me. I have had to ask myself—' is it worth it?'"

It is probably for this reason that the ancient university institutions in Kemet—now Egypt—had identified only one major theme or core agenda, the primary requirement of education by which they evaluated how one is educated. That was: "Know Thyself!" Attributed to Socrates, Know Thyself was a key concept that refers to self awareness. Self awareness refers to the ability to first know yourself and then to be able to manage one's emotions. It is the ability to motivate oneself in whatever form of emotions, ability of recognizing and to advantageously put to use the emotions in others, and finally the ability of handling relationships with oneself and other people and environment around you.

In words of David Orr,[50] developed from the Greek concept of Paideia, "The goal of education is not mastery of subject matter, but of one's (own) person. Subject matter is simply the tool. Much as one would use a hammer and chisel to carve a block of marble, one uses ideas and knowledge to forge one's own personhood. For the most part we labor under a confusion of ends and means, thinking that the goal of education is to stuff all kinds of facts, techniques, methods, and information into the student's mind, regardless of how and with what effect it will be used. The Greek knew better."[51] The fifth quality in Draper Kauffman's six areas of competence that could comprise a possible future curriculum, he identified this first quality as: "Understanding the individual and society." Is it important, this ideal? Let us see.

In an article "The Educated Slave,"[52] Dr. Person-Lynn Kwaku wrote that: "One of the most miscalculated assumptions is that when a person receives a college degree, whether undergraduate or graduate, that individual is now educated." This is wrong. It is true that that individual is qualified to apply for various positions or professions where a particular degree is required. However, if one were to evaluate being educated by the first requirement, most would not be considered educated. …. If the principle of "Know Thyself" alone was applied to today's college graduates, most would be considered illiterates, because they basically don't know who they are," concludes, not this author, but Dr. Lynn Kwaku.

---

[50] *What Is Education For? Six Myths About The Foundations Of Modern Education,*
And Six New Principles To Replace Them by David Orr: adapted from a commencement address to the graduating class of 1990 at Arkansas College

[51] *What Is Education For? Six Myths About The Foundations Of Modern Education,*
And Six New Principles To Replace Them by David Orr: adapted from a commencement address to the graduating class of 1990 at Arkansas College

[52] *http://whgbetc.com/ifbm/educated-slave.html*

The point I am trying to impress upon you is this: instead of our schools focusing on professions or work skills, they must first emphasize the education of the self or self concept. Education should help the learner first to identify his inner person. Self concept gives one a sense of direction. For instance if colleges and schools taught their learners about themselves, if the learners realize importance of knowing who they are, we shall take knowledge base to tremendous infinite heights. When we reach this stage when our schools emphasize first the education into the self, then the learner will muster an eager want to study biology for instance in order to know how his body functions. And that's not the end. He shall then find within himself the push for learning anthropology for instance order to learn about his genealogy, his background. That is not enough though.

He will then find within himself the need to know his own history—to know where his ancestry came from—how he ended up becoming who he is today. That is how he will begin studying history to know his past. Such is how he will know why we look as we do. Why some are black, orange, or yellow or white and others colored? As I enumerate these areas, think of the white men in south Africa, the Mulatoes in Zanzibar, Tabora, or in any deep village or township such as Rulenge, Katera, or Kiijongo, in Kagera, Tanzania. Again as you ponder about this narrative think of such Irish men and women in America or even Barack Obama. Ask yourself why you or me look the way we do? Why do you, or I, resemble someone in SA, Nigeria or Congo or Ethiopia or Uganda? Why are men of all races in all these countries, races to which you and I belong? By doing so, you will get a clue about diversity of human population. By doing so, you may be led to understand that we are all sojourners whose future we are yet to know, and the past only a mist of history of our forefathers who migrated either from North, East, South or West. The recent and well recorded Ngoni migration to Tanzania from South Africa helps to put that into context. History suggests that the Nilotes and Hamitics settled in this part of the continent from North, as the majority Bantu moved from the Congo.

By analyzing our history, we can reconcile ourselves with our differences. We can as well learn how slavery, colonialism and neocolonialism still divide us in order to rule us. We can as well have our eyes opened to the fact that our differences are fuelled by our politicians wishing to rule with ease and without end. That's how we can come to terms with religious differences, which together with ethnicity, have been used to tame us, causing so much blood bath when in fact we are one and same folks despite the different ethnic or religious orientations we embrace. So far the world of races and faith is merging toward one another with growing interracial marriages and belief in but one mighty loving God, and not like one of the malicious self-doubting gods of the dark ages, gods that were fond of hate and revenge and blood bath—with or without ubiquitous prophets every society may choose to profess. The study of how the typical future American will look like—The Changing Face of America, available at http://ngm.nationalgeographic.com/2013/10/changing-faces/funderburg-text, by Lise Funderburg and Photograph by Martin Schoeller—has helped to put that into perspective.

In the wording of the study, "We've become a country where race is no longer so black or white," That is civics. This kind of study will then take you into the study of geography for instance and therefore environment that surrounds you. But you will not end here. You will go a step further by studying how your mind works; how best you can interact with others and do so advantageously and so on. That's social science. That's the same way how you will find yourself engaged in all sciences. That is a starting point.

The mistake we make is to begin with biology or history, for instance, without the goal of doing so or a sense of direction. Indeed by doing so, students or learners don't see the connection or reason why they should spend their valuable time and resources on education. If we can answer to questions such as who are we, why are we who we are, when and how we became who we are etc., we can take education to far greater heights! It is not enough to tell our students that education is important. We need to tell them why, how. And to tell them how is only possible if we can begin with such notions as what is education and importance of self concept. Our society weeps for an education that will help to introduce our students to their immediate selves as well as their other selves—the buried self—the inner person. And what is surprising is that it is these other selves—not the body but the intellect and soul—that hold keys to the secrets of prosperity.

THE INDIVIDUALITY WITH THE COMMUNITY
Yes you have got to create harmony within yourself but if you have to have peace and harmony within and without and to therefore be self confident and able to embark on a life's journey successfully, you must first know who you are. Knowing who you are—which is self same fact that you and I are all sons and daughters of the same Almighty God, individuals who are blessed and capable and endowed to do and be and achieve whatever we want—of course within limits, individuals whose individuality is only meaningful in a community and hence a new perspective into the sense of

one's own person viz: in relation to Mwalimu Nyerere's view, "What gives humanity to our individuality is a sense of community...", the ideal scholar understands he just a part of a big whole and in African perspective he cannot escape the extended family, or even the neighborhood in which we live. He goes beyond the foregoing spirit. He regards himself as a provider and not a receiver of favors. This new outlook will give you pride to recognize you aren't an underling over others. It will set you free to know that you are equally blessed and crafted and that your destiny is in your hands, as well as those around you are now willing to support you not to stifle your efforts. We have heard of people who preach that we should forget the past—or others. That's not only wrong but it is immoral. Our past history as well as the others around us form, not only our present or even our future—either of which is more than important—our own persons, and character.

Certainly the mistake—the mistake to ignore, to look at your past and others indifferently or even hate your past and others around you—stems from a misconception embedded in the definition itself—the definition of what constitutes our humanness, our *person*. We aren't complete without all about us as we shall see shortly. With this positive pride in oneself, one's history and all about him, it is possible to harness your potential and be yourself and thus gain the self-esteem and self-confidence to the max— the self- esteem and self-confidence you have always lacked but desired. Truly if our graduates have mastered economics—like this author—or even rocket science, but they don't know who they are, the people around them, the environment or ecosystem and biodiversity around them and how they affect t one another, Aldo Leopold asked: "then what is education for?" This is the principal quality without which no one is whole, or the ideal scholar for that matter no matter the number of years he spends in classrooms, or degree papers he has under his belt.

Because of the importance of the concept of *Know Thyself* and *The Educated Slaves* as concepts, we are certain we will revisit them time and time again along the way.

8. SELF-ESTEEM: LOVING ONESELF AND THE QUEST FOR PERSONAL LIBERTIES

"When history is erased, people's moral values are also erased!"
—Ma Jian

Developed by this author from the Socratic concept of *Know Thyself*, the ideal scholar loves himself. This is what we can call positive pride in oneself, or self- esteem. It is an inner power that protrudes, or brings out its face in the form of self-confidence. This assertion calls for further explanation. Let me explain further. Because the ideal scholar or graduate has great self-awareness, it follows therefore that having known that though you and I were made of different clay or timber and therefore have different skin color or morphology but all of us were made in the image of God. And that he was not born an accident—or by it— and that he is here by plan—and for a purpose, which means he was not created as a mere sort by the Gods, the ideal scholar appreciates that he is here to accomplish something really significant—something that is life changing, something different from the others.

In other words, he knows he has a different job description commensurate with his talents, his big dream and a calling as destined for him since creation. With the foregoing knowledge, knowledge that though we are diverse and have diverse roles to pay, the ideal scholar accepts who he is. Emerson said: "You cannot run from yourself." But that's not all. Knowing too well who he is, he realizes that he cannot but be himself. With this knowledge at his disposal, he then loves himself and loves himself so dearly. Because he loves himself, the ideal scholar has high self-esteem.

This ideal is a quality that is especially highly desirable today for instance in Tanzania as we are moving toward EAC. Internationally, nations should find this ideal highly sought-after because of globalization, ICT and ever increasing economic and political blocs or regional integrations. We in Africa could do with self-esteem as a quality to fall back on when facing self-doubt. Self-doubt and low self-esteem are almost innate to any society with the history of slave trade and colonialism, which together killed self-pride among the people, robbing them of their self-confidence and self-love trapping them into faceless people with no background or history.

Besides, today arts and sports such as athletics, boxing and football no longer serve as only entertainment but as sources of lucrative employment. Without self- esteem we shouldn't expect our youth to triumph however much instructed they can be in the ways of professional or technical skills—not even when they are highly talented or gifted. Probably more than any other of our neighbors, we in Tanzania could do more with this quality following our history of Ujamaa policy or socialism. During Ujamaa, competitiveness and resilience among our people were stifled because of communal property mentality. Having ruined competitiveness and resilience, this policy then in turn ruined self pride or self- esteem among our people.

Doubtless *Know and Love Thyself* is what Abraham Maslow called self-actualization. According to Abraham Maslow, persons who attain self actualization have become psychologically healthy and mature. And this to him is what generally sums up the goal of education: to produce a healthy and a happy person who can accomplish, grow, and actualize his and her human self. Self actualization and a sense of personal fulfillment are what a learner and schools or education therefore should strive for. These are what teachers therefore should emphasize. Maslow characterized such persons as: having an efficient perception of reality; being at ease and comfortable with themselves and with others; not overwhelmed with guilt, shame or anxiety; relatively spontaneous and natural; and problem centered rather than ego centered. It also means self love, higher self consciousness, psychological health, ego identity and anything that suggests maximum self realization.

CHRONIC IDENTIFY PROBLEM, LOW SELF- ESTEEM AND ALTENATIVE SOLUTIONS

We all are born without identity. We take on other people's identities. We prefer to conform and bond. We conform or bond with our parents, guardians, adopted parents, etc even when we cannot confirm our real parents. I've never heard of a child who dragged his or her parents to a DNA test! It is unheard of! Few wish to part ways with their parents after they realize that their parents have actually failed them. That's how they begin seeking their own personal identities. We are all in it! Think about Balotelli's excellent footballing career. Yet aside from children born to surrogate mothers and a few cases such of child adoption as the Madonna's Malawian adopted children, Balotelli offers a very typical chronic identity problem. And mark my words: we all at some point in time tend to have some chronic identity problems of one kind or another.

Now Balotelli is a black Ghanaian by birth. But he was adopted and brought up by a white Italian couple. He plays for Italy. He in fact has scored key goals for Italy. Yet Italians have booed him severally, calling him names. Put yourself in his position. Would you really feel you are Italian in that situation? And this isn't about Balotelli alone. I've seen people who have lives they can't call theirs. They cannot claim to have future they call theirs therefore.[53] To gain self-confidence and self- esteem, we need to belong to the kind of people we belong to. Otherwise we will always be haunted by a question Jackie Chan directed not to anyone else but rather to himself, a question that bears the title of the same film: "WHO AM I?"

Besides Balotelli's case, one can consider the case of the black Americans as a clear case in point of such identity problem. To solve such a psychological crisis, one has to ask oneself, how am I who I am? How did I or my forefathers find themselves here? In the light of the knowledge that their forefathers arrived in America by slave boats as abducted slaves from Africa, a continent that apart from the color of one's skin remains alien, he will feel comfortable with himself and bring the matter to a closure. The Indians who find themselves in Africa fall in the same category. They arrived in Africa in masses as coolies or casual laborers and porters during construction of railways etc. the Tanzanians with Asian decent should also reconcile with the fact that they are Tanzanians for instance despite their color because of the intermarriage following the settlement of the Seyyid said and later slave trade agents who settled on the coast and later in the mainland especially along the slave trade routes or among the rhinos and elephants hunting zones.

The Bantu, the Nilotes and Hamitics of Tanzania for instance should reconcile with the fact that their forefathers arrived in this part of the

---

[53] *Adapted from Vintage Stuff by Tom Sharpe p.222*

beautiful continent at different times in search for better productive land and better life thereof. The Ngoni people provide us with one of the highly distinctive and most recently recorded history of how one can reconcile with one's origin or why he may seem a little different from the others. We all have learnt in history at school how the intertribal wars among the Zulus in South Africa forced the Ngoni factions under Zwangendaba and Mputa Maseko—among others—to move further north and finally they settled in different south western parts of modern day Tanzania.

FIELD MARSHAL TONGO LANGA AND SELF- ESTEEM

Referring to the concept of "Know Thyself," Emerson said, "You cannot run from yourself." Many of people with low self- esteem have a tendency to look over the shoulders and find a reason to blame themselves. Most graduates today don't know who they are. As a result they look at themselves indifferently and as a result they tend to fall in love with personalities or nationalities that appear to be better off. To know yourself you must appreciate your background as well as your present and finally where you want to go. Yes it is about the outward person but more so the inner person you are and one you desire to be —your accomplishments. I've myself forced myself to fit in other people's personalities. It is self-torture. It is vandalism of the self. I've tried it, I know how it is. You can't change who you are—from even such meaningless and useless attachments as tribe, color, size, height or even history.

But that's not Field Marshal Tongo Langa. That's not right. And that's one of the major answers to low self-esteem is knowledge. You must ask yourself why am not confident or happy with myself? Among reasons why you may have low self-esteem are your levels of education and affluence, your race, nationality or tribe. With knowledge that you are who you are because of reasons not much under your present jurisdiction, things like races or tribes which you cannot change, nonetheless which don't account for superiority or inferiority one has to have, besides knowledge that if it is a question of education or wealth you can work hard and make it, this is how knowledge sets you free. This is how you once can again make you fall in deep sincere love with who you are—your own person. In short, with this knowledge, you will strive to change the few things you don't like about yourself especially character, while accepting the things you can't change—things like your background.

A good dose of self-esteem makes you accept who you are no matter what others may think or say. Self-esteem makes you accept who you are no matter what is your education, level of affluence, race, nationality or tribe—the things which often haunt the weak variety. Indeed self pity accompanied by fear form one of the major symptoms of low self-esteem. That's why I've an enormous admiration for Field Marshal Tongo Langa. It is not a certain big army general I am talking about here. He is a musician—a Tanzanian musician.

Knowing his background, that he belonged to a tribe which many may not regard so highly for many of their own reasons, many people tend to cower and hide in their shells. But that's not Field Marshal Tongo Langa. Instead he loves his tribe enormously. He loves it so much that he doesn't feel ashamed or haunted to be a Makonde. Despite what many may consider to be a disadvantage to be a Makonde in Tanzania because the Makonde are mainly a Mozambican tribe, Field Marshal Tongo Langa knows that tribes were there before nation states were formed. He knows that tribes or even races are nothing when it comes to nationality. He knows that only borders determine one's nationality.

How do we know? We generally know that most people from the tribes that are from the borders with other countries like the Haya, especially the Baganda Kyaka, a tribe in Tanzania that bears the name of another nation, the Wanyambo especially the Wahima of Kyerwa and Karagwe, the Wahangaza and Washubi of Ngara, the Ha people and the Bembe of Kigoma, the Kurya and Luo of Mara region, etc., may fret because of association of their tribes or background with those across the borders, Tongo Langa chose to compose and sing songs praising his tribe. In his songs he doesn't have to bury the fact that the Makonde belong to both Tanzania and Mozambique. While accepting that his tribe has great association with the neighboring Mozambique, but in his own way he concurs with Professor Haroub Othman.[54] Field Marshal Tongo Langa is therefore bold about being proud as a Makonde, albeit being delightfully happy as a black African Tanzania first. His boldness and pride come from knowledge we have discussed above.

HAMZA KALALA AND BANTU GROUP BAND

That's what Hamza Kalala did. While not necessarily you or I crave to belong to the Bantu as a race, but that is you or me. That is not Hamza Kalala. An African himself, and therefore the question of being a white man being out of question, but as well not hailing from among the Nilotes,

---

[54] *Adapted from What Makes People Rich and Nations Powerful*

Hamitics, or Cushites, he chose to name his band Bantu Group whether or not his race was traditionally regarded as finer among African races. But that is only what the others say—or believe. Not him! Big idea, is it not? Accepting who you are!

THE MANYEMA

The Manyema were smart also. This is a community or tribe now in Tanzania which originally came from the Manyema province in Congo during both the intercontinental trade and especially the Arab slave trade. On arrival in Tanzania, they probably didn't like it at all. But as days went on and found they had no more close family connection in Congo, the Manyema decided to put that behind their history and fit in. they didn't cower at their background though. They retained their identity as Manyema naming the streets where they settled Manyema or Congo, such as Congo Street here in Dar es Salaam. These men were so self confident. They even formed football clubs and they named them Manyema Football Club.

THE HIMA AND THE HINDA COMMUNITIES IN TANZANIA

Very recently , a group of communities associated with the Hamitic ancestry, the Hinda and the Hima ethnic groups and their sympathizers in Tanzania met to discuss what they considered as a plight they had to solve once and for all. Why? Following the shortly-ended tribulation against the pastoral communities in Tanzania in 2014 to 2015, these communities were forced out of their lands and their cattle annexed from them on the ground that they illegally grazed in the land when they were not Tanzanian citizens. Yes, not all cattle herders were Tanzanian nationals, and yes with ethnic or background and language connections with neighboring communities like elsewhere—albeit intermarriages that have long since diluted the sense of such ethnicity identities in East Africa, it is hard to distance such communities from cattle herders who illegally cross over from the neighboring Rwanda, Uganda or Burundi—culprits who had had long since been ordered out of the country on political, environmental and security reasons.

These poor fellows, the Hinda and Hima, least educated only concerned with their cattle; they believe they have long since been putting up with the authorities on a sustained regularity. In such operations, they reported, some of the administrative individuals joined hands with the local manipulators to forcibly annex their ancestral lands and flock using intimidation and deception. The author also noted a sense of growing resentment among cattle herding communities elsewhere that the administration considers animal husbandry as second rated economic activity, and the herders as second class citizens. Though the author doesn't believe that the government deliberately discriminates cattle and cattle herding, I think it is not any wiser, or safer, to permit such sentiments to grow. As such, if the flock herders were least important in the sight of God, the angels wouldn't pass on the tidings of great joy concerning the coming of the messiah first to the herders and their flocks 2000 years ago apart from the fact that livestock contributes to about 50% of total agricultural contribution to GDP in some countries! Indeed, "Africa is at war with herself," aptly said PLO Lumumba in his illustrious speech, "Africa's Worst Tragedy: Economic Disorientation–A Case of South Sudan!"

The author also noted that because of their disadvantage academically following their forefathers' bad choices and poor decisions or inaction and indifference towards the changing world order, a group of learned men and women among these communities—and their sympathizers—convened to draw a roadmap toward the lasting solutions thereby weeding out such plight once and for all. If this was true, it was clear to me that the misfortune among Hima, the Masai and Hinda was indeed a result of economic and political battle if there was no an iota of any element of reprisal on this pre-independence wealthy and ruling clan on the part of the perpetrators.

In naming their organization or association, which is my message, many suggested moderate inclusive names. But one delegate didn't like it one bit. He emphasized that they were forming an organization to stand for the rights of the Hima in Tanzania. Without mincing his words, he suggested they name it a Hima Association. Period. I didn't like it too. But with a little thought, decided that I liked both the idea or confidence and the guy. His name is Emmanuel mwene Bhuta Bhwela. I looked in his eye and saw self-esteem that is indeed short in supply in our society today. Indeed I discovered a true ideal scholar in him. In fact I could conclude that *"God was with us,"* as his biblical name connotes. Didn't Emerson say that you cannot run from yourself? Now one question remained: did, or indeed do, they have ground on which their argument rests, in as far as their resentment is concerned? Let us rationalize together.

To do that analysis, knowing how Tanzania, or even the rest of EA is a diverse society amongst major three ethnic groups, i.e., the majority Bantu, the Nilotes, and the Hamitics—itself an unreasonable classification of the population having excluded the Hazhabe, the Twa or the Kwa and such human endangered species who are in fact the first humans to dwell in this land—communities that can fit well in each of these countries because of the presence of the same communities elsewhere, the author decided to do a little research. Following that little research, I have now the 2011 official diary of the Immigration Department in Tanzania before me as I write.[55] It reveals very intriguing information about each of the East African states economic status, religious structure and population figures. What intrigues me most is the segment called Ethnic groups. Here I want you to ponder about it as you read.

For Kenya it indicates the following figures: Kikuyu 22%, Luhya 14%, Luo 13%, Kalenjin 12%, Kamba 11%, Kissii 6%, Meru 6%, Other African 15%, non African Asians, European and Arabs 1%. For Uganda it indicates Baganda are 16.9%, Banyankole 9.5%, Basoga 8.4%, Bakiga 6.9, Langi 6.1%, Acholi 4.7%, Bagisu 4.6%, Lugbara, probably Amin's people, 4.2%, Banyoro 2.7%, Other 29.6% according to 2002 census. You will probably notice one setback in this form of segmentation. It tends to perpetuate tribalism and sectarian sentiments in the population. Take a break now! And a deep breath! Now Tanzania: and I want you to watch it closely.

Whereas for Zanzibar it simply indicates Arabs, Africans and mixed Arabs and Africans; the figures for Tanzania mainland simply indicate that the Mainland population consists of 99% of Africans whose 95% are Bantu consisting of more than 130 tribes; other 1% consisting of Asians, Europeans and Arabs. Such blanket categorization of tribes and communities such as the diary indicates for Tanzania has the advantage of detribalization by concentrating on major ethnic groups in the population. And it is probably more convenient because of an enormous number of small-small tribes there are in Tanzania. This is understandable. One setback remains unsolved nonetheless.

What I am saying is this: If the preparers of the data for Tanzania above used the Kenyan or Ugandan pattern, in Tanzania we would see Sukuma, Washubi, and Wanyambo, Wahaya etc., only a handful out of 130 and more tribes. But instead we are placed in what others call races, viz. Bantu, Hamitics and Nilotes aside from Asians and Europeans. Truly the Bantu are the majority, but you cannot ignore the 4% of your citizens in such an

---

[55] *The figures are also available at* https://www.cia.gov/library/publications/the-world-factbook/fields/2075.html.

official diary overlooking the injustice they may go through overtime without officially being recognized as indigenous citizens.

Take Kagera or Arusha for instance and all round Lake Victoria. In all three countries we see all three races of Bantu, Hamitics and Nilotes. I used to think it was bad to trail the path of races. But with an accidental exclusion of the Hamitics among them Hima or Huma and Hinda, and the Masai and Nilotes or the Luos on the part of the preparers of the diary, leads me to ask who are this 4% of the population? Notice that if you subdivided Kenya or Uganda in such racial groupings the figures would probably read that Bantu were 70% and Hima and Luo communities around 30%; a substantial figure huh?

Were it not for the quest to Know Thyself, they wouldn't have learned that indeed they were part of the 4 percent that wasn't registered in the diary. It is for this little insight that I truly believe they have ground on which to register an association in their tribal or racial community for that matter to safeguard the interests of their community.

This is the importance of to, *Know and Love Thyself.* To know yourself you must find who you are. By doing so, the Hima or Masai, should be proud of their past glory but not get intoxicated with ancient good-for-nothing-glory. Instead it should help them to affirm their love for themselves and their country much as they will seek to transform their social economic as well as political situations through investment in education and both national and international businesses. John Dalberg-Acton, 1st Baron Acton was right: "Liberty is not a means to a higher political end. It is itself the highest political end!" Ayn Rand cemented the point I want to stress thus: "Individual rights are not subject to a public vote; a majority has no right to vote away the rights of a minority; the political function of rights is precisely to protect minorities from oppression by majorities…"

THE LAMENTATION OF THE SELF-PITYING SON OF THE GODS
Did I ask if the Hima or even the Hinda had the ground to lay down their claims? Let us see. The trekking south of Ruhinda the First from central Uganda through southern Uganda and later settling and ruling most parts of the north western Tanzania especially in Kagera with filtration of a smaller faction deeper into Sukumaland, Ukerewe, Kome and Unyamwezi explains why the first European explorers met the Hinda rulers in the Lake Region. That's how Speke met King Rumanyika of Karagwe. That's why the American Henry Morton Stanley had to meet King Kibogora of

Bushubi while seeking permission to cross over Bushubi—in modern day Ngara district—to Ujiji seeking Dr. Livingstone. That's how Bauman met King Rwabigimba, Kibogora's son in Bushubi. That's how the Iron Age was introduced to this side of the continent from the north. Such is how in Kagera we have villages like Ntungamo and Mitoma named their ancestral villages back in Uganda just like the Kurya named a village the settled in Kenya Manyori, or *Little Kenya* here in Tanzania, or how the English immigrants named their settlements in America after their hometowns.

That's how we have had Ankole cattle in the Lake Region. That's how we have such regalia as drums and iron spears and clothing similar across the North West Tanzania and South Western Uganda. That's how we have a lake named Lake Katwe and villages called Mitoma, Isingiro etc. in Karagwe, in fact the capital of Ruhinda the First, besides a village christened Buhima in Ukerewe islands names that existed long before independence. Recently the author met a group of colleagues from back home in Kagera. In this get together party o some kind; the author introduced himself as a Hinda. A little after the meeting, one of the delegates followed the author and almost dragging him, pushing him into a hideout, told him almost rebuking him "I am also a Hinda," he said. Before an answer, he added, "But we never mention it. We keep it to ourselves!" I didn't get it. I asked why? "They don't like it!" he said mournfully as if it was a bad taboo. "Who?" I asked, already suspecting that he was about to cry in agony, and in open without shame, like an infant! "The majority!" he replied somberly. "And what else can we do?" he lamented! An attempt to provide answers to this question is the burden of this chapter.

The point I am trying to say is that you cannot run from yourself. No matter whether he disowned his past, no matter whether he did plastic surgery, he was still his own person. Yes our forefathers were rulers, I thought to myself watching him almost trembling, yes they might have been brutal to their subjects, yes they may have intermarried from amongst different communities, and therefore resemble and relate with the tribes or communities from neighboring Burundi, Rwanda, Eastern D.R. Congo, Uganda, Ethiopia or Somalia, but which single community doesn't relate with, or look like one or another ethnic group elsewhere? The Masai, the Luo, the Kurya, the Makonde, the Bembe, the Nyasa people, to mention but few communities (Please refer to What Makes People Rich and Nations Powerful). And yes, though the beauty is in the eye of the beholder, but who doesn't sing praises to the beauty and courage of the same community (https://gakondomedia.wordpress.com/2012/08/04/the-cwezi-people/)?

Yes they may have become more backward because of the bad choices and interfamily wars for the reins of power such is in Bushubi as it is in Karagwe for instance, reasons that escalated rivalry among the ruling families, setting them farther apart inciting hostility that even forced the author's forefathers to go into exile in Burigi in 1800's; yes they may have long since been stiff-necked by not taking their children to school concentrating with herds of cattle and unwisely finding pride in marrying dozens of wives instead, yes a few of the same clansmen intoxicated in glory of their past may have been a little less intelligent to keep looking to the past with pride, instead of looking to the future with pity; yes they may be minority, but what about their past glory—the glory of ruling such vast land from Bunyoro, in Uganda down to northwest Tanzania. In fact, tracing the origin of this family tree in the Suez, from which the dynasty's name stem viz. Cwezi, or in Bantu tongues, Chwezi, according to the web page https://gakondomedia.wordpress.com/2012/08/04/the-cwezi-people/.

Again, according to the Encyclopedia Britannica (http://www.britannica.com/place/eastern-Africa#ref418922?), radioactive carbon dating suggests Bigo in western Uganda was occupied from the mid-14th century with evidence that around the turn of the 15th century the Chwezi moved to, and ruled the south under rulers of the Hinda clan beginning with Ruhinda the First, beginning with Nkore in Uganda and later in Karagwe, Buhaya, Biharamulo and Busubi (i.e., Bushubi), and around to the southeast of Lake Victoria in modern day Tanzania.

And what about the contribution to the civilization and introduction of Iron Age and establishment of the first forms of government—pre, during and post colonial eras? And thus isn't only based on this author's baseless sentiments. No sir! Addressing the nation on the 35th Tarehe 6 liberation anniversary at Kololo, President Museveni put it into context when he said that the country had not been at peace for 500 years following slave trade, colonialism and intertribal wars down to general Amin era where kingdoms such as Toro fought Buganda, Buganda fought Nkore or Rwanda (wars that extended to Karagwe and Bushubi) until when NRM came to power, excepting of course for the period during which Uganda (and part of Tanzania) was ruled by the Chwezi dynasty.

That's in part why the author felt sorry for his distant cousin brother recognizing the magnitude of the identity problem and low self-esteem he had had. The author couldn't say a word but just thanked him, wondering if he, the author, should follow suit and disown his background with such glory, albeit ancient one, and probably a little useless, and though itself not personally earned, the glory of belonging to such a family of such names as Kibogora, Rwabigimba, or Rumanyika, and Ndagara, individuals and clan or family that was believed to have powers over the sky, the rain, the sun, and the lions and all predators, the glory that even makes the author a son of the gods, himself being the descendant of Ruhinda I, Wamara and Ndahura,[56] even the gods worshipped among the believers of the Chwezi religion until as I write! I decided that it just didn't add up! If others disowned their background whether Hinda, Hima, Twa, Bantu, Iru, Nilote, though my distant cousin brother beside me had endured the collapse of the Hinda dynasty and kingdom with great pity, and though he felt uncomfortable to be identified as such, I was going to accept my past and myself—albeit with humility, modesty and humbleness, because I didn't contribute to this past glory! Yes I was not going to look to the past with pride, but I was as well going to look to the future with pity! Does the glory the author talks about mean nothing to the reader? Well, it meant something to Mr. Malimbu, himself the author's tribesman, a Mshubi, and his former teacher at Kahororo Secondary School. I recall when once the author introduced himself to his teacher and tribesman, knowing he came from Ngara, he exclaimed saying: "Yewee, kumbe ul'umuganwa?" literally meaning, "Hey, I didn't know you belong to this great clan!"

Why then did I write this narrative? Did I write about it to impress myself, this brother, or anyone else? No sir! I didn't write it to impress anyone. Instead, this book has been written to inspire all worthy men and women who are still encased in the deep self-pity, and low self-esteem—which is indeed the greatest malady that this nation is suffering from. And as a nation we suffer from it because of the history of slavery, colonialism and divide and rule strategy that the modern colonialists amongst our own brethren use to set us against one another, and in the process, allow them to rule us with ease—and without end! So, really, this is not about the author, or his distant cousin brother. It is about you, yes you, the reader—the common citizen! This is bout you because it makes you rethink about your own history. Do you know it? Do you care, anyway? "When history is erased," said Ma Jian, "people's moral values are also erased!"

---

[56]*https://gakondomedia.wordpress.com/2012/08/04/the-cwezi-people/, http://www.britannica.com/place/eastern-Africa#ref418922*

ALTERNATIVE SOLUTIONS

We have seen how one can be self pitying no matter where he shouldn't. To mitigate the situation, we can learn from the most striking recent cases of identify problem are the cases of Makonde and Zigua tribes from Mozambique and Tanga in Tanzania, respectively. A group of Tanzania Bantu tribes among them Zigua settled in Somalia where they found themselves for various reasons, among them business and labor. This population has grown and mixed within the Somali population but being Bantu they remain a little different and far detached from the traditionally Cushite or Hamitic Somalis. Their fate has not been addressed in full. And I know what I say having personally run a training among refugee students of higher institutions sponsored by the UN and DAFI, among who were Somalis facing the same fate I narrate.

Aside from the recent example of the generous German and Swedish governments that have granted Syrian refugees the status of citizenship, the exemplary case in point here in EA is a decision by the Kenyan Uhuru Kenyatta's government to officially grant Kenyan citizenship to a group of the Makonde and registering the tribe as one of the tribes of Kenya after the Makonde had settled there for many years back such that they had established in their mind that Kenya was their mother country. Tanzania has severally granted citizenship to Burundian and Rwandan refugees. Another president with Kenyan blood on the western hemisphere in America has also only recently enacted laws to grant American citizenship to the 5 millions of the undocumented Latino immigrants in America. Failure to do so, puts the decision makers in the same class as Botha and his apartheid regime or the extreme South Africans who cannot accept the white settlers after they have settled in SA for centuries now no matter the color of their skin—which so far they didn't choose—whether that color is venerated or demeaned today.

COUNT YOUR BLESSINGS

Aside from identity problem, to fortify one's self-esteem, one has to count his blessings. However that brings with it another dilemma. How do you count something that doesn't exist? To count your blessings you need to work and get results or achievements that we can fall back on. When we have some sort of accomplishment, we gain self- esteem, self-confidence and self love.

How does it happen? I mean how does accomplishment help to bring about self-esteem and self love? It is purely scientific—purely biological. We know from biology that for the body to function well, it excretes hormones that support growth of , or stimulates the body and mind. Again because we don't engage in futility and self torture such as sleeplessness, we actually use optimally the little energy and resources we have at our disposal. As a result we sleep well, and wake up healthy and strong by the dawn. To accomplish something significant, is not always an easy thing. That's why few actually do so. In order to do this, start where you are and begin with painless tasks. Then proceed to bigger goals.

Indeed, courage acquired from our own accomplishments and plans injects into us more energy than that consumed during work itself. And as a result of the same, we come out smiling happy and rejuvenated. Many people did know that when we make such accomplishments, we get out smiling but only few did know how. The foregoing is the explanation. Besides, such accomplishment gives us a great sense of command over our own selves. It multiplies our purpose reshaping it and spreading and deepening its reaches. Certainly you have heard of Oliver Mutukuzhi he is one of the greatest African talented musician of the generation. He is from a shattered country—a country shattered by economic embargo. He hasn't emulated American artists. He has remained himself in his black skin. He wears inconspicuous cloths and at times a hut that does more than add harm to his looks than add decorations. What does he say about it?

Recently attending the music festival in Zanzibar in 2011 he declared something, in an interview and in my own hearing, something I'll try to present as best as I can. He was asked something like why he doesn't change and try to look like other artists who seem to concentrate with their looks. He said: "I'm who I'm and you be who you are. I'm not competing with anyone else. I'm Oliver Mutukuzhi. That's who I am. There's no other!"

In other words, to put things more plainly, he seems to have said: "I'm Oliver Mutukuzhi. I'm Zimbabwean. I'm a Musician. I'm black and tall. I wear a hut. I know better English but I choose to sing in Shona and Ndebele. This is who I'm!" You cannot run from yourself. Endeavoring to do so, to run from yourself, to be another person is futile. It destroys you than it does to build you and the relationship with the people you deeply intended to bond with. It will destroy your potential to think and relate. It kills your personality and thus limits your success.

Therefore accept who you are. No one is better or inferior. We are just one big family whether of different color, race, nations or tribes. The people we see as superior today were so positioned because at some point in time they worked hard. Really you have got to *Know Thyself,* a concept whose central part is to recognize that you were not born to fail. You were rather born to win. Only know thyself and identify the kind of victory you were born to champion. If you do so and follow through, then you are almost already a winner you were born to be. The following chapters were written with this end in mind. It was written that in the end you may reclaim what is yours which is endless victory and limitless abundance. In the final analysis, failure to know that you were born a winner will kill all ambitions left in you. With the death of ambition in you, the desire to be top will be butchered. With the passing away of the desire to be top, the self-confidence in you is stifled. The circle goes on and on until when you are deprived, or rather when you deprive yourself of your self- esteem. In the end, after self-esteem has been butchered, the whole thing goes on to kill, well, to kill you—finally! Sadly, a staggering 97 percent of all of the people you meet fall into this category.

The strongest African slaves in Arabia were castrated to tame their invincibility. And it worked. If you doubt if it worked, visit any costal city in Africa where slavery was prevalent. The men there are still very tame when it comes to any association or discussion about Arabia long after formal slavery was abolished. Long after its abolition, you will still find a great mental slavery still as strong as it was in the 19th century when slave trade and brainwashing thrived. In these cities you will still find the heathen and the civilized mentality of the slavery era where black Africans were heathen and brown Arabs the civilized—civilized slave traders! The lion or a leopard is a very fierce animal. But castrate it and you will, in no time, tame it that it will, with great docility, follow you in your evening strolls wagging its tall—like a dog! And this isn't my personal imagination.

"Destroy the sex glands," aptly concluded Napoleon Hill in his wonderful book Think and Grow Rich, "Destroy the sex glands, whether in a man or a beast, and you have removed the major source of action. Sex alteration," he continued, "takes out of the male , whether man or beast, all the fight that was in him. Sex alteration of female has the same effect,"[57] he concluded as if warning the Kurya tribesmen of Tarime, Tanzania. Try it. Here is another thing. There is also mental castration.

---

[57] *Napoleon Hill 205*

In the mainland where the Europeans ruled, still the black Africans regard the White Fathers as Gods! I have given you an account of my elderly auntie who trembles when her eyes meet their opposite numbers from a white man or woman—no matter whether he or she is an Einstein or an idiot. Yet she, rather innocently, admits that it makes her happy to always be in the company of a white man or woman, in spite of the fright her body, soul and mind feel in such an environment. Why? I man why she is frightened but she still feels happy in this weird atmosphere? Because she believes, they are a superior breed. Period. You agree this is nothing but deep-rooted colonial mentality or indoctrination, don't you?

SYMPTOMS OF LOW SELF-ESTEEM AND THE ROLE OF THE GOVERNMENT

By now you should have realized that self confident person will surely love his country. He will work hard. He will not endeavor to partake in graft or to sabotage his people and the nation as a whole. Even though it is within us to be self confident and proud of who we are, the government has to set the house clean at the top as should we the parents at household level. If there is cleanliness at the top, and conditions are good and convenient to working and making money and grow here at home, people will be patriotic. They will work hard to attain what they desire. They will not go file to go abroad for better lives.

The escalating number and instances of people seeking and destroying their passports immediately after they set foot abroad in order to seek refuge identifying with troubled countries like Somalia or Burundi or even Darfur is probably the major sign of low self-esteem. It is to surrender to the thought that one cannot do anything to change his life. If poor counties did census of the passports issued to its citizens, the nation would go mad! Passports are rubber stamps they simply need to cross borders after which they are not in fact useless but fatal and therefore destroyed first thing.

No wonder in such countries people read hard about foreign languages which is another sign of low self-esteem if you look so closely. In Africa today people tend to learn to speak languages and intonations not of the traditional American English of French? Noooh! Nah. they learn to speak Congolese or Kirundi. Once they are abroad they begin learning to speak like they are real black Americans or Jamaicans. Others will try to speak like true English people.

Do you want to know another symptom of people with low self-esteem? If you do, very good. I will tell you. Such people tend to hate themselves. They hate their languages and indeed their own persons. Such is an example of many of our youth today. They speak slang, dress like 2 Pac Omar, hang the US flags than that of their own nations, they prefer foreign music or anything imported from outside etc. his parents hailing from Ngara in Tanzania a place bordering Burundi and Rwanda, the author knows how most people there feel proud to drink Amstel and not safari lager. Having lived and worked in Kigoma a region in Tanzania that was once a Congolese territory before the Belgians and British swapped it back to Tanzania, the author knows how people in Kigoma prefer Congolese music and speak Congolese accent believing it gives them a kick of some kind.

Yet I've always fascinated by why I never see Yoweri Museveni trying to speak American slang even when he hosts Clinton or Bush or Obama, nor have I seen him dress like 2 Pack Shakur. He didn't even try to patch up things even in his single hip hop You Want another Rap?! There is one little secret I will tell you about Museveni. Though he is proud of Ankole blood, he comes from a very lowly Siita clan. Notice also that curiously even when Siita are not highly regarded among the Huma clans both in Uganda and Tanzania, he still prides in this lowly clan—lowly in other people's eyes—not Museveni. What the Hinda or other clans say is their opinion. He doesn't have to take it and feel the same. I've rarely seen Museveni dressing like Tupac or Jay Z. He will often wear his suit and out a palmer hat on his upper dome instead of a cap like 50 Cent. A person who does so is doomed. For I sure tell you even these people you try to model around, most aren't themselves aware of—and therefore happy with—who they are!

Other major symptoms of low self-esteem include self consciousness, lack of poise and extreme fear—fear of nothing really genuine. There is also inferiority complex, reckless spending and wastefulness trying to impress others while agonizing inside. Other major symptoms of low self-esteem include self consciousness, lack of poise and fear of nothing real. There is also inferiority complex, reckless spending and wastefulness trying to impress others while agonizing inside. Other symptoms include fear of self expression due to the fear of making mistakes or lack of ambition. In extreme cases, indifference to self expression is due to accepting one's fate as final and therefore surrendering or accepting defeat without striving—without guilt why one has failed—the guilt that would otherwise push for a second attempt. Truly, the trouble is inevitable but misery is optional.

HOW DO YOU IDENTIFY A PERSON WITH HIGH SELF-ESTEEM?

Probably this is the easiest task ever of all I have accomplished. Just trace the sense of self love in that person. A person who genuinely loves him own person is at peace with his own person. He is consistent in his behavior and plans. A less self confident person will not be at peace with himself. He will not be consistent is his attitude and behavior. His plans will too be haphazard for he is easily influenced by the outside world. Because of his deep self hatred, he will find delight in an environment which causes fear, terror and horror or fright to people around him.

If he is a manager he will terrorize his assistants and peers. Just watch around this person. If you find his people is running away from him or perspiring in his company dreading his presence than delight that's first sign? When his subordinates make some slight mistakes such as spilling a few drops of coffee on the table or even unintentional typographical errors, he will erupt in rage unspeakably horrendously as if life was at stake because of such a trivial mistake. I'm not writing this to support sloppiness—mind you! His eruption is far more horrific than that of Vesuvius or even Oldonyo Lengai volcano. Fury will be his constant company, and resentment to his people. There will develop antagonism in the team.

Without self awareness this person is insecure. Like elderly people, when you don't know who you are, you lose hope and tend to be quite conservative and a bit suspicious of any supposed advancements or opinions of the others, especially those junior to you. Such a person, in his department there will be very little talk and things will be too formal. There will be strict rules under his charge and failure to observe to the letter summons tough penalties. He is not ready to learn from others fearing to display his ignorance. That's why he will not learn anymore. That's why he will know only that what he already knows which is, I am afraid, very little! He is not ready to train or pass on any of his work skills or knowledge to others at work. He cannot do so. He is unsafe and selfish.

I've worked with MT. It is sufficient to call him MT. I know how it is to be in the presence of an insecure leader who lacks self-confidence. He is envious. He doesn't believe in equitability. Fairness isn't in his books. He wants to be a God. He is uncompromising at this. Self confident persons, those with high self-esteem accept others have strength they may be lacking. Brutus acknowledged the greatness of Julius Caesar's. Comparing himself with Mwalimu Nyerere his predecessor, President Mwinyi in Tanzania said he was like an ant-hill before the mighty Kilimanjaro. Not only Clinton but also Barack Obama has habitually referred to Lincoln or

Jefferson when explaining something that required thought. Almost all writers including the immediate one cannot conclude their works without referring to the most apparent and "Immortal" Ralf Waldo Emerson—as politicians in this part of the world prefer to refer to Nyerere, Nkrumah or Mandela! John the Baptist announced without an iota of pity, or shame, that he wasn't even worth to loosen the messiah's shoelaces.

Conservative old minds fear that the world is running out of resources. They tend to accumulate wealth by any foul means possible fearing the future will be terrible. They forget the true resources are in-built and within humans mind and brain. Indeed we are richer internally than we are externally.

Instead, people with self awareness are more confident that they believe in more personal freedom and development. They believe in a fairer sharing of wealth and power within society. They are liberal. Liberal people respect and tolerate different opinion beliefs or behavior. The ideal person is humble. Humility to him isn't miserable but instead knowing we didn't accomplish all by ourselves but by people around us and environment in which we were. "There, by the Grace of God Go I," he will sing. Indeed the wisdom wrapped in the Proverbs—Pride goes before destruction and a haughty spirit before fall—is spot on. A wise person recognizes that when pride comes, then disgrace follows in its footsteps; but humility brings forth wisdom. If you find a person so much full of himself, a person who prefers to look down his fellows eager to expose them as weak, that is the first sign of insecurity stemming from his own distrust in his own abilities and self worth. In Think Big, Ben Carson wrote thus: "Generally when …the more confident of their abilities …persons are, the less they feel compelled to tell others of their achievements."

You recognize however that I'm not trying to say every other way we are made is advantageous to us—all the time! No! We may have handicaps we may need to change be that physically or mentally. It is customary that Huma people have white teeth unlike the northern Tanzanian people whether that is from the composition in the waters or milk they drink I have no way of knowing. But it isn't a bad thing for a person with brown truncated and disordered teeth to whiten them a little and reshape them if he feels that that will make him happy and his looks better. Take Michael Jackson for instance. I've learned from him to seek what I want if it real resonates from within me. He didn't like his nose alright. So he modeled it in the way he wanted it. He had money and a plastic surgery saved the purpose. He wished he were a little bit light colored, he went ahead and reshaped his skin! That's why we have sciences! Of course I wasn't there when he did undergo plastic surgery, but I know his feelings from lyrics of his songs such as Heal the World or even in It Don't Matter Whether You Are Black or White.

Yet if you have ever faced agony such that you contemplated suicide, you are on the extreme opposite of an unfortunate weak person who knows and loves oneself. Always be yourself. Love who and what you are. It makes you unique—which is what you are. Do not get carried off by a few areas or instances you truly believe you could do without or with better gifts. I know it is tempting to slip back into self-condemnation or self-hate. A good example is among persons who stammer. It shouldn't embarrass you even when sincerely you and I agree that you could become a good speaker without it. But notice that even emperors had some of their own weaknesses. The kings and queens have some of their own persons they would have wanted to change. A prudent thing to do is to make a close analysis of your own person. What do you see? What do you like or hate about you? Why? What's your company? Which are the places where you find yourself getting into your true element? Who are the people or places where you find yourself going back into your own old spoilt self? Could it be a drink? A club? To be honest my clubbing friends have a tendency to influence me into getting more into it—much as are my smoking friends. Avoid such a place or company.

Of all things, be you yourself and love yourself. Don't ever try to be another person. You will, as we shall learn more on the nature of how Lady Opportunity conducts herself, how you can ruin your potential and worse more, endanger your personal freedoms. To benefit from your true potential or freedom, be yourself. Accept yourself. You should know you are very special. You were born for a purpose. You are unique and did come to accomplish greater things. You are in God's future plans. God didn't engage in the endeavor of creating you as a mere sport. No! You are God's own minister and missionary. Don't lose hope or surrender to the situation—however discouraging that situation is. It is part of your path toward the greatness that was long prepared for you.

Find your strong and weak qualities. And don't stop there. Analyze and increase your strengths and reap from them while you must as well take and maximize opportunities while weakening weakness and doing away with your threats by turning them your opportunities. It was Lincoln who said, "I destroy my enemies by making them my friends," wasn't he? His enemies didn't only cover breathing humans. They covered demons too.

These demons are habits and emotions that work against you and me. To be yourself if you are an artist, remember the world gets used and bored to present qualities. Dig deep and wholly get your new self that is not influenced by the other persons. When you produce something new, something you are , then you are heading for a fortune and a big future. The economic law of diminishing marginal utility applies in this analysis.

Besides, you have got to be yourself, for indeed Dale Carnegie was right in How to Stop Worrying and Start Living: Nobody wants a fake coin. No one likes to buy counterfeit products. "Nobody," said Angelo Patri, "Nobody is so miserable as he who longs to be somebody and something other than the person he is in body and mind." Why? Let's see. You lose freedom. You have tension fearing to slip. You are always under comparison measuring up if you are he or still lacking. You are a laughing stock. Worst of all you will never achieve as he did for you are a second rate he. Besides you will never ever reap from your own strength which is what you can only reap because you are not trying to reap from your deep reservoirs? It further exhausts your energy for you use a helluva of energy trying to be a bit of someone else.

To prove it, try to mimic somebody. Then be yourself and speak as you always do. What's the difference? Embarrassment. Too much waste of energy, very poor results. Don't be like that. Be yourself. Afterall you are something special. Not because you better than others but because you are what others cannot compete with and triumph over. You were given special values and traits to bring to life and speak for. No one can ever try filling that role but you. Dale Carnegie in how to stop worrying and star living gives the best admonition. You are something new in this world. Be glad of it. Make the most of what nature gave you.

In the last analysis, all art (you included) are autobiographical. Dale Carnegie was right. Try hard as you can but you can only write, sing or paint only what you are. You can only be and present a person you truly are. Indeed "Envy is ignorance," Emerson was right, "and imitation, it is suicide...the power which resides in him is new in nature and none but he knows what that which he cannot do nor does he know until he has tried!" To supplement Emerson, Napoleon Hill concluded that envy is foolish because we become what we decide upon our own being. He was right. What people are, is what they decided or chose to be—by their own action or inactions—long time ago. We become who we are because of the difference we crave to make or how we choose to remain indifferent in whatever we do. In terms of one's true calling, we are all at the disposal of same-same opportunities in greater and broader extent just as are all successful people. But the difference lies in the decisions or choices we make in terms of our actions. As a writer you can write only what you are. You can only write your experiences. You can only tap from your heredity or background environment etc. these are the things which shape you. Stay home. That's where you can make the most and the best of every accomplishment you ever dream of.

HOW TO CREATE HARMONY WITHIN YOU: FINAL COUNSELS INTO THE REORIENTATION OF THE MIND TOWARD SELF-ESTEEM

You cannot have harmony with yourself, within, without accepting yourself. And without accepting yourself, you cannot be at peace with yourself. And if you are not at peace with yourself, you cannot have self-esteem. That's the first and doubtless the prime condition. But since self-esteem is not outward but an inner emotion, it all begins in the mind. Therefore to remain at peace with yourself, think and act like a man. Entertain only good positive and elevating thoughts both in public and private. Do your manly duties both in public and private. The statement, *Think and Act Like a Man*, means nothing but to really think and always respond to life with vigor, energy and dynamism. We talk of diversity and interdependence or even reciprocity but a man has to be a man if he should remain one. Strive to retain your *manhood* or dignity in order to regain or retain your humanity. Have you ever observed the castrated animals? They have lost that sense of pride that was natural to them. Self-confidence or self-esteem is impossible without this sense of pride that natural to man, to humans.

Also notice that there is no one like you. Each one of us is in his own ways superior to one another. That's God's plan that we complement one another. Shakespeare said, "self love, my liege is not so vile a sin, as self-neglecting." Indeed it is torture. Self-hate is the worst form of disgrace! Thus be yourself. Choose to accept who you are. Yet it is not something from without. That's why it is called self- esteem. In the ultimate, we need each other. Love yourself, for indeed it is not merely self—ridicule to hate yourself. It is ingratitude and defamation to God the Maker. So take time to know thyself.

Make a great deal of personal inventory and learn to recognize who you are. Do it with great enthusiasm. Know your strengths. Study your weaknesses. Capitalize on whom or what you are. And this can be done by pursuing self enhancement or self development using your own person as an advantage. At society level, recognize who you are—as a society. Learn, understand and love your history. You cannot change it. You ought instead to love it because by doing so you can improve your person, your life and how you relate with the others and nature. Getting hold of your history helps one to meet ones aspirations.

You also have got to take note of the fact that what we may account as weaknesses in one society, may actually be strength in another. What you have got to do is to find ways to use your persona in bettering your situation or station in life; you must use it to increase your mastery over the nature, or rather to work advantageously in harmony with nature. In your personal self censorship, don't forget to learn from others: their strength, weaknesses, etc. Japan Tobacco's business culture is summed up thus: "By capturing the best of both Japanese and Western business culture we have the potential to flourish as a business the world over. We blend the best of our tradition with innovation and new thinking. We are anchored by our heritage rather than hampered by it."

There is also a problem many may wrongly entertain. I don't. Recall that a mention has been made about the term "nigger" and how it was used to put down the black people in America. To heal prejudice that is eating into our society, we must learn what the Black Americans did to avert such subjugation. This is an important point because the same thing—albeit in different scope and magnitude—is happening in every society. For instance when cattle were precious medium of exchange, the cattle herders looked down on the crop farmers. A typical case happened in Uganda especially in Ankole as well as in north-western Tanzania, in Kagera. Cattle herders called non cattle herders names. They called fishermen Abalobi and crop farmers Iru. The author is not certain if it tasted well with the traditional crop farming communities or their brethren fishermen. But he knows the Iru then called the cattle herders *Abalalo*.

With the ancestors who were traditionally cattle herders, the term didn't go well with the author. But growing up, he realized it was stupid to hate a mere nomenclature. It was rather the right term for my ancestors were indeed *Abalalo,* or the kraal people, a term for cattle herders coined from the kraal, an English word for a *Kilalo* or cow pen, a traditional fencing that was common only among the herders of Kagera as well as the Masai. The crop famers didn't need one. I have learnt that the crop farmers too, shouldn't feel embarrassed with the term Iru, which represented nothing but crop farming in the region. In the end—and watch me—in the end both names mean so little today. Firstly, inter-tribal marriages have watered-down the morphological differences. Number two, possibility of diversifying vocations among communities and individual families and persons has stripped and left both the prejudice and names bare. Some traditional crop farmers or fishermen have moved to cattle herding (such as Bitainesha—and his son Kabalyenda—a famous crop farmer in Siina, Katera, Kyerwa, Karagwe, Tanzania who switched to cattle herding), as the Hima and the Masai traditional herders who now switch to crop farming or move to the city, leaving cattle and kraals behind. Eleanor Roosevelt was right: "No one can make us feel inferior without our permission."

Here is another point concerning loving yourself. Indeed what you may aspire to be, what you may consider as strength may be regarded as weakness or a laughing matter in another society. A light-skinned black woman is cherished in Sukumaland but despised among Huma or traditional Hamitics. Excepting milk of course, super-black people were highly cherished among the Hamitics such as the Hima of Uganda and Tanzania, the Tutsi of Rwanda, Burundi and Congo, the Nilotes of Uganda, Tanzania and Kenya, the Masai of Tanzania and Kenya and yes among the Ethiopians and Somalis. The author knows some of the Hima and the Hinda very closely being the heritage of his forefathers.

They loved everything black. They reared a black bull to generate black cattle. They smoke milk to make it sweeter. They prefer to roast the meat to make it more romantic. They revere a woman with black gum in the mouth—a complete reverse of the European culture or reality. For them typical ideal man was black, like king Rumanyika and Ndagara of Karagwe, Kibogora and R of Bushubi, or Edward Sokoine—if I have to present the most recent and handy image I am talking about. And I am writing about the value of the black color to the real African perspective with something close to a religious emotion. The author's father was always singing the beauty of the darkest skin of Augustine Kambarangwe, his Super-black father.

While the western culture reveres skinny women especially in their cat walks, it is traditionally the big woman with curves and big limbs, like a hippopotamus that is highly attractive to African men. Gordons, the Nigerian comedian was right. There is no need to emulate everything western thinking because it is western then it is the best culture. As such we shouldn't be blinded by the cat-walk and dieting. He emphasized that the cat was not the only animal. There were also elephants and hippopotamus and they are more graceful than the cat. A few years ago in

Tanzania they glorified the nation's true nature when they staged Miss Bantu competition, representing the majority of the population's typical woman with rounded figure and all the curves natural the black woman. That was first-class. That was an attempt to be themselves.

Identify, therefore, your strong points and take advantage of them. Certainly that is why Dr. Johnson said that "The habit of looking on the best side of everything is worth more than a thousand pounds."[58] Probably you and I should take advice from Jack Johnson the first black world heavyweight boxing champion. His bitter fight was not one in the ring for he was champion. His worst and toughest fight was one he fought himself! He didn't love his color. He actually despised it. Then he knew better that he was shooting himself in the foot and thus said: "I'm Jack Johnson, heavyweight champion of the world. I'm black. They never let me forget it. I'm black all right! I'll never let them (let me) forget it!"

I'm no angel. Like you the reader, I the author, am human too! Many times he was ashamed of himself when he watched the Japanese Sumo wrestlers, or even the American mighty basketball or base ball players the author is not physically anywhere near a Japanese sumo wrestler. He cannot ever dream to compete with the weakest Japanese sumo man! He would love to be compact and tough like Mike Iron Tyson. But when as I grew up, and now as I think about it, I tell myself: "Festo Michael Kambarangwe, look here! You were born a Hinda! You aren't Japanese. You are made to be who you are! You are not too tall, nor are you too black. Your hair is not too tall or too short. It is not too straight or too crooked only a little shaggy. Your nose is not too extremely blunt, or as pointed as Zlatan Ibrahimovic's. It is somewhere in between. This is who you are!

You aren't privileged to resemble President Mkapa much—well forget that. Yes you could also do with a muscle. You aren't Mike Iron Tyson much as you aren't Bill Clinton! You are who you are. That's who you are! It's not a curse of course. It's a fact. Love it." Trevor Noah, a South African comedian wondered why mixed people like himself were called half-breed—or half caste. He suggested they rather were recognized as full-breed because they have half-half each from each of the major breeds thus becoming complete whereas the rest are half full without the combination from another breed. Isn't it sensible? With all keenness to the

---

[58] *How to Stop Worrying and Start Living by Dale Carnegie p. 150*

ideals we teach in this book, the author cannot however engage himself in the prejudice involving color, race, religion, tribe, or even the size or morphology because he is mature enough to know he has no control whatsoever over the color, race, religion, tribe, or even the size or morphology over the next generation even of his own posterity. The author is sharp-eyed enough to even view it can only be advantageous to many in the long run. As for the uninitiated and skeptical reader, it is as such that probably God sent down the Obamas, who knows?

The right education or correct reorientation of the thought should lead a person to identify with and love for one's background. The right education is the one that tells you where you come from, where you went right, and where you went wrong—and why. Dr. Lynn Kwaku suggested the following: the parents should not leave the whole task of reorientation of their children to the schools and the teachers. In an essay he wrote about the educated slave, he wrote that, "Parents…can prevent mental slavery of next generation (after they are themselves emancipated)…by making sure their children are exposed (to this facts), addressing their history and culture, including relevant videos and DVDs (and books like this one), monitoring television usage, taking them to events that expose them to their own culture, being actively involved in children education, insisting the curriculum including history, and he added something of major importance which is my central message in this book: but at same time not relying on public or private education to provide quality information…that should be done in the home after school or weekend educational programs. The dinner table is a perfect venue for these discussions." We have to know where we come from but as said Val de Wall, "Look no back in anger nor forward in fear but around yourself in awareness."

To create harmony within, harmony within a you, you need first to know who you are. When you know thyself, you will really love yourself. You will because that's who you are, that's what you were meant to be. And that's the real stuff. Ensure also that you guard the thoughts that pervade your mind. Related to the foregoing suggestion, choose friends that will have positive impact and influence upon you and your goals. These decisions will help you to avoid negative emotions such as fear, worry, doubts and unbelief. Wattles wrote thus :"Guard your thought …as your beliefs will be shaped…by the things you observe and think about…it is important that you should carefully govern what you give your attention." When you observe this canon to the letter, you become balanced and harmonious with yourself. You become genuine to yourself and others, body and soul. You will then begin to be authentic in word and deed.

When a certain community, tribe or race is debased, it is in the main not because of its hereditary or genetics, color of its skin, height or financial status. All these are just temporary situations and often a function of inaction, your past poor choices and wrong decisions by itself or its forbearers or ancestors. It therefore follows that instead of striving to change their situations, this community, tribe or race eyes consumed with hate indulge in revenge—but against the wrong victim. It was our forefathers who made mistakes somehow that we all in Africa were first enslaved, then colonized and now victimized by the world order. Envying, let alone killing all Arab slave traders and colonialists—or aptly their offspring—or even the ruling class or the wealthy people in your community is rather unreasonable as a strategy to wealth. It was by some kind of head start from their choices and decisions at the time when the powerful met the weak that made one wealthy and another poor. It was one's wealth and good choices thereafter that that gave one community access to education, resources and power. We know the fall of the Hinda, Hima and Masai cattle herding communities alongside the fortunes amongst, for instance, the Iru in the Southern Uganda and North West of Tanzania, as was among the Bantu crop farming communities elsewhere is a result of resistance toward change on one hand, and resilience on the other. The fall of the Hinda and the Hima and the Masai is due to their wrong choices and decisions on forfeiting education and continued culture of overgrazing of their highly cherished cattle. Should the Hinda, Hima or Masai hate their counterparts or the progress they are now enjoying because of their prudent investment in education for their children and in business, things that put them in political powers today? That would be foolish. We know since Museveni ceased power in Uganda, he helped in redirecting the Hima away from resistance to change and we know that the Hima of Uganda now have gained class and dignity once again unlike in Tanzania—with or without ceasing power. Envy is indeed foolish and in a different perspective from Emerson's, when, and only when used wisely, imitation is wise.

LESSONS FROM AFRICAN AMERICANS

Talk about accepting your circumstances, and accepting who you are, and therefore the possibility of raising your head and walk with importance, is one of the greatest lessons you will ever learn no matter your circumstances. Take black Americans! They were demeaned and called names. Among these names was NIGGER! Did they accept nigger as happily as their own class? No! They fought it. They fought back and called non black people names such as zombies and skin deficient but it wouldn't help. Instead they fought in rings and athletics and won a name and money and fame. They even began upholding the term NIGGER! Instead of considering it as an abusive language, they used it to signify a greater buddy, and a very successful person, one they respected so highly!

Therefore true niggers had to be world champions, like Muhammad Ali, Michael Jordan, Usain Bolt, Barack Obama, Colin Powell, Condoleezza Rice, Nelson Mandela, John Pombe, Ben Carson, Julius Nyerere, Ellen Johnson <u>Sirleaf</u>, Bob Marley, General Muhammadu Buhari, George Weah, Martin Luther King Jr., Tiger Woods, the William Sisters, Ronaldo de Lima, Zinedine Zidane, Beyonce, etc. In the same light, any great personality, a person with conscience and superior brains is also a nigger. That's makes the following people NIGGERS: Bill Clinton, Albert Einstein, Hillary Clinton, Marco Polo, Yuri Gagarin, Galileo, Harun Rashid the ancient ruler of Baghdad, Socrates, Lionel Messy, Sharuhk Khan, Jack Chan, Amitah Bachan, Bruce Lee, Hu Jitao, Bruce Lee, Steve Jobs, Bill Gates, Mahatma Gandhi, Alfred Nobel, Pope Francis, Angela Markel, Abraham Lincoln, Jesus, Pope Saint John Paul, Jack Ma and Vladimir Putin—among others. Through the proceeding chapters, we are going to see closely how even our handicaps don't make us inferior. And if we are smart enough, they make us even more important and in some ways superior!

We in Africa need so badly to learn from African Americans. By the same forces, forces of the law of the jungle where the fittest survives, they became slaves. But they knew that they were slaves not because they were born differently or were inferior to Arabs or Europeans by birth, but because their forefathers were poor economically and technologically at the time of their meeting the slave traders and the colonialist. It follows therefore that defeat in the raids for slaves and their ultimate slavery and exportation to the America was quite natural especially during the barbaric eras of the time. It was therefore natural that Africans were called names among them Negros or niggers which was simply an insult, a half human or human animal. Did the black people in Arabia survive? Very few—if they ever did. They were castrated into eunuchs. The population of black people ceased to exist. In Europe and America however they were allowed to breed and therefore grew in population. They counted this as a positive thing and were glad they were ferried to the American or European cost and not the other way round. Black people today form ten percent of the American population. As far as we know yes they hated the slave traders and the slave masters—Arab or European. But upon a thorough thought and counsel, they didn't go on engaging in killing or plotting to cleanse the wealthy white population.

Yes some did revenge but it wasn't to the extent of total mass action. Talking about right actions, true, they began by rejecting themselves. They even fought when someone called them blacks. A few wrangled and fought against the being called niggers. Some even went to the extent of bleaching their color of skin to be white. Some struggled with their hair to make it long and even blonde. But the majority brave blacks accepted their color and heritage and thus the name. They knew nigger was not an insult in its original sense. It simply meant black—which is what they were alright. They didn't stop here. They went a step further. They turned an insult into a victory song. They began taking pride in the name nigger. A great guy was called a nigger. A great buddy was termed as a nigger—my nigger. This then helped restore their self-esteem. That's how they began winning in athletics, in boxing, baseball, and all sports in general—an only area in which overtime they were allowed to compete. Soon they were winning in all sports. The great winners were then called niggers, be they black or white! Today it is no longer an insult but a praise to be a nigger.

LOVE YOURSELF: YOU WERE BORN A WINNER
Before we end this chapter, let me recall what we identify as symptoms of poor low self- esteem. It is poor dressing and low attention to one's body and therefore or rather thereupon, his mind and soul. A good mind thrives in a good body. Therefore love you body. Dress it well. Look after it. Recall also that your body is indeed the temple of God. Far from neglecting himself, he will instead love himself and properly dress both his inner and outer selves. St Ann's Schools here in Dar es Salaam, Tanzania have a slogan that sums up this ideal so brilliantly. "Cleanliness is near holiness," so goes this school's slogan.

A woman walked up to a little old man rocking in a chair on his porch. "I couldn't help but notice how happy you look," she said. "What's your secret for a happy long life?" she added. "I smoke three packs of cigarettes a day," he answers. "I also drink a case of whiskey a week, eat fatty foods, and never exercise." That's amazing?" the woman said adding thus: "How old are you?" now see the answer: "Twenty six," he said very proud of himself. When I first read this story in a January-February 2007 Jambo in-flight magazine, I muttered than this woman should have muttered, "idiot!" The ideal scholar will look after his body, intellect and soul. He won't indulge in over drinking or smoking, nor would he or she indulge in over eating or fornication or anything that ruins his body, mind and soul, much as he will avoid negative thoughts, badmouthing and gossip, bad actions, inaction and bad intentions. Isn't this what we were taught to pray in confession at the church before baptism? He will also choose to be and live in an environment where he accesses only the fresh air and clean water, an environment that has hygiene. He will thereupon constantly take a good care of himself avoiding any such irresponsible self-neglect. Indeed a healthy, wealthy and happy person is conceived out of a healthy body—and vice verse.

Finally, all my research has shown that no one major killer of self-esteem is as powerful as is worry—or fear. Surprisingly they are both symptoms and causes of low self-esteem. Kill the habit of worrying immediately. Do away with it in all its forms. Indeed Napoleon Hill was right. "Nothing which life has to offer is worth the price of worry." Now what will you get indulging in worry? He who does away with the habit of worrying is set on a victorious life. For with this decision come self-confidence, a new bearing in life and personal dignity. With it come peace of mind and calmness of thoughts. With the foregoing blessings, you get happiness and new vitality. You get new vigor to confront life. Truly fear destroys your thinking capacity and erodes your brainpower and thus faults your actions.

To enhance self-esteem, count your blessings. To multiply your blessings, you need to work hard and get results, or some form of accomplishment to your name. But the question is many will ask do I have any worthy record of achievement to fall back on for my self-confidence? I'll tell you yes you do. No matter how small that accomplishment is it is an accomplishment. It is the beginning. Every great success story started with a humble beginning. Do you realize that even your own life, something you consider to be most precious of all: and indeed a miracle of all miracles, beginning with your birth. That is indeed the greatest success story that proves that you were really born a winner, a real hero.

You, yes you the immediate reader was born a winner. No matter whether you are a blue color worker, a junky or drug addict, you have something in common something you share with the kings, queens, presidents or a even a holy pope. You all share one unique and primary great success story—a story that confirms that you were born a winner. It is only the circumstances that have eclipsed you and thus making you to lose hope imagining you are a loser. No. You are naturally a winner. And here is how. You were born when only two people, man and a woman, met and mated for but few seconds and that set in the motion you're the making of—yes, a You. This act, their union, resulted in a race or competition among a million finest sperms. And when I said it was a miracle it was serious. Think of such finest agent—very fine such that a million of them can dance on the point of a needle—and how only one of these generated you.

Do you really realize that only one of these finest units was indeed the real you, you who can not only run a train or fly a Boeing, but indeed create one? All these sperms were aware of the trophy the winner would get and the penalty the losers get. The winner would go on to fertilize the female egg and form a union that would be stronger and live on for very long time enjoying an open air life where freedom abides. The losers die in their custody. But unfortunately, the rule of the game provides that almost every time only one in a million wins and the rest lose the race—and they lose life and any hope for freedom.

Despite all this cut throat competition, you, yes you were the only one in a million, you are that lucky individual who beat a million other competing peers to have arrived at the finish line before the million other eager competitors met the female egg, that female being your mother, before others and that same same second, the beginning of the making of you was set in motion, launching your new state in your mother's womb where you started a new life for nine moons before your outcry of joy when you first set foot here on earth on the day you were born. So you see. You were naturally a winner. Every time you feel any sign of inadequacy and low self-confidence pull this paragraph into your mental screen and reread it. You are a winner. Otherwise you wouldn't be here. With this primary victory in mind, count and see! Indeed you may wonder at how abundantly blessed you are but only that you have been naïve or indifferent to your talents and gifts.

9. EDUCATION: A CONCEPT UNKNOWN EVEN TO THE MEN OF EDUCATION AND WHY OUR SCHOOLS PRODUCE ILLITERATE GRADUATES AND EDUCATED SLAVES

"Who dares to teach must never cease to learn."
—*John Cotton Dana*

The ideal scholar comprehends what education really means. Is this important? Certainly! How can you set out to successfully find that what you don't even know? So to begin with, the ideal scholar comprehends what "education" really means. And that's not all. He recognizes the goals and roles of education; and therefore his own responsibilities as a man of education. But since our graduates assume the leadership role in the society, they must not be people who simply become certified based on pass mark.

What then is education therefore? Really! Do we know? I've asked even the learned and they didn't seem to respond properly to what did education mean. Expecting that someone will come out of school successfully when not only he, but also his teachers don't know exactly what it was that he was looking for in school, much as his teachers didn't know what or why they taught him what they taught him may surprise anyone who is a little sensible. How can you set out in search of something you don't even know, in the first place? Endeavoring to write this book, the author asked numerous people what really education meant but none offered a satisfactory answer—and among them were highly respected men of education.

Congruent to the foregoing assertion, in answering what were schools for, or generally why should we develop curriculum, Allan C. Ornstein and Francis P. Hunkins in their magnificent book Curriculum Foundations, Principles and Issues (3rd Ed, pp.33-34) aptly said: "There can be no serious discussion about philosophy until we embrace what education is. When we agree what education is, we can ask what schools are for then can we pursue the philosophy, aims, and goals of curriculum..."

What I am trying to say is this: when we take our children to school, whether they aim at it or not, in the end they graduate and become graduates—or scholars. According to Cambridge Advanced Learners Dictionary the word Graduate, especially in UK, means: to complete a first university degree successfully. But what does it mean to be successful? What is success?

Dictionary.cambridge.org defines the term *Scholar,* as a person who studies a subject in great detail, especially at a university. It also represents someone who is clever or good at learning by studying. According to i.word.com/dictionary he is a person who has studied a subject for a long time and knows a lot about it: an intelligent and well-educated person who knows a particular subject very well. It is also a person who has done advanced study in a special field: a learned person. Unfortunately all these definitions confront the modern educated man with defiance. We are addressing both this person and another one which is also another definition of the term scholar: a person who attends a school or studies under a teacher.

The second definition is especially commonly used in the US: to complete school, college or university correctly. It also means to advance or improve. It also means a stage you reach when you receive your degree for completing your education or a course of study. I prefer completing *correctly* than *successfully*. In this case, the term that stand for *correctly* include fittingly, suitably, appropriately etc. But all these words don't adequately describe who is a true man of education defined from his character and personality... Besides, all these definitions do not define what does completing education successfully or correctly connotes. Also, we find that no mention is made on what does to improve or advance means of doing work, or even to establish what is intended to be improved. The role of education in advancing good things is good, but because the descriptions given are silent about these things, we are forced to ask—and retrace—what are these good things we intend to advance anyway? In advancing them, how do we advance them and relative to what—or which yardstick? There is deafening silence about such important info!

Moreover, synonyms for the term "graduate," include regulate, adjust, modify, accommodate, adapt, mark off, measure off and divide up. Here we come close to truth. But we cannot come to truth without actually defining what the ideal graduate—or scholar is. The ideal scholar is a person who is properly educated. That's why ordinarily we need to draw up a picture from which we shall mark off the educated person or for that matter, the scholar. The foregoing statement makes this book even more significant.

They, the Chinese, say that a good picture is worth a thousand words. They are right. Below is a short story "Luck," written by Mark Twain and adapted for Special English program, American Stories, by Harold Berman. Through this story, the reader come across the description of the handicap of education beginning with the failure of establishing what really does education mean, hand in hand with the weakness of establishing the realistic yardstick to benchmark who really is the ideal scholar, an educated person or a man of education.

To illustrate the foregoing dilemma, here' a story that sheds light on the importance of the ideal scholar concept.

"LUCK" A STORY BY MARK TWAIN[59]

Here is a story by Mark Twain, a story that illustrates what we have just discussed.

"I was at a dinner in London given in honor of one of the most celebrated English military men of his time. I do not want to tell you his real name and titles. I will just call him Lieutenant General Lord Arthur Scoresby.

---

[59] *"luck" a story by Mark Twain adapted for Special English Program, American Stories, by Harold Berman (http://learningenglish.voanews.com/content/short-story-luck-by-mark-twain-118657939/114335.html).*

"I cannot describe my excitement when I saw this great and famous man. There he sat, the man himself, in person, all covered with medals. I couldn't take my eyes off him. He seemed to show the true mark of greatness. His fame had no effect on him. The hundreds of eyes watching him, the worship of so many people did not seem to make any difference to him. Next to me sat a clergyman, who was an old friend of mine. He was not always a clergyman. During the first half of his life he was a teacher in the military school at Woolwich. There was a strange look in his eye as he leaned toward me and whispered — "Privately — he is a complete fool." He meant, of course, the hero of our dinner. This came as a shock to me. I looked hard at him. I couldn't have been more surprised if he has said the same thing about Napoleon, or Socrates, or Solomon. But I was sure of two things about the clergyman. He always spoke the truth. And, his judgment of men was good. Therefore, I wanted to find out more about our hero as soon as I could.

"Some days later I got a chance to talk with the clergyman, and he told me more. These are his exact words: 'About forty years ago, I was an instructor in the military academy at Woolwich, when young Scoresby was given his first examination. I felt extremely sorry for him. Everybody answered the questions well, intelligently, while he — why, dear me — he did not know anything, so to speak. He was a nice, pleasant young man. It was painful to see him stand there and give answers that were miracles of stupidity. I knew of course that when examined again he would fail and be thrown out. So, I said to myself, it would be a simple, harmless act to help him as much as I could. I took him aside and found he knew a little about Julius Caesar's history. But, he did not know anything else. So, I went to work and tested him and worked him like a slave. I made him work, over and over again, on a few questions about Caesar, which I knew he would be asked. If you will believe me, he came through very well on the day of the examination. He got high praise too, while others who knew a thousand times more than he was sharply criticized. By some strange, lucky accident, he was asked no questions but those I made him study. Such an accident doesn't happen more than once in a hundred years.

"Well, all through his studies, I stood by him, with the feeling a mother has for a disabled child. And he always saved himself by some miracle. I thought that what in the end would destroy him would be the mathematics examination. I decided to make his end as painless as possible. So, I pushed facts into his stupid head for hours. Finally, I let him go to the examination to experience what I was sure would be his dismissal from school. Well, sir, try to imagine the result. I was shocked out of my mind.

He took first prize! And he got the highest praise. I felt guilty day and night—what I was doing was not right. But I only wanted to make his dismissal a little less painful for him. I never dreamed it would lead to such strange, laughable results. I thought that sooner or later one thing was sure to happen: The first real test once he was through school would ruin him. Then, the Crimean War broke out. I felt that sad for him that there had to be a war. Peace would have given this donkey a chance to escape from ever being found out as being so stupid. Nervously, I waited for the worst to happen. It did. He was appointed an officer. A captain, of all things! Who could have dreamed that they would place such a responsibility on such weak shoulders as his! I said to myself that I was responsible to the country for this. I must go with him and protect the nation against him as far as I could. So, I joined up with him. And anyway we went to the field.

"And there—oh dear, it was terrible. Mistakes, fearful mistakes—why, he never did anything that was right — nothing but mistakes. But, you see, nobody knew the secret of how stupid he really was. Everybody misunderstood his actions. They saw his stupid mistakes as works of great intelligence. They did, honestly! His smallest mistakes made a man in his right mind cry, and shout and scream too — to himself, of course. And what kept me in a continual fear was the fact that every mistake he made increased his glory and fame. I kept saying to myself that when at last they found out about him, it will be like the sun falling out of the sky. He continued to climb up, over the dead bodies of his superiors. Then, in the hottest moment of one battle down went our colonel. My heart jumped into my mouth, for Scoresby was the next in line to take his place. Now, we are in for it, I said…

"The battle grew hotter. The English and their allies were steadily retreating all over the field. Our regiment occupied a position that was extremely important. One mistake now would bring total disaster. And what did Scoresby do this time—he just mistook his left hand for his right hand…that was all. An order came for him to fall back and support our right. Instead, he moved forward and went over the hill to the left. We were over the hill before this insane movement could be discovered and stopped. And what did we find? A large and unsuspected Russian army waiting! And what happened—were we all killed? That is exactly what would have happened in ninety-nine cases out of a hundred. But no—those surprised Russians thought that no one regiment by itself would come around there at such a time. It must be the whole British army, they thought. They turned tail, away they went over the hill and down into the field in wild disorder, and we after them. In no time, there was the greatest turn around you ever saw. The allies turned defeat into a sweeping and shining victory. The allied commander looked on, his head spinning with wonder, surprise and joy. He sent right off for Scoresby, and put his arms around him and hugged him on the field in front of all the armies. Scoresby became famous that day as a great military leader — honored throughout the world. That honor will never disappear while history books last.

"He is just as nice and pleasant as ever, but he still doesn't know enough to come in out of the rain. He is the stupidest man in the universe. Until now, nobody knew it but Scoresby and myself. He has been followed, day by day, year by year, by a strange luck. He has been a shining soldier in all our wars for years. He has filled his whole military life with mistakes. Every one of them brought him another honorary title. Look at his chest, flooded with British and foreign medals. Well, sir, every one of them is the record of some great stupidity or other. They are proof that the best thing that can happen to a man is to be born lucky. I say again, as I did at the dinner, Scoresby's a complete fool.'"

Who is the educated person? How do we measure credibility of graduates? This is one of the greatest weaknesses in the education system today. We cannot fairly define a man of education without first establishing what does education really mean. What then is education? Or what is learning or to learn? How do we learn—or how do we get education? A very good and relevant question! Education comes from the Latin word *Educo*—which means: *To draw out or develop from within.*[60]

This is a very important point and all that we learn and teach—me and you—tend to mainly echo with this definition. Much as we have already introduced this idea, much as we shall revert to it, time and time again, Educo is what the English named *To Educe!*

The second most important remark from the author is that much of what you read from this volume is a result of the same kind of education—the author being no a holder of a PhD. This leads us to the key point. What should education teach, or address? Education must address six major areas of learning or education. Number one, It must address us about us—our

---

[60] Source: *Think and Grow Rich* by Napoleon Hill, also at www.answerbag.com/q_view/480273

physical domain. Number two, it must address us about the mind, the intellect. Number three, it must address us about the soul or spirit. Number four, it must address us about the people around us. Number five, it must address the environment—the ecosystem. It must do so for all these affect us and without this knowledge, what then is education? But it must also make a note about the unknown. If it cannot, how then can we create, invent, innovate and learn the unknown? How then can we connect our own being with the Source of Life and learning itself? Much of the failure of our present day education, and why it is called Miseducation resonate with this secret. It resonates with addressing—in the main—the physical person. Plato was probably the first to make this note when he indicated the failure among the medics, the failure of attempting to heal the body without healing the mind, whereas they are one another's halves, and affect one another. You have and still will meet the same sensibility now and again.

Through meditation, Gandhi attained wisdom unthought-of, as our witness. Ronald Doll seconded this idea when he identified sources of ideas that should undergird curriculum designs as: science, society, eternal verities and Divine Will.[61] The ideal scholar strives to know what education really means to him, to his environment and people around him. What does it mean to be educated? The ideal scholar also discerns the goals, roles, or the difference education, education must bring.

Indeed *Learning,* as a term, is defined by dictionary.cambridge.org as to get knowledge or skill in a new subject or activity. To be learned is defined as to make yourself remember a piece of writing by reading it or repeating it many times: while to educate is defined by the same dictionary as: to teach someone, especially using the formal system of school, college or university: to be educated is defined thus having learned a lot at school or university and having a good level of knowledge that's where we go wrong. "Education isn't knowledge (and knowledge per se) as wrote Dale Carnegie in his splendid book: How to Win Friends and Influence People. "It is action," he said. Furthermore our problem as a nation isn't lack of knowledge as graduates but inaction. To learn is according to the dictionary.cambridge.org as to be told facts or information that you did not know. All these definitions are but commonplace. We need more

---

[61] Source: *Ornstein and Hunkins 3r ed. p.234*

description of education. But look at this which is much better. To learn is "To start to understand that you must change the way you behave."

We also were required to know how we learn—or how we get education. A very good and relevant question! To respond to that question, we know that many people have heard that you cannot teach a man anything but you can only show him how to. Many people have heard what Bernard Shaw said. He said that: *If you teach a man anything he will not learn.* But very few souls know why. Here's why. To learn effectively one must gather information from inside out and not otherwise. Because no one can go into the deep bowels of your heart and soul you can only go there and find information and ways to learn commensurate with your own person. Education comes from a Latin word educo meaning to draw out from inside. From yourself. Alan Alda in seconding the opinion said: The creative is the place where no one else has ever been. You have to leave the city of your comfort and go into the wilderness of your intuition. What you'll discover will be wonderful. What you'll discover is yourself. Having dropped out of school both for financial reasons and intuition, Steve Jobs seconding the assertion above, said in a commencement speech to graduating students thus: "And much of what I stumbled into by following my curiosity and intuition turned out to be priceless later on." Jesus said the kingdom of heaven is in us. He also said that what you take into your body will never effect much as that what comes out of your own person. In other words He was saying you and I get blessings not from what we take into but from what gets out from the heart, the thoughts or the mind. Any teaching methodology that simply imposes instructions upon the learners leaves a lot to be desired! We are also required to answer to the question about who is an educated person. How do we know? By use of mere papers? Mhhh! Technology and quick fix stand between certificates and reality. Today it seems we don't have the right indicators.

Without establishing clear and comprehensive meaning and indicators of being educated, certificates and degree papers will push us deeper into the stupor of paper work, most traditional schoolmen boast of, thereby losing sight on the true expected end: practice, action and actual delivery of results. The performance of our scholars should thus be judged on criteria that relate to their ability to respond flexibly, creatively and competently to work after graduation; to national development and to the needs of the employer or the workplace.[62] They should be judged by skills and character

---

[62] *The Promise by Maliyamkono and Mason (1982) p. 426.*

they exhibit beyond the classroom examination results. Thus, "In basic terms," analyses The Promise, a book by Professor Maliyamkono, "education is (and should be) perceived not only as infusing knowledge but also as equipping citizens with the ability to understand and unravel problems within the society caused by the ever changing economic, technological, and social environment in which we live." And failure to produce graduates who respond to the above call is essentially one of the major characteristics of any failed education system. There cannot be a better KPI or key performance indicator of how successful the education system is working! With rampant fake schools and counterfeit certificates the foregoing statement is probably one of the best ways to identify or judge between who is an educated person and who's not.

Truly we can best judge a learned person by the change or results he brings with him. The performance of graduates should therefore be judged on the criteria that relates to their ability to respond flexibly creatively and competently to work after graduation to national development and to the needs of the employer. Today it seems we don't have right indicators. Without right indicators certificates and degree papers elude us such that the real indicators of or candidates get marginalized as quick fix finds its way by the day. When students understand what education really means, they will become independent intellectually. The foregoing statement is a precondition that predates financial freedom. With the latter, they will be free from private and public employers. They will be employable, hard working in schools and productive at workplaces. Indeed education and knowledge are no longer one and same thing. Education doesn't represent knowledge, nor does knowledge by itself mean education. Here is an important note to make: Any knowledge isn't of any significance whatsoever until when it can be applied and applied to produce tangible results—results that help to add value to life for the individual humans, the community and the nature as a whole.

Napoleon Hill said (as we adapt it here) that true education comes from "mind development from within... it is therefore a mixture of both the mental and the spiritual..." And he didn't stop there. "Experience has proved," he continued, "that the best educated persons are often those who are known as self-made or self-educated. It takes more than a college degree to make one a person of education. An educated person is the one who has developed faculties of his mind that he may acquire excellence in any career or vocation of his choice and improve his life as well as lives of his family and people around him without violating rights of the others."[63]

True education is therefore that kind of education that initiates the learners in the specific brand of knowledge which he furthered thus, leads to "understanding—understanding of the self, (and) understanding of others understanding the laws of nature, and recognition and understanding of happiness." and it is important to mention here that because of his understanding of himself and laws governing nature he is not superstitious which is a symbol of fear of the unknown. Ideals are connected! He will therefore work hard as well as smart respecting yes the importance of others but as well that life is in his own hands. To achieve this feat, a person should reverse the pattern of his life. This he can do by changing his thoughts—and his thought pattern. By doing so, he will then find one major area of specialization which he likes to be part of his life. Having decided so, that's where he will specialize. He will then keep on studying, advancing himself to meet the ever changing realities. If you do so you won't be a slave as are majority of our graduates today.

ROLES OF EDUCATION / SCHOOLS
What then are the roles of schools or education in general? Education or generally learning is a human activity. It is not a machine driven process engaging people as cogs in the wheels. In response to what schools are for, Ornstein and Hunkins stated that: "The school's first responsibility is to the social order (pp. 33-34)." They also inserted that the sense of individual growth and potential as paramount as wrote Dewey thus we not only wish "to make (good) citizens and workers, (but also) to make human beings who will live life to the fullest…" Ornstein and Hunkins (p.34) concluded then that this duality—allegiance to the nation and fulfillment of the individual—is a noble aim that should guide…the means to the ends…"

Ornstein and Hunkins stated that: Education must build an individual to function well as a free person in a free society. Education must also respond to the needs of the society. With the culture of laissez-faire and inaction pervading our society today, education should instill into our youth and the society as a whole the desire to, and the culture of working hard. Indeed for the most part the problem with our graduates is not knowledge but inaction. And it is wrong for our graduates from any level

---

[63] *Think and Grow Rich by Napoleon Hill page 137*

of education to believe knowledge is power. It is not. It is when, and only when, used tangibly to bring significant results.

That's why this form of education and methodology is very fundamental to Tanzania and most young nations. Why? Ours is a very young economy whose growth depends on the knowledge of what resources we have and how to go about leveraging from her natural and human resources. These resources will depend on the average man and woman and the information about everything has to be attained from the scratch. That's why our schools should engage in research and data collection. According to Ornstein and Hunkins (1998): "The schools should also be considered as a major data source for knowledge..." Therefore,: "Faith, equality and a sense of community and not individualism are important concepts embedded in the belief that all people were important and that in order to survive each had a job to do despite different backgrounds. The belief that each had the capacity and responsibility to improve his or her life is not only an important message but an indispensable one. Mass education was not only important but also necessary for intelligent participation in political democracy. The later is a key element because people don't work hard enough under dictatorships and nepotistic systems.

Schools should teach innovations which are—according to Ornstein and Hunkins in their book Curriculum Foundations, Principles and Issues 3rd Edition—*required for tomorrow's technological world.* With fast changing world trends, on the other hand, education has to equip our people with technology. Indeed today a person is not considered to be literate if he is no technologically literate. Schools and education must enhance or promote sciences being the most practical subject for survival of the individual and the society...Schools and education as a whole should teach our children how to think and how to solve problems and not what to think. *"The individual,"* rightly wrote Ornstein and Hunkins: *"The individual, in modern society must learn to live with computers, robots, lasers, telecommunications, and space exploration. A truly educated and well rounded individual will be able to function in an accelerating world of science and technology."*

Without innovation and constant pursuit of evolution and advancement outside one's own space, because of the law of nature only intelligent and productive populations would adapt to environmental changes. Less intelligent weak or lazy people would slowly disappear.[64] If an individual person, household, institution ,organization community or nation shouldn't adapt to the changing world no matter how top it is today, it will not be too long before in words of Boyd bode; *"it is circumvented and left behind."*

---

[64] *Allan C. Ornstein and Francis P. Hunkins, Curriculum Foundations, Principles and Issues 3rd Edition p. 71*

10. SELF-ADVANCEMENT AND THE ILLITERATE GRADUATE

"Any man (or woman) who stops learning is old no matter whether he is 20 or 80!" — Henry Ford, founder of Ford Motor Company was right.

The ideal scholar pursues self-advancement. He seeks excellence in his life and all that surrounds him, by ceaselessly seeking continuous improvement. And this isn't something new that should you should think twice to adopt. The successes of Japan, a country with no significant comparative advantage whatsoever in terms of natural resources—the land, minerals, gas and oil, etc.—but which has remained number two world economic power for a very very long time, resonates with the same principle or virtue. They call it Kaizen. So, what is Kaizen? Kaizen is the practice of continuous improvement. Kaizen was originally introduced to the West by Masaaki Imai in his book Kaizen: The Key to Japan's Competitive Success in 1986. The ideal scholar knows that, as was John Dewey posits: Education is a journey and our intentions however phrased must inform the learner that the attainment of a waypoint enables him or her to proceed to the next. Ends for a particular point are essentially the means for striving to another point another destination toward another intention. Indeed he commented saying that ends are, in fact, literally endless, forever coming into existence as new activities occasion new consequences.[65]

The ideal scholar, a truly educated person is therefore one who can use his imagination and intuition to generate useful knowledge from his own

---

[65] Allan C. Ornstein and Francis P. Hunkins, *Curriculum Foundations, Principles and Issues* 3rd Edition p. 269

environment to advance his own life and that of the environment and people around him. In Think and Grow Rich, Napoleon Hill said something I have paraphrased thus: "An educated person is the one who has developed faculties of his mind that he may acquire excellence in any career or vocation of his choice and improve his life as well as lives of his family and people around him without violating rights of the others."

With the foregoing quality you realize that the ideal scholar can never become what is termed as illiterate graduate.

CATEGORIES OF ILLITERATE GRADUATES

It is doubtless an important step in understanding the illiterate scholar concept to try to breakdown the types of the illiterate scholars or graduates. The first category consists of those who became illiterates right from the beginning of their degree courses. The typical example is the Nigerian illiterate graduates we have already presented in this very book. How did this happen? They simply maneuvered through and managed to complete their term at the university without actually getting educated! The second category consists of those who qualified nicely at the graduation but simply stopped learning what they were taught in school and so they simply forgot everything. Most folks falling in this category become illiterates when for instance they lose themselves in their present career and its routine, the god diggers fighting to climb the career ladder, those who throw all cautions to the wind provided they get promotions at work and make money. And such folks are ubiquitous among our elites who cannot stop selling anything to climb a ladder or make money by selling anything from their own bodies, their liberties and dignity; to selling or buying albinos—dead or alive! This is indeed the easiest to illustrate for indeed not all they do to achieve such ambitions are educative! For such folks that is the end of the road whether they know it or not!

The third category consists of those who are the majority today, a group of folks who because they took no notice of ICT and the rapidity of the pace of technological and social economic changes; because they didn't heed the importance of self-advancement in terms of reading and staying up to date, tend to often shorten their shelf life—whether they know it or not. Truly there is no end to learning. Education is a process. It is not an event with a sharp end just after graduation. Indeed Henry Ford, founder of Ford Motor Company was right. *"Any man (or woman) who stops learning is old no matter whether he is 20 or 80!"*

THE EDUCATED SLAVE

The plight of the illiterate grad is incredible even when he doesn't notice it. His demise doesn't end there—sadly! These illiterate graduates have another tragedy in store for them—and their families and community—as a whole! They become slaves! Read on! It could help you catch up with prosperity and the craving for the reading of books!

You certainly have heard of those countries they call third world. These are the countries which indeed are sick in nature and their sickness is almost impossible to heal. They are slave communities–slave nations. We don't need to illustrate this concept any further with the publication of our previous book, *A Sick Nation: How to Heal It*.

Indeed Erich Fromm was right: Why should the society feel responsible only for the education of the children and not the education of the adults of all ages? Developed from Abraham Maslow, education or learning is a lifelong process. It is experimental, its essence being freedom and its outcome being full human potential and reform of society.[66] The sixth quality in Draper Kauffman's six areas of competence that could comprise a possible future curriculum he identified this quality as: *Enhancing personal competence*. The Phi Delta Kappa Honor Society[67] identified the eighth quality for the American graduate. Thus he should be able to: "Develop a desire for learning now and in the future." Paraphrasing what Ornstein and Hunkins remarked on page 46 in their great book Curriculum Foundations Principles and Issues 3rd Edition, "Teaching is, in fact, the art

---

[66] Allan C. Ornstein and Francis P. Hunkins, Curriculum Foundations, Principles and Issues 3rd Edition p. 125

[67] Delta Kappa Phi, established in 1899 in America as a fraternity with the purpose that can be summed up as the advancement of the interests of its members in acquiring a thorough education in engineering, the sciences, or the liberal arts whereas according to http://www.kdp.org/membership/, Kappa Delta Phi (KDP) International Honor Society in Education, is a membership organization founded by Dr. William Bagley in 1911 at the University of Illinois to foster excellence in education

of stimulating discussion and the inherent rational powers of the students. The school can transmit the culture of society while it prepares the students for the changing world because either reality is always changing."

The foregoing assertion is pivotal to someone aiming to remain on top of his own life and his life's affairs. Part of being on top of your life is to conquer fear. Human beings fear what they don't know. Indeed it is impossible to separate fear from ignorance. To be yourself—I mean to grow into a person you were born to be—to accomplish your dream and achieve your true potential, you have to conquer fear. To conquer fear you must conquer ignorance.

But since we seem to be constantly under the siege of ignorance, to conquer ignorance we must constantly read and write and advance our understanding on a daily basis. If you do so: "Then you will know the truth, and the truth will set you free," rightly recommended Apostle John.[68] The Association for Supervision and Curriculum Development identified this quality among its ten major goals or qualities for American youth as the fourth quality i.e. encouraging interest in and capability for continued learning. Why? *Knowledge acquisition should be a lifelong process. Sooner or later any sensible man realizes that schools provide only a preliminary and temporary base of knowledge that is eventually superseded by different forms of education. Other learning sources such as books, newspapers, television, videos, computers, World Wide Web, social media, peers and superiors and mere observation assume greater importance and more influence than textbooks or other educational materials for continuing the education. Their experiences extend beyond schools. They acquire most new learning, in fact, outside the school settings.*

FINAL NOTE ON SELF-ADVANCEMENT

Are you then pursuing personal self-improvement as you should? Do you have any plan about it anyway? It is to your advantage much as its reverse is going to ruin you if you don't. Besides, self-advancement is not time consuming as such. Moreover, you don't have to forgo your job or abandon your family or your social commitments since you only need even

---

[68] *John 8:25*

one hour in your day. If you program your day such that, you would be able focus and give maximum attention to your program. "Although this amounts to only one hour of study per day," wrote Bob Proctor another great advocate of the foregoing approach to self-advancement, "if you were to follow this schedule rigorously, in a relatively short span of time you would stand among your peers like a giraffe in a herd of field mice. In fact, "continued Bob Proctor, "when you really think about it, you will soon understand there isn't any competition at all, because there're so few people in the race, that even the losers are winners. Therefore, you need not do a tremendous amount of studying to gain the understanding you require, because again, the difference between knowledge and ignorance, may be as fine as "The Razor's Edge."[69]

He will take into account such information as the job he is doing presently and ask himself the following questions: "How good am I at what I am doing?" "How much better could I be?" "What do I need to get there?" "How much time am I putting into it?" "...resources I am putting in my personal or career advancement?" It only takes commitment to attain one's true potential, a person must always try to be conversant with what goes on around him.[70]

He has to know who he is: his past history, education, the recent advancements in technology and how it affects his life etc. This person understands that the limit of knowledge or therefore of success is the sky. This person will never accept to be uneducated, uninformed, ignorant, self-righteous, dependent!

Very recently I overheard an argument between two of my siblings. They argued about what's best for a young man to do after graduation. Daudi emphasized importance of great attention to details, self-advancement and continuous improvement as another one said, certainly representing the views of the majority, that he wasn't worried a bit about the future as long as long as he had a job and was earning a living. That's not all. He said that, which is my message, he didn't bother about continuous improvement as long as he wasn't deteriorating.

---

[69] *You Were Born Rich by Bob Proctor p. 1162.*

[70] *Source: Adapted from Ben Carson's book: Think Big*

Now here is the point to the lazy herd. Daudi said that that was impossible and misleading. He said that as long as you are not increasing, you are deteriorating. You are deteriorating because you can never remain static. Static is a state that is unattainable. You are, he said, at any point in time, advancing forward, or backwards. Static was impossible. Why? The world was always changing. If you didn't do anything to advance your situation you are deteriorating. You either create or disintegrate. Bob Proctor was right when he said that, "I believe you are all aware of this fact: everything in the universe is governed by a basic law—"Either create or disintegrate. Therefore, it follows that, if something is not in the process of growing, it must, by the law of its being, be dying." That's why we need to always be on the go; to always be advancing. This explains importance of great attention to details, self-advancement and continuous improvement.

11. THE IDEAL SCHOLAR READS (AND WRITES)

> *"For what else is there that can guide mankind better—something that sets man far apart from other organisms—while as well, timelessly reserving the same precious priceless wisdom for the future generations?"*—Author (Festo Michael Kambarangwe) in acknowledgement of all authors, writers and publishers (The Ideal Scholar)

The ideal scholar reads—and writes. And this is a key ideal that should probably be sitting at the top of the tree. For indeed what else is there that can guide mankind better—something that sets man far apart from other organisms—while as well, timelessly reserving the same precious priceless wisdom for the future generations? And yes what else is there that separates mankind from animals, for instance? We breathe, they breathe. We eat and excrete, they eat and excrete. We love our lovers and reproduce; they too love their lovers and reproduce. We think, see, hear, plan and communicate; they think, see, hear, plan and communicate. We love, have feelings, and affection; the animals also love, have feelings, and affection. We stand on two feet and walk, kangaroos, dogs, cows (when necessary—such as in the pursuit of reproduction), and penguins regularly stand on their two feet and take a walk—swaggering as they converse. We all live—and then? We all pass on—we all die! Afterlife? That's what we say? What do their prophets say? Do we know—or care to know? If you are worth it, find and read the book: The Fall of Man and the Return of the Beast. And yes, who knows? If animals, for instance, knew how to read and write, we wouldn't be taming them anymore, would we? Wait and see the major strategy the slave master used to tame the African slaves in America! I promise you that you are going to be shocked not far too long from now!

Passion for reading and writing as a hobby, and duty, is his culture—the culture and vocation of the ideal scholar. The ideal scholar recognizes that writing and reading as a culture, doesn't start and end with the mere ability to write and read news feeds on Facebook walls or twits on your Twitter account, or even ability to post something on Instangram. Patricia, my daughter now a couple of months before she cerebrates her fourth birthday can do that. A reading and writing scholar is far better than that for a word on its own doesn't mean a thing. What does it say to us? Yet, that is also insufficient. The ideal scholar learns and puts to work, or interprets what he has learnt through reading and writing into his life. In words of Ornstein and Hunkins, "...analysis, interpretation, and evaluation of the problem are insufficient; commitment and actions...are needed."

With reference to the modern-day graduates—graduates whose pastime is in drinking, clubbing and bodily pleasures—or what we can generally categorize as leisure—the Ideal Scholar reads—and writes. And he doesn't do this only for self-advancement? No! Not even only for the development of his body, intellect and his spirit? For him reading or writing is not merely duty to him. It is also his pastime. Therefore to see him with a book or having regular visitations to the public library is common. On the contrary his opposite number, the mediocre common man of education, finds a library as Witch's Den, or a Hall of Nightmare. That's why when the ideal scholar feels excited when he is about to read a book, when the opposite shrinks from a book, let alone a library. That's why Lincoln said: "A person I call a friend is the one who gives me a new to read."

The German philosopher Johann Freidrich Herbart maintained that the chief aim of education was moral education... And therefore the need was *to educate the good person who had diversified interests and a balanced perspective on life.* And this is not new or simply something that I and only I advocate. Being the first in Draper Kauffman's six areas of competence that could comprise a possible future curriculum he identified this quality as: *Having access to information.* Is reading and writing that important? "The word," aptly said Don Miguel Ruiz, "The word is not just a sound or a written symbol. The word is a force; it is the power you have to express and communicate, to think, and thereby to create the events in your life."

Is the foregoing true? Let's see. *The New York Times* reported that, "In 1975, a herd of prime beef cattle was destroyed by accident in Chicago. A feedlot worker couldn't read the labels on the bags that he found piled in

the warehouse and fed poison to the cattle by mistake. He thought that he was adding a nutrition supplement to their feed basins..."[71]
In his inaugural address as governor of Georgia, a future President of the United States proclaimed his dedication to the crisis of Illiterate America. 'Our people are our most precious possession ... Every adult illiterate ... is an indictment of us all ... If Switzerland and Israel and other people can end illiteracy, then so can we. The responsibility is our own and our govenment's. I will not shirk this responsibility.' Today the number of identified nonreaders is three times greater than the number (6) Jimmy Carter had in mind when he described this challenge and defined it as an obligation that he would not shirk.

I visited St. Augustine Secondary School in Mbezi, Dar es Salaam, Tanzania recently, and the school motto—Tolle Lege—caught my attention. And here are the words I read, word that describe the meaning of the motto. "Tolle Lege is a Latin word that stands for: "Take and read," the description began. "Take and read; words that... (were to inspire their readers) St. Augustine (who) was in Milan, Italy, attempting to find the truth. In his confusion, unaware of what to do, one day he heard a voice of a kid singing repeatedly: "Tolle Lege," "Tolle Lege," "Tolle Lege," trying to recall whether he had heard anything like it during his childhood games but to no avail. Then he believed it was a small voice from God asking him to read the bible...." I am Christian, but I say read everything. Read the bible. Read the Koran. Read the Bhagavad Gita. Read the books. Read magazines. Read the newspapers. Read anything on walls or clothing, or even on the public buses. In short: read, read, read!

Is reading—and writing—that important? Let's see! The Koran set aside two books on the topic: one is Al-Kalam and another Iqra, meaning the pen, representing writing, and read respectively. But that seems a little unconvincing. Let's try another one. Accordingly, according to DoSomething.org,[72] 2/3 of students who cannot read proficiently by the

---

[71] *http://eserver.org/courses/spring97/76100o/readings/kozol*

[72] *https://www.dosomething.org/facts/11-facts-about-literacy-america*

end of 4th grade will end up in jail or on welfare. Over 70% of America's inmates cannot read above a 4th grade level. 1 in 4 children in America grow up without learning how to read. Students who don't read proficiently by the 3rd grade are 4 times likelier to drop out of school...As of 2011; America was the only free-market OECD (Organization for Economic Cooperation and Development) country where the current generation was less educated than the previous one. Nearly 85% of the juveniles who face trial in the juvenile court system are functionally illiterate, proving that there is a close relationship between illiteracy and crime. More than 60% of all inmates are functionally illiterate. 53% of 4th graders admitted to reading recreationally "almost every day," while only 20% of 8th graders could say the same. 75% of Americans who receive food stamps perform at the lowest 2 levels of literacy, and 90% of high school dropouts are on welfare. Teenage girls between the ages of 16 to 19 who live at or below the poverty line and have below average literacy skills are 6 times more likely to have children out of wedlock than girls their age who can read proficiently. Reports show that the rate of low literacy in the United States directly costs the healthcare industry over $70 million every year. In 2013, Washington, D.C. was ranked the most literate American city for the third year in a row, with Seattle and Minneapolis close behind. Long Beach, CA was ranked the country's most illiterate city, followed by Mesa, AZ, and Aurora, CO.

Concerned with the weaknesses amongst the youth and purposes of education, in 1994, the (US) Education Policy Commission, formulated ten aims (or in our case ,goals or purposes) of education in what was called education for all American youth. In this document we find emphasis, and mention of, among others, the importance of: *development of capacities to appreciate literature...and to read.*[73]

Ornstein and Hunkins emphasize that: *"(To continue acquiring) Knowledge (one's efforts) should comprise the basic tools. This," they continue," includes reading writing, arithmetic, and oral communication."* The Phi Delta Kappa Honor Society as its second quality of required the American student to:*"develop (not only) skills (but also interest) in reading, writing, speaking and listening.* As a society we must recognize that as Ornstein and Hunkins indicate that textbooks for much of this

---

[73] Allan C. Ornstein and Francis P. Hunkins, *Curriculum Foundations, Principles and Issues* 3rd Edition p. 270

century have been the linchpin of the curriculum...Textbooks are the curriculum. Ask teachers and public alike what the curriculum is and they most frequently will point to a textbook...what is emphasized by text gets included in the tests and taught by teachers. Reliance of textbooks (as well as its companion, the workbook) is consistent with the stress on written words as the main medium of education...[74]

In most schools, the textbooks used frequently determine the curriculum. The power of the textbook is particularly evident when we realize that nearly 75% of the students total classroom time is spent engaged with instructional materials. An even greater percentage of time, 90%, is spent with instructional materials when students are doing homework. What students know therefore usually reflects their textbooks content.[75]

Attention to details together with continuous self-improvement are almost impossible without constantly reading and writing, especially today with fast changing world trends vis a vis our non reading and the writing culture in countries like Tanzania. You need to build and nurture the culture reading and writing especially in a country where after one has graduated from the university, asking him to buy or read a book—other than mushrooming tabloids—is considered punitive. The sight of books or anything scholastic or educational frightens away the typical Tanzanian—youth or adult. Indeed students would rather be anywhere else but in class where some exchange naked erotic images of women or constantly gossiping on facebook, Instangram or Twitter as the sessions go on. The same *scholars* export the same habit with themselves wherever they land after graduation. Predictably, asking even members of the parliament or government officials to read government bills or investment contracts is considered nothing but penal. Predictably, the only two unfortunate MPs were caught on CCTV in India not only watching porno and on the iPad but also others were caught in Karnataka and in the parliament where they

---

[74] Allan C. Ornstein and Francis P. Hunkins, Curriculum Foundations, Principles and Issues 3rd Edition p 358

[75] Allan C. Ornstein and Francis P. Hunkins, Curriculum Foundations, Principles and Issues 3rd Edition p

227

were caught on camera taking bribes for asking questions as the parliamentary session was on[76].

The journalists also reported thus: "Narendra Modi party members watching pornography total 15 BJP MLA's caught on CCTV cameras." You can watch the evidence for yourself at http://youtube.com/watch?v=rjlu9EwAMTk. Unsurprisingly, we have failed to revoke even the scandalously discreditable contracts we have signed locally or internationally. The radar contract saga that was debated on with great enthusiasm in the UK parliament, looking into whether the UK government should refund Tanzania, or not, the billions of the British pound sterling following a bribe motivated contract involving senior government officials, leading to the resignation of the secretary for the UK department for international development, Claire Short, in protest. This is not my good guess. You can witness it for yourself at www.theguardian.com/world/2010/feb/06/bae-tanzania-arms-deal. There is also the outcry on the mining contracts and IPTL saga here in Tanzania which together offer generous exemplars of the foregoing—the fact that our leaders don't read or they are indifferent about it. For a country like ours to develop, we need a new emphasis on leaders who are readers—and readers who become our leaders. Truly I cannot overemphasize importance of reading and writing. Probably our people don't read because our people don't write. In other words they don't read probably because there are relevant books to read—books that resonate with the people's lives and realities.

Many people know that America is the wealthiest country on earth but few know why. They read and write—and they read and what is relevant to American Dream. Period. It didn't come as a miracle. The policy makers and the educators and writers sat together and prepared material that would elevate the sense of America: the pride of America as a new nation, a nation destined to overcome and thrive over others. They also value readers and writers. When books are opened, relevant books, mines of education and wisdom are laid bare for any person who is eager to learn, and advance his station in life. Nations that read conquer poverty, dependence, exploitation and obscurity. Having risen from obscurity and the shadow of poverty, a story told in full in the book What Makes People Rich and Nations Powerful, and further lessons from this experience now

---

[76] *m.firstpost.com/politics/gujarat*

wrapped in the upcoming book, another volume in this series: A City in Your Mind, A Dream from My Childhood, the author recognizes that this statement cannot be truer.

Indeed, the early American society did not want an illiterate class to grow...they feared that such a class might comprise of dependent poor, an underclass ,...which they wanted to avoid...unable to read and right, many of them grew up to be subsistence farmers like their parents before them...the curriculum...consisted of reading writing and arithmetic...and lessons designed to develop manners and morals... the student would be admitted into college upon examination whereby he could show competency to read (among others)...[77] and thats not all. Not only do they put money behind reading and writing but they vote in readers and writers. Barack Obama became president after writing his two books. Not everybody who writes will be resident but for Obama that was a strong point to prove his worth. And it's no joke. Kennedy won nomination yes with the support of vast other reasons, but he had to work out and publish a book about which he made a big deal during his campaigns. Did he win? You bet it! We can indeed evaluate how a nation is developed by analyzing the kind of leaders that country votes in. We in Africa, in general, and Tanzania in particular, have another problem. In words of PLO Lumumba, we tolerate "An Africa that does not tell her (own) stories; an Africa whose story is told by Europe and America—the CNN, Radio Deutsche Welle, Radio France," etc. It is the Hollywood and media that structure the minds of such a people. We in Tanzania can easily learn from the experience of popular music in the country by comparing the era of Radio Tanzania, Dar es Salaam and an era of FM radios beginning with Clouds Fm Revolution. Jim Morrison was right. "Whoever controls the media, controls the mind!"

HOW THE VOCATION OF READING AND WRITING BOOKS IS ALMOST HOLY

Did I say that reading (together with writing) was divine? Forget it! I meant to talk about importance of reading and writing. I mean to somehow validate why the slave masters feared the slaves with books than those with guns. Here is why. In the spring of 1871, a young man picked a book and read twenty-one words that had a profound effect on not only his own

---

[77] *Allan C. Ornstein and Francis P. Hunkins, Curriculum Foundations, Principles and Issues 3rd Edition p. 63-65*

future but to lives of many people not only in America but right here at home in Tanzania. At the time he was a medical student at the Montreal General Hospital.

According to Dale Carnegie in his book *How to Stop Worrying and Start Living,* there was a young man "who was worried about passing the final examinations, worried about what to do, where to go, how to build a practice, how to make a living." Dale Carnegie explains that the twenty-one words that this young medical student read in 1871 helped him to become the most famous physician of his generation. He became the regius professor of medicine at Oxford—the highest honor that can be bestowed upon any medical man in the British Empire. He was knighted by the king of England. And that's not all.

We made a mention that the waves of his reading the 21 words didn't only help make him famous and change his life and lives of those around him in America two centuries ago the same waves have helped millions of people in far different many ways including training of the highly talented students in medicine and neurosurgery in our times—people who have saved lives of the millions of people who would otherwise be condemned to death or handicaps maimed all their lives. When I say this I am certain of what I say. It is this hospital where the famous Ben Carson was trained and finally was able to rescue the lives of many. That's where the first separation of the Siamese, or conjoined, twins was finally, finely accomplished by Dr. Ben Carson. You probably already know the name of that hospital. It is the same hospital that has only recently saved the life of our president Jakaya Kikwete. It was these same-same twenty-one words he read that led the foundation of the famous John's Hopkins School of Medicine—and hospital thereof. Dale Carnegie adds that when he died, two volumes containing 1466 pages were required to tell the story of his life. His name was Sir William Osler.

Those words he read in the spring of 1871—twentyone words from Thomas Carlyle that led to all this success could look so commonplace to you or me. I know. But the truth is you and I have different talents and inspirations. We have different aspirations and things which make us tick. And all us can find what makes us tick in almost every other book. But what is important here is that without having Thomas Carlyle writing that book containing those twenty-one words without him reading those words he probably wouldn't have been the sir we know today. We certainly wouldn't have some f the best medical experts on the planet recommend our president to go to John's Hopkins. We don't what would happen otherwise. Still want to hear those words? Here: "our main business is not to see what lies dimly at a distance but to do what lies clearly at hand."

Forty two years later after he read those words he was invited to speak to the students of the Yale University one of the top four universities at the time. He told the students of Yale that a man like himself who had been a professor in four universities and had himself written a popular book was supposed to have brains of a special quality. He declared that that was untrue. He said that his intimate friends knew that his brains were "of the most mediocre character." What then was the secret of his success? You bet it. His secret springs from one major and only secret. And this secret was born in Thomas Carlyle and was manifest in his writing a book that he, William Osler, read as a student; a book that breathed life into William Osler beginning with the twenty one words. And here is the most beautiful thing about this story. In fact it is the cream of the whole thing—about John's Hopkins—beside having treated our president. We all know that it was Cana where Jesus discharged his first miracle—a place where he turned water in to a magnificent wine that even the host had to ask whence this magnificent wine had come.

We have indicated that it is here at John's Hopkins that the first miracle of the separation of the Siamese or conjoined twins was finely accomplished by none other but Dr. Ben Carson. Now who is Dr. Carson? He, young Dr. Benjamin Carson, was disadvantaged black in slaving America, grandchild of one of the black slaves prohibited to read and write books. It is the same man who also has done many more miracles in writing books that have helped many children to change their lives throughout the world. Probably you have read some of them including *Gifted Hands* and *Think Big*. It is no wonder for first time in the American history that some elements in the conservative white slave masters Republican Party did even tip Dr. Carson for presidency of the United States. This unprecedented because it is traditionally the democrats that have chemistry with black men and women.

Recently the BBC Hardtalk program interviewed Werner Herzog about the secret behind his spectacular successes in the film industry, the advice to anyone wishing to stand out in whatever he does; Herzog a person a German film director, producer, screenwriter, author, actor and opera director, a man according to Wikipedia,[78] the French filmmaker François

---

[78] *(http://en.wikipedia.org/wiki/Werner_Herzog),*

Truffaut once called Herzog "the most important film director alive,"http://en.wikipedia.org/wiki/Werner_Herzog - cite_note-3 and the American film critic Roger Ebert said that Herzog "has never created a single film that is compromised, shameful, made for pragmatic reasons or uninteresting. Even his failures are spectacular," and guess what his answer: "Read, read, read![79]" Ben Carson was right. When you read and write books truly you can "be a baseball player, lawyer, a Neurosurgeon, president of the United States, and a writer—and in that order!"[80]

Now here is my last point about Dr. Carson. Whether he is finally elected as Republican Party nominee to eventually contest with the Democratic Party nominee, whether he wins the nomination and ultimately become president or not is not an issue. What is important is that as I write, he is leading in the presidential race. What's important is that the Republican Party and millions of Americans who have supported him have helped to illustrate the importance of reading and writing. Truly, what books can accomplish does more than astonish me! Indeed, aside from Ben Carson, thinking about Mwalimu Nyerere, led me to a realization that, **readership breeds leadership.**

The recent prosperity of Malaysia in the past decade is appreciated and revered as exemplary. But one of the reasons why it is so revered, is the nation's widely English speaking population. Reading and writing doesn't only help in real terms it helps to shape the mental and cultural fiber of a people. The prosperity of the modern day America began with a philosophy and policy of high ranking attention on reading and writing during the earliest settlements and first school establishments. Indeed it was made binding by the act of 1647 that every town of fifty families to have a teacher in place who taught the people to read and write.[81]

Indeed as a student he cannot acquire the best unless he reads extensively. One of the greatest minds of our time who rose from obscurity to extraordinary accomplishments and fame drew from his experience and it

---

[79] http://www.bbc.co.uk/programmes/b051rd39

[80] Adapted from Dale Carnegie's How To Stop Worrying And Start Living Revised edition Pocket Books p. 4

[81] Adapted from Allan C. Ornstein and Francis 1998, P. 63

is none other but Ben Carson who summed it up thus: "Students who excel academically read (and write) extensively!" We therefore ought to inspire students and every other citizen to read and write extensively. Mwalimu Nyerere stands for such a person. We all know his brilliance whether in his speeches or writing. But for sure it was sharpened by intense reading and writing. Nelson Mandela knew it and though he didn't specifically refer to Mwalimu Julius Kambarage Nyerere but the assertion fits so unerringly when he said that "A good head and a good heart are always a formidable contribution. But when you add to that a literate tongue or pen, then you have something special."

Reading and writing, as a value, is such an imponderably essential contribution that I believe the researchers and academics of the future will have to dig deep into how it works. In the book A Sick Nation and How to Heal It, I narrated how I went to a doctor with clear symptoms of the disease I had contracted. I could have thought it was malaria or anything else being medically naïve or lay. But not this specialist doctor! He should have seen my illness or its symptoms. He was a doctor afterall. But instead? what did he do? He did something that made me think he was wasting his, and worst of all, my time. He should have just spelt down the medication I needed and let me go. Instead what did he do? He took a pen and a notepad. Then he jotted down what I had told him as if h would forget it instantly. Then he asked me some more question at my annoyance. It was until he had filled the several notepads in front of him that he let me go have more checks before I was prescribed with right medication. Think about it.

Talking about Ben Carson, it clicks in my mind that reading and writing should have already transformed this very author, if it did so to Ben Carson, and to Osler. "Here," said Dale Carnegie referring to importance of writing. "Here is the point I am trying to make. Neither you nor I nor Einstein nor the Supreme Court of the United States is brilliant enough to reach an intelligent decision without first getting the facts. Thomas Edison knew that. At the time of his death he had 2500 notebooks filled with facts about the problems he was facing.[82]" As the body needs exercises, I believe you and I need reading and writing not only for sharpness, but indeed the health of our mind. Abu Bakar was right. "Thinking is the food of the mind." In the same line, he aptly said, "knowledge is the life of the mind."

---

[82] Dale Carnegie; *How To Stop Worrying And Start Living* page 40-41

Besides, if you think about it, we need more of mental exercise than that of the body for truly the mind governs the body. A Novel Idea suggests rightly that books are the quickest and most constant of friends; they are the most accessible and wisest of counselors, and the most patient of teachers!"[83]

As for writers our message doesn't fade away. It can be preserved and reread and perhaps most importantly experienced simultaneously by great numbers of men and women across all sexes, races, religions, nations, and ages in places and spaces near and far. In Pecuniary terms, a diligent writer's success is just a mouse click away! But truly for most true writers there is nothing great as to wake up one day and find that you are truly a published writer. For such few honest writers and authors writing is itself more valuable than material or financial gains thereof. It is the noblest thing noble men and women—men and women who have the best interests of the others and the future generations at heart. And the reason is plain. When the books are opened, mines of wisdom are laid bare and set before all worthy men and women who wish to change their lives—men and women who are still struggling to free themselves—and other people around them—from the iron chains of ignorance and poverty. Indeed Clarence Day couldn't be more right. "The world of books is the most remarkable creation of man; nothing else that he builds ever lasts. Monuments fall; nations perish; organizations grow old and die out after an era of darkness. New races build others; but in the world of books are volumes that live on still as young and fresh as the day they were written, still telling men's hearts of hearts of men centuries dead."

Reading and writing therefore, together, form one of the most important sources of knowledge—how one can gain knowledge for himself and how it can be passed on. Knowledge is transcendental and transgenerational. That's why no one becomes a professor without reading and writing or publishing scholarly works. This criterion is very crucial if someone has to be truly academic. Why. If one has to teach others he has to keep abreast with ever emerging changes. He has to remain at the top and on the go. For this to happen, one has to gather, conceptualize and record his lessons or new insights. One of the key qualities apostles of the messiah had to write—they kept on writing a number of epistles to deliver the message home and teach lessons. The companions of Prophet Mohammad recorded

---

[83] *August 2010 Dar Guide p.50*

his teachings in what today we hail as one of the official teachings of this religion—the hadith. Tony Blair, President Clinton, G.W. Bush and Julius Nyerere—among others leaders—published books when their terms of office were over, endeavoring to fill gaps, to make up for what they couldn't accomplish.

Recently Fidel Castro materializing on his first ever public appearance after a long time in exclusion after a long illness wouldn't come out with nothing for his citizens. He had the best gift for future of Cuba, and for himself, a lifetime accomplishment. What was it? In his pair of jeans he presented it. What was it? It was a book with a thousand pages, a book with ideas his publishers had to convey in two volumes. The reporter hinted that the renewed Castro looked gratified than ever before. What did he say about it? He said jubilantly that that was his gift to the Cuban people. He accentuated that he was exceedingly contented to have finally accomplished that feat. He would finally rest in peace knowing the cause for which he dedicated all his life would live on.

Paul apostle and Mwalimu Nyerere present leaders who constantly reminded their audiences about their goals and roles in life through writing—aside from speeches. We are constantly reminded of how to really live, the real importance of self-reliance through Emerson's self-reliance. Through Shakespeare, the early English civilization—and thereupon the future's—has been neatly wrapped up and preserved even for our generation and generations to come. Ezra Pound was right. Literature is news that stays news. Joseph Stalin said *Writers are the engineers of the human souls*. Thomas Carlyle said that *Literature is the thought of the thinking men*. John Wolfgang von Goethe said that: *The decline of literature indicates the decline of the nation.* Ben Carson's book *Think Big* sums it up thus: "I want to be a baseball player, lawyer, a Neurosurgeon, president of the United States, and a writer. And in that order!"

Probably paraphrased from Cicero's Ad Atticum 4.8: "postea vero quam Tyrannio mihi libros disposuit mens addita videtur meis aedibus", which means, "Moreover, since Tyrannio has arranged my books for me, my house seems to have had a soul added to it," which means: "A room without books is like a body without a soul." The impact of writing quite beats me! I met Julius Mitinje, an acquaintance of the author and his brother's, when I'd just accomplished my first three books and was about to go back to working. He commented about something I consider genuinely as a reality. He said I would make an ideal worker, a productive employee. I was purposeful and intended to see life and productivity at workplace improving.

You can probably understand importance of reading and writing from Desiderius Erasmus. Why? How? Here is his astounding remark about how reading was important to him. He said that: *When I get a little money, I buy books; and if any is left, I buy food and cloths.* Born in a log cabin and working as a grocery store clerk, a young unlearned American man found himself in presence of a set of unclaimed items among which lay some law books. He bought nothing else but the books which he read devouring them with the vengeance of a fat hungry nursing lioness in the Serengeti. A few years later he became a lawyer. His upward journey didn't end there. Guess what! He claimed the highest office in the greatest nation of the time down to ours. You already know that office. He became president of the United States of America only a few years later. His writing and speeches distinguished him as nothing else but a philosopher. You must have heard about him—I am sure. His name is Abraham Lincoln.

What is really happening on the ground? Kids are encouraged to pursue sports and entertainment than education. We build interest and affluence with short term benefits forgoing association with education. As a result, serious studies appear boring and meaningless in eyes of our children. Just as much fault, however," writes Ben Carson in Think Big "is our allowing science to come across as boring and uninvolving. We put too little money into true education preferring to spend larger and larger amounts on football and basketball. Favorite nonfiction TV fare centers around programs such as Lifestyles of the rich and Famous and …Home Videos…," laments Ben Carson. "We find virtually nothing from those who want to make our environment comfortable, provide us with fantastic inventions and to your knowledge and encourage research so that we can live longer and healthier lives," counseled Ben Carson, "I'm not opposed to popular entertainment," he continued, " I do however, at least urge balance…crying "Here's the treasure chest of the world, the public library or a bookstore."

Are we in Tanzania any better? When I look at our priorities, I marvel. I marvel at the magnitude at which we import into the country the famous entertainers and artists thus promoting art and entertainment. I'm not opposed to entertainment but if we brought into the country Dr. Ben Carson or even Bill Gates and Steve Jobs and learned from them, acquiring such things as character and attitude that made them special we would reap more than tenfold. The entertainers or entertainment in general is not claptrap on the whole. But they only provide short term benefits whereas writers and experts and inventors offer long term benefits not to one person but they create lasting impact and role models.

In his book Think Big Ben Carson stresses that: "People with high visibility or great influence in our society have a responsibility to improve the society. Such individuals frequently have significant insights concerning the necessary developmental factors involved in success. The acquisition of sound in-depth knowledge is clearly one of the most important factors that these individuals should feel a responsibility to stress. To do otherwise is not only selfish and irresponsible but unwise because if they allow the society to deteriorate their offspring will also suffer the consequences. Because I feel strongly about this I want to go on record with as strong statement: if we would spend on education half the amount we currently lavish on sports and entertainment we could provide complete and free education for all students in this country. The dividends that we would ultimately reap would be phenomenon. America (or Tanzania for that matter) would quickly rise to prominence as an intellectual nation. Once again we would be the nation that the rest of the world yearns to imitate in terms of creativity and economic prosperity…Students who excel academically read extensively!"[84] This is my massage to both the parents and students. I'll repeat it, "Students who excel academically read extensively!"

THE ROLE OF THE GOVERNMENT AND MEDIA IN PROMOTING READING AND WRITING CULTURE

The government has a responsibility in building a reading and writing culture. Sadly, the government and corporations in many countries do not only take the back seat in building this culture, but also they lavishly fund sports and entertainment by far than activities that support reading and writing. the ideal leader should shout aloud with a clear message that reading or generally education is a key activity if we have transform our lives as individuals and the nation as a whole, whereas people behind promotion of reading and writing (in any discipline) are the true role models as persons. Books give us positive thinking. They guide us into further reading or into other sources of knowledge. A better reading in the

---

[84] *Paraphrased from Think Big by Ben Carson*

end produces better readers, readers who become better leaders in the true sense of leadership, i.e. in terms of knowledge and character.

Mwalimu Nyerere is undoubtedly one of such leaders. And this is not something I have concocted. Writing in remembering the greatness of this personality in the Dar es Salaam Guide magazine for November 2008, Saidi Ibrahim wrote thus: Mwalimu spent most of his time reading, writing and learning. He, Mwalimu believed that the purpose of going to the university was to learn and acquire more and broader knowledge and not to read and pass exams—for he knew he would pass anyway. As a result? We produced for ourselves the great statesman and a great role model. Abraham Lincoln and Thomas Jefferson add to the tally. If these are old timers, think of Dr. Ben Carson. Think of Barak Obama. Truly I cannot enumerate all the advantages human societies and individuals gain from reading and writing. Take patriotism for instance. While many people know that we are probably a less patriotic people, few actually know why. No un-informed citizen is ever patriotic—let alone hardworking! This is the secret only known to few! That's why it is the mission of this author and this work to make this nation a reading, writing, hardworking and a patriotic nation.

We cannot bring about the culture of reading and writing, unless we begin with students in our schools. The nation or the government can promote reading by investing in infrastructures that support this endeavor. The government can as well identify and support our local writers through access to capital and promotional platforms, such as book fairs and national awards for publishers or literary works, as we see our government promoting music and musicians or beauty and beauty queens, things that are of far less importance when compared to reading and writing. Such fairs can be used as a national platform to display and glorify the local talents for instance during any national or international exhibition. The government should go further by enacting laws and by laws requiring all schools to store books by local authors. Government ministries, our embassies and state house should keep in their libraries every one of the local books. They should find means to provide for reading among all offices and workplaces. The government can also provide training and development besides sponsoring locals in international book fares and all others exhibitions.

The ministry of education should encourage the use of the local home grown books into the education system. The ministries of Foreign affairs and East Africa must take the books and writers to the Diaspora. The recent unfavorable international contracts signed by our leaders, men and women we can call elites, well, in connection with chief Mangungo who sold the nation to the Germans by signing a document he couldn't read besides the processes involving the constitutional reforms have helped to put the importance of reading and writing in the right perspective. If we cannot read the contracts or write and read our own constitution, should we then hire the Ugandans, Rwandans or Kenyans to come down and help us? Only thinking of it already shames me!

Reading and writing competitions not only among schools and students but also adults should be encouraged and funded. Winner in national secondary schools essays completion, the author himself knows how a generation ago reading and writing were highly valued and financed among our schools in the country. A Novel Idea, a renowned book seller suggests rightly that books are the quickest and most constant of friends; they are the most accessible and wisest of counselors, and the most patient of teachers![85] It is no wonder St. Augustine Secondary School in Dar es salaam, Tanzania chose Tolle Lege, or Take and Read as its motto!

To develop the rational person, schools must teach, as their role, the children to read. In the early American society reading and writing together formed the most important subject for civil spiritual and moral grounds. Indeed legislation was passed in 1642 requiring parents and guardians of children to make certain that their charges could read and understand in general the principles of a decent living. In 1647 an act was passed requiring every town of fifty or more families to appoint reading and writing teachers.[86] Indeed reading and writing culture was necessity if a person or society has to develop. Einstein said "...knowledge must continually be renewed by ceaseless effort, if it not be lost. It resembles a stature of marble which stands in the desert and is continuously threatened with burial by the shifting sand. The hands of service must always be at work, in order that the marble continue to shine in the sun. To these

---

[85] *August 2010 Dar Guide p.50*

[86] *Allan C. Ornstein and Francis P. Hunkins, Curriculum Foundations, Principles and Issues 3rd Edition p. 63*

serving hands, mine shall also belong.[87] But that simply doesn't say it all. I mean the above importance of reading and writing doesn't say it all. Because of the nature in which the written word can liberate and elevate man, in the slave America, the children of the black slaves were forbidden to read or write. Why? Let's see!

Ornstein and Hunkins (1998 p. 64*)* only added that) and were relegated as the underclass of the plantation system. But it was more than that. If they knew how to read and write, they would fight and rid themselves with the status of the underclass and of the oppressive ancient Slave American plantation system. Teaching a person to read and write is, in fact, the enterprise of stimulating inquiry— the strength of mind of questioning, the spirit of asking Why Not?—and therefore stirring the inherent rational powers of the learner. Reading and writing can transform and transmit the culture of society as it prepares the learner for the changing world inspiring the learner to recognize that reality has already changed and is always changing.

SLAVERY AND THE MAKING OF AMERICA
When I say reading and writing is an important quality I mean it. Erasmus didn't reach a decision to proclaim his conclusions about reading and writing as a result of mere sport. To rationalize what we say, let's review the ACTS against education of slaves South Carolina in 1740 and Virginia in 1819 cited in William Goodell: The American slave code in theory and practice pt 2 New York; America and foreign anti slavery society 1853 dinsmore documentation classics in American slavery.[88]

DOCUMENT DESCRIPTION:
Fearing the black literacy would prove a threat to the slave system—which relied on slaves' dependence on the masters—whites in many colonies instituted laws forbidding slaves to read or write and making it a crime for others to teach them.

TRANSCRIPT:

---

[87] *Einstein on education in 1954:gabrielatardea-development.blogspot.com/2010/01/albert-eisntein-on-knowledge-phylosophy.htlm?m)*

[88] *Adapted from http: //www.dinsdoc.com/goodell-1-2- 6 htm.*

Excerpts from South Carolina Act of 1740
whereas, having slaves taught to write, or suffering them to be employed in writing may be attended with great inconveniences; Be it enacted that all and every person and persons whatsoever ,who shall hereafter teach or cause any slave or slaves to be taught to write, or shall use or employ any slave as a scribe, in any manner of writing whatsoever, hereafter taught to write, for every such person or persons shall, for every such offense forfeit the sum of one hundred pounds, current money.

Excerpts from Virginia Revised Code of 1819
That all meetings or assemblages of slaves, or free Negros or Mulatoes mixing or associating with such slaves at any meeting—house or houses, … in the night; or at any SCHOOL OR SCHOOLS for teaching them READING OR WRITING, either in the day or night for whatsoever pretext, shall be considered and deemed UNLAWFUL ASSEMBLY; and any justice of the county, &C, where in such an assemblage shall be either from his own knowledge, or information of others, of such assemblage ,&c. may issue his warrant, directed to any sworn officer or officers, authorizing him or them to enter such house or houses where such assemblages, &C., may be, for the purpose of apprehending or dispensing such slaves, and to inflict corporal punishment on the offender or offenders, at the discretion of any justice of the peace, not exceeding twenty lashes.

Well, does this astound you? Several African Americans faced even more severe punishments among which some were executed or poisoned only for teaching their family members how to read and write. Truly this revelation demonstrates how reading and writing as an ideal is indeed the powerhouse. "The enemies of a people," said Thomas Sankara, "are those who keep them in ignorance!" And this is no fiction. You can read the whole matter for yourself at (www.pbs.org/*wnet/slavery/exe*perience/*education/docs/docs1.html*).

12. THE IDEAL SCHOLAR DOES NOT ONLY HAVE A DEFINITE NOBLE PURPOSE OR GOAL IN LIFE, BUT HE ALSO AIMS HIGHER

> *"If you do what you love you stay young!"* —Omma, an Indonesian elderly lady in interview with BBC Outlook Program Jan-Feb 2016

With self-awareness as his virtue, a person who knows that he was not born by accident or as a result of the mere sport by the gods, but one born for a mission, the ideal scholar is a person with a definite concise purpose or goal in life.

A MAN WITH NO PURPOSE
Say what you want to say, but without purpose in life there is no life. A very good example of a man with no purpose—an unfortunate situation in which we find most of today's youth—is the man I personally met in Kigoma, the land of Lake Tanganyika. I worked with Tanzania Breweries at the time. The moment of truth—the moment that would give me leads toward a kind of a purposeless person he was happened at a promotion session for our new beer brand—Bia Bingwa. During the happy hour, we served our customers with free beer—and a lot of it. What's more, this was a tasting session to introduce the brand. Not everybody took the advantage of the event? No! One person in particular, consulted his watch in the middle of event and— to the amazement of many, excused himself and left only after he had had only two bottles. After we had closed the promotion, and that was the same day, the same evening, I bought a couple of beer to the customers who were still there for it was near my home in Mjimwema before I went home to bed.

Now the next day, as I drove to the office, the next morning, not far from the same grocery store, before me I saw something unusual. It was a figure that appeared like a dead body. It laid half way on the road and its other half, in the ditch! I put a foot on the breaks and got out of the car. I wasn't going to kill him even if it was a dead body already. My religion and conscience are against it. As I recall the event, I feel proud not to have been a disciple of Jihad John. Well, he wasn't dead afterall. Lucky him! He was breathing his last—I told myself. He was conscious. Who was he? I recognized his face. I recognized his clothes. It was him! The same man whom I'd offered a couple of free beer a night before—both during and after the promotion. I regret it of course, for I am partly taking the blame for over dosing this innocent man, but he had responsibility over himself, over his soul. So he hadn't managed to make it home! A few people came to the scene and helped me unload him fast and first from the road.

Yet after he was raised from dead, he fell back in the ditch. It was the baptism of the cold albeit dirty water that resurrected him. To the amazement of everyone, he began staggering on the road albeit the road to nowhere. I went back to my car and I heard someone cursing saying, "what a loser!" He was a loser indeed—like everyone with no goal in life! I wrote this chapter and book because I believe that if we can guide every child and every adult to identify and affirm his calling, we can help and lead each one to his or her true and noble goal in life. When we do this, when one realizes this judiciousness, he has reached a point where he will realize his powers over his aspirations. Indeed that's why a person who has a goal in life never fails.

A MAN WITH A MISSION IN LIFE
Whereas by now some of my readers already reckon that a man who has a mission to accomplish always wins, few actually know why. He wins not because of hereditary. No. He wins because he knows what he wants and goes out for it. He pursues his goal with the vengeance of a hungry breastfeeding lioness. He never hangs out for nothing like the Kigoma loser. A winner is not like a hyena. A hyena, because of its failure to plan its own life, has a tendency of escorting a walking man hoping the hands will somehow fall off. Potential winners have obsession to win. Take Serena Williams or Ronaldo de Lima, for instance. When winners succeed, when they win, they don't simply shout or punch the air. Not only Ronaldo, but also Serena wept publicly unashamed after her first victory in her series of attempted comeback after long series of injuries, and wept as an infant. That's what all the greats do. They burn with desire to win.

When the averages already are brooding the winners already dream and plan and work toward their comeback.

Does this apply to school or work performances? Very much so! Students who pass at the top of their classes aren't necessarily or always different from the others by birth. They have no better tools at their disposal. No! They aren't even necessarily the genii. Employees who exceed their targets or expectations are not always people with greater talents or the ones with the finest tools or resources. They simply have obsession to achieve a goal—to make a mark. They are habitually the people who know they do what they do for their own good. Such people know they depend on their present commitments, be that the school or employer. They know to get what they want they have to give their all and so they gather momentum to stand on their feet and acquire whatever they wanted in life—in that very moment—as they work toward bigger goals. If someone tells you I am not working hard because I am not in my kind of job or vocation, or because my boss hates me, he is nothing but a loser. He is a loser even if he asks you to "wait and see when I am in my element." Don't believe him. Don't even waste your time to wait to see. He will never change unless he begins to change from that same moment when he recognizes that he is not in his kind of job or vocation; when he recognizes that his boss doesn't favor him. This man will not change unless he endeavors to seek or identify—and pursue—what he wants in life. And now here is the question. What do you want in life? We will come back to that.

OPRAH, SHARUK KHAN AND FORTUNE

Born in, and surrounded by people who had surrendered to poverty and mediocrity, Oprah Winfred set her sight to bigger things. As a young girl, her grandmother endeavored to train Oprah to conform, and live the standard average life. She didn't agree with her granny. She had her bigger plans and knew where she was heading for. Recalling one event, in her own words Oprah said: "I remember a specific moment, watching my grandmother hang the clothes on the line, and her saying to me, 'you are going to have to learn to do this,' and me being in that space of awareness and knowing that my life would not be the same as my grandmother's life." Probably Miss Winfred's example is farfetched! But that's almost what Fortune did. That's what you too ought to do no matter what the people around you think, do or say. And I know this is true because Fortune is my own brother. When he curiously failed to impress in his junior school exams, he didn't shrink when mother confronted him. Instead, knowing himself too well than anyone else does, with faith in himself and devotion to big dreams he called "Jumboism" he didn't shrink one bit despite his apparent disappointing performance. Indeed he said to mother: *"Utaona!"* Just one word! *You will see!* I was astonished by his response at the time for I was there. But that is how though he did a far less impressive work then, he went on to sit at the top his class at high school. And he didn't end there. At the time of graduation at the University of Dar es Salaam he was at the top of his class. How impressive that was! And that's not all about his trajectory—his Jumboism. Whereas everybody else settled for a small piece of land, or an average bungalow, he got for himself several acres of vast land, and built a story building—something out of ordinary I must say. Did he have more resources at his disposal than the rest at the time? A big NO!

Truly, it really doesn't matter where you are now. All that matters is where you are going. And that is in the mind. It doesn't matter who you are today but who you want to be tomorrow. Also you can't establish who you want to be if you don't know who you are today. Not all winners began as winners. But winners know they would somehow win. Asked about his successes, despite all odds, how he made it to the top as a Bollywood Actor, one closing in on the ranks of the Bollywood maestro, Amitah Bachan, a feat few even dream of ever entertaining , Sharuhk Khan answered: "I always felt I could win." The secret? Why? Because he knew what he wanted—and wanted big things—and did what he liked to do and be. You cannot win in, or thrive at anything you despise—something you don't enjoy doing. And there are reasons for this. Because a potential winner has a major goal or purpose in life, one that is noble and big, a dream he is so much fond of, he will give his all to make it happen.

Almost everybody has heard of St. Bernard. What made him special to be canonized a saint? Travelling along the shores of Lake Leman, and noticing neither the azure of the waters nor the luxuriance of the vines, nor the radiance of the mountains with their robe of sun and snow, but bending a thought-burdened forehead over the neck of his mule, burdened by the sins of the world and the judgment day, (he was) unaware that they(the shores of Lake Leman, the azure of the waters, the luxuriance of the vines, he radiance of the mountains with their robe of sun and snow) were sight worthy,[89] he only focused on his mission and alert only on this one mission of serving God, and saving his soul; but blind, and deaf and numb in all

---

[89] *A metaphor adapted http://history-world.org/renaissance.htm*

other things. Think of that intensity! Can such a man fail? No! Naturally he will accomplish anything he sets out to do, get and be. Married couples can go back in time and recall the concentration they bestowed on the sheer desire of being together. If they do so, they can probably learn to transmute the same experience and energy in achieving anything they want. And this is no some game of chance? No! It is science. Once a person has a goal, and is obsessed to achieve it, and that goal being a big noble goal, his whole being tends to marshal all his energies and focus toward this one major goal. With all his senses focused upon his goal, it follows naturally that his body, mind and soul will rally behind this one major goal. There is also a supernatural law that then descends to ally with a person with such an attitude especially now that his is a noble goal, such that all forced of nature seem to conspire to pull resources—human, financial and material—and at the same time creating environment that together facilitate the accomplishment of his goal.

Part of the reason why a person who has a major goal in life, a person who dreams big, succeeds is that he habitually reaches the decisions promptly, and of changing these decisions very slowly—the characteristics of almost every single person who ever accumulated a fortune or became successfully in any undertaking he is in. Those who fail in life, without exception, have the habit of reaching the decisions, if at all, very slowly, and of changing these decisions quickly and often.[90] With this attitude such a person wastes time and with little concentration, his accomplishment per unit time is miniature. Behind this flaw there is *Indifference*. What is indifference? Jarrod Kint concluded that: "When faced with two equal tough choices, most people choose the third choice: to not choose!"

Truly, all successful persons are men who have a major fixed goal or purpose over a period of time. That's why they succeed. They have a direction. Without a direction, if you don't know where you are going, you will end up where you are going—which is nowhere! Why? How? Here is how it works. You cannot know where you are going, and therefore you will not know the direction, how can you find the destination? With self awareness and having a major goal in life, you give yourself a sense of direction. By giving yourself the sense of direction, you bring harmony to your body, mind and soul and your whole being will rally behind you and your goals. What's more, and even more tantalizing is the fact that once

---

[90] *Source: Adapted from Napoleon Hill's Think and Grow Rich*

you choose what you want in life and fix your attention on, or by focusing on achieving it, the forces of nature seem to collude to make conditions right for you to succeed. Before you know it, when you are certain of what you want to do, and set out to achieve just that, nature's forces seem to throw themselves beside you, along with them, attracting all favorable agents—agents that are in harmony with your conduct and goals whether human or material, tangible or intangible—which together conspire to accelerate the speed, and facilitate your achieving the goal in question. That's why purposeful, succesful individuals, people with goals in life, eventually succeed, whereas those without, even when the latter are more gifted—in the long run—they fail.

YOU CANNOT HIDE; CAN YOU?
Potential winners, people with big—good or bad—dreams are conspicuous. It is science. A person obsessed with an idea, is noticeably conspicuous. Our intentions or ambitions are transparent. A person with big dreams, big noble dreams, can be spotted from the herd by not only how he walks or talks, but by the aura around him—the energy he radiates. A man walked in a bar and I quickly hid behind a wall and ran away before he shot in the air and asked everybody else to lie down, and collecting their monies and all he and his friends could lay hands on. No one wants a bad guy and seldom can one hide. Coupled with the fact that people and environment tend to fall in love with potential winners, persons with big dreams, and because they are also always on the lookout for such a person since afterall such persons are scarce in supply, they will spot him very easily before they pledge allegiance to him personally and to his mission. How do I know? Here is my testimony. Almost every member of my family and friend who happens to know Nafro, my wife, closely tends to whisper to us saying that we are best suited to each other—and with prayer, I thank God for her. But how did I spot her from a herd? Well, why almost immediately after setting my eyes on her, I asked her hand in marriage—despite all conventional reasons why we shouldn't have married? She accepted despite all reasons against conventions considering that she is from the Mohammedan family and I am Catholic? It is long story. Briefly, a person's character is transparent if you choose to open your eyes—inner eyes! You can read about it on your own in MOHHAMEDANS: VILLAINS OR VICTIMS?

On graduation from the University of Dar es Salaam, the author got hired even before his final results were out. He didn't have to validate his abilities or the impact he would bring to the company by presentation of the mere certificate papers. No. He relocated from one better organization to another and another until eight years later when he resigned for good from being employed without ever having displayed his degree papers. Why? I mean why did he present them papers? He had not yet collected them from the university–where they are still looked after until as I write. How then did they hire him without any papers? When Rajiv shortlisted the author for a final interview for Smith Cline Beecham sales rep position, he whispered to me: "Don't miss the next interview. I know you are going to be selected!" how did he know??? Snyman, a South African regional manager at Tanzania Breweries helped to put that question into context. I can recall that moment as if it is just yesterday. Though there were a couple of newly hired souls in the room, he approached the author after a range of interviews and interactions, and holding my hand firmly he said: "I know you are going to work so hard. I can see it in your eyes!" The author left the company when he served as the deputy sales manager, and the region's employee of the year. So forget that you can fool people.

There's one more thing about this person. Such a person doesn't need supervision from anyone else. He doesn't need it at all. Why? He is a dutiful kind of person who fills his present position. In his present job he is a person who can cover for two or more people. And this is no magic. For unless a person is insane, otherwise if he knows what he gains from his work, something that accomplishes or leads toward accomplishment of his lifetime goals and desires, certainly he will work hard. He will certainly be super productive. A sane person will also recognize that the bottom—drudgery as a result of poverty—isn't a better station wherein to camp for life. If you don't know what you desire in life, if you have not achieved finality of purpose—poverty and drudgery are your only twin foreseeable companions your whole life. Talking about having goals in life, poverty is not one of the goals you should aim for. I have been there. I know what I am talking about. That's why one has to solidify his desire for prosperity i.e., aiming higher and rejecting poverty rather than entertaining indifference to it. This is so important ideal or virtue that we chose to give it enough time and space in our upcoming book, also written as Volume III in this series also titled: A CITY IN YOUR MIND: DREAMS FROM CHILDHOOD!

WHAT WE WANT IN LIFE
The first thing to do if you intend to thrive in whatever you do is to establish what you want to do, get and become. But yes you must have an understanding of what you need to give in return. And so have your wish list before you give them weight to ascertain the scale of preference. With this scale, you will then be able to establish which is high on the list, and

so on. That's how you will rationally make choices between two things. This isn't mere verbalization. It is Economic Science. It is probably why Roy Disney concluded that: "It is not hard to make decisions when you know what you values are!" The foregoing statement wraps in it the definition of what success means to you if you want to make any success. On the contrary Wallace D. Wattles rightly said in his wonderful book Science of Getting Rich: "Once you have clearly formed your vision, the whole matter turns on receiving!"

So, really, what do you want in life? Do you know? Does your traditional classroom teacher, or parents or even superiors at work know what they themselves want? How is this incorporated in our curriculum? I have asked many people during the training sessions, people from all academic levels, but rarely did any register exactly what he wanted in life. That's why though we give general ends we want in life, we know each individual has his specifics when it comes to personal goals-or objectives that lead to such great ends.

WHAT YOU AND I WANT IN LIFE
This is a very crucial moment in your life! I suggest that you spend adequate time to ponder about this section. Indeed no matter how many times we discuss this matter, every time this comes up you and I ought to give it our maximum attention. These are the reasons why we forgo other luxuries of life to send our children to expensive schools. It is why you and I wake up early in the morning and go to work through the night! So what really do we want in life? It, I mean this question, may look so innocent and simple question but I have, several times without number, asked graduate students among my trainees of our training programs about what they want in life and many failed flat. Some of the author's friends with advanced degrees failed on this one too. To expect much from our present schools or students if our curriculum, education system and teaching methodologies remain as they are today would be self-deception.

Now back to the sessions, this is how I conducted myself and the questioning. I always give pens and papers or notebooks to all trainees before the session. Then first thing I ask them—under strict timeline—to answer to the following questions after which every question they exchange their answer sheets and become one another's examiners. Here are the questions. What's your name? In which class are you? Which course are you doing? Who is the world footballer of the year? Who is your favorite teacher? What's your favorite food? Name the person other than your family whom you love most? Who is the president of the country? And that of the US? Now to all these questions they get the answers right and on time. However for the following question, there is a little twist. Most get their answers on time but most of their answers are wide off the mark. And the question is this: Mention five things you want in life. Why they fail? Take your time and give me your answers too.

Now these are the typical answers I ordinarily get. "I want a car." "I want money." "I want a job." "I want to be a manager at work." "I want," well you can enumerate as many such types of answers! It doesn't matter how long our list is. These answers are wrong. Now how do you expect a person who doesn't know what he wants in life to know what he wants in school? How do you expect him to make a difference in his life and the lives of the others and environment around him? And you cannot blame them. Their teachers too seldom know what they want and therefore seldom do they know what they teach or to be a little fair to them, they don't know why they teach what they teach. Here now are the things you and I want in life. Here, as I have already mentioned, are the reasons why we forgo other luxuries of life to send our children to expensive schools. It is why you and I wake up early and go to work through the night! It is why we go to church! So what really do we want in life?

We want, well, that's cheap. We crave breathing fresh air; we crave food and drink (not beer); we want shelter and warmth; we crave sleep and comfort; we die for freedom, safety and peace of mind (not drugs). We also crave harmony with the employer, co-workers and neighbors; we want business success or promotion at work; we want wealth, affluence, prosperity; we crave love and belonging-- being cared for or having somebody devote his or her time and attention to your needs. We crave familiness, affection, strong relationships, etc. We want to raise healthy, bright and happy children; we want friendship and being surrounded by true friends. We want harmony with ourselves; we want to have self control—to be in charge of our own persons and to keep our bad desires in check. We crave victory and accomplishment—accomplishing everything good we set out to do, get and be.

We crave affection and harmony in marriage. (Now if you are unmarried, skip the following sentence.). We are rather ready to die for marital gratification and contentment it fetches (a reason probably why female folks weep more bitterly than their male counterparts when their spouses are called to heaven). We want a name, influence, fame, recognition. We crave lasting legacy—a legacy that can envelope our children and their next generation. Aside from all these successes, we want to be healthy and to live forever young—if that was possible. We also, and with most touching sentiments, we crave afterlife. We know people we can call whatever names, people who are ready to die, to take their own lives away if believing it can pay for their ticket, and book and a nice spot in, heaven. Think about that kind of audacity! Truly if you don't want these things in your life, things that give your happiness and make other people's lives better —then stop here! Don't waste your time. This book is not for you.

MASLOW'S HIERARCHY
Developed from Maslow's Hierarchy of Needs, here're human wants or what we want in life. But before we describe them or rather streamline them, here's the typical Maslow's Hierarchy of Needs as reads from http://www.businessballs.com/maslowhierarchyofneeds5.pdf. Biological and Physiological needs: basic life needs—air, food, drink, shelter, warmth, sex, sleep, etc. Safety needs: protection, security, order, law, limits, stability etc. Belongingness and love needs envelope family, affection, relationships, work group, etc. Esteem needs: achievement, status, responsibility, reputation. Self-actualization: personal growth and fulfillment.

Here let us now realign the human needs based on Maslow. Basic life needs: these are four-fold. First, breathing and presence of fresh air. Secondly, you need food and drink. These two go together. Thirdly, shelter, warmth, sleep and comfort. Fourthly, physiological and psychical needs specifically spiritual or personal internal harmony and a very noticeable need, a need that is only reserved for the married adults, of course discriminately excluding Roman Catholic priests, bishops, the pope, nuns and monks, i.e., sexual gratification which too covers affection. Safety needs: This is generally a state in which or a place where you are safe and not in danger or at risk. In its basic definition it is security, protection and wellbeing etc. In its secondary level, it covers order, law and stability, etc. The first class of safety needs is what we really need but the second group is important because it is what maintains the first class of safety needs. Love and belonging: Love can be simply defined here as being cared for or having somebody devote his time and attention to you in ensuring the rest of your needs are attended to etc. Esteem needs: accomplishment or achievement, status, responsibility, reputation. Self-actualization: personal growth and fulfillment. It may also include the craving for continuation of a safer and secure prosperous life for oneself and his or her offspring. Afterlife: When we say continuation of life whereas we know we die at some point in time we mean humans crave for an everlasting happy living.

You realize, don't you, that the above are engines of whatever we do here on earth? They are the catalysts of whatever emotions we bear and actions that are transmuted from these emotions. They are indeed what we interpret in the material or worldly possessions and accomplishments we crave or achieve in the physical form.

WHAT DOES SUCCESS MEAN TO YOU?
We all know people who die young from the workplace tension striving to climb the career ladder. We also know other who die young from hypertension because they stretching themselves to the limit striving to turn a business into a "world Class" organization, people who don't their spouses anymore, not to mention their children and themselves too. What does really success mean to you? In his wonderful book, The Power to Influence People, Dr. O.A. Batista aptly said: "There are two common ways that people mistakenly look upon success. 1. They feel they are successful as soon as they are sure that others look upon them as being successful. 2. They assume they are successful because they feel superior to others." But no one succeeds big time by centering his goal on other people's goals. The center of your goals is but you! Your biggest competitor today is, but you! To be best, to earn the best, to perform the first best like Usain Bolt, the Jamaican reigning world Champion and today's superman, an all-time champ revealed his secret of victory and why he regularly seems to be in the race of his own even though the running lanes are parked with other top world sprinters, fellow national and world class world champs. This is his secret also even when he breaks world records some of which are his own, is because he competes with but himself! I recently watched the London Olympics and the commentator remarked that Usain Bolt didn't bother about the others. His eyes were on the clock competing with his own record—striving to break it. "Envy," said Yevgeny Yevtushenk,"envy is insult to oneself." Muhammad Ali was right: "Champions aren't made in gyms. Champions are made from something they have deep inside them: A desire, a dream, a vision. They have to have last-minute stamina, they have to be a little faster; they have to have the skill and the will. But the will must be stronger than the skill."

No wonder he cannot fail. He cannot fail simply because he has a goal in life, and is devoted to that goal, a goal for which he is ready to lay down his life. When a person knows exactly what he wants in life and benefits accruing from such an endeavor, whether it is a gain he gets immediately or over time—which is the value he gets in return, when he knows the cost of losing it, but when as well he has full knowledge of the cost involved, the value of what he has to give back, he will not sleep but work hard until he gets it into his obsession. I can assure you such a person will also work hard to retain it. Notice also that because he knows why he chose that goal in life he is committed to whatever he has chosen to do and be and gives it his all.

When I say the cost of what he has to give, I want you to consider the fact that few individuals who excel to the max, are only those who are ready to give even their lives in return. And this is no hoax or some form of amusement. Call to mind the reverence Socrates and Jesus retain to date. These two souls had had opportunity to escape death, but chose to die rather than tarnish their convictions. But since that seems a little ancient and farfetched, let's take another example. Almost everybody knows how Nelson Mandela was idolized across all continents of the earth, how he was celebrated amongst all races and all tribes; how he was revered among all nations whether they were Christian, Hindu, Mohammdan or non religious. Why? Why did the earth get paralyzed by Nelson Mandela—as he once personally asked the interviewer? Here is why. He had given not only his career or family. He had given his all. For a democratic and free society in which all persons lived together in harmony and with equal opportunities, Mandela told the jury: "I am prepared to die." Now tell me. How can the world fail to lie low or tremble before such unprecedented devotion—the kind of devotion? Now here is a question. How can a person with such devotion—solid devotion—in his present state of mind fail to make a mark whether in the classroom or at work? You wanted an answer? That is why the earth got paralyzed!

CONCLUSION

The ideal scholar doesn't only have a major goal in life, he has the burning desire to succeed, an obsession for prosperity. He is not indifferent to poverty. He aims higher and loathes poverty rather than entertaining indifference to it. That's why he will always acquire anything he sets out to achieve. But beyond having goals in life, average goals, or merely having obsession to acquire what he sets out to do or achieve, his aims are big noble goals—goals that are human and environment friendly. It is not thus enough to have a goal when that goal is so too ordinary, or even evil. The same goes for an obsession for an ordinary goal or even an evil plot. This goal should not be only big but also a noble one. This is what differentiates winners from losers. It differentiates heroic scholars from mediocre scholars. This is what differentiates men from animates. It is what differentiates civilized men from heathen. It is the quality that separates top winners from average ones. Failure to grapple with this secret is the reason why some of our highly educated men and women remain in the middle when they should be leading in their chosen vocations.

It might not be one of the greatest testimonies on the part of the author to cite such simple exploits, I know that! And though we have highlighted a set of things we want life, we are going to revisit what success should mean to you or me shortly before we wrap this book up. Also notice that though I refer to a few of my long time accomplishments, it is not about me. It is rather about you, yes you, the reader. That's why these examples are recalled—however humble they may appear to be. Having said so, let me now announce that it was because of immeasurable desire to prosper, a desire that was enveloped by a sense of taking risk, the risk that was persistent, but one coupled with self-advancement that made it possible for the author to rise from obscurity to become probably the first among his peers to appear on television when he became a brand manager for Carlsberg. It must not, however, go unstated that though he trembled before the camera for the first time at the news conference, something no one amongst his peers had ever done before—and if there is one, he has skipped my mind; yes he trembled before the camera when he first held a press conference, but he was alright a little later having recollected his experience in public appearance drawing out from his experience as the main speaker and chairman during inter-school debating sessions at Kahororo Secondary School, and later as school secretary general at Ihungo High School. That's what having a goal in life, a goal that is associated with burning desire, persistent effort and determination to succeed, the obsession to transform and elevate a person's life and the lives of the people around him can do to you. It was the same thing that helped the author to acquire one job after another when many were struggling in interviews. It was the same desire that afforded the job that placed at the author's disposal a personal car as a sales development officer when many thought it was impossible. It was the same desire that made the young man in the author's person rent a big house in the top end neighborhood and acquire a television set and a refrigerator when many happily—which is the issue at stake—settled for any affordable single rooms without electricity or flowing water.

Indeed, as humble as these testimonies may seem to be to you, but it is the spirit embedded in such humble dreams whose accomplishments help us to become who we are today. It is as such that the author resigned from a good job in the upcountry to move forever to the city when many didn't choose where to work or live. It was the same pursuit of quality that led the author to publish his books in The States when many settle with something else. And what of the choice of your spouse? When many men settle for an average spouse whom they can "control" do you push the boundaries and select a learned person, or advance her? It was the same spirit that pressed the author to resign as a sales manager to become national brand manager. It was the same spirit that pressed the author to resign as a marketing manager to write books—and create training and educational programs such as the one being presented to you now. It is in such small humble accomplishments that we connect the dots in pursuit for bigger things. "The tragedy of life," said Dr. Benjamin Mays "doesn't lie in not reaching your goal. A (real) tragedy lies in not having a goal to reach for. It's not a calamity to die with dreams unfulfilled. It is a calamity not to dream. It is not disaster to be unable to capture your ideal…it is a disaster to have no ideal to capture. It is not disgrace not to reach the stars, but it is a disgrace to have no stars to reach for. Not a failure but low aim is Sin!" aptly said Clarence Day.

Finally, do I still have to explain why the ideal person cannot fail? Do I still have to substantiate why the ideal person is self motivated, focused? Or why he works, or should work hard? Though I don't have to, still I will. "Forget everybody," wrote Bill FitzPatrick in his Action Principles. "Forget Everybody: Not everybody wants to do business with you. Not everybody wants to be your friend. Not everybody wants world peace. Not everybody wants to work hard. Not everybody wants to be president. Not everybody is smart enough to be a rocket scientist. Not everybody is fast enough to run in the Olympics. Who is helped by pretending otherwise?"

13. THE IDEAL SCHOLAR PURSUES SPECIALIZED TRAINING AND IS SELF-TRAINED

> *"Adam Smith pointed out that there were three things that make us more prosperous, in a general sort of way: freedom to pursue our own self-interest; specialization, which he called division of labor; and freedom of trade."* —P. J. O'Rourke

The ideal scholar recognizes and pursues specialization and self-training. Why? Specialized training is a form of training that is targeted. It is specific and spot on. The traditional form of education is more of general knowledge. Linear form of education has failed. Let us see how dictionary.cambridge.org defines it. Linear measurement is relating to length, rather than area or volume. You see. It isn't anything to do with cumulative or rather bulging or radiating form of education but simply crossing a number of years or series. It is something involving a series of events or thoughts in which one follows another one directly.

What is not written here is that the linear form of learning or education rarely goes back to pick up from where it began. It never reconciles itself with the other lives or rather it never reconciles itself with the reality of life even when it is just in the vicinity provided it is on its east or west. Linear form of education is on its track obediently following either its premeditated or predetermined track even when it always is a road that leads but to nowhere. The great writers of the great dictionary added something so spot-on—something the men in guard of the old don't want to hear or put in practice. It says to break the linear thought pattern you need "… mental exercises…designed to break linear thinking habits and encourage the innovation," that is needed to break away. Our youth need to know the truth.

Such truths include the fact that there is budding unemployment. And this cannot be solved in an environment where there are only a handful of job creators—and therefore low job creation. Also the despair on personal incomes is on the rise. There is greater demand for better and new education. They, the youth, don't need—don't need? No! That's not the right word: They hate old school education. They want to know what really drives their lives—what governs prosperity. They abhor the time-consuming, linear form of education.

What is not written here is that the linear form of learning or education rarely goes back to pick up anything from where it began from. It never reconciles itself with the other lives or rather it never reconciles itself to the reality of life even when it is just in the vicinity provided it is on its on its east or west. It is on its track obediently following either its premeditated or predetermined track even when it always is a road that leads to nowhere. The great writers of the great dictionary added something so spot on that I would like to share it with you. This is what the men in guard of the old don't want to hear or put in practice. It says to break the linear thought pattern you need, "…mental exercises…designed to break linear thinking habits and encourage the innovation that is needed for innovation…" *Truly,* our youth need to know what does really drive their lives as a society, but more so and particularly, what drives their individual lives.

Specialized form of education is different from general or traditional education in that it is derived from the need to understand a specific skill or expertise—the skill or experience that aims at a specific end. This is what triggers the concept of self-training as we shall see soon. The general knowledge we receive in classrooms today is different from specialized education in that here education starts and then the student or trainee goes, and often left to fit in. This form of education is limited. Specialized training is boundless and transcendental. That's why it accommodates everyone's talents or calling and goals in one's career or life. We shall however, because of relevance of this concept and connection with one's major goal in life and therefore choice of one's vocation, advance this concept through the upcoming chapters or works in this book or series.

SELF TRAINING
Knowing what he wants, the potential ideal scholar chooses his areas of specialization. Again, though he can't learn it all by himself despite internet and libraries that are bursting with all kinds of education he may need, he will organize and direct his training program. Why? It is he who knows better that anyone else what he needs and how he needs to learn it. That is why indeed the ideal scholar is *typically self-trained*. There is also another reason, and a bigger reason at that. The conventional education,

sadly, rarely concerns itself with such personalized needs; itself beefed up as often one size-fit-all. In need to learn how to enter a specific field of work, or pursuit of one's calling, a calling or vocation that is not, and indeed couldn't, or aptly cannot be, addressed by formal or conventional education, the significance of self-advancement and continued pursuit for education vis a vis time constraint and his urge to make, get and become more and better, the ideal scholar pursues self-training. That is probably why the Phi Delta Kappa Educational Foundation cites specialized knowledge as the 7th quality of a good education.

Aside from developing and availing good environment for specialized training and self training, how do we institute it in our system of life as a society? Someone wants a position in an office be that private or public we should ask him the same question. He or she must prove and provide a detailed and binding commitment to this promise as a token or *promissory note* of his intent before we bid him enter. An investor wants to come to invest in the land we must ask him the same question. He must provide the same elaborate answer—and to the letter—about what he wants to do for the country. Someone applies for higher education must duly explain what he wants to do for the country. Students who boycott in the higher learning institutions are a result of failure of the education system. They, the people, aren't to blame. Do they have specific goals to achieve?

Why then have we remained in the middle when we should be leading? The problem is that we don't specialize in whatever we do. We don't seek further knowledge and skills after we finish schools. Yet conventional education is only general knowledge. It cannot help much in your profession. To sharpen your skills, you have got to specialize and that can only be done by pursuing self training—organizing the kind of education you need commensurate your goals and choice of vocation. Yet do we have the priorities as financiers and leaders at household, workplace and government level? Is there any sure means or machinery to enforce action? Truly, with these revelations, beginning with the awareness that what we miss is to have major concise goal in life and aiming higher, the schools' poor facilities or even the low allowances to higher learning students are not the real problems that should give us sleepless nights. Not even areas from which lasting solution shall come. The problem is twofold; the new culture among the youth in the country and indecision among both leaders and students. Students lack or have altogether lost ambition for everything let alone schooling as the leaders are distanced from real situation. To succeed we have got to have a dream. A dream acts as a map and compass of our direction. Mary Martin was right when she sang: *"If you don't have a dream, if I don't have a dream how are we going to make a dream come true?"*

Our people must be inspired toward self-advancement. They must be assisted to nurture the spirit of self reading as a tool to self-advancement. We need some form of education that our youth as well as adults need during and after formal college education. Such an education must address public speaking, self-employment and innovation. We know people who discover themselves after they drop out whether willingly or by circumstances. Henry Ford had no college education when he invented and brought the modern form of cars to us in his own name. Such individuals need some form of education to bridge their educational gaps and make their impact more profound and far reaching. However the culture of self-advancement and the tradition of reading and writing books as a whole are impossible without developing the obsession for, or obsession for success, prosperity and to be top, to thrive.

Our curriculum must take note of the fact that some students develop during primary or grade school, while others develop their capabilities later in high school. Truly we cannot tell with all confidence what a child at tender age will be. Hence supporting and giving every child a chance to be and choose what he or she can be and a chance to specialize later on can only be advantageous to all. With an army of street children and dropouts we need the kind of a curriculum that addresses special education for such a cadre of our youth. Though this doesn't in any way mean to advocate or promote dropping out of school, and though a mention has been made about it before, but we recall the same question: did you ever know that Albert Einstein was a failure in the formal school system? The great inventor Thomas A. Edison never had any college education. Abraham Lincoln had no formal education having crossed no more than the fourth grade in his education or training, thus serving in a restaurant until when he began reading books. But finally, through self-advancement, he became a great president of the great country and doubtless a philosopher. And the foregoing illustration explains why education and the curriculum must accommodate those in our society that have been academically displaced.

Indeed giving the children and adults a chance to try time and time again is not a favor. The ideal educator or any one engaged in the transformational pedagogy knows that it is his moral duty to encourage the weak and the disadvantaged for afterall they are the majority; and education should never be for the few privileged if it has to transform the society. With the experience of the past when we had fewer schools and colleges the times when many resumed classes and reseated to qualify for further studies, and following the recent extent of dropouts and girls leaving schools on pregnancy, the importance of the efforts to seek ways and means to fast track the return or reappearance of the displaced cannot be more noteworthy. Indeed such dropouts aren't reseaters. They are returnees we should be happy and excited to welcome home in the analogy of the biblical parable of the prodigal son.

Bringing such wrongly condemned folks back into the system is like reclaiming the lost value back into the system and society in general. We must consider that they just passed through schools simply as a routine, or sport, and therefore with no specific goals or dreams to achieve, and therefore naturally they didn't see the meaning of education and hence didn't find any excitement in the classroom, failed and then naturally dropped out. This is why we should offer them a chance to return after they mature and find the need to return. In the same spirit, we must bid enter those young girls who leave school because of pregnancy or the children who do so having lost their parents from HIV/AIDS etc. Education is the only hope for the majority of our people. To do otherwise, I mean to deny the dropouts and returnees a chance to return increases the individual household and the nation's dependant ratio and thus poverty. Resisting the efforts to bid the returnees enter is therefore to choke the possibility of our nation to stand on its feet. It is also important now that we learn from the 2012 and 2013 secondary education results, that we would not even manage to fill a handful of openings amongst our high schools and colleges following perverse school performances. As if that's not all, we have witnessed many stakeholders of education voicing their discontent shouting aloud lamenting that the government has had to doctor the national wide pass marks to accommodate the persistent collapse of schools and school performances. And we must do so for otherwise should we let them stay underutilized or import people from beyond our borders? They are both no better options. Only we must find ways to protect the freshers through alternative grading system that they may not be victimized by the returnees as we safeguard the rights of the returnees to return. To do this is in the interest of the nation, not of the author!

Such efforts ought to include or think of differentiation in pass marks and creation or promotion of special seats for them among existing colleges such as vocational colleges or developing special courses learning from the way the medical department developed courses for clinical officers and assistant medical doctors. Calling them Assistant Medical Officers is nothing but nomenclature. They are indeed medical doctors who for whatsoever reason, they circumstantially couldn't go through formal or linear education. And I speak about this area with experience. I know how a couple of my closest relations now serving as Assistant Medical Officers are worshipped by their patients and employers. Truly it is even unbelievable to narrate how in the medical line, they give their all to their immediate patients and employers in terms of their commitment and passion which together help them achieve a far greater feat than *more* qualified superior medical doctors. In fact some employers and *customers*[91] indicate that our professionals who follow the traditional channels of education albeit with *superior* opportunities and education tend to develop academic arrogance which curtails discharge of their duties. This isn't my creation or cynicism. You can read for yourself such articles as What Do Employers Want From Graduates (escalate.ac.uk/downloads and www.geos.ed.ac.uk/), British Graduates Branded Arrogant... (graduatefog.co.uk). Many Tanzania Graduates Suffer From Certificate Arrogance (www.ippmedia.com), etc.

We must have in place some courses to supplement whatever gaps there are and in the same or different approach reward such returnees. And this is not something idealistic that only this author sits here and *dreams* as a possibility. No! Article 13 of the African Youth Charter—which is part of the United Nations initiatives—indicates that the State Parties should among others: "revitalize vocational education and training relevant to current and prospective employment opportunities and expand access by developing centers in rural and remote areas; …. establishing distance learning centers of excellence; avail multiple access points for education and skills development including opportunities outside of mainstream educational institutions e.g., workplace skills development, distance learning, adult literacy and national youth service programs; allocate resources to upgrade the quality of education delivered and ensure that it is relevant to the needs of contemporary society and engenders critical thinking rather than rote learning; adopt pedagogy that incorporates the

---

[91] *A customer is, in this definition, a person who uses not only goods but services you provide. In an organization settings, there are external customers and internal customers. External customers of an organization are those that not directly connected to that organization and the reverse is generally true with the internal customer; i.e. stakeholders, employers, employees, peers etc.*

benefits of and trains young people in the use of modern information and communication technology such that youth are better prepared for the world of work; encourage youth participation in community work as part of education to build a sense of civic duty; introduce scholarship and bursary programs to encourage entry into post-primary school education and into higher education outstanding youth from disadvantaged communities (and, which is a point that prompted recalling of the African youth charter); promote the equivalence of degrees between African educational institutions to enable the youth to study and work in State Parties..."[92] Need we say more?

We must also find ways to honor and bring on board inventors or innovators and thinkers and writers from different fields. But if we have succeeded in the most sensitive field of medicine or even writing, and I am a witness, how can we fail to do the same in laws, or even engineering? We have Lincoln and Ford for our greatest success stories for the mentioned disciplines respectively. We also have Bill Gates and Steve Jobs as top world class most successful school drop-outs! The foregoing assertion emphasizes availability of motivated teachers and the spirit of apprenticeship as a key factor to big results in schools. Performances in schools for both groups will then reflect at the workplace later when the same trainees enter the labor force. We should recognize that teaching doesn't end when students leave classes. Students must be assisted to choose friends. Parents must also play part in establishing and educating their children in terms of their innate abilities and calling. On the other hand the students and parents have the right to take sides and therefore pursue ideas or paths that seem to be more relevant in responding to their needs. Today students must be taught to desire great successes—to succeed morally and materially—to be independent, self reliant and thus self employed. We have got to encourage them to be self starters, hard workers, and creative or innovative people who team up to get more for everyone involved. We have got to promote self reading and the spirit of self-advancement among our people.

We all are witnesses of how parents seem not to cooperate with our conventional education system. We have seen many parents redirecting their children outside the formal education system. Why? They say: We study and get degrees and get back to streets with no tangible change but

---

[92] *www.africa-union.org*

age and some green or grey sheets of papers you call certificates which are nothing or meaningless as they don't add any value to our livelihood. Why pay such fees? Why waste time in schools? Why waste money and time? Educators must answer to parents who ask: We study and get degrees and get back to streets. Why pay such exorbitant fees—money down the drain? Why waste money and time? Today students must be taught importance and how to acquire knowledge. It begins with the skills to acquire the obsession for success. A potentially successful person craves to be independent, self reliant and self employed. They therefore demand to be trained into being self starters, hard working, creative and innovative. We have got to help them to discern importance of interdependence and the spirit of cooperation. They should be able to team up and work together. This can be done through sports and different games that illustrate significance of working together like football or rugby. The children and the youth ought to be assisted to stand on their feet, think, make choices and decide rightly. Having decided which path to follow, they must be made able to muster courage to pursue or execute their decisions so reached with diligence and perseverance. Such games like scrabble tend to help build a healthy mind and nurture ability to think. We must recognize that a healthy body thrives in healthy mind—and vice versa.

Talking about the pursuit for self-advancement, we can—and indeed must—surely learn from the traditional society. The traditional society taught mainly that what was useful and meaningful to its livelihood commensurate with its environment. The author is not that naïve, however, not to expect the challenge he is apt to face from most of his readers who are pro-modernity. Truth be told: the traditional society had no such formal schools we have in place today. But the society organized itself such that, a farmer learnt how to farm better from within the society. A hunter learnt how to be one from experience. A cattle herder chose his area of specialization. For skeptics, here is my answer: Not everything more modern is equally more relevant to every society. And everything modern began in some crude unconventional way. Search and see. "Modernization," wrote Carmen Jessica De Menech in *Inclusion and the Inuit Experience: The Legacy Of Residential School Perspective In Contemporary Education an essay* featured in *An Exercise in Worldmaking* (2007: 27), "Modernization promotes certain beliefs and ways of doing as superior and 'the right way' just because they are 'modern' (Sutton, 2000:77). It is inherently biased against other ways of learning and teaching." Indeed the ideal education or rather educational experience is determined by the learner's environment. One major reason why self-training should be promoted is our budget constraint. As such self-training is self-help. It is self-reliance.

We can't agree more with Erhard Berner and Benedict Phillips in their paper: LEFT TO THEIR OWN DEVICES? COMMUNITY SELF-HELP BETWEEN ALTERNATIVE DEVELOPMENT AND NEOLIBERALISM. "It is now widely agreed that the poor are not passive in the development process. Participation, once radical and controversial, is now mainstream management theory. Harnessing self-help potential is the order of the day. Properly 'empowered' or at least 'enabled', the poor are assumed to be able to overcome deficits of infrastructure and services and exhaust their tremendous entrepreneurial potential," they said. "...Evidence on the futility of top-down interventions is overwhelming, and a return to government-led development would not help the poor," they concluded albeit emphatically stressing the importance of support and empowerment (http://n-aerus.net/web/sat/workshops/2003/papers/docs/5.pdf).

STEVE JOBS COMMENCEMENT SPEECH AT STAMFORD UNIVERSITY 2005

"I dropped out of Reed College after the first 6 months, but then stayed around as a drop-in for another 18 months or so before I really quit. So why did I drop out? ...I naively chose a college .... After six months, I couldn't see the value in it. I had no idea what I wanted to do with my life and no idea how college was going to help me figure it out. And here I was spending all of the money my parents had saved their entire life. So I decided to drop out ... It was pretty scary at the time, but looking back it was one of the best decisions I ever made. The minute I dropped out I could stop taking the required classes that didn't interest me, and begin dropping in on the ones that looked interesting... And much of what I stumbled into by following my curiosity and intuition turned out to be priceless later on. Let me give you one example...

"Reed College at that time offered perhaps the best calligraphy instruction in the country....Because I had dropped out and didn't have to take the normal classes, I decided to take a calligraphy class .... I learned about serif and san serif typefaces, about varying the amount of space between different letter combinations, about what makes great typography great. It was beautiful, historical, artistically subtle in a way that science can't capture, and I found it fascinating. None of this had even a hope of any practical application in my life. But ten years later, when we were designing the first Macintosh computer, it all came back to me. And we designed it all into the Mac. It was the first computer with beautiful typography. If I had never dropped in on that single course in college, the Mac would have never had multiple typefaces or proportionally spaced fonts. And since Windows just copied the Mac, it's likely that no personal computer would have them. If I had never dropped out, I would have never dropped in on this calligraphy class, and personal computers might not have the wonderful typography that they do.... You have to trust in something — your gut, destiny, life, karma, whatever. This approach has never let me down, and it has made all the difference in my life.

"My second story is about love and loss. I was lucky—I found what I loved to do early in life. Woz and I started Apple in my parents' garage when I was 20. We worked hard, and in 10 years Apple had grown from just the two of us in a garage into a $2 billion company with over 4000 employees. We had just released our finest creation—the Macintosh....and for the first year or so things went well. But then our visions of the future began to diverge and eventually we had a falling out. When we did, our Board of Directors sided with him. So at 30 I was out....I didn't see it then, but it turned out that getting fired from Apple was the best thing that could have ever happened to me. The heaviness of being successful was replaced by the lightness of being a beginner again, less sure about everything. It freed me to enter one of the most creative periods of my life.

"During the next five years, I started a company named NeXT, another company named Pixar, and fell in love with an amazing woman who would become my wife. Pixar went on to create the world's first computer animated feature film, *Toy Story*, and is now the most successful animation studio in the world. In a remarkable turn of events, Apple bought NeXT, I returned to Apple, and the technology we developed at NeXT is at the heart of Apple's current renaissance. And Laurene and I have a wonderful family together. I'm pretty sure none of this would have happened if I hadn't been fired from Apple. It was (an) awful tasting medicine, but I guess the patient needed it. Sometimes life hits you in the head with a brick. Don't lose faith. I'm convinced that the only thing that kept me going was that I loved what I did. You've got to find what you love. And that is as true for your work as it is for your lovers. Your work is going to fill a large part of your life, and the only way to be truly satisfied is to do what you believe is great work. And the only way to do great work is to love what you do. If you haven't found it yet, keep looking. Don't settle. As with all matters of the heart, you'll know when you find it. And, like any great relationship, it just gets better and better as the years roll on. So keep looking until you find it. Don't settle.

"My third story is …..When I was 17, I read a quote that went something like: "If you live each day as if it was your last, someday you'll most certainly be right." It made an impression on me, and since then, for the past 33 years, I have looked in the mirror every morning and asked myself: "If today were the last day of my life, would I want to do what I am about to do today?" And whenever the answer has been "No" for too many days in a row, I know I need to change something.

"Remembering that I'll be dead soon is the most important tool I've ever encountered to help me make the big choices in life. Because almost everything—all external expectations, all pride, all fear of embarrassment or failure—these things just fall away in the face of death, leaving only what is truly important. Remembering that you are going to die is the best way I know to avoid the trap of thinking you have something to lose. You are already naked. There is no reason not to follow your heart…..Your time is limited, so don't waste it living someone else's life. Don't be trapped by dogma…living with the results of other people's thinking. Don't let the noise of others' opinions drown out your own inner voice. And most importantly, have the courage to follow your heart and intuition. They somehow already know what you truly want to become. Everything else is secondary. (Finally)…if you were so adventurous…Stay Hungry. Stay Foolish. …And now, as you graduate to begin anew, I wish that for you. Stay Hungry. Stay Foolish.

Thank you all very much."[93]

LAST WORD: GATES JOKES TO HARVARD GRADS: "I'M A BAD INFLUENCE"

While Steve Jobs created a start-up in his parents' garage and built it into the world's most valuable company, you should not lose sight that Bill Gates is another special self-trained person. Before he dropped out, he

---

[93] *http://news.stanford.edu/news/2005/june15/jobs-061505.html*

spent most of his time studying the things he wanted about computers. Many years later, he continued to self-train into what he had started—the computer science of his own, apart from learning how t run a business and manage people. In his own words he admitted that while at the campus, he didn't know much about the world outside his area of study albeit unrelated to his course, most important nonetheless. "I left campus knowing little about the millions of young people cheated out of educational opportunities here in this country. And I knew nothing about the millions of people living in unspeakable poverty and disease in developing countries," he said in his commencement speech at Harvard. "I'm just happy that the Crimson has called me 'Harvard's most successful dropout,'" he added. "...But I also want to be recognized as the guy who got Steve Ballmer (who was Microsoft CEO and director) to drop out of business school. I'm a bad influence. That's why I was invited to speak at your graduation. If I had spoken at your orientation, fewer of you might be here today," he stated. But truth be told, and David Orr was right (please go back THE IDEAL SCHOLAR CONCEPT—AND HOW IT WAS HATCHED UP), should such lessons be addressed when students are graduated and therefore when it is already too late to learn such important education, or during their orientation? And if they are graduated without such important knowledge, or skills, what then is the meaning of education, or graduation for that matter?

"Experience," concluded Napoleon Hill, ""Experience has proven that the best educated people are often those known as self-made or self-educated. It takes more than a college degree," he continued, "to make one a person of education. Any person who is educated is the one who has learned to develop faculties of his mind that he may acquire excellence in any career or vocation of his choice and improve his life as well as lives of his family and people around him without infringing rights of the others.[94]"

---

[94] Source: *Adapted from Think and Grow Rich By Napoleon Hill's Think and Grow Rich*

14. THE IDEAL SCHOLAR IS FUTURISTIC AND FOCUSSES MORE ON THE FUTURE RATHER THAN THE IMMEDIATE CAUSE

"Show me the way, show me every possibility,
Others got plenty, others no opportunity,
Show me the way, how to live out of calamity,
Show me the way, How to live better, how to live greater."

— Chorus, Wale song lyrics by Jose Chameleone

Here's a story of a person who had set his mind on the future rather than short term gains. I write this story to advise you, my readers, never to give up on your ambition; and never give up on a resilient and futuristic person. This is no work of fiction. No! It is a true story about a person I know. I present it because I know it is a true story. It is about a person I know so well because we were at the same campus at the university. Besides, he and my brother were close friends and in the same class. The last time I met him was about ten years ago. That's in the upcountry where I worked about six years after they had graduated from the university.

Having no reason to brag about such a trial matter, and with no motivation for personal gain or to humiliate anyone let alone Meshack, the author can now proceed with the presentation of the facts as they are. And I do so for the sake of inspiring others to learn from Meshack. Having graduated in a completely different profession—environmental studies—a discipline that is a little distanced from his chosen future career, he realized that though he had a job, he only scraped, and his big dream could never be met. He decided that such form of life was not for him. To accomplish his dreams with ease and speed, he had to quit his job even when jobs were not readily available—albeit how low paying they were—another reason why he had to find lasting solution. A sense of duty to his family and community came in handy, settling upon his already overburdened shoulders. Yet he had few options: cower and keep on scraping the rest of his days, or change the society—however long that might take, considering the magnitude of work ahead. Fewer children had access to education, albeit meager that education was, not to mention access to water, health care etc.

I can now safely say he had no fame, money or even a job commensurate the big dream he had had to fall back on when he staked his life on the dream of his future. I know he looked like a person who was desperate, one who needed support for he had no car or any significant property to his name. This is a position in which I last found him in. he, on his part, was a contented person. He knew everything had price. This was the price he had to pay. But Meshack was a natural leader. He was destined to succeed. I knew he would because he had rallied students around common agenda when he was minister in the university government. What I have narrated happened long ago when his ambition looked soooo bleak, when many thought he was daydreaming, days when he walked the thorny path towards his glory in the days to come.

I realize now that he began gathering relevant skills and personalities around him. He read books and trained himself in areas of his new career; one he knew was on its way coming his way. He took extra courses and classes to prepare himself for the challenge ahead—for he didn't want to fail his dream or the people who had confidence in him at the time when he spent his meager resources on self-advancement. He learned some IT skills apart from having some leadership training courses. Some people doubted his ambition. Others looked down on him gossiping that he was so full of himself, believing he should settle for what life had presented to him. "Who does he think he is?" And what about Meshack? True to his spirit, mocked, he didn't react; laughed at, he didn't despair. He only focused on what needed to be done to land at his destiny. Twelve years down the line, what do you suppose he has become? I will tell you how I knew this is true.

I was driving through the city center when an image of a person I seemed to know very closely rose from a very expensive imported big brand new 4x4 car. That wouldn't shock me. But everything about him seemed to indeed be bling-bling to my disillusion. It couldn't be him. The person before my sight looked like a very, very wealthy, and a very confident person. These facts contradicted one another. The wealthy image resembled just like the deprived classmate of my brother's! I immediately called my brother. He confirmed it was he, the person who once needed—and the author among others—afforded him some pocket change! Did he stick with the same political party? No sir! They were vehicles and not the final destination. Was he rich at the time? Not so, now that you know the facts! He was indeed in a not so inspiring position and probably a reason why he struggled politically over a period of over ten years. Though things looked dismal for him, it was only on the surface. In his heart he had a very strong foothold. Today, the rest is history now that he stands tall as a hero to all of you who have dreams. The question that remains unanswered is his full name. It is Honorable Meshack Opulukwa, MP, member of the Tanzanian parliament, and policy maker.

With realization of his dream, the dream to be a member of the parliament, he counted it as a stepping stone to address the weaknesses in the society, weaknesses our children and communities face; setbacks our young graduates endure so that they can stand and meet the challenges to support themselves, their families and add value to the society going forward. And what about his attitude today that he is there? Success, money, fame: all have not changed him. He is still humble and a man of the people. Is it guess work? No sir. Meshack's own long time friend and classmate who happens to be the author's own brother witnesses that his *sudden* success and fame have not gone into his head. That's what he learned when they met recently. As they both were crossing to Kigamboni from downtown Dar es Salaam. When they met, and though Meshack had now the status of the honorable diplomat, he conducted himself the same way he did when they were students at the university. With such a character, vision, and interests of his people at heart, it's no wonder he would be given five more years to represent his constituency once more.

LESSONS FROM MESHACK OPULUKWA

The ideal scholar is futuristic, i.e., has his attention focused on the future. According to http://dictionary.reference.com/browse/futuristic, the term futuristic is an adjective that represents, "of or relating to the future," or "ahead of the times", "advanced!" Is this virtue important? Why? Within the long term goals, are a person's immediate needs or interests—and vice versa. In other words, he knows that when one focuses on the immediate needs, he is risking the big future goals. But he has another reason. He knows that life's realities, social as well as scientific dynamics change over time. That's why the ideal scholar is never a stiff-necked fool who clings to the ideas or beliefs that he already knows. That's why his attitude is futuristic. He is therefore a person who will never say NEVER knowing how changes in our lives are bound to happen. By this insight, we put emphasis on the fact that the ideal scholar is keen on the changing world trends, and is therefore attentive to details; and is therefore continuously engaged in personal self-advancement.

And this is not my own idea. According to Alvin Toffler, "Nothing should be included in the required curriculum unless it can be strongly justified in terms of the future. If this means scraping a substantial part of the future, so be it." That's why: "While we honor traditions to some degree we are always challenging it and thinking of ways to *bring it forward.*"[95]

TECHNOLOGY AND THE FUTURE

It is no more secret that the author is convinced that we need new kind of education—an education that embraces a changing man in a changed world. The Association for Supervision and Curriculum Development names such a quality as *Coping with Change*. In words of Ornstein and Hunkins (p. 150.): *Having modal beliefs (or ideals for that matter) doesn't erase the fact that the particulars of the society are changing*. Here are a few insights into how the world is really changing according to Warren Ziegler: (1.) More mathematics has been created since 1900 than during the entire period of history. (2.) Half of what a graduate engineer studies today will be obsolete in ten years, and (3.) Half of what a person learns is no longer valid at the time he or she reaches middle age. Ornstein and Hunkins added that nearly half of what we will need to know to function in scientific or technical jobs by the year 2200 is not even known today, by anyone. Knowledge taught therefore should be futuristic.

With almost all future hopes and promises placed upon the world of technologies—excepting of human wisdom of course—schools must innovate themselves and be able to innovate and teach how to innovation. With the constantly changing world, we are convinced in a large part that Herbert Spencer was right. Without innovation and constant pursuit of progress because of the law of nature only intelligent and productive populations would adapt to environmental changes. Less intelligent, weak or lazy people would slowly disappear![96]

---

[95] *Adapted from Allan C. Ornstein and Francis P.142-143*

[96] *Allan C. Ornstein and Francis P. Hunkins, Curriculum Foundations, Principles and Issues 3rd Edition p. 71*

Concerned with the weaknesses amongst the youth and purposes of education, in 1994, the (US) Education Policy Commission, formulated ten aims (or in our case, goals or purposes) of education in what was called *Education For All American Youth*. In this document we find emphasis, and mention of, among others, the importance of: *understanding the methods of science*, the influence of science *on human life*.

Writing about the American society Ornstein and Hunkins wrote thus: Considering that we live in a highly technocratic and scientific society one in which knowledge has great impact on our standard of living and in a world in which the push of a button can have enormous impact on our lives, the enrolments in science and mathematics have serious implications for the future of our country. A similar concern was voiced over 30 years ago when our standard of living was increasing more rapidly and when we were more influential as a superpower. Then James Conant stressed that students needed to enroll in more courses in science mathematics and foreign language…and there is the same feeling of urgency. Our failure to heed to Conant's warning continues and is viewed by some as one reason for our decline as the leading political and economic giant of the world, and for the general decline of our manufacturing capability and standard of living (p. 151). Schools and education must enhance or promote sciences being the most practical subject for survival of the individual and the society especially now that it occupies little or minimum space in the curriculum because impractical and ornamental traditions prevailed…

6. Education must as well impart democratic moral duty to our citizens. That goes for technology. Indeed today let alone in the future a person will not be considered to be literate if he is no technologically literate. "The individual," rightly wrote Ornstein and Hunkins in their book Curriculum Foundations Principles and Issues (1998), *"The individual, in modern society must learn to live with computers, robots, lasers, telecommunications, and space exploration. A truly educated and well-rounded individual will be able to function in an accelerating world of science and technology (p. 153)."*

Likewise, nothing should be held as sacred education by the graduates and scholars unless it can be strongly justified in terms of the future. Again, if you're present profession or career does more to hamper your efforts to transform your own life and the future of the society, then you have to reevaluate your options. If this means dumping your degree papers or abandoning the most of your old education or profession, so be it. Indeed if the education or knowledge you have is of no use to you, your family, employer or community, what then is it for? The point I am trying to make is that whatever we do in developing learning and education in general, we must keep in mind the intent or the goal of our efforts. In the end, whatever we do we do it in the spirit of attempting to improve human life and our humaneness. In words of Ornstein and Hunkins concluding a chapter on Psychological Foundations of Curriculum, "We are not machines and the mind is not a computer...humans are biological beings influenced by their biology and their cultures. Our intellect is an ever changing dynamic complex...so that we...can create educational programs that will nurture more advanced, more total, more complete human learning."[97]

The graduates of today therefore put themselves and their successes at peril if they ignore the social dynamics of the society in which we live. To transform themselves and the society, they need to continue reshaping themselves and the society as a whole. The modern world demands that we keep redefining ourselves, our education and our roles in the society constantly. That's exactly what Meshack did.

CONCLUSION
Though there are many shining illustrations than one I have reported here, but I chose to include the story of Mr. Opulukwa for a couple of reasons. One, I know him personally, to substantiate what I say; Two, his was a humble beginning, something that can inspire many of the youth from the disadvantaged majority; Three, persistence; Four, focus on the future rather than short term gains—something that author strongly upholds; Five, and certainly of more significance, is how he has humanized his education in line with Renaissance. Renaissance, or the age of enlightenment named the voluminous subject-matter of scholarship, Litterae Humaniores or, "the more human literature", the literature that humanizes.

Having highlighted about the attention to the future, the reader must have probably learned through the foregoing narrative that our ideal scholars must not only have dreams but as well advance the sense of community and interdependence if they have to survive, let alone thrive. We must emphasize that each of us has a job to do despite different backgrounds;

---

[97] *Ornstein and Hunkins p.130*

and that each of us had the capability—and work to do. Each of us has responsibility to improve his or her life as well as that of his family and community and the nation as a whole. With the culture of laissez-faire and inaction pervading our society, we only have education as a tool that should instill into our youth the desire and culture of working hard and to focus on the future. Like every young economy, our growth depends on the common or average man. It is therefore the mind of the same man we must advance. But since it all begins with the mindset, our education should not be only skills based. It must inspire and encourage learners to focus on the future rather than short term gains. It must illustrate that everyone can do, have and be anything he chooses, only if he is focused and has his eyes set on the future, and not today, like Meshack Opulukwa.

15. PERSISTENCE AND DETERMINATION

"Changes that last a lifetime begin in a moment. With persistence, only time stands between you and your goal." —Bill FitzPatrick

The ideal scholar is a persistent person. Why? How? The ideal scholar has a definite, concise and a noble goal to accomplish in life. He has a mission in which he is obsessed. That's why it follows therefore that he is a persistent person—a person who patiently perseveres in pursuit of his goals, obsessed to accomplish what he sets out to do, get or be. Persistence is in the firmness, resolve and determination to do, get or be anything on which you set your sight. Persistence is a fruit of having a goal in life, a mission to accomplish—a mission conceived in self-awareness and knowledge of what one wants in life. With this awareness parallel with faith and conviction into one's abilities and choices, the desire to acquire what one pursues turns into obsession, a state in which a person is ready to give his all to acquire what he pursues. A person's faith is however crystallized when it is mixed with emotions—positive inspirational emotions. Such faith or conviction, though hard to quantify algebraically, and hardly written about, brings firmness, urgency and consistence. This is why when you know what you want, and are prepared to pay the price—when you are ready to stake your life behind one noble goal—you can never fail!

Is this an important reading? Ideal? Well, nothing is so common, something that is behind most big failures as is the lack of persistence, a habit of easily giving up. Giving up is a result of indifference. This study is therefore important because of the nature of most of our people. 99 out of a 100 people in this society tend to throw in a towel and give up at the first encounter of opposition. For them opposition is synonymous to defeat. A persistent person will strive to make the best of a bad deal, and still come out smiling. This is a major turning point that sets winning and losing apart, a turning point that sets apart winners and quitters. These two personalities, a quitter and a winner, are two extreme opposites whose relations defy the magnetic law—they repel from one another. The two are bad bedmates. Wherever one is another cannot be. We can enumerate all great achievers, all great men in history, and they all share one major same-same character. In words of Napoleon Hill, they are "immune to fear and blind to the possibility of failure."[98]

KING OF THE WORLD: MUHAMMAD ALI AND THE RISE OF AN AMERICAN HERO

On November 5, 1963, Liston and Clay signed to fight. The bout would be held in Miami Beach, Florida—on February 25, 1964. Few believed Clay could beat Liston, and he was made a seven to one betting underdog. In a poll of sportswriters before the fight, 43 of 46 pick Liston to win. Later in the game, the Power Punches stats seemed to establish the predictions: Liston's stats showed thrown punches 159 with 63 landed punches against Cassius Clay's (Muhammad Ali's) 62 thrown and only 25 landed. Clay worked himself into frenzy during the official examination and weigh-in the day of the fight. His antics (or behaviours) were so wild that the commission fined him $2,500. Clay's heart rate registered at 120 beats per minute and his blood pressure was 200/100.

Dr. Alexander Robbins, The chief physician of the Miami Boxing Commission, determined that he was "emotionally unbalanced, scared to death, and liable to crack up before he enters the ring." He said if Clay's blood pressure didn't return to normal, the fight would be cancelled. A second examination conducted an hour later revealed Clay's blood pressure and pulse had returned to normal. It had all been an act. Clay later said, "Liston's not afraid of me, but he's afraid of a nut." Yet even before the fight, Muhammad Ali was upbeat to win. For instance, he bought a bus and had "Sonny Liston Will Go in Eight" painted on the side. "Round eight to prove I'm great!" Clay gave his prediction before the fight, adding that, "If Sonny Liston whups me, I'll kiss his feet in the ring, crawl out of the ring on my knees, tell him he's the greatest and catch the next jet out of the country," He told a pre-fight press conference.[99]

The fight began with Clay showing a lot of movement, using his fast and effective jab and quick combinations, making it difficult for Liston to score with his slower jab and heavy punches. In the third round, Clay opened up

---

[98] *Napoleon Hill in Think and Grow Rich page 169*

[99] *https://www.youtube.com/results?search_query=muhammad+ali+vs+liston+1*

his attack and hit Liston with several combinations that caused a bruise under Liston's right eye and a cut under his left. During the fourth round, Clay coasted, keeping his distance. However, when he returned to his corner, he started blinking wildly and complained that there was something burning in his eyes and that he could not see. Angelo Dundee rinsed Clay's eyes with a sponge and pushed him off his stool to begin the fifth round, telling him to stay away from Liston. When Ali asked his manager to call the fight off, Angelo Dundee reported later: "I said, 'whoa, whoa, back up baby. C'mon now, this is for the title, this is the big apple..." That was round four. But the eyes and probably the exhaustion ate at him, Ali's odds to go on, let alone win the fight was sceptical. The commotion wasn't lost on referee Barney Felix, who was walking toward Clay's corner. The challenger, Ali, his <u>arms held high contemplating surrender</u>, was demanding that the fight be stopped and Dundee, fearing the fight might indeed be halted, gave his charge a one-word order: "Run!" Clay managed to survive the fifth round.

By the sixth round, his eyes had cleared and Clay landed several effective combinations, seemingly at will. Then the bell rang for a break before round seven. Though Muhammad Ali's team were still keen appealing to him to persist, it was obvious enthusiasm had waned, and the possibility of throwing in a towel accepting defeat eminent. Then something unprecedented unfolded! On his stool following the sixth round, Sonny Liston told his corner-men that he couldn't continue, complaining of a shoulder injury. He failed to answer the bell for the seventh round and Clay was declared the winner by technical knockout! Clay sprang to the centre of the ring and did a victory dance with his hands held high. He then quickly ran to the ropes and began yelling at the ringside media, saying, "I am the greatest" and "I shook up the world!" The Ring named the Clay-Liston match "Fight of the Year" and would later name it "Fight of the Decade" and "Upset of the Decade!"[100] Muhammad Ali eying the reporters said, "Eat your words!" shouting at reporters after the fight. Who won the

---

[100] *Adapted from*

http://boxrec.com/media/index.php/sonny_liston_vs._cassius_clay_(1st_meeting)
, http://www.history.com/this-day-in-history/cassius-clay-defeats-sonny-liston,
https://www.youtube.com/results?search_query=clay+vs+liston+1

fight? Well—let me rephrase my question: what won the fight? You bet it! It was persistence—persistence, patience and determination—on both the fighter and the team! Vince Lombardi said: "It's not whether you get knocked down; it's whether you get up." I must add one more point. What so astonished me is the power of persistence. It gives one the super confidence after he has triumphed, that it astonished him also. Having won the first bout against the invincible Liston, the rematch was rescheduled, against the backlog of fans and media saying Sonny was probably not in his element in the first round. What happened? Watch from yourself at You-Tube https://www.youtube.com/results?search_query=muhammad+ali+vs+liston+2 . Liston was knocked down only in the first round!

That's it! Sportsmen and teams which win trophies don't do so because of mere talents or skills and resources at their disposal. No! They do by sheer perseverance. Marriages are saved—and you can quote me—by sheer perseverance, sheer emotional commitment. With my many years in the institution of marriage, I can say with certainty that if anything can work in a marriage, and oh yes, I know that if anything can work in a marriage, it can work elsewhere. Indeed time is a great healer. So my friends blessed and happy are ye when you persevere and faithfully await your time of triumph. While you do so, nonetheless, act. Don't sit there and do nothing hoping for miracles to unfold. "The answer to prayer," rightly observed Wallace D. Wattles in his magnificent book Science of Getting Rich, "is not according to your faith while you are talking, but according to your faith while you are working."

Does it work in business? If you are a salesman you will register how severally it is hard to wait for the shop owner to place an order. You will register how often you hear a person inside saying, "let's go. We are wasting our time here. These people are imbeciles. They can't keep us waiting all this long. Who are they? Bullshit. They don't know how valuable my time and my products are. Idiots! How many people out there are waiting for me? Call it quits and go with or without order, with or without farewell." You will also recall your conscience as saying: *"Please wait*, wait a little longer!" a little voice from within counsels: "You depend on this job. If you get more orders you will earn more at the end of the month as your commission. Afterall you have family to look after." I have found that this kind of reflection has always been a shot in my arm. It allows you to wait a little longer. I have learned from experience that often such patience pays notwithstanding the need of prudential algebra of what is patience and impatience.

The headmistress at Lutengano High School called me once asking me to visit her so that we could arrange to demonstrate the training programs we offer at KI. With confirmation of my appointment, I travelled to Mbeya only to find the headmistress had evacuated herself from the neighborhood of her school. The second master tried his own contacts but she was nowhere to be reached. Did I curse her? I didn't. Did I fume? I didn't. I put on my best smile, not for the second master or the academic master who smiled back? No! I did it for me! I chose instead to take them through the brief of what we do in absence o the headmistress after which I saw myself out of the school compound and drove off back to Dar es Salaam. Was I saddened? Oh no! Was I victorious? Yes. Contact had been made. I only had to demonstrate the best we could offer which could pay off in the future. Well. That's not the right phraseology. Let me rewrite it here: *I was privileged to have a rare opportunity to demonstrate the unique services we offer, which would certainly pay off in the future.*

Then a month later, I received a call from the headmistress. I went back and ran the training for a week. Leonard Kitoka was right: *Every contact matters!* This was his credo to the customer contact team when I worked with him. He was right. Every contact matters—whether it is successful on the first go or not. Lasting relationships demand patience. To win you must be ready to lose something–well, that's not the right wording. To win you must give something in exchange—among which is to forget all other "better" alternative ventures. That's the difference between the winners and failures. Winners don't quit even after defeat. They change strategy. Winners respond with new force and vigor—albeit with a change on strategy when it deems necessary. The difference between the two is not whether they make mistakes or even meet temporary failures! No! They both are apt to make mistakes and to meet failures. The difference is in how they respond to these challenges. The quitters don't persevere. They simply quit. Don't! When a misfortune shows its face up, understand in it there's an equivalent or even an opportunity of far greater magnitude to seize. In my life I've learned that even in biggest crisis you need to be thankful for through it you benefit by learning from it and thus avoiding a bigger mistake yet to come. In fact I've been transformed such that I tend to worry when there's no crisis in my life. I've grown to love crisis and miss them when they are not frequent and close apart. And this is not my own creation. I mean it doesn't only work for me. It works for many other worthy men and women. Napoleon Hill writes thus in Think and Grow Rich: "All who succeed in life get off to a bad start and pass through many heart breaking struggles before they arrive. The turning point," continues Mr. Hill, "The turning point in the lives of those who succeed usually comes at the moment of some crisis." that could be a reason why Publius Terence concluded that: "Fortune favors the brave." The foregoing assertion is worth more thought and clarification.

When a person has persistence as an ideal in his possession, he is more likely to benefit from whatever circumstances that are forced upon him. The super obsession to excel usually comes at the moment of some crisis through which a person is introduced to his other self—his other self that is even more defiant to the opposing forces. It is during such threatening moments—moments when his mission is threatened—when he realizes how priceless his mission was. It is during the same moments, moments when one faces apparent failure, when he realizes what he ought to have done better. It is this change that leads him to simply not give up—come what may. When a person knows exactly what he really wants, and wants it badly, he forgoes everything else choosing instead to stand behind one major goal in life. And this change—the change in which defiance in him soars—turns out to give him an upper hand against circumstances that conspire to pull him and his enthusiasm down. No one has ever succeeded with too many contrasting goals. Contrasting goals result in divided attention. With one undivided attention, attention to serve one mission, such a person tends to burn all the bridges toward surrender, closing down all the tunnels toward escape—leaving the person with no option but to fight back with all forces he can muster—if he, or his mission has to survive. That's why persistence, as an ideal, is the way to success. That's how persistent people stand out.

NELSON MANDELA: THE ICON OF PERSISTENCE

We know there are so many moving analogies on persistence and determination. Because, however, this book is about persistence of a certain way, humanistic scholarly persistence, let me introduce to you a brief story of Nelson Mandela. What you are going to read is yes, defiance against apartheid, or color-bar, but the lessons aren't irrelevant to our society in Tanzania, and elsewhere today. Though Mandela and co., fought against color-bar in South Africa we share the rationale to fight back—and with the same vigor. The majority of our people are naturally barred from certain stations in life, career, or choice of profession, residence, health services, or even schools, not because of color-bar though? No! It is because of income-bar. The ideal scholar, citizen or leader this country weeps for, is the one who shall help to bring down apartheid of the few, thereupon preparing their minds—the majority's minds—to receive, retain, and enjoy, their Godly given rights, by spreading the hope and means, making independence or freedom a reality to the majority who are ready, the majority who still suffer in the darkness of hopelessness: ignorance, diseases and paucity. That's why though this discussion should have ordinarily been placed at the end of the book in order to leave the reader with a full feel of the lesson thereof; I chose to put it here to inspire the reader to think as he reads through the rest of the chapters.

Born black in an apartheid South Africa, he, Nelson Mandela, found himself in the struggle that would encroach half of his valuable lifetime. Committed to his cause, he ultimately rose into the ranks of the ANC and as well as in the struggle that finally led to his arrest and imprisonment. Intimidated to stop inciting the blacks against the system, he didn't budge. Arrested and behind bars, the white minority didn't feel any better. The fire of his cause had been fanned, and his defiance multiplied. Kill him? If they did, the white men rationalized, more blood would be shed and violence would hit the roof and that was the last thing the white minority wanted at the time. They bribed him, it didn't work. They even pledged to release him but on condition that he renounces his political agenda, but he didn't agree to that proposal either—stubbornly clinging to his one major demand—free and equal prosperous South Africa literally with his molar teeth.

Here, in his own words, is an account of his defiance and the price he had to pay: To forgo his wife and children, his career and "freedom" for he had to live like a fugitive, and yes, the ultimate imprisonment—the cost he had to pay to gain one most important goal, one lasting treasure. Mandela's lawyers urged him to leave out the final statement, lest it provoke the judge into sentencing him to death, but Mandela refused. He spoke for some three hours, before concluding with the often quoted passage: "I am prepared to die." While delivering the last line of the speech Mandela looked the judge, Quartus de Wet directly in the eye, the last eye contact between the two during the trial. On 11 June 1964, at the conclusion of the trial, Mandela and seven others—Walter Sisulu, Govan Mbeki, Raymond

Mhlaba, Elias Motsoaledi, Andrew Mlangeni, Ahmed Kathrada and Denis Goldberg—were convicted. Mandela was found guilty on four charges of sabotage and like the others was sentenced to life imprisonment.

NELSON MANDELA'S STATEMENT FROM THE DOCK AT THE OPENING OF THE DEFENSE CASE IN THE RIVONIA TRIAL: PRETORIA SUPREME COURT, 20 APRIL 1964

"I am the First Accused. I have done whatever I did, both as an individual and as a leader of my people, because of my experience in South Africa and my own proudly felt African background, and not because of what any outsider might have said. In my youth in the Transkei I listened to the elders of my tribe telling stories of the old days.... those of wars fought by our ancestors in defense of the fatherland....I hoped then that life might offer me the opportunity to serve my people and make my own humble contribution to their freedom struggle. This is what has motivated me in all that I have done. ... I do not, however, deny that I planned sabotage. ...I planned it as a result of a calm and sober assessment of the political situation ... many years of tyranny, exploitation, and oppression of my people by the Whites.

"I admit immediately that I was one of the persons who helped to form Umkhonto we Sizwe, and that I played a prominent role in its affairs until I was arrested in August 1962...I, and the others who started the organization, did so... as a result of Government policy. ...there would be no way open to the African people to succeed in their struggle .... and we were placed in a position in which we had either to accept a permanent state of inferiority, or to defy the Government. We chose to defy the law. ... (The ANC) sent delegations to the Government in the belief that African grievances could be settled through peaceful discussion and that Africans could advance gradually to full political rights. But White Governments remained unmoved.... In the words of ...Chief Lutuli, ... President of the ANC in 1952, ... later awarded the Nobel Peace Prize: "Who will deny that thirty years of my life have been spent knocking in vain, patiently, moderately, and modestly at a closed and barred door? What have been the fruits of moderation? The past thirty years have seen the greatest number of laws restricting our rights and progress, until today we have reached a stage where we have almost no rights at all." .... Pursuant to this policy the ANC launched the Defiance Campaign, in which I was placed in charge of ...I and nineteen colleagues were convicted for the role which we played in organizing the campaign.... the penalties of imprisonment and whipping .... Despite this (imprisonment and whipping), the protests continued .... In 1956, 156 leading members of the Congress Alliance, including myself, were arrested on a charge of high treason ....

"In 1960 there was the shooting at Sharpeville... and the declaration of the ANC as an unlawful organization. My colleagues and I, after careful consideration, decided that we would not obey this decree. The African people were not part of the Government and did not make the laws by which they were governed. We believed in the words of the Universal Declaration of Human Rights, that 'the will of the people shall be the basis of authority of the Government', 'and for us to accept the banning was equivalent to accepting the silencing of the Africans for all time. The ANC refused to dissolve ...went underground. ...to preserve this organization ... built up with almost fifty years of unremitting toil. I have no doubt that no self-respecting White political organization would disband itself if declared illegal by a government in which it had no say.

"In 1960 the Government held a referendum which led to the establishment of the Republic. Africans, who constituted approximately 70 per cent of the population of South Africa, were not entitled to vote, and were not even consulted about the proposed constitutional change. All of us were apprehensive of our future under the proposed White Republic, and a resolution was taken to hold an All-In African Conference to call for a National Convention, and to organize mass demonstrations .... I was the Secretary of the conference ...As all strikes by Africans are illegal, the person organizing such a strike must avoid arrest. I was chosen to be this person, and consequently I had to leave my home and family and my practice and go into hiding to avoid arrest.... (as the minority government chose to) introduce new and harsher laws, to mobilize its armed forces, ... armed vehicles, and soldiers into the townships ... to intimidate the people.... was an indication that the Government had decided to rule by force alone, and this decision was a milestone on the road to Umkhonto (ANC's Military wing).... I went to jail in 1962 ...What were we ... to do? ... give in ..., or ... fight it and, if so, how?

"We had no doubt that we had to continue the fight. Anything else would have been abject surrender. Our problem was not whether to fight, but was how to continue the fight...fifty years of non-violence had brought the African people nothing but more and more repressive legislation, and fewer and fewer rights. ...our policy to achieve a nonracial State by non-violence had achieved nothing, and that our followers were beginning to lose confidence in this policy and were developing disturbing ideas of terrorism.... Thirty-nine Africans died. ... violence was the only way out—it showed that a Government which uses force to maintain its rule teaches the oppressed to use force to oppose it...a way that it could not hope to achieve anything other than a loss of life and bitterness....at a time when the Government met our peaceful demands with force.

"This conclusion was not easily arrived at. It was only when all else had failed, when all channels of peaceful protest had been barred to us, that the decision was made to embark on violent forms of political struggle...We did so not because we desired such a course, but solely because the Government had left us with no other choice. In the Manifesto of Umkhonto ..., we said: "The time comes in the life of any nation when there remain only two choices—submit or fight. That time has now come to South Africa. We shall not submit and we have no choice but to hit back by all means in our power in defense of our people, our future, and our freedom."...I can only say that I felt morally obliged to do what I did....As a result ...the ANC heritage of non-violence and racial harmony was very much with us. We felt that the country was drifting towards a civil war in which Blacks and Whites would fight each other. We viewed the situation with alarm. Civil war could mean the destruction of what the ANC stood for; with civil war, racial peace would be more difficult than ever to achieve. ...The avoidance of civil war had dominated our thinking .... We did not want to be committed to civil war, but we wanted to be ready if it became inevitable...Already scores of Africans had died as a result of racial friction. ...twenty-four of a group of Africans ... were killed by the police and white civilians. In 1921, more than one hundred Africans died in the Bulhoek affair. In 1924 over two hundred Africans were killed ...On 1 May 1950, eighteen Africans died as a result of police shootings during the strike. On 21 March 1960, sixty-nine unarmed Africans died at Sharpeville.

"How many more Sharpevilles would there be in the history of our country? And how many more Sharpevilles could the country stand without violence and terror becoming the order of the day? And what would happen to our people when that stage was reached? In the long run we felt certain we must succeed, but at what cost to ourselves and the rest of the country? And if this happened, how could black and white ever live together again in peace and harmony? ...Experience ...decided ... the possibility of guerrilla warfare. At this stage it was decided that I should attend the Conference of the Pan-African Freedom Movement for Central,

East, and Southern Africa, which was to be held early in 1962 in Addis Ababa, and, because of our need for preparation, it was also decided that, after the conference, I would undertake a tour of the African States with a view to obtaining facilities for the training of soldiers, and that I would also solicit scholarships for the higher education of matriculated Africans. Training in both fields would be necessary, even if changes came about by peaceful means. Administrators would be necessary who would be willing and able to administer a non-racial State and so would men be necessary to control the army and police force of such a State.

"It was on this note that I left South Africa to proceed to Addis Ababa as a delegate of the ANC. My tour was a success. .. I was promised support by such men as Julius Nyerere, now President of Tanganyika; Mr. Kawawa, then Prime Minister of Tanganyika (among others) … I started to make a study of the art of war and revolution and, whilst abroad, underwent a course in military training. If there was to be guerrilla warfare, I wanted to be able to stand and fight with my people and to share the hazards of war with them…. I approached this question as every African Nationalist should do. …I also made arrangements for our recruits to undergo military training. …The first batch of recruits actually arrived in Tanganyika when I was passing through …. back to South Africa… and whatever happened the training would be of value… early in April 1961 I went underground to organize the May general strike. My work entailed travelling throughout the country, living now in African townships, then in country villages and again in cities. During the second half of the year I started visiting the Parktown home of Arthur Goldreich, where I used to meet my family privately. Although I had no direct political association with him, I had known Arthur Goldreich socially since 1958.

"In October, Arthur Goldreich … offered me a hiding place there. A few days thereafter, he arranged for Michael Harmel to take me to Rivonia. I naturally found Rivonia an ideal place for the man who lived the life of an outlaw. Up to that time I had been compelled to live indoors during the daytime and could only venture out under cover of darkness. But at Liliesleaf (farm, Rivonia), I could live differently and work far more efficiently. For obvious reasons, I had to disguise myself and I assumed the fictitious name of David. ….. I stayed there until I went abroad on 11 January 1962. … I returned in July 1962 and was arrested in Natal on 5 August… Whilst staying at Liliesleaf farm, I frequently visited Arthur Goldreich in the main house and he also paid me visits in my room. We had numerous political discussions covering a variety of subjects. We discussed ideological and practical questions, the Congress Alliance,

Umkhonto and its activities generally, and his experiences as a soldier in the Palmach, the military wing of the Haganah... the political authority of the Jewish National Movement in Palestine.... The ideological creed of the ANC is, and always has been, the creed of African Nationalism. It is not the concept of African Nationalism expressed in the cry, 'Drive the White man into the sea.' The African Nationalism for which the ANC stands is the concept of freedom and fulfillment for the African people in their own land. The most important political document ever adopted by the ANC is the 'Freedom Charter' ...open up fresh fields for a prosperous African population of all classes, including the middle class. ...

"I joined the ANC in 1944... the ANC was formed and built up, not as a political party with one school of political thought, but as a Parliament of the African people, accommodating people of various political convictions, all united by the common goal of national liberation. I was eventually won over to this point of view and I have upheld it ever since...I turn now to my own position. ...I have always regarded myself, in the first place, as an African patriot...Today I am attracted by the idea of a classless society, an attraction which springs in part from Marxist reading and, in part, from my admiration of the structure and organization of early African societies in this country. The land, then the main means of production, belonged to the tribe. There were no rich or poor and there was no exploitation.

"...I have been influenced by Marxist thought. But this is also true of many of the leaders of the new independent States. Such widely different persons as Gandhi, Nehru, Nkrumah, and Nasser all acknowledge this fact. We all accept the need for some form of socialism to enable our people to catch up with the advanced countries of this world and to overcome their legacy of extreme poverty. But this does not mean we are Marxists. The basic task at the present moment is the removal of race discrimination and the attainment of democratic rights on the basis of the Freedom Charter. ...The Magna Carta, the Petition of Rights, and the Bill of Rights are documents which are held in veneration by democrats throughout the world. I have great respect for British political institutions, and for the country's system of justice. I regard the British Parliament as the most democratic institution in the world, and the independence and impartiality of its judiciary never fail to arouse my admiration. The American Congress, that country's doctrine of separation of powers, as well as the independence of its judiciary, arouses in me similar sentiments. I have been influenced in my thinking by both West and East. All this has led me to feel that in my search for a political formula, I should be absolutely impartial and objective. I should tie myself to no particular system of society other than of socialism. I must leave myself free to borrow the best from the West and from the East...

"Our fight is against real, and not imaginary, hardships... poverty and lack of human dignity... South Africa is the richest country.... But ...the whites enjoy what may well be the highest standard of living in the world, whilst Africans live in poverty and misery. Forty per cent of the Africans live in hopelessly overcrowded and, in some cases, drought-stricken Reserves, where soil erosion and the overworking of the soil makes it impossible for them to live properly off the land. Thirty per cent are laborers, labor tenants, and squatters on white farms and work and live under conditions similar to those of the serfs of the Middle Ages. .... Yet most Africans...are impoverished by low incomes and high cost of living. ....Poverty goes hand in hand with malnutrition and disease. The incidence of malnutrition and deficiency diseases is very high amongst Africans. Tuberculosis, pellagra, kwashiorkor, gastro-enteritis, and scurvy bring death and destruction of health. The incidence of infant mortality is one of the highest in the world. ...tuberculosis kills forty people a day (almost all Africans), and in 1961 there were 58,491 new cases reported. These diseases not only destroy the vital organs of the body, but they result in retarded mental conditions and lack of initiative, and reduce ... concentration. The secondary results of such conditions affect the whole community and the standard of work performed by African laborers. The complaint of Africans, however, is not only that they are poor and the whites are rich, but that the laws which are made by the whites are designed to preserve this situation. There are two ways to break out of poverty. The first is by formal education, and the second is by the worker acquiring a greater skill at his work and thus higher wages. As far as Africans are concerned, both these avenues of advancement are deliberately curtailed by legislation. The present Government has always sought to hamper Africans in their search for education. ....

"There is compulsory education for all white children at virtually no cost to their parents, be they rich or poor. Similar facilities are not provided for the African children.... African children, however, generally have to pay more for their schooling than whites... approximately 40 per cent of African children in the age group between seven to fourteen do not attend school. For those who do attend school, the standards are vastly different from those afforded to white children....The quality of education is also different. This is presumably consistent with the policy of Bantu education about which the present Prime Minister said, during the debate on the Bantu Education Bill in 1953: "When I have control of Native education I will reform it so that Natives will be taught from childhood to realize that equality with Europeans is not for them …. People who believe in equality are not desirable teachers for Natives. When my Department controls Native education it will know for what class of higher education a Native is fitted, and whether he will have a chance in life to use his knowledge."

"The other main obstacle to the economic advancement of the African is the industrial color-bar under which all the better jobs of industry are reserved for Whites only. Moreover, Africans who do obtain employment in the unskilled and semi-skilled occupations which are open to them are not allowed to form trade unions …. This means that strikes of African workers are illegal, and that they are denied the right of collective bargaining which is permitted to the better-paid White workers. The discrimination in the policy of successive South African Governments towards African workers is demonstrated by the so-called 'civilized labor policy' under which sheltered, unskilled Government jobs are found for those white workers who cannot make the grade in industry, at wages which far exceed the earnings of the average African employee in industry….

"Our complaint is not that we are poor by comparison with people in other countries, but that we are poor by comparison with the white people in our own country, and that we are prevented by legislation from altering this imbalance. The lack of human dignity experienced by Africans is the direct result of the policy of white supremacy. White supremacy implies black inferiority. Legislation designed to preserve white supremacy entrenches this notion. Menial tasks in South Africa are invariably performed by Africans. When anything has to be carried or cleaned the white man will look around for an African to do it for him, whether the African is employed by him or not. Because of this sort of attitude, whites tend to regard Africans as a separate breed. They do not look upon them as people with families of their own; they do not realize that they have emotions—that they fall in love like white people do; that they want to be with their wives and children like white people want to be with theirs; that they want to earn enough money to support their families properly, to feed and clothe them and send them to school. And what 'house-boy' or 'garden-boy' or laborer can ever hope to do this?

"Pass laws …keep husband and wife apart and lead to the breakdown of family life. Poverty and the breakdown of family life have secondary effects. Children wander about the streets of the townships because they have no schools to go to, or no money to enable them to go to school, or no parents at home to see that they go to school, because both parents (if there be two) have to work to keep the family alive. This leads to a breakdown in moral standards, to an alarming rise in illegitimacy, and to growing violence which erupts not only politically, but everywhere. Life in the townships is dangerous. There is not a day that goes by without somebody being stabbed or assaulted. ... People are afraid to walk alone in the streets after dark. Housebreakings and robberies are increasing....Africans want to be paid a living wage. Africans want to perform work which they are capable of doing, and not work which the Government declares them to be capable of. Africans want to ...live where they obtain work, and not be endorsed out of an area because they were not born there. Africans want ... to own land in places where they work, and not to be obliged to live in rented houses which they can never call their own. Africans want to be part of the general population, and not confined to living in their own ghettoes. African men want to have their wives and children to live with them where they work, and not be forced into an unnatural existence in men's hostels. African women want to be with their men folk and not be left permanently widowed in the Reserves. Africans want to be allowed out after Eleven O'clock at night and not to be confined to their rooms like little children. Africans want to ... travel in their own country and to seek work where they want to and not where the Labor Bureau tells them to. Africans want a just share in the whole of South Africa; they want security and a stake in society.

"Above all, we want equal political rights, because without them our disabilities will be permanent. I know this sounds revolutionary to the whites in this country, because the majority of voters will be Africans. This makes the white man fear democracy. But this fear cannot be allowed to stand in the way of the only solution which will guarantee racial harmony and freedom for all. It is not true that the enfranchisement of all will result in racial domination. Political division, based on color, is entirely artificial and, when it disappears, so will the domination of one color group by another. The ANC has spent half a century fighting against racialism. When it triumphs it will not change that policy. This then is what the ANC is fighting. Their struggle is a truly national one. It is a struggle of the African people, inspired by their own suffering and their own experience. It is a struggle for the right to live," said Madiba, as he drew to a close. Then there came his concluding words, monumental statement that rocks the mind of every worthy reader and every worthy man and woman, a spirit that the author seeks to sow among all worthy leaders and all scholars in the country, the spirit of the true scholar:

"During my lifetime,' he continued as he closed his speech in defense of his actions and those of his fellow prisoners, "During my lifetime, I have dedicated myself to this struggle of the African people. I have fought against white domination, and I have fought against black domination," he said as he concluded, before he inserted the following line which is the cream of the whole thing: "I have cherished the ideal of a democratic and free society in which all persons live together in harmony and with equal opportunities. It is an ideal which I hope to live for and to achieve. But if needs be, it is an ideal for which I am prepared to die!"[101]

This was the moment that the Mandela brand had been sown. It was the moment that led to his lasting impact. His persistence to reject bribes or drop his cause in exchange for his ouster watered the plant he had sown. His patience of 27 years ripened the fruit that had developed. It wasn't surprising when 27 years later, itself a lifetimes among many communities, 27 years spent in jail, Madiba was finally taken from the jail and led to the statehouse as the first black president of the multi-racial South Africa—winning a Nobel Peace Prize in the process, besides lessons that his life teaches many, and yes a name that shall endure forever. That's why and how later July18 was declared by the UN as the Nelson Mandela International Day for freedom, justice and democracy in honor of his life's cause—and character. "Changes that last a lifetime," wrote Bill FitzPatrick in his Action Principles, "begin in a moment. With persistence," he continued, "With persistence, only time stands between you and your goal." And what a great piece of news that is!

---

[101] *Abridged and adapted from: http://www.anc.org.za/show.php?id=3430*

16. THE IDEAL SCHOLAR IS A HARDWORKING RESULTS FOCUSED PERSON

"How can I slow down when there is still a lot to be done?"
—Jane Goodall: responding to a BBC interview on her busy schedule even at age 84

"The more I practice the luckier I get."
—Arnold Palmer

"If I don't work, I feel lonely!"
—Omma, an Indonesian elderly lady in an interview with BBC Outlook program Jan-Feb 2016

The ideal scholar this country weeps for is results focused, a hard working person who judges the education he had had not only by what he can do with his education, but as well, and most importantly, what he actually does with it—rather than the certificates he holds—the certificates he is not ordinarily fond of. Is it important? "Education," said Herbert Spenser, "Education is not knowledge but action." That's why the ideal scholar is a person who gives his work all his attention in order to deliver the most and the best results in everything he chooses to do—a person who when a day goes without any accomplishment becomes a great embarrassment to him. We all have heard the successes of Newton. We heard how he oftentimes forgot his meals when he was busy working. Such a person will never go to bed without accounting for, and evaluating his day's accomplishments—while setting the next day's, from the lesson thereof—the quality that in this country—and especially in this generation—is weeping from being murdered. With invention of high tech gadgets, today we experience a society and generation living in extreme indolence. And with social media and cell phones, our people today tend to spend a good proportion of their day chatting, gossiping or watching porno videos both during private time as well as during work hours. This is not insinuation or something the author saw many years back. No! He sees it every day. I am probably the only surprised author now living, who has seen too many people, and in too many ways as they can think how, do too little work, and yet, without shame, they organize demonstrations to claim salary increments, and paid vacations outside the locality, and they still get away with it!

The ideal scholar doesn't expect to achieve his life's goals through quick fix approaches—approaches such as lottery or dodgy deals that leave the country on its knees with public funds in hands of the few and no action is taken—as most of our present day *men of education* do. Wondering how on earth we allowed this situation to happen in the first place, and then let it blossom to an extent that it is becoming a national culture—a culture that has left the newly elected president Magufuli with a hand on his mouth when he recently addressed the judges saying "Hii ndio Tanzania," i.e., This is Tanzania; when I hear politicians talk of doctored growth data, or the number of school buildings and finalists we produce year by year; when I look at how our men and women have creatively found ways to give impression that they are busy, all the time on the run pretending that they have important appointments or that they are doing something important, all lying to one another with straight faces when in fact all know the truth that nobody is doing anything tangible; when I look at the low levels of literacy and readership in the country; when I ponder about skyrocketing unemployment, inflation, per capita income, dependence ratio, etc.; when I look at how we have remained poor and dependent on foreign donor funds, funds that come with the price of losing our freedom and dignity from the skyrocketing national debt and its vicious circle; and when I look at how our politicians blow their own horns enumerating the number of begging tours they have successfully managed to accomplish 55 years after independence; when I look at how our curriculum is filled with everything else including fine art, drama—you name it—but one that remains a little silent about working hard and focus on big and quality results as an important ideal in its place praising the rich without questioning how they got wealthy or positions of power among which conning, robbery, corruption, killing for money or for potion as is in the case of albinos, I realize with something close to desperation, that, in words of Cathy Williams in her sweet novel Wife for Hire, our workplaces have been like "an activity of a gerbil frantically turning circles on its little wheel, moving quickly but going nowhere!" And my shame cannot be more pronounced.

The ideal scholar knows too well that from his toil he shall eat—a person who knows that his life is in his own hands. Through his analysis of the characteristics of money, Bob Proctor explains why, through his magnificent book You Were Born Rich. "Money is an effect and it must always be earned!" The idea scholar recognizes that the rewards which you will receive in this life, material or psychic, will not come to you because of your talents or skills, but rather, because of what you can produce, or inspire others to. Bob Proctor went on to say that: "Money is an effect and it must always be earned. Believe me," he counseled, "there're no free rides in this life and the only people who are making money the easy way either work in the mint or are on their way to jail, if they have not already arrived there. Therefore, always bear in mind that while 'good fortune' is a factor in financial success, it must always be coupled with effort and hard work!" Having read this magnificent point severally, yet every time I reread it, I can't stop from asking myself: How is the foregoing statement reflected in our education and society today? "All the text books of western countries" said Mwalimu Nyerere in Nyerere of Tanzania (p.21-22), "talk about rights, rights, rights and no duties. The charter of the United Nations is a charter of rights. Very good. This is very good. You can't state it better. Schools, churches talk about rights all the time. And duty is usually defined as "obey law." The minimum! And a large number of crooks do obey the law. I think the opposite must be established before a balance can be reached. There's something all nations need: a stress of duty!" Isn't this critical to any thinking man? Nancy van Pelt warns that; "some (men and) women tend to live in a dream world…and imagine that one can live on love alone. Although romance is sweet and good, a cake made from nothing but sugar would soon dissolve."

The ideal scholar recognizes that when leisure is preferred to labor with frequent regularity, the society is sowing long term tragedy, and it won't be far too long before it faces the music it orchestrated—and that's where I see happening in this country—and indeed president Magufuli's speeches during his first 100 days say much about the foregoing statement. That's why our ideal scholar is not fond of quick fix. He knows quick fix makes one fail to think differently. It kills not only imagination—a mind activity that is very important such that Napoleon Hill christened it "The Workshop of the Mind," it also kills innovation. Make a good analysis of any person who is used to getting free rides or even one working with a big company and gets such perks as housing, healthcare, transport, free lunches etc. Such people breathe their last and release the ghost without delay after they retire! That is one side of it—the side that doesn't exclude a lame duck employee who waits for his retirement benefits. There is another magnitude which is worse still. It is during such levels that the greed for quick money creates the unfathomable desire for the ill-gotten money. The tragedy is this: ill-gotten money is intoxicating. Once you drink of its cup, you become addicted—and that's the beginning of the end.

In a society where the majority of our workforce is fond of quick fix or exercising the *Intellectual Discipline of Schoolmen*, the ideal scholar distinguishes himself only through the positive change he brings to the workplace team or society. This is a very relevant ideal to our society that ought to have been at the top of the tree of our curriculum in the country. We are a too wordy people. Actions? Naught! We may have incredible ideas but have too little actions and too few results to exhibit. We have so many of the invaluable ideas we have tabled so well, but left them on the flat surfaces of the tables untouched, unattended, and without interpreting them into actions. We can plan better than anyone else. We can have best thoughts or visions. We are blessed with best intentions. But our problem is action—the ultimate end. Indeed the ultimate end of any planning session is to get to the process that leads to getting the final results. Therefore to launch into the actual process or work itself is what is key—something shockingly missing among most of our scholars. We indicated that the Association of Tanzania Employers complains of our graduate employees as being ineffective at work, didn't we? What it means is that we can't, instead, seem to finish anything leaving most of these plans half done, even when we are always a busy herd, *moving too quickly but going nowhere!*

And behind all this failure is one handicap. Our scholars today are a swollen-headed types. No wonder they usually cease learning—and working. Why should they? When it comes to learning, don't they already know everything in their field (or assume they do)? On the other hand when it comes to working, aren't they the thinkers? And you can't blame them. Didn't our economics professors at the university tell us that they were training thinkers? So the scholar-managers or even employees are thinks and the rest, their subordinates, the unlearned, their working hands or tools! Yes the ideal scholar ought to think, but his thinking must be channeled toward actually getting results. Yes he must initiate ideas, yes he must plan the activity, but he must also show the way work has to be done and coach his juniors. That's why they cease learning. They forget to learn from our greatest leaders.

Here is something worth more of the reader's time, and the author's space—something we are therefore going to repeat from his speech to the jury that convicted him to a life sentence, a great leadership secret our scholars ought to catch a glimpse of: "I started to make a study of the art of war and revolution," he said admitting his role in the war struggle, "and, whilst abroad, (I) underwent a course in military training." Why? "If there was to be guerrilla warfare, I wanted to be able to stand and fight with my people and to share the hazards of war with them.... I approached this question," he continued in conclusion, "as every African Nationalist should do!" back to our misled scholars, they forget that despite their talents, such people lose their usefulness—and ultimately their talents. Such people have another handicap. They tend to do too little work but think of themselves so highly that they tend to imagine that they deserve a big pay. A person is not paid commensurate with his education or even potential but what he actually brings into being, or how he inspires others to do so. That's where our youth and most men of education go wrong. They emphasize knowledge, knowledge, and knowledge! The problem we face in this country is not knowledge. No! Our problem is inaction!

On the contrary, ideal scholars are greatly employable. That's not all. They are indeed the diamond in the ruff! They are hard working at home and in their studies as they are productive at workplaces. These are the kind of people every employer is looking for. They work hard because they seek to be more independent financially, besides retaining their freedom of thought and dignity. Indeed education is not knowledge and knowledge on its own. It isn't of any significance until when and only when it can be applied to produce tangible results—results that help to add value to life for the individuals themselves and society as a whole.

The ideal scholar knows too well that: "Even if you are on the right track," as said Will Rogers, "you'll get run over if you just sit there." To acquire wealth therefore, and have in his possession the right to life, wealth and liberty, and pursuit of lasting happiness i.e., living a wealthy and happy life and still be able to age in dignity, the ideal scholar recognizes that it is he himself who has to make it happen. To acquire the above rights the ideal scholar knows he has to be on the ground, thinking, actioning, working, making things happen. Yet he knows not all work is work. No. No. No. There is work and there is mediocrity—something today which is almost unthought-of.

Probably the key indicator to know if you are putting enough into your work is what Frederick W. Taylor discovered in How To Do More Work Without Getting Tired. It is from his lessons that "I measure my accomplishments not by how tired I am at the end of the day, but how tired I am not. When I feel particularly tired at the end of the day, or when irritability proves that my nerves are tired, I know beyond question that it has been an inefficient day both as to quantity and quality."[102] Notice also that when we say action we mean more than someone's presence at his job station. It is more than that. The ideal scholar is, yes, faithful and loyal as a person. He is faithful to his work and the nature in which the Supreme Force works, but as well, he knows that faith and loyalty mean more than just sitting there in prayer expecting God to shower manna as he did in the Sinai. The ideal scholar the family, employer and the nation weep for recognizes that: "The answer to prayer," as aptly said Wallace D. Wattles in Science of Getting Rich, "is not according to your faith when you pray but an answer to your faith when working," he said. "Oral prayer," continued Wattles, "is well enough and has its effects especially upon yourself in clarifying your vision and strengthening your faith. But it's not your oral petitions which get you what you want. In order to get rich you don't need a sweet hour of prayer; you need to pray without ceasing… and by prayer I mean holding steadily to your vision with the purpose to cause its creation into solid form…"

The ideal scholar's actions are quick and decisive. A potentially successful person acts very fast. This is because he has no doubt in his mind about whether what he is doing is right or wrong. He knows he is right for he had given it a good thought and had planned well before hand. That's also why when he makes decisions he sticks with them he is not indifferent and undecided. He is not a kind of a person influenced by the public opinion or alcohol without whose influence he will reverse the order of his priorities. Not all advice is good. The third party's advice always lacks thorough thought. It often may also glister with malice. That's why you don't have to go on tossing your ideas everywhere. This may only give the game away. To prosper you must always be in constant company with your life's major goal. Then, "you must do, every day, all that can be done that day, taking care to do each act in a successful manner," once again, rightly counseled Wallace D. Wattles in his magnificent book, Science of Getting Rich.

When the author talks about action, or actioning, let not the reader imagine that it is something of little consequence elsewhere. Very recently, the Republicans accused President Obama, of all the citizens! What was their

---

[102] *Quote credited to Jocelyn w. Daniel, in Dale Carnegie's book, How To Stop Worrying And Start Living Rev. Ed, p.242, also excerpts available at http://www.oldandsold.com/articles35/why-be-tired-2.shtml*

accusation this time? of talking too much and delivering too little. They emphasized that they wanted results Referring to their hesitation in funding the government bailout plan, saying: "We want actions; we want results; achievable, accomplishable results. We want a concise plan, a comprehensive plan—not a speech. We want a plan. We haven't seen that," Smart Americans! They didn't want even a fine speech. They wanted action. Period. Again, recently BBC reported how an American investor pulled out his plans to invest in the northern France. Why? Because they, the Frenchmen, according to a very recent BBC program, talk too much as they do too little work. What's surprising is that this seems to be a national culture the Frenchmen uphold so dearly. Indeed when he inquired why things were so slow, the head of the trade union didn't mince his words. He stated pointblank that, "that is the French way!" Call it anything, technique, manner, path, or way, it has not helped France to thrive when the great nation has all reasons to come out as a pinnacle nation.

SUMMARY

The key word in this ideal has been action—well, actions that lead to intended results! Why? This is one of the greatest handicaps in our society today. Truly we don't lack knowledge or good will. We are known generally as good people. Many of our academicians are internationally acclaimed as some of the most Africa's highly qualified academicians. Our politicians are known not to lack in good visions, goodwill. Our problem is not all that. It is inaction. Inaction comes about because of our indifference to situations we find ourselves in. It may truly have its root in our history: slavery, colonialism and bad perception of socialism on the part of the people, not Mwalimu's! But the ideal can't keep on lamenting about the history 55 years after independence—if he craves it; I mean if he craves to be independent, and not tamed. "While we value efforts and good-will," Lafarge couldn't state their work ethic better, "we are convinced (that) accountability is ultimately about delivering results!" Truly, "A society will collapse," rightly admonished Karl Marx, "if it ceases to produce material wealth!"

We suggest, in as far as this ideal is concerned, that with action, into the mix you should then add faith, purpose and imagination—or positive emotions. These three have an influence on the will—which influences the action and quality of your efforts. I've seen several times without number that I am forced to take a halt in order to bring myself to the point of having my whole self, body, mind and soul entangled together, rallying behind one goal. This is what I call harmony. I've never been in my element, nor have I accomplished anything noteworthy when I was not in this state. And the same applies to you—whether you already know it—or not!

Finally, because of the significance of this ideal, a society where quick fix abides, a society where what is termed as Ujanja-ujanja, Uswahili, or the Cunning Discipline of Schoolmen and workingmen count more than the real work result, we ought to look more into how we can change this mindset. The bible says: You will reap what you have sown. If you don't work hard, if you don't get results, tangible results, you are then working hard to be poor, or a run of the mill. If you don't change, you will naturally remain in the middle, if not in the tail, when actually you should be leading. How then can one change, and make a difference, getting significant results that enrich not only he himself as a person, but the whole organization and people around him? Let's see!

HOW TO INSPIRE YOURSELF AND STIR ABILITIES TO PERFORM A TASK AT BEST

Nothing happens as a miracle. Everything is an effect, an outcome of a certain of cause. It follows therefore that we are poor because we don't work hard. We don't have a belief in, or honor work ethics. The successes of America as a big world economy didn't simply descend down as a miracle from High Heavens. It is a function of the culture ingrained in the American people. The United States is not the vastest country in the world. The US is not the most populous country in the world. America is not the most endowed country when it comes to natural resources. You can as well think of Japan or Switzerland or Botswana, or recently, Rwanda. Why then is the United States the most powerful country on earth today? Let's hear it from the horse's mouth as wrote Ornstein and Hunkins in their book *Curriculum Foundations, Principles and Issues* 3rd Edition: *"It is often heard that Americans are the hardest working people on the earth. As a nation we have the least amount of time for vacations from our work usually two weeks compared to six weeks of paid vacation time in Germany. We instill in our youth the importance of work... Work hard now and you can play later. As a people we tend to separate work and play. Work is necessary and purpose driven. It need not be enjoyable although we do esteem to be changing on this point. Work is so integral to the American culture that we frequently we classify ourselves and others by the work done...we are task oriented people and we believe that if you work hard you will attain success.*

What about the others? Tanzania? Please go back and reread how our youth perceive work or time, through our previous works such as How Universities Under Develop You, What Makes People Rich and Nations Powerful, and especially A sick Nation and How to Heal it. In short, our people prefer quick fix and there is a sea of *Mission Town* or what we could brand as *Middlemen* if not Con men. We also know that the recent worldwide economic crisis was a result of unprecedented shift from the work-hard mentality to the quick-fix worldwide and specifically at the Wall Street in the States. Indeed this author is the firm believer in that in the end no one is safer if basic principles of growth, growth drivers and success factors are compromised.

For a person to perform a task with his greatest abilities, whether that task if purely physical or—and most conspicuously—mental, a state of total harmony to pursue the task in one's body, soul and mind, a state also known as enthusiasm, there has to be a very high rate of vibration in his inner mind space, a state triggered by a great intensity in one's desires towards the task—or its byproduct. This state can be attained when he knows exactly what he wants both in life and of course in the immediate. The question now is one to ask oneself if one has specific goals in life. Once a person has a goal to achieve, enthusiasm sets in. "Once you have clearly formed your vision," radiantly observed Wallace D. Wattles in Science of Getting Rich, a work that subconsciously connects with Napoleon Hill's book Think and Grow Rich, "the whole matter turns on receiving." going forward, we shall further this discussion through the proceeding chapters in this book and series.

On the individual level, we have to focus on what makes a person perform or underperform. Here we must address the agents or factors which stimulate the mind to vibrate at the highest rate such that a person's enthusiasm or one's desire to perform a task is intensified, or "keyed up" to employ the exact word used by Napoleon Hill, notably a person who worked so extensively on the subject—and thereupon call the reader to read Think and Grow Rich. We have categorized these agents or factors as internal and external stimuli.

THE INTERNAL STIMULI

In his superb analysis of the working of the subconscious mind, Napoleon Hill identifies seven major positive emotions: desire, faith, love, sex,[103] enthusiasm, romance, and hope. The seven major negative emotions he included fear, jealousy, hatred ,revenge ,greed, superstition and anger.[104] Love, sex and romance are closely related and their influence of one's desire to perform a task and not only perform it but at best can well be studied and established in the desire for and effect of man to please a woman. "When driven by the desire to please a woman, based upon the motive of sex alone, a man may steal, cheat and even commit murder."[105] What is also remarkable is that the concentration one's mind has on the idea, has a tendency to intensify or incite a person's enthusiasm to perform a task—whether that task is a fine or terrible one That's why you don't have to entertain any stimuli indiscriminately, for stimuli like alcohol and narcotics can show temporary results, but in the long run, they do more harm than good.

On the contrary, however, true love at home, compassion, mutual support and harmony help a person to rediscover his inner capabilities—to exceed his own expectations. That's why the ideals we present in here are connected—in this case, a family person, one who cares much about his family, one who is also cared for by his spouse and children, will work hard to elevate his own but more so, the station of his spouse and their children.

EXTERNAL STIMULI
Here is where the external agents or stimuli come in. These include narcotics and alcohol. The environment in which you are also counts a lot. Researches show that many of those who stumble upon a hunch, if they ever do, do so when travelling especially in a public transport. That's why

---

[103] *A mention has to be made that when we refer to these stimuli, we attach them with appropriate age. Not everyone is eligible for nicotine, alcohol or sex*

[104] *Source: Napoleon Hill in Think and Grow Rich the unabridged edition Embassy Books, p. 234- 235*

[105] *Source: Napoleon hill in Think and Grow Rich the unabridged edition Embassy Books p. 221*

I prefer public to a private one. A timely vacation can also create such an environment. Whenever I am writing, every time I go to the toilet to attend to the natural call, long or short, I have seldom walked back without a new fine idea—which I jot down very quickly before I leave the lavatory. I have thereupon developed a tendency of attending the natural calls with a pen and a notebook. With recent high tech environment, and more and more as we go paperless, , I have even found myself walking to the lavatory with a mobile Phone or a tablet into which I record down every new ideas that pop up during the event of relieving myself. The most economical use of time, isn't it?

HOW TO UPLIFT THE RATE OF WORK AND OUTPUT

People talk about recreation as a means to uplift productivity. It hasn't helped me much, or my work either! Here are few tricks toward getting things done—tricks toward getting bigger results, results that will help to elevate your productivity, and thereupon, your station in life. Seek the vocation you love. No one does what he doesn't love ever did the most and best of it. So seek and work in a vocation or profession and company you are fond of; the air and people you love to surround yourself in. there is secret behind this. We normally perform our best when our frame of mind feels good to do something. Now ought we to wonder why many of our today's graduate employees underperform at work? No sir! Since we perform our best when we are in the mood to do something, woe to those who are not in their chosen professions, vocations, calling, job, company, department or employer, for seldom will they perform anything worthwhile!

I have found that when I am writing I get removed from the physical world. I have severally on the verge of shouting like an insane madman when my wife or even child interferes with the new spiritual world I find myself in. I often go to a great trouble to control myself to accommodate such situations. I have gone to the toilet with a piece of meat or bread, or even a cup of tea to save my reading and writing time. I have pulled a book or pen using a foot to not stop from reading or writing. I have severally found that my bladder near the bursting point when reading or writing. And this—consciousness to time—is not something I promote singlehandedly. This is a lesson I learned at the University of Dar es Salaam where Professor Shayo walked with a tea flask. Read What Makes People Rich and Nations Powerful. I have once (I must confess: recall I smoked occasionally) looked for my cigarettes but to no avail even when I knew I had kept them somewhere safe: on the table, or in the cupboard.

But in the midst of writing, I completely forgot where I had put them. Then I combed the whole house—to no avail. Then, I decided to have some cold water instead.

Now here I am. I approach the refrigerator. I say let me check if I put them on its head. They are not there. I knew then that my wife didn't like my smoking. All fingers pointed to her. I chose to go ahead with my cold water and go back to work. With a glass in hand, I opened the cooler. I couldn't believe my eyes. The packet of cigarettes was impeccably packed in, and now very peacefully slumbering on a small fancy cabin in the freezer, cooling down to ice! Think of that concentration. The intensity of thought—and dedication to one goal! Was the work error-free? I bear responsibility on errors admitting that it might not have been the best edited work ever. But what about the novelty of the idea? Inventiveness and the innovation in such a work like this one? Did Newton forget his meals? Well, I used to think it was a hoax. I was immature—and lost—albeit lost inside my own domain! (Well, never say never.) Could the foregoing account help you to register whether you are in your own vocation that God planned for you? May be!

Think, therefore, of what you want to achieve in life. Then connect it with what you will gain on accomplishing such a goal. Then connect all these with the fact that you cannot accomplish all these without your job or work. That was on the psychological level. On physical or practical level do the following against the rumor that stressing out is good. It is not for them who advocate it nor is it good to you. The difference between those who do most and best comes from one's concentration. So find an environment you love, an environment that allows you to concentrate. Personally I prefer to write in a solitary environment. That's why when I want to concentrate I prefer to shut both my mind and the windows, creating an artificial night—my best writing time—when I write in a broad day light. By coincidence, some writers for instance, prefer some of the times, to write in the open bar environment, albeit a peaceful one. BBC interviewed an author, who admitted that she preferred to write or create a plot of a book when in bar or restaurant.

Notice also that no one ever concentrates when he is exhausted and tired in his body but especially in his mind. So take vacation every day. Don't wait to do so at every end of the year or week. If because of physical exhaustion you cannot stand up, sit down, if you still can't sit, lie down but the bottom line is your mental fitness. No physical exhaustion should deter you from working. I have personally managed to write for a very long time and sometime through the night because I don't force myself to write seated on the chair. If I can write seated it is fine. If I am exhausted, I change positions by going to bed and write right there flat on the bed. It helps me not to tire. When I think of it I believe that if I had only written and read all the works I have written and read books that together can fill the whole room, I would be now paralyzed in the feet, the back and certainly in the brains. It is this trick that has rescued me so far. This is not strange, is it?

In his late sixties down to his seventies, Winston Churchill led the war efforts for the Great Britain awake 16 hours a day but never tired. An extraordinary feat, huh? His secret? He woke up at 6.00 A.M, had coffee in bed from under his bed sheets. But he didn't arise or stand or sit. He conducted meetings and directed war generals from inside his bed sheets until 11.00 A.M when he arose and went to office and immediately dictate responsibilities and. At noon took a nap ten minutes and woke up fresh to get feedback before he, himself, reported to his superior. That was time for lunch at 1.00 P.M another nap, another meeting, the slept in his sofa for another hour in office. He would wake up for follow up and any necessary briefings then. Then he went back to his bed once again. And these aren't my words. It is no fiction.

Dale Carnegie reports about his work schedule in his book How to Stop Worrying and Start Living thus: "During the WWII, Winston Churchill, in his late sixties and early seventies, was able to work 16 hours a day, year after year, directing the war efforts of the British Empire. A phenomenon record. His secret? He worked in bed each until eleven O'clock, reading reports, dictating orders, making telephone calls, and holding important conferences. After lunch he went to bed again and slept for an hour. In the evening, he went to bed once more and slept for two hours before having dinner at eight. He didn't cure fatigue. He didn't have to cure it. He prevented it. Because he rested frequently, he was able to work on, fresh and fit, until long after midnight." That's was Dale Carnegie's assessment of the marvelous record of Churchill. "The original John D. Rockefeller made two extraordinary records. He accumulated the greatest fortune the world had ever seen up to that time and he also lived to be ninety eight. How did he do it? ...his habit of taking a half-hour nap in his office every noon. He would lie down on his office couch—and not even the president of the United States would get John D. on the phone while he was having his snooze!"

In his excellent book Why Be Tired, Daniel W. Josselyn observed: "Rest is not a matter of doing absolutely nothing. Rest is repair." With that observation, Dale Carnegie added: "There is so much repair power in a short period of rest that even a five minute nap will help to forestall fatigue!" Eleanor Roosevelt said that before meeting a crowd or making a speech, she would often sit in a chair or a Devonport, close her eyes, and relax for twenty minutes.[106] Dale Carnegie reports that he interviewed Henry Ford before his eightieth birthday. He reports that he was surprised to see how fresh and fine he looked. "I asked him the secret," says Dale Carnegie, "I never stand up when I can sit down; and I never sit down when I can lie down."[107]

SET STANDARDS AND GET OVER IT

We emphasize quality as an ideal and value we must observe. However perfection can be a stumbling block. That's why we must set certain standard as a pass mark, a mark at which we can decide to get over it, and put the processes to closure in order to move forward to other things, other challenges. Many of the potential winners are drown into failures, the potential rich who are drown into poverty, end up there only because they either fear to try, or fearing to wrap-up, craving perfection. To illustrate, I know a person who is now well over 35 years old but is still unmarried, unsure of who to marry. Not because he is short of potential spouses? No! On the contrary he had several of them. The reason is that he has failed to establish what he wants in a fiancée. As result he has had many short lived and often simultaneous relationships. Recently he came home and told me he had good news for me. I knew it was about marriage plans for I had pressed him about it for some time. He told me with great enthusiasm that he had finally made his decision. I rushed and brought a bottle of Champaign and we toasted to his big idea, a life changing decision he had made to finally get married. Then after gulping down his drink, he turned to me with glittering eyes. I was happy for him.

Being Catholics I knew how it was courageous to finally choose one girl out of a million to be your one and only wife, to love and honor in richness and in poverty, in health and in sickness until do you part. Did it work out well? I was shocked out of my mind to find that the cerebrations were

---

[106] *How to Stop Worrying and Start Living the revised edition Pocket Books by Dale Carnegie, p. 232*

[107] *How to Stop Worrying and Start Living the revised edition Pocket Books by Dale Carnegie, p. 232-234*

premature. Why? He hadn't made his decision, yes. But the decision was only that had narrowed down his choices to only two! But it was an opportunity I was not going to lose. I rose to the challenge and decided I was going to help him make a decision right then and there. He talked briefly about the two contenders for his soul and I saw the boy was in love! His face lit with great fire as he narrated how he met them and how he is finally about to getting married. In fact we went ahead and made a call to one of the two. Then finally I asked him if she was the one. He said he was still not sure if he had dumped the other one. I thought it wasn't so bad anyway because between the two he would choose one and we close the deal.

Now one question remained. Which of two had more chances—if he had not yet made his final decisions? None of them! He explained mournfully how each had strengths—irresistible to any sensible man. Whereas one of the two was more attractive and more agreeable, the other was more industrious, more learned. But we had to reach a decision. So I cornered him for one last time: so whom do you choose and we begin the formalities? I waited for an answer but it was not forthcoming. Instead he scratched his head. I gave up! Until as I write it is three years down the line and he is not yet married! This time I am not shocked to know both are married to some other persons whereas this time he is shocked how they could do this to him!

When I, the author chose writing as my vocation, I shut out all other unrelated vocations. There is also another lesson to it. Though I am fond of the books I write, though I am obsessed to make my books perfect, though I crave to only see my name on a spotless clean book that is error-free; but I strive to make the most and the best I can. Yet I will be deceiving myself, and you the reader, if I imagine or state that the books I write have no errors in them. Yes I am privileged to be a writer, and published author, but I am human, aren't I? The editors are humans too. Much as we may try to perfect the books, some errors will still be hard to spot—on the moment.

Yes, I know there is the second edition, and the third, editions that are likely to resolve the error making we endured during the first edition, I tell my student friends, that my greatest fear is not to make mistakes; that rather my greatest fear is to do nothing; that rather than staying there endlessly doing one thing forever, not accomplishing anything at all! I believe in doing something, at the best of my capability, and fear little about mistakes or perfection. They ask why? Saying that, that is probably the same same old biblical teaching philosophy: *Do as I say and not as I do!* I say it is not. I say I don't fear to make mistakes, because in making mistakes, I make things happen, while opening a room for others—the reader included—to improve the work of my hands.

17. THE IDEAL SCHOLAR TAKES RESPONSIBILITY OF HIS LIFE AND THE LIVES OF THE OTHERS

"The greatest gifts you can give your children are the roots of responsibility and the wings of independence." —Denis Waitley

The ideal scholar is a responsible person. By this we mean he is a person who takes responsibility of his own life as well as the responsibility of people and environment around him. Indeed, anything that can enhance this quality to our people and the youth especially is more than welcome especially with irresponsibility pervading our society today. This is a very important ideal especially in this country where nobody feels responsible not only for the public utility but also those of his employer. Indeed such people are irresponsible even for themselves their own lives. You and the author are witnesses of the extent of carelessness in our society today. We have both witnessed the national electric company and the telecoms separately lamenting of the events when individual citizens pull down the transmission wires, cutting them down and selling them to various individuals who use them for minor works such as fencing etc. The water taps are flowing with water down the drain in the busy streets and nobody cares; one leaves the room or the office when the power is on and no one cares; the teachers and government officials go clubbing, as the lecturer or the doctor roll into the class or surgery room roaring drunk is not frowned at by the society or immediate carefree supervisor, and no one in the senior ranks cares. When the services are very poor and the national debt on the rise nobody seems to be doing anything about it. Those who are now in power, those in the positions of authority, people who gain from the anarchy, chaos or disorder are often short-sighted and indifferent, forgetting their actions, or inactions, are at the expense—and indeed the peril—of themselves and of the future of their own posterity.

People relieve themselves along the road side open spaces and on the walls of houses like heathen cattle—and leave their droppings all over the place in the city and nobody cares. They throw all kinds of litter—wastes, garbage or refuse—anywhere, anyhow, at any time of the working day, and no one cares; they spit anywhere and blow their noses in the public or even in a restaurant and nobody cares. And when I say this, someone says this isn't a big deal. But indeed they forget that the dirty on the outside is the manifestation of the dirty we carry on the inside. It is the symptom of the sickness—the sickness of dirtiness and hopelessness we have on the inside. Again, those who believe this is no big deal, (they) forget that this is how the trend grows into a habit, and culture; and in the end the people engage in street fights or any other antisocial activities such as rape or robbery, and still nobody cares; children aren't in schools and with their infant siblings on the streets begging and nobody is concerned. Slowly they begin ambushing and killing innocent people only because these other people worked so hard and made money; or even—and probably the most contemptible form and magnitude of carelessness—they kill albinos to sell their body parts to people who believe in witchcrafts and quick fix approaches to wealth and nobody cares.

There is also a growing culture of complaining we need to heal. We were prone, initially to self belief, then to self-recrimination, and finally, in many occasions, to complete denial of all blame by placing it squarely on whomsoever happens to be handy, usually, pointing a finger to our juniors or alternatively, our superiors.[108] Everybody—the leaders and the led—complain of mismanagement and carelessness—but who cares? Today employers complain about employees, as the employees complain about employers. Teachers complain about students and students complain about teachers. Parents complain about the children, as the children complain about their parents. On the other hand, the leaders complain about the led and the led complain about the leaders. This situation then leads us into a situation where, while in fact we should be working together to serve the common end, we are right now working against one another. We should be working together to serve the customer—which is us again—the society. The (American) Association for Supervision and Curriculum Development identified this quality as: *Becoming responsible members of the society*.

Being responsible, the ideal scholar or model personality expects less—if any—from others while expecting a lot from himself. I was recently travelling to Dodoma, Tanzania where I was scheduled to run training

---

[108] *A statement adapted from Wife for Hire, novel by Cathy Williams*

session for the university students from UDOM and St John's, when I witnessed how taking responsibility disarms even the evil men. I am not trying to say that the police force is a gang of evil men and women? No. my own wife works with a department within the ministry of home affairs, a department that is not far removed from the police force itself, besides having attended the police force training college herself. So what I say is not out of malice or simply from being misinformed about this forces duties and responsibilities. But I have witnessed how some of the men and women within this force—like any other persons or deportments—may lack the sense of responsibility. . We had just arrived in Morogoro when the driver packed the car under a shade to collect some supplies. No one warned us or the driver that that was a wrong parking.

Then immediately after the driver had committed the *dreadful* offence of parking the car at the wrong space, all of a sudden, a resentful heavily bearded traffic policeman materialized on the scene. Then with the vengeance of the angry devil, a display of authority, wrath and greed all wrapped in his person, he began: "Where's the driver?" he asked without salutations. We said he was fetching some supplies following the fact that we had a long trip to Dodoma. He wasn't listening. He already was exhaling brimstone. Then the driver arrived. "Why did you park here," thundered the authoritative responsible disciplinarian. "I went for supplies as you can see," said the driver displaying his merchandize among them mineral water and a few snacks. "Are you really a driver? Where's your driving license," a not-so-unexpected question under such circumstances, which is then annexed by the police force. "So you cannot read? What does that sigh in front of you say?" Lo! There was a signboard reading, *"No Parking!"* the driver was paralyzed. He couldn't talk one word. He began trembling. That made matters worse. Fear did completely disarm our driver. Then I saw the police officer reaching for some documents as he firmly held the drivers license.

I felt compassion for the driver. I had not seen the signboard myself. It was itself hidden in the midst of the tree branches under the shade the good driver had compassionately parked the car—mindful of his passengers. Notice also that the important sign board was hidden, but no one cared about it—not the road authorities, the municipal council, the traffic police department, you name it! Not even the people—to be fair to the authorities! Seated in the rear, I cackled to lighten the things up. Then I said that we who were in the car were all fools too! How could we have not noticed the sign board or even allowed him to park there in the first place! Then addressing the officer, I said, "I'm a driver myself, and I feel ashamed for the slip-up," i said. I said and meant it was a shared offence, it wasn't the driver alone, but all six people in the car had committed the offence! The traffic immediately loosed up and returning the license, without a word, off he returned to the hiding place whence he had come!

The sense of responsibility should be ingrained in a person as his own credo. At work, he is responsible hard working and result focused a person who exceeds his employer's expectations, a person who outcompetes himself. At home he helps with kitchen work, or even homework. As a son or daughter he takes care of the domestic chores and cleans the home and utensils regardless of his or her sex. as husband he helps his wife in a range of domestic tasks including cleaning dishes, child upbringing and cleanliness; reads books for the children, and is responsible with the social and community based services; at the church he volunteers to teach Sunday school, or even shares his wisdom and finances, and has moral and spiritual stronghold as a role model to others—much as man or wife, one will not shy away from his or her marital obligation besides conducting oneself as a desirable role model for his or her children—and the neighborhood.

PRISCILLA'S CASE STUDY
Here is a true event that I hope describes the foregoing sense of responsibility. It is a letter we wrote and sent to the headmistress and sent a copy to the class master of our daughter, a letter we wrote with great intensity following the written end of term report of the poor performance of our young daughter of four years. Notice also that we enjoyed great relationship with the school administration for many reasons. But that didn't stop us from shouldering our responsibility. What do most people do in such cases is to point fingers believing that after paying such high school fees, the school should do the rest. That's not us. In fact we called and thanked the headmistress and the class master for letting us know—letting us know that if our daughter's poor performance persisted, if she didn't improve, she would be thrown out of school. I am copying it here that you may shoulder the responsibility of your life. I included this ideal so that you may recognize that you are on your own.

As you proceed through these lessons, I believe you recognize that what I'm presenting here about taking responsibility of your life is not my own invention. It isn't my own creation. The message in this book is as old as creation itself. Indeed when I meditate about it, I realize it is the Creator's will that you manage your own life. I included this ideal so that you may recognize that yes we need to be good to others because we depend on the people around us, but that in the end you and I are on our own. And I suggest that you believe and conduct yourself and your affairs accordingly because it was not this author who instituted this—call it law or ideal. Yes he also wrote so widely and taught about it, but it wasn't Mwalimu Nyerere who crafted and taught the importance of taking one's responsibility or self-reliance for the first time. Ralf Waldo Emerson wrote about and taught self-reliance too. Saint Francis of Assisi lived it but it wasn't his creation also. It was God himself who instituted it. The book of Genesis says, *"With your toil, you shall eat of the land."* So you realize that when Emerson stated that: "Nothing shall bring you peace but yourself," he was not inventing a new ideal, nor did Karl Mark teach a different creed when he declared that: "A nation shall cease to exist if ceases to produce material wealth!" Indeed, when we moved from Ujamaa to market-led economy, a country we should have addressed competitiveness, entrepreneurship, punctuality and attention to time etc, the ideals that deficient in our society today! We also needed to start addressing the fact that success or prosperity isn't about luck or chance but burning desire, determination, planning, consistence and action.

Now read the letter we wrote concerning shouldering responsibility that was ours. It is probably worth to note that after it was received—and read, this note promptly a call from not only our daughter's class teacher but also the Headmistress Sr. Sleeva Metu herself. It also prompted the granting of the special amnesty for our daughter, one we wouldn't obtain if we didn't accept full responsibility. Here it is before you. It dated and read as below. Read the whole thing for yourself.

Date: 11.05.2010
RE: PRISCILLA'S UNFORTUNATE POOR SCHOOL PERFORMANCE

"Dear Headmistress,

"We thank you for the support we get from you—and your staff—in the education and upbringing of our daughters Princess and Priscilla. Over the course of the few months, we have seen how they change to be better both in the classroom and life skills. They have also grown in loving God! These are invaluable assets in our daughters' future—career and personal growth. Thank you so very much! As for Priscilla, she was so slow but slowly she is catching up. Take princess for instance, she started from far behind but now—we would like to share our heartfelt gratitude for their performance at school and home. Princess now scores As from Cs and Bs. Yet we know she started from behind.

"Together with appreciation for you personally, we also recognize commitment from the class teacher, Ms. Elizabeth! As an example, a few weeks ago, I'd come to attend some school meeting and I requested the teacher to take her home in my own car than wait for the schools bus, one that may delay her en route, hungry and fatigued, and though it was past class hours, the teacher denied sayings he wanted to take her through some corrections. We are writing this letter, together with appreciation, but to express how we suffered for her recent poor performance this last week's exams. She has not progressed. We write to say we accept responsibility. We sent her to exams knowing she was sick from a strange disease of skin lashes, a malady that weakened her. Again, we accept responsibility because Tr. Elizabeth had asked us through her diary to prepare her for upcoming exams. We regret we didn't. We must admit we forgot to give attention to her school work throwing all cautions to the winds. We have had so many failures recently—and are glad to learn from them.

"For instance we made another mistake of over confidence in her exams of the last month where she had scored above seventy in each exam. That was a mistake we made. Scoring A's doesn't mean she is ok in every other area. We would send a word of mouth to you about this or write to you but we went to a great deal of printing this letter to clearly demonstrate our concern—and our distress. Going forward, we commit ourselves to look after her and her sister's school work and keep a watch on their progress on daily basis! We further plan to engage somebody else as a hand in tutoring her and her sister.

"Notice however that we, I mean her mother and I, are not angels either: we know that! At college we too, occasionally failed in some exams. But when we got poor marks, severally we went to see the professor, and expressed guilt and that we requested to redo the exam. Severally, they were ready to offer such a privilege under condition that we accept the outcome no matter whether the results improved, or turned out to be poorer. In some cases we accepted to reseat and got lower marks. We request the same favor. We plead for this favor because we are guilty. Besides, we saw her face when she learned about the content of your letter. We saw sadness, regret. We also learned that she was haunted the whole day she received her papers. That gives us courage that she also regretted and determines to do better going forward. That is why we are certain she didn't fail; we failed. We failed her! We write to request a chance to offset our slipup.

"Kindly allow her to reseat and take any results even if they turn out to be worse than the first ones. Kindly give her and us a chance to hope for the future and courage to fight back. We request to redo what we didn't do. Kindly help us help her grow without feeling guilty of her but especially our own past mistakes. Together we can help her overcome low self-esteem—which she will go through if we don't patch up things. Help us to "grow" without suffering in our hearts for having failed her. We can together bring change of attitude to one more child; and to one more set of parents and then one more child and one more parent may help change others—going forward. We recognize this is a supreme favor but morally it is justifiable and a prudent deed. It is for good reasons for after all we are in a learning process day by day; learning to understand and learning to keep learning further! Here's a chance for your student and her parents to learn to be better students and better parents—respectively. We thank you for this privilege. Sincerely and faithfully, thanking you,

"It is us Festo and Nafro Michael Kambarangwe, parents of your scholar Priscilla."

That says it all; doesn't it? Now the good news about taking responsibility is that, as a principle, it pays off. In some cases its rewards are immediate in coming while in others it is slow and longtime in coming. That's why many people lose hope in its delays and turn to quick fix. I have made this additional comment to counsel you that you guard yourself against such anxiety. Three years later in front of school parade Priscilla was summoned in front of the long and wide lines of students at St. Ann's with an announcement by the Headmistress thus: "the first student in Class Three is Priscilla Festo Michael Kambarangwe."

As a final point, the central part of being responsible, comes from the sense of duty the ideal scholar finds in his heart to have and live up to his ideals. What happens when, especially in the corporate settings, the assistants make mistakes? Most of us tend to distance ourselves from such unfortunate men or women. But that's not being responsible. After his aides had slipped up, Barack Obama didn't distance himself. Instead he told the nation: "The buck stops with me." That's a true mark of a responsible person.

CALL FOR ACTION
Finally, notice the critical part of your responsibility to yourself, indeed a major indicator whether you—yes you—the reader are now responsible is

to make informed personal decisions, decisions to do what it takes to win—to be a winner. And the beginning is right here and now. With these ideals now at your disposal, we hope your journey has just begun. Notice however that the information we place before you isn't completely new to you—or many other people who now seem to be condemned to eternal depravity and dispossession. These ideals are known to many—at least in the very least—but actually lived only by not so many—the few who now rule of the others.

18. GRATITUDE

> *"Gratitude is the sign of noble souls."*
> —Aesop

A person with exceeding consideration for people around him, a self-reliant person who expects nothing more significant from the others than from himself, being responsible, and knowing his life is in his own hands, the ideal scholar is person who is not short of gratitude. Ingratitude is never his favorite suit. Besides, he doesn't entertain it knowing that ingratitude breeds malice, regret, disappointment, loneliness, and self-neglect and generally anti-social behavior. Gratitude, like all sweet fruits, must be cultivated. On the other hand Ingratitude is natural like weeds. Gratitude is like a rose. It has to be sown, fed and watered. It has to be cultivated and protected. Dr. Samuel Johnson was right. "Gratitude is a fruit of great cultivation," he said. "(That's why) you don't find it among gross people"[109]

THE TRUE NATURE OF MAN

As we are now launched into the true nature of man in relation to gratitude, the author is not concerned with the feeling of the fragile reader who will judge this as one of the gloomiest chapters ever written by man in the recent recorded history. I say so of course, with memory of the lamentations of Jeremiah! Of course that was written over 2000 years ago. But there is nothing I can do about it because that's the true nature of man. That's why I fearlessly chose to present it raw as it is.

Here is a story of the true nature of men I heard of many years ago. She was the reverse of her husband. He was selfish. And most people are. That's why ideal scholars are still few. That's why few are scholars who are successful and happy, fewer and far apart in terms of time and space. This couple was travelling through the wilderness to another part of the

---

[109] *Adapted from How to Stop Worrying and Start Living by Dale Carnegie*

country. In those days, the human population was still scanty and communities lived distant apart looking after flock and farms while in between the animals navigated freely. Yet rarely predators were harmful for game was plenty. So people always walked unarmed. Then as they arrived in the midst of the jungle a tragedy struck. As the man went round the shrub to attend to the natural call, but all of a sudden he began shouting: "Please help. Help me my dear wife." When his wife turned, she saw an awful picture. His husband half naked in the midst of his call of nature, was struggling to free himself from the jaws of a hungry lion. They wrestled and wrestled but the match was still goalless draw. But eventually the man had begun losing the ball possession. So slowly the lion began having an upper hand and probably tasted some juice blood from the hand of the man holding jaws of the predator in self defense.

Under the influence of adrenaline, all of a sudden, she ran and began pulling the lion by its tail. This was a strange thing to him as it is to any lion. Rarely anyone ever made the lion's tail a spot! And what a force! So as the man fought to rescue himself from the jaws of the beast the woman pulled with vengeance and the lion was perplexed. He didn't know what to do. Should he concentrate with the delicacy in his mouth or the strange tragedy that almost tore apart his balls? He chose to let go of the delicacy, and thus freed the man so the he could concentrate with the force behind it. He turned with full force and the woman did stick to her guns. Round they turned and the lion didn't know what to do. The semicircle he had managed was more than he could stretch. You can bluff with a happy woman but not an angry one, a typical woman determined to protect what hers— or revenge against his was suffering. On his side the man on being freed, charged like a bullet renewed with a new force from the more powerful trigger. Usain Bolt wouldn't follow his heels.

There, finally he was secure, settled high among the tree branches. Though I wasn't there at scene, I guess he had taken cover in the highest most powerful branches, while his voice down a giant of a thorny tree gravely admonished his wife to fight on vigilantly, on her own. Repeating to her, I mean to his wife, the words of encouragement, he shouted eyes shut: "Yes you can! You saved me, and so you can save yourself." This was in response to his wife who was shouting saying: "come help me, my husband." But then regardless of their might, determined women are humans nonetheless. That was as far as she could go. Poor woman! She gave in and surrendered to the pressure of the struggling angry roaring lion. That's how she finally let go of the tail of the astonished predator!

Then the strange thing happened! The lion didn't attack. As she waited for her end, praying her final prayers like Jesus in John 19: 3 saying, "it is finished," she cited Luke 23 verse 26 saying, "Father into thy hands I commit my soul." Then she gave up and closed her eyes resigned to her exit from the earth in to the lion's intestines. She therefore didn't see, hear or feel anything around her domain except a few pounding feet. She turned and saw the lion taking to heels. The lion had concluded that he couldn't take it anymore. He had escaped, running for the safety of his soul.

The lion had, for first time in its mature life, met a powerful enemy. In fact the lion ran cursing the enemy for playing a foul game. Then she looked up the tree and told his husband come down. He is no longer here. We are safe. Let's run away as fast as possible before he comes back with a platoon of lions. Atop the tree, the dignity a fading star decried him. Perspiring and trembling, he came down to face the music. He couldn't answer the next question. "Why did you leave me to fight the beast on my own?" he couldn't answer. Instead he hung his head in deep humiliating pain, recalling how his wife had just risked her own life to save his. But as once said Mwalimu Nyerere, some of the sins we commit here on earth, don't wait the final day to be repaid. Such sins are settled right in the process here on earth. Married myself, I know a defeated man can stop at nothing to reclaim what is his. Since then they swapped their functions in their home. Save for his manhood, he became her wife and he happily rose to the opportunity. It was the only way he could serve in return. It was the only way he save his face and marriage.

One evening, the author was driving home when he met a team of young men carrying wailing man on their shoulders. He stopped the car to hear the guy on their shoulders wailing in deep pain. He had been fractured in the street football game and therefore had no aid at all. The credo of such games is play at your own risk. They were almost six guys. I revered and drove him to his home and his family took him with me to the hospital. Only Two months later, one of the six men I had relieved from the weight of a giant footballing brother a friend—just by coincidence—reminded me I had offered them a hand. I had probably rescued him from amputation of his leg. Who knows if they delayed him or caused more harm by mishandling him? The other five have never come back to me. The person who was injured is living a stone throw from where I am writing this book now in your hands and I meet him almost every day. But he has not yet come to me or to say one word about it. And that's not all. Six months later he finally came back only to ask me if I could hire him as a driver. I was not shocked enough!

A year later, I refused to board a car my neighbor was driving. Why? Probably because I was very close to my house, but there was another reason I hadn't yet been able to decipher. Though I am writing about gratitude as an ideal, but I would like to insist that these ideals are connected and at work all the time. Now recognize that my instincts had warned me against boarding that car, yet after repeated pleas from the three of my colleagues, I budged—and that's when the trouble—which is my lesson began. Having given in, against my will though, he dropped me at my house as I left him behind reversing his car to go home, a few meters from my house in Mbezi. But a few minutes later, as I was preparing to go to bed, I learned that he hadn't moved an inch. His four wheels had failed—and the car slipped. I decided to be mindful of his needs as part of gratitude on my part following goodwill on his part. My young brother and I push the car. It moved. We push with vigor and it crossed the obstacle. But with it, his car tire ground my toe on the left foot. I can sit here and see the event as it happened.

Now I am at the scene. The car vanishes as I use the tail lights to inspect my toe. It was all mushy and the nail sifted! But now my point is this: did he stop to thank me? Nope! I went to hospital with support of my wife and brother that same night. I paid the bill myself. Four months passed by and he hadn't come to see me. Didn't he know about the event? Yes he knew it. I had sent word through his son, my brother and the other neighbor, and all had informed him about it. It is six months now as I write, and he hasn't come to see me even though he lives a stone throw from my house. But I shouldn't have been shocked by his attitude. No! Indeed I bought him a drink a few days later when I met him in the nearby hotel bar, ashamed of myself!

Teaching about human nature, in his book How to Stop Worrying and Start Living, Dale Carnegie wrote thus: Marcus Aurelius…wrote in his diary one day; 'I am going to meet people today who talk too much—people who are selfish, egotistical, ungrateful. But I won't be surprised or disturbed, for I couldn't imagine the world without such people." The author has learned this grave distressing human mistake of expecting gratitude from men. But instead he is grateful for the lesson. And here is how he learned—albeit the hard way—that not you or me should expect gratitude. Many years ago, he took a boy as his domestic helper. But then he found out that he was from a very poor family. He had also been actually selected for secondary school but his parents couldn't afford it. I sacked him from my services immediately. Why? I sent him to school. Then he graduated and got a job. He disappeared. No letter or call.

Then one day we met. I asked him why he had deserted on us, for he didn't call or write back. He said he was busy at work. That's understandable. I didn't even shudder when he told me that he was a grown man and had his life and he will look after himself. But I wouldn't be more shocked if he had slapped me in face when he told me that he didn't need my "bullying!" anymore, and that, "if it is about the money I had spent on him, he was going to pay it—right away!!!" he said this with his hand going into his hip pocket, returning with a thick wallet in his hands. I turned and fled. To say I wasn't disappointed would be inexcusably insincere on my part. I was not even angry. That would be understatement. I was mad, suicidal madness did suddenly engulf me. But in that instant, I recalled the following story—a story you can find at *academictips.org*:

There was a blind girl who hated herself because she was blind. She hated everyone, except her loving boyfriend. He was always there for her. She told her boyfriend, 'If I could only see the world, I would marry you.' One day, someone donated a pair of eyes to her. When the bandages came off, she was able to see everything, including her boyfriend. He asked her, 'Now that you can see the world, will you marry me?' The girl looked at her boyfriend and saw that he was blind. The sight of his closed eyelids shocked her. She hadn't expected that. The thought of looking at them the rest of her life led her to refuse to marry him. Her boyfriend left her in tears. Days later, he wrote a note to her saying: "Take a good care of your eyes, my dear, for before they were yours, they were mine." This story worked wonders for me. I realized, for the first time, the fact that only very few souls remember what life was like before, and who was always by their side in the most painful situations. That's how finally, and I thank him for letting me learn this truth about men and life. That's why I refused to be angry. That's how I came out smiling. I was a happier man to learn a lesson of my life. Think about it. He had no shelter, I sheltered him. He was underdressed, I dressed him up. He was under fed, I fed him. He was sick and I looked after him. And of most importance, he had neither the hope, nor the vision for the future, and by the grace of God, I gave it to him! I have learned to thank God and feel proud in myself in the service I do than the returns I get from my services to mankind whether it be my sibling, wife, children, neighbor, or strangers, save for my mother and father. Rabindranath Tagore was right when he said: "<u>I slept and dreamt that life was joy. I awoke and saw that life was service. I acted and behold, service was joy.</u>" I have learned to deepen my gratitude—to question my own level of gratitude. It is from this lesson that I began looking for opportunities to honor and reward anything—small or big—someone does for me or others. That's how I changed. You too can learn from the nature of men.

As character, gratitude is a blessing in itself. It guards you against one of the most ruinous habits—the habit of playing the blame game. As such, playing the blame game is not only a fruitless but a costly business. It consumes both your physical and inner resources or energy—resources or energy you would use productively in other areas. Come to think about it, it is not a sensible thing to do—I mean to expect gratitude. Indeed, it is not a sensible thing to do—I mean to expect gratitude. Jesus healed ten lepers. How many do you think came back to thank him? Only one! He, Jesus, had lived his life providing for the twelve chosen men, men he trusted with his life, and unto whom he unfolded all his wares and mysteries; men he fed day and night and gave them drink as he paid for their government taxes. That was not all. He even healed some of their dead. But what happened? Let's observe the records.

When the Jews plotted evils against him, they realized they wouldn't succeed without someone who would betray him. Who do you think betrayed him? It was Judas Iscariot one of the twelve chosen and most privileged Israelis of all time. In fact I can say without doubt in my mind whatsoever that they were the most privileged humans who will ever live. In fact Judas was the most highly paid of all disciples being the treasurer himself. You don't have to search the scriptures or archives for this information. Just compare the salary scales of the teachers, such as the preachers Peter and John, with that of the Revenue Authority officials even here in Tanzania. And at what a price did he betray Jesus! It was only at thirty pieces of silver. Think of it. And that's not all. Peter, Simon Peter who was in fact his right hand man amongst his disciples, disowned him not once but three times only the first day of his seizure even after Jesus had warned him of it besides having replaced the ear lobe of the Jew that Peter had cut off.

There was another man. His name was Thomas. Though he had experienced all the miracles Jesus had done before his own eyes, when Jesus stormed into the house in which they were for the second time, despite Jesus having promised to do so, he did what amounted to nothing but insubordination when he asked to touch the spots on the body of Jesus where the Jews had nailed him on the cross. It was then that he believed. Think of it. Three out of twelve which is one of four returned what amounted to ingratitude to Jesus why should you expect more? To do so is not only ridiculous but also self defeating. It will create enemies and miseries for you and finally break your plans before it completely breaks you down.

Among his twelve disciples, people he had lived and shared with almost everything he could concoct free of charge of course three betrayed him. Think about it. Judas sold him out for only thirty pieces of silver. Simon Peter denounced him three times. And there was another one.

Though Jesus had beseeched and did all that was necessary to win loyalty from another one of his disciples, but when Jesus resurrected and returned to the house in which they were meeting, even when all the doors were closed, he disbelieved him insisting he had to touch his scars to prove it was he. You know his name. It is Thomas. If now three out of twelve trusted friends and protégés , didn't return gratitude or trust, but instead betrayed him, if Jesus had healed ten lepers, but only one came back to thank him, why expect more for yourself? Besides, YAHWEH had rescued and fed the Israelis with manna and cool most hygienic water from the Sinai rocks for forty years without tilling the land or collecting in the barn but instead they treated him with an endless litany of curses shouting saying: we had better go back to pharaoh. What kind of God is this? they seemed to ask. They wanted more. That's the nature of human mortals.

But I have realized that gratitude is a very hard human trait. "Thank you, dear God," said Garrison Keillor, "for this good life and forgive us if we do not love it enough," he continued. "Thank you for the rain. And for the chance to wake up in three hours and go fishing: I thank you for that now, because I won't feel so thankful then." Like weeds, bad character such as ingratitude in natural. So to be people of gratitude we have to cultivate that habit. Now you probably by now recognize that it is to your advantage to have gratitude in whatever happens to you. To be successful in whatever you do, you need to have inner harmony. But inner harmony is almost impossible without a sense of faith and gratitude, amnesty and clemency toward others. In his magnificent book Science of Getting Rich, Wallace D. Wattles counsels thus: "Also, faith is born of gratitude. The grateful mind continually expects good things, and expectation becomes faith. The reaction of gratitude upon one's own mind produces faith, and every outgoing wave of grateful thanksgiving increases faith. The person who has no feeling of gratitude cannot long retain a living creative method... It is necessary, then, to cultivate the habit of being grateful for every good thing that comes to you and to give thanks continuously...because all things have contributed to your advancement."

The ideal scholar is a man of gratitude—gratitude and thanksgiving—in all things. It is the quality of that though it is also in him as one of his values and moral duty, but the ideal scholar recognizes that gratitude sows seeds of love and kindness. And since it is a rare trait among men, he will be the first to ever show gratitude without expecting it in return anyway knowing the nature of man. It is futile to expect gratitude from the people. Because it is futile, and because hunger for gratitude from other people ruins the person himself, it is safer to return gratitude yourself in everything you do, and yes in everything others do for you.

19. THE IDEAL SCHOLAR IS TIME CONSCIOUS

"Punctuality is the politeness of kings." —Louis XVIII

The ideal scholar is time conscious. He knows we are all given almost every other ability and equal number of hours but the difference is how we use our time productively. Time consciousness is an ideal badly lacking recognizing that time is the only resource that cannot be renewed. Soon is no longer enough. How soon is soon? And by the way, how do other people see us as a nation? Sloppy, carefree and indifferent. The author hails from Ngara and knows how the clock never ticks there deep in Bushubi! A group of tourists visiting Tanzania were interviewed and witnessed that they loved everything in the country but mournfully disclosed that they disliked the levels of punctuality in the land! What can this habit add to our investment opportunity? We don't seem to know our prospects! Zero! In its ten points as aims or goals or qualities of the American youth issued by the Education for All American Youth report, the eighth emphasizes the same sense of time consciousness. It says the ideal American youth should have the best ability to:*"use ...time and budgeting of it wisely, balancing activities that yield satisfaction to the individual with those that are socially useful."*

We have, through the book a Sick Nation and How to Heal it, indicated how our society today—and the youth especially—almost completely loath wearing wrist watches (with an alibi that the Chinese watches have substituted the wrist watch. It is a fabrication) but instead they put on bangles and bracelets that display the cool brands of Fubu or Nike and those of the top European football teams of Chelsea, Barcelona, Madrid, Man U, Milan or Arsenal. Probably it would do us justice—the developed nations and some of the prosperous few—to compare our levels of progress with those of the United States with an eye on how we revere or loath time. Indeed whereas we in this country begin our weekend on Wednesday and watch midnight football Monday down another Monday, and our radio programs and entertainment media such as DSTV— indeed the most preferred brands in the country—are loaded with "Hakuna Kulala" programs. That is, don't go to bed; just enjoy, go clubbing etc, forgetting that: "Time and tide wait for no man!"

In contrast to the popular view, Ornstein and Hunkins write thus: *"...work is so essential to our cultural fabric...revealed by how we look at time. Time is money. Don't waste time. In academics we have such concepts as academic time on task and total allowable time to educate students to the importance of time...those...in the United States...are firm believers in the work ethic and in the precise management of time. We,"* continued Ornstein and Hunkins, *"We like planes that depart on time. We like people who are punctual in keeping their appointments. We expect* (anyone) *to arrive on time for their days work. We even regulate our leisure with an eye toward precise time... It would not feel right,"* listen closely to this contrast; *"It would not feel right to have Thursday-night football."* And *"Most people would feel naked without their wrist watches. The tick of the watch is almost the pulse of America."*

Need we then ask why one person, community or country is prosperous on one hand and another remains a beggar, deprived and a low income?

What is your true measure against this ideal—I mean what is your performance indicator against time consciousness? As for me, considering the average life span and the vast and high goals I have set for myself, I have often gone to bed with my laptop. Also if I had to make a prayer it would be to have four eyes and four hands. Recognizing that that is long shot, I have always prayed and exercised with the left hand to make it work equally better as the right. I would as well pray to have one eye awake as another goes to sleep. I would pray to have one eye awake at a time so that I could have twenty four hours to read and write more books. And this is no joke. When I am obsessed with my work I have found myself accumulating urine in my bladder sometimes on the brink of bursting to waive the frequency of leaving my work. I have never gone to the toilet or washroom; call it anything, with no preplanned or premeditated task.

I choose instead to use this precious time of relieving myself—whether that is a short or a long call of nature—to grab a cup of coffee, or a piece of snacks drinking or munching something right in the toilet in order to put my now idle hands, the mind and the mouth to good use. I also use this time rationally as apart from eating, or brushing my teeth, on meditating upon the topic I am writing about, or even read a page or two of the book or manuscript before me to meet the deadlines. This all helps me to save precious time that would otherwise be wasted in an activity of such trivial importance, the activity of dropping unwanted materials from my person. Indeed when I concentrate, rather than leaving my books, if I concentrate with a story I am reading or writing something, I have often found myself using my leg to pull the pen, papers, a book or something else I need lest I leave my work.

I often wash my feet with cold water, or even take shower to be fresh, to add more hours on my working day. I regularly wash my face to remain not awake, but also to keep my eyes fresh and I have found that it helps me. But that simply washes the outside of the eye. That's why I haven't stopped thinking, wishing there was some ointment clinically made to wash the cornea, the lenses, the iris and retina in order to keep the eye not only fresh from exhaustion but also to prolong its active working hours. Obsession with what you are doing can be intoxicating, and damaging too! I have once heard something knocking something down in the kitchen, an incident that ordinarily throws me on my feet. But because I was under my own obligation to finish a certain number of pages, I ignored what was happening, only to responding when the crash continued. What about you? As for me, not once when I had deadlines to meet with my publishers, a deadline that I had to honor the same night, or else incur additional cost. It is often a significant cost for a self employed full time writer. Yet coincidentally, I had accepted a very important appointment I also had to honor at 8.00 a.m. I concentrated with my manuscript until when I penned off, and after I had attached the document to the publisher, I pressed the send button only to realize it was already 12.00 a.m. I rushed, brushed my teeth, grabbed a cup of strong coffee, put on my suit, and switching on the car, I drove off to meet my appointment in the city center 15 kilometers away. To say you cannot meet deadlines—for whatever reason—is unfounded! Whatever reason one may give is an alibi. This is a culture or tradition that you and I ought to, and can break.

20. SELF-RELIANCE AND PURSUIT FOR PERSONAL LIBERTIES

"You may look like a Goddess Miss Mayberry, but be assured that I can exist quiet well without you!" —Spencer, Lord Beecham in Catherine Coulter's novel, The Courtship

The ideal scholar, knowing who he is, and what he wants in life, and having learnt how to get what he wants in life, is a free person with a great sense of, and pride in, personal liberties. In his Action Principles, Bill FitzPatrick was right: "If there is one gift that you can give yourself that will enhance the overall quality of your life, it is self-reliance." A person who chooses to work for someone for the rest of his life is not educated no matter how high ranking his position is in that someone's company. It is not for failing the company, no. it for not doing more, such as creating employment for others rather than occupying some executive space. That's why a person willingly sells his labor and initiatives in return for a salary is actually selling his first-born's birthright for a morsel of bread, and that's why he is not educated no matter how many years he has been instructed, or a position he holds.

Yes, we know everybody has to work for someone somehow, and yes we know that not all of us have the same talents, and yes we know we need every other profession and vocation, but because talents can be learnt, and because we are certain such most menial job descriptions are going to be filled by robots, from today on, put your credibility under the microscope if you have still chosen to relinquish the rights for a higher purpose, willing to cheerfully serve as someone's employee all your life. The love for personal liberties, freedom, or independence, is what almost determines the rest of your future, the prospects for your success or failure. It is in it that there is persistence and determination, or low self-esteem, indifference and total surrender to circumstances. A mention has been already made concerning how God created man, and gave him dominion over his own life, the Garden of Eden, and all the earth and all that dwell in it. He indeed gave him dominion over the universe i.e., the earth (the land, the waters and air and all that dwell therein) , the sun, the stars and all in between. This ideal is therefore nothing else but the attempt to reclaim that which was his birthright since the beginning of creation. Isn't therefore this a central ideal?

He is therefore independent at thought, and therefore in decision making, viz., which actions he should take in whichever situations. He is a person who has his life in his own hands and has power over his destiny. This is probably one of the greatly missing ideals among our scholars today. Lack of it can be identified by indecision and indifference one exhibits. This weakness is a result of, or effects of slavery, colonialism and deep-rooted poverty or inadequacy. Indeed slavery was the worst and longer evil system ever perpetuated on any group of people. But today an educated slave is worse than a slave (trader and slave) masters of old...[110]

Educating our people into this ideal through our schools, households and workplaces could heal the society against major weaknesses among our people—weaknesses including self hate and mediocrity or slothfulness. It can help increase the desire to excel and therefore to work hard—themselves more important ideals. It can help them to acquire wealth and therefore have in their possession—or more aptly make it part of their lives—the right to life, liberty, and pursuit of lasting happiness and be able to age in dignity. But a person who really strives for personal liberties, is as well striving for the liberties of the people and all about him. And this is a very important assertion. Why? "For to be free is not merely to cast off one's chains, but to live in a way that respects and enhances the freedom of others," aptly said Nelson Mandela.

That's why the ideal scholar is a self reliant person, and often self employed, I must add, after a certain level of career development. And he has a reason to pursue self-reliance. He strives for self-reliance because he craves abundance of material wealth and freedom; personal or moral liberties, knowing too well the nature of mankind—selfishness. He understands that if one wants something and wants more and better of it, he has to work for them, to think out of the box, push the boundaries—whether that is about intellect, traditions or time and space. That's why the ideal scholar is a man of ideas and imaginations. He knows as wrote

---

[110] *Adapted from an article Illiterate Graduates by Dr Lynn Kwaku; The Citizen p.7 Dar es Salaam Tanzania February 13, 2010*

Napoleon Hill that, "The idea is capable of yielding an income far greater than that of the average doctor lawyer or engineer whose education required several years in college." He is an entrepreneur in nature, a person who seeks more but in a fair way. He therefore seeks to increase the size of the pie instead of battling everybody else for a larger share of the same bread.

When we say he is self reliant, we mean he strives to attain maximum self-sufficiency. But since to be self-sufficient is almost impossible now that we no longer live in the Robinson Crusoe's times, and that we live a world of coexistence and interdependence today, the education must construct a person who has something to give so that he can get back for himself. To be able to do this, he must first realize how pivotal is the foregoing statement and in essence paramount for personal and national growth. Such a person will therefore bring fulfillment to himself and people around him everlastingly. In summary he is a kind of a person who more than fills his own personal present position or responsibility knowing too well that in any society there are more dependants than productive responsible individuals.

Recently I watched a television program ran by Nation Media Group in Tanzania. It was about growth agenda for Africa in general, and Tanzania in particular. Two things surprised me. One: attention to medium term but secondly associating growth with foreign input in terms of technology, skilled manpower and capital. No growth agenda can come from a short term perspective based on imported manpower. Any natural and thus lasting growth must come from the people themselves. How can you build innovative workforce and grassroots growth path when the psychology behind your model is that of the ancient angels who descended down to earth from high heaven and did some miracles and then immediately ascended back to whence they had come. Experiences from our recent privileges on cancelation of national debts on one hand and lessons from China and Botswana prove otherwise.

Mineral or fuel-rich countries of Africa or Asia have not realized any significant social or economic advancement from the Descending White Angels. Instead of smelting gold or diamond into wealth for the local people, the human angels of today tend to ascend back to whence they had come with not only gold and diamond or gas and crude oil, but also preconditions for grants. And that's not the worst case scenario. The worst thing is that they ascend back with local self-confidence and self-esteem thus leaving behind not only waste materials such as underground useless holes and heaps of underground soils but also overused polluted rivers and contaminated air and overused polluted minds and souls. What I am trying to say is that we can only progress through grass root strategy, strategy that leads to advancement and evolution of our own people.

Nigeria, Congo D.R and Tanzania generously offer a conspicuous example of dependence on external sources of growth—and markets. Nigeria leads in drilling mineral fuel from the bowels of its rich soil apart from the local market of more than 150 million people. DR Congo like Tanzania is richer in diamond and gold. Tanzania is the only mining home to Tanzanite—hence its name. While Nigeria enjoys the pride of leading as exporter of fuel her leadership is only in crude oil. As a result Nigeria has to import its own gasoline and diesel from oil importers of its own fuel only this time more expensively.

Nigeria has had to subsidize its fuel for its local market as a result. Refining it at home would accrue with it economies of scale involved that are presently enjoyed abroad. On the part of Tanzania as it may be same for DR Congo or any other mineral rich country, Tanzania is probably third in gold mining but earns only a shamefully minute proportion of its revenue from its gold and diamond. What happens is that the soil is hauled and exported overseas to be extracted for ore abroad and then philanthropically the miner determines what he will give back. Countries that follow this model of investment will be poor and get poorer as the sun sets each day eternally until when he comes—he who shall judge the earth and its arrogant occupants. Amen.

Probably you recognize we are probably a leading country in coffee production in EA but Uganda leads in exporting it to foreign markets. Why? I don't plainly whether it is due to proximity or pricing but in Karagwe one of the leading coffee growing districts in Tanzania farmers exports coffee to Uganda. Tanzanite is mined only in Tanzania hence its nomenclature. Surprisingly Kenya and India lead in Tanzanite business worldwide. We are source of Kiswahili in Tanzania but few Tanzanians benefit from it whereas Kenya exports a flock of teachers and lecturers for Kiswahili Language as well as news presenters to the Voice of America, BBC, China or even Radio France International. Why? Benny was right. There's a deep problem in the society which calls for immediate attention. We may say this author or Benny is just so skeptical a person and that the problem is so insignificant. But that's how all catastrophes begin. They begin with slight episodes.

Earth quakes are caused by nothing but a slight collision among the tectonic plates which them form a slight rift or crack deep in the core of the earth. Then all of a sudden a volcanic eruption or a Tsunami hits before suddenly its cousin Katrina follows right in its tracks claiming tens of thousands of lives. I am saying if we cannot stop it, let us evacuate our people and our female folks and children and then try to reclaim some of our properties. Indeed "Our life is an apprenticeship to the truth that around every circle, another can be drawn," said Ralph Waldo Emerson, emphasizing that: "That there's no end in nature, but every end is the beginning; and under every deep, a lower deep opens!"

IS SELF-RELIANCE IMPORTANT?
Self-reliance is not only important. It is indispensable—yes it is so especially as you mature. And when I say you, I mean you as an individual person or society. This is a key quality in the true sense that people don't care about you or your troubles. That's how other people don't either care about me or my troubles. They don't even think about you or me. Don't waste your time. They only think about themselves morning, afternoon and before dinner. Someone's flu matters so much to him than the flooding of River Ganges claiming a thousand of innocent Indian souls. A nagging wife is a calamity to a husband than an earthquake on the other side of the ocean that devastates lives of a million people.

An insider during General Amin's rule in Uganda, a person the author knows at personal level, confided with the author that the secret service unit, in which he served, ceased and put any person they suspected into the safety of their car boots and locked him safely as they drove during the night patrols. And that's not all. They would, with much regularity, park at the night club and order a few drinks which they would drink with great enthusiasm and dance to the tunes of the song that was famous at the time, a song with lyrics that went like this: "Omukwano Omutono Muwanvu, Bamulete Bamu..." completely paying no attention to the souls of the unfortunate people in the bonnet of the dusty car outside the pub in the air tight car boot, otherwise known as convicts. But most of these victims were often political—or personal rivals.

You now realize that no matter what, you have got to make yourself and your children to stand on one's own two feet. Writing about life being in your hands Emerson wrote in his essays on Self-reliance thus: "A political victory; a rise in rents; the recovery of your sick, or the return of your absent friend; or some other quite external event, raises your spirits and you think good days are preparing for you. Do not believe it. It can never be so. Nothing can bring you peace but yourself!" Indeed ,"Therefore let no man glory in men. For all things are yours (1 Cor. 3:21)!" When we are not independent, when we are not capable to run our own lives— think about it—we have no options. We tend to be domesticated and intellectually castrated. We cannot think straight. We cannot do anything by ourselves. And we are the old thing we hate to recall: slaves.

May I therefore suggest that you make reference to the book How Universities Under Develop You! You are going to realize that after a certain point in time you have to look at your options. Such is how I was over joyous when I first got myself employed.

I can still remember that day vividly. I can still visualize everything as is it was only yesterday. What I am trying to tell employees is that, time comes when you have to retire even when you love your job and the company. I cannot find words to describe how it felt good to start my first job. In fact I was about to lose it outright after I missed my sleep the whole night before my appointed date and therefore running the risk of arriving at the office when the sun was already over head. I went to work and worked so hard, giving my all to the job and company. As such, not only Snyman, Rajiv or Godfrey Mugambi noticed my passion and gave me several opportunities. Indeed I was nominated the best employee severally.

And I remember one more important moment—the moment when I relocated. In this company, I was given an impressive title The General Sales Manager! On that day I smiled at every passerby I met; I laughed at every conversation I was engaged in; I cheered every speaker who spoke; I had kissed goodbye every old foe, the house and old neighborhood. I'd smiled at everything my old boss said! Then, bracing myself for a set of new responsibilities, I rushed to the city center and purchased a few new additions to my wardrobes.

With this euphoria, I imagined that I was on top of the world. I acted—or tried to act—professionally. I spoke with dignity and changed my tone. I assumed I was indispensable and that all company's future depended on me! It was like all the expectations and future hopes of the organization, its employees and their families had been heaped upon me and I had to shoulder them. I had had work to do. Oh how I loved responsibility! But after a few months into it, oh my gods! My enthusiasm took toll and began to fragment yet again. Soon that everything no longer tasted sweet any more. I realized. I wasn't any significant in the future of these parties. I could be fired anytime and the company wouldn't collapse. I could be defaced or lame through accident and lose my dexterity and my job. I could as well be outcompeted in my quest to give my all.

What is hilariously similar about donor funds and employment, is the fatigue—i.e. donor and employer fatigue. The employer or any philanthropist can change his priorities, thereby stopping you from enjoying the blessings that you imagined were yours for life. As for employees, time comes when you have to retire even when you love your job and the company. I went to work hard giving my all to the job and company such that Not only Snyman, Rajiv or Godfrey Mugambi noticed my passion and selected me for various openings but I was nominated the best employee severally. But soon that was no longer sweet any more. I soon found out I'd traded my wife, my life, and children for the trophy of the superior slave in an oppressive system otherwise known as career! I agonized in my heart and began hitting the bottle—before I began thinking of other ways— ways to get a better living—without slaving. Soon I hit the edge. I was jumpy! I was nervous! I was powerless and completely exhausted!

The fact that I would soon be forty five, fat, frumpy and frail; with my bulging belly threatening the buttons off, terrified me most. For first time in my mature life, I questioned my existence. Indeed, I felt like I was a hundred years old Eskimo living in some godforsaken remote areas in Alaska only surrounded by the Eskimos, facing only the Russian icecaps and missiles! And I hated the truth that was downing on me! I hated my job and wanted to quit. But what would I fall back on? Nothing! On the brighter part, I realized I'd nothing to lose. I wasn't any wealthy. I wasn't any happy. My family wasn't well provided for. It wasn't any happy. The future was bleak. I'd no option. You don't. I resigned! I couldn't see myself running behind my boss all my life. I was running an empty life; a useless marathon of life, nourishing the ego of the others on company funds using some of us as guinea pigs. I couldn't go on working in such a drinking culture waking up drunk every day, squandering my precious time and energy with the recklessness of the fifteen rum-drunken sailors in the fables of John silver. It wasn't easy to resign from my job. Resignation meant to cut off the lifeline of my existence and the livelihood of my family. But more than anything I needed to be free. And when the thought of freedom that comes with such a decision, freedom that came with taking responsibility of my life in my own hands, I felt an overwhelming sense of dignity. This was the motivation that kept me going.

So really the time comes when you begin to reevaluate your priorities if you happen to mature—in the brains. But what's so disappointing is that to most people, when you do you are already old and exhausted and aren't any trained in the ways of managing yourself and your own business. That's when many collapse and die prematurely. As I thought of these facts, I realized that I was indeed insignificant to the organization. I realized that if I was any significant I was in my own livelihood as well as in the lives of my children and wife. I'd gone through transformation. I'd grown up now. I needed new and better reasons to stay on now that I had better reasons to move on.

Recalling the life I lived at the time, I realize now that I was either a genius, or all happened by God's own design that I resign, for indeed my predictions would've come true if I had not changed the course of my life. Truly I was heading for trouble. And what was worse, my family would have followed along with me. I truly needed to change. I had lost my sense of direction. There was no more future in that kind of life. Indeed even if I stayed on, and thus knowing where I worked, fearing to begin afresh, I was lost in the inside of the company, like many employees today. In fact having lived both lives, I know how getting lost in the inside is much more painful than getting lost on the outside. You realize that when lost on the outside, at least you have some space to wonder about! That's not the same when you are lot on the inside. That's why I decided that I needed change—the change that would pave the way for the future I wanted. I needed the change in the way I worked. I'd to work like the sun, not like a candle. I was living a life to make my employers and superiors happy. My life was geared toward making the people around me accept me: my peers, the community around me and some of my family members who didn't understand why I had to cross over. It was time to think about me. My life had proved a complete reverse of my expectations after I had graduated. It was a life filled with miseries. I hated the meals I could afford. I loathed the cloths I could afford and houses I could rent. I knew somehow I could do better than that—I knew I deserved better things. It wasn't afterall a loss in any way if I lost my job. I wasn't losing anything so far if you consider what was at stake.

The crossover also gave me a chance to try something new and novel. At my age I stood good ground. I was a little under forty—if things didn't go well, I'd have learned my lessons. I would then return to my job a better person. If I succeeded I would say bye-bye to misery: deprivation, mosquitoes, bugs, jiggers, black and white lice, flies, rats, maggots and cockroaches that roamed all over my body and house. Really faced with such a situation, you have only two options at your disposal: fight with the pests and bugs; or burn down the bed. I chose the third—the unthought-of! I burnt down the house altogether. I decided I was going to build or buy a spacious house free from insects fleeing from clogged toilets and smell that rambled all over my house. I also was fed up with the empty life. I lived a life that was meaningless. That's why many devote their lives to a drink or drugs when they lose meaning in life. I feared about my future without meaning in my life. It was time to make decisions before it was too late. For, as wrote Cathy Williams in her novel *Wife for Hire,* "whoever reaches eighty and thanks their lucky stars for amount of time they have devoted to their work?" I wanted to reach eighty and wring my hands thanking God —and my decision—for work well-done.

As I recall the situation at the time, I can still see many of my self-appointed advisors who came in handy to warn me against the decision I was taking. But are they themselves in the right calling or in their dream vocations? I wasn't going to settle for any job. I was not ready to start looking for another job—file my application letter —take any job according to my credentials. I was not ready for a marketing or sales job in any organization. I wasn't ready to stoop that low and flow with the waves as do the lifeless, soulless boats. I hated to be an employee, to work for someone for the balance of my lifetime. It wasn't different from slaving, was it? I hate to be a slave. On the whole, the lifestyles of my ageing superiors didn't do much to inspire me into lifelong employment. Most of the lifelong employees are stunted and perpetually in their adolescence, weak, and insecure except in their mothers' laps. They are forever boys and girls in their inner most selves unable to dare to stand on their feet and always afraid of dangers and risks of free world.[111]

Why people tend not to concede when faced with a situation which can never change is something I cannot still understand—despite all rich talk about perseverance. But truly one perseveres when he has a goal in sight.

---

[111] *Adapted from Vintage Stuff by Tom Sharpe*

Miracles don't happen anymore. Such individuals don't fail to recognize the fact that "at some point (in time), state services end for everyone, including the president." Medvedev, the then Russian president and now premier was right in answering to the dismissal of the head of upper house of the parliament, Sergei Mironov. I look at such men and feel sad. If they have done same things for ten or twenty years and they have not yet achieved anything significant, how do they expect the results to all o a sudden change in the future? That's insane. Albert Einstein was right. "The definition of insanity is doing same things everyday and to expect different results." Indeed, they forget the cost they incur in pursuit of such a path. "The cost of a thing is the amount of what I call life which is required to be exchanged for it immediately or in the long run."

On the contrary, "All successful people, men and women are big dreamers," Rightly observed Henry David Thoreau. "They imagine what their future could be," said Brian Tracy, "... they work every day toward their distant vision, that goal or purpose." These praiseworthy individuals, are able to scan the landscape, and to determine what could be done, when and how. Shutting themselves from the outside pessimistic world, they look at the possibilities and decide the way forward rather than concentrating with negativities. Like these great men, and as I analyzed deeds of such men and women, I recognize that all great achievers became so because they always expected to do greater things. And they didn't only dream. They went on ahead and acted on their dreams.

I had the confidence of making it—of succeeding! I had studied and come to the conclusion that only great men who could dream and act on their dreams often transformed their lives and the world around them—albeit only a few men and women have so far achieved this feat. I was certain because I knew the tremendous power that there is within all men who choose to use these powers. "The ultimate creative capacity of your brain may be, for all practical purposes, infinite," Rightly observed Dr. W. Ross Addey, of the Space Biology Laboratory of the Brain Research Institute at U.C.L.A. The same capacity is in the same way infinite in me as it is in you.

I could feel it now as I did long time when I was super enthusiastic about life. I don't know what happened in between but I wasn't going to lose it now that I felt it in me once again with the same entity as it was long ago when I was young. Pablo Picasso discovered that "All children are artists. The problem," he said, "is how to remain an artist once he grows up." I dreaded to get old and have my talents gone. Truly writing and training are a set of an ice cream in the desert in this country! It created an uncomfortable private domestic scene of biblical proportions when I resigned to pursue this goal. I cannot blame those in my family who weren't happy about my decision to resign. People seem to be fond of business as usual. Lillian Hellman said: Decision by democratic majority vote is a fine form of government, but it's a stinking way to create". But I had another advantage. I had a deep desire to leave. I had an enormous desire to pursue a new career.

How is it advantageous then? Indeed it is. Whenever there's a strong desire to do something, it is proof that there is capability to do it. I also had a premonition that in life or in any decision i have to make, I have two forces opposing one another. Only the stronger of two lives on. Now what are these forces? One is desire to please others, to conform. The second is the desire to be yourself, to give your own person full expression. If your desire to please others and conform is stronger than desire to find and please your noble goals, you will end up as a failure. The reverse is true. So I normally choose to align my actions with my goals. To conform you have to have low aims and act even less. For so are majority. . I wasn't going to conform. In Self-reliance Emerson had said: "And that the Society everywhere is in conspiracy against the manhood of every one of its members. And that indeed who so would be a man must be a nonconformist."

I must admit there was much turmoil in my mind. I was going to forget what others say, and follow what my heart tells me to do instead. I wasn't going to conform. To hell. Martin Luther King, Jr. said that "human salvation lies in the hands of the creatively maladjusted." It was indeed a little later that I learned that even my closest people thought I was out of my mind. But if they said i was crazy, it didn't matter. Niels Bohr said: "Your theory is crazy, but it's not crazy enough to be true. Nietzsche said, "You need chaos in your soul to give birth to a dancing star." Oscar Levant observed that "There's a fine line between genius and insanity. I've erased this line." Napoleon Hill in Think and Grow Rich reveals something that will "interest you to know that Marconi's 'friends' had him taken into custody and examined in psychopathic hospital, when he announced he had discovered a principle through which he could send messages through air without the aid of wires or other direct physical means of communication." Professor William James said: "Genius means little more than the faculty of perceiving in an unhabitual way."

MEET JULIUS

Indeed all major changes have been effected yes with the cooperation from many other people but there has always been one person behind every social change. Think of Julius Nyerere Abraham Lincoln or Mandela. Rosa Parks, Jesse Owens, Jack Johnson, Barack Obama, Martin Luther King Jr., Mahatma Gandhi or Julius Best Kambarangwe and a few others, names that can fill this and a few other pages, are people who decided to make hard decisions, decision that meant life or death, but decisions that would lift up the lives of the rest of their family members and fellow citizens. When we mention such names like Nyerere or Mandela, may seem like cutting the average person off. And it is understandable. I'll be the last person to do that nonetheless. I say so because I know without the audacious choices and decisions Julius made in his very humble position that many went to the university. How did he manage to do this? It all began with the decision he did when like Abraham in the holy bible departed from his father's household leaving almost everything behind to set up his own life—a life that multiplied and gave the others not only a home and put food on the table but also schools fees and therefore education and livelihood.

To try to show you the audacity of this person, he had had a dream for education when being the elder brother at home at the time; his father didn't want to lose him. He wanted him to work in his farm and manage his cattle and goats. But he had bigger dreams than being a goat herder. After pleading with his father many times without number, and failed, he packed his few clothes and walked away once and for all. This was not a simple decision—though? To give you a picture, he had signed a document to disband any financial and certainly moral affiliations with the only conceivable source of financial and certainly moral means—which was his wealthy father. This was a decision that changed the whole family. I know this is true because Julius is my brother. The author also know that at the time this family's resources were getting depleted at a supersonic speed due to drought and indeed many mouths to feed his father had created at the time, all which together demanded a shift from old ways of living.

Is this a mere fiction? Nay! I know this story is true because Julius is my brother! It was this major decision he made that the author went on to accomplish his secondary school education and—thereupon—the university. It is through the work of his hands and innovation of his mind that I managed to pay for my school fees. It was through Julius—literally that I extended the same lessons and deeds to my younger siblings. It was the same initiative that extended the same lessons to the rest of the extended family and the whole of village of Katera and whole neighborhood. In fact I can say without shame—I can say it selflessly that it was through my brother's efforts and lessons—after he had been a good student of my mother's—that many of us today learned lessons into indispensability of the ideals or character, self-reliance, and that hard work and imagination pays off. This was vivid to me after the severe famine of the eighties and nineties, alongside the dwindling of my father's wealth, the two sad experiences on which you cannot put a blame: the vagaries of nature, or my father's multiple wives; when through my brother Julius therefore that the idea—and ability—to write the book you are now reading was set before me about twenty five years ago. It is probably most appropriate to say without Julius, this book you are now reading would not be written! And I am not a seer to determine what you—or especially what I—would otherwise be doing right now—praise God!

Let me end this narrative now with two more insights about Julius.One: When I talk about the hand hoe, it may sound like a trivial matter to many. But it was different to Julius who had lived a prosperous life during his early life. To such a person it is different! Trust me. Two: Just a few days ago, I called him over the phone but he couldn't quick the phone. So I drove straight and went to see him because he was not very far from Mbezi where I live here in Dar es Salaam City. And remember the events I narrated above happened only about twenty five years ago back deep in the cattle plains of Igabiro and the village of Kifuye in Katera, Kyerwa, Tanzania. I couldn't see Julius even though the matter I needed to discuss with him was urgent because he was attending an even more urgent task, for he was in the theater. Mind you he wasn't in a music theater? But instead he was in the hospital theater room not because he was sick and getting operated? No sir. It was he who was doing the surgery to a very seriously ill patient! Think about it! It didn't come out of easiness though? He had to sustain himself and others by tilling the land with a hand hoe, and becoming a goat herder—projects from which a few farm produces and a couple of heads were sold to pay for my fees—long before he became a doctor—and mentor.

IS THIS ABOUT ME?
Though what I have written above may seem to be like a biography of an author who triumphed over worst misfortunes, it is not about me. It is not even about my brother. It is rather about you—yes you—the immediate reader! That's why I believe we need to look at our education system. We can't go with a system of education within which people may though pass exams, yet majority doesn't get employed. And we can't go on with an

education system where though only a handful gets employed, what's more, those who get employed, aren't any productive, or happy. This can be evidenced by the turn over of the employees everywhere among a few companies that still believe they can turn the tables around. Many have already submitted to only breaking even. They believe they can't do any better. Back to our graduates and education in general, we cannot go on with an education that leaves majority of our scholars misallocated only to be disillusioned far too long when they can redo their lives.

Napoleon Hill in Think and Grow Rich was right when he said that: "There's something radically wrong with a civilization and a system of education which permits 98 percent of people to go through life as failures." No nation ever progressed without building industry and innovation. No nation ever developed without progressing or advancing its middle class for otherwise you will fill the country with foreign cheap goods while little or no trickle down effects in terms of technology or capital from watered down foreign investors or expatriates. No country ever developed without developing a sense of self-reliance. You cannot develop if you are dependent. Dependence begins when you can't be self employed as a people. It is people who are self employed that build big businesses and bigger middle to upper class.

In the main, this failure is a seedling of the culture we are tolerating: mass indecision, lack of ambition, low aim, and quick fix; I've got news for you. All these are a set of bad habits which habitually begin in youth stage. At the head is the tradition of indecision and lack of stimulation of ambition. As for indecision, it begins during young age. Combined with lack or absence of desire for success and choice of vocation, this habit grows as one gets through secondary school—unguided—then through wrong choice of a course and cause—that is inappropriate course and cause—then the natural thing happens: one gets through high schools, college or even university without definite purpose. Isn't that logical? Nothing else can be more natural—indeed!

Is this unique or, natural to Tanzania alone? No. It isn't a unique problem to us alone, but we ought to mind our own problems first. The major weakness of most educational institutions is that they neither teach nor encourage the habit of identifying ones abilities and choosing to have one major definite purpose—which transmutes into lack of decision making, poor jobs, low earning, low self-esteem and absence of or low levels of practice, low or absence of critical thinking, creativity, and total collapse of free enterprise—and life after college etc. It is no wonder formal educational instructions in schools, even at the universities, all under develop talents of the students. Schools don't inspire or train students to seek and pursue one's vocation or calling. We must teach them to dream and imagine whatever they crave to achieve in life is possible. It begins with imagination. Henry Van Dyke summed it up thus: "I hold it true that thoughts are things; they're endowed with bodies and breath and wings. And that we send them forth to fill the world with good results, or ill. That which we call our secret thought, speeds forth to earth's remotest spot, leaving its blessings or its woes like tracks behind it as it goes. We build our future, thought by thought, for good or ill, yet know it not. Yet so the universe was wrought…"

Talking about self-reliance and empowerment or capacity building, only recently writing this chapter, when I saw a poster hanging on a wall in a restaurant where I was taking a retreat and it attracted my attention. It was created by Twaweza a local NGO dealing with enlightenment among the local people in Tanzania. What did attract me was, yes, the pictures of famous people smiling back to me with a sigh of confidence and self assurance spreading across the huge poster, but as well the layout. Yet there was something more about it that forced me to take a ballpoint pen and a diary and copied the content of the poster. The pictures lined up the most famous living personalities of this generation, people you would agree that they stand out as the Kilimanjaro among the ant hills.

They are an assortment of academicians, political leaders, sports stars and among them a handful of writers. From right to left the poster lined up faces of president Kikwete of Tanzania, Dr. Asha Rose Migiro, then the deputy secretary of the UN ,the famous opposition leader and presidential candidate in Tanzania, dr. Willbrod Slaa, Prime Minister Mizengo Peter Pinda, speaker Mrs. Makinda, the then opposition party leader and professor of economics Professor Ibrahim Lipumba, an academician and former UN Habitat Boss and now as I write member of parliament and minister for lands Anna Tibaijuka, Zitto Kabwe, a young and probably most famous upcoming opposition and youth leader and role model for many, former premier and member of parliament Edward Lowassa, former premier and OAU general secretary and former UN candidate for general secretary and one time presidential hopeful Salim Ahmed Salim, parliamentary opposition leader and president of the leading opposition party CHADEMA, Freeman Mbowe and finally a leading solo and probably most successful music artiste in the country Lady Jaydee.

Well, quite an impressive list huh? But before I take you into what was written on the poster as its ultimate message, let us turn the page. I turned the page and I saw the pictures of Barack Obama, Bill Gates Koffi Annan, Didier Drogba, Queen Elizabeth, Ban Ki Mun, Dalai Rama, Nelson Mandela, Wayne Rooney, Lady Gaga, and Mo Ibrahim. Now underneath these great names, on the rim of the poster the note in italics which is my message, read thus: Je Nani Atakukomboa 2012? Je Utakaa tu Kusubilia Mwaka Mzima au Utajikomboa? It meant: Who will set you free? Are you going to sit back and wait for salvation from elsewhere the whole year round or you are going to free yourself and choose the life you want and go ahead and take it? Indeed you will wait for an eternity if you wait for salvation from all four grid references. You can choose any politician but that's the end of it. They forget. Don't waste your time. And I speak with experience. The Arab spring beginning with Tunisia illustrated how not Ben Ali, Mubarak or Gadafi was working to promote the interests of the people. When I look at the struggles between the West and East or North and. South, I realize that few are men in power that have the interests of the people at heart. That's how few have already realized that politics is sham, and democracy a hoax. That's why typically, "In a sick country," aptly observed Bernard Malamud, "every step to health is an insult to those who live on its sickness!"

I once took a pen and many papers and counting my enemies, I jotted their names down. I had an impressive list of my enemies—the sadists—and people who let me down, people who came between me and prosperity I craved and deserved. They were the people who came between me and my goals—the goals to excel, to be successful. And how I loathed and cursed them? I wouldn't have poured water on them if hell fires were burning them. In fact I am ashamed to admit that I wouldn't have been disappointed if at the time they were in the death list in the hands of the messenger of death! Then as I pondered about what everyone had done to derail me, I noticed I had forgot one person—one great enemy. He was actually the one who was responsible for my miseries—one senior enemy and the most meanest of all. Yet his name hadn't appeared in the list. Do you know who that person was? It was the man in the mirror—a me—a Festo Michael Kambarangwe. Ralph Waldo Emerson was right in his Essays of Self-reliance when he said: "A political victory, a rise in rents; the recovery of your sick, or the return of your absent friend; or some other quite external event, raises your spirits and you think good days are preparing for you. Do not believe it. It can never be so. Nothing can bring you peace but yourself!"

Knowing too well that he has but to be self reliant the ideal scholar is a taker of risks—calculated risks. This is an imperative trait if one has to succeed as a self employed entrepreneur. After all he reckons that nothing ventured, nothing gained. The king's guards' motto in ancient Greece went thus: "All people have fears, but the brave put down their fears and march forward; sometimes to death but always to victory!"

Among the goals of education for all American youth, the (US) Education Policy Commission issued as its third aim, or goal or purpose of education in our definition stipulated as the first of its ten qualities that all youth needed in order: *to develop skills and attitudes that enhanced saleable skills and those understandings and attitudes that make them intelligent and productive participants in economic life*; and number five seems to also emphasize the same notion thus: *the knowledge of how to purchase and use goods and services intelligently, understanding both the value received by the consumer and the economic consequences of the their acts.*

The Association for Supervision and Curriculum Development summed this up as being informed about participating in the economic world of production and consumption. Education should therefore allow students to have an upper hand on what they want to be. *"the choice is the individual's, and the decision leads to his or her own self- definition and in doing so makes his or her own essence,"* said the two concluding beautifully that; *"We are what we choose to be (*Curriculum Foundations, Principles and Issues 3rd Ed, p.36) ." "The most important kind of knowledge is about the human condition and the choice that each person has to make...* (Curriculum Foundations, Principles and Issues 3rd Edition p. 36)." *(Also), "Education is a process of developing consciousness about the freedom to choose and the meaning of and the responsibility for ones choices* (Curriculum Foundations, Principles and Issues 3rd Ed, p.36)." Education must produce *self-actualizing people,* in Maslow's words, or *total humans* in Roger's...."[112]

---

[112] *Curriculum Foundations, Principles and Issues 3rd Edition p 47*

21. THE IDEAL SCHOLAR IS MONEY CONSCIOUS

"I wish it grew on trees, but it takes hard work to make money." – Jim Cramer

The ideal scholar is not only time conscious, self-reliant and self-employed person. He is money conscious! Though by money conscious, we may mean he is economical, yet we don't mean this person is—or should be—a miser. Instead he knows the money, its kind and characteristics, much as he is able—and willing—to tame both the money and himself. The latest word or quality is pivotal since if he cannot control himself, he cannot control anything else let alone money. He is therefore a person who sets out to find money, gets it, keeps it and enjoy it. He enjoys his money because he is on top of it—he is in charge. Yet this is mistake our curriculum does so well. It never concerns itself with mastery of money. And men of education do the same mistake. They learn how to acquire money but fail to learn how to keep it, and so they enjoy it only temporarily. How? They successfully find money but fail to keep it. This is why we question if such a person is really educated. The proverbs say: the fool and his money are soon parted.

When it first came to my notice that if somebody wins a million dollar in lottery, the Gaming Board requires that he is prepared to handle both himself and the money before his money is handed over to him in most advanced parts of the world, I was shocked! I couldn't believe it. Today I know why you have got to be money conscious. I didn't reckon that failure to do so leads to the money, however torrential it may come over to you, yet like water it may flow back to whence it had come right through your fingers leaving you penniless.

This lesson is important because with mastery of the rest of the ideals, we are certain if you put them to full use, money will flow to you. In fact it will, until when you will wonder where it had been hiding before; or you may not understand why others scrape for a living while you have it in abundance. Truly if you put to use all ideals in this program, ideals such as determination, faith and standing behind one goal, you will, with little effort, see how money starts flowing in—almost with vengeance.

Recognize therefore that prosperity, or its opposite number, begins in the mind. To prosper, you should transformation your mindset. Why? Negative mindset is natural. And like sin, you must not entertain it. Bad mindset is like bad friends. Entertaining it is like quartering a wolf in the sheep's pen. indeed considering the importance of this subject and the fact that they don't teach it at the university, instead preparing you to serve as someone's accountant or auditor and scrape the rest of your life it confounds me how mankind spends time and resources irrationally!

I see how we spend years in school learning how to balance books of accounts than learn how to actually attract money and sigh! When I think of how irrationally Televisions, governments and corporations stash money in sports, music and entertainment than in books and reading or sponsoring writing exhibitions I agonize so deeply. I agonize because most of it goes down the drain. And that's not all. Such bad moneys destroy its receiver, leaving him with stress, hypertension and in the end addiction to alcohol and drugs. Hip-hop music , modeling and film industry are some of the exemplary rich soils where drug abuse and depression thrive. That's the doom of man. He is naturally a politician. He does things to please the majority of the less intelligent folks in order to win their praises, their votes—or both.

That's why it is not enough to learn how to make money. The painful truth is that earning big money and keeping it are two different things. I submit that you read a magnificent book by Bob Proctor titled You Were Born Rich. In this book we are astounded to learn the following astoundingly painful facts—facts that are true nonetheless. In 1923 eight men controlled more money than the United States' government at that time. Naturally, irrefutably these men had found, as Bob Proctor put it, "The secret of earning money." Now let's see where these men were twenty-five years later: The president of the largest independent steel company, Charles Schwab, lived on borrowed money for five years before he died bankrupt. The president of North America's largest gas company, Howard Hopson, went insane. The greatest wheat speculator, Arthur Cutton, died abroad, insolvent. The president of the New York Stock Exchange, Richard Whitney, was sent to Sing-Sing Penitentiary.

To add a little flavor on Sir Richard Whitney, according to money.cnn.com/2008/12/16, he was paroled in 1941 after serving year's sentence after which he became the manager of a diary farm supervising three farmhands and only 25 cows. Imagine. A member of the President's cabinet, Albert Fall, was pardoned from prison so he could die at home. The greatest "bear" on Wall Street, Jesse Livermore, died a suicide. The head of the greatest monopoly, Ivar Krueger, killed himself. The president of the Bank of International Settlement, Leon Fraser, also died a suicide. Each of these men learned well the art of earning money, but it would seem that not one of them had ever learned how to live the "rich life", which was their birthright."[113]

Let us make a few more reflections from our own lives. Now think of Mike Tyson or Michael Jackson. These were people who earned a fortune in their career life. Severally they lost more money than they earned it. Let the American idols free. Talk about our senior executives and politicians here at home. What about our artists and sportsmen? I have met personally an Ex-government minister wearing torn sandals and drinking the hardest liquor he could lay his hands on—or one offered by any generous citizen. I have seen too sports men who are beggars today as I write. But why? This is what I can call a Mr. Nice syndrome. Mr. nice was one time the author's best artist. He was adored by many as is his name. He made a fortune but soon he was outcompeted and sidelined and drained of his fortune.

When most of us especially our artists in the country have earned a significant amount of money, and fame, they spend it extravagantly, thoughtlessly. Many spend long hours in clubs for leisure rather than in creating music or performing—things which brought one wealthy and famous—in the first place. As a result? A footballer grows bulky, fatigued and unfit. The artist falls in the charts and he loses his earnings. He can't create music or perform any more. And that is his end. You will find many retirees who earn more than two hundred to three hundred million shillings on retirement. But do they prosper afterwards? Nay! They run bankrupt and soon too soon they are back on the streets chasing mediocre jobs. It is no wonder we emphasize the training in self-reliance and entrepreneurship which together help to prepare employees before they retire. It could also be of great benefit if people had big picture and spread their earnings over

---

[113] *Source: You Were Born Rich By Bob Proctor*

the long period of time rather than living like kings or queens today and die as beggars on the streets a couple of years later. That's the story of the author's father. The author, for instance, is a witness of the almost same-same verity following experience from his own father.

Before he died almost a pauper in the eyes of people who did not know he had other assets, assets that did not readily translate into money, Michael Kambarangwe Sr. had accumulated a sizeable fortune. I was young then but I can close my eyes and almost touch several suitcases stuffing bank notes of various currencies at the time when coins were an ice cream in the desert. I can now even see I witnessed long queues of men and women who came to change money or seek jobs and livelihood at our doorsteps. Dad was not a money changer but I guess he had excess over what he needed then. Anyone who knew him at the time cannot describe his wealth in this sub county of Katera failed by words. It was a spring in summer. Now look around you. I have had to use the first person account to emphasize the fact that what the author says is true. Now forget about my father for now. Afterall no money can sustain a family of fifty children and ten wives for long. What about you? What are you planning to do to mitigate this prevalent disaster?

CHARACTERISTICS OF MONEY

This discussion is meant to help my reader to make money. And having made money, this book intends to help you keep it and keep the benefits money brings to our lives. We are very soon going to discussion how best money can be made and keep because we have seen that making millions isn't enough. One making millions, needs also the discipline to keep it. But unless you have knowledge on what is money and its characteristics, you cannot have an upper hand over it.

Bob Proctor suggested rightly that money was important. "Nothing can take the place of money in the arena in which it is used! Don't listen to some folks who say money doesn't matter. It matters a lot. Money is an effect and it must always be earned. You must work hard, you must plan to get it. But getting it isn't enough. You must keep it. But to keep it, Money must circulate. Money is not meant to be hoarded. Rather, it is meant to be used, enjoyed and circulated. Money is a servant. Always remember, money is a servant; you are the master."[114] But to these three I would like

---

[114] *Adapted from You Were Born To Be Rich by Bob Proctor*

to add the fourth characteristic of money. It is intoxicating. One a person has money, he likes to spend it. Not for the pleasure of it alone, but for the good things money does to its owner. The problem to this attribute of money is that the desire to spend is unlimited. A wise person will control his desire to spend and increase his desire not only to save but to get more money. The principles of economics teach us that income is equal to the proportion you consume plus what you save. The principle further states that what you can invest is proportional to what you save. We are therefore advised to manage what we consume much as to save and invest our savings in profitable ventures. The authors of the proverbs knew this truth when the concluded that the fool and his money are soon parted.

Though not all who lose their money are fools, but because many of us are unwise when it comes to money, we are going to dedicate a few minutes discussing how you can respond to the forgoing characteristics of money, with the quest to make more of it and spend it as much as you want but as well be able to keep it—which is your greatest handicap you want to tame. In short we are going to study how to tame rather than being tamed by money. We are going to learn the difference between a mediocre scholar and the ideal scholar: one puts his money where his mouth or the zipper is, as another hoards it, invests it.

HOW JOHN D. ROCKEFELLER BECAME—AND REMAINED—THE RICHEST MAN IN THE WHOLE WORLD

John D. Rockefeller, Sr. had accumulated his first million at the age of thirty-three. At the age of forty-three, he had built up the largest monopoly the world has ever seen—the great standard Oil Company. But where was he at fifty-three? Worry had got him at fifty-three. Worry and high-tension living had already wrecked his health. At fifty-three, he "looked like a mummy," says John K. Winkler, one of his biographers.

At fifty-three, Rockefeller was attacked by mystifying digestive maladies that swept away his hair, even the eye-lashes and all but a faint wisp of eyebrow, "So serious was his condition," says Winkler, "that at one time John D. was compelled to exist on human milk." According to the doctors, he had alopecia, a form of baldness that often starts with sheer nerves. He looked so startling, with his stark bald dome that he had to wear a skullcap. Later, he had wigs made—at $500 apiece—and for the rest of his life he wore these silver wigs.

Rockefeller had originally been blessed with an iron constitution. Reared on a farm, he had once had stalwart shoulders, an erect carriage, and a strong, brisk gait.

Yet at only fifty-three—when most men are at their prime—his shoulders drooped and he shambled when he walked. "When he looked in a glass," says John T. Flynn, another of his biographers, "he saw an old man. The ceaseless work, the endless worry, the streams of abuse, the sleepless nights, and the lack of exercise and rest" had exacted their toll; they had brought him to his knees. He was now the richest man in the world; yet he had to live on a diet that a pauper would have scorned. His income at the time was a million dollars a week —but two dollars a week would probably have paid for all the food he could eat. Acidulated milk and a few crackers were all the doctors would allow him. His skin had lost its color — it looked like old parchment drawn tight across his bones. And nothing but medical care, the best money could buy, kept him from dying at the age of fifty three.

How did it happen? Worry. Shock, high-pressure and high-tension living. He "drove" himself literally to the edge of the grave. Even at the age of twenty-three, Rockefeller was already pursuing his goal with such grim determination that, according to those who knew him, "nothing lightened his countenance save news of a good bargain." When he made a big profit, he would do a little war dance—throw his hat on the floor and break into a jig. But if he lost money, he was ill! He once shipped $40,000 worth of grain by way of the Great Lakes. No insurance. It cost too much: $150. That night a vicious storm raged over Lake Erie. Rockefeller was so worried about losing his cargo that when his partner, George Gardner, reached the office in the morning, he found John D. there pacing the floor.

"Hurry," he quavered. "Let's see if we can take out insurance now, if it isn't too late!" Gardner rushed uptown and got the insurance; but when he returned to the office he found John D. in an even worse state of nerves. A telegram had arrived in the meantime; the cargo had landed, safe from the storm. He was sicker than ever now because they had "wasted" the $150! In fact, he was so sick about it that he had to go home and take to his bed. Think of it! At that time, his firm was doing a gross business of $500,000 a year — yet he made himself so ill over $150 that he had to go to bed.

He had no time for play, no time for recreation, no time for anything except making money and teaching Sunday school. When his partner, George Gardner, purchased a second hand yacht, with three other men, for

$2,000, John. D. was aghast, refused to go out in it. Gardner found him working at the office one Saturday afternoon, and pleaded "Come on, John, let's go for a sail. It will do you good. Forget about business. Have a little fun." Rockefeller glared. "George Gardner," he warned, "You are injuring your credit at the banks—and my credit too. First thing you know, you'll be wrecking our business. No, I won't go on your yacht—I don't ever want to see it!" And he stayed plugging in the office all Saturday afternoon.

The same lack of humor, the same lack of perspective characterized John D. all through his business career. Years later he said, "I never placed my head upon the pillow at night without reminding myself that my success might be only temporary."

With millions at his command, he never put his head upon his pillow without worrying about losing his fortune. No wonder worry wrecked his health. He had no time for play or recreation never went to the theater, never played cards, and never went to party. As Mark Hanna said the man was mad about money. "Sane in every other respect, but mad about money."

Rockefeller had once confessed to a neighbor in Cleveland, Ohio, that he "wanted to be loved," yet he was so cold and suspicious that few people even liked him. Morgan once balked at having to do business with him at all. "I don't like the man," he snorted. "I don't want to have any dealing with him." Rockefeller's own brother hated him so much that he removed his children's bodies from the family plot. "No one of my blood," he said, "will ever rest in land controlled by John D."

Rockefeller's employees and associates lived in holy fear of him, and here is the ironic part: he was afraid of them—afraid they would talk outside the office and "give secrets away." He had so little faith in human nature that once, when he signed a ten year contract with an independent refiner, he made the man promise not to tell anyone, not even his wife! "Shut your mouth and run your business" — that was his motto. Then at the very peak of his prosperity, with gold flowing into his coffers like hot yellow lava pouring down the sides of Vesuvius, his private world collapsed. Books and articles denounced the robber - baron war of the standard oil company—secret rebates with railroads, the ruthless crushing of all rivals.

In the oil fields of Pennsylvania, John D. Rockefeller was the most hated man on earth. He was hanged in effigy by the men he had crushed (i.e. the men he had crushed made a doll of Rockefellers and hanged it in a great jubilation). Many of them longed to tie a rope round his withered neck and hang him to the limb of a sour apple tree. Letter breathing fire and brimstone poured into his office—letters threatening his life. He hired bodyguards to keep his enemies from killing him. He attempted to ignore this cyclone of hate. He had once said cynically, "You may kick me and abuse me provided you will let me have my own way." But he discovered he was human after all. He was puzzled and bewildered by this new enemy —illness —which attached him from within. At first "he remained secretive about his occasional indispositions," tried to put his illness out of his mind. But insomnia, in digestion and the loss of his hair —all physical symptoms of worry and collapse—were not to be denied.

Finally, his doctors told him the shocking truth. He could take his choice: his money and his worries —or his life. They warned him; he must either retire or die. He retired. But before he retired, worry greed; fear had already wrecked his health. When Ida Tarbell, America's most celebrated female writer of biographies, saw him, she was shocked. She wrote: "An awful age was in his face. He was the oldest man I have ever seen." Old? Why, Rockefeller was then several years younger than general Mac Arthur was when he recaptured the Philippines! But he was such a physical wreck that Ida Tarbell pitied him. She was working at that time on her powerful book which condemned the Standard Oil and all that it stood for; she certainly had no cause to love the man who had built up this "octopus." Yet, she said that when she saw John D. Rockefeller teaching a Sunday-school class, eagerly searching the faces of all those round him—"I had a feeling which I had not expected, and which time intensified. I was sorry for him. I know no companion so terrible as fear."[115]

---

[115] *Source: How to Stop Worrying and Start Living p.329-35*

22. ORDER

"To love rightly is to love what is orderly and beautiful in an educated and disciplined way." —Plato

With order as a quality or virtue, the ideal scholar is a disciplined person. Being orderly he recognizes, and reconciles, his life, and actions, with the fact that the universe is principled. He recognizes that nothing happens without a cause, and nothing happens without a certain order. The sun rises from east and falls on the west on a certain strict way. The day follows the night as winter with summer. The heavenly planets and stars rotate in their orbits without colliding, each maintaining its proper place, path and relationship with one another. The foregoing verity doesn't simply skip the ideal scholar. That's on one level. On the other, ORDER summarizes a situation where a person conducts oneself in a certain way; he lives his life in a certain specific way of life. It is a kind of one absolute and though supple, yet a definite way or path. A certain way has something to do more with character than with work skills or one's talents or gifts. This is about which principle architects carefully put two bricks together. Alexander Pope concluded saying that: "Order is heaven's number one law." [116]

Being orderly, the ideal scholar plans his day. He plans and knows his long term plans subdivided into shorter medium and daily plans. To him meticulous planning is his strong suit. For such a person, tedious patient planning is his way of life. He plans tediously long before he endeavors to act.

---

[116] *Please make reference to the chapter on the principled universe, or in the book* A Sick Nation *in this very series*

That's why when he acts, he does so with quite a speed. Besides, after he has made a decision, he never changes his plans quickly. If he ever amends the plans, he does so very slowly—very cautiously. Talking about life of a certain way or the verity that the universe is principled, he recognizes that success or prosperity isn't about luck or chance but about purpose and standing behind one major goal in life, burning desire to achieve—to excel; determination, planning, consistency.

When we say the ideal scholar is principled, some of the readers will imagine that this is one of the easiest ideals or character to observe. They are wrong! To be principled requires that you submit to the principles even when the right actions may apparently seem to present situations that are themselves dangerous—situations that seem to be perilous to you. Take David for instance. I mean King David. Soon after the God of Israel had turned his back on king Saul, and having therefore anointed David as the future king, Saul began hunting him down, intending to kill him. During such secret missions, severally David found Saul in his hands.

One of such dramatic moments was when Saul left his army commanders a distance away and entered in a cave to relieve himself—a cave in which David and his men were hiding. Did David raise his hand against his sworn enemy—the king? No. He didn't empty his gun on him. An unprincipled dishonest gunman would have left holes all over King Saul's body. Well, they didn't have guns those days, but it makes no difference. He should have smote him to death with one mighty spear. But that's not David. You or I would have killed the enemy. You or I would have chosen to hasten the takeover. The situation was even tougher for David because of his loyal army men—the men who were with him day and night running from cave to cave, eating abhorable things when they knew the opportunity to end their miseries and enter into the glory had presented itself!

"Kill him. The Lord God has presented this moment for you," they pressed him. And it was true The Lord God has presented this moment for David. But only with a different intention—to put him to test. His answer was: "I can't raise my hand against the Lord's anointed." He didn't give in to quick fix. He knew there was time and season for everything under the sun. He knew there were dos and don'ts. He knew there was good and bad choices. It is no wonder he earned loyalty from not only his army commanders, but God himself again not only because he refused to take advantage of an enemy but also because he refused to raise a hand against the anointed of God.

And what of Socrates? Though he was accorded a chance to escape and probably live on well enough in the exile elsewhere, he declined to escape his death penalty, saying he would not run away if it was the will of the Gods and the community that he dies. Besides, running away would go against the ethics and morality he stood for. It would like to say he didn't mean what he said. "Let it be then, Crito," he said in response to his decision not to run away,"and let us act in this way, since this is the way the God is leading us." Then with indifferent look in his eyes, he drank a cup of poison—and died.[117] Yet, to be principled means one will not be dragged into doing something or reach a decision even when the body or mind, or even the status quo says otherwise.

Finally, does order have anything to do with wealth or prosperity? We know that there is a principle or law governing everything under the sun. This is true in business much as it is in biology such as in reproduction and in astronomy etc. In words of Napoleon Hill: "We are where we are, because of our own conduct," he said. "If there is a principle of cause and effect, which controls business, finance and transportation," he continued, "this same principle controls individuals and determines their financial economic status." Indeed if there is a law or principle that governs the prospects of the individual person or business entity or institution, we can thereof safely conclude that either the same law or principle, or another controls nations international standing and economic and political power. If this is true, then there is no other study in the universe that dwarfs the one we are presenting right here—and now.

---

[117] *www.moyak.com/papers/socrates.html*

23. THE IDEAL SCHOLAR IS WISE AND SENSIBLE—AND THEREFORE HAS PLANS AND A SET OF PRIORITIES

"Always plan ahead. It wasn't raining when Noah built the ark."
— Richard Cushing

Proverbs 4:7 (KJV) states that: Wisdom is the principal thing; therefore get wisdom: and with all thy getting get understanding." When we say the ideal scholar is wise and sensible, we mean he is sane, levelheaded, reasonable, rational, wise, prudent, practical, judicious and farsighted. Google.com defines sensible as (of statement or course of action) chosen in accordance with wisdom or prudence as something too of benefit to the future." Acting with care and thought for the future. Cambridge advanced learners dictionary defines the term "wise" as approving possessing or showing the ability to make good judgments, based on a deep understanding and experience of life: Its reverse is being foolish which is the same as being unwise, ridiculous or lacking in judgment.

As I write on, indeed as you are reading this statement, I know there some of my readers now saying that this is the part of the book that could be skipped to save the time of the readers and resources of the author. I refuse to accept that an initiation into wisdom is meaningless altogether. Indeed though you may imagine prioritization is a simple thing to do, but we seldom go right in doing our prioritization. All of us. Is this ideal that important? Yes indeed! It is the few who can ignore the trifles and focus on the big issues, the big picture, it is these who can walk the fine line, it is these that set themselves aside; that stand out from the crowd. Let me illustrate.

Before I narrate how I personally stumbled upon the importance of having prudent priorities, let me first say that being wise, the ideal scholar has priorities—prudent priorities. What then does it mean? Dictionary.cambridge.org defines priority as something that is very important and must be dealt with before other things. That is why the ideal scholar plans ahead. This is no big deal to him because he already knows what he wants in life. But there is another motivation to have priorities. We all know we are facing time and resource constraints. There's a limit to what anyone can achieve not only in a specific duration of time but also in your lifetime because of prevalent scarcity of resources. With our desires covering an endless list which unfortunately cannot all be met at a time, there is a need to make choices. We encourage people to seek and pursue the fundamental goal in life. The ideal scholar is wise. What does it mean?

Dictionary.cambridge.org defines the term wise as an approving word for possessing or showing the ability to make good judgments, based on a deep understanding and experience of life. It follows therefore that the ideal scholar is a person with the ability to make good judgment about matters or affairs that need attention or priorities. It is also important to mention that though he is able to make good judgment, but he is not judgmental about personalities. He is not a person with only technical skills but he has analytical and conceptual skills: knowing what to do, how, when, why, and with whom; he therefore is a person with right priorities.

Knowing time and resources are always scarce, he will plan his work and goals to attain the best and the most he can. In words of Ornstein and Hunkins, "Everything about us competes for our attention or motivation. When we pay attention to something, it usually means we are not paying attention to something else. All of us…must make choices on how we dispense our attention and time." Henry L. Doherty valued this ability so highly that he remarked thus: "These two priceless abilities: *first the ability to think. Second the ability to do things in the order of their importance.*

Now let me tell you that I've been in worse financial situations severally to be able to know the importance of having priorities. Indeed I have been severally forced to do thorough scrutiny before I consulted my thin wallet. As I am about to tell you my story, I am certain you will laugh at me, and I agree I was a fool. That wasn't right priority or choice or decision making. Here's the story. I was much unprepared when I was first posted outside Dar es Salaam on graduation in 1998. With scarce resources and alone and lonely in a hotel in Mwanza city I made sure I ate a huge proportion of food in the afternoon mostly Ugali-Samaki which is the food made from corn flower with fish. I went back to the office and worked before I returned to Kishamapanda Hotel. Then comes dinner time. I normally consulted my wallet and would find two thousand shillings worth two dollars. What did I do? Bet on it. Buy chips? No! That would ruin my whole day.

After a hard search of mind and choice making and weighting entertainment arrived at the head of priorities. I wouldn't just sit alone in a hotel locked up like prisoner. I was young and a river of insulin flowed through my whole body. I found myself walking to a nearby vibrant pub. I can't blame myself. I was idle as I was afraid of sugar mummies who would ruin my life but still wanted to avoid loneliness and so I found myself in a pub. That was the right place for me. How could a night fall on me on my own alone and frustrated? I suspected suicide wasn't far away! You don't know how it feels to be a graduate with only two dollars on your name in your pulse! It is a predicament. It was agony, anguish!

From where I sat I could smell nice beef or chicken across the pub but either pretended I didn't or tried to cancel that sense from my system. Did I succeed? My mouth watered until it dried up. Then I'm there watching some TV programs or football. That was true sincere company from evening to around ten when went back to Kishamapanda and sleep thoroughly well. The trouble is I wouldn't be left to sit on a TV without ordering something. So I ordered a Safari brand of beer popularly known as Mtikira for reasons I didn't know then. I paid a five hundred. Then should I eat? No. what will I do for the rest of three hours? I chose another Mtikira which I sipped carefully to avoid gulping half of it in a single gulp. That would leave me in a very bad state. And remember this was a graduate of economics who because he was alone and lonely in Mwanza, he wouldn't have dinner but a couple of beer bottles! Think of it. Now come night fall. My visit to the urinal increased and left me with an empty stomach.

My brother's choice was, and still is, by far much better. He liked milk as a young boy. Very much. Whereas I chose to buy beer and go to bed with an empty roaring stomach, he bought milk. Long time ago he returned home on graduating from the national service where he got allowance of the monthly allowance of three hundred shillings. When mother asked him how he used the money he said it was very difficult life. He said one had to squeeze so much to survive. He had saved a penny and that's no news. You would not expect to save anything from an allowance that didn't even manage to buy a single decent meal in a three star hotel. The news is what he chose to buy. Where others chose to buy sandals and others yes another awkward choice beer or women he said the money was truly so little that after buying such necessities as the shoe polish he could only manage to buy milk! He didn't buy anything whatsoever but milk. His was nobler choice than mine.

I'm not the only person who has had poor priorities. Here is a man I will introduce as Patios for anonymity. His was worst priority. And I know it is true because it was I who had given him a job as a driver in a company where I served as a manager. I knew him as far as his poor priorities were concerned but because I knew his family I felt compelled to help now that he had no job and he needed anything for his livelihood. His poor priorities had made him unemployable and unbefriendable. I took the risk nonetheless because so far we needed extra drivers for our extra fleet of sales trucks. After a week in his employment, I met him and inquired if the job was helping him knowing the wage he was paid was very little. I told him that I knew he didn't make enough money for his livelihood, but at least he had a beginning after he had been jobless for a very long time. Truly, it wasn't a great job but he could make a living.

Say what you want to say, but even mediocre dim-witted people have their strong points. His was honesty. He was an honest person. He told me how he spent his money without any grain of shame. He said yes it wasn't a lot of money but he could afford a modest meal and:"after paying my rent, I can afford a prostitute!" That's not rational prioritization, is it? It can never be a prudent choice, don't waste your time to think about it. To be clear about his daily budgeting exercise, from the five thousand that he received as his daily wage, he bought a few cigarettes, a long neck of a strong beer brand to see him through the darkest hours of the night; and the balance he set aside for the purchase of anything cheap walking in a skirt.

Yet he wasn't the only person with poor priorities. Poor priority or choice making—almost on an industrial scale—was announced on radio in Tabora. Men had chosen to use mosquito nets provided by their dear government to protect themselves and children from rampant ubiquitous mosquito and malaria in the land but they *"wisely"* used them as fishnets and chicken barns. The extreme is in the fashionable trendy Congolese.

Recently BBC unearthed the fact that in remote Congo—Congolese are a fashionable and trendy smart people—the creative Congolese chose to shine the shoes using the oily condoms otherwise freely supplied for HIV AIDS. Quite creative. Smart people, huh! For them, elegance and classiness begins and probably ends on the clean shining shoes. Thus they must clean and shine the shoes. But due to vastness of the country, inflation and poor infrastructure such as impassable roads, they cannot access shoe polish. So think of it. They shine shoes so that they can attract girls, so what? Indeed they run the risk of going unprotected! Indeed how men can make terribly irrational priorities does more than shock me!

What then is good priority making? I've a plaque in my house hanging in my living room reading thus: Have goals but choose the right ones. Such is a credo for good priorities. A good example is what I saw at a school where my children attend. At St. Ann's the domicile for the catholic sisters who also serve as administrators and teachers, is still a work in progress. It is a story building which for almost ten years now still hangs with only its ground floor. What's so conspicuous is that instead of a fancy home for the sisters, they have chosen to increase classes and the number of teachers. When I joined Kahororo Secondary School, I discovered that because the school was only a few feet from the level of the Lake Victoria, the land was always wet.

The second discovery I made was that there was only one storey building. Why? It was because of altitude and almost a number of dormitory buildings drowning under the underground Lake Victoria waters, the administrators chose instead of housing the headmaster, finance department or even the priest into that conspicuous building. Instead that building houses the school library—to keep the books safer! This opened my eyes. I realized how we all have lack of resources at one time or another. As a nation we have lack of adequate resources to finance education properly just as are households and individuals. So too are schools and organizations. This then requires that we walk with great concern before we spend the little resources at our disposal. "Your achievement can be no greater than your plans are sound," rightly observed Napoleon Hill in *Think and Grow Rich*.[118]

PRIORITIES AND EDUCATION

---

[118] *Napoleon Hill in Think and Grow Rich the unabridged edition page 113*

You recognize that in this book we are concerned with the kind of education we have in the nation and the world as a whole. But the question is this: why education? Why should we now be engaged in this discussion about education? Aside from importance of education in transforming lives of individual persons, communities and nations in general, it all comes down to our unlimited wants subject to scarcity of resources as recommend the principles of economics. The point is this, we have so much to do. Our country has so many problems. Every ministry and almost every department is faced with budget deficiency—every department from that of defense, to the ministry of health, ministry of agriculture, ministry of labor, that of gender and the genuine rights of the deprived women and children —albeit a curious platform for cantankerous activists, etc. What should we attend first? Where should we invest our scarce resources? That's where priorities come in. that's where choice making is necessary. That's where weighting these unlimited wants to filter among them the urgent needs from inconsequential wants—wants that are so inconsequential that they may be considered as luxuries—and therefore allowing us to separate chaff from wheat!

On discussing the legacy of Mwalimu Nyerere, a re-known scholar and lecturer at the University of Dar es Salaam, Dr. Ayub Rioba, said recently, that, yes Mwalimu identified the three major challenges facing the nation: poverty, diseases and ignorance. We would like t fight all these three if it were possible. But with scarcity of resources, we cannot afford to do that. Instead we must consolidate our resources in the fight against ignorance. Why? He observed that if we do so, we will have also fought disease and poverty. Education affords a person the abilities and initiatives to improve his standards of living. Therefore to concentrate our efforts in fighting ignorance, or education is paramount! In 1997, President Clinton indicated in his state of the union message that education would be a primary focus of his second term.[119] Ornstein and Hunkins indicate that he also renewed the call for continued work on national standards. With establishment of national philosophy or standards the battle lines for individual persons, households, organizations and the nation as whole have already been drawn. And you realize that the same should be drawn around education. That's why this chapter, and major part of the remaining book, will focus on education.

---

[119] *Ibid p. 355*

The foregoing analysis, you recognize, describes the importance of the ideals or certain values in uniting the people and cementing national unity—and cause. This is the new order. A nation that should progress must unite first internally and later externally with other nations. Without developing national ideals or standards this is impossible. According to Wikipedia (https://en.wikipedia.org/wiki/), *E pluribus Unum* is a Latin slogan for "Out of many, one or alternatively translated as "One out of many" or "One from many" (https://en.wikipedia.org/wiki/E_pluribus_unum - cite_note-4) —is a phrase on the Seal of the United States…Never codified by law, *E Pluribus Unum* was considered a *de facto* motto of the United States until 1956 when the United States Congress passed an act (H. J. Resolution 396), adopting "In God we trust" as the official motto.

Much as the ideal scholar has priorities, the ideal family unit, business organization and nations must have priorities to accomplish too. That's why we forced to ask ourselves if our priorities are right? Do we have any—anyway? And looking at how as a nation our children have failed so badly in school today, we have to provide answer to such questions as what is behind this mass failure? Is it wrong priorities! Certainly! Such as? Indecision, lack of one major goal to fulfill in life; and indeed misinformation that is generally due to mis-education.

The failure we experience in education will be here to stay unless we address the need for long term goals among individual persons, households, schools or institutions, corporations and the nation as a whole. And that goal can be anything specific. Not money or wealth as a general term. As for the youth it underlines having a goal in life and a big heart to pursue it, the desire and ability to have a choice on one's career or vocation during school, and ability to diversify or diverge if it needs be. Not everybody will prosper or be happy in every form of career or vocation. Not even Michael Schumacher or Usain Bolt, persons with vast talents, would succeed in everything else. Mwalimu Nyerere himself once declared his greater capability for science subjects such biology but he chose to specialize in such subjects as history and political economy because he knew where he wanted to go. Well, he had decided long ago that he would go into politics.

Let's face it. The aspiration to build a strong middle class as a key to growth especially today with globalization seems to be a popular policy among our leaders, economists and policy makers. But it is vague as a strategy. But a country that should progress should start with the empowerment of the youth. Ours remains to be an attention that is less rich, less meaningful to the youth and as such it is unlikely to bring the needed impact our society craves. There is almost absolutely nothing that a dynasty or nation can do to prevent itself from collapse or extinction if the lifeline of that society—the children and the youth—isn't empowered. When I talk of getting the youth empowered, I mean to enable them to have the will and capacity to be self-reliant and productive; to be willing and able to make meaningful choices and pursue the vocation of their choice. But that state starts with the desire to prosper. Indeed, any form of education that ignores this precondition or a condition *sine quo non*, is good for nothing. It would do a greater service to a family unit and the nation to enlighten the youth how responsible they ought to be.

Come to think of it, it does the same to the corporation that empowers its fresh employees and those in the lower and middle ranks. Lack of the sense of responsibility and personal leadership is the greatest form of ignorance. This is where the author's father and mother invested well. This is where Kennedy Sr., Jack Kennedy's father, invested. That's where all top football clubs and European and world champions invest in. That's where America invested in to be a pinnacle nation we see today. This is what one could associate with the American dream. Solution? Priorities! Education first! Of course we are bound to further this discussion through the proceeding chapters and series. On independence Mwalimu Nyerere identified a nation he craved to build. I can paraphrase his words as: A *free nation that is literate (writing and reading), self-reliant, prosperous and equitable society.*

But what is education—if we have schools and children attend classes in masses—isn't that education? Students today don't concentrate with their studies anymore. Teachers don't push them anymore. Classes and education aren't necessarily one and same thing anymore. Talk about actioning, Mwalimu, invested in education. Not only this but he took it is his moral duty to read and write books. A couple of handful authors the nation has managed to produce for itself are a result of free education and probably one of model reading and writing citizens that the *Father of Nation* aspired to see as the future model Tanzanian youth the next generation would look up to. Not only in the field of writing, but he created a sizeable group of empowered youth that has helped bring us to where we are today.

When we say education first, we mean that, if we fight ignorance, we will have fought all the other enemies: disease and poverty and the collapse of family institution, enlarging stock of street children, youth unemployment, drugs trafficking and drug addiction, alcoholism and dependence as individuals and a nation as a whole. It is inevitable therefore that we focus and allocate the better share of meager resources we have got in fighting against ignorance—first! As educators we have got as well to emphasize qualities of character, intelligence and personality far more than…educational background. Addressing the Rich Management Club (www.rich.co.ke) in Nairobi Kenya recently, president Museveni referred this lack of sense of priorities to the paraphrased quotation of Mathew 23:23: "We have left undone those things we ought to have done, and did what we ought not to have done." This is the verity behind this mass failure—and indeed the reason why we have reached where we are today. So truly it is as said Apostle John (1 John 1:8), "If we say we have no sin, we deceive ourselves, and there is no truth in us. (We have lost).

HOW YOU CAN MAKE PRUDENT OR GOOD CHOICES

We make choices by establishing what is more important between two or three things. We do this by putting different weights on different needs and then we arrange them in order of their weights. That's how we can then be able to allocate time and resources without pressure for we will first endeavor to get the items high in the order of ranks. Indeed life without purpose, passion and plan is like a ship sailing without particular destination. With weights in place, he can then establish what time or resources he will spend on each task or item. Notice this is not weight-weight if you know what I mean. It is not the weight we measure algebraically with the beam balance. No. It is prudential weight. The imaginary weight corresponding with the satisfaction it will give us.

Notice also that this weight is different to each individual. With a clear purpose in life and weighting of all his goals, the ideal scholar has a tendency to choose and then stick with what he chooses to do or accomplish. In the end for a person to be happy with who he is and his achievement—to acquire happiness—a person must have a purpose, a goal to achieve, a record to break, a timeline to meet, a challenge to overcome—if he has to really be genuinely happy. For indeed as Harry Emerson Fosdick said, "Happiness is not mostly pleasure; it is victory!" This is prudence. It is good sense. And if you look at closely, happiness therefore, is a presidential providence only available to the ideal scholar.

And here is another thing. If you want to accomplish many things at one time you must many times accomplish one thing at a time. With plans in place backed by a clear mind of what he wants and obsession to acquire the same, from the onset, his is a battle half won. Is this ideal important? When the Lord appeared to King Solomon at Gibeon (call him Suleiman or Solomon) …at night said he told him thus, "Ask what I'll give you!" The king answered, "Give me understanding." He didn't ask for wealth or leisure! Or even a thousand years of his own life! But understanding! Wisdom! which is worth more than anything else!

In the first book of Kings, chapter three, it is written that it pleased the Lord and God said "because you have asked this and you have not asked for yourself a long life or riches or lives of your enemies but have asked for understanding, behold I now do according to your word. And you shall be wiser than anyone before you and none shall arise after you. I give you also what you have not asked, both riches and honor," said the Lord, "and if you shall keep my commandments," delighted, continued the Lord Almighty, "And if you shall keep my commandments," I'll even lengthen your days (life)!" The holy book goes to great heights to emphasize significance of wisdom. The proverbs state that a wise young man is better than an old and a foolish king! Many people have read this verse but few know why. And it is why. The old foolish king— in spite of his seeming greatness—is fast losing not only his wealth but his throne not because of his age but because he was unwise and his has got little time and sense to mend his ways.

24. THE IDEAL SCHOLAR IS A SOCIABLE AND MORAL PERSON

> *"And the chief sign that a man has any nobility in his character is the little pleasure he takes in others' company."* —Arthur Schopenhauer

> *"Since belief determines behavior, doesn't it make sense that we should be teaching ethical, moral values in every home and in every school…?"* —Zig Ziglar

Understanding that life is not work and work alone, the ideal scholar is a sociable person and thus balances career and social life. He knows that his family and the world around him want more from him than mere bread and butter. He will therefore try to strike a balance between career and social obligation and therefore harmonize his routine to ensure he lives a balanced life socially religiously and intellectually.

I visited Hindu Mandal Hospital and one doctor prompted me to add this quality to the ideal scholar. My aging mother had been consulted to undergo a wide range of serious medical checkups including that of the heart. It was considered that she needed urgent treatment or medication. Then a few minutes on top of the hour the doctor vanished, abandoning patients. Why. It was time for prayers. I questioned the doctor's faith or rather common sense not only for my mother's sake but for even more serious patients. They were all abandoned for not less than an hour. Jesus chose to break the Sabbath to heal a sick person against extreme observance of the Mosaic Law.

Abdullah bin' Amr bin al Aas narrated thus: God's Messenger entered upon me and said, "Have I not been informed that you offer prayer all the night and fast the whole day?" I said, "Yes." He said, "Do not do so; Offer prayer at night and also sleep; Fast for a few days and give up fasting for a few days because your body has a right on you, and your eye has a right on you, and your guest has a right on you, and your wife has a right on you. Abu Tha'labah al-Kushanee—Jurthoom bin Nashir said that that the Messenger of God said: Verily God has laid down religious obligations, so do not neglect them; and He has set limits, so do not overstep them..."[120]

Being sociable on its own, doesn't make a person's character ideal,. The ideal scholar is a moral and ethical person. Morals are defined by dictionary.cambridge.org as standards for good or bad character and behavior. On the other hand ethics, according to dictionary.cambridge.org, is a system of accepted beliefs which control behavior, especially such a system based on morals. This is what forms the good winning character. Dictionary.cambridge.org defines character as the particular combination of qualities in a person or place that makes them different from others.

Ralph Waldo Emerson taught that "Character is higher than intellect...A great soul will be strong to live, as well as to think." The human whole transcends his physical body. *Indeed human nature transcends bodily and intellectual needs or concerns. Thus the goal of education "is to develop the rational person and to uncover the universal truths by carefully training the intellect. Character training is also important as a means of developing one's moral and spiritual being."*[121]

With recent trend in our society where modernity is considered to be synonymous to rebellion—especially among the youth—hand in hand with ICT and globalization, moral education has to receive increased attention. Today we cannot guarantee what our children will learn before the sun sets. We the parents and teachers and priests can no longer control or even monitor the interaction our children will make at the end of the day. The television and the mobile handsets will all bombarded them with breaking news and information they cannot but watch, hear, and engage with. You can try to control your children but what about their interaction with their peers outdoor? To be brief, with ICT, gone are the days when you could build walls and fences to protect your children from interacting with the other children who would teach them deplorable habits.

---

[120] *Hadith no 67 (ahadith.co.uk)*

[121] *Allan C. Ornstein and Francis P. Hunkins, Curriculum Foundations, Principles and Issues 3rd Edition p. 38*

The point I am trying to make is this: we live in a society that is facing more than just the challenge of obtaining our daily bread and no wonder therefore the moral education has begun gaining superior attention from amongst the parents, the teachers and priests and all teachers in the spiritual field more than before. It is for this that the contemporary curriculum demands that we address morals or ethical values—despite missing homogeneity in its definition—to enable our children and the youth to engage in right actions develop those competencies and dispositions and therefore to act in a way that will not only advance their livelihood but also the wellbeing of the whole society.

In words of Ornstein and Hunkins: "...as a nation we...realize that the challenges to our society are more than just economic and academic. Many of our problems relate to shortcomings in our morals and character or at least in our willingness to play what we essentially know as proper action. We can certainly raise the scores with the new curricula. We can be more effective in the world economic theater with new courses with higher standards. However, we are beginning to realize that we must be as dedicated to raising our moral standards as well. We must nurture those ethical ideas as justice, faith, hope and charity if we are to reach the heights of good ...national and world community."[122]

Talking about the diversity of the definition of what is good and what is bad, indeed the source of contention when the discussion of moral values is discussed, we find ourselves compelled to attempt to answer what is good and what is bad. I believe the Golden Rule does more than answer to that. The good thing is that which I want others to do for me. The bad thing is its reverse. Prophet Muhammad taught his companions in the Middle East that "a good deed is the one that leaves a smile of joy in the face on another person."

The hadith or the teachings of the prophet Mohammad taught about the good thing as the one that you are not only willing but proud to do in the open, put simply, plainly. Ornstein and Hunkins wrote that: "a moral person is driven by more than warm feelings for herself and others. A moral person has awareness, understanding and appreciation of those

---

[122] *Allan C. Ornstein and Francis P. Hunkins, Curriculum Foundations, Principles and Issues 3rd Edition p. 370*

values and ideas that are essential for productive relations with other and for the meaningful and authentic constructions of our own persons. As Selznick denotes, a moral person has both commitment and competence. It is here that a challenge exists for Curricularists. We need , and more people are demanding , a curriculum that allows students to learn about moral values and ethics and the competence aspects and to experience such knowledge in ways that ignite in them a desire to put what they know in meaningful action.[123]

When we say we should to reintroduce the moral education in our schools, some of our most accomplished cynics or doubters will suggest that I am attempting to teach my own religion. Far from that. That is a bogus claim. Schools and teachers besides parents have a conscientious commitment to teaching morals or ethical values. Recently Priscilla came from school asking me to tell her more about Ben Carson's story. It was her teacher who had asked them to emulate Ben Carson. Everybody knows Ben Carson. I don't have to reintroduce him. So I will only introduce Priscilla. She is the author's daughter. Now you realize that by teachers narrating the life of a poor boy brought up by single mother, who then rose from obscurity and valleys of darkness to global limelight not only because of his accomplishments as a neurosurgeon who separated Siamese twins, which was unprecedented at the time, but also a world accredited author of such magnificent books as Think Big and Gifted Hands among others.

His morals and personal conduct have brought him affluence and fame not only as Dr. Benjamin Carson we all know today, but also as a man the Republican Party have scratched their heads considering him for presidency—which he turned down until much later. Think about it! The first black Republican Party presidential majority candidate for the United States! He was teaching them to work hard and to love and have confidence in themselves and God, knowing that if they work hard and respect others and relate well with everybody else regardless of race or gender or even religion he was teaching them morals.

That's not Christianity. It is not Catholicism. Teachers and schools teach moral values also through the organization of the school and classroom where each student and teacher acts with awareness of the impact or effect

---

[123] *Allan C. Ornstein and Francis P. Hunkins, Curriculum Foundations, Principles and Issues 3rd Edition p. 371*

of his or her actions to the others. We also know that schools and teachers reward good deeds in classrooms and at school on daily basis beside end of term or year ceremony. By doing so they project what is considered as good manners or morals. Through English literature of bible studies or even the hadith the children learn from great deeds or rather moral values of the biblical heroes. We know many of them but Daniel and Meshach Shadrack and Abednego showed constancy to their moral values. Moses was a boy who had a chance of becoming king in Egypt if he detached himself from his people but chose to sacrifice wealth for the good of the others. We know that though he was the first born, Reuben was denied his first-born's birthrights. Why? because he slept with his father's concubine. Simeon and Levi didn't get the blessings from their father or reinstate them as his successors or heirs because they had killed a man.

However we know that Judah had been blameless. That's why his name stands to date. We know also of Joseph. He was courted by the wealthy and powerful woman who promised him wealth and power if he became her lover. He chose to remain poor rather than break his moral values. We know that in the end however, he triumphed and became prime minister. We know and see (as was originally was recorded by Jackson, Boostrom, and Hansen in their work the moral life of a school) "the signs and bulletin boards that are placed in the school environment, such as signs saying *Just Say No!* Or *Just Wait!*"[124] We have so many of such exemplars but suffice to say here that the teaching of morals has been in existence before history itself. What I am attempting to do is to streamline the lessons and organize its teaching or reading that it becomes more spontaneous and probably plainer. In the end recall we said that though it is hard and very debatable on what are the good and bad and therefore what is right or what is wrong and that we said the Golden Rule and the hadith attempt to tell us what is good and what is bad in the end in words of Ornstein and Hunkins: "it is essential for us all to realize that for societies to exist they must be bound by a core of powerful, shared beliefs.

As Wynne and Ryan note , these beliefs and values should be such that citizens are motivated to make great personal sacrifices for the general

---

[124] *Allan C. Ornstein and Francis P. Hunkins, Curriculum Foundations, Principles and Issues 3rd Edition p. 371*

good. Individuals must have goals that extend beyond immediate self interest." Ornstein and Hunkins add ed that "if our nation fails to educate students to a commitment to a common morality it is likely to experience social chaos." in the book *The Abolition of Man*, C.S. Lewis indicated that many of his ideas reflect the thinking of many cultures through time: *Babylonians*, ancient Egypt, old Norse, Greeks, Romans, Chinese, Indians, Christians, Hebrew, Islamic, Anglo-Saxon, and Americans. To his list naturally are included other cultures from Europe, Asia and Africa.

Thus we can present moral values according to C.S. Lewis as adapted by Wayne and Ryan as follows: An effectively functioning society requires of its members human kindness; Individuals in the society owe a social love and loyalty to their parents; They owe a social love to and responsibility for themselves and their own families; Its citizens exhibit some degree of honesty; All members of society have an obligation to help the poor, sick, and less fortunate; Its citizens respect basic property rights; Its citizen's respect the personal rights of others. The view of our personal lives and our mortality influences how we view life and its meaning.[125]

But how does the moral person work? Or, alternatively, how is he different from the herd around him or her? A moral person, person of good character, knows the difference between good and bad, knows the basis for his or her behavior, and chooses right over wrong, action that is of benefit to the person and society over that which is not. There is the difference between…behaving rightly and behaving morally. The latter implies an awareness of the bases of action or nonaction…possesses moral competence …consciousness about action and the values that guide it. Moral competence also means…capacity for moral inquiry. A person with moral competence has the will and ability to seek goods that are genuine and enduring not superficial and transitory.[126]

Achievement therefore on its own is not enough. How did one get wealth or position one has. According to Ornstein and Hunkins getting or having

---

[125] *Adapted from Edward a. Wynne and Kevin Ryan Reclaiming Our Schools 2nd edition from Allan C. Ornstein and Francis P. Hunkins, Curriculum Foundations, Principles and Issues 3rd Edition p.372*

[126] *Allan C. Ornstein and Francis P. Hunkins, Curriculum Foundations, Principles and Issues 3rd Edition p.373*

an education must be sold on a more solid base than its economic clout...we need to achieve by attaining the human values for others, an appreciation of diversity, and by attaining higher levels of spirituality. We need to direct our attention away from self-gratification and more to the welfare of others. Economics should no longer constitute the driving force of public education...this vision is more than having the good life; it is being a good person in this life. This vision of possibility is connected to the spiritual nature of humans. In real sense the argument for celebrating possibility is giving new testimony that people can live full lives that are not measured by material objects...but rather by the inner selves. People are coming to accept more completely that we should be judged by the quality of our character.[127]

Indeed in as much as we have the moral right to that which furthers our humanness, we have responsibility to our fellow men and the environment that shelter our rights. Education should therefore be into context with moral values. It should help create the moral fiber and establish individual household standards as well national ethics Bill FitzPatrick was right. By now you: "You do not need lessons to act civilly. You do not need prompting to help someone in need." Finally, it should be conspicuous to every student of this, or any other worthy education, that: Moral courage is needed more often than physical courage. Moral courage may mean the challenge to stay with a belief when your position may not be the most popular. Moral courage can be standing tall against bigotry, prejudice, unfairness, and bullying behavior. Moral courage is a challenge to do what is right, regardless of the personal consequences. Moral courage may ask you to forgive," concludes Bill FitzPatrick in his Action Principles. *"The greatest danger in teaching knowledge,"* aptly counseled Allan C. Ornstein in his work *Knowledge is hange, "The greatest danger in teaching knowledge is to ignore the values that shape the individual and society; this is teaching in vacuum and without vision."*[128]

---

[127] Allan C. Ornstein and Francis P. Hunkins, *Curriculum Foundations, Principles and Issues 3rd Edition p140*

[128] Allan C. Ornstein and Francis P. Hunkins, *Curriculum Foundations, Principles and Issues 3rd Edition p.154*

25. IDEAL SCHOLAR IS A GOOD COMMUNICATOR

"Speak when you are angry—and you'll make the best speech you'll ever regret."
—*Laurence Peters*

"The single biggest problem in communication is the illusion that it has taken place."
—*George Bernard Shaw*

To be effective as a scholar, the ideal scholar is leader, role model, and a good communicator. To communicate effectively, to lead others, the ideal scholar recognizes importance of interdependence. He knows he cannot achieve anything big with the support of the others. Napoleon Hill said rightly that, "the story of practically every great fortune starts with the day when the creator of ideas and the seller of the ideas got together and worked in harmony. For some of you who already question the universality or validity of the foregoing statement based on the fact that you probably are not in business but in any other endeavor that seems far removed from business you say this ideal doesn't concern me. You are wrong. Every other profession or endeavor in life such as a house wife, a student or even a catholic priest to mention but a few areas that seem far removed from business is practically a business transaction like any other typical business transaction.

What is different is the kind of returns one expects from these two categories. Whereas a businessman expects financial gains, something his counterpart professionals such as a house wife, a student or even a catholic priest—don't look forward to, but if one has to succeed in either category, he has to influence and win people to his ideas. This is what communication really means. No one ever succeeded in anything without good communication skills, skills that transcend technical skills, skills in human nature and character and attitude that makes people tick.

To communicate effectively the ideal scholar is articulate viz: coherent, expressive and communicative, but to be such good communicator, he has to think and communicate clearly. To communicate effectively, such individuals know how to engage themselves and others not only in the conversation but in the plans. By this we mean to speak out concerning the plan of action, listening effectively, and giving constructive feedback. They know why to say what, to whom, when, and how. "To relate effectively," said Stephen Covey "To relate effectively with a wife, a husband, children, friends and working associates you and I must learn to listen. And this requires emotional strength. Listening involves patience openness and desire to understand-highly developed qualities of character...."[129] What then would you gain if you learned to listen? "Your life would be longer, richer, more fruitful if you only spend a greater share of it in the tranquility of meditative listening. We are such a noisy lot that most of what we say goes unheard and unheeded," said Dr. O. A. Batista in The Power to Influence People.

From the foregoing statement, we conclude that the ideal scholar reckons importance of learning to listen. Listening is indeed an important element of communication. I can suggest that in order to become a great orator, or communicator, one must first become a great listener! A good dose of such a skill can be gauged against how one listens with complete concentration without preemptive notions or judgment. Indeed people who speak too much rarely have anything to say, or otherwise what they had to say could be packaged in few sentences and uttered in a fraction of the time they take to say it. In his book Think and Grow Rich, Napoleon Hill was right: "Those who talk too much do little else. If you talk than you listen you not only deprive of yourself many opportunities to accumulate useful knowledge, but you disclose your plans and purposes..." I could add to Napoleon Hill's counsel that you turn people away from both you and your ideas.

Listening has become a very important virtue especially in an individuality and world that has become too noisy, preferring to talk without heeding what the other has to say or if he has even listened to what he so dearly

---

[129] *The Seven Habits of Highly Effective People by Stephen Covey p. 37*

meant to convey to his audience. It is why we redefine communication introducing relationship building into the traditional communication skills. Why? Communication doesn't simply mean passing on the information. It is rather how you relate with yourself and others. Indeed, "it is a mark of an educated mind," said Aristotle, "to be able to entertain a thought without (necessarily) accepting it!" This is why Gardner called this quality as interpersonal and intrapersonal intelligence. The former refers to: *The ability of an individual to understand other people—what makes them tick, and how they work and how one can work with them,* while the latter is: *Correlative ability.* It is a reckoning of how cooperation or interdependence or reciprocity are pivotal in growth at personal and group such as work teams and the society as a whole.

To communicate effectively, if he has to thrive in his profession, and as a person, recognizing that he has useful knowledge and skills that many didn't have the privilege of acquiring, knowledge and useful skills that are apt to transform the society and make the world a better place, the ideal scholar volunteers to lead. But he cannot lead effectively, if he is not an inclusive leader, a leader whom people will follow willingly, if he cannot be of service to others—of service to others by thought, word and deed. Thus he knows he has to submerge in other people's hearts and needs. This is what others call empathy. Empathy is nothing but to enter into another person's shoes in order to be part of their feelings and emotions if he to win their trust and support and therefore to be able to rally them behind the common agenda. One of the BBC programs, has recently helped to put this concept of giving into the right perspective. It was brought to my attention through an interview in which this British diplomat described how as a diplomat one has to dance according to the tunes. She said this insight became vivid to her when she served as a British ambassador to Russia. It was during that time that she learned that often times you have got to do the unprecedented to win others over. One of such self sacrifices happened one day when she had to have a typical Russian breakfast—whiskey served with vodka!

PAUL: A SERVANT TO ALL
In order to respond to what we have presented above, consider a catholic priest who may assume that the foregoing assertion is none of his business, let's bring in here what Paul apostle wrote to Corinthians—. Paul is indeed one of the greatest winners of people. Here is what he wrote concerning winning people to your way of thinking. It was the greatest weapon he used to win all nations unto his mission. He wrote that, "For though I am free from all men, I have made myself a slave to all, so that I may win

more. To the Jews I became as a Jew, so that I might win Jews; to those who are under the Law, as under the Law though not being myself under the Law, so that I might win those who are under the Law; to those who are without law, as without law, though not being without the law of God but under the law of Christ, so that I might win those who are without law. To the weak I became weak, that I might win the weak; I have become all things to all men, so that I may by all means save some. I do all things for the sake of the gospel, so that I may become a fellow partaker of it."[130]

The Foundation for Advancement of Teaching and Carnegie Institute of Technology uncovered that even in such technical lines as engineering only about 15 % of one's financial success (or any other success) is due to one's technical knowledge and about 85% is due to skills in human engineering—to personality and ability to lead people. Concerned with the weaknesses amongst the youth and purposes of education, in 1994, the (US) Education Policy Commission , formulated ten aims (or in our case ,goals or purposes) of education in what was called Education for all American Youth. In this document we find emphasis, and mention of, among others, the importance of: *growth of their ability to think rationally, to express their thoughts clearly, and to read and listen with understanding (Ornstein and Hunkins 3rd Edition Page 271)*. "Everyone," wrote Bill FitzPatrick, "Everyone admires the bold, courageous and daring; no one honors the fainthearted, shy and timid." It is undoubtedly what the Association for Supervision and Curriculum Development identified among the ten major goals for American youth as the second quality i.e. understanding others. The third quality in Draper Kauffman's six areas of competence that could comprise a possible future curriculum he identified this quality as: *Communicating Effectively.* The Phi Delta Kappa Honor Society identified this quality being its second:*"...to get along with people who think, dress, and act differently."*

Though we have mentioned the idea of submerging in others people's needs and wants, because of its importance, we are going to single it out as an important quality of the ideal scholar. It is for the same reason that we are going to dwell a little more sacrificially into it one more time right here. Thus the ideal scholar not only reckons importance of cooperation or interdependence and reciprocity but indeed goes out of his way to cooperate with the people and environment around him.

---

[130] *1 Corinthians 9:19-23*

But is this ideal important? Is it worth the reader's time? Maybe someone is already imagining that this could be one of the discussions I should have skipped. Wrong. This ideal should even have been at the top of the tree of life considering its importance to a person's success or failure in life. We know that the communal man realized that to be able to conquer nature or at least be able to fight against odds, had to work in collaboration with his fellow men. Yet with the today's interconnected or rather interdependent world, cooperation or reciprocity is pivotal to growth than any factor now than during any other time. We can no longer today live in an island or isolation like Robinson Crusoe. Yet even Robinson had Friday to give him company only a little while later just like how Adam had Eve. It is from this verity that the ideal scholar recognizes personal growth or the growth of the individual in the team and the team as a whole depends on every member in the team. Let's observe our day to day life in relation to the present discussion.

When you wake up early in the morning, in a house built by some masons you don't know or even care to know of, who used the materials you don't know who produced them, then rising from a bed and beddings made by some carpenters or factory somewhere in the city or even from outside the country, themselves having used trees and glue and nails on one hand, and cotton on the other, products manufactured by some other men and women they didn't know or even care to know anything about. You will then slip into slippers made by somebody else and a towel by another before you pick a tooth brush and paste made by another 'incognito', a complete stranger to you. Then you would need a bath. You would then need some flowing water. You object and say I would simply swim in the pond. But you didn't create it too. Leaving it at that, you would need a towel, a soap and clothing. You use water supplied by someone you don't know or care about through pipes made and fixed by different people you don't care to know, or who you don't necessarily love to meet in person.

You will have your breakfast whose combination is a miracle you cannot dare explain; from tea leaves, water, sugar, the cooking pot, the cup, the spoon, the electricity or even coal, all are made and manufactured or produced by so many different people whom you and I cannot even figure out how they look or behave. You would alternatively have fish, banana or some vegetable soup as part of your breakfast; and even if you grew them in your farm but you cooked them in a pot you didn't manufacture or used power or fire you didn't naturally possess. If you used the firewood you burnt it with fire using a match box from some factory in some outfit somewhere you didn't know or own. Banana itself or vegetables grew because they were showered with rain and stuck in rich soil both you didn't create or dare to explain how it was created.

You will then dress up in some suit made somewhere in Italy by some funny Italians; and probably drive an imported car made by some skinny Japanese men and women you don't necessary love, a car that arrived by ship made by a thousand men and women whose crew of hundred men and women you don't know or mind to know.

Recognize that we are engaged in the discussion of how you and I are interdependent. Now think of the modern world in which we live today now that we are no longer hunter-gathers, you would then be ready to attack the office work miles away. You would then need transport. You will drive either in your own private car or commuter bus for you cannot make to the office on time fifty kilometers away unless you did fly through the air but you would then need heavy clothing or some umbrella to avoid cold or rain or else freeze mid air. The workplace is not your own. Some of my readers will probably be saying: what if I am self employed?

If you are self employed, you would also need employees, suppliers and the market. You would also need the government of some kind; for otherwise you would lose your peace of mind and possessions under anarchy through thieves and surrounded with uncouth, uncivilized, insane, barbaric goons who would swiftly break into your house combing the house and leaving nothing except free flowing air thus arriving home to an open cold air now that not you, the president or even this author can lead the model life of Robinson Crusoe. Even so, Mr. Crusoe was delighted when Friday came into his life—just like God made up for his initial pitfall of having created a lonely Adam in the Garden of Eden!

At the office you will need a secretary and a doorman. You will also need some stationary and electronics etc. There is a telephone and a number of machines you need to work effectively not forgetting the chair you sit and the toilet you go to, made and cleaned by other men. At the end of the month you will be paid a salary in bills and coins made by some men you know not. Then you will need the services of the doctor, an accountant and a lawyer. You would also need the teachers and of—well, it is a long list— lists I cannot exhaust strive much as I can. All these are things without which your life is not complete, lovely or meaningful, things and services your own existence depends on but which are produced and procured by— and through—others to your doorstep. Think of how you would procure them by walking to the nearby house, shoo, city, or even by swimming to India or china for the same. Think of the time you would spend to go and com back if at all you would manage to.

You cannot be a pilot and a crew at the same time. You cannot be a driver and a passenger at one and same time. Here is another analogy. Airplanes are flown by pilots, excepting of course the American drones. Yet pilots need air-hostesses—beside copilots. The public bus, a Daladada or a Matatu needs the services of the bus driver but he needs the conductors! Trucks have helpers beside their drivers—we are the truck helpers. There is a referee or an umpire in almost every game but there is an assistant referee. In athletics, for splinters to perform at their top, even Usain Bolt himself—have pace-Makers. Today we can no longer live in an island or isolation like Robinson Crusoe. Yet even Robinson had Friday to give him company only a little while later just like how Adam had Eve. Parents are two for everyone—excepting Jesus of course. But even so, the services of Joseph were inevitable—even in the upbringing of the messiah!

It is tick-bird and rhino relationship; it is complementarity between butter and bread. Indeed we need each other—in all circles of life. Cooperation. Collaboration. Interdependence. Reciprocity. Interdependence. I read on the facebook wall, something I am going to paraphrase and report here because I believe it is worth revisiting. Did you realize that: "Your car could be German; your vodka Russian; your pizza Italian, your kebab Turkish, your democracy Greek, your coffee Brazilian, your movies American, your tea Tamil, your shirt Indian, your oil Saudi Arabian, your electronics Chinese, our numbers Arabic, your letters Latin? And you say you are on your own? Pull yourself together buddy."[131] Lily Tomlin was right. Indeed, "Sometimes," in the vein of Lily Tomlin, "I (the author) worry about being successful in a mediocre world." Why? We depend on each other. Really!

We must as well emphasize that openness and readiness to share information is paramount. There're two major reasons behind secrecy. One

---

[131] *Adapted from https://cafewitteveen.wordpress.com/tag/your-car-is-german-your-vodka-is-russian-your-pizza-is-italian-your-kebab-is-turkish-your-democracy-is-greek-your-coffee-is-brazilian-your-movies-are-american-your-tea-is-tamil-your-shirt-is-i/*

we believe by discussing our differences we will blow a hole into our warm relationships. Wrong. We must know what to say and how to say it. We must use diplomacy. We must not expose and revile others. We must avoid such stance and speeches that dictate or declare a state of emergency. We must use soft language and pleading. We must suggest that there's a need probably to assess how best we can relate. And that we depend on our peers. We must engage them and suggest they must take time to think it over. Other people are slow to reach decisions. Think of work places and of a marriage. We are different everywhere. We must do it in the spirit of cooperation ready ourselves to lose so that we may gain in the process of better relations. The other fellow must see his benefits. In any such discussions remember one will ask what is in it for me! Show it! Show what wares you have and how connected you are and can help others. Many people believe information is wealth and true to their belief information is wealth only when it is shared with right people. These people hold to their information and never disclose it. Many family problems stem from a no information situation. No communication at all.

I've had a very big albeit a silent but straining misunderstanding with a person so close to me. Over the years we grew up and everybody took his time and career and lived in different cities. Then as days passed we met and stayed together for a couple of long hours. I was able, through that meeting, to cover the ground on which we differed in the past—the difference that threatened to wreck our relationship for ever. After looking at the other side of the story, he admitted that he didn't know other facts, adding that: "I blamed you for nothing." Indeed not only misinformation but also lack of communication breeds distrust. How do you break this gap? First lower yourself. Expose part of your treasured information and do it easily as if you have no intention of cracking down the walls of communication between you two. You will see slowly he or she will start believing in you and he or she will get down to his part of the story. People who are today successful in every other aspect—thieves, conmen, suicide bombers let alone priests, wives and politicians and prostitutes—are all regarded as champions in relating with the others. They do so knowing that there's what is known as Win-Win situation when only a few know that to arrive and stay there, one needs to know and practice what the author discovered and termed as Lose-Win relationship.

Rajoelina was a mere DJ in Malagasy's capital Antananarivo but he soon influenced the whole city and became the record youngest mayor ever at around 30. A couple of years later this young man shocked the helms of power when he stood up with the multitudes of the public and armed forces forcing the commander in chief and president Ravalomanana out of office. Who do you suppose took over! You are right. Rajoelina! Love him hate him, call him names, call him DJ as once did Bernard Membe at the time when he served as foreign minister in Tanzania; that's not who he is today. That's charisma. That's a knack on winning people to your side, to your point of view. Instead of cursing this charismatic young man, we should instead be lining up like ants to learn from him.

But the question is this: What did he, Rajoelina, do? It is in this very book. Just remember everyone's asking what is in it for himself. He questions his, or her, own stake and that's all. Though the author doesn't in anyway endorse or advocate a coup d'état, yet if you study the biography of one young man in the rank of a sergeant, indeed a sergeant who outshined the generals and the men in power aside from all Liberian academics and to then go on and be the president as a teen, and I mean sergeant Samuel Doe, this young man Rajoelina himself still not anywhere far from a teenager, entered the palace and served successfully as president when compared to the host of the ubiquitous mediocre graduate presidents whose names cannot be farfetched. It is not fair nor is it justified to downplay this young man's inner power—and education, human knowledge—afterall the master key that can unlock all doors when science and conventional education and all military might have failed.

When I look at human anatomy and reproduction as a whole, I can't but find that the locations and the interdependence of the reproduction system or even the love affair prove God loves negotiation and understanding. When asked by Cosmo magazine that what do you think makes you popular the interviewer suggested could it be your ordinariness Sharuhk Khan had this for his answer. There're two ways you can be a star (that's to be successful in this case. You could either be someone people want to be like Amitah Bachan or some great sports super star. Or (secondly) you could be someone people can relate to. I think I belong to the latter category he said. How does it work? How does it influence others? Mothers and little girls think of me as a son they would like to have or the guy they would like to marry. I've always been very simple and ordinary...I believe in the gentleness...

Coca Cola Company back in Atlanta knew this secret, and they declared that, "the secret to our success lies outside the bottle," that is, outside the drink; in people—in employees and customers! Reginald Mengi, a leading businessman and media mogul in East Africa recognized this secret earlier on and asserted that: "The human mind is our fundamental resource," said

Mr. Mengi. "Our business is composed not of land or buildings," continued the businessman, "not even of the capital invested, but the caliber of our people...A group of people who work a little better every day in products, services and ideas."

Through the theory of Economics we are taught the notion of cooperative and absolute advantages. But really there is no such a thing as absolute advantage. The Adam smith's emphasis of doing the best at an individual level was hugely misconceived and misrepresented—unfortunately. His model of *Individual Ambitions Serves the Common*; and therefore *Everyone for Himself* is erroneously conceived. The best comes when everyone in the team strives to; and gets the best as an individual first. But that's not all. Everyone in the group has to do or earn the best yes, for himself first, but he has also to strive to and earn the best for the group.[132] That's how we all win—together. Besides, the forces of the group that works toward a common goal are far greater than the individual's. The essence of interdependence works to check the undue competition among individuals in the team. In fact this is the basis for each individual to compete with himself first and foremost. By 'competing with oneself', we don't mean that we shouldn't evaluate our achievement or accomplishment matching with the others'. No. It rather means we don't get in each other's way. And we don't stop there. We keep looking in the ways of doing the best for ourselves and the team.

Until as I write, everybody knows that under José Mourinho Chelsea became a force to be reckoned with but few know why Chelsea rose from fifty years of deep sleep to be a force to be reckoned with in English premier league. In a letter to his players fresh as manager at the Chelsea Mourinho wrote to his players the following note he disclosed much later to the public domain—and was the key of success at Chelsea as it is to the immediate reader.*"There is history made by each of us that leads to that final victory. It is that history in its entirety that turns us into champions. From here,"* he said; *"each practice, each game, each minute of your social life must center in the aim of being champions. First team,"* he continued; *"first team will not be a correct word. I need all of you and you need each other. We are a team."* If anyone fails, if Mourinho himself doesn't somehow accomplish such a feat, it is probably because he has just walked away from the same principles we advocate.

---

[132] *Adapted from a movie, A Beautiful Mind*

Have you not learned that, from the theory of comparative advantage, we grow and get maximum value, when we concentrate with that endeavor on which we have cooperatives advantage over the others as we exchange what we produce efficiently with what others can happily produce easier and at low cost.

26. EXCELLENCE AND QUALITY OF WORK

> *"If a man can make a better mouse trap than his neighbors, though he builds his house in the woods, the world will make a beaten path to his door!"* —Ralph Waldo Emerson

Though the ideal scholar is hard working; a person who produces results about which he knows the result by itself isn't sufficient anymore. This is another set of weeping trait in this country—and in general in the world today. It indeed stands close to the head of the badly missing qualities among our people. And this is for obvious reasons. It is innate to us because of our history, beginning with slavery, colonialism and the Ujamaa Policy or socialism, the form of social life based on common property. The ideal scholar should instead be a person of quality—or excellence. Yes the ideal people are hardworking and produce results, but they know a result by itself isn't good enough.

The ideal scholar or employee does his best to get the best of his job in terms of quantity and quality, and does it in the spirit of responsibility and not coercion, not even out of the sentiment of supporting one another but cooperation. He therefore spends sufficient time at work and observes quality of his work constantly asking oneself that same old question that Jesus asked his disciples: *what am I doing more (and better) than the others?* This is an important ideal because as said Vince Lombardi: "The quality of a person's life is in direct proportion to their commitment to excellence, regardless of their chosen field of endeavor." Indeed because of our history, beginning with slavery, colonialism and the Ujamaa or colonialism, this ideal should be at the head of the attributes which we should initiate amongst our people in this country. Today competitiveness and pursuit for quality in terms of how one conducts himself—or his character one exhibits—and products or services he produces are key qualities if a person has to excel—the qualities that remain scarce in supply amongst our people.

How did it start? As a slave, one doesn't crave for quality. By this assertion I mean slavery butchers the craving for quality beginning with butchering personal dignity. With colonialism, one had to do just the necessary. With Ujamaa and common property, one didn't have to compete for superior work or quality services. That's how ultimately the whole society became prey to this handicap. Indeed that's how such communities began producing mediocre professionals, and a society that breeds with bleeding mediocrity. Training our people into becoming quality focused is very essential especially today with globalization and competition worldwide. Quality is not only expensive any more. It's invaluable! That's why we must increase the quality of our own persons as well as of our own products and services. We must do so because afterall, a person who gains most from this transformation is, not anyone else. It is you. In the end it is you who will benefit most. But it all begins in the mind—as we are about to see. That's why we began this book with personal analysis—the reflection on your own life to enforce the reader to cultivate mindset change and overall paradigm shift.

And if facts be told, to become quality focused is not an uphill task. All that is needed is only an extra effort. With the spirit of empathizing with the others, by putting yourself in the shoes of the others: your customers, employers or associates by putting in only a part of you into what you do, by giving your all into whatever you do, your superiors, customers or audience will be thrilled that they are ready to give anything in return. In the end you will stand out from the crowd only by mere extra effort beyond average man's standards.

The second point which is equally significant to remember is that people love winners. So since you will win through empathy and therefore extra effort and quality of services, not to do is self defeating. It is not enough to say one has accomplished something. What is its quality? What is its stand against competing close substitutes whether that is a product or service? How was it produced? We know with coercion people can produce quality products but that will not be long enough before they sabotage everything you stand for. Quality is an ideal that in this country stands close to the head of the badly missing attributes because of our history during slavery and colonialism before independence. During independence, Ujamaa demonized competitiveness and industriousness. As such a slave doesn't care for quality. With colonialism one had just to do the necessary. With Ujamaa and common property, one didn't have to compete for superior work or quality of products or services. Indeed, when we moved from Ujamaa to market-led economy, we should have addressed industry and industriousness, competitiveness, punctuality etc, as a few among the key ideals in a contemporary society! We also needed to address that success or prosperity isn't about luck or chance but burning desire, determination, planning, consistence and action.

HOW DO YOU ACHIEVE SUCH A FEAT?

In order to be able to acquire *Quality* as your constant ideal or virtue, you have to build it as a culture or tradition. For the ideal scholar, one who aspires for excellence, anything less is indeed mediocrity. You have to acquire that sense quality in whatever you do, as part of your personal conduct. That's why we made an emphasis on the question of mindset change—and paradigm shift. You can do this by having principles and abiding by a certain set of standards—high standards in whatever you do. The second method is by aiming higher constantly and in daily basis. If you do so, you never have to think about what to do over and over again. Things are at your finger tips. Sometime you just need to force yourself to slow down in order to be in your element. So, take time to consider what you are supposed to do or achieve in the long term broken down into medium and short term. Then keep sight of the class or quality of your end product. The higher the attention to quality the more the attention you will give to the process. The degree of achievement you get determines and impacts your future. All this preparation is done in the mind. You can call it meditation. You can call it reflection. It is nothing but a constant and consistent attention to the bottom line quality standards but at the same time flexibly keeping an open eye and ear for an improvement or enhancement of the said quality standards.

Here now comes an assertion which will make whatever you produce, sell or stand for—products, personal services or ideas not only saleable or marketable but hot cake. It is an assertion that makes whatever you do tick. And what's more, you can charge the premium price for it when its close substitutes in the market are rotting on the shelves at throw away prices. With this quality, you simply get a privilege of determining the price as your product, service or idea become indispensable. It then follows that your posterity gains a name and spirit of high standards in whatever they do. The standards you set stand as KPI or key performance indicators going forward. Wouldn't you agree then that it is an advantage to keep on seeking excellence? Here now is a major motivation for you to keep seeking excellence—which is my message. Think of tomorrow. Competition is ever on the rise and standards ever rising. It's not the excellence of your products today that will guarantee your sustainable profitability. Excellence in character is the only means to sustained quality.

Think of yourself as the buyer and not seller. What does a buyer look for? If you orient your mindset in this regard, you will always seek to offer the best. But that is not enough. The ideal scholar recognizes that the term best is a relative term and extremely under the influence of time, trends and technological advancement. It's not fixed, and never will it be.

A true scholar recognizes that what is worth doing at all is indeed worth doing well, as goes a wise English saying! In Ecclesiastes, which is one of the highly prized books in the bible records thus, "whatsoever thy hand finds to do, do it with thy might.[133] But what do most of us do. We just pass time. We just want to get away—to do with it. We do the average work and assume it is over. We prefer to pass on the buck such that the leaders tend to throw the entire burden to workers as workers say we are just workers. As leaders we imagine we aren't concerned with quality. We place the burden on the supervisors as supervisors point the fingers to the workers.

Astonishingly, most managers or supervisors will say we are just managers or supervisors. To get the most we need to lead by example. Jesus was more than right when he asked his disciples thus: "What are you doing more (and better) than others?" Barack Obama was right. "As a society we have got to internalize the idea of excellence. Not many people try to achieve excellence." There is no shortcut to top success. Madeline Bridges said: "Give the world the best you have and the best shall come back to you." This is a constant reminder to you that to succeed, the ideal scholar will always strive to beat or outdo and surpass or outperform your own present standards every time you are at it. You should not only meet but always exceed your goals as a worker, and constantly beat your customers' expectations as a tradition. To do this, to achieve this feat, you must always strive to outcompete yourself. With this in mind, a person who strives to achieve the most and best of everything he is doing, is on his way to great accomplishment.

HOW PRICELESS IS QUALITY AS AN IDEAL

Not only men prefer quality results. When God prepared the house of Israel to leave Egypt he asked them to give an offering of an animal and not a

---

[133] *Think Big by Ben Carson*

lame or weakling cow or goat or lamb. It had to be yes an offering of animal but a strong and fit and healthy animal probably the best of all. Cain was cursed because when he went to sacrifice to the Maker he looked at the best sheep and at a second thought chose to offer a weak and probably sick animal which he didn't offer too for he said I've few and I specialize in crops so I'll offer crops. But when he saw the best and first class produce of his farm he said no! I'll just offer the second class and probably third class of cereals and olives and beans for he said afterall God has more than he needs in his lifetime which is itself a wrong idea. God doesn't have a lifetime. He is timeless for God's sake. "God is so selfish," he protested. "He has more than he needs. It is a waste to give him anything when he has more than he needs. I'll reduce the waste by offering the least needed crops," He counseled with himself. On the contrary, Abel ,his brother, selected the best sheep and cattle and went straight and offered to the Almighty without thinking about his lack. God praised Abel publicly accusing Cain. Cain then envied the favors that God had pronounced for Abel that he killed him in a cold blooded murder. Enough of metaphors.

Quality as an ideal is a do-or-die value if we have to prosper. Among the human species, it is the female folk that tend to marry a successful person to perpetuate prosperity and quality of life. To continue a strong generation male bees must compete in the field and the strongest will meet and mate with the queen in the spaces. The dogs too. They fight and bounce against one another as the female watches closely, judging between her suitors, deciding who is more powerful. And that is final judgment. No beauty her. It is the most powerful, not the most gorgeous fine-looking, male dog that she will offer her booty. The Chicken too. They tend to act likewise. They tend to surrender to the wishes of sturdy men among the males in the chicken species.

The lions will kill the weak males to ensure a sustained strong generation. Only the bees, unlike lions, don't kill the adversaries during infancy in fear of competition which is unfair competition for the young and weak members of the community. Not Lionel Messi or Einstein would survive if either of them were mothered by a lion. They were weak and not anywhere near what you could call competitive in their earlier lives. I can add Steve Jobs to the list. This author too wasn't that promising to a man who had a family of forty-plus children as a young man, unlike the lions—male lions that tend to wipe out all males in the herd fearing completion—bees engage in a very fair competition than the rest of the species. Like the lions who wipe competition partly out of selfish reasons why many of us today have envy and are jealous and they are ready to kill, or think of, or plan all adversities against the people who are prosperous instead of blaming it on ourselves. The prosperous became so by giving the best instead of expecting the best from the others.

Let me illustrate. When Bastard, my short story, came out on the observer in 2006, at the time when I was at the university (authored by Festo L. Michael, a name you can still search in The Observer at the university library, University of Dar es Salaam under the same title) though I have already mentioned this in another book, but because it was presented in wa different context, I feel compelled to repeat it here. So far as Apostle Paul said, it is not irksome to me to repeat it and it is beneficial to you. So why not recall the event. After I had written a short story I named Bastard, a story that was the second in my fiction works, I presented it to the paper's head offices in Mwenge, Dar es Salaam, Tanzania. That was on Friday. On Saturday, the three of us: a relative of mine in the name of Leonard, my brother and I, visited the paper's head offices for the payment for the works we had published a week before. This was on Saturday. Though we all had presented some more articles, the editor revealed to us that due to space only one of the stories we had presented was selected to be published immediately after it was presented while the other were published a week or two later. Its title? Bastard!

Asked why?—and notice not out of envy? Oh no! It was rather out of curiosity—and the editor simply said, "It has content." That's probably why when the Bastard was published, I saw Fortunatus reading the pages with great intensity. He in fact read it with deafening silence. When he finished, oh my God, was I listening right? Whether he said these words after a deep thought or whether the words escaped from his mouth, I have no way of knowing! But I can still recall the moment. The words still ring in my ears as if it was a whisper, a whisper I heard only yesterday. He said, or rather words escaped him: "You must be a genius," he said eying me for the first time—and with the same intensity he had shown when he began reading the paper. One thing was certain. The words were so genuine. They came from deepest part s of his heart. Not from the mouth. That's why I indeed had to restrain myself to hear the words properly. After I had digested the words, it was my turn to be open-mouthed. But he was dead cold and serious. He was not doing me favors I guess, nor was he shilly-shallying. Besides notice that Fortunatus is my big brother and accordingly consider the fact that it is out of the ordinary for siblings especially mature ones to regard highly the estates of their own brothers abilities—an unfortunately deep rooted tradition among the Kambarangwes.

If we can retrace where we began in this analysis, and recognizing that I didn't retell this Bastard story for self gratification, but rather to learn from it, here is the question: what did I do, or rather, what had I done to achieve such a feat? You can read it for yourself in the book How Universities Under Develop You, but let me pick another illustration—an illustration that will describe what I had done to achieve that feat. To be brief, I had given it my all.

Certainly you have heard of Sharuhk Khan. Probably you have not missed his successes in Bollywood movies. He is an Indian internationally renowned movie star. His secret? Submerging in what he is doing and indeed endeavoring to do so for the sake of his audience, as well as with the hindsight that that's how he can make it to the top. As for me, I needed money and needed it bad! I needed money for my family back home, and knew to get it, I had to produce something good for everyone, that it could add value to the editor and the paper—on one hand—and on the other, excite and enlighten the reader, as I could earn the money. He gives his all such that he is like a person who keeps on disintegrating himself leaving his part in the film he makes. How do we know this? Again Cosmo magazine interviewed him on what was his greatest fear; and he publicly declared that: "Every time I do a film …I feel that I leave behind a certain part of me!" How can such a person fail to succeed? Impossible. It's not a joke.

WITH QUALITY PEOPLE DON'T CARE ABOUT WHO YOU ARE

Indeed it is to your advantage to be of value to others. I've never seen people as insane as to dishonor somebody who fed and clothed and sheltered them constantly excepting of course the biblical Israelis. The Israelis were ungrateful. God provided for them but still they denounced him at Sinai. Over and over again he gave them manna, healed and fed them and they said they wanted a human king and not an unseen God seated in some heaven in the clouds above until God gave them the brutal King Saul. They were indeed an ungrateful people them Israelis. Jesus didn't only feed or heal them but resurrected some of their dead. Yet they killed him. That's an extreme case.

But overall, to succeed in everything you do, you must follow the Wallace D. Wattles credo: "In following the certain way…, you are getting continuous increase for yourself, and you are giving it to all with whom you deal. Convey the impression of advancement with everything you do, so that all people shall receive the impression that you are an advancing personality, and that you advance all who deal with you. Even to the people whom you meet in a social way without any thought of business and to whom you do not try to sell anything, give the thought of increase."Indeed build a better mousetrap, and the world will beat a path to your door." alternatively, Ralph Waldo Emerson said: "If a man has good corn or wood, or boards, or pigs, to sell, or can make better chairs or knives, crucibles or church organs, than anybody else, you will find a broad hard-beaten road to his house, though it be in the woods."[134] Thus indeed if you are of significant value to people, instead of beating you, people will beat a path to your door, for indeed, "nobody kills a goose that hatches golden eggs!"

Is there any explanation for this credo, for this verity? Why is this so? Let us ponder a little about it.

Overall, as humans, we seek more and better things: more food in many varieties, more and better cloths, better and safer shelter, more luxury, more beauty, more knowledge, more leisure and pleasure. We seek more life. And the recent study shows that the beasts too aren't removed from the league. Every living organism is under this necessity for continuous advancement. And this, it seems to me, is a God's way to perpetuate life, for where increase ceases, dissolution and death set in at once. Man instinctively knows this, and therefore he is forever seeking more. This law of perpetual increase is set forth by Jesus in the parable of the talents: Only those who gain more retain any; from him who has not shall it be taken away even that which he has. The normal desire for increased wealth is not an evil or a reprehensible thing. It is simply the desire, an aspiration, or inspiration for more abundant life.

And because it is the deepest instinct of their natures, all men and women are attracted to those who can give them more of the means of life. Indeed men have the same trait but as my brother Fortunatus concluded, young men seeking girl friends beware. Married men aren't any safer too for

---

134

http://en.wikipedia.org/wiki/Build_a_better_mousetrap,_and_the_world_will_be at_a_path_to_your_door women folk express this attribute better than another species. That's why he remodeled the Kiswahili saying thus: *Mkono Mtupu Haulambwi na Mwanamke* viz. a woman lover can never lick an empty hand. Men shouldn't take this as a liability but as an asset and an incentive being divinely ordained as the provider of the family.

THE UGANDAN EMMANUEL OKWII'S DISTINCTION

Though I'm not a fan of Simba Football Club, I cannot make myself not to bring up what happened when they arrived home at the airport after defeating the desert foxes of Algeria. Though all ten other footballers of that club persisted and even though they lost two to one based on an away goal rule they qualified for the second round. Now why write about the club I loathe myself being a fan of their rivals Yanga? Here's the point. The goal was scored through personal efforts of one and only one player. Notice again that this player isn't a local boy to woo the author's favors. This man is a Ugandan and his name is Emanuel Okwii. Now with the qualification in the bag the team headed south toward Mwalimu Julius Nyerere airport back home. When they arrived now Okwii was, the only man every camera cited. He was the only man every fan crowded around. Indeed every fan wanted to touch the helm of his garment and get healed after many years of football shame. Astonishing? Embarrassing? No! The crowd was all Tanzanian yet they didn't care about their own countrymen. Indeed they seemed to completely ignore them.

Indeed, when we have something worth to offer, no matter whether we are pale, white as paper or black as charcoal. It doesn't matter if we are tall or short, massive or slim. Success overshadows all other qualities. I've a newspaper before me, and notice that is one among numerous others, with a colossal photo of Emanuel Okwii standing tall amidst tiny ubiquitous local boys displayed on—mind you not on Ugandan papers but—all national papers that whole week. "If a man can write a better book," said Ralph Waldo Emerson in another version of the same piece of wisdom, "preach a better sermon or make a better mouse trap than his neighbors, though he builds his house in the woods, the world will make a beaten path to his door!" That is the argument. Let us illustrate a little bit about what we are presenting here. Let us picture it for you to grasp the point I'm trying to make here. When David killed Goliath, people literally threw themselves on his feet. To put it in another way, when king Saul let David fight Goliath, he was establishing him as king over his own kingdom. After he had killed the giant, the people sang, "Saul has killed a thousand, but David ten thousand."

The traditional society rewarded winners too. It was quality in its truest sense that caused King George I, to come spontaneously to his feet in an ovation to the outstanding performance of the song Hallelujah! Why did King George stand in an ovation? He stood in an ovation to the historic song Halleluiah in recognition that, though he, King George, was king, he knew somehow Handel—even his own subject—was somehow superior to him, the king, himself. It was the reflex recognition of the quality of that piece of music Hallelujah that King George gave way and rose to the custom of the audience standing in ovation to an outstanding performance. What does this say? The king's reaction, his first reaction, was to stand up in an ovation and recognition, that is to say: "In one way, George Frederick Handel was greater than King George himself!" so quoted a BBC program![135]

HOW TO PROMOTE QUALITY AS A NATIONAL VIRTUE
Quality, I mean the sense of quality is a virtue, and unlike vice which is natural like weeds, it has to be cultivated, it has to be nurtured. Arnold Palmer Said: "The road to success is always under construction." The road to excellence is a process, and therefore always under construction. It requires concentration. What is concentration? Arnold Palmer referred to his quality at golf by the same formula. "What do I mean by concentration?" he asked, "I mean focusing totally on the business at hand and commanding your body to do exactly what you want it to do." In his book What They Don't You at Harvard Business School, Mark McCormack illustrated that: A carpenter who ends up becoming a foreman is the one who drives a nail straighter. The hunter-gather society rewarded the best hunters and fighters.

Besides a lion's share of the meat, they were promoted into the leadership of the society. I have lived among the hunter-gather communities back in the days in Karagwe in Tanzania. During the hunting sessions, I learned that a man who hit the animal first got the lions share as a law. He in fact got for himself the whole of a hind limb as a person who was the second to hit the animal got for himself half of the animal's front limb for an assist. To make sense of how the traditional society encouraged action and excellence, no matter whether they were ten or twenty hunters, the rest of the band shared the remaining portion. In Things Fall Apart, a novel by

---

[135] *Further reading on this quality can be found in the book What Makes People Rich and Nations Powerful.*

Chinua Achebe, Okwonkwo was promoted to the status of the Egugwu, or spirit-elders, while he still was almost a young man. Why? Because of his courage and character. In football world games are won by scoring goals. It is natural therefore that the world footballers of the year awards go to goal scorers in ninety nine out of a hundred.

How does the government or even organizations respond to this challenge—or opportunity? The Emirates airliner declares that there is no need of making an effort to choose between the best fares and best services. That is whatever the package—economy or business class—quality is at the forefront of the service delivery. On August 4, 2013, in an interview with the Turkish newspaper *Hurriyet*, former Pink Floyd member Roger Waters stated that: "I was about 15. In the middle of the night with friends, we were listening to jazz. It was "Georgia on My Mind", Ray Charles' version. Then I thought 'One day, if I make some people feel only one twentieth of what I am feeling now, it will be quite enough for me.'" But for long term far reaching change, quality shouldn't be privatized. It should be nationalized! Paul apostle said,"But we beseech you, brethren to honor those who labor among you…and admonish you…to esteem them very highly in love because of their work!"

Parents, teachers and leaders of men amongst us ought to promote quality as a virtue, setting high standards for themselves and their children. And I know it works. For instance, the author came home having come out second in one of his annual exams at Kahororo Secondary School. Did mother pamper her son—yes her son? "You have failed so terribly. How can you fail like this?" I know you have now joined the gangs and bad boys at school. I am going to even tell your brothers. This is unacceptable!" she wanted her son to remain at the top of his classes—and God knows my boyhood-self did I on the whole—at least from that moment on until I graduated from high school four years later.

Now having said so, I want to insert a comment. I didn't give this account to "raise" my own status or standing before the reader. No! Nor do I narrate about it to brag about my academic credentials of the past which mean nothing anyway. No! Instead I am writing this account to admit I had walked away from my traditional path, dragged into the popular conduct. In fact I had even joined some groups of boys who went out to girls' schools nearby for either dancing or to make friends with girls. I had begun wasting my precious time on useless matters. My mother taught me to impress the most important people in my life—and that's myself, my mother and family and of course God. It was this change of attitude that led the same boy to go on to graduate from the university in economics—the discipline that his father, Michael Kambarangwe, revered so much. And that's not all! The author has a small secret he wants to confess—without shame!

He went on to refrain from the girls and got himself buried into the books. As a result? he went on to graduate from the university almost ten years later, untainted, having—in the metaphor of the Song of Lawino—had his manhood temporarily crashed by the book volumes he read. That's how the author graduated a virgin, and certainly the same reason and moment—that moment that mama scolded me—that also reclaimed the books you are now reading, the seventh of the books authored by the same boy who had begun walking away, apart from dangers of HIV/AIDS, the disease whose prevalence remains untamed in that part of the country—and I thank mother for it! Notice, however, that the author doesn't write the forgoing to claim sainthood? No! The difference is that a real scholar will reckon he has fallen short of the glory of God, as the fool will celebrate his fall. So far I am writing to inspire you to do good. I am not writing and not to persuade you otherwise.

You recognize this little declaration is important especially today when vices are praised, regarded as a cool thing to do whereas virtues are despised as outdated and out of place! One last remark! Concerning giving our services to the most important person in our lives, the author's classmate named Richard, alias Abbas, was immovable in the way he conducted himself. It was no wonder when my boyhood-self walked away he rose to the number one spot in terminal exams that year. He, Richard, didn't change much even after secondary school. He knew who to serve and where to direct his energies. That's why when he graduated from high school, his mark was unbelievably high—it was 4 points! Do you want to know where he is now? On graduation from high school, he went to the seminary, and now he is in Rome, Italy. Not Italy-Italy, if you know what I mean? He, Reverend Father Richard Tiganya, is in the Vatican, having chosen to bestow the entire balance of his life to God!

27. ATTENTION TO THE CUSTOMER: A DARK SCAR IN OUR SOCIETY, AND A BARRIER AGAINST BUSINESS GROWTH AND FOREIGN INVESTMENTS

"You don't run a business solely dependent on finding new customers."
—Bill FitzPatrick in Action Principles

Through the foregoing discussion on quality—or excellence as an ideal—we brought up a phrase adapted from Napoleon Hill in Think and Grow Rich: "The spirit in which products or services are offered, or delivered," didn't we? We did so not because we either wanted to make this discussion expansive or expensive. No. We did so because of the greatest mistake we do so well, not only in this country, but also in all societies corrupted by slavery and colonialism. One can give all good reasons in all Christendom about why common property is good as a policy, but it also has a tendency to breed indifference that chokes delivery of results in terms of quantity and quality.

Many people and indeed many corporations mistakenly consider customer care and customer services to the customer as secondary function in an organization believing that the production of the products and services they sell, marketing or even advertising are more important so long as they have quality product and services. It is massively wrong. We brought this discussion because no matter how useful is the product or service you offer in terms of its intrinsic value, no matter how colorful it looks in terms of how it is packaged; no matter how functional is the product or service: but if the spirit or character in which it is being offered at the time and space the customer or buyer comes into contact with the seller is awful, if the attitude of the salesman is unwelcoming and his conduct disagreeable, you will naturally put him off.

What does this say? It says that your efforts—energy, time and resources—to produce, market and advertise the quality product or service was indeed meaningless and indeed total waste!

In fact the author himself having served as a sales and marketing executive and manager for a significant duration of time, and therefore being on familiar terms with the egos of men, I can go on record to state that: given two combinations of the same product or service in which one combination is composed of the product or service with the top quality but offered with the cruel, insensitive, cold, heartless, unfeeling, unsympathetic spirit in an unfriendly environment whether because of naivety or ignorant self importance because of the high quality of the product or service one offers, on one hand; and another combination of the same product or service constituting the average quality but offered in the 'bestest[136]' manner or in the most empathizing character and spirit in a very friendly environment at the contact point, nine out ten buyers will opt for the second option. We have discussed that quality or competitiveness is another set of weeping trait among our youth. And the true quality of your products or services can only be best measured by the degree of how it is accepted by its consumers. So you have to work with them, you have to labor in listening to them—and indeed responding with the right answers.

CHARACTER AND CUSTOMER SERVICES
We have highlighted that that mindset and character cannot be substituted by technical skills; haven't we? This is one of the greatest secrets of great services. Trainers into customer services should build the services culture or character. It should start from reorientation of the people's mindset. Sadly that's what all customer care trainers don't know or ignore. Here's the difference. You can successfully force the donkeys to a well, but however dumb are they, that's only as far as you can go—for you cannot force them to drink the water. Unless they have reasons to do anything, until when they see how they personally benefit, you cannot be successful to sell a product, service or idea. And if you cannot do so, you can as well

---

[136] *The term is coined to mean the first best or the top most quality*

forget success or affluence. Among the benefits, personal dignity and the nourishment of one's ego are key.

We have witnessed how external failures have been responsible for the economic crisis and organizational failures across the globe. That's right, only in part though. With a keen analysis, the author came to a conclusion longtime ago that the internal factors count more to such failures than the external ones. Most organizations fail not because of poor distribution or the quality of products or services they offer. They fail because of poor internal communication both intra-personally and inter-personally. As we advise you to follow the book What Business Leaders Should Know But they Don't, for more on the matter, beware of the fact that most failing organization fail because of poor communication skills and character or attitude. They fail not because of financial reasons. Far from that! They fail because of selfishness and disharmony amongst the stakeholders, among them the owners or employers, employees, suppliers, the government and customers or retailers and distributors—and more to the point, the end users or consumers. Because of the same attitude, the same people, the stakeholders who should be working together to foster each other's needs and interests, failing to understand they depend on and need one another, they instead engage in self seeking discord tearing one another apart. They forget a house divided against itself cannot stand.[137] It is why we advise you to recall the immediate preceding ideal of communication and cooperation.

Indeed it is due to internal environment (an elephant in the room—a skeleton in the cupboard) that one country cannot improve her economic situation even with financial support or grants. We know most countries in Africa including Tanzania had their debts lifted but only a few years later most are worse than before. We all know that a checkbook cannot answer to all our problems, no? Let the skeptic recall what in Tanzania was termed in Kiswahili as *Mabilioni ya Kikwete*, namely the President Kikwete's Billions, under which small businesses were financed by the government. Where are they? Who is it that is today rightly rich only because of the same investment? We have seen already—haven't we?—how the research by the Carnegie Institute concluded that "even in such technical lines as engineering, about fifteen percent of one's financial success is due to one's technical knowledge and 85% is due to skill in human engineering...!"

---

[137] *Source: The Proverbs*

We are witnesses of how companies which invest wonderfully in expensive adverts and even build very wide shop floors and show rooms, parked with, displaying world class modern high tech value for money products or services waited for by beautifully dressed customer services agents who are sadly not trained how to treat a customer right: agents who don't listen empathetically to him or her, and responding appropriately; and in spite of all this investment, these well and expensively dressed, highly paid customer services agents end up blowing a hole into your intended warm relationships with a customer, and therefore ending up forcing the customers out of the shop (along with their wallets)!

We see a disturbing tendency of "business as usual" growing incredibly. Also though not necessarily a sign of dissatisfaction on the part of the staff, we have seen customers who grumble about less than true optimal customer services. That is why in this country we need a fresh, tailored customer care and customer services program—a program that best delivers to the customers with the *bestest* experience, if I may coin a superlative phrase, on and off the shop floor—a different employee based program that should help to transform into a consumer-led organization—and nation. In short, being consumer-led, as you know, is an art and culture of commitment to respond to the consumers and, to heartily listen to, communicate with and respond to their needs. Why is it important? Such examples such as the rise of China as the top global exporter or even the rise of under-dogs in every other sector from sports, music, telecoms, beverages or banking in Tanzania say it all.

Coca Cola Company back in Atlanta knew this secret, and they declared that, "the secret to our success lies outside the bottle," that is, outside the drink—in people—in employees and customers! Reginald Mengi, a leading businessman and media mogul in East Africa recognized this secret earlier on and asserted that: "The human mind is our fundamental resource," said Mr. Mengi. "Our business is composed not of land or buildings," continued the businessman, "not even of the capital invested, but the caliber of our people…A group of people who work a little better every day in products, services and ideas."

By now you have probably begun to realize the fact that, for many reasons than those described above, attention to the customer is a very important quality, especially in our society today. We are witnesses that the mindset or character cannot be substituted by technical skills. Yet, one of the greatest handicaps in our society today is customer care and customer services—or attention to the customer—as our previous works have revealed![138] Why is this so important to business corporations wherever they operate—and in this country in particular? No business can operate profitably or aptly sustainably if it cannot satisfy the egos of the customers or buyers but their own. As an economy, we cannot attract adequate foreign investment without improving customer services. Besides, with ICT, globalization and ever emerging and strengthening of the regional economic blocs such as EAC, SADC or even EU, great quality and customer services build great workforce—the workforce that is more productive—and competitive. That's briefly why you cannot successfully discuss QUALITY—or EXCELLENCE—as an ideal, without bringing up a phrase "the spirit in which products or services are offered,"[139] into the mix.

THE CUSTOMER IS THE KING AT BARCLAYS—A RARE PRECIOUS CULTURE IN TANZANIA

This change can come into effect when the employer and the employee come together to work for the public they serve. If you look at it so closely, the modern day employer is the customer, in whose presence the employer and employee ought to tremble. This secret was recently presented to the author when he visited the Barclays Bank in Dar es Salaam, Tanzania and coincidentally, Honorable Nimrod Mkono, a distinguished lawyer, businessman and Member of Parliament traced his feet toward the counter. Everything seemed to turn upside down. The regular services seemed to halt for a moment. I witnessed the bank managers from almost every other department literally sprinting scrambling to welcome him and listening to him. Then I saw a convoy of men and women gluing their ears to the important entrant as they led him into a private spacious room. Five minutes later, a not-less-than a presidential convoy began on its way out, literally creating an in-house bank stampede, albeit protectively, leading the most important customer to a place where he had parked his big 4x4 car! I learned later that, with a very significant deposit in this bank, honorable Mkono was one of the very few top customers. But since he, hon. Nimrod Mkono is certainly above

---

[138] *Please make reference to the books How Universities Under Develop You, What Business Leaders Should Know But They Don't and What Makes People Rich And Nations Powerful*

[139] *The term is traced back from Napoleon Hill's book Think and Grow Rich*

the average citizen, the average reader is likely to be misled into believing that such services are only special for the big boys only. Wrong.

"No matter how small the transaction," said Wallace D. Wattles in his magnificent book Science of Getting Rich, "even if it be only the selling of a stick of candy to a little child, put into it the thought of increase, and make sure that the customer is impressed with the thought. Convey the impression of advancement with everything you do, so that all people shall receive the impression that you are an advancing personality, and that you advance all who deal with you. Even to the people whom you meet in a social way. Without any thought of business and to whom you do not try to sell anything. Give the thought of increase." Arrogance among the businessmen as a policy is now passé. Napoleon Hill was right. Such a policy "has now been supplanted by the "we-are-obligingly-at-your-service, sir," policy… Today, "businesses managed by courteous men who do everything short of shining the customer's shoes, have pushed the old time merchants into the background. And make no mistake, time marches on! Courtesy and service are watch words of business today."[140]

I also hope that by now you have become conscious of the verity that we did not bring this additional discussion on only the grounds of either wishing to make this discussion expansive or even expensive.

Yet when we talk about the weakness of the customer care and customer services in this country, ours is a unique case. Our problem with customer services in Tanzania is a deep- rooted problem. It began with our history.

After the colony mother, Germany, was defeated by the Great Britain and her allies, Tanzania—as a case study—was placed under trusteeship of the GB. She was not a colony like her neighbors of Kenya and Uganda. GB was only entrusted to guide Tanganyika until when she was able to govern herself. It was natural therefore that the colony mother wouldn't invest so much is such a trusteeship. This explains why we have had fewer investments in terms of social economic infrastructures such as educational facilities, health, railways and road networks, banks etc. here at home as compared to the investments GB has had in Kenya and Uganda. It was also

---

[140] *Adapted from Napoleon hill in Think and Grow Rich the unabridged edition page 131*

natural that disarray in the long term economic plans would occur having stifled the initial physical investments and plans by the Germans.

The same explanation is the reason why we have English language barrier here in Tanzania. My grandfather and dad, for instance, could speak some German because my grandpa served as a teacher during the Germans. But soon the British took over, the little German my father had begun learning became useless and obsolete as he began getting instructed in English. That's how language barrier we see amongst our people today began. It is no wonder a very recent research on English language proficiency among African countries revealed that Uganda was top on the list, whereas Kenya was third amongst the proficient English speaking countries in Africa. I worked feverishly trying to trace my Tanzania but I couldn't find her goon name even in the top ten. I gave up!

Poor customer services in this country also stems from the foregoing handicap, viz., language barrier. Language barrier contributes to poor communication skills, the latter of which contribute to low self-esteem, which then contributes to poor customer services. That's why it has never gone well with me when some of our activists campaign against English as a medium of instructions in our schools. Without more attention to the mastery of languages, we accelerate our situation from bad to worse.

One of the reasons why we have poor customer services in the country as a culture, is the post independence socialism or Ujamaa policy. Because of Ujamaa, our education emphasized the socialist conviction that competitiveness was entirely evil. This belief stifled the spirit of working hard among our people. Why should they? Work or don't work the generous government would still provide for you and your family. The author enjoyed some of the last benefits of the Ujamaa free-of-charge services. And when I say Ujamaa killed self initiative and competitiveness and quality, it is not fiction. Eva Mendes, the Cuban superstar said: "I love sleeping. And if there were Olympics for it, I would take Gold," she said, "I'm Cuban. We like to sleep." Indeed everybody likes to sleep. The difference resonates from possibility of living on other people's or government's resources and the desire to be wealthy. Notice also that such priceless attributes: individual self-reliance, hard work, industriousness, innovation, quality and excellence, competitiveness, the desire to excel—to be wealthy etc., are not only nonexistent or only discouraged among socialist culture? No. They are stifled!

No one has ever thrived without good relationships with the people they serve. You can only grow by delivering the best product, offered excellently in the spirit of giving service—the spirit that cares more about building relationships with customers than making money on the backs of uninformed customers. And it is this kind of relationships that can help you to move your customers along the loyalty ladder thereby turning once-off prospects into buyers or customers, who then, with the best customer experiences, revisit your shop for repeated purchases thereby becoming regular customers. Regulars customers normally become clients, who then become your advocates and in the end your business partners. You need a training program that helps your staff to do this on their own. This is only possible with behavior change or personal transformation in terms of character and attitude among our people —a change of attitude toward themselves, work, their peers and managers as well as the customers. You need a program that outs emphasis on self awareness among the people while motivating and inspiring them to build a new drive or spirit towards team work and eagerness to generate more and better results with less resources per unit time!

Briefly, I trust you that with your experience with your children, your spouse, your siblings, your coworkers, your employers, your neighbors or even the strangers you meet—your customers—you must have already realized that today customers are now more demanding than ever before—demanding solutions, services, value, attention, recognition, involvement, wider choices, change etc. That is why the right training in customer services must cover marketing communication and we highlight sources of brand contact including product related sources, service contacts, planned and unplanned contacts. As part of customer services training, you need a training program in communication skills covering how to build lasting warm relationships, listening skills, presentation and conversation skills. A customer services program that doesn't resonate with the culture within a particular society is doomed to fail right from the onset!

28. THE IDEAL SCHOLAR IS A THINKING MAN—AN INNOVATIVE AND IMAGINATIVE PERSON

"Poirot," I said. "I have been thinking."
"An admirable exercise my friend. Continue it."
— Agatha Christie, Peril at End House

The ideal man thinks. Why important? Thinking is the food of the mind," aptly said Abu Bakr. If you can't think the mind will give up the ghost. Thinking is the lifeline of the living man. "And therefore if Africans are to begin to make a contribution in their affairs, they must begin to think. But the question is: are we thinking?'" asked P.L.O Lumumba. Really, do we think? This is a global infection but our culture and history make us the most favorable habitat for this malady. And this isn't my good guess. "Five percent of the people think," observed the inventor, Thomas A. Edison, "ten percent of the people think they think, and the other eighty-five percent would rather die than think!" This is nothing less than a tragedy.

We are not thinking and are not encouraged to do so by our masters, the slave masters and colonialist. Neither does our curriculum, nor teaching methodologies, nor how exams are set encourages us to think. Ujamaa or state socialism too had its setbacks where the vanguard few did the thinking for the population. Today we see the same system among our corporate, academic and political structures. Take any third world country like Tanzania, and put it under the microscope. IMF and World Bank tell our leaders and economists what to do. Donors tell our politicians what they should with the monies. Our patrons in education send us books to read for free, and our academics feel happy to be relieved from such a strenuous work of thinking and writing books much as partying politicians celebrate to have been saved from the headache of procuring books.

Go to any corporation: employees are directed from abroad. Why? These companies are multinationals. They are branches of big corporations abroad. It is no wonder all marketing or even production strategies at companies like Tanzania Breweries, Serengeti Breweries, Celtel, Vodacom, Tigo and Coca Cola are top down. They are imposed from above with the net effect of undermining our people's abilities and dwarfing their mental and moral capacities. Among such corps, local people may have big names title-wise but that shouldn't deceive you. They just names. Most are coolies; they are there only to implement and report on how things went as directed. They are not thinkers or inventors. Our education and strategies must address this area should we heal the inherent problem of graduates who cannot innovate or think. Not only academic but also economic revolution is impossible without reorientation of our mindset—and of our curriculum—an empowering curriculum, one that will make people think. "The one real goal of education," said Max Beerbohm, a British Critic, Essayist, and Caricaturist, "is to leave a person asking questions." That's why this is not healthy in terms of our people's creativity and innovation. It is a challenge we must respond to.

The author is a witness that when he began working with TBL, a subsidiary of SAB/Miller, and later with a Pan African telecom giant, his imagination was soaring and very active. When the merger with the SAB a giant SA brewer came into effect, all plans were imported from SA or UK. We were given sales targets to achieve, targets we didn't know whence they came, how to achieve them or why. My instincts didn't like it one bit. It wasn't far later when we were provided with banners and various decoration materials, a package that was perfected with an imported tool boxes whose contents may shock you: nails, glue, scissors, and harmers! We were no longer required to think but to "Just Do It!" we went to work. We began hammering the bar walls, and gluing colored beer posters, and with towels we began to wash coolers and beer bottles in every bar we visited. This was a new job description for the graduate officers in positions of marketing officers and sales and marketing managers—and that's how performance appraisals were made. That's the way promotions were determined. I didn't like it. I raised the matter in a senior regional meeting with national directors explaining that it was why morale was low among the staff and productivity and sales falling. Here was why.

We hired university graduates, albeit themselves handicapped by the teaching methodologies aside from outlines model of answering questions, but we hired thinkers to think and plan and manage execution but instead we turned them into mason and carpenters and drivers and coolies. The senior management turned their ears deaf, as some of my compatriots suggested that it didn't matter as long as they remained in the payroll; they were ready to do anything. This response put to rest any doubt I had had that such minds had been conquered—the situation I dreaded to happen to me. This, mind you, is by no minute measure, a fiction story? No! You can read it in this author's previous book What Business Leaders Should Know but They Don't (www.amazon.com)! But then the whole thing became evident to me when the company began hiring rugby players and celebrities in the top ranking positions—people who didn't necessarily have the ability to think. That's when typical South Africans like Malcolm came in. Such senior managers worked so hard to promote the Nike slogan, "Just Do it! Don't," don't think!

Doers were promoted, and thinkers dehumanized! I knew that's not my kind of job, or place. I quit.
"Why must we remind ourselves of these realities?" rightly asked Prof. Lumumba in his illustrious speech: The tragedy of Africa. "Because throughout the ages, the battle has been always the battle of the mind. And if your mind is conquered," he continued, "If your mind is conquered, then you are going nowhere." Because we were going nowhere, I disembarked my own person from that bus! Notice, however, that not everybody was insensitive to what was happening, no! Gideon Mkama, 55 at the time, was my superior and ally. He confided with me counseling me suggesting that I quit. "Your brains are still active and are bright. Quit this place before you turn forty. By then you will be like us—we have reached to a point of no return!" he admonished. Did I quit? I did! Did the move make a difference? Well—without such a decision, you wouldn't be reading the book now in your hands!

THINK FOR YOURSELF
Addressing a group of young graduates, fresh scholars and members of TANU Youth League during the early years of independence, Mwalimu Nyerere counseled the congregation asking them to think. "Think for yourself!" he told them point blank. "Think about your future, your children and your children's future," he said. Referring to the work well done—the struggle for independence and efforts he and his colleagues were doing in rebuilding the nation, he said, "And every generation must choose its duty. Yours is to think. They, the imperialists, will tell you thinking is a very big problem, and that don't do it," they will tell you, he said, "we will do it for you. Don't accept."

IS THINKING OR IMAGINATION IMPORTANT?Is thinking or imagination an important ideal? Should our schools begin to teach such subjects as thinking and imagination? Let us rationalize together. How many times we have woken up to the echoes of bad deals, deals in which our representatives have signed documents unthinkingly, giving away our national treasures away on a silver platter? Cases of ESCROW, EPA, the radar saga, mining contracts, wild life and many others speak for themselves. Our men of education today aren't any better than Chief Mangungo who signed a document handing over his country and the rest of Tanzania to the cunning German Carlo Petro, alias Carl Peters, are they? And what of the Radar saga? Whereas the British Parliament was engaged in a bitter debate on the matter having unearthed that some British businessman had colluded with the Tanzanian officials leading to an inflated sale of outdated radar, what did we do or say? Wasn't it Claire Short, the British cabinet minister who resigned in protest of such a bad and disgraceful deal and not our officials? This isn't the author's concoction.

According to http://www.theguardian.com/world/2010/feb/06/bae-tanzania-arms-deal, Cabinet ministers Claire Short and Robin Cook had tried to stop the sale of the hugely expensive radar to the poverty-stricken Tanzanians...The World Bank and the International Civil Aviation Organization judged that the 2001 purchase was unnecessary and overpriced. But the £28m deal started to look even worse when the SFO discovered that a third of the contract's price had been diverted into secret offshore bank accounts. The SFO believed that this money was used to pay bribes to Tanzanian politicians and officials... Short, who resigned from the government, said: "Every way you looked at it, it (the deal) was outrageous and disgraceful... "It was an obviously corrupt project. Tanzania didn't need a new military air traffic control, it was out-of-date technology, they didn't have any military aircraft–they needed a civilian air traffic control system and there was a modern, much cheaper one...

What about rampant quick fix, low rate of self employment? All these together with religious radicalism we experience today are results of failure in thinking and imagination.

But we can positively consider importance of thinking and imagination knowing that success factors and growth drivers change over time the ideal scholar is imaginative, inventive, innovative, and has initiative. He is curious and has an inquisitive mind: a trait we badly need today especially with the fast changing world in terms of technology and indeed business drivers and success factors. This is undoubtedly what the Association for Supervision and Curriculum Development summarized as: Enhancing Creativity. Indeed, the proverbs couldn't be more right; for truly: "As a man thinketh, so is he!" As a society, only a little while ago we had no mobile phones and there was no internet. So people communicated by way of letter writing. Beside letters there was telegram if you had an urgent message which would be delivered in two to three days. A very efficient way, huh? It was really efficient when compared to the letters that arrived if by chance in a month's time and the hot news no longer any news to the other party.

Telegrams were so popular that they even formed a topic in mathematics. Such questions were as follows: If a standard telegram is ten words and it costs a hundred shillings. If every extra word is charged ten shillings what will be the cost of 208 words cost. The world is really changing so fast. When I think of the changes that have happened in the world of reading and writing I can't see how one can stop changes. The first or original letters were oriented by God himself on stones. Then men discovered tree backs and papers before they discovered typewriters and today soft copies literally writing on air. Innovation has made life easier. If the medium of storing writings remained to be stones; think of the burden and budget of keeping or reading a book this size. How many rocks would you be required to carry in order to read the whole text? Think of the how many days you would travel from one continent to another without flying airplanes.

Innovation is possible. Invention is reality. Creation is indeed ordained to man as co-creator of all things around him, such as the rest of discoveries we associate with science. Indeed in this assertion there is a point of great importance. In this statement we solve the all time contradiction and confrontation between the two aspects of creation, namely, religious aspect and the scientific approach to the origin of life.

The ideal scholar is a man of ideas and imagination. He knows that the idea or imagination is capable of yielding anything in life. He knows as wrote Napoleon Hill that "the idea is capable of yielding an income far greater than that of the average doctor lawyer or engineer whose education required several years in college." Through this ideal or faculty, man has been able to be a master of his destiny, and an umpire of his own game. "Through the aid of his imaginative faculty," wrote Napoleon Hill in Think and Grow Rich, "man has discovered, and harnessed, more of Nature's forces during the past fifty[141] years than during the entire history of human race, previous to that time. He has conquered air so completely, that the birds are a poor match for him in flying."

There is also penicilium and other vaccines etc, all which have helped check diseases and made life longer and a little more predictable. Innovation has lengthened life span and lowered the child mortality rate. It has indeed made life better. No wonder Exim Bank declared rightly that "Ugunduzi ni maisha;" that is to say innovation if is indeed life. It is "Making life better," as a Celtel slogan suggested. Schools therefore ought to produce daring minds. We need to transform the nation into one home to many of Christopher Columbus, Yuri Gagarin, Albert Einstein, Newton, Edison etc. Through education we must transform the nation into one home to inventors and writers and risk taking entrepreneurs. This is the nation we must focus on building. This is the kind of a nation our education should aim to enhance.

---

[141] *It is now about a hundred years since this statement was first put on paper.*

29. THE IDEAL SCHOLAR HAS A BEAUTIFUL MIND: HE IS A CRITICALLY THINKING OPEN MINDED PERSON

"The essence of the independent mind lies not in what it thinks, but in how it thinks."—Christopher Hitchens, Letters to a Young Contrarian

Through the previous chapter we learnt that the ideal scholar is a thinking man. We also saw a few areas in which a person or society that is unthinking Is apt to lose much as a thinking person and society gains or contributes to growth or in the prosperity of the country and making the world as whole a better place. In this chapter we want to extend lessons into thinking or mindset, with the intent of addressing quick fix, extremism, low self-employment and why some people prosper when others are trodden in poverty. And the explanation is simple: It is all in the mind. That's why the ideal scholar has to have a beautiful mind: a person who thinks critically but also is open-minded—a positive thinker, a man with a positive mindset. Thus the ideal scholar has emotional intelligence or strength and therefore is levelheaded. Being emotionally intelligent, he knows how to unleash the power within but also how to tame thoughts and emotions. Beyond all, he knows the primary battle ground is in the mind—and not on the outside.

Very recently, the Indian policy makers indicated that the new government under the Narendra Modi, had, among other priorities, planned to provide new and clean trains and toilets. Why? India didn't lack toilets, trains or resources to put the same in place. No sir! The existing ones didn't inspire users because they were so dirty and tarnished. Now the question is this: would the installation of the new toilets or train cabins solve the Indian problem on the same? No madam! That could doubtless be off-mark! Probably all the prime minister and his government needed to do, and do it first, fast and furiously, was to change the mindset of the vast majority of the Indian masses—the masses who would not fancy using toilets; individuals who don't mind spitting, urinating or dropping human wastes on the new train walls etc. And you know what? What I write for Mr. Modi, his administration, academics and policy makers, I also write for Tanzania and all worthy peoples around the globe, people craving to advance their own situations and stations in life and in world affairs. And this analogy is transcendental. That's why any individual wishing to progress, ought not to trace his failures or priorities from without. The primary battle is waged in the mind. The foregoing assertion is a life changing message and therefore it calls for a little more thought and reflection.

AS A MAN THINKETH SO IS HE

"As a man thinketh so is he." That's not me. It is the bible. Reading this preamble, some of my most accomplished skeptical readers will say that: Now this author is going to waste my time with this useless religious pap. It is not merely religious. It is reality. Indeed what we put our minds as mere abstracts, when we supply them with manure, air and water, it soon returns to us crystallized in real form. And I am a witness. Two men were walking when we they saw a man coughing and his nose wet dripping with flu walking in their direction. One of them told his friend that he was susceptible to flue, and that he was certain to contract the disease. Soon after they had crossed, he began coughing. Two minutes later he was dripping with flu unable to continue with his class. I know this is true. I know they couldn't of course avoid the man because they were crossing the Academic Bridge at the University of Dar es Salaam. I have no doubt it is true because I am that man who predicted that he would contract the disease.

On the birth of her first born, a woman back in Karagwe Tanzania, began singing thus: "Chamuzala, chamuleta, akafuraude, akana kamweee, Chamuzala, chamuleta, akana kamwe..." he song and the voice rambled on, literally meaning, I have only been given just one kid and no more. What happened? Whereas her husband fancied having many children manifested by his record: one of his senior wives had twelve children to him, another had eleven, another seven and no one had less than four (much as others who came after her gave birth to several children) her words came to pass. This is not fiction because this young mother was the author's father's wife. The author knows a person who fancied raising cattle and becoming a great family man of many wives and children. But then the Kagera war broke, after which the war in the neighboring Rwanda followed in the former's steps. During these wars, he talked so much about the war, weaponry, prominent generals such as Silas Mayunga, Msuguli, Museveni, Kayitare, Fred Rwigema etc. Where is he today? A farmer—the vocation he fancied? No madam! You bet it right. Emerson said, "a man is what he thinks all day long." Norman Vincent Peale concluded from experience that, "You are not what you think you are. But what you think you are." Marcus Aurelius said that "our life is what our thoughts make it."

We all are equally blessed. And this assertion is true because we are all equally able to tap from the pot of gold that's indeed three feet from where you stand right now. And that's also equally within the reach of us all. This pot of gold is our thoughts. Those individuals who are positive in their thoughts always tend to look upon the brighter side of life. With their faces turned toward the sunshine they attempt to see the good, even in the most awful situations. Such individuals habitually think thoughts of a positive nature. And unlike the law of magnetism, the positive minds attract positive minds. And the negative personalities, on the other hand, habitually look upon the dark, gloomy, and depressing side of life. Even the good holds some bad for them. They dwell on the bad and the negative. They think about it, foresee it, and almost look forward to it, and most certainly receive what they have been on the lookout for—albeit unawares. Due to the negative vibration which they submerge in, they of course attract other miserable personalities to them, and that perfects their negativity.

According to Bob Proctor, "Negative personalities are depressing to everyone around them. Their faces take on the expression, in physical form, of the negative thoughts which they are holding in their minds...No cheer, no joy radiates from them—just gloom, frowns and hostility. Having created their own hell for themselves, they seem to enjoy wallowing in it." What is so bad about such a habit is that it doesn't end with the person who opens his doors to negativity. No! The negative vibrations one emits are apt to affect everyone around. So beware with such men. Do not have anything to do with such men. They will kill your inner heath and ruin you before you know it. Nothing good comes from such men but hatred, miseries and calamity we see rocking the world today. I know a person who hired a guard, and with photos of his own negative siblings and pessimistic acquaintances he had the misfortune of ever meeting, or relate with, with instructions never to bedtime enter.

Is this ideal important for any learner, or scholar? Let's see. In his book As a Man Thinketh, James Allen wrote thus: "A man will find that as he alters his thoughts toward things and other people, things and people will alter toward him…let a man radically alter his thoughts and he will be astonished at the rapid transformation it will effect in his material condition of his life. Men do not attract that which they want but that which they are…the divinity that shapes our ends is in ourselves. It is our very self…all that man achieves is a direct result of his thoughts…a man can only rise conquer and achieve by lifting up his thoughts. He can only remain weak and abject and miserable by refusing to lift up his thoughts." Supplementing the above lines he picked from James Allen, Dale Carnegie wrote something to which I am a witness. "The longer I live," he wrote, "the more I'm convinced of the tremendous power of thought."

In the end, because now we reckon how important the thought is, must we not guard ourselves against what we think all day out? What is the best way to do that? The best way to control and govern our thoughts is to manage what you take in. You must avoid negative inputs. Always stay away from negative people. They will transmit the same thoughts or feelings, thoughts or feelings that will influence you negatively. To avoid doubts remember you only have to be your best and let the future take care of itself. As long as you did your homework and you chose rightly, as long as you keep working and meeting any situation as it comes, you will face no obstacles on your way to great success. And if you meet them, you will overcome if you stay cool. Try to meet them as they come. This will help to keep your cool disposition which in turn will help you to avoid negative thoughts while nurturing the positive ones.

Let's now learn from a person who transformed himself into an open-minded person. Whereas everybody knows that Ben Franklin had a beautiful mind; a man who remains one of the most gifted persons in America to date—a world-famous figure that he was even appointed the ambassador to France, one of the most important posts at the time following the post world-war balance of power and thus France regarded as the major American ally at the time—very few know that he was not so as a young man. According to an extract from his biography as recorded by Dale Carnegie in his fine book, How to Win Friends and Influence People, Ben Franklin was a blundering youth, and as a result he never put much of his innate talent to meaningful use. His is an example to all who wish to change their lives by altering how they think. Here is how he conducted himself and the consequences he suffered—consequences any person who behaves the same way is apt to face.

So how did he conduct himself? He was impossible. His opinions had a slap in them for everyone who differed with him. His opinions had become so offensive that nobody cared for them. His friends found they enjoyed themselves better when he was not around. He knew so much that nobody could tell him anything. Indeed, no man was going to try, for the effort would only lead to discomfort and hard work. So what were the consequences? He was not likely ever to know anymore than he did then, which was very little!" [142]

Can we change? Is it worth it? Ben Franklin changed his attitude after a little scolding that brought him to his senses. He began learning to learn or listen from others, and to refine how he conducted himself, thereupon dropping his judgmental nature. That's how he regained his beautiful mind. "I made a rule," said Franklin, "to forebear all direct contradiction to the sentiment of others, and all positive assertions of my own. I even forbade myself of every word or expression in the language that imported a fixed opinion, such as 'certainly, 'undoubtedly,' etc… (How to Win Friends and Influence People, Dale Carnegie, p. 129)" It is as such we realize that a person is the final creator, architect, producer, manufacturer, the workshop and marketer of his own reality. With this final note, you realize that you have only yourself to blame when you fail for indeed we can be rich or poor, slave or master, we can be rulers or ruled–but God forbid. I hate the both later conditions. I don't fancy being a ruler or to be ruled over. But we can also be beggars or givers. We have indeed been accorded with all powers to take in our possession whatever we want in life. We were given dominion over the whole enormous universe. What mighty loot! We can take the whole of it or just a portion. The choice lies with you and me! Your destiny lies with you—yes as an individual but more so as a society—if only the leadership realized this secret—both at personal and national levels.

Indeed we live in the world where every ideal person, every ideal citizen, and every law abiding citizen who plays around the governing rules enjoys the freedom of thought and freedom of deed unequaled anywhere in the world. Sadly most of us have never taken inventory of the advantage of this freedom. We have never compared our unlimited freedom with curtailed freedom in other countries. We have freedom of thought freedom

---

[142] *Adapted from How to Win Friends and Influence People, Dale Carnegie, p. 129*

in the choice, and enjoyment of education, freedom in politics, freedom in choice of business profession or occupation, freedom to accumulate and own without molestation all the property we can accumulate: we have freedom to choose our place of residence, freedom in marriage, freedom through equal opportunity to all races, freedom to travel from one place to another, freedom for choice of food and freedom to aim for any station in life for which we have prepared ourselves and our children even for the presidency of the United Republic, something that John Pombe Magufuli has helped to put in perspective.[143]

THINKING VS. EMOTIONS

Here is another fact about our thought pattern or mindset. The truth is, your emotions affect your mindset, or thought pattern. When we think of intelligence, we think of intellectual intelligence. The IQ is it not solely a function of—nor is it only shaped by one's education—traditional classroom education. It is also a function of his thought pattern, his mindset. But since one's thought pattern or mindset is affected by his emotions, a person's actions or behavior are affected by his emotions. That's why "…a view of human nature that ignores the emotional aspect of human is shortsighted. Indeed, some argue that if we neglect the *Emotional Mind* of individuals, we may do them a greater disservice than if we shortchange the development of their rational mind. Certainly, both rational and emotional aspects of individuals are crucial to complete living…Emotions strongly influence how we relate to people or treat certain information, or even construct meaning.

Coleman states that the root of the word emotion is *Motere*, Latin word for: *To Move*. The prefix "e" suggests away, thus emotion suggests: *Move Away*. Emotions contain power to affect actions… (thus an) increasing *focus on emotions or …emotional intelligence….* Emotions are what Gardner called interpersonal and intrapersonal intelligence. The former refers to: *The ability of an individual to understand other people—what makes them tick and how they work and how one can work with them,* while the latter is: Correlative ability. Individuals with this ability can look inwardly, can develop or possess the capacity to form an accurate inner sense of one's self, and can use such understanding to operate effectively in life (Ornstein and Hunkins, 3rd Ed p. 114-115). Unless knowledge

---

[143] *Adapted from Napoleon Hill p146 147*

relates to feeling, it is unlikely to affect behavior appreciably (Ornstein and Hunkins, 3rd Ed, p. 153)."

OPEN MINDEDNESS AND CRITICAL THINKING

And yes the ideal scholar is also a critical thinker. To be a critical thinker he must first think clearly. Schools and education as a whole should teach our children how to think (or how to solve problems) and not what to think.[144]

Part of new sciences and technologies the future demands includes the science of thinking. It demands knowledge of the working of the mind—and how we relate with one another. This isn't my creation. You can find and read for yourself the chapter on the future directions for curriculum in their magnificent book *Curriculum Foundations, Principles and Issues 3rd Ed. By Ornstein and Hunkins* Is it important? Very! To prove it is, I have had to consult a book I now declare to be not an ordinary literary work, but a scientific book—a book about the science of human nature—a book by Dale Carnegie it is called *How to Win Friends and Influence People*. I have also had to read other books in the same category: The Power to Influence People by Dr. O. A. Batista, Bob Proctor's book *You Were Born Rich, Think Big, A Sick Nation and How to Heal It, What Makes People Rich and Nations Powerful,* and the two most influential books by Wattles and Napoleon Hill respectively, the books titled Science of Getting Rich and Think and Grow Rich respectively, books the author now beatify as *Science Books*. They are no longer what they were used to be regarded–Inspirational Books. They are Science Books—the science of the mind—and of the soul. They are the books of the future which for a few began long time ago, whereas for many they begin today. these are the books that ought to be read more by the youth and adults, students or employees and businessmen and to be read so closely than the mainstream academic books.

In this category of scientific writers are Ben Carson, Earl Nightingale and a number of other outstanding authors. Probably you will also endeavor to find and read the book *What Makes People Rich and Nations Powerful* by this author to realize in full what I say. All education starts in the mind—and all success is a function of how we relate with the people and

---

[144] *Allan C. Ornstein and Francis P. Hunkins, Curriculum Foundations, Principles and Issues 3rd Edition p. 71*

environment or nature around us. Indeed, "There is a danger to individuals," aptly said William van Til, "and to society in an education which accepts uncritically and thinks unthinkingly...the danger is that some forces which mutually reinforce each other may take us down roads contrary the...ideal of the individual who is free, morally responsible, and important. Some tendencies of the times, if uncritically accepted and implemented by education, could lead to the powerless man in the powerful society."[145] The second quality in Draper Kauffman's six areas of competence that could comprise a possible future curriculum, he identified the same quality as: "Thinking clearly." That is not to say he must be eloquent. Yet he should have the quality of expressing thoughts and feelings easily and clearly.

So how does a person think critically, but remains open minded? How do you combine the two seemingly opposing ideas? Ennis identified 13 attributes of critical thinkers: (be) open minded; take a position (or change a position) when the evidence calls for it; take into account the entire situation; seek information; seek precision in information; deal in an orderly manner with parts of a complex whole; look for options; search for reasons; seek a clear statement of the issue; keep the original problem in mind; use credible sources; remain relevant to the point; and exhibit sensitivity to the feelings and knowledge level of others. Lipmann distinguishes between ordinary and critical thinking thus: Ordinary thinking is simple and lacks standards whereas critical thinking is more complex and is based on standards of objectivity, utility, or consistency. such a person is removed from guessing to estimating; from preferring to evaluating; from grouping to classifying; from believing to assuming; from inferring to inferring logically; from associating concepts to grasping principles; from noting relationships to noting relationships among relationships; from supposing to hypothesizing; from offering opinions without reasons to offering opinions with reasons; and from making judgment without criteria to making judgment with criteria.[146]

---

[145] *Allan C. Ornstein and Francis P. Hunkins, Curriculum Foundations, Principles and Issues 3rd Edition p. 143*

[146] *Allan C. Ornstein and Francis P. Hunkins, Curriculum Foundations, Principles and Issues 3rd Edition p. 118*

TESTIMONY: THE MIND IS THE SOLE DETERMINANT OF OUR FATE

Imagination is self-manifesting. I dreamt that I bounced into a glass window and had picked up a wound on my hand—the one with which I tried to protect my face. I woke up the next morning with genuine pain in the same hand. Imagination is real. It manifests itself in our lives like everything real. I had a very bad quarrel with my wife. It was the worst argument in over ten years of our marriage. In fact the quarrel threatened to break our marriage. Frankly, I am convinced it would break if I didn't wake up that night—waking up from that dream! It was a dream! Yet I remained so angry the rest of the day—angry of her. You see! It is all in the mind. In other words, the mind is the master. It is the master because it determines our destinies. Be therefore conscious of that what you put in your mind, for that is what you get out of your life. Guard yourself against negative emotions. Pamper positive thoughts or emotions. They work like manure. But since not all that comes into the domain of our minds is all good, be a critical thinker—now that you know how to be one.

Yet much as we need to be conscious of what we put in the mind, you must, with the knack on self-control—at least to a certain limit, and with awareness of how winning opportunities sometimes come dressed in the attire of the pauper, allow your mind rivers to remain navigable. Different inspirations sail through different streams. To be open-minded is to think critically, to let the new ideas sink. That's why you need to let the inspiration penetrate and permeate through, for we don't know which part of us the hunch will touch to generate, or stir the desired effect. Henry Van Dyke summed it up thus: "I hold it true that thoughts are things; they're endowed with bodies and breath and wings. And that we send them forth to fill the world with good results, or ill. That which we call our secret thought, speeds forth to earth's remotest spot, leaving its blessings or its woes like tracks behind it as it goes. We build our future, thought by thought, for good or ill, yet know it not. Yet so the universe was wrought..."

I have given a couple of personal experiences of how the mind is the master as the testimony of the power of the mind—but also how and why you should be in guard of whatever is going in, and coming out of you mind. Indeed I am convinced that if you haven't gone through such experience, probably you haven't yet matured enough in the ways of the working of the mind a lesson that probably represents the most dramatic illustration of the foregoing assertion, the fact that the mind is the sole determinant of one's fate. This can be summed up by the tragic story of

Mary Baker Eddy. This is not my invention. In her own words, words recorded in her autobiography, she said, "Their spiritual signification appeared; and I apprehended for the first time, in their spiritual meaning, Jesus' teaching and demonstration, and the Principle and rule of spiritual Science and metaphysical healing,—in a word, Christian Science... The miracles recorded in the Bible, which had before seemed to me supernatural, grew divinely natural and apprehensible..."[147] Those years of Bible study eventually led to her writing the definitive textbook on Christianity scientific healing, called Science and Health with Key to the Scriptures. The last 100 pages of this book contain testimonials of people who were healed—mentally and physically—simply by reading Science and Health. First published in 1875, it has today sold more than 10 million copies worldwide and has been translated into 16 languages; healings experienced by readers of this volume continue today.[148]

It shouldn't therefore surprise you to know that those who train in a Course in Miracles are taught that: "Psychotherapy is the only form of therapy there is. Since only the mind can be sick, only the mind can be healed."[149] But this is a good ending of her discovery. How did Mary Baker Eddy stumble upon this revelation? Well, it is a long story, whose beginning you can read for yourself in Dale Carnegie's great book: How to Stop Worrying and Start Living. "The dramatic turning point in her life occurred in Lynn, Massachusetts," narrates Dale Carnegie. "Walking down one cold day she slipped and fell on the ice pavement—and was knocked unconscious. Her spine was so injured that she was convulsed with spasms. Even the doctor expected her to die. If by miracle she lived, he declared that she would never walk again. Lying on what was supposed to be her deathbed, Mary Baker Eddy opened her bible, and ... read these words from saint Mathew: "And behold they brought to him a man sick of the palsy, lying on the bed: And Jesus said unto him...Arise, take up thy bed, and go unto thine house. And he arose, and departed to his house." These words of Jesus she declared, produced within her such a strength, such a faith, such surge of healing power, that she "immediately got out of bed

---

[147] *Retrospection and Introspection, p. 25*

[148] http://christianscience.com/what-is-christian-science/mary-baker-eddy-discoverer-founder-author

[149] *www.miraclesofmind.org/healing--psychotherapy.html*

and walked," she testified. "That experience," Mrs. Baker declared, "was like a falling apple that led me to the discovery of how to be well myself and how to make others so… I gained the scientific certainty that all causation was Mind, and every effect a mental phenomenon." this is the mistake educators do. "The greatest mistakes physicians (and most academic instructors) make," aptly analyzed Plato, "is that they attempt to cure the body without attempting to cure the mind; yet the mind and body are one and should not be treated differently!"

30. THE IDEAL SCHOLAR IS A JUST PERSON AND MINDFUL OF OTHERS

"I want people to remember me as someone whose life has been helpful to humanity."—Thomas Sankara

The ideal scholar is a just person—a person who embraces, enhances and advances justice. He is therefore a considerate person who is always ever mindful of other people's needs. In other words, as a just person, he seeks to grow without infringing other people's rights. Yet this quality is impossible if the person is not honest. The ideal scholar is therefore loyal, honest, and trustworthy or dependable—a man of his word—a man whose words match his thoughts and deeds.

Recall that the ideal man is a responsible person and therefore a person who will do more for himself and others while expecting less from the others? In this case, to the truest ideal scholar, responsibility transcends work or promotion at work. This ideal also transcends our actions, or inactions. For instance, the Proverbs 3: 27-28 says that: "Do not withhold good from those to whom it is due, when it is in your power to do it." The ideal scholar thus has love for others as his credo, principle or philosophy of life. Why important? Because man doesn't expect much from himself, and as such, it can be said that he expects less from others, recognizing his life is—and of those around him are—is his own hands. This decision on the part of such a person is important because Mankind is so selfish. Whereas a typical human isn't ready to serve others, he or she often tends to expect others to do far more greater things for him or her, than he himself or herself is ready to do anything for oneself. The ideal scholar is responsible to himself, serves others and recognizes that part of doing his best, is to make sure that not only he or she does his or her best for oneself and others around him? He or she will also see to it that everyone in the team does the same, and gets, the very best for himself, and others in the team.

Is this whole scheme about being ever mindful of other people's needs—the quest to live by the spirit of the Golden Rule: "Do unto others as you would have others do unto you,"—realistic? I know some of my readers will already be saying the foregoing is nothing but religious pap! No! It is not! Recall Pope Francis. When he was elected cardinal and years later when he became pope, he relinquished the luxurious house and car given to him, instead went on to live with his juniors in something close to servant quarters—not to mention that he did away with a golden staff and a majestic golden chair. But you will say that is a different thing altogether because he is pope. Navigate into this very book and reread the life of Patrick Njoroge, a newly elected Central Bank of Kenya, a man who has done almost the same being no priest. But since he is a member of a Christian Church that observes strict fellowship, let's recall the life of Samuel Milton Jones whose factory needed only one policy—the Golden Rule. That's what governed his business—and he dramatically nailed a plaque with that phrase to the factory wall. He paid his employees very fairly at fewer working hours, better working conditions and paid vacations, did away with bosses and time keepers, and held employee picnics. So it pays to do justice and become ever mindful of other people's needs. So does it pay? Let's explore more. To the surprise of many people, his business thrived.

But that's not all. "By the end of 1800s, he became mayor of Toledo, and served four terms becoming the city's most respected and popular political leader and achieving fame across the nation and around the world," records Wattles. "As a mayor, he championed the public park system and public ownership of utilities. He also replaced policemen nightsticks with walking sticks and refused to prosecute the so called morality *laws*, which he felt were unfair to the poor." Applying the same Golden rule to his business and politics earned him immense respect and affection as well as his nickname—Golden Rule. Now the reader will be saying why he didn't then become president of the United States if he had earned such fame — if it pays to follow the Golden Rule!? In his book Science of Getting Rich, Wattles records that: "In 1904, at the age of 57, Mr. Jones died suddenly while still in office."[150] He was saved from the agony of death many people

---

[150] *Adapted by this author from Wallace D. Wattles' book Science of Getting Rich; for more reading, find Wallace D. Wattles—I must add, an extremely magnificent book—Science of Getting Rich, or else for some insights into the story, go to* https://en.wikipedia.org/wiki/Samuel_M._Jones.

suffer! I know the skeptic will say that's long long time ago, claiming that times have changed. Let's now present another most recent person who lived the Golden Rule nonetheless.

JOSE MUJICA

It's a common grumble that politicians' lifestyles are far removed from those of their electorate. Not so in Uruguay. Meet the president who lives on a ramshackle farm and gives away most of his pay," reports Vladimir Hernandez for BBC, Montevideo, in a 15 November 2012 news report. Vladimir Hernandez went on to report: Laundry is strung outside the house. The water comes from a well in a yard, overgrown with weeds. Only two police officers and Manuela, a three-legged dog, keep watch outside. This is the residence of the president of Uruguay, Jose Mujica. He has shunned the luxurious house that the Uruguayan state provides for its leaders and opted to stay at his wife's farmhouse, off a dirt road outside the capital, Montevideo. The president and his wife work the land themselves. He donates about 90% of his monthly salary to charity.

"I may appear to be an eccentric old man... But this is a free choice," he said. "I've lived like this most of my life," he says, sitting on an old chair in his garden, using a cushion favored by Manuela the dog. "I can live well with what I have." His charitable benefit donations, which poor people and small entrepreneurs, mean his salary is roughly in line with the average. All the president's wealth has is a 1987 VW Beetle. In 2010, his annual personal wealth declaration mandatory for officials in Uruguay, was $1,800 (£1,100), the value of his 1987 Volkswagen Beetle. Elected in 2009, Mujica spent the 1960s and 1970s as part of the Uruguayan guerrilla Tupamaros. He was shot six times and spent 14 years in jail. Most of his detention was spent in harsh conditions and isolation, until he was freed in 1985 when Uruguay returned to democracy. Those years in jail, Mujica says, helped shape his outlook on life. "I'm called 'the poorest president', but I don't feel poor," he says.[151] Is Mujika some person farfetched because he is from South America? Well, what about our very own, Julius Nyerere? Julius Kambarage Nyerere, well–there is no single moment I have ever tried to analyze this great man's life, without being driven into more thought and reflection. It is for that reason that we will give a closer look at his life and impact in more details a little later. So stay put!

---

[151] *Adapted from http://www.bbc.com/news/magazine-20243493*

EMPATHY AND FORGIVENESS

Justice and being mindful of other people's needs transcends actions we do. It envelopes our response to what unjust and selfish people may do, or may not do to us which was our right. Being a just person and mindful of other people's needs, the ideal scholar is an empathetic, understanding and therefore forgiving person. Dictionary.camabridge.org defines empathy as the ability to share someone else's feelings or experiences by imagining what it would be like to be in their situation. Because he is a person who is ever ready to step in the shoes of the others, he is always willing to forgive in the Lincoln's gold standard, "with malice toward none, with charity for all." Being forgiving and empathetic therefore, he is a self restrained person and is patient with others. Before he condemns others as in natural to raw people, he will candidly pray the Sioux Red Indians prayer: *O Great Spirit, keep me from ever judging and criticizing a man, until I have walked in his moccasins for two weeks.*[152] Being mindful of other people's problems, the ideal scholar recognizes that his wellbeing or freedom is entangled with that of the others. "For to be free," aptly said Nelson Mandela, "is not merely to cast off one's chains, but to live in a way that respects and enhances the freedom of others."

Thinking about it brings two names to mind. Pope John Paul was knifed in the ribs by a Turk man Mehmet Ali Agkar. He was rushed to hospital as Mehmet was sent to custody. When he was once again conscious he called upon his assailant and they were left alone and they conversed over his hospital bed and John Paul did not only forgive Mehmet but blessed him. If you say that holds no water because he was pope, what about Mohammed Ali Nur, the Somali ambassador to Kenya? More than twenty years back, a group of buglers stormed into the house where he lived with his parents and wife and children. They stole a fortune and not only did they mistreat them but killed his young baby girl. It is only a couple of weeks now as I am writing since that September Sixth 2014 when he was at the beach in Somalia on a official duty enjoying his cup of cappuccino with a colleague who was sipping coffee when suddenly a man approached him asking him if he was Mohammed Ali.

---

[152] *How to Stop Worrying and Start Living by Dale Carnegie*

He thought about it for a moment fearing that probably he could harm him but decided to acknowledge his identity. The man said he was asking for forgiveness. Why? For he was one of the three men who had stormed into his house and robbed at gunpoint killing his baby girl twenty years back. It was like bomb shell. He was drawn back on the day. He recalled his baby in his hands as he laid her in the little grave back in Mogadishu. And that thought made him weep so bitterly. He couldn't stop from thinking about everything for a while recalling his little baby girl in his hands…and then forgave the killer. Asked whether he did forgive him, he said he had to not only because of the teachings of the holy Koran but also because—in his own words: "My anger wouldn't return my baby." And he was right. For so is what he had to do. So far that was what the Koran teaches. Mahatma Gandhi was right. "Hate cannot be ended by hate but by love." His exemplary courageous gesture is all that the war-torn Somalia needs. Somalia needs reconciliation in his words in line with Rwandan and South African truth and reconciliation.

Part of the responsibility of the ideal man is to owe no one anything, except to give himself for the good of the others. That's why the ideal scholar strives to achieve success without coming between the others and the good that they deserve. Wallace D. Wattles aptly said: "The right motive in life is more life for all and less to none." Loving one another fulfills the law (Romans 13: 8)." Aristotle said: "The ideal man takes joy in doing favors for others." Prophet Mohammad said: "A good deed is the one that leaves a smile of joy in the face of another person." Wattles said: "What is good for me is good for others." Ben Franklin said, "When you are good to others, you are best to yourself!" Daudi Michael Kambarangwe said: "I will do what is good for others." Jesus taught thus: "Do unto others as you would have others do unto you!" Put humanly, we can say, "What is good for me is good for others." Indeed, as aptly wrote Wattles, "The very best thing you can do for the whole world is to make the most of yourself…" Ben Carson wrote that: "We do not have to compare our achievements with those of the others." We need only to focus our lenses on ourselves.

What can we then say to be the measure of selflessness? I know one author who had two younger children born at the time when he was confined in his farm house writing a set of his book manuscripts. Now because of fear of mosquitoes as it is common in the tropical Africa, though yes he covered the bed with a mosquito net all the time and made sure to cover the babies when his wife was away—for his wife worked for the government—but that was not enough. While revising his own manuscripts, he would position himself beside the kids but remained uncovered, exposing his own person to the lingering ever-hungry mosquitoes. As a result? Often they found him fast and first. When they began biting him, did he wave them away? Nope! He let them bite him enough first so that it could be easy for him to get and eliminate them than let them wonder about and find the kids. That's how he protected his kids. But that doesn't mean this author was a saint. I know he is not, and I know this is a true story because Patricia and Prince are my kids! In fact it can be said that the author's actions cannot, and shouldn't be considered as a clear sign of selflessness. However dramatic or incredible that can be, he did it for his own kids. Selflessness must cross such borders. How? Here are a few questions for you!

"Can you give a dollar to a beggar? Can you lend an ear to one avoided by others? Can you work an extra shift for a parent who needs to be with a sick child? Can you visit a shut-in? Can you speak up and defend a poor soul being teased or bullied? Can you treat all people as your brothers and sisters? Your example may become contagious. Even as one, your example can make a difference."[153] A man came up to Jesus and asked, "Teacher, what good thing must I do to get eternal life?" Jesus set a true mark of how selflessness we should be when he told this wealthy man Jesus replied saying that, aside these, "'You shall not murder, you shall not commit adultery, you shall not steal, you shall not give false testimony, honor your father and mother,' and 'love your neighbor as yourself,'" he told him, "Go, sell your possessions and give to the poor, and ...then come, follow me." Read Matthew 19:16-20.

With all these lessons we come to a conclusion that doing good, love and charity to others define someone's religion. Indeed, Abraham Lincoln said: "When I do good, I feel good. When I do bad, I feel bad. That's my religion." Zig Marley sung thus: "Love is My Religion." That's why selfishness is an unscholarly virtue. Look: if all of us neglected ourselves submerged in the service for others, we would all in the end be better off in our later state than the former. Lesley and Biddle noted that, social value,

---

[153] *Source: 100Action Principles, by Bill FitzPatrick, www.success.org*

common good or public wellbeing is only possible once individuals are willing and able to look beyond themselves.[154]

Talking about being of services to others, Saint Francis of Assisi had decided and prayed thus: Lord, make me a tool of your peace; where there is hatred, let me sow love; where there is injury, pardon; where there is doubt, faith; where there is despair, hope; where there is darkness light; where there is sadness, joy; O, Divine Master, grant that I may not so much seek to be consoled, but to console; to be understood as to understand; to be loved as to love; for it is in giving that we receive; it is in pardoning that we are pardoned...!"

ROBIN HOOD

I am, from experience, radically convinced that before a man becomes a philanthropist, he must first experience dearth. Though I am not suggesting that we become poor, but I know that it is hard to feel compassion for the poor, one unless you stand in his shoes. You must have heard a story about a man who deliberately engaged himself in stealing sprees among the wealthy people in the neighborhood in order to distribute the loot to poor people. Strange, is it not? He was strong enough to work among the building sites. His wages were enough for him and his family. What about elderly people? What about the needy? he reasoned. That is how he chose the new vocation. This isn't a religious pap. It is real. His name was Robin Hood. You can search about this story on the World Wide Web on your own. The man wasn't nuts! He was compassionate. If Robin Hood story is so ancient, here is a recent chain of events in which a bank manager stole from rich customers to debit the needy as reports the daily mail: "A bank manager behaved like a real-life Robin Hood by taking millions of pounds from rich clients and giving it to needy customers. Benedict Hancock, a 39-year-old father of two, channeled more than £7 million into the accounts of companies in trouble. Astonishingly, the unassuming Royal Bank of Scotland senior relationship manager did so for 'an entirely altruistic motive', Blackfriars Crown Court has heard." Still in doubt? You can read more: http://www.dailymail.co.uk/news/article-1056746/Robin-Hood-bank-manager-stole-7m-rich-clients-gave-needy-customers.html#ixzz3b6Unq3Oi

---

[154] *Allan C. Ornstein and Francis P. Hunkins, Curriculum Foundations, Principles and Issues 3rd Edition p. 397*

CHE GUEVARA

You have obviously heard of Che. I mean Che Guevara. He fought a war of independence for his country Argentine with vengeance. But immediately after the victory, he didn't stay home to claim power as many do. He did stick with the reasons why he fought for independence. It was to free his people. This didn't end with independence of only one country but all the people who suffered the same way. That same night he did sleep conceptualizing his next challenge. The next morning, off he set out toward the jungles in the outskirts of Havana in Cuba and fought along Fidel and Raul Castro and their gallant militants until when the Cubans regained their independence. Did he rest then? No. That could be you. Not Che. He had experienced oppression. He had lived it. He knew how it hurt. He wanted to wipe it out and thus chose to dedicate his life helping any people who fought colonialism. He set out for his next journey. That was in that was in Africa—in Angola where he joined forces to fight the Portuguese colonialists before he returned to South America to fight alongside Bolivian people. That's where he was captured and flown to the states where he was killed. No wonder Che is most popular in Africa and his portraits probably more ubiquitous than even some heads of states.

The author hails the respect Che is accorded, but believes he deserves more. He is more than that. He is a saint in his own way. Our media houses today have purported lies concerning entertainment. Chelsea Football Club, Manchester United, Real Madrid or Barcelona; or Ronaldo, Brad Pitt, Angelina Jolie, Kim Kardashian, Leonardo di capriole, or most other Hollywood TV heroes don't represent the same values western media have purposely overstated. Indeed the value isn't in entertainment we gain but a new living we gain from someone's life or work. We should value instead those who give more of themselves even part of their lives to make ours a little better. Indeed Arthur William Beer was right. Che gave his life in the service to his—I repeat to his—people. Political position to his cause and especially the west may call him names such as he was a communist, a terrorist, a fanatic etc but he was more than that. We can see that in his last words—words he told his captors and killers. "Tell my wife to remarry and try to be happy," he said. And then krrrrrrr: a trigger was pulled, and Che began his trail to meet His Maker. Amen!

Well, back to the same question: does it pay to be of service to others?

We have made a mention about The Golden Rule and Golden Rule Jones. Walace D. Wattles wrote rightly thus: "And because it is the deepest instinct of their natures, all men and women are attracted to those who can give them more of the means of life. Toward the end of the 1800s he became mayor of Toledo, and served four terms, becoming the city's most respected and popular political leader and achieving fame across the nation and around the world." Lao-Tse taught the same in an incredible way. Lao-Tse rightly observed and taught thus: "The reason why rivers and seas receive homage of a hundred mountain streams is that they keep below them. Thus they are able to reign over all mountain streams. So the sage wishing to be above men putteth himself below them, wishing to be before them, he putteth himself behind them. Thus though his place be above men they do not feel his weight. Though his place be above them they don't count it an injury!"

We are going to furnish this answer with more flesh before we end the qualities of the ideal scholar.

A CLOSING WORD
Here's an event that really happened to me—the event that has since left me a despondent person. It happened in the year 1996. The author was still in a boarding school at Kahororo, in Bukoba, Tanzania. He was himself underprivileged financially, but in better condition than at least one "gentleman." And this is how it dawned on me. I had some pocket change to fall back on aside from guarantee of breakfast, lunch and dinner at school, besides having loving senior siblings and parents—who stood by my side, one or another. Now as I was picking some coins to pay for a few goodies I had purchased from the roadside merchant near the Bukoba Town market, I stashed the 50 shillings' bill in my left pocket behind my dungarees pair of trousers, I felt something creeping inside my pockets. I turned only to find a shadow behind me—and his hand searching my pockets. I regrettably checked my pockets to find that his scheme had failed. My 50 shillings bill was safe and intact. His face and dress betrayed him. He was very hungry and very very hopelessly poor. When our eyes met, embarrassment washed through him as he turned and retreated into the midst of a multitude. He was a pickpocket? No! He was needy! No pickpocket stole from a teen. He was rather a beggar who, for personal pride, didn't want to beg from a teenager. I didn't shout or call attention to what had ensued, because my money was safe. Now the question is, "What would you have done in boyhood self's position? Who was to blame for this man's self conduct and character?"

Mature and more thoughtful today, I try not to put blames on the shadow, but rather I censure the author's boyhood-self. I put the blame on him for denying, first, the hungry man a privilege to dinner; but secondly, for denying me the opportunity for charity and the opportunity to brag about it today. Today I know I should have pretended as if I hadn't noticed anything letting him pick the 50 shillings bill, and letting the pickpocket retreat delightedly that he'd not been found out. Many years later, the author learned to better himself. And this is how.

Through this chapter, the reader had been led to an account of the times when the author began his writing career, and he wasn't very rich then to enjoy all the trappings money can fetch. The reader was led to how he learnt to expose himself to the mosquitoes, letting them bite him rather than bite his kids. But this cannot be judged to be a peculiar act on the part of the author; can it? Certainly every sane father or mother would do this, and the author doesn't have any reason to brag about it. But what about going to the university exams without having had meals? And this didn't only happen because he didn't have the money in the first place. No! He had sent his meal allowances to his siblings back home. Probably he didn't do anything bigger. It was the culture in his family, especially at the time. I must, nonetheless, admit I was a better Christian, a true Catholic, at the time. As such, at the time I prayerfully skipped my meals during the whole 40 days Christian fasting period. Oh how I struggle to go back to my roots!

Being mindful of other people's needs was really innate to us as a family. Probably, the second letter of Paul Apostle to the Corinthians 8:9, says it all: "For you know the grace of our Lord Jesus Christ, that though he was rich, yet for your sake he became poor, so that you, through his poverty, might become rich." This is a culture that elevated this family. It was the same virtue that the neighborhood acquired and changed their lives for good. If this nation and the rest of the world—Christian or not—acquired and developed this culture, extending the same spirit to all our homes, schools, workplaces, and churches or mosques and temples, we could make everyone better off without making any worse off—a situation that seems to be a prerequisite today in this era of the law of the jungle and the vicious circle of ills it creates as we experience in Syria, Iraq, Libya, Nigeria, Somalia etc. With this tradition, we can for sure make the world a better place for everyone now living and millions yet unborn.

Giving—and I mean giving without calculated personal motives--I mean giving for the sake of giving, helping—is probably one of the top ranking ideals, but certainly one of the most hidden secrets of success. Mr. Bakura was school headmaster at Ihungo high school when I schooled there. He used to counsel his students that we should always be ready to: "die a little, so that others could live a little longer—and better." And you and I can do that. Yes we have different gifts and responsibilities but have reservoirs within us that are rich with giving. I know we can, I know it is possible having lived that credo on the first person account. Besides, whatever portion of our possession we may choose to give out, we will not become worse off if we work hard since the universe cannot be depleted with resources. We also know that to win—whether it is to win the respect of other, or gain materially—we must lose somehow somewhere. It is in losing that we gain, and it is in losing that we win for ourselves. That's how we build what is called win-win situation—a situation that must nonetheless be preceded by a lose-win situation, something more obvious among the parents in relation with their children, if not with strangers.

As we come to the end of this chapter, recognize that I included this last part of the chapter to emphasize why, and how, our curriculum should address compassion to the less fortunate in our society. And mind you I am not unaided in this matter. David Purpel also spoke about educational crisis. In his six points educational credo, the fourth, fifth and sixth emphasized nourishment and development of: "cultural mythos...to participate in creation of a world of justice, compassion, caring love, and joy; nourishment and development of ideals of community, compassion and interdependence within the traditions of democratic principles and; nourishment and development of attitudes of outrage and responsibility in the face of injustice and oppression.[155] This is indeed Desmond Tutu's credo. The retired Anglicans church arch bishop of Cape Town in SA said that:"If you are neutral to situations of injustice you have chosen the side of the oppressor." In the end as Wallace Wattles wrote: "Social obligation is valueless—and this obligation impacts to our people's minds and the quality of their lives."[156]

---

[155] *Allan C. Ornstein and Francis P. Hunkins, Curriculum Foundations, Principles and Issues 3rd Edition p.394-5*

[156] *Adapted from Science Of Getting Rich by Wallace D. Wattles*

From the foregoing assertions, we JUDGE that the ideal scholar strives always to be better off without making other people, or environment around him, worse off. And to transcend oneself and be mindful of other people's needs is not baseless. "Students (or ideal scholars for that matter) …need to go beyond their narrow self-centered views; they need to transcend themselves—at least to see themselves as part of the community (local, state, national international) of people. (And to recognize that) what we do can affect others, and often does and what others do affect our lives."[157] Truly, "If you light a lamp for someone else," so goes a Buddhist saying, "if you light a lamp for someone else, it will brighten your path (—someday)." Indeed, "Part of the fragrance the flower, remains in the hand of the giver!"

Finally, being mindful of other people's needs is not only the ideal scholar's moral duty. No! It is also his way of life. As for an average person, he should do so knowing too well that, "If one wants to establish himself," analyses a Confucian saying, "he should help others establish themselves first."[158] He should also recognize that, "Doing good to others is not a duty," said Zoroaster,"…it increases your own health and happiness.[159]" And, "when you are good to others, said Benjamin Franklin, "when you are good to others, you are best to yourself.[160]" What then is a good deed? A good question. There are many good deeds you can do to enhance this ideal that I cannot enumerate each one of them. But let Prophet Mohammad sum it up for us. He said a good deed is the one that brings a smile of joy in the face of another. Jesus taught his congregation to do the same five centuries before that. His teaching was summed up in the Golden Rule. Do unto others as you would have others do unto you. The ideal person looks beyond himself and his own needs. Indeed, "Success means nothing, Wrote Bill FitzPatrrick, "If you are a doctor who is abusive at home. Success means nothing if your sole aim is to make your own life easier," he concluded. "They are not educated," snapped Dr. Nicholas Murray Butler, president of Columbia University. "Those people

---

[157] *Allan C. Ornstein and Francis P. Hunkins, Curriculum Foundations, Principles and Issues 3rd Edition p. 394*

[158] *Judy C. Pearson et al 2003*

[159] *Dale Carnegie How To Stop Worrying And Start Living page 181*

[160] *Dale Carnegie How To Stop Worrying And Start Living page 181*

who only think of themselves. They are hopelessly uneducated. They are not educated no matter how instructed they may be!"

31. OTHER QUALITIES: LOYALTY, PATRIOTISM, FORGIVING AND EMPATHY

> *"Without patriotic political education, a soldier is only a potential criminal."*
> —Thomas Sankara

The ideal scholar is honest, loyal, and patriotic. Yet, this quality, the threesome, is impossible if the person is not honest. The ideal scholar is therefore honest, trustworthy and dependable. He is honest to himself and to others. He is honest in private as well as in public. This is challenge to many politicians. Rarely is a politician a person who says what he means and mean what he says; a man whose words match his thoughts and deeds. This must be both in word and deed. The ideal scholar is honest in public as well as in private. What most people say in public isn't what they do in their private lives. This is one of the greatest human handicaps education must heal. But is honesty any praiseworthy? Let's see. Take Gordon Brown. He acted as an honest man in public, but he was just a politician—like many others. That's how he was caught whispering to a colleague despising an adult woman, a woman who was not a mere stranger but a 66 years old lady and labor party member, named Gillian Duffy, after she had pressed the prime minister for performance, to which reaction he praised her in public. The contrast between him patting her on her back and praising her for being from a 'good family' and trashing her in the privacy of his Jaguar, caught off-mike and off camera, saying, between a laughter, that he just said that, and patted her, only to hearten her; and that he didn't mean what he had said horrified everyone!

And that's not the ideal the British people expected from their leader. That's not the scholar, an ideal scholar we look forward to. What was the victim's reaction? Gillian Duffy only said: "I'm very disappointed. It's very upsetting. He's an educated person. He wants to lead the country."[161] That was the moment that Gold stopped being radiant and turned brown, the moment when Gordon Brown began to lose ground leading to events that led to his ouster. Honesty is not only celebrated in such areas as humanities only. It has the same impact in business. We know that most beer brands are packaged in opaque bottles or containers that obscure the contents. Now when Heineken rebranded and packaged its drink in a see-through glass bottle, they came out with a slogan I loved! "We hide nothing!" they challenged their peers—as they demonstrated their keenness on quality and their degree of honesty. It is no wonder Heineken remains the number one premium beer in the world.

LOYALTY

The ideal scholar is loyal. He is loyal to his spouse, family, employer, community and the country. His opposite number is one who ridicules his spouse, denounces his family, betrays the trust bestowed upon him by his employer, let's down and shames his community and country. Such a uselessly instructed person is disloyal, promiscuous and knows no fidelity as a moral, is fraudulent and corrupt. Being loyal to the country, employer, business partners, friends, family and spouse, the ideal man is also indeed loyal to himself in that his wellbeing depends on the wellbeing of the country, employer, business partners, family and spouse. Being loyal to himself he maintains chastity and celibacy as a young unmarried soul knowing it in his good to look after his body and that if it is tainted, it taints the rest of his whole—his intellect and the soul—and he has therefore come between himself and success he craves and deserves. If he is married, fidelity to his spouse is absolute.

Thinking about chastity and fidelity, I recall the Golden Rule. If we considered what or how our parents wanted us to be or behave as children, but as young unmarried adults, or even what our spouses wanted us to be like, we would refrain from having sexual relationships—with or without unwanted pregnancies or HIV and AIDS. Our lives are intertwined much

---

[161] *Source: Adapted from*

http://blogs.telegraph.co.uk/news/benedictbrogan/100036874/the-gaffe-that-could-kill-off-gordon-brown/

as the body, mind and soul are. If one is tainted, naturally the other gets tainted. Being loyal, the ideal scholar fulfils his promises and pays his debts, taxes and dues to others. Loyal to his values, and being a moral or ethical person, the ideal scholar is not afraid to pledge allegiance to values, ideas, decisions or actions he believes to be right.

Think of a country or community where all individuals fulfilled their duties!

PATRIOTISM

The ideal scholar is patriotic. The term *Patriot* is defined by dictionary.cambridge.org as a person who loves their country and, if necessary, will fight for it. Patriotic is an adjective for a person showing love for his country and pride in it. For instance many Americans felt it was their patriotic duty to buy bonds to support the war effort. Being patriotic, the ideal scholar doesn't only know his civic or civil rights and accountabilities, but executes them. He is therefore always politically active. He is so recognizing he has a role to transform the society and the leadership by voting rightly, or standing for a position that he believes he can use to transform his wellbeing but as well his community or nation. He is active knowing that yes, politics affects his life as well as that of his family and generation, but more so the prospects of his posterity. But what do most of us do? We elect incompetent people only because they are our friends or especially our tribesmen. Ask any politician in Africa.

They play with numbers—which tribe has more heads—and alliances are thereupon formed. Recent elections in Kenya offer such a conspicuous illustration. Two men contested for the school chairman when I was at Kahororo. One was from my district, and of course my protector, as another was a complete stranger. Whom do you think the author's boyhood self voted? Who won? The author's boyhood was embarrassed when his man lost, but had clean conscience every time the weak leader blundered! Yet the biggest mistake is committed when we accept financial bribes—surprisingly bribes worth a once off lunch, or even in-kind gifts like a bottle, or two, of beer—and then we give a five year mandate to the wrong people. Indeed, Prof. Patrick Loch Otieno Lumumba was right: "We are co-authors of our own misfortunes...we elect hyenas to take care of goats; and when the goats are consumed, we wonder 'why?'"That's not patriotism. Patriotism, I mean enlightened patriotism, is when think beyond a day's challenges but long term solutions, forgetting our personal gains placing national interests before our own.

However, you realize that patriotism isn't a small thing. It transcends mere compassion and lip service. The ideal scholar loves his country and loves it so dearly that he loves the country, and works hard to improve her situation, to advance his fellow citizens intellectually, socially, culturally, security-wise and economically. Among the goals of education for all American youth, the (US) Education Policy Commission issued as its third aim, or goal or purpose of education in our definition, *understanding of the rights and duties of the citizen of a democratic society, and those necessary to serve as members of the community and citizens of the state, nation, and the world.* Being the first in its list, the Phi Delta Kappa Honor Society stipulated that the American student should:*"*Learn how to be a good citizen.*"* That's why Dewey considered the school as a miniature democratic society in which students could learn to practice the skills and tools necessary for democratic living.*"*[162]

Now, as we close an analysis of these ideals, let us rationalize if—and how badly—a country like ours needs such qualities as honesty, loyalty and patriotism. Firstly, with the culture of *Uswahili*, we are society that is carefree, untroubled, relaxed, free from care and lighthearted. We are a people who say what we don't mean and mean what we don't say. We don't also keep our promises or commitments. We are a wasteful people who trick our employers and the nation into big pay or into conferences and trips within and especially outside the workplace and abroad without a fair return on the part of the employer or the country. We have witnessed a rise of out and open corruption where our private sector and government officials have severally betrayed the trust we bestowed upon them when negotiating contracts and as a result they have failed us by entering the country into bad deals such as the purchase of items beyond their shelf life, or inflate the price and reap off the 10% that stashed in offshore accounts—as the recent president Magufuli's credo, a social economic incision and drainage of corruption, irresponsibility and anarchy, lawlessness, chaos and disorder both in the government and the public domain, popularly known in Kiswahili as "Kutumbua Majipu," has helped to put the foregoing assertion into perspective. With increasing trend of our youth who not only have lost pride in their country and all that is Tanzanian, the youth who praise European Football Clubs and footballers, foreign books and films rather our own, the people who renounce their

---

[162] *(Ornstein and Hunkins, 1998 p.46*

citizenship sailing to SA or Europe as Burundian or Congolese and Somali refugees burning down their Tanzanian passports to ashes; when I see how fidelity is on the downhill in our society today, the time when HIV/AIDS' prevalence and promiscuity are on the rise and especially among the married group, among other reasons, to say we need to educate and pass on these ideals to our youth—and the nation as a whole—is important is an understatement. It is indeed an emergency.

32. THE IDEAL SCHOLAR IS KEEN TO OPPORTUNITIES, CONSCIOUS TO FAULT AND A RISK TAKER

"Ekyashamile ototamu e'kyala!" —a Kihaya saying, meaning: Never put your finger in an open-mouthed deadly beast (With tributes to Pancrace Binamungu, former 2nd Head-Master at Ihungo School)

The ideal scholar is keen to opportunities and conscious to fault. This, however, doesn't mean that reader should aspire to be a shameless opportunist, a gold digger. No! Just go back to the qualities of the ideal scholar above and you will see why it cannot be. Being sensible, moral, and hardworking, a person who knows who he is and all around him, a person who is self-reliant and takes responsibility of his life cannot be an a shameless opportunist. He already knows that those who succeed, do so by following a certain path, living a certain way. And part of a certain way is choosing what to do and what not to do. This choice itself is risk taking by itself, for if you choose to do one thing, you cannot do another at the same time. That's where the aspect of risk taking comes in. but often we are frightened to choose fearing to lose an opportunity somewhere else, and as a result we end not choosing, and so taking the risk of losing everything altogether. So there is way you can avid to take risk.

Here is a true story of my life, the beginning of how I became who I am today, a reason why you are reading this book right now. It began when the opportunity came knocking on my door, an opportunity that would transform my life. I was serving as a deputy regional sales manager at the time. As I recall this event, I realize it was a kind of a NOW OR NEVER opportunity—an opportunity I could not afford to lose! But truth be told: how many times we fail to rise to the opportunities? Churchill was right. "Most men occasionally stumble over the truth (or opportunity), but most pick themselves up and continue as if nothing happened." While we stumble upon opportunities, what do we do about it? We procrastinate fearing to decide between staying on, or rising to an occasion. Indeed it is almost a tradition today that everyone envies successful people instead of putting blame on himself.

ONE afternoon ten years back, a call came in inviting me to attend an interview a 1000 miles away in Dar es Salaam. I was in the upcountry at the time. But I had one major problem—well, two! One, I was supposed to head a meeting with the team I managed at the time when I served as deputy regional sales manager with Tanzania Breweries in Shinyanga Tanzania. Two, my life and family's future depended on the same job I loathed. Truly, I'd quite a few options: fret and stay, or take the risk and transform my life. I was fed up with the brewery, and the beer culture. I wanted a break. I needed—and deserved—a nobler job. Notice the fine line between truancy and obsession to change, to rightly transform your life—and reclaim the dignity you deserve! Yet, some of the peace-loving members of my team had already convened in Ngara town, a couple of days earlier. This was where we had decided to hold our meeting.

Besides, I must add that I had sentimental attachment to this trip! The author's forefathers hail from Ngara, and part of his family still lived there. But the hunch was so strong that I couldn't risk it. Indeed never had been a hunch so much a risk. I cancelled the meeting and sent copies to my colleagues and my superiors as I boarded Boeing to Dar es Salaam. Did I get the job? What would be my fate—and that of my family—if the job interview aborted? Did I come back? Well, it is a long story, but to be brief, I did the interview but the decisions were not made on time that my superior sniffed the possibility that I was away. When I was back in Mwanza, he summoned me and we had a small chat which made me notice his suspicion. I wasn't much worried anyway. I had staked my job, my livelihood and family's on one major, but also nobler cause.

Naturally, I was staking my future on one toss of a die, one that I decided I couldn't afford to lose. Before my superiors made decisions or investigations, I received a call the same night, I resigned sent a farewell note, and off I flew back to Dar es Salaam where I signed my appointment docs as national brand manager-cum-sales manager for Carlsberg. You are now aware that there are costs involved in any decision you and I make. Indeed, "The value of decisions," aptly said Napoleon Hill, "depends upon the courage required to render them. The great decisions, which served as the foundation of civilization," continued Mr. Hill, "were reached by assuming great risks which often meant the possibility of death." Lincoln and Socrates offer such exquisite examples. As for me, you recognize that by this decision I was staking my job—indeed the only source of my, and my family's livelihood on the decisions or choices I was making. I was risking not only my reputation but also the goodwill and friendship I enjoyed with my workmates besides promotion that seemed to be already in the bag.

I have been a risk taker that severally I have been misunderstood, ridiculed, and dumped by my peers at work, friends and family members. When I resigned as a sales representative for Hedex and Panadol, my peers raised their eye brows. Then I was hired by Tanzania Breweries, a subsidiary company of Sab/Miller, as a sales development officer and served as sales manager. Now at the time TBL was the *toppest* employer in the land. When I resigned at TBL then, everybody thought I was mad. Then I was appointed as national brand manager cum sales manager for Carlsberg. When I resigned, my former peers and superiors thought I was finished again. Then they knew a bank had hired me as a marketing manager before moving on to another top telecom company at the time, Celtel. When I resigned again, the same men and women laughed: "Ha, ha, ha! He has messed up again!"

Many must have suggested that I wouldn't make a comeback this time. Many said, and few prayed, that I would face the music. "He has screwed up again?" In fact on two occasions, my friends summoned meetings to counsel the author suggesting that he was daydreaming to think of things that would never happen. Briefly, almost everybody lost any balance of hope that he had in me—except few of the few among whom was one person—Peter Louis. Louis was my boss at the Tanzania Breweries. Then my books got published! Louis sent me a note saying: "Everything you touch seems to flourish!" Why? Here is the answer! I risk! I take calculated risks. And I know that. That's why every time I fall, after falling, I have always gone back to where I started and began my trail once again. And I must add that this trick has always helped me to rise again every time I fall. That's probably why in the end, I have always been considered as a person who has always been at the top. It is not true! The truth is this: I have mostly been at the bottom climbing back to the top. It a reason that led Baker Mwinyiheri, my former workmate at TBL to suggest that I was lucky! It was also a lie also! I risked. And that is standard—the SI unit of someone's success potential. I wasn't the first.

And here is that standard: to every good or service we need there is a price! Bill Gates forfeited his University education for the timing of the business idea he had had. For Bill, the rest is history. Yoweri Museveni was a teacher when he abandoned his family and career to buy a few arms and gunpowder to the bush to fight Amin. Notice that we cannot avoid taking risks in our everyday life. That's why we should always be keen to opportunities and consciousness to fault. Think about when we choose to plant a tree for shade. The tree may occupy some space we would need somehow, and so we may—supported with logic—decide to leave it altogether; or rather than planting a tree for mere shade or for its colorfulness such as are flowers, we can as well choose to plant a fruit tree: a mango tree, an orange tree, an apple tree, a banana tree, or even surround the fence with healthy passion fruit plants.

Back to my absence without leave, I never returned to meet my accusers, for I was appointed for that bigger job in the city. In retrospect, I realize that if I didn't make the decision I made then, my life wouldn't have been the same as it is today. For instance, instead of writing the book you are now reading, I would be now in a grocery store selling and at the same time drinking alcohol somewhere in the midst of small districts in the upcountry. I was not lucky. I risked. This is what Thomas Sankara called madness. That's why the only persons who were close to truth were those who suggested that I was mad—mad and out of my mind. "You cannot carry out (any) fundamental change," aptly observed Thomas Sankara, "without a certain amount of madness. In this case, it comes from nonconformity, the courage to turn your back on the old formulas, the courage to invent the future..."

What I am trying to say is this: yes you could be one of the people who have a knack for sniffing money! However that isn't enough. Action is required if you have to make a difference. And to take action, you must take risks—calculated risks—focusing on the gains to be achieved. But since everyone wants the gains associated with any opportunity that comes their way, why then so few rise to the occasion? Fear! They fear to lose what they already have, whether a job or capital, deciding to remain static rather than risk and face the music—fearing the bad. With the gains involved at the back of your mind, go forward and take a chance. "To diminish a fear," wrote Bill FitzPatrick in his Action principle, "you must first face it. The one hundredth skydive or speech won't be as traumatic as the first. The best way to deal with first fears is through a combination of logic and bravery. Logically, most people who jump from planes or give speeches don't die."

Concomitantly, not every person who resigns from one job seeking another, or even, a person who quits employment altogether dies out of starvation or ridicule. This explains why many of the mushy pilots who contemplated being blown up and so "played it safe" died during World War than the risk-takers who didn't entertain any negative thought. People who become successful in any endeavor—politics or business—are the ones who don't contemplate failure, people who invest unthinkingly as far as risk is concerned. William Shakespeare was right: "A coward dies a thousand times," and the brave never dies. "All people have fears," so goes a King's Guards' motto in the ancient Greece, "All men have fears, but the brave put down their fears and march forward; sometimes to death but always to victory!" People who try to do something fearing to fail, end up failing. Those who do anything certain of accomplishing it, seldom fail. What did Jesus say? "(it is) because of your unbelief: for verily I say unto you, if ye have faith as a grain of mustard seed, ye shall say unto this mountain, 'remove hence to yonder place and it shall remove; and nothing shall be impossible unto you!"

It explains why businessmen who risk investing in any opportune business that comes their way make it when those who tremble at the sight of a new opportunity either run bankrupt, or stagnate. Personal experience has revealed to the author, not as a proposition but as a scientific, or even a divine, law that bravery—informed bravery—seems to strike a chord with God; and that God seems to throw himself beside the brave men and women who have a noble cause to accomplish. And this is not my invention. It is neither exaggerated. Doesn't the bible say; "If we are with God, whom should we fear then?" the reader must, nonetheless, be reminded that preparation is key. Preparation gives a person hands-on agility aside from solidifying his faith in himself—and in his mission.

Timing is also important in reaching the right decision. They say time and tide wait for no man. With the present rapidity of pace of change, good decision yesterday may not be as good today. Notice also that there are people who say that there is no hurry in Africa. It is wrong. As the planet turns around, Africa remains no static. It turns with the rest of the planet. You will miss opportunities if you don't act—and act now. Indeed it is safer to get ahead into life earlier on. By the law of average, the more you attempt , the bigger the probability you have of winning. Besides, the more time we take to enter into a business, the moiré difficulties are likely to arise due to such changes as the government policies and competition, technological changes etc., and thus less and less favorable conditions for new entrants. Besides, having got into life earlier on than many, whereas many were still struggling to get a job, a car or a good apartment, the author had had enough of all that. That's why he resigned earlier on to pursue more rewarding exciting opportunities elsewhere.

You now realize that when you see an opportunity, when there an opening somewhere somehow, then rise to the occasion, fill the gap. Being keen to opportunities is to go against shortsightedness such as restricting your thinking within some boundaries. Instead push the boundaries. Go outside the box. You must do because there're vast new sources of wealth or expansion somewhere, somehow and it is possible anytime we think afresh. Businesswise here we can talk of inventing or innovating new products, new approaches, new markets, hiring new people, bringing in new extensions, new uses, promoting new deeds, and new ideas, such as new cost approaches and thus allowing you to capture new market and new segments etc. But many people let the big moment, their big moments, pass by! We can identify the opportunity by all reasons possible but as well by analyzing if we are still part of the team and the mission. If you doubt about it begin looking out for new spots. But as we are also going to learn further in the forthcoming chapters, we must always consult the inner person—that strongest person in us. By heeding to it by listening to the little voice in us we know where we stand, we know if there is an opportunity calling. And if so our task is to respond with enthusiastic actions. Pastor Chris Oyakhilome was right. Failing to comply with spiritual instructions is foolish and misleading approach without being aware.

HOW TO TURN USELESSNESS INTO USEFULNESS
Napoleon Hill observed rightly that when the opportunity comes, if it ever comes, it makes its appearance in a different form and often from a different direction you may not be expecting. Take a writer as an exemplar. And I can exactly fit my shoes into this illustration. I write books, and without a doubt, I've already gained through writing. But the biggest break may come from elsewhere—from a place I never imagined. That's one of the tricks of opportunity. "It has a sly habit of slipping in from the backward door and often it comes disguised in the form of misfortune or temporary defeat. Indeed perhaps this is why so many fail to recognize opportunity. And when faced by these temporary defeats, the natural thing to do by many men is to quit. Winners have faith and determination and try and hope and are hard working. They have imagination and are intuitive to accept failure by face value. They know failure takes delight in deceiving people when success is knocking and at their door steps. Very few folks who see it see it crawling in so quietly, hidden in a queer look.

Opportunity often makes its appearance in shabby attire while misfortune in *bling-bling*. "[163]

The term *Opportunity* is defined by dictionary.cambridge.org as to collect something, usually after much work or with difficulty: it requires thinking. But probably the slyest part about opportunity is, before success comes in, you will surely meet with necessary temporary defeat and certainly failure of great magnitude. This certainly explains why so few people ever hit to the top when majority of very capable men and women remain in the middle when they should be leading. Opportunity may also come dressed as a disadvantage. It is there in your apparent disadvantage that *Opportunity* abides.

THE AUTHOR'S UNFORTUNATE CAT: OUR INFIRMITIES HELP US UNEXPECTEDLY

Furthermore, if you analyze the biographies of all successful individuals, you will realize as rightly observed Emerson: "Our infirmities help us unexpectedly." Accepting your situation is the beginning of finding harmony with yourself. Accepting your situation is not to surrender. It is prudence. It is pragmatism. It is to be realistic. Besides, it gives you a new outlook of your own person and opportunities commensurate with your person and environment. I've a cat at home, a cat I decided to love and care for. She bore four children you may call kittens. One of its babies was born handicapped. One of his legs was lame and he couldn't walk but crawled. He was always late when the mother came to breastfeed her children.

As they grew up, we started providing them with milk and food. But again this "unfortunate" young fella was always late and found all fatty and juicy portions of meat grabbed away by his stronger siblings. He grew weaker and weaker. But this prompted as a benefit from its handicap compassion from my whole family beginning with especially Priscilla who quite strongly took it as her duty to come in her defense. We also began setting aside some fatty portions for him. Soon like a miracle, his leg healed up but he was still a little less powerful as compared to his siblings. It should have been so to benefit this poor young fellow. That's how when my neighbors came for the kittens—which we gave away for I wouldn't turn

---

[163] *Adapted from Napoleon hill in Think and Grow Rich the unabridged edition*

my house into a den of cats—the stronger siblings attracted the new adopters. So the stronger siblings were the first to evacuate leaving their mother's milk and love all to the disadvantaged kitten besides all juicy catches of fatty rats the mother hunted.

In the heart of your disadvantages, the circumstances are preparing you for a cause! For instance, I know a young man who grew up to be risk-taking as a person, which explains why he even resigned from a lucrative job at almost a very tender age! Why? How? I will explain.

As I analyze his background back during his birth and childhood, I realize he is a product of the nature of his family and indeed the timing of his birth. He is thirteenth to his father, third born to his mother, fifth wife to his father of fifteen wives. He was born when his father had had a bride for himself. Now himself married, the author knows how the bride occupies the groom, keeping him busy. I can say without doubt whatsoever that during this young man's childhood, he didn't see much of his father. Mostly looked-after by his mother, he therefore grew up a little freer than his elder siblings—free from his father's airtight authority. It is therefore safe to say that his personality is in no small measure, due to his unfortunate freedom and independence from his father!

Distanced from his father, whether by the wall of his new bride, or a dozen of elder siblings, or even his father's busy schedule, I have no way of knowing. But I know it had its cost. Because of this environment, he wasn't one of the most favorite kids, and so never his father's pet. But in retrospect, his background paid dividends in some strange ways. Being a sincere writer and mentor, I will count myself a dishonest person if I don't give an account of this narrative for in it is enlightenment, and education—especially to all who count themselves disadvantaged as children, whether orphans or children born to poor single mothers.

It is again safer to say that by virtue of his birth, he grew up to be rebellious or rather courageous—call it anything. To say the least, because of somewhat circumstantial non-compliance to authority, disobedience, rebellion, or even lawlessness, call it anything, it was an innocent environment or personality that developed from persistent independence so that he found himself doing most of the things others wouldn't dare attempt! And it, probably, is for this reason that he stumbled upon some ground others wouldn't have—albeit the many other enviable advantages his senior siblings have enjoyed themselves—advantages he will never have himself. But because we are concerned with how to turn disadvantages into opportunities, we will concentrate with this less advantaged sibling. As such, one of the biggest advantages he enjoyed as a toddler was that he began seeking, practicing, and experiencing, to be himself—albeit support from his elder siblings and well-wishing friends. That's how he desired to be self-sufficient and self-reliant! That's how later on he got himself into work as early as it was almost impossible. He got for himself a couple job appointments during the time when he was supposed to be doing final University Exams.

The thing is, when many of his buddies were concentrating for final EUs, he did both—he concentrated for EUs, and applied and attended job interviews—and got three from which to choose. That's how he grew into career earlier when others were still struggling. That's how he resigned from work earlier on—that is—only about eight years into it. How do I know all this? That it is true? I know it is true because concerning that young man, I am he.

Though I love the above account, and I believe it is, by itself, fitting, I must insert one comment nonetheless. Yes the narrative above may seem to blow the author's horn. I know that. But that's not my intent, and yes, the whole account is not about me. It is rather about you. I could find a thousand examples of people who turned disadvantages into advantages, but I would not be that free to go deep into someone's private life as I can on my own life, would I? As such, suffice to say here that indeed in every adversity, there is an equal and opportunity of the same magnitude if you choose to focus on either of the two. I know a couple of successful people, successful in their own ways whether at individual or family level, professionally or in career, people I know personally, if I shouldn't talk about Steve Jobs people who rise to the top despite all the disadvantages they seem to bear. Just look around you.

You, the reader, too, know many other persons who have their lives lifted probably because of the matching circumstances I have narrated above. Okay? It is probably Messi's small size that makes him fluid on the football pitch. This is probably part of the secret why he has won the prestigious world footballer of the year award four times in a row, a feat that not even Ronaldo de Lima, a football whom many recognize as the most successful footballer of this generation—could accomplish partly due to series of injuries he picked because of his size. It was Jericho's size that helped him to escape blows than do huger wrestlers in WWE. Though I am not in any way advocating or even suggesting that you go and chop your legs off or pluck your eyes out, but it was Nzigo's infirmity—for both had one smaller leg and therefore had to use a pole to walk—that gave them acrobatic and most famous and highly venerated individuals in the whole of Kahororo and Ihungo schools in the eighties and nineties. It was Steve wonder's blindness that made him produce the exceptional tunes and lyrics in music. On the other hand, Hasheem Thabeet's extra ordinary size and height is partly what made him the first ever Tanzanian to lay in the NBA and now probably the highest paid Tanzanian, albeit a mismatch for most genuine beautiful girls Hasheem may have wished to approach. And when I say this I know what I talk about. His is a unique size of a habitual Tanzanian.

I was visiting Clouds Fm Radio at the time when this famous radio station was housed in the NIC Building downtown Dar es Salaam city centre in Tanzania. When I got out, immediately I met a stampede he had caused. I had no way of knowing what his mission at the building was, but one this was clear. A thousand souls had gathered choking the whole parking space and the roads nearby bewildering at the immense size of Hasheem Thabeet. He should be proud of it too. It was probably why on his visit to Tanzania president Obama mentioned one Tanzanian in his speech. You know who it was? Yes you are right. It was he, Hasheem Thabeet.

In addition to accepting yourself, accept your situation. Cursing yourself because of your circumstances doesn't help you in anyway. It is a waste of time, energy and resources that would otherwise be used optimally in other productive endeavors. If you change and begin to love your circumstances—loving it in as far as you have to work from the same situation if you have to transform your life— will elevate your spirits and with this change, you will change your circumstances and of those around you. Is it possible? Lie. You say. Okay. You need proof. You may be right.

It was his imprisonment that helped Paul apostle to write the best and vast epistles that cannot be outnumbered or outsmarted by any. I have in fact learned from Paul apostle's experience and took myself from the world, imprisoning myself into my home to write the books one of which you are now reading. It was Julius Nyerere's upbringing as a village boy that gave him a human heart than many other humans with hearts of the beasts of a heart of stone. It was Nelson Mandela's imprisonment that made South Africa Free, and him an icon with an enviable timeless name. It is probably from my father's huge family of fifty children less four in addition to the seventy-plus grand children that I draw inspiration in my writing.

That's the tricky part about opportunity. It prefers to shepherd, accompany or chaperone failures as opposite poles attract one another. Now because failure is so arrogant and pompous and dressed in more colorful clothes, success or opportunity seems to be overshadowed by its opposite number just like the lunar eclipse! Dressed in pale and inconspicuous attire, opportunity lets the most arrogant part and showmanship of the failure go before it. How Opportunity can be so cunning does really strike me!

Yet, when Lady Opportunity proves that you are a persistent guy, she doesn't just come in crawling anymore. She will flow, pouring in, flooding in torrents towards your tent. In fact she may astound you and flatten your innocent expectations as it keeps moving in your direction, continuously and effortlessly like torrential rains which then may seem to be so sudden or too large amount and uncontrollable. If I can manage to insert-in any further advice, here it is. Be yourself and love it. Stay home. That's where your chances are. That's where you can make the most of your vast talents. You can accomplish more there than elsewhere. Stay home. That's where your mind is more likely to be in its element. That's where you will find your luck, that's where you will coincide with it if at all there is anything called luck. That's where you are likely to succeed. Period.

I must insert one last admonition nonetheless. Staying home, notice however, doesn't mean staying where you are. It means finding and going back home. It means work—working on yourself, your own person—and working on work itself. The foregoing statement is of significant meaning to majority—for the majority doesn't know yet where they belong. That's why we talk of Know Thyself! To attract or somewhat recognize Lady Opportunity if she comes at all, don't wait for her to materialize. Don't even wait for her to be fully ripe before you pick it up. What I want to say is that don't wait until when it is ripe for the picking that you should start associating with it. Start now. Get yourself introduced to it. Offer a hand of friendship. Pay her a visit. Let her be a regular social contact with you. Learn from her. Yet there's one advice I want to share with you, yes you, if you should be able to find and tap into your true potential. And here it is. Yes I know you are a busy person. You are truly busy and it is for good reasons. You don't want to dissipate your resources and most of all time. You know time is money. And that's very good. But to make use of your time so wisely, you have got to halt or a moment and take an inventory of what you have real accomplished with your time and resources. Also during this time try to observe and analyze how others are growing while you don't or whereas others lead you remain at the bottom. If you do so, you will , in the light of where you stand, learn whether you have to work harder or smarter. People who do not do this tend to move on blindly without realizing they are heading for a wrong direction and it will not be too long before they are discouraged. This explains why and how people fail and cease trying.

HOW MUHAMMAD ALI USED THIS FORMULA TO BETTER HIS WINNING CHANCES

You can as well use your handicap to better your circumstances. Cassius Clay, the world boxing heavyweight champion joined Islam and changed his name to Muhammad Ali after he had judged that Christianity at the time did nothing to save the black people from humiliation, Christians or not, while Islam safeguarded interests of the blacks among which interests, the top was personal dignity. Now it was the time when he was about to fight in the ring. Paterson was his opponent. In the psychological warfare before the bout, Paterson denounced not only Muhammad Ali's decision to join Islam, calling his actions ridiculous during the pre bout interviews, he also called him Cassius Clay, the name Ali had dumped as a slave name. Naturally Muhammad Ali didn't like it.

So he went into the fight with a determination to teach him a lesson. He hit hard and every time he hit him? He kept asking him: "what's my name?" "What's my name?" "What's my name?" in his own words in an interview with Sam Pollard, Muhammad Ali said "I took the offensive and said "I am going to whoop you till you tell me my name. During Round One I said, What's my name. He didn't say nothing. So round two, round three, I hit him with my right hand , (asking him what's my name and) he said: Muhammad, Ali Muhammad Ali. That was not all. When he, Muhammad Ali, fought Henry Cooper, he fought with the vengeance of the wounded buffalo only because the white controlled media had pronounced that the white man would triumph over the inferior black man, that inferior black man being Muhammad Ali. That's how he knocked him out flatly.

JESSE OWENS

Jesse Owens was insulted by Hitler and denounced him refusing to shake hands with him during Berlin Olympics in 1936. Did he, Jesse Owens, whine? Did he sue and complain and grumble? Oh no! Never! Not Jesse Owens. Instead of whining or indulging in self hate, as an average person would have done, he used it to intensify his desire and determination to win as the only better way to put Hitler to shame. Of course the author wasn't at the Berlin stadium when this happened, or even he couldn't go into Owens' heart or brain to see what transpired there, but I suspect he said to himself: "I will show him!" What happened? Let's see. For Adolph

Hitler and the Nazis, the 1936 Berlin Olympic Games were expected to be a German showcase and a statement for Aryan supremacy. Most notably, Hitler lambasted America for including black athletes on its Olympic roster.

But it was the African American participants who helped cement Americans success at the Olympic Games. In all, America won 11 gold medals 6 of them by black athletes. Jesse Owens captured four gold medals for the 100 meters the long jump 200 meters and four hundred meter relay breaking two Olympic records along the way with his long jump record to last for 25 years until 1960 when Irvin Robertson broke it. Now after Owens had won the 100 meter event, a furious Hitler stormed out of the stadium.[164] Hitler's shock was premature. Jesse Owens went on to win all four gold's in which he participated.

When people despise you, when people scorn or deride you, when everybody else mocks you, remember it is because probably you have not done enough. It could as well, and mostly, because there is something in you, something that makes you superior to them—something that incites envy or jealousy. Why otherwise should they attack you? Dale Carnegie was right. No one kicks a dead dog. It is their envy that gnaws at their inner persons inciting them to stab you, to put you down. Never allow their intentions to happen—to put you down. Here is what I do when confronted with such a situation. I ignore what they say. But I don't take it at face value. I reevaluate my character determined to become even a better person. I have also, surprisingly, found it to be an inspiration for me to find within me more energy, more force, more courage, more determination, more resolve, more tenacity, and more willpower to double, or even triple, my efforts. And as if it is not enough, I find inspiration to keep on keeping on, to make sure I succeed, so that I can prove a point. Surprisingly, I have found that I look forward to meeting such gross people for the inspiration I draw from their actions. That's what Muhammad Ali did. That's what Jesse Owens did. That's what makes champions. That's what makes heroes. And I have got news—good news—for you! The same kind, and in the same magnitude, of heroism abides in you—only more abundantly.

HOW THE AUTHOR PUT HIS HANDICAP TO ADMIRABLE ADVANTAGE

---

[164] *Adapted from www.biography.com/people/jesse-owens-9431142*

Probably you are saying that that is third party information. You say it doesn't hold water. You are right. If I were in your position, I would feel the same way. Now here's the first hand information you requested. (Note: The narrative you are about to read is serious personal information I considered withholding but I decided to share it in the spirit of emphasizing the point I am trying to make. So really it is not about me. It isn't for me. It is rather for you—yes you the immediate reader).

When I went to secondary school I was not well provided for in terms of school requirements. First my father was already getting aging had retired and had a big family to look after. He couldn't supply all of our school requirements. I depended on papers and exercise books I got from friends but that wasn't a lasting solution. There was one option—one option that was lasting one. I had learnt that every term, the top three students were awarded with school requirement, the support which covered from pens, school books and exercise books. That was at Kahororo and Ihungo respectively.

Really I'd no option. If I'd to keep studying successfully, I'd to be first in my classes to get the maximum of the academic support the school provided to the three winners per class per term—the academic support I badly needed. Looking back, I realize that I was not a genius. It was coming to terms with my situation, an understanding of my deprivation, the verity that I'd no other options but to win this support. I could let such an opportunity silo between my fingers. So I went for it. This indeed explains why during the whole period of about eight years of my schooling beginning with class six to high school through secondary school I came out top of my classes with exception of two or three times of course when I came out number two. Really, "The most important thing in life is not to capitalize on your gains," said William Bolitho, "any fool can do that. The real important thing," he continued, "is to profit from your losses. That requires intelligence and makes (real) difference between men of sense and a fool!"[165]

A MAN WHO TURNED SNAKE'S DEADLY VENOM INTO PURE GOLD

When I first began working, and that was with Pepsi, thanks to Mahendra Patel, my first paid official visit took the author to Arusha City, home to

---

[165] Source: *Source: How To Stop Worrying and Start Living By Dale Carnegie*

East Africa Community headquarters. I can say therefore that, so many things intrigued me. But one thing remained with me many years later, wondering how on earth a person could turn deadly snakes into a thriving business. This was after visiting the Snakes' Park. I saw people paying cash, as foreigners paid in dollars to have a look at the snakes that roamed about in the park coiling and uncoiling themselves moving from one branch of a tree to another. I must admit I am not fond of snakes and they have never won my good graces. Never—since Adam and Eve! But this man did! Yet out of shock, I couldn't interview the man to know how he could even imagine such a thing. Here is how I got a hint—and that was many years later after reading Dale Carnegie's book, How to Stop Worrying and Start Living. What did he do? How? Well, I cannot make myself dare to water down by explaining what the gifted author did so splendidly. I advise you, instead, to read the book on your own. However, for the want of options, coupled with the breathtaking lessons thereof, let me here attempt to sum up the story.

A man bought a piece of land planning to run a farm for livestock and agriculture. But unfortunately, that piece of land turned out to be useless for ordinary farming. It was infested with ubiquitous poisonous snakes! There were vipers roaming about in the farm. Rattle snakes hissed across from the land. You name all kinds of snakes. They simply occupied the land that normal farming was impossible. What would he do? He had thrown all his monies into this farm and had no any other options. What would he do? What would you do?

He had no any other option left for him but to turn it around. He turned it into a tourist attraction. This was indeed a man of sense. When I first read about this narrative, I thought it was pure fiction until when I visited the snakes' park in Arusha Tanzania. This man of sense gathered the snakes and put the outfit to serve as infrastructure for the snakes and tourists. Then he went to work. He read and studied what made snakes thrive. He provided the facilities and services to the serpents. They blossomed.

Soon he discovered snakes meat made wet the mouths of the Far East human species. He rolled his sleeves and went to work more feverishly. He installed machinery and a small factory in his farm. Then he began canning snakes "at the dismay and a chorus of criticism from everybody else," narrates Dale Carnegie. He quietly sold them to tourists at a good price. Soon his farm was a national phenomenon. He became an idol. A man who canned snakes! He had turned a piece of land infested with snakes into a tourist attraction! Snakes which everybody in the neighborhood considered as nasty pests, he had turned into admired money makers! You realize that now in this God-forsaken, poverty-stricken, serpent-infested neighborhood, there stood now a factory that canned serpents! Besides doing away with the dangers of snakes that roamed about the neighborhood threatening lives of the inhabitants and their livelihood, this countryside was now a top end part of the town.

The factory also began providing employment to the local folks. It was because of this man's audacity to do the unthought-of, pushing the boundaries such as canning the snakes, that even the new and better infrastructure such as roads were built in the area creating more employment and social facilities to the community such as banks, hospitals and schools for the children of the employees. The economies of scale set in. The small village grew into a township which grew into a city in no time still attracting more opportunities for many people who lived and more generations yet unborn. I know some of my readers are already imagining this is a fiction story I concocted to entertain my readers! Wrong! It is the true story, a narrative as it was handed down by the eye witness. His name is Dale Carnegie, and this is his story, a story you can read for yourself in his wonderful book How to Stop Worrying and Start Living.

"I," he began, "once visited a happy farmer down in Florida... The land was so wretched (that) he could neither grow fruit nor raise pigs. Nothing thrived there but scrub oak and rattlesnakes...To everyone's amazement, he began canning rattlesnake meat... I found that tourists were pouring in to see his rattlesnake farm at the rate of twenty thousand a year. His business was thriving...poison from the fangs of his rattlers...shipped to laboratories to make anti venom toxin;...skins...sold at fancy prices to make women's shoes and handbags; saw rattlesnake meat...shipped to customers all over the world...(and) the village... had been rechristened rattlesnake Florida in honor of... (this great) man..." Now you be the judge. Isn't this man the icon of the ideal scholar, ideal citizen? Well, sorry! It is wrong. He is more than that. His is a true fabric we should use to build the true scholar we crave, indeed a celebrity I wouldn't be shocked to see nations go to war to claim as their citizen. This isn't a mere imagination. It is reality. Have you not heard how nations dispute over talented sportsmen?

33. THE IDEAL SCHOLAR HAS THE THIRD EYE AND THE SIXTH SENSE

"If 'seeing is believing' what happened to taste, touch, sound and smell? Did our creator really intend to favor sight over the other senses? I don't believe so."
—Alex Morritt, Impromptu Scribe

When everybody else knows that humans have two eyes, and five sensory organs, but only 4few recognize that all men have a third eye and the sixth sense. What is so tantalizing is that only few of the few put the third eye and the sixth sense to use. The Ideal scholar sees things or reflections in the form of hunches, instincts or hears small voices, or even experiences visions others cannot see. This is the intuition—it is in the form of instinct or a hunch. He knows it is at work—and he readily therefore puts it to use. What then is the sixth sense? Is there really anything known as the sixth sense? It is an extra kind of sense beyond the established five physical senses. So far science has not yet been able to resolve what it really is, but simply put, it is a form of sense that is available to us from other sources outside tradition physical sensory organs. Recall the meaning of education, as having been derived from "Educo," or to educe, to draw out from within. This is indeed the major source of all education.

In Think and Grow Rich, movingly Napoleon Hill suggests thus, "The sixth sense is the medium of contact between the finite mind of man and the Infinite Intelligence," he said, "and for this reason," he continued, "it is a mixture of both the mental and spiritual. It is believed to be the point at which the mind of man contacts the Universal Mind... Napoleon Hill wrote that "human beings receive accurate knowledge through other sources other than the physical senses." He also observed that, "Through the aid of the sixth sense, you will be warned against the impending dangers in time to avoid them, and notified of opportunities in time to embrace them. There comes to your aid...a "guardian angel" who will open to you at all times the door to the Temple of Wisdom,"[166] he concluded.

To put the sixth sense to use, the ideal scholar is meditative, and listens to the little voice—the inner voice. He knows there is an inner power within him that guides him. Many people will tell you that reasoning is greater than intuition. I object. Most of human reasoning is biased—and therefore unreliable. To the contrary, the sixth sense gives us easy and seamless access to relevant information existing somewhere we may not know, the information that decides rightly for us without our ever having learned or reasoned about the problem or solution. When you need solutions to your problems, listen first to your heart. And I didn't get this from the moon. I have experienced it. Many times reasoning has failed me. But when I succeed, and I talk about big time success, it oftentimes comes from unerring instincts. The reason for this is that the faculty of reasoning is a conformist as a servant. It will always respond to a person corresponding to what are his expectations. If you expect a yes for an answer, the faculty of reasoning will go to work to concoct every reason to justify a YES. That's how it works. That's how it fails many. Intuition, on the contrary, is unerring. "I don't feel comfortable here. I don't like the sound of this. This doesn't look right to me," etc. That was how Bill Fitzpatrick describes how the sixth sense communicates—and how unerring it is—in his Action Principles.

The sixth sense or intuition on the other hand is not a conformist as a servant but a rebel. With it you will never fail. It never fails you because it pays no attention to your opinion and doesn't bother whether you like it or not when it gives you counsel. It has another advantage. Because it doesn't need to conform, it is instant. It is instant because it wastes no time in thinking about your opinion or reaction. The best example of how intuition works is in the settings of the car accident. Many drivers will tell you they responded accurately and spot-on to accidents without much of their reasoning or will. And this is how it works. When it appears, it will appear as a hunch or inspiration into your mind. Napoleon Hill went further. "This inspiration may be considered as a "telegram" or message (sent down)

---

[166] *Napoleon Hill in Think and Grow Rich the unabridged edition page 250*

from the Infinite Intelligence," he said. When it comes, he said "treat it with respect and act upon it as soon as you receive it.[167]"

It was the sixth sense that made Pirate's wife to warn his husband of not involving himself with judging the innocent Jesus. It was the same sense that made Columbus sail the unknown waters to discover America. It was the sixth sense that came in handy when Bill Gates, whom The *Harvard Crimson* called the "Harvard's most successful dropout" —the rest of the world just calls him ridiculously rich. For more than a decade, Bill Gates has been one of the wealthiest, if not the wealthiest, men in the world,[168] chose to drop out of Harvard to form what we now know as Microsoft. It was the same little voice that sang in Steve Jobs' ear before he dropped out of Reed College in Oregon due to lack of direction. And 17 years later he enrolled and dropped again from Stanford to pursue self-training form of education in typography and the rest remain as history.

The author has also learned through experience that whenever reasoning fails him, he simply lets go of the reasoning mind. And no sooner has he let go of it, resorting to meditation instead, thereby simply letting the subconscious generate the answers than a hunch, idea or solution began falling in place. Truly, more than anything, through meditation, or rather going back into your inner self makes it possible for the intuition or the subconscious mind to generate one of the most powerful energies, energies that join hands to give an answer in no time, an answer that is correct if we only listened. It is no wonder intuitive and meditative people are likely to accomplish anything they set out to achieve.

With intuition, you have guarantee of the permanency, or constancy, of unfailing knowledge—unfailing knowledge that has stood the test of time. We are very strong inside except that we have forgotten we're. It is based on universal knowledge or on the society's truest cherished values—values that have intellectual, moral, spiritual as well as bodily constancies and existence through different times. Through intuition a person is able to access his or her creative thinking and to generate a holist perception of reality thereby individuals inner and outer worlds tie in his or her inner self

---

[167] *Napoleon Hill in Think and Grow Rich the unabridged edition by Embassy Books page 71*

[168] *content.time.com/time/.../0,28804,1988080_1988093_1988082,00.html*

to the environment.[169] Furthermore these persons are critical learners—individuals able to take self initiated actions and responsibility for those actions—capable of intelligent choices and self direction. They are also capable to approach a problem situation with flexibility and intelligence, and to work cooperatively with the others. They are internally guided with regard to their socialization process; they don't wait for or work for the approval of others.[170] Indeed we are very strong in our innermost selves than we already imagine or know.

I know we are stronger inside than we already know. I got that secret through a very grave life style I lived when I worked with the brewery that I am ashamed of it. Yet, though I am ashamed of it, I am delighted that I went through it that I learned this secret. I say it was fatal because during the time, we ran beer promotions and drinking sessions oftentimes going well past midnight. Returning home then, I would completely dose off and fall into deep sweet dreams. But that was only in terms of the physical body for I drove with an alert mind. I would close my eyes and drive back home and pack the car and walk eyes closed to the door, turn the door knob and lead myself to bed and—then collapse—with or without locking the door. Why bother! Though I was mute in the body but in the inside I was whole and complete. I was alert and at peace with myself —and creator— probably than ever! I'm not—mind you—suggesting you do try it out!

I admit it was fatal, and I regret it of course. But I am only narrating how I arrived home safely to hoot at the right gate and not running over my young brothers who opened for me, then after packing the car in its place, I often walked eyes closed to the door, and retraced my bed room where I collapsed until when I resigned from this damned job. It was a good experience because though I was highly paid, I learned that money and money alone isn't enough. I learned there is more to life than material things. I learned there is an inner person whom many choke in pursuit for material wealth ignoring the inner huger and more powerful self. I have predicted to accomplish certain things and they came to pass. I heard from deep inside that money or any property wasn't lost and though my wife

---

[169] *Adapted from Allan C. Ornstein and Francis P. Hunkins, Curriculum Foundations, Principles and Issues 3rd Edition p. 256*

[170] *Adapted from Allan C. Ornstein and Francis P. Hunkins, Curriculum Foundations, Principles and Issues 3rd Edition p. 206*

never trusted me in the beginning, but regained the money or property; more often than not I didn't follow the popular choices however enticing they looked and people laughed at me at first only to say much later that you were right and we were wrong. These are few examples of how it works. Intuition also works as a warning or sign post that there is danger ahead. Intuition also comes in handy in identifying opportunities or becoming conscious to fault. The educated person is therefore a person who can use his imagination and intuition to generate useful knowledge from his own environment to advance his own life and that of the environment and people around him.

Because I am certain of availability of such exciting testimony on the existence and working of the sixth sense, I am not going to dwell much on the subject. Instead I submit to you that you read the book: What Makes People Rich and Nations Powerful by Festo Michael Kambarangwe, and Think and Grow Rich by Napoleon Hill.

Finally, for you to harness the power inside you, you need quiet time in your day when you do nothing but to immerse in your own thoughts. It is pursuit for serenity. And it can be harnessed in a variety of ways. Let us listen to Bill FitzPatrick: "It can be traditional Zen or transcendental meditation, but it can also be taking a walk, gardening, making a pot of tea or taking a long, hot shower. You may wish to pray. Each day, take twenty minutes to stop, reflect and enjoy being who you are. Think about the past, present, future or nothing in particular. Relax by yourself and you will feel renewed. Tranquility will re-energizes you. Without trying, you will be amazed at how your subconscious mind releases so many good ideas. As you reflect upon the true sense for your existence…"

34. THE IDEAL SCHOLAR IS A FAMILY MAN

"If you cannot get rid of the family skeleton, you may as well make it dance."—George Bernard Shaw

Excepting of the Roman Catholic priests, monks and nuns, of course, the ideal scholar is a family man—or woman. He is a man of a wife—and a woman of a man. He is a man or woman who respects his spouse and children. He is man who looks after his family and his children such that they are well provided for bodily, intellectually and spiritually. He doesn't only focus on his today's needs but also on their future needs. Is this an important ideal? The family unit is a primary educational and economic entity. A family man shapes his family, sets standards for the future, they both—he and his family—shape the neighborhood, and he or she is also shaped—and during old age—and looked after by his or her family, and possibly by the state.

We must, nonetheless, cautiously, add that there are men and women who, on their own accord, choose celibacy as a lifestyle, whether based on one's religious code, or for any good social or religious reasons, cannot be distanced from the same gold standard. Just like how Pope Francis chose to relinquish his papal mansion in the Vatican, the newly appointed central bank governor in Kenya, a celibate, Patrick Njoroge, who was offered a fleet of cars, high-end smart phone, and a mansion in Nairobi's most exclusive area, but Kenya's new Central Bank governor, a member of Catholic sect Opus Dei, has turned down every one of them, instead, chose to lead an almost monastic existence in an Opus Dei religious commune in Nairobi, sharing with them part of his generous salary and benefits, since most of its members are poor lay people aside from modest priests under the bishop.

"His refusal to take his turn to eat is surprising," says Business Columnist, Otieno Otieno. Opus Dei, which means "work of God" in Latin, is a branch of the Catholic Church that teaches that ordinary life is a path to sanctity.

Members aim at "humility, justice, integrity, and solidarity" and to work "hard and well, honestly and fairly," believing that "in God's eyes, what matters is the love people put into their work, not its success in terms of money or fame." Patrick Njoroge seems to be from a different planet altogether. His "refusal to take his turn to eat is surprising" <u>says business columnist Otieno Otieno in the Daily Nation</u>. While <u>Victor Nyakachunga writes in the Standard</u> "many were challenged" by him opting for the simple life. Kenyans are used to senior government officials leading lavish lifestyles. His character has attracted offers of marriage and admiration on Twitter. "And then, that new #CBKGovernor just made me re evaluate my life goals....man is so humble and content," <u>tweeted an inspired Anthony Mbugua</u>. His colleagues are equally taken by him. "Totally devoid of ego and instinctively averse to self-advertisement," is how a senior treasury official and long-serving central banker described him. Kenyans hope his austere nature means he will keep their luxury-loving politicians in check and safeguard their economic future.[171]

Besides, the term family is larger than the term wife or husband especially in traditional African sense. It covers father, mother, brothers and sisters, grand pas and grannies, nieces and nephews, aunties, uncles, neighbors, etc. etc.

Article 8 of the Youth Charter promotes protection (and reverence) of the family. It states that: (One,) the family, as the most basic social institution, shall enjoy the full protection and support of States Parties for its establishment and development noting that the structure and form of families varies in different social and cultural contexts. (And two,) young men and women of full age who enter into marriage shall do so based on their free consent and shall enjoy equal rights and responsibilities.

Having cleared the mist of doubt that did hang on the matter, now the author can go on with the analysis of the ideal scholar as a family man. Talking about protecting family as a basic social, educational and economic unit, its protection whose importance is priceless, the family requires that the ideal scholar be a man of an undivided love and loyalty to his or her spouse. He or she understands that his or her accomplishments in

---

[171] *http://www.bbc.com/news/world-africa-33414351*

life begin with getting a good spouse. Identifying, and eventually marrying, a good spouse is not an event nonetheless. It is a process.

Indeed a good family is priceless. It is an insurance against all maladies of the body, the intellect or mind, and the soul or spirit. Above all, it is the insurance against financial unhealthiness. Indeed a good family never becomes poor or miserable. And I know what I am talking about. Yes even a good a family, a good union, may struggle for sometime, but in the end it comes out smiling. The truth is: it is in the becoming. You have heard this saying for sure: "To every successful man there is a good wife." The same goes for a woman! For a very successful and happy woman there is a good man beside her.

The ideal scholar therefore is a person who cares for his spouse and their children—well with or without the latter. He is keen with the upbringing of the children—if and when they are blessed with that gift. With good upbringing, he raises great children and a great family. He is focused and responsible at work and at home. He puts in more hours and concentration into his work to earn more for the company and his family. He gives a helping hand whether he is a father, mother or as son or daughter. It is not surprising that he partakes in cleaning the home and utensils regardless he is a male or female; as husband he helps his wife in managing their home, cleanliness and in child upbringing; he reads books for the children, and through his actions, he strives to build a responsible family, a family whose members are responsible in public as well as in their private lives—responsible at home, work, in church and community.

MATHIAS AND THERESA (ALSO KNOWN AS MKAKA): THE TESTIMONY OF ONENESS OF THE BODY, INTELLECT AND SOULS OF THOSE IN TRUE LOVE

Surprisingly, love for, and attention to one's spouse and family is something you cannot counterfeit. You can never fake it. A couple that is truly in love lasts together and dies at old age but not too distant apart. This assumption takes into consideration a few genuine reasons where couples had better part—of course we too have to give provisions for Roman Catholic priests and some strong men and women who decide to dedicate their lives for a higher cause—like mother Theresa of Calcutta. I think this is so because of the sanctity of love, of matrimony. Yes there are many ways to do so, but here is one an astounding indicator I have got to share with you from lifelong commitment of a couple that I know at personal level.

Here's a true love story. It is how Mathias died because of the agony of losing Theresa, his dear wife. How do I know it is true? Well, Matthias and Theresa (alias Mkaka) were so much in love. They had worked through many things together and they had grew to have their lives entangled and fixed together that when Theresa passed on, Matthias concluded that he couldn't live anymore—nor did he need to.

How do I know? Or even why am I concerned with this man's life? Why shouldn't I? He was my maternal grandpa. I know it is true because they are my maternal grandparents. I am sure he died manly and happily having fulfilled his promise to understand and striving to provide for each other's needs, to love, comfort, honor and keep…in sickness, and in health and forsaking all others to keep oneself only unto each other so long as you both shall live.

And it was grandma who went first. Grandpa was not too old not to live any longer. He was very strong and enthusiastic with the future now that the family livelihood had improved and the cattle growing in numbers as his daughters—already properly married—were doing better, and we his grand children growing up, his relief was suddenly mounting. The two elder of all his grand children had proved to be very intelligent and outstanding. Josephine, the author's niece was already at the university. Her brother Joseph was a rising star. Julius, Fort, Alex and the author—among others—had also proved to be promising. Yet when grandma got sick, he, grandpa, was very anxious. As I tell this narrative, I do so mournfully. He and his wife were my sanctuary longtime ago when I was young.

Indeed I can still see him beside me. I can right here close my eyes as I wrote and see grandpa, protectively holding the little hand of my boyhood self as we regularly walked together toward the kraal. I can see the evergreen scenery over the whole land as we escorted his cattle in their pastures. I can see and admire his admiration of his black and white cattle he raised. I can certainly see yes an old man by my side but I can see he is upbeat and proud. I can still see grandma handing over warm natural rich milk immediately after we returned home. I can see her bathing me and enveloping a thick blanket around me—caring about me. I can see true love from a true caring family. I must admit I still cherish these little old moments when we visited grandpa and grandma because quite frankly I kind o missed such attention back home in Kilembe where dad worked—or back in Karagwe. And it is understandable. Dad had a big family. He had several wives and numerous children. I couldn't have expected much attention when dad had even younger children—and wives.

To cut the long story short, grandma died almost at once. That's when trouble ensued. And that's my message. Grandpa lost confidence in life and fell back into depression. His lungs stopped supplying enough oxygen. The liver problems ensued. He lost appetite. His heart failed to pump blood through thinning veins and arteries. Then the inevitable happened. Mathias died within two weeks of his wife's death. She was not only his wife but also his life. He depended almost solely on her breathing much as she depended on him. Those who were near him realized something was wrong. And that something was his life. His life was in danger. Without her his audacity was put to test. She was emotionally the things that held him and his life together. He was no longer in one piece. His other half had gone—forever. He couldn't live in one piece anymore without her. He couldn't take it anyhow anymore. He chose to rest in peace by her side. I wept so bitterly for my grannies when mummy reported to us this story for first time when she returned home. For now I can only say; rest in peace grandma and grandpa.

Now, if we can do a little postmortem of the whole story, doctors with the support of high-powered machines, concluded that that couldn't find anything serious that killed my grandpa. It was the emotions—the desperation. He had vowed thus: "I can do nothing than surrender to your demands—your wishes are my commandments." And that, "I can't but count myself privileged to be yours and to share a—well, to share me—my whole self and my whole life with none but you until do us part."

LESSONS I HAVE RECENTLY LEARNED FROM MY BOYHOOD SELF

The ideal scholar doesn't blindly look after his family with great care. He does so not only because it is his responsibility, but he takes pride in doing so knowing it is a two-way traffic. I say so because as we grow up, we all need some kind of family support. I know this is true having had looked after an elderly step grandmother. But the ideal scholar also knows the unequaled pleasure we derive from being there for our families and people around us. If you read the book What Makes People Rich and Nations Powerful, you will come to terms with what I am talking about. The ideal scholar also looks after his family with utmost love and heed, knowing that not only do the Gods want him to be good to his family and people around him, but it is for his own good. Besides, the greatest thing a father or mother can do for his or her family is to provide for them. And when I say to provide for them i mean to raise them in a proper way that all the body, intellect and soul is looked after and cared for such that the person grows up to be exemplary—a diamond in the ruff—in terms of his character and how he conducts himself towards people, work or life's pleasures and wealth! A father or mother has a duty to give them a good name. And, "A good name," so goes an English saying, "is worth more than riches."

Notice also that if we give our children good upbringing, we help pass on the education and knowledge that was passed down to us, plus our own life experiences, that help to shape them as future leaders of, and role models to, others. By doing so, we give this nation the future leadership our nation is weeping for, making this nation and the world as a whole a better place for the majority. We all know that under the today's trend, only the rich get richer and fewer as the state of pathetic poor get poorer and colossal. By transforming our families and households we transform the whole nation. The ideal scholar recognizes that by advancing social mobility of his offspring, he so advances his next generation above his or her existing levels. And recognize by shaping his family, he is making them role models and teachers of the others in that community and thus besides himself, his family, and offspring become change agents. We all know the reverence the Kennedy family enjoys in America. It was work that transcended individual selfish gains. If you want to prove this verity watch every other past but especially the <u>2013 Presidential Medal of Freedom award ceremony</u>.

And when I write about this sense of duty in the big picture perspective of course, I know it is possible. Human as he was, I have seen how Michael Kambarangwe transformed the whole village by slowly modernizing the village that was almost ancient, and any modernity or modern person alien. The whole village spoke only vernacular languages, leading traditional life, believing in Mbandwa and traditional Chwezi Gods, uncultured and running away from classrooms. Only a few years later, after he had chosen to retire and returning home to the village, the whole village began becoming a universally Kiswahili speaking country and people began enrolling their children to school albeit skeptical. He brought modernization and civilization by the way his family dressed and the attire he put on. He introduced—literally speaking—money economy, changed the perception people had over education, as he helped doing away with superstition having had education at Rubya seminary; he detribalized the village by marrying from different tribes and clans, certainly a knack from Ruhinda the First his ancestor, marrying many wives from different tribes yet keeping his family cohesive and as one and hence bringing the sanctity of the family institution into something close to impossibility.

He helped bring the sense of diverse economy into the village by running agriculture as well as business hence bringing the sense of thinking out of the box rather depending on hunting and gathering or cattle rearing and crop farming only. This is how he did stir innovation and new ideas in the village. I hail the old man for that's why we are born and brought here on earth. We are born for a purpose. We are born to be change agents. We are born to help advance or contributed to fineness of creation. In fact I wouldn't be surprised if one day the whole of Katera village, or at least some street was named after him for he deserves recognition of some kind as human as he was.

Recently I heard Princess and Priscilla my daughters cross examining one another and I was impressed by their discussion on family. Priscilla asked "what is a family!" Princess replied "a family is a group of people living together closely related to one another! It is papa, mummy, you Patricia and I!" Prince Ruhinda, their junior brother was yet unborn. This intrigued me and though I was writing and pretended I was not conscious about their discussion, I roughly jotted down their conversation eavesdropping across from the living room. "The family helps people know one another. They assist one another in times of need; and the family is core for the closest friendship. It creates relationship," they continued reading and rehearsing from their notes as I shorthanded their conversation down, "and respect for one another. Economically," they continued, "they work and hoard wealth together. They then in assisting one another become closer proving for one another and develop and advance one another," their class on family institution I was sailing in had docked. Later that same evening I learned they were revising Civics for Standard Three, a book used in their school curriculum by Edward N. Nyema.

Hearing this lesson, I had but to recall how Julius or Fort and mother had been there for me; how Candida, Maria Augustina, Clement, Monica, Margaret, Domina and Leonidace Rugambwa (RIP) had helped steer me to various heights in a range of other ways. Then I, humbly, saw in retrospect, how I had helped transform the lives of those who are junior to me and reckoned in African perspective that a family is beyond father, mother and sister or brother. I saw how clement, Monica, Regina, Domina and Margaret had always covered for me and one another. The family does really serve as shock absorber. They provide principles and ideals by which to go. The family builds culture and attitude and character. With these ideals, family prosperity and continuity are guaranteed.

Therefore when the unity within the family unit is weak, or its cohesion in shambles, all members are likely to be shaken and weakened—in the long run. With unstable or loosely connected family members, which is disunity, it brings negative effects to especially the children and later to the whole family which fails to meet their needs of a decent life, they lack direction and hostility arises. In such circumstances, there's no cooperation which leads to distrust between parents and ultimately separation. With separation? With separation HIV and AIDS come in and thus premature deaths and a nation of street children we see on rise today. With separation and lack of leadership, indiscipline and lack of character settle in. By the foregoing statement, we mean immorality, theft, drugs, prostitution, lawlessness, nationally and poverty which together lead to high dependence ratio and short miserable life spans.

The ideal scholar, the ideal man is as adapted from what Gauri Karan (Cosmo Magazine): He is a man who makes a conscious decision to surround his or her family with endless love and understanding (Cosmo Magazine). Truly nothing makes one richer than that. Indeed as I grow up I learn to be especially loyal to my wife and family. I've indeed vowed to love through seven lifetimes and not stopping. People who vow to love in seven lifetimes, but only soon to review it in seven days end up bringing sorrow, poverty and miseries to many people than the couple itself. That includes their children and their families and friends of both sides etc. This commitment between couples however must be a two-way traffic. Yet you shouldn't wait for him or her to start. Be the one.

Couples who are able to grow and change together, striving for common goals and dreams, have the best marriages. On the other hand, "A lot of couples fall into trouble not being on the same page," warns US based psychotherapist in his book Things You Need to Know before Getting Married (Cosmo Magazine). Couples should help one another, submit to one another in quest to satisfy one another. What happens today is the reverse. the Guardian in June 2011 reports of the boy who indulged in theft, shoplifting and robbery and one evening his father called him and enquired about the report that he had grabbed and sold the neighbor's property, the boy said let me come. It was not long time in coming. He returned with an axe and chopped off his father's head—just like that! That isn't the kind of a son you or I hope for.

As parents we need to prepare our children to meet the future challenges readily. Such an ability as this—meeting the challenge with class and dignity—is impossible without preparation on the part of the parents. Children have got to be well mannered and cultured such that they respect and relate well with people. When the children have had good upbringing, which by the original plan of the Almighty, is to have the children raised by their father and mother, living under one roof, given good care and upbringing, they will attract good friends as magnets attract iron firings—and the reverse is true. They will make good friend and become wealthy. Can we prove it? I mean can we prove that the ideal son or daughter attracts people and possessions even as a young man or woman? Let me illustrate.

When we were but young boys, Julius, Fortune and I were such highly classed and good mannered children. Mother used to tell us that if you behave yourselves, the whole world and all that is it are yours. Dad emphasized that he had come from a noble background. He said he wanted us to reflect that to people around us. He heeded us against roaming around on the streets or picking fights. He taught us however rarely that was, that as Christians we must love all and forgive. One of such most remarkable memories I've is during the same time when we were still in Uganda where my dad worked then before we returned home. The first time we went to the Kyanjuki market, I could feel the intensity of the group of merchants that looked at us with interest. I didn't disclose my feelings, but I sensed they watched closely how a trio of us walked and talked. Mama was so strict in a way during those days. We were made to be prayerfully respectful. He had set a gold standard for our character. I guess it was the only weapon one would complete in polygamous family like ours.

Later on, as we grew up, we were afforded with some pocket money for our favorite fruits which were countless at the Kyanjuki market over the Ruwenzori. We visited this market quite a few times. So slowly we made friends with our admirers and we would soon be bringing home more than the value for our Ugandan shillings. As we kept visiting and buying and communicating respectfully, we started bringing home ripe assortments of fruits and several other goodies—most of them free of charge of course. This didn't fascinate mama. She in fact began doubting if we were given excesses or simply we stole them. When we returned with stocks and our moneys in full as it was with the biblical Joseph's brothers on returning from Egypt, mama didn't like it. She demanded that we take her to these merchants. We were only six, five and four respectively. We had no objection. Mama took us and we walked up the Ruwenzori to Kyanjuki market.

We took her straight to the merchants and introducing her, Julius, my brother introduced mama. She was skeptical but extended her gratitude for our friends saying she came to thank them for befriending us her children and—of course—for the gifts! I could sense she was tricking them to say they didn't give us any gifts. Instead they thanked her for taking her time to come and visit them. We kept quiet. I was in particular eyeing the fruits and sweets again and wishing mummy would buy some more. This time they did the unprecedented thing that left mother ashamed of herself. They literally swept their stocks collecting assortments from each one of their buddies one with banana gave us banana one with oranges gave us oranges and one with passion gave us passion fruits as other gave sweets until when we couldn't collect them all.

We arrived home but mama was panting with the load we had collected! She didn't say it but she was happy with how we made friends and indeed our character. Mama began limiting our visits there of course fearing to be so overburdening. Then, weeks later, we were visiting with these merchants. They came home at Kilembe and got them introduced as our friends as we too visited their hilly homes and their families among the Konjo people who live high over their ancestral Ruwenzori even when they were considered at the time as a less modern if you know what I mean! We were connected with their children and young brothers as our new friends. We were also introduced to their sets of friends.

Finally the circle of our friendship kept enlarging and we began learning many things from them as they learned from us. I believe our friendship would ramble on if it were not for General Amin's extreme revulsion for the Tanzanians which prompted our returning home to Tanzania. To be honest I don't know what would happen if we grew up there. I am not sure, only if God doesn't appoint spouses for his creation now that we are all married, I am not sure if we wouldn't be married from among the Konjo people of the Ruwenzori mountain—primitive (in the white man's eyes) or not. Really I don't believe love can be modern. In fact I imagine that modernity has helped to garrote true love. I wouldn't regret a primitive true love if God had instead used my rib to form a mountainous Ugandan Konjo girl. From this experience I learned that great people, young or old, ideal persons represent passion, charm, hope, enthusiasm, courage, friendship and happiness to, and for the others. Who would not reward such a person? We were young and aliens but that didn't stop us from making friends, thanks to mama. The English people say so wisely: "Kill not the goose that lays the golden eggs!"

35. SELF CONTROL: THE IDEAL SCHOLAR IS RATIONAL, TOLERANT AND SELF-RESTRAINED

"I count him braver who overcomes his desires than him who overcomes his enemies." —Aristotle

The ideal scholar is person who has self-control, a person who is well balanced and self-restrained. He is sober and always alert. He is a person who has control over his destiny. He is not drunk or picking up fights or addicted to some habits. He will never chase women or make a drink his master. He will never pick habits and will never seem preoccupied with cash or inclined to grandstand. He has self-respect and respect for others.

Self-control is the will power or ability to consciously do something or to avoid doing it altogether. It is to have a firm grip on yourself. But notice that self-control doesn't simply mean you should ignore danger signals or avoid risky environment. No! Self-control doesn't mean as an ideal that you should not run or stay away from vice or evil. The Nyambo people of Kyerwa, Karagwe Tanzania have a fitting saying: "Embwa k'ezanisa orukobha, elurya!" that is to say, when a dog plays with a rubber in the end it eats it. Thus don't ignore the danger signals and risks that surround you, risks such as drugs and alcohol or even promiscuity, i.e., never entertain environment that triggers such habits—habits that are addictive.

The back label on the Tusker Lager's bottle puts that point into perspective. When you open a bottle of Tusker Lager,"—well, you become: "Friends Forever!" why? "Every...mouthful summons up the taste,"—the addiction! Safari Lager beer didn't beat about the bush. "Safari Moja Huanzisha Nyingine," i. e., one bottle of Safari summons another! So? be forewarned. Don't try it. And concerning this warning, I know what I say. I have worked in brewery for eight years. I saw new employees who came to the brewery as saints but ended up as alcoholics that they were sacked in a short period of time. What I don't know is whether they were sacked to save the brewery—or the victims. Working as a sales representative in a brewery, I visited and worked with night clubs and brothels to see virgins who began working as pure angels but ended up as whores. Jesus himself taught his disciples thus: Put us not into temptation, but deliver us from evil…"

Self control is impossible without positive mindset. Indeed as parents and schools we have got to help children and the future generation to learn to be on top of their life. And it is possible. Addiction to alcohol, nicotine and even physical pleasures aren't above one's ability to manage if he has to live long and acquire a rich meaningful life for himself, his or her family and people around him. The proverbs say that: "The path of the just is as the shining light, the light that shines more and more until the perfect day…"

As a parent or guardian, school or teacher, as well as the manager or leader of men at the workplace, one needs to give his charge leads and guidance on how to refuse poverty, failure and sickness. And it is possible because this is the question of making decision—to decide to pluck such attitudes and in their place load victory, health and generally positive mindset. When we instill in young generation a sense of self-control, it allows them to gain a strong spirit, one that is regulated and has mastery over one's mind and body. Is it possible? Indeed. That a person can fully control himself was brought to my attention in style during my formative years, sharing a room with someone else. When most of us cannot control ourselves when it comes to sleeping or waking up, I recall vividly how on different occasions when I was in boarding school, severally I experienced that a person can choose to sleep and wake up at will. This is how it happened especially during the exams preparations the times we spent long hours revising the notes.

Then one day, one of my friends ask me to wake him up—only as precaution though—before he would summon up the sleep and then go to bed and start snoring in a deep peaceful sleep every sane man craves. Sleeping, recall is one of the top human desires. I remember I would then sit there and watch these two privileged men before I awoke them up just as arranged at the fifteenth minute on the dot. And then one would dart into the shower and dress up and brush, before he darted once again into an examination room. How can such people fail in an exam! No wonder my brother and Francis went on to score on top of their respective classes. And that's not all. They went on to top their peers in their chosen vocations. And this is for a simple reason. Such people are purposeful, hardworking, focused and they can work innovatively and productively for very long hours. Where are they now? You ask! Francis was a chairman when the author served as school secretary and now is a CEO with a top organization in EA as the other has just returned in the country from Nigeria having been poached by the UN, craving such unique human abilities and workmanship. Who wouldn't need such a person in his team? And there is more to such a quality.

Without self-control, a person, short tempered, is reduced to a beast. Self control could define the highest form of humanity. Fortune my brother has exceeded that human standard. He was once asked what would make him lose his temper. He simply said: "if you put a finger in my eye." Is it realistic? Is it a lie? Engaged in a hot argument, a group of employees pushed and tossed their otherwise haughty fellow in the river. But that's what they assumed—that he was so full of himself. And they had reason to believe so. He was a German. Spotting the danger signals, a few others allied with him. When he got out, dripping with water and mud, he presented a picture that was less inspiring. Most on lookers held their breath, waiting for the spell to break. It was like everyone was waiting for his response—and they suspected it wouldn't be anything saintly. Do you know what his response was? His answer to all these questions about his being humiliated, his dignity? He just laughed! And this is not fiction. Read it for yourself in Dale Carnegie's wonderful book How to Stop Worrying and Start Living. Do you still wonder if it is realistic that ever since I learned this lesson, whatever of the sort happens to me, I JUST LAUGH? Yes I laugh, and yes you can control your anger, and your all person since it all begins in the mind. Such a person has his spirit regulated and has gained mastery over his mind and body, brings his or her thoughts, will and emotions and physical senses into subjection and control by an inner person, the real you, your conscience. , "He who rules his spirit," so counsels the proverbs (proverbs 16:32) , "is better than the one who takes the city." Prophet Mohammed said: "The strongest person is not the best wrestler, but it is he who controls his anger!"

Dale Carnegie wrote elegantly thus: According to the book of Genesis the creator gave man dominion over the whole wide earth. A mighty present (huh)? But I am not interested in any such super royal prerogatives. All I desire is dominion over myself —dominion over my thoughts; dominion over fears; dominion over my mind and dominion over my sprit. And the wonderful thing is that I know I can attain this dominion to an astounding degree anytime I want to..." Indeed, there is more benefit to self-control aside from conquering dangers of a drink, drugs, or HIV and AIDS. "A diligent person," so quote the proverbs, "A diligent person shall sit with the kings."

Is self control that important? The bible—through the proverbs—teaches us thus the strongest person is not the one who takes the city. Rather it is the person who controls his anger and has his desires in check. Knowing too well that the spirit is indeed willing but the body is weak, the ideal scholar has learnt to tame his inner person or self. He also knows the luxuries of the world cannot end or endure. Isn't the ideal scholar temperate? also, knowing too well that vices are natural like weeds, and that it is in the nature of the beast to be selfish and antisocial, the ideal scholar is a person with mastery—of all things—over oneself. The ideal scholar therefore has great self control. He is a person who is always striving to keep his ego in check. Self-control is a stubborn quality to tame. I know some of you will assume because have self control because you have yes controlled your beer levels or cigarettes. It isn't enough if fail to control yourself when it comes to chastity or fidelity; or even when your greed for money is unfathomable. And what about your self control when yes you control beer and women but have a bad temper like the wrath of the ancient God s? If you can't control your anger or tribal and racial smugness against others, you are not a self restrained—you have no self control! Indeed, spiritual integrity "can no longer be proven by drinking orange juice. There is more to self control as it is to true religion.

THE IDEAL SCHOLAR IN THE DIVERSE SOCIETY

Temperate and well balanced person, the ideal scholar is not socially, religiously or intellectually skewed toward any extreme. And this is not a lesson he gathered from any hard subjects. It is not rocket science. It is our day to day reality. And it is not a good guess work by me. No. In their analysis on the Social Foundations of Curriculum Development in their book Curriculum Foundations, Principles and Issues, 3rd Ed., Ornstein and Hunkins rightly conceived that: Never has there been a period in our history when the people within our borders have reflected such a diversity of customs, beliefs, values, languages, religions and social institutions. The current and emerging times require Curricularists…to understand the social foundations and to grasp the social implications of the nature and purposes of education… Schools exist within, not apart from, social contexts…Schools…can alter society and the society can mold the school and its curriculum. We cannot meaningfully consider the development or delivery of the curriculum (or education) without reflecting on the relationship, of schools and society.

And it is possible to completely control your own person. This is a very important ideal because if you cannot control your own person, then I have bad news for you: You will never be able to control anything else and instead you will be controlled by persons and circumstances around you; you will never amount to anything worthwhile and you will never be whole as a person. Indeed the World Health Organization defines health as: "not merely the absence of disease or infirmity but (instead and indeed) a state of complete physical, mental, and social well-being!" Therefore to be complete, to walk toward perfection, a person must learn to control himself, which must begin from the mind. And if it is so, this is something you can build through conscious effort concentrating on the morrow than on the immediate romanticism. This is one of the greatest mistakes the conventional education does.

Knowing too well that we are created naturally as diverse persons, beginning with being created men and women, and that even if we are born the same way, our temperament and therefore our characters are shaped by the environment we face, and that we become black or white men or women not by our choices, the ideal scholar is rational—and tolerant therefore. He recognizes the global reality or nature of the diversity of the world today. He will therefore accept all people and traditions as equals in the sight of men for that is what pleased God. For if God—for instance as once questioned Mwalimu Nyerere—didn't love the Chinese (their looks, traditions, their language, religion, communism and their eyes) why would he create them in their great quantity in the first place? But He created them in big numbers than any other people and let them and their traditions, their language, religion, communism and their eyes or brains thrive.

Very recently, watching European football in a public outfit, the author was taken aback at how we really are influenced by what we are accustomed to. Living in a community with majority of people with not so much long or pointed kind of nose, and therefore generally accepted as universal, one spectator shouted denouncing Ibrahimovic's, as too long and pointed! I have since failed to discern whether Ibrahimovic's nose was too pointed or this young man's was too toooo blunt! He couldn't make good judgment based only on his neighborhood. The Indians in these East African countries tend not to marry from amongst the native Africans considering themselves, the Indians, as superior to the locals regardless of the caste system back home. What about the indigenous people? Rarely do they seek a hand in marriage from amongst the Indians. Why? Whether it is because they abhor the reek most Indians exude, or the skin color I have no way of knowing. Again, whether that reek is in-born amongst the oriental population, or cultural; i.e. from the perfume they wear, or the meals they eat, I have no clue!

Mind you I haven't written the preceding statement to oblige you to wed someone you don't love—or care about! No! A big NO! I am only saying wed anyone you love regardless of her religion or the color of his or her skin. Napoleon Hill raised something that is worth more thought and reflection. The Chinaman looks at your eyes, if you are African, Arab or European among others, as if they, I mean your eyes, are off slant. But what do we say about theirs? It is not different from the white men who look down at blacks as unacceptably too dark skinned whereas blacks see the whites as too pale with skins which not fully formed. In fact when the first white men set foot in Africa and in Bunyoro to be particular the Africans concluded they had or first time come in contact with the ghosts and the ghosts really existed and no more a myth. When Gulliver landed in Lilliput, the people of the land wondered at how giant a five ten inch tall Gulliver was. But he became dwarf in another community.

From the above assertions, you realize that to true ideal scholars, tribes or races and color are outward values that don't count much anymore. Globalization and ICT have blown the lid off the value the traditional agrarian or even medieval human placed on tribal, religious, racial significance or importance of color of the skin and we may never need to replace it—I mean that lid. As we of different tribes, races, faiths and backgrounds interact almost on the daily basis, we learn from one another, and in due course appreciate the good things there are among one another's communities and no wonder they finally intermarry. We then become one people. They say the world is a village today. It is true. But it is even going to be truer in the future. In the future the world is going to be just like a household—an extended family.

A Chinaman works and lives deep in Bushubi in Ngara Tanzania building the roads and bridges intending to further connect Tanzania, Rwanda Burundi and Congo; as an American runs a factory in China. a Chagaman from Tanzania, a Kikuyu man from Westland in Kenya or a Bangladeshi from not only Dhaka, the capital city, but also one from the most remote towns like Chittagong or smaller village in Gobindaganj; or a man from Kathmandu Nepal pops on and off to Guangzhou, China for the merchandize he sells in Lusaka Zambia—places where he has homes—the people among whom his son or daughter takes into marriage. To prove me right or wrong just study the politics of the US and you may be astonished to learn that not only their president they voted by sweeping majority in an open ballot, granting him four more years in the White House is a son of an East African who just went for scholarship in the US, but also and of more significance, those people who considered themselves the majority and ideal Americans are now the minority. It could turn out to be the same in your country during your lifetime! With an interracial background—races as they existed in this continent, and married to a beautiful wife who hails from a Mohammedan family while I am myself Catholic, I feel proud to sing *that resounding line from Walt Whitman's "Song of Myself": "I am large, I contain multitudes."*

Taking about being rational and tolerant, the ideal scholar is not simply gender tolerant but a believer in the sense of gender balance. This is so serious a matter that we cannot simply brush, and just let it go—just like that. That's why we shall find some space to broaden our discussion on the matter.

As for the love affair, the act of love, the ideal scholar will approach such an affair as the means to augment mutual interests: affection, love, social and economic interests, reproductive and moral reason etc; and he or she will approach it with discipline, and in great moderation. How astounding that most animals respond to the call of sex in harmony with the laws of nature and moderation whereas the male human, aside from their opposite number engaged in commercial sex, seems to declare an open season to this most important but delicate matter. We cannot be more primitive than are beasts, can we? "A sex madman is not essentially different from a dope madman," concluded Napoleon Hill.

To emphasize the foregoing point, I couldn't but consult what a person who identified himself as Akanyihayo Amon Chopper posted on the facebook: WORDS FROM A FATHER TO A SON ABOUT MARRIAGE (from which this author developed the following golden advice about gender relationships).

My son, a woman could be a good wife to you…, could be a good mother to your children; but if you've found a woman like a mother to you, your children and your family, please don't let her go. Son, don't confine the position of your wife to the kitchen, where did you get that from? Even in our days, we had farm-lands where they worked every morning . . . that was our office. Son, if you want to have a long life, let your wife be in-charge of your salary... Son, don't ever beat your woman... Son, under the cocoa tree that I did meet your mother, could be your eateries and restaurants of nowadays, but remember, the closest thing we did there was to embrace each other... Son, when I threw little stones or whistled at the window of your mother's father's house, to call her out, it was not for sex, it was because I missed her so much. Son, don't ever compare your wife with any other woman, there are ways she's enduring you too and has she ever compared you to any man?

Son, I didn't send your sisters to school because I was foolish like many to think a female child won't extend my family name, please don't make that mistake, the kind of female achievers I see nowadays have made the male-gender an ordinary tag. Son, your mother has once locked up the cloth I was wearing and almost tore it because she was angry. I did not raise my hand to beat her because of a day like this, so that I can be proud to tell you that I never for once beat your mother. Son, remember I bought your mother's first sewing machine for her, help your wife achieve her dreams just as you're pursuing yours. Son, don't stop taking care of me and your mother, so that you too may expect the same.

LAST WORD

Before we turn the page, here is the verity about love. A man who is loved and is certain of the love of his wife, works miracles not only within the family domain, but also beyond—and the converse cannot be truer! To love and consummate love is, yes, to the good of both, but whether for of biological reasons, or for the social or gender settings, the female folks stand to gain more by showering love to their partners. I would like to emphasize that—with all greatness we talk about the female folks, regardless of all the reasons on earth why we should praise the female folks, no matter how much we revere female folks being our mothers, sisters, and daughters besides being our spouses, our better halves; despite the indispensability we all confess to, concerning the female folks—the female folks should never be indifferent concerning the true nature of the male folks, and remember I am addressing the married couples, much as I prepare the future couples, if they should effectively discharge their obligations, and maintain their reverence.

And as such, the foregoing assertion lays emphasis on being realistic when it comes to the biological and cultural nature of the male folks, much as the male folks should do the same. To give an example, recently BBC reported about a project NASA is working on. They want to send off a group of men and women to the Mars—to see if life could thrive there. Besides, the envoys wouldn't return on earth for good once the space craft arrives there, for it cannot complete the back trip in their lifetime. Now the BBC reporter visited a couple from which one candidate was shortlisted. Though I have no way of knowing whether they were Catholics, or not, she was married–and that's my point. During the interview, her husband pledged his commitment to support her, to make her dream come true—the dream to tour the spaces. It was an ambition filled with love and good intentions. But that's what triggered the reporter to ask something that intrigued the author. Would she, or wouldn't she, remain loyal to her husband while in the spaces? And what about her husband's fidelity during his wife's lifetime adventure in the sky, given the circumstances? What is your take on this matter? In the end, considering gender differences not as a liability but an asset to complement one another, the ideal scholar recognizes what the bible says, and the same is the oath of the marriage institution: "What God has joined, no man should set asunder!!" This—I mean the equation of gender and marriage—demands more thought and reflection.

36. JUSTICE TO GENDER DIFFERENCES

"The most important thing that a father can do for his children is to love their mother." — Bill FitzPatrick, in Action Principles

The ideal scholar recognizes the equity of the sexes. What does this mean? Recognizing that, generally speaking, no sex is better than another, the ideal scholar knows that every person of every sex or gender has the right to life, liberty and pursuit for happiness. He also recognizes that people have an alienable right to have personal freedoms and individual expression. That's why he recognizes that no one sex should be given special privileges over another. That's why the ideal scholar is not simply gender tolerant, but a believer in the sense of gender balance. He considers female folks, not as tools for personal male desires, or material gains, but as indispensable life's partner whether they be daughters, or spouses. He recognizes that every person, man or woman has the right to life, liberty and pursuit for happiness. Yet equity doesn't mean as individuals we don't have differences in terms of our talents, race, and religion or sex nonetheless.

According to dictionary.cambridge.org, the term *Equity* simply means: *When everyone is treated fairly and equally: a society based on equity and social justice.* According to Ornstein and Hunkins: *Equity doesn't mean that all will be the same or attain the same...success will depend largely on the energies of the individual...Individuals have the right and chance to experience that which is necessary and meaningful to them for their benefit and the good of the nation at large...Equity for most Americans refers to the right to be able to participate in the American dream not to live out the dream to a limited conformity (Curriculum Foundations, Principles and Issues 3rd Ed.).*

Recall that we began by saying that the ideal scholar recognizes that he has individual responsibility not only to himself but to the people around him and community as a whole. That's why the ideal scholar therefore reveres the different strengths one gender has over the other and therefore deeply appreciates mutual and harmonious coexistence in the spirit of advancing complementarity. Writing for The Citizen in his corner, *"A Chat from London"*, Fred Macha in an article *"We Should All Speak out against Female Genital Mutilation,"* quotes Professor Doctor Ruth Meena in her essay *"Women and Sustainable Development"* in which she argues that women in Africa contribute 80 percent of labor while only owning ten percent of land. Fred Macha goes on to radiantly write what Dr. Meena writes paraphrasing Mwalimu Nyerere: *"It would be appropriate to ask our farmers especially men how many hours a week or how many weeks in a year they work. The truth is that women in the villages work very hard 12 to 15 hours in a day. They work even on Sundays and public holidays. Women in the villages work harder than everyone in Tanzania. But men in the villages are on a leave for half of their lives."* Why must we discuss this matter? Is it important?

As I write about this ideal, I am absolutely certain there is a reader out there who probably is suggesting that this ideal could be skipped. I refuse to agree with such an idea. And here is why—and you will be shocked by the news that was reported on The Daily Post by Seun Opejobi on May 21, 2015 under the title: *Angry Man Strangles Day-Old Baby To Death For Being Born Girl.* The report reads thus: "A certain Bello Rabiu has been dragged before a Senior Magistrate's Court in Katsina for allegedly killing his new-born baby girl. Bello, 35, was said to have strangled the new baby to death and buried her in his compound after she was given birth to by his wife, Fatima Bello. According to report, the accused had eagerly waited for a male child but his expectation was dashed when after delivery, the baby turned out to be a female *(*http://dailypost.ng/2015/05/21/angry-man-strangles-day-old-baby-to-death-for-being-born-girl./)."

Moreover, only recently, BBC reported the highest level of gender ignorance in India where a young woman, Gunja Devi, was kept in custody in small room for three years only to be rescued by police. And not only that but also she was denied contact with her daughter who was then three years old. Her crime? She hadn't finished paying the dowry and number two she had given birth to a baby girl. According to the website m.bbc.com/news/world-asia-india-29127425, her torture escalated when she gave birth to a girl in a culture where boys are valued. It was reported that thousands of women are killed each year in India due to dowry-related disputes. Isn't this objectification of women? Does this happen a million miles away from us? Oh no! Just look around you! The foregoing challenge reminds the author of the event that took place many years back when his father took into marriage a Mnyankole woman adding to the tally of the author's step mothers, themselves from a diversity of tribes and races across East Africa. Nkhuhe was a very rich and powerful man. For the send off he slaughtered two bulls.

At the send-off party, they sang to the effect in Lunyankole thus—which is my message: "Iwe Mwana Joy, Iwe Mwana Joy, Iwe Mwana Joy, washangwa otali waitu…iroko ojende, iroko ojende, iroko ojende, washangwa otali waitu. Iroko ojende iroko ojende, iroko ojende nyamwishichi tabha mwojho," literally meaning: "You poor Joyce; oh you poor Joyce; you don't belong here. Go, go, go, go! …You don't belong here with us. Go your way; a girl is never a boy!" Who sang the song? The bride's brothers, sisters, her parents and the whole village sang along, including the village authorities' men.

Women in traditional society were considered to be simply useless—simply put! What astonishes the author is that we choose what to see and as a result we stop thinking about indispensability of the other gender or sex. And this isn't a problem only womenfolk face in Tanzania alone. In Saudi women cannot drive a car. They cannot sell in shops. They cannot travel alone. They can never sit on the throne as female king conveniently known as queen. But that is not all. They cannot vote. Caught in the act in Arabia and some societies in Africa an act which a woman can never commit alone she is stoned to death while not only a man is set free but he is also praised for his manly hyper libido and power of persuasion! In the neighborhood from where I'm writing this chapter women are mutilated before the age of marriage to reduce their sexual desires so that they can serve one master called husband who does everything in his power to heighten his sexual libido in order to meet his obligation for a school of wives he is entitled to marry. And this is a major factor among males in that part of the country Tarime! Many Indians shops and businesses are named such as Singh And Sons Co. Limited. When I read one such a registered business name I thought of opening one myself and call it Kambarangwe and Daughters Company limited. But let us now shift our focus. What do men gain by domesticating others?

Well, I don't want answers for now, for I know such gains are short lived. It is to your advantage to favor women as for now and vice versa for the foreseeable future (please make reference to What Makes People Rich and Nations Powerful on gender). Many people know that the old said to every successful person there's a strong woman but they don't know why. The above is a direct connotation and connection. There's also an indirect relationship. Women tend to influence a man to find within himself to be big and great and more powerful. That's is how it was since of old when men hunted down a big game or wrestled the invincible wrestlers and triumphed. They were ready to risk lives only to make the secret master happy. Many societies today earn more income from informal sector than formal. It has been recognized that over 75% of the sector is led by women! By promoting women in terms of education and inheritance we promote morale for them to work even harder and better. With their numbers, if empowered academically and financially, women form the major internal market. Indeed they are a new source of skilled labor and entrepreneurs and therefore a new source of growth!

In the same-same way, women ought to know both sexes have strength and weaknesses of their own. Today we recognize the fall of morale for women to care for their traditional roles in a family from home chores to children. They truly have all reasons to explain this mishap, but they shouldn't forget the influence they have on their children or even their husbands and the future of the family, the country and humanity as a whole. The love in a family, sense of belonging and compassion, harmony in a household, besides reproduction among others are impossible without the cooperation of especially the woman though the wellbeing of the members in a family depend on each other. Hillary Clinton said human and women rights are one and same thing. Why? One sex is part and parcel of the other.

We cannot do virtually anything without mutual harmony and union of thought and deed. Well it is true that some men—and lately and on an alarming scale women—bully their spouses, or children. But such insensitive actions are like homing pigeons. They always come back home, and in the end will kick you back. Afterall we have said before that there's neither a superior sex, nor tribe, even when our parents are different. For afterall we are made up of 48 chromosomes—chromosomes which you and I know that your, and my, father and mother contributed apiece in the making of you or me. Probably you haven't asked yourself why children resemble fathers so often than not! Men use this to justify male dominion over women but that reasoning is counterfeit. Bogus? Sham! I'm not the old prophets for I should have written thus: God told me he did this purposely to illustrate that men have part in creation of this child, for otherwise, how could a man prove he had a child? A woman doesn't need proof. And no wonder Prince Charles is an heir to the throne in the UK while his ancestors came from Greece. And it's no secret anymore that the Brits are intelligent. They have once more helped to take a lead in putting such sexist notion to bed, notions that in this day and era are not only irrelevant but also troubling and self-defeating. Once more they have passed a bill ordering the first born of the king or queen to be the right heir to the throne whether it is a baby boy or girl, following Prince William—the third in line—and his wife Searches Related to Prince William's wife, Duchess of Cambridge, Catherine's expectation of their first child!

Asked so (what's) your final message to women from 18 to 80. Sharuhk Khan a great Indian actor responded that: *I think you are the best thing God has made. Irrespective of what anyone else says about you or tries to demean you just remember this and I truly believe this. God has created the women in His own image. I believe women are the gentlest intelligent and sweet creature ever created.* Remember there's no life without women. Let me introduce Mpogazi. He was a mere demeaned shorter gentleman who had married a very tall woman. Dwarfed he wasn't respected among male dominated Karagwe men. But unlike Ntimba he had a sense of justice for the other sex. He knew he was scorned because he was too lenient to his wife and often times he happy accepted orders from his gigantic wife yet he once declared courageously and openly amidst insults that "Bitali Byukubeha Umwana nu wu mukazi." That is without telling lies or bullying a child belongs to his or her mother. Finally women have been trained for many generations to be givers and not getters. This alone suggests they fit far better for any position than men from politics to business or simply as employees. The changes in the world today have passed through the era of go getters and probably we will never return to that era once and for all.

Gone are the days when companies hired people who went out to get for the companies. With customer supremacy and globalization, ICT and customer awareness and attention to trends and indeed the fact that products and services are readily available anywhere and time you want it besides attention to quality and customer services along the door to door marketing, today companies need a person who is ready to give more of himself than he takes out of it. This is a kind of people the companies seek today are called go-givers, not go-getters.

That's a quality that is purely a female trait. Yes, we male folks can learn to do and be so, but it is innate to women. Male folks are never generous unless they have an agenda whereas for typical female individual, it is natural to give for the sake of giving. Also women are a more orderly than their opposite number. In consideration with many households, family income is in safer in the hands of a woman, while it weeps fearing to be butchered in the evil hands of men. May be we need more youths and women in the parliament or leadership than are men today for afterall they are majority and more active in matters of the family and therefore growth and development, matters that touch real life, and them, than it is to adult men now choking all such positions of power. I've never seen a woman MP sleep between sessions dosing off the liquid lunch in the parliament. For a skeptic, let him recall if it wasn't it the male MPs who were caught by CCTV in India watching porno between parliamentary sessions?

So borrowing it from Shaggy, this chapter, "This one goes out to all women, my strong women, among them my granny Theresa Mkaka, my mother, my wife, my sisters, my good daughters and all women folk whose grace and strength make the world go round!" And my admiration for womenfolk cannot be more pronounced. That's why Shaggy sang in the praise of a woman wondering how so amazing this world was made. He saw the gift of life and the generosity of the world, and so comparing it with how a woman gives life and how she will protect you like a child enduring constant pain, and refused to accept that GOD could be otherwise. Indeed, "Just picture if you could what life would be," he sang concluding that it would be worse "GOD, bless the ground beneath her feet." And bless "The strength of a woman!"

Here is another revelation about sacredness of women. A man approached the Holy Prophet and asked him who was the person he was supposed to honor than any other on the earth. Give it a thought. Do you think it was the kings or any mighty commanders of the great armies? No! It wasn't even the prophet of God himself! In his own words the prophet said in response: "(Honor) Your Mother." The man asked the second time. Who the next should I honor? Prophet Muhammad in answer said: "Your Mother." Alright: the man said. Then who is the next I'm supposed to honor most. The prophet repeated: "Your Mother." This didn't add up in the man's mind. He didn't understand it and decided to ask for the last time. "Who then is the next person to whom I should bestow honor?" This time a different answer was forthcoming. You guess who the next person was! Do you know who then the next person was? Yes you are right. "Your Father." These aren't my words. It was reported by Abu Huraira and here in his own words he said that a person came to God's Messenger and said: Who among the people is most deserving of a fine treatment from my hand? He said: Your mother. He again said: Then who (is the next one)? He said: Again it is your mother (who deserves the best treatment from you). He said: Then who (is the next one)? He (the Holy Prophet) said: Again, it is your mother. He (again) said: Then who? Thereupon he said: Then it is your father. Indeed, Bill FitzPatrick was right: "The most important thing that a father can do for his children is to love their mother."

Recognize that I have gone to a great deal of trouble to trace the strength of women, not because men are weak? No! Our society is still narrow-minded and unfair to female members of our society. Yes, women still have a mountain of work to do to make it happen, for it is the female folks that should begin to reject cheap mindset or favors. They are the ones who should be rejecting such typical less stress inducing cheap cadres of positions traditionally filled by female folks, disgraceful vocations, nonetheless which they fill astonishing ubiquity: cleaners, waitresses, customer care agents, airhostesses, front desk attendants, nurses, copy typists—among others—as natural to females. Marketing is also slowly giving way, becoming a typical average-female profession. On the other hand, super females or he-females, call it anything, have begun turning down nursing, call centers and anything average such as secretarial job descriptions etc., turning instead to engineering, rocket science, geology, economics or even serious national and international politics.

And mind you! This doesn't mean that other vocations are simply rejects or not required in the society? No! But these female heroes of mine have begun to exercise their birth right as ordained to them from the Most High, the rights to freedom to choose, whether that is a vocation, position at work, a station in life—or even a spouse. But as well female folks should stop complaining but instead stand on their two feet and champion the struggle for their rights i.e. rights for women and girls. They should as well start taking charge in planning and executing their responsibilities to the male folks and the society as a whole if the rest of the society must rally behind, or even beside them. The (US) Education for all American Youth report put emphasis on: *"Respect for other person's insights into ethical values and principles and the ability to live and work cooperatively with others."*

Finally, is all this chat some kind of humanistic conversation intending to display civility, or is it some form of politically motivated pap? Oh, no! Far from it! Having been privileged to be a father of three wonderful daughters, and I couldn't ask for a different gift, (of course God, also, blessed the author and Nafro with two sons, and yes we could have more of the other but didn't because of choice and not out of want), I mean what I say! Besides, I have a mother and sisters and nieces I empathize with. In the author's family are five female folks, and two men: my wife, three of our daughters and a house keeper, aside from the influence of the author's mother and his mother in law against the author and his son Prince Ruhinda. It is five—or seven—not the two who run the show! Because of numbers? Several few years back when the author began working and was still single, he stayed with four of his brothers and one sister—and all of them were students. Who do you think ran the show? Yes the author was the bread winner; yes the men had the advantage of numbers, but it was Vicky who ran the show. And she was younger to everyone except one. "The revolution and women's liberation go together," aptly observed Thomas Sankara. "We do not talk of women's emancipation as an act of charity or out of a surge of human compassion. It is a basic necessity for the revolution to triumph. Women," he continued, "Women hold up the other half of the sky!"

37. THE IDEAL SCHOLAR AND ECOSYSTEM

"A true conservationist is a man who knows that the world is not given by his fathers, but borrowed from his children." —John James Audubon

The ideal scholar is a friend to the environment and cares for animals and vegetation. He is in love with nature not only as duty vested upon him in the creation, but because he appreciates the beauty of nature. And that's not all. He also recognizes the ethical right of the animals and vegetations to independent life beside collective responsibility and duty to protect nature i.e. animals and vegetations and therefore soil and air as part of ecosystem, to which his or her life depends. Yet statements like these alone aren't good enough. We must call for action. Protection of environment should transcend our everyday's breathing life.

I've a novel before me as I write, and on the first page as you open the book, the publishers demand all future publishers and printers to operate in an ecosystem friendly environment. Gopsons Paper limited of India had to include a statement of greater concern for environment and I can read it from here as I write. It reads thus; "Papers used by Random House are natural recyclable products. That was great but not all. Just see the next comment. It wasn't just enough to give instructions. This instruction must be specific. Gopson had to add that the natural recyclable material must be from wood grown in sustainable forests. (Then) The manufacturing processes (should) conform to the environmental regulations of the country of origin." And that's the States! Vegetations, insects and even microbes—which include microorganism, bacteria and germs—are indeed the sustainers of life. They manufacture oxygen we inhale without which we die. How? You ask? This is how. To answer you! These microbes are in fact engineers of oxygen we inhale. Whatever we eat comes either directly from the green vegetables nuts or peas or from meat of animals feeding on grass. Chlorophyll! Grass cannot grow without insects and microbes which chew compost itself a product of grass again into fertile soils.

By now I imagine you are beaming saying, "Oh I see!" You see that vegetation cannot grow in deserts or on rocks except those of Kitonga in southern Tanzania. It is the microbes that sustain environment and growth of vegetation and of animals we eat therefore. They are the bearers of oxygen therefore because plants are ones which emit this life giving gas without which we die. They are bearers of beef and of chicken we crave. How? Chicken eat insects and inhale oxygen to grow fat before we cut off their heads and pluck off their feathers and roast them mixed with some binjal, onion, tomatoes etc themselves vegetations dependent on microbes for a nice dish which is already watering your mouth as you read. So you see! Microbes are indeed the bearers of our lives. You and I have got to love them. Love all around us. You shouldn't be ashamed of it. I'm not! In fact I'm a lover of environment. If there's any strong reason why I wouldn't regret to be appointed head of this state, the environment; the trees, the peacocks, the surrounding untouched piece of forest amid the tall story Magogoni white house apart from its ubiquitous wide windows and a huge extensive balcony at the head of my reason—that would make my life that of a picnic every day. Then I would work hard to make sure I win five more years; but who has ever failed to run for both terms in the country? I would then go on to have a ten years term of sheer leisure—one close to a heaven's own time off. I would also indulge in some reading. I would surround myself with nice books under shades of big mahogany trees I would add to the tally, and I would even dine surrounded by peacocks!

Adapted from his commencement address to the graduating class of 1990 at Arkansas College, following the human negligence of environmental education, David Orr analyzed the handicap in our education thus:" First, all education is environmental education. By what is included or excluded we teach students that they are part of or apart from the natural world. To teach economics, for example, without reference to the laws of thermodynamics or those of ecology is to teach a fundamentally important ecological lesson: that physics and ecology have nothing to do with the economy. That just happens to be dead wrong. The same is true throughout the entire curriculum… For example, we routinely produce economists who lack the most rudimentary knowledge of ecology. This explains why our national accounting systems do not subtract the costs of biotic impoverishment, soil erosion, poisons in the air or water, and resource depletion from gross national product. We add the price of the sale of a bushel of wheat to GNP while forgetting to subtract the three bushels of topsoil lost in its production. As a result of incomplete education, we've fooled ourselves into thinking that we are much richer than we are.

"If today is a typical day on planet Earth, we will lose 116 square miles of rainforest, or about an acre a second. We will lose another 72 square miles to encroaching deserts, as a result of human mismanagement and overpopulation. We will lose 40 to 100 species, and no one knows whether the number is 40 or 100.

Today the human population will increase by 250,000. And today we will add 2,700 tons of chlorofluorocarbons to the atmosphere and 15 million tons of carbon. Tonight the Earth will be a little hotter, its waters more acidic, and the fabric of life more threadbare. The truth is that many things on which your future health and prosperity depend are in dire jeopardy: climate stability, the resilience and productivity of natural systems, the beauty of the natural world, and biological diversity." The fourth quality in Draper Kauffman's six areas of competence that could comprise a possible future curriculum he identified this quality as understanding humanity's environment (Ornstein and Hunkins 3r Ed.)."

38. DOES THE IDEAL SCHOLAR BELIEVE IN GOD?

"There are Known Knowns, Known Unknowns, and Unkown Unknowns!"
—Donald Rumsfeld

"All I have seen teaches me to trust the Creator for all I have not seen."
— Ralph Waldo Emerson

Before we end this analysis, the analysis about the ideal scholar, here is another key and core value for the ideal scholar. But before we fully launch into it, brace yourself. For we now bring you one of the most controversial qualities of the ideal scholar. Now do we have to, or rather should we, as ideal humans, believe in God? Before we answer that question, here is a related question: does the ideal scholar have to have a religion? Which one? Now back to the belief in God, I believe we should. Yes we may quarrel over his forms and names; We may disagree over whether God is even genderless; or whether he is White, Arab, Indian, Chinese, Cheyenne, Eskimo, or if he is a Jap, Aboriginal, or Black African (again, if he is black, is he Hamitic, Bantu, Nilote?); but apart from these differences and multiplicity of names and perceptions, watching and listening and feeling what we are discussing now, or what we are hiding from one another, the breathing God is alive and kicking. I know there is a host of individuals who believe that because they are educated, they have no time or space for religion—or God, for that matter. Yes, the author is not close-minded as to condemn those who question the form of God, or research in the beginning of existence of man, or the universe.

I have had to raise this matter because of its importance. To such men who dispute over the existence of God, here is their answer. Yes, I agree no one can describe the form, and nature, of God fully. Yes I know we can get hints, mere hints, from the Christians, and partly the other Abrahamic religions, who believe in the scriptures, which say in the book of Genesis thus: "Let us make man in our own likeness," as a hint about the form of God; yes we have another hint from the Gospel where Jesus says: "No one knows the father except one who has descended from the heaven, "But what about the image of the gods of the Hindu? What is the explanation of the Hindu, for instance, people who don't necessarily believe in Abrahamic holy books? Yet, failure to explain something doesn't disqualify its existence. We know many people with apparent credible education who line up logical arguments for the inexistence of God, logical analysis they will cultivate as if to prove they are really men of education. I am not going to argue with such desperate yet *clever* men and women. But simply put, if life I real, that reality that life is itself real, if this doesn't prove the existence of God, it is itself—I mean life—unrealistic. On the other hand, probably these other forces of creation our argumentative men of education seem to profess are some form of God' hands—one way or the other! Who knows? I cannot, frankly, attempt to raise an argument about the features, views, plans and intentions of the Maker without a feeling of helplessness!

But one thing is certain: Religion brings "spiritual values," aptly said Dale Carnegie. With the same sense of helplessness, I will attempt to report what a couple of distinguished men and women said in response to the same argument—views they gave from many years, and lots, of meditation! "I know men who regard religion (belief in God) as something for women, children and preachers. They pride themselves on being He-men," wrote Dale Carnegie in his book How to Stop Worrying and Start Living. "…How surprised they might be…!" Wise men, genuine He-men submit to God. Professor William James of Harvard said, religion gives you and me: "A new zest for life…a larger, richer, more satisfying life."

Yes we may not know every puzzle behind religion or multiplicity of them and the gods, but sensible men will respect religion for what it does toward many sensible full-grown men and women. In words of Dale Carnegie in How to Stop Worrying and Start Living: "It gives me faith, hope and courage. It banishes tensions, fears, and worries. It gives purpose to my life—and direction. It vastly improves my happiness. It gives me abounding health…creates…oasis of peace… (Indeed) conflict between science and religion…no more. Dr. A. A. Brill said: Anyone who is truly religious doesn't develop an autolysis. If religion isn't true then life is meaningless. It is a tragic farce. Today even many psychiatrists are becoming evangelists. As an example…read The Return to Religion by Dr.

Henry C. Link. Professor William James, father of modern psychology wrote to his friend Professor Thomas Davidson saying that...he found himself less and less to get along without God. Truly, as said Francios Bacon 'A little philosophy inclineth man's mind to atheism; but depth in philosophy bringeth men's minds about to religion (How to Stop Worrying and Start Living).'"

Yes part of this quality the ideal scholar wedges, which is the belief in the existence of God, the ideal scholar understands that no one is certain about the form of the Almighty. In conjunction with the foregoing assertion, he recognizes that not Jesus, Moses or Prophet Mohammed, or even Buddha went to the Amazon or made any effort to evangelize the Choctaw or Sioux or Cheyenne Indians in Spokane, Tennessee or Wyoming. He will understand why then these good people may not only recognize, but also—and most importantly—that most may not care one bit about Christianity, Judaism or Hinduism or any other religions.

He will realize that it is neither reasonable, nor any Godly to chop the heads off the Choctaw Indians only because they don't believe the same way as he does! He will question his civility and faith as to why while he judges the Indians, they don't bother about converting him to their traditional religions or even think it is necessary to absorb others into their own way of life. He understands and respect diversity of cultures and religions. If the ideal scholar therefore wishes to evangelize the others, he will do so in a certain way. Among these ways, he will, aside from writing and making available online, or in any other socially agreeable, pro-life ways, he recognizes that through genuine work of charity and his character, he disposes as the reflection of his true faith, or religion. He understands that actions speak louder, and we can best be judged by the harm or blessing we dispose to others—and not through religion!

With this insight in mind, the ideal scholar is an agent of peace. He therefore respects other peoples' cultures, traditions and religions or faith, recognizing that not you or I who chose to be who we are not only in terms of our traditions, cultures and religion, but also the color of the skin, gender or sex and the place of birth. Most of us are who we are not solely because of our personal efforts, but because of where we were born—and to whom. Barack Obama's biography stands in the witness podium testifying for what I have to say right now. Writing About multiplicity of the Gods in his work *A Catalogue of the Gods of the Hindoos* by Alexander Dow thus: "Such is the strange thing about religion throughout ages... There's one thing however to be said in favor of the Hindu doctrine...it teaches the purest morals....Systematically formed on philosophical opinion. Let's therefore, he continued. "Let's therefore no longer imagine half the world is ignorant than the stones which they seem to worship. Rest assured that whatever external ceremonies of religion may be, the self-same infinite Being is the object of universal adoration. (I am going to repeat this statement.) "Rest assured that whatever external ceremonies of religion may be, the self-same infinite Being is the object of universal adoration. The ideal scholar therefore knows no one chose to be who or where he was born which determines race and often religion he will tolerant of the others perception of God and will never coerce others into his faith. But will do so by the character he disposes toward others and his deeds and how he relates to his family, gender and people and the environment around him in general.

I have realized that near death we experience God. My beloved nephew was seriously ill when he taught me this great secret. At only four years of age and in his death bed, the age when we know so little about God or religion—however genius you are, which he was—he saw God I suppose. He was so ill and couldn't speak. But when he opened his eyes for almost the last time and saw his father and family around him wailing sobbing in deep grief, in his Christian faith, he opened up his mouth and spoke what were his last words—words I suppose inspired from visions he saw walking on his last fine line between earth and heaven. He didn't say the words with anger or sorrow. He even almost smiled as he said it. "Kwanini mnalia? Msilie. Msali." Those were his words he spoke in Kiswahili. "Why are you crying," he counseled the elders of his family, "you shouldn't be crying. You should be praying." Those were his last words—words from an infant! Then he closed his eyes as his soul ascended to heaven. Weren't they almost the same words Jesus did speak on the cross when he said: "don't cry for me?"

People who were with Steve Jobs at his death bed reported to have seen his face light up and shouting almost triumphantly: "Oh wow!" three times. You recognize that that kind of expression signifies victory or vision. He repeated those words three times before he let go of his ghost. I was travelling with Fr. Valentine from Biharamulo to Mwanza when suddenly a huge tame animal, it was a cow, crossed the road. Deep in conversation, we didn't see her coming. Father Vally who was behind the wheel is a Roman Catholic priest, who in fact inspired me to write this book. it I from the discussion centering at the disclosure I had made as to why I had resigned from work to write and create training that he loved we had had earlier as I reported in my previous book What Makes People Rich and

Nations Powerful, centering at the quotation I had made that if you haven't find something to die for you are not worthwhile to live

Now in deep conversation we didn't see clearly the animal that suddenly was crossing the road. He knew it was all over. He had to make his last appeal. It is what his subconscious response that coincide with the foregoing witnesses. I am certain he couldn't have thought for himself. It was some truth in him that told him to make an appeal to God when he shouted saying: *Mawe Bikira Maria* viz. Holy Mary, mother of God. In the early 60s, Ray Charles had a near-death experience after the pilot of the plane he was riding in lost visibility. On the way from Louisiana to Oklahoma City, the windshield of the plane become fully covered in ice due to snow and the pilot's failure to put on the windshield defroster. The pilot made a few circles in the air before he was finally able to see through a small part of the windshield and land the plane. Charles had a spiritual interpretation of the event, claiming that "something or someone which instruments cannot detect" was responsible for allowing the small opening in the ice on the windshield that enabled the pilot to land the plane safely.

I've lived enough to see enough: to see how well the works of God work in his own ways. The earth hangs in the sky and the stars too; but they never fall. The planets go round the sun but never collide midair with one another; how huge the sun is and how hot that can be but has never burned us down to ashes. I've seen how when drought is severe He sends water to cool the land and shower fresh water. I've seen how when we get tired He sends night for us to sleep. I've seen a lot of troubles that would mow you or me down but soon He pulls us through. I've grown to know God is in charge and that when He is, we should not worry an iota. If we do, we only have to place our problems upon his laps, there we have the answers—and peace of mind—if we be wise enough.

THE IDEAL SCHOLAR AND RELIGIOUS EXTREMISM
There is also a growing sentiment on faith or religion. Besides afterlife, instead of the original role of religion as a tool for peace, it has now turned out to be a tool to gang up gangs of men and women to kill and claim material wealth, or a curious form of hardheartedness. Lack of this quality is what Napoleon Hill termed as: *Intolerance*. "The person with a 'closed' mind on any subject," said Napoleon Hill in Think and Grow Rich, "seldom gets ahead. Intolerance means that one has stopped acquiring knowledge. The most damaging forms of intolerance," he continued, "are those connected with religion, racial and political differences of opinion," he concluded.

Aside from extreme forms of ubiquitous radicalism on every other religion or denominations as we have recently witnessed in West Africa, Middle East, East Africa, Europe, and the States, cases that claim lives of hundreds of people in the name of a Deity, recently in Sudan and Pakistan, in different occasions, different couples—and their families—respectively sentenced and stoned to death their own daughters. The crime? They had married from different faiths. Francois Rabelais was right: *Half the world doesn't know (or have a sense of) how the other half lives (or feels)*. Ours is a very subjective, irrational world. The ideal scholar recognizes that most of us became Christians, Hindu, Mohammedans, pagans, atheists, spiritists, or Chwezi not in the main because of our prudent choices or decisions, but because of our different histories or background such as the place of origin. Very few Eskimos and Aboriginals belong to the major three Abrahamic religions unlike most of the Middle East and its neighborhood such as the coasts of the rest of regions where indigenous people had trade relations with the Middle East. Dale Carnegie's suggestion is very relevant here.

You and I are who we are, i.e., we are not rattle snakes but humans not because of personal efforts but because our parents were humans and not rattle snakes. In Think and Grow Rich, Napoleon Hill said rightly that, "We foolishly believe that our limitations are the proper measure of limitations. " With these facts in mind, the ideal scholar therefore, is a broadminded tolerant person. He is a person who strives to understand other people, their faiths and customs; and will not try to impose or forcibly convert others to his faith or traditions. Indeed when Apostle Peter tried to fight for Jesus, the Lord commanded him shouting at the top of his voice saying: "Put your sword away." If God wants to fight for you or Himself he can send a powerful regiment of commandos in the form of angels to fight his own cause. "For such as God leaves to stray no one can guide. And as such as God guides there can be none to lead astray (Az-Zumar 39:36-37)."

Indeed if He wants anything done, the ideal scholar understands that He, God, will take matters in his own hands. Indeed the ideal scholar recognizes that God is the disposer of all affairs (Surah An-Nisaa verse 4: 171). You and I can be proud of ourselves as a pious creation of His might if we put trust in His might believing that He is not a weakling that needs your or mine in disposing God's affairs. You be the judge, if to believe otherwise is, if it is not blasphemous itself, then is it not something on the edge of the same? With the faith in the same credo: that God is disposer of all affairs, Padre Pio used to counsel himself and others thus: "Pray, have faith and don't worry!"

In the end, let me admit that, yes, I may not be the ideal human myself, yes I may not be infallible, just like all humans big and small, but I do have my own ideals and virtues—ideals and virtues I follow—ideals and virtues by which I hold myself accountable when they are broken! Ultimately, I love a sense of patience, self control and a cool, tolerant and self restrained heart the faith gives to me. I am frightened to become faithless. A faithless person—one who doesn't believe in some Supreme Powers—is apt to be a monster. A faithless person, an individual who doesn't believe in some form of divinity, or a Deity that is powerful than all armies of the world, is not in sync with the will of the High Powers and is desperately ready to harm others for even a very trivial matter—to whom it matters most. Read the holy books. If you do, you will learn that God Almighty doesn't need any arsenal—well not the arsenal football club? I mean machine guns, Kalashnikovs, atomic bombs, or even bombs, spears, arrows and bows and machetes to fight his wars. It wouldn't indeed astonish the author if a faithless person ate his fellow men alive. Faith is hope. It is belief in the possibility. With this kind of belief, a person tends to be temperate, hopeful, good hearted and generally more prayerful; a person who knows God is in charge—and if anything, He, God Almighty, is invincible and ever most powerful who doesn't, in any way, need your intercession to execute his missions. Are these the words of the author who is only too wordy? Oh no sir! Let's see, let's rationalize together!

When Jesus sent his disciples for a mission, to preach the word of God, he asked them to carry neither the machetes nor any monies. When Simon Peter picked up a sword and cut off the ear of the soldier to whom Judas Iscariot had betrayed his Lord, what did Jesus say and do? These aren't my words. We read in John 18:11 as Jesus commanded Peter saying: "Put your sword away!" He taught his disciple, Peter, that God had a better armory than Peter's, and could pursue His missions with or without Peter, or his sword. That's how he simply grabbled both the sword and the earlobe of the Italian puppet, throwing away the sword, literally disarming his only army visible, handing away the only arsenal at his disposal to the enemy, as he attached the earlobe back to whence it had been chopped off by the stubborn Peter? He taught him that God has a more powerful army than all armies of the enemy and of those who were loyal to Him—the kinds of Peter put together? He literally told him God didn't need him to perfect His works—or His glory.

Didn't he, Jesus, teach that if God wished adoration from indignant humans, He could make the rocks sing his praises? According to the *Hadith*, didn't Abu Dharr say that the Prophet said that He, God, said: "...O My servants, you will not attain harming Me so as to harm Me, and you will not attain benefiting Me so as to benefit Me. O My servants, if the first of you and the last of you, ... were all as pious as the most pious heart of any individual amongst you, then this would not increase My Kingdom an iota. O My servants, if the first of you and the last of you, ... were all as wicked as the most wicked heart of any individual amongst you, ... this would not decrease My Kingdom an iota!"???

Now because faith is such a complicated idea, can we go further into attempting to redefine it? What really is faith, or religion? By faith we mean what Professor William James referred to as: faith is one of the forces by which men live and total absence of it means collapse (Source: How to Stop Worrying and Start Living). Paul Apostle wrote the same thing beautifully thus, *"Now faith is evidence of things hoped for, things not seen." It is the conviction of the things not yet received but certain of receiving them,"* in author's own paraphrased wording. Is it idealistic, unrealistic and therefore immaterial to discuss about faith if it cannot be algebraically proven to be true or false? Let's see. On the contrary, Lincoln said, "To believe in the things you can see and touch is no belief at all; but to believe in the unseen is a triumph and a blessing."

Indeed "Faith," Clarence Smithson said, "is the ability to see the invisible and believe in the incredible and that is what enables believers to receive what the rest think is impossible." It is indeed catastrophic to live without faith. As a young man the author lived in pre-civilized Karagwe and saw Kabwitonzi stick a knife between his brother's ribs, and taking his life away for a small piece of land supposed to be inherited by both during their father's funeral. Why? He alleged Rwamlumba, the deceased, as a person who had killed Homanya, their father, in order to claim the property. Not Kabwitonzi or Rwamlumba could inherit the farm. One died at the hand of another, as the other ran away before he was jailed.

Wishing not to judge anyone, I am proud to live among the men of faith and community—looking at how imposters who call themselves faithful people massacre one another in hundreds and thousands in the name of the Gods and religions whose meaning is no longer under scrutiny anymore. Such people aren't men of faith and their Gods and religions are not any Godly no matter how long they spend their time in the temples of the said

Gods. They are neither ideal humans, nor ideal scholars, nor ideal neighbors. They are neither religious, nor are they faithful to God those who kill one another for property or for disagreement in matters of the religion; or for any other reasons whatsoever no matter how much religious verses they may profess, or how religiously clothed they present themselves—or even how frequent they go on their knees in their prayers everyday invoking God.

I have a friend named Beda Minja. This man, sober or not, successful on the day or not, he will shout at least eleven times a day in Kiswahili: Acha Mungu Aitwe Mungu! That's to say: Let God be! He is God! Realizing the probable meaning, and the importance of faith; and the fact that faith is in the heart and not in the temples of the modern religions—or of those of the past—no matter whether the person in question is in Israel, Middle East or in the Amazon jungles, God is! And that is the deep meaning of faith! So if you or I wished to perfect God, let us always reread these few notes. An intelligent person I know, Amos Benjamin is his name, a person who is a friend of the author's—named his daughter Faith (or thus, Imani, a Swahili word for Faith). Talking about perfection of man through education, Alfred Adler wisely concluded thus: "God who is eternally complete, who directs the stars, who is the master of fates, who elevates man from his lowliness unto Himself, who speaks from the cosmos to every single human soul, is the most brilliant manifestation of the goal of perfection."

39. THE IDEAL SCHOLAR LEADS OTHERS—AND LEADS BY EXAMPLE

"Readership breeds leadership."
—Festo Michael Kambarangwe (in The Ideal Scholar)

"Readers are leaders."
—Willy Jolley

"Leadership and learning are indispensable to each other."
—John F. Kennedy

Having gone through all but one last quality of the ideals, having understood the difference the ideals can make to the individual, his family, his business, schools and the society as a whole, the ideal scholar takes the lead—and therefore a leader of others in inspiring change and meaningful living. Is this ideal important? It is more than that. "The demand for leaders," wrote Napoleon Hill in Think and Grow Rich, "has greatly exceeded the supply. (Yes) some of the old type of leaders will reform and adapt themselves to the new brand of leadership, but generally speaking, the world will have to look for new timber for its leadership," concluded Napoleon Hill hinting that, "this necessity could be your (yes you the immediate reader's) opportunity."

Leadership could mean so many things. It could mean control, headship, management, direction, or guidance, but the ideal scholar, the ideal leader helps only to give direction of where to go from the present station, suggests how and guides throughout the way. He cannot do this well if he cannot first himself know the way or how to get there. Not only that but also he cannot succeed if he cannot win the people to his way of thinking. To win the people to his way of thinking, he must have will and ability to engage others in his ideas and plans—let alone implementation of the said plans. That's why for a leader to succeed, it begins with himself, by which I mean, he must first be a person who successfully provides leadership to oneself before he can lead others. Indeed you cannot lead others if you cannot lead yourself.

To lead others, he knows that he needs first to have a grip on himself. He has to be a person with such qualities as self-control, focus, attention to details, discipline, selflessness, passion for overall transformation in the society and an awareness of what it takes to bring change. Napoleon Hill sums up the qualities of the good leader as including but not limited to: unwavering courage, self-control, a keen sense of justice, definiteness of decision, definiteness of plans, the habit of doing more than paid for, a pleasing personality, sympathy and understanding, mastery of details, willingness to assume full responsibility, and cooperation.

Taking about cooperation, "There are two forms of leadership. Leadership by consent and eldership by force…leadership by force cannot endure," said Napoleon Hill. "The downfall of kings and dictators is so significant…people will not follow forced leadership indefinitely. The world has entered a new era…which very clearly calls for new leadership in business and industry (and in politics). Those who belong to the old school of leadership by force," he continued, "must acquire an understanding of the new brand of leadership (viz mutual cooperation and partnership) or be relegated to the rank and file of the followers. There is no way out for them.

Mwalimu Nyerere said that leadership is showing the way. To show the way is first made possible by knowing the way. For a leader to be effective and efficient, he ought to have and continue gathering knowledge which he uses to govern and improve the direction of the society, the direction that leads to the improvement of the livelihood of the society. In other words leaders have got obligation to enhance and prolong long, happy and meaningful lives of their people—and prosperity of the society.

Here is another quality of an ideal scholar, indeed the ideal leader. A good leader is the one who doesn't pursue leadership motivated by the trappings involved, but to see transform the society through implementation of certain ideals that he believes would guide the society toward the desired destination—with or without him at the helm of power.
If someone else can lead the society, with the assistance of the said ideals, it is fine with him, for he knows too well that the society counts more than the individual. He also knows that he is not indispensable, and therefore as a leader, he attempts so hard to do away with indispensability. The ideal scholar recognizes that it is his character and contribution to the society, beginning with his family and community that the people distinguish him from the herd, and if necessary that he leads, they will take him from the senate and put him in the White House. The recent rise from obscurity to

power when John Magufuli was elected the presidential candidate for CCM in Tanzania helps to put the foregoing assertion into context.

Furthermore, the ideal scholar, the ideal leader, doesn't emphasize title or authority. He knows political powers vested upon him are from people and that they are his employers. The ideal leader is open and transparent, afterall what is he hiding and from whom? Napoleon Hill says, "The doors to the office of the new leader are open to all who wish to enter and his working quarters are free from formality or ostentation." We in Tanzania do not need more illustrations about the foregoing statement beginning with the first president, Mwalimu Nyerere, and now the impression we already have from President Magufuli. To be a good leader one must be selfless. The ideal leader is not afraid to take low profile. "He who has never learned to obey, said Aristotle, "cannot be a good commander." Benjamin Disraeli, the British Premier said: "I must follow the people. Am I not their leader?" Mandela said, "It is better to lead from behind and to put others in front especially when you celebrate victory, when nice things occur. You take the front line when there is danger. Then the people will appreciate your leadership." The ideal leader is confident in himself—and the people. "A leader…is like a shepherd," said Nelson Mandela in his book Long Walk for Freedom. "He stays behind the flock, letting the most nimble go out ahead, whereupon others follow, not realizing that all along they are being directed from behind," analyzed Madiba. The ideal scholar is clean in his body and his heart. "Appearances matter," continued Madiba, "—and remember to smile," he counseled.

Now because I find that the rest of the points in the foregoing qualities of a good leader seem to be plain enough to need no substantiation, except the last one—appearance—and therefore calls for more attention and reflection. And a person who comes to mind is Francis Nanai. The first time I the author met him was Ihungo High School. Francis came to school a couple of weeks after everybody else had joined Form Five. That made him somehow conspicuous. And there was a reason for it. But what's more, which is my message is that when everybody dressed casually, the moment he made his first appearance at school, he wore a jacket. Though true leadership qualities are more on the inside than on the outside, and though Francis has more of an inner glow than what we present right now, yet no sooner had he set foot on the school compound that everybody judged that we finally had found the school chairman. You bet it! A few weeks later he was elected president. The author, himself also elected school secretary general, was privileged to serve and learn from the heaven-sent school chairman.

I suppose our relationship was cordial enough such that three years later after we had graduated from high school and military national service, he visited the future author at the Pepsi factory in Bukoba where I served as sales supervisor at the time. What surprised me is that Mr. Nanai hadn't walked away from his true self. When almost everybody else hanged their hands dressed in American Jeans and branded T-shirts, he put on a nice Italian pair of trousers, a nice long-sleeved white shirt and–watch it–topped it all with two more simple but extras that set him apart: A very fashionable handbag in which he carried all his credentials, and a very, very, very nice necktie. You couldn't doubt that he had positioned himself for a very high station in career and life. Do you want to know where he is today? Managing director or CEO for Mwananchi Communications Limited, a member of the Nation Media Group, a leading media house in this part of the continent succeeding a very, very senior personality, Tido Mhando—onetime BBC Swahili service director.

Because the ideal leader is confident and knows what he wants and goes for it; and because he is confident, in himself and others, he respects others irrespective of their age, size, race, wealth or sex. He speaks when necessary and does a great deal of listening. "A big man," said Mwalimu Nyerere, "A big man doesn't keep shouting that he is big. A clever man doesn't keep shouting that he is clever. It is the small and stupid who constantly reiterate their claims to size and intelligence, hoping to convince themselves if no one else, and of course earning derision in the process."
As we inch to the end of the chapter, here is a counsel not only for those with the intent or aspiration for leadership but also everyone who so aspires to make his ends meet and lead a noble honorable life, and be able to age in dignity. They should realize that leadership is critical especially today with scarcity of true leaders or leadership. Thus the reader must realize that any individual with such details on leadership as we present them here, if that individual aspires for leadership and has will and knowledge, even if he didn't have charisma many natural leaders have had, since charisma is inborn, ad of course not everybody will be a Julius Nyerere, but with these little trick, he will now be emboldened to lead because it is his duty as the ideal scholar, and having been emboldened to serve, and having been provided with tricks of the game, he is now confident to interact with the others and lead. In fact, with self-confidence, something near charisma will arise from deep within and help to bridge his natural handicap.

SELFLESS LEADERSHIP: A CASE STUDY OF ABU BAKR'S SELFLESSNESS

They say a good picture is worth a thousand words. Here, let me briefly paint the picture of a good leader, a selfless leader. Why it important? The author has had to include this touching account because of the ever-increasing selfishness amongst our leaders today—leaders who don't have any other agenda but to amass wealth for themselves and their families. Because of their self-centered agenda, such leaders never step down in order to protect their ill-gotten loot, and in doing so, they cause more mischief to the nation and humanity as a whole. Marshal Mobutu Sesseko has succeeded, quite in style, to make a name for himself, as a typical leader who only thought about himself—and nothing about the people.

Notice also that aside from presenting other qualities of a good leader, this example is exquisite because selflessness is a key leadership quality. Why? A selfless leader will learn—and put to use—the rest of the qualities at will, and therefore augment his standing as a leader of men. Again, though this is something we rarely talk about, or even when we do, we do so only mutantly, most average minds have been swayed to believe that nothing good—but terror—can, or has ever come, from Arabia, and everything good must, and has always, come from the West, especially following the recent terror associated events in the Arab World, forgetting that that land has contributed so much to modern civilization. We in Africa, and Tanzania in particular, even now experience the same negative stereotype—a stigma we need to address.

Good ideas can, and have always, come from anyone else and anywhere else. The problem is not someone's background, but our bigotry, especially among the elite. This is the major source of human self-defeat and therefore the downfall of human civilization. Henry Ford, Thomas A. Edison, Lincoln—you name it—didn't go through college education. Saint Apostle Paul was only a prisoner when his wisdom skyrocketed, and his writing talent manifested. Yet because the latter looks more biblical and hence more ancient evidence, let me present another prisoner—a prisoner who had been locked up for 27 good years, years associated with hard labor. You know his name. Mandela was in prison serving a life sentence with backbreaking labor, and not at the campus of some top university working on his PhD, when his imagination and wisdom went sky-high.

Having reconciled ourselves with the background to the choice of our case study, I can now go on to state that, being judicious, and therefore with no religious sentiments or affiliations, or even conflict of interest with one of the sects among Mohammedans or any other religious denomination, the author pledges to present an unbiased exemplar of the ideal leader, one who has the interests of his people at heart, the quality that today is becoming scarce in supply, day by the day. We in Tanzania present Mwalimu Nyerere's life as an absolute example of such leadership. No doubt about it. But because more has been said, and will still be presented about Mwalimu, the author chose to pick a model from a completely very different angle. That's how we picked Abu Bakr, the first caliph (according to the majority of the Ummah) and an heir to Prophet Mohammed. Here is a narrative we have adapted from the Hadith, which represents the teachings and traditions of the holy prophet (PBUH) and biographies of the first caliph. Here we go…

"The first problem before the people (after the death of the holy prophet) was the election of a new leader. There had to be a head of the State (for otherwise things couldn't work). The need was too urgent to allow delay," the hadith takes us back in time. We learn from the hadith that addressing the problem and the people, though he was senior to the others in many ways before the people as the prophet himself had so manifested, but he didn't elect himself. Mwalimu Nyerere was right. No one should fight or cry for this high office if he be genuine! "If you are a genuine person, leadership is like being laden with a heavy load," Mwalimu confessed. Back to the hadith, during this congregation, one man who was senior by all standards, Abu Bakr took podium and said: "Friends, I think either Omar or Abu Obaida should be the Caliph. Choose one of these two gentlemen," he said as the heads turned. "Hearing this, both Omar and Abu Obaida jumped to their feet, and exclaimed, "O Siddiq, how can that be? How can anyone else fill this office as long as you are among us? You are the top man among the first followers of Prophet Mohammed. You were the companion of the holy Prophet in the Thaur Cave. You led prayers in his place, during his last illness. Prayer is the foremost thing in Islam. With all these qualifications, you are the fittest person to be the successor of the holy Prophet. Hold out your hand that we many pledge loyalty to you," they concluded. "But Abu Bakr did not stretch out his hand. Omar saw that delay might lead to the reopening of the whole question. That could easily create difficulties. So he himself took Abu Bakr's hand and pledged loyalty to him. Others followed his example. Men from all sides rushed to pledge loyalty to the successor of the Prophet. Abu Bakr became Caliph by the general consent of the people…

"On the following day (after he had been elected caliph), Abu Bakr went to the Prophet's mosque. Here people took the general oath of loyalty. When this was over, Abu Bakr mounted the pulpit as the Caliph... Then he spoke to the gathering as follows: "O people, I have become your leader which doesn't (necessarily) translate that I am greater and better than you. If I do good," he continued, "If I do good, help me. If I go wrong, please rescue me...," he said. "You should obey me," he continued, "as long as I obey God and His Messenger. And if I disobey God and His Messenger, then I have no right to your obedience." Like Mwalimu Nyerere, Abu Bakr had several sons and many near relatives. For public offices, he did not choose anyone of them though. He rather chose other people who were fit for public service. He had to nominate his own successor to prevent quarrels. But his choice fell on none of his own relatives. His choice was rather the man whom he honestly believed to be the best among the Companions. All the same, he did not force his choice on the people. He put his proposal before the Companions. When they had agreed to it, he put it before the people. Thus Abu Bakr, the first Caliph, left behind a noble example of selfless service. He lived and worked for his people to the last breath. And for his tireless labors, he sought no worldly reward.

Now after careful thought, he chose to nominate Omar. He put his proposal before the leading Companions. Most of them liked the proposal. But someone said, "Omar is no doubt the best man, but he is rather too strict. To this Abu Bakr replied, "As soon as the burden of Caliphate falls on his shoulders, he will become milder. When all Companions agreed, Abu Bakr called Othman. He dictated to him Omar's nomination. It was read out to the people. It said: "This is the will of Abu Bakr, the Caliph of the Holy Prophet. He is making the will when he is about to leave for the next world. This is the time when even a non-believer begins to believe and even a sinner begins to trust in God. I appoint Omar bin Khattab as your ruler. In appointing him, I have kept your welfare fully in mind. I hope he will be truthful and just. But if he leaves his path and becomes unjust, I know nothing about the unseen; I have only the well-being of people at heart. Everybody is responsible for what he does." The will was read out to the people. After this Abu Bakr went to the top of his house, supported by two men. Addressing the people he said:

"My brethren in-faith, I have not appointed any of my own brothers and relatives as your Caliph. I have appointed a man who is the fittest person among you. Do you approve of him?" he asked. "Of course we do," went up a shout from hundreds of men. Next he called Omar to his bedside and spoke to him thus: "Omar! I have nominated you my successor. My parting advice is that you fear God and work for the well-being of the people. Remember, Omar, the duties you own to God are to be discharged at the proper time. Some of these are to be discharged at night and some during the day time. First things must come first. On the Day of Judgment only those will come out successful whose good deeds are weighty. Those, whose evil deeds out-weigh the good deeds, will have a terrible time. For success and salvation…when you read about the dwellers of Paradise, pray for being one of them Omar, if you follow the path I have chalked out for you, you will find me by your side." When Omar had left, the dying Caliph raised his hands in prayer and said: "Lord! I have taken this step in the best interest of the people. I feared disunion among them, so I took this step, the consequences of which are best known to You. After careful thought I have appointed a man who is the sincerity and the most energetic worker for the well-being of the people. I am at death's door now, so help the people, Lord after I am no more. They are Your servants. Their future is in Your hands. Lord, keep their rules on the right path. Make Omar one of the noblest Caliphs and help the people help him."

CONVENTIONAL LEADERSHIP STYLES AND BEHAVIOR
Though we have talked about leadership in general, we know that almost every leader has a different way of leading. It is for this reason that we seek to consolidate good qualities from each leadership style. According to Rhea Blanken, if you're leading well, you won't have just one leadership style. You'll mix and match to engage your team and meet your goals. That's why despite making a mention about his eight different leadership styles, namely, Charismatic, Innovative, Command and Control, Laissez-Faire, Pace Setter, Servant, Situational and Transformational leader, we believe there is a strong point in each leadership style that needs to be learnt and adapted to the situation as it comes—albeit setting principles of leadership and the organization right. Again, though we believe we are born with different mixes of talents, including leadership, talents which beat one another amongst different individuals, but Rhea Blanken, was right. In his article: 8 Common Leadership Styles, he says: "There is no such thing as a born leader. Leadership is an acquired attribute that begins early…" Again, situations change, and the leader ought to alter his way of managing situations and the people, if he has to remain on top of things.

Learning from the article 8 Common Leadership Styles above, we believe that when success comes, 20 percent comes from knowledge and 80 percent from behavior. And because we believe leadership is dynamic, we have adapted the leadership behaviors or strengths from each style above to present specific ways in which the leader conducts himself specifically in relation to his role as a leader. Recall that to be successful in his role, one must provide leadership to first himself, and then the others. Having presented how he generally conducts himself as a person, i.e., how a person provides leadership to oneself, i.e., outside the role of providing leadership to others, which can be said to be a summary of the rest of the qualities of the ideal scholar, here are, but not limited to, the behaviors one needs if he has to be an effective and efficient leader of the others.

Therefore the leader: Will influences others through power of personality; Acts energetically, motivating others to move forward; Inspires passion; Puts the team first, but understands that the team is a collection of individuals and hence knows that the attention to the self is important; Grasps the entire situation; respects the standards but is not bound by any of the standards, and therefore goes beyond the usual course of action—when necessary; Can see what is not working and brings new thinking and action into play; Follows the rules—even when not bound by them—and expects others to do the same; Empowers the people but is keen on what is happening even when not directly involved in everything. Alternatively, (he) directs and supports, while empowering and coaching; Keeps his word and trusts others to keep their word; Monitors performance, gives feedback regularly; Links behavior with group's readiness—when necessary; Puts service to others before self-interest; Includes the whole team in decision making; Provides tools or means to get the tools to get the job done; Stays out of limelight, lets team accept credit for results; Sets high performance standards for himself and the group; Epitomizes the behavior sought from others; Expects and helps the team to transform ; Counts on everyone giving their best; Serves as a role model.[172] Finally, a true leader is identified not by the number of people who serve him though? No! But those he serves. "This I know," said Dr. Albert Schweitzer, "Those among you who will be happy are those who have sought and learned to serve."

---

[172] Adapted from http://www.academia.edu/7060161/8_Common_Leadership_Styles

Governing Dynamics

40. THE IDEAL SCHOLAR IS IMPACTFUL; A REAL "HE-MAN" WHO TOUCHES THE LIVES OF THE PEOPLE AND ENVIRONMENT AROUND HIM

"The thief cometh not, but for to steal, and to kill, and to destroy: I am come that they might have life, and that they might have it more abundantly."
—Jesus in John 10:10

The ideal scholar is impactful. Being impactful, he is a he is a person who touches the lives of the others, the people with whom he comes into contact. He does so by vast ways, whether it is to encourage, give hope, teach new ways of thinking, living or doing work, etc. his actions embody the zeal to bring positive transformation. By doing so, this person leaves behind the positive life-changing legacy. A true ideal scholar recognizes that there is more to life than acquiring wealth and the bodily pleasures of life. But before the foregoing conclusion, it is important to insert one important fact about impactful people. While average people crave to live longer lives, but giving life, bringing life out of your existence—is all that counts! The foregoing is nothing other than having modeled your life such that at the time of your departure, you can be sure to have already served your purpose in life. "And in the end," said Lincoln, "in the end it's not years in your life that count. It is life in your years—that matters." This is a critical analysis of a person's life. It is a key milestone in a person's self-censorship.

You must have heard of the heaven and hell. It is rather a curious admission that I believe a close look at the face of a corpse can tell whether his or her soul will rest in peace or not having served or not one's purpose or not. Indeed I can fairly suggest it is easy to know whether a person is a credible candidate to enter heaven or not by looking at his final days and his face at the time of his death. Probably it is same science or connection from which the Roman Catholic Church finds insights into declaring someone a saint or not. Is this is a new science? Have I just introduced something new for the future minds to expound? Nonsense! In his book *What Life Should Mean to You,* Dr. Alder wrote thus: "All that we demand of a human being and the highest prize we can give him is that he should be a good fellow worker, a friend to all other men and a true partner in love and marriage." Probably the best analogy of being impactful is described by R.L Sharpe. "Isn't it strange that indeed princes and kings and clowns that caper in saw dust rings, and common people like you and me are builders for eternity?" This is great and I am going to repeat it, in italics, *"People like you and me are builders for eternity!"* and an important last remark, "Each (one of us) is given a bag of tools, a shapeless mass, a book of rules (like this one you are reading now!), and each must make—ere life is flown—a stumbling block or a stepping stone!"

"The American Scholar" is Ralph Waldo Emerson's work in which he established a new way for America's fledgling society to regard the world. Sixty years after declaring independence, American culture was still heavily influenced by Europe, and Emerson, for possibly the first time in the country's history, provided a visionary philosophical framework for escaping "from under its iron lids" and building a new, distinctly American cultural identity.

In summary, he said: We are all fragments, "as the hand is divided into fingers", of a greater creature, which is mankind itself, "a doctrine ever new and sublime;" An individual may live in either of two states. In one, the busy, "divided" or "degenerate" state, he doesn't "possess himself" but identifies with his occupation or a monotonous action; in the other, "right" state, he is elevated to "Man", at one with all mankind; To achieve this higher state of mind, the modern American scholar must reject old ideas and think for him or herself, to become "*Man Thinking*" rather than "a mere thinker, or still worse, the parrot of other men's thinking", "the victim of society", "the sluggard intellect of this continent"; "The American Scholar" has an obligation, as "Man Thinking", within this "One Man" concept, to see the world clearly, not severely influenced by traditional or historical views, and to broaden his understanding of the world from fresh eyes, to "defer never to the popular cry." The scholar's education consists of three influences: Nature as the most important influence on the mind; The Past manifest in books; Action and its relation to experience; The last, unnumbered part of the text is devoted to Emerson's view on the "Duties" of the American Scholar who has become the "Man Thinking." Oliver Wendell Holmes, Sr. declared this speech to be America's "Intellectual

Declaration of Independence." It is probably in the same sequence of events that Winston Churchill prophesied that the empires of the future would be the empires of the mind. In fact Ornstein and Hunkins quoting Alvin Toffler in his book Poweshifts said that Churchill's prophesy had actually come to pass (Ornstein and Hunkins 1998 p.382).

Here's another fact about being impactful. Impactful people are naturally nice people. They don't do good to flatter or appease people. They do it as personal and moral duty. That's the difference. Here is another fact you should know. Many people recognize that nice people last longer but few know the secret behind this universal law. We cannot accomplish anything without support from other people. I can see you already question the preceding statement. The thing is when we say success or prosperity we mean one attained by sincere long-term plans of course not denying the fact that there are some fortunes along the way. But how can you be lucky seated in your room? When we say success we indeed mean long term success. When we choose as our principle, to always do good we tend to be rewarded threefold and more. That's where they end. No. They imagine some ancient Gods send their holy angels who in turn descend the skies with showers of blessings. Never! God blesses you through other people around you. When you are good to people not so long whereas you are only one person many people you helped come scrambling to give back to you. The purpose in life should be to do good and help elevate other people's lives, not only in terms of quantity but also the quality of life. Jesus himself identified his mission in John 10:10 thus: "I came so that everyone would have life, and have it in full." That is the mission of the ideal scholars.

In his, I must add *magnificent*, book, Seven Habits of Highly Effective People , Stephen Covey summed up the quest to be impactful thus: "I sacrifice: I devote my time, talents and my resources to my mission," where that mission is one in line with John 10:10. The ideal scholar will vow thus: I seek to inspire others, to teach by example that we are all children of one same heavenly loving God and that we all can overcome and prevail; I seek to be impactful; that whatever I do makes a difference in my own life as well as in the lives of the others. As a husband or wife, I make my spouse not only to feel but realize that he or she is the most important person in my life. As a father or mother, I help my children experience progressively greater joy in their lives. As a son or daughter, I seek to learn to be better and seek to frequently be there for support and love. As a big brother or sister, I seek to be responsible and supportive to my parents, my young brothers and sisters. As a creation of God, I seek to make sure God—in his whatsoever form or state—counts on me to keep my covenants and to serve and love others in my family and neighborhood; to fulfill the Golden Rule and the Greatest Commandment—to do unto others as I would have others d unto me.

If you ask me, this is what you should do to reclaim this quality—the quality of being impactful. To my neighbors, I seek to be inspirational and to make God visible through my actions toward myself and others. I seek to be a catalyst and agent of change; seeking to develop high performance and productivity in any work and organizations I work with. As the ideal scholar, a person seeking to touch lives of the others, I seek to learn new things and explore, and apply new ideas in my every day's life. Indeed the right motive in (life) …is (to avail) more life to all and less to none as said Wallace D. Wattles. Truly when you become a leader, you are called to serve. Success in leadership, therefore, cannot be measured by a number of people who serve you, but rather a number of people whom you serve— Pope Francis said recently in Havana Cuba, allegedly addressing the Castros, emphasizing that: "If you can't serve others, then you are useless!"

It is your vow as the ideal scholar that: I commit myself to searching, observing, documenting the knowledge from my own experiences and those of my generation, and to pass them down to the next by reading and writing books. We all know the impact of the gospel or Koran. We know the influence we have from Charles Darwin. We know Emerson and William James for the impact they left to the world from their writing. Shakespeare, Einstein, Newton, William James—among others—impact our lives until as I write. Truly impactful people are noble people. Certainly this is what Pastor Chris in Rhapsody of reality of November 2008 said that: "Responsible people are noble people," says Pastor Chris, "learning to take up responsibility takes you off the sidewalk and reveals greatness and nobility in your character."

I can already, even at this juncture, sense you are already attracted to this personality—the personality of the ideal scholar; aren't you? Why not!

How then can one become really impactful? Pastor Chris in Rhapsody of reality of November 2008 said: "responsible people are noble people," says Pastor Chris, "learning to take up responsibility takes you off the sidewalk and reveals greatness and nobility in your character." It is therefore through good deeds. But that is a long shot without genuinely having good thoughts such as love for others. Impactful people love others. They give their lives to others. And this isn't religious. It is natural to humans. Look at how a mother gives to her child. It is natural to men to give life and love.

Apostle Paul wrote that: If I speak in the languages of men and of the angels, but have no love, I'm a noisy gong...And if I've prophetic powers, and understand all mysteries and all knowledge and if I've all faith to remove Mountains but have no love, I'm nothing. (For) Love is patient and kind; love is not jealousy or boastful; it is not arrogant or rude. Love doesn't insist on its own way; it is not irritable or resentful; it doesn't rejoice in the wrong but rejoices in the right. Love bears all things, believes all things, hopes all things, and bears all things. Love never ends...." (Cor. 13:1-8) It is a circle!

Is it possible to identify such a person? Yes you can identify such a person. You can because actions speak louder. The facts speak for themselves. You don't need certificates to prove someone is educated or impactful. He is a contented and joyous person. He never hungers in his spirit. Why? He lives a responsible and giving life. He isn't demanding or expecting anything from others than from oneself! He is one who brings class and dignity to any undertaking he is engaged in. he is a person who brings excellence to anything he does and brings blessings to all about him such that whatever his hand touches flourishes. He sows confidence among the people around him and brings results of high order to his family or team in a school or at his workplace.

That's why as a leader, teacher, a responsible father or loving mother and a writer, the ideal scholar, a potentially impactful person, is a caring person, one whose work resonates with making the world a better place. He is never a gold digger whose attention is to make money and money alone; and having made the money, all he craves is to have fun and pleasures his money can buy. The impactful person also never complains believing in what Lincoln seems to refer to as; what you do with your life. "And in the end," said Lincoln, "it's not years in your life that count. It is life in your years—that matters." The author has indeed come to the realization that while average people crave to live longer, but instead giving life is all that counts! Probably one of the best analogies of the impactful is described by R.L Sharpe when he said "Isn't it strange that indeed princes and kings and clowns that caper in saw dust rings, and common people like you and me are builders for eternity?" This is great and I am going to repeat it, in italics, *"People like you and me are builders for eternity!"* and an important last remark, "Each (one of us) is given a bag of tools, a shapeless mass, a book of rules (like this one you are reading now!), and each must make—ere life is flown—a stumbling block or a stepping stone!"

Here now is a word of caution. However invaluable these ideals are—all of them—but one ideal alone however top in the list it could be cannot make you an ideal person. You need to study and combine all of them and that's where trouble begins.

Finally, in biblical terms, the ideal scholar or person is one that Mathew chapter five writes about thus: "Blessed are the poor in spirit, for theirs is the kingdom of heaven; blessed are those who mourn for they shall be comforted; blessed are the meek, for they shall inherit the earth; blessed are those who hunger and thirst for righteousness, for they shall be satisfied; blessed are the merciful, for they shall obtain mercy; blessed are those who are persecuted for riteousness'sake, for theirs is the kingdom of heaven; blessed are the peacemakers for they shall be called sons and daughters of God ; blessed are you when people revile you and persecute you and utter all evil against you falsely on my account…rejoice and be glad for your reward is great in heaven…"

Again, here is another way of distinguishing ideal scholar from the ubiquitous cunning schoolmen. Good people, ideal scholars don't hide. They aren't cockroaches. I have observed that cockroaches are pick pockets—and robbers. They don't till or make a living by legal means. They come in the night to steal. If they have to get out in the broad daylight, they will almost like a canon; they will hide on any dark spot. That's not the spirit of the ideal scholar. To this Jesus said, "You are the salt of the earth…you are the light of the world. A city set on a high hill cannot be hid!" And so far why hide if you are that clean? Even General Amin knew this. He once warned his ministers saying, "If I see a person who is not confident I immediately know he is hiding something." Heineken beer knew this secret too. When they launched a see-through transparent bottle, they bragged about it big time, saying: "we hide nothing!"

This analysis looks more biblical, more religious, I must admit! So let's take some more humanistic definitions as defined by other individuals in more secular lines of attack. In her wonderful novel The Courtship, Catherine Coulter describes her ideal man as: being marvelously degenerate and lecherous," she said referring to total commitment from the man of her choice, "in short," she continued, "a man of vast competence and talent...I want a man who can control himself, who can decide what to do and get it done; A man who sets his sight on a goal, and won't give up, until he has attained it...so he doesn't ever find himself in the end or the middle when he should be leading...a man who performs continually at the most rigorously high standards to keep himself in business. I want a man of charm and a bit of wit and endless experience. I want a man who can set a goal and figure out how to gain it, a man who can separate the chaff from the wheat...a fine strategist, (who) can organize details well, and...always perform at high level!"

Ben Carson—though without mentioning the term *Ideal;* said he or she is "as far as I am concerned," wrote Ben Carson in Think Big, "The money and what it buys are insignificant. Achievers are going to have these things anyway! What is important-what I consider success-is what makes contribution to our world...success means putting more into life than we take out. I think success is reaching out and helping other people in specific ways. This can be as simple as a father who inspires his children to make the best of their lives-being a mother who guides her children to faith in God and confidence in themselves—or being faithful to whatever enterprise one undertakes, and doing it with determination to be the best at that task."

Dr. Nicholas Murray Butler said, "They are uneducated those people who only think of themselves. They are hopelessly uneducated (and) they are not educated no matter how instructed they may be!" Mwalimu Nyerere said: "Those who receive this privilege of education have a duty to return the sacrifice which others have made. They are like a man who's been given all the food available in a starving village in order that he might have the strength to bring the supplies back from a distant place. If he takes this food and doesn't bring the help to his brothers," what is he? "He is a traitor!"

Here we are talking about a person who has confidence and faith in himself and the powers that control the universe. It is the positive mindset and trust that keeps the person's heart merry and his face glowing with an ever ready smile knowing that all these possibilities are only a mouse-click-away! You can never persevere in doing something, or accomplish or become anything impactful if you are pessimistic or selfish. Emerson summed it up excellently thus: "To laugh often and love much, to win the respect of intelligent people and affection of children; to earn the approbation of honest people and endure the betrayal of false friends, to appreciate beauty, to find the best in others , to give one's self; to leave the world a little bit better whether by a healthy child, a garden patch or a redeemed social condition, to have played and laughed with enthusiasm and sung with exultation, to know even one life has breathed easier because you have lived—this is to have succeeded!"

But then before we sum up, let us establish how we can identify him. Well, his work, or impact, cannot be hidden. But Jesus said it so nicely that it worth to repeat it here when he set down how to establish if someone is the impactful person. He said: "You are the salt of the earth…you are the light of the world. A city set on a high hill cannot be hid!" Talking to Pele, the footballer the world recognizes as the all time best footballer, president—mark my word, president and not president of a corporation but of once again not a small nation hidden in obscurity of poverty and darkness such as Haiti, but the president of the United States of all countries and who is that? Of all presidents Ronald Regan who had had all fame as a Hollywood star said: "My name is Ronald Regan. I'm the president of the United States of America. But you don't have to introduce yourself because everybody knows who Pele is!"

Probably a definition by what Bill Clinton defined as the American hero describes the ideal scholar, person or employee, or even the ideal citizen— perfectly! He or she is—one Clinton called American hero, whom I call Tanzania hero. "The real American (or Tanzanian) hero of today are citizens who get up early in the morning and have the courage to work hard and play by the rules; the mother who stays up the half extra hour after a long day's work to read her child a story, the rescue worker who digs with his hands in the ruble as the building crumbles about him; the neighbor who lives side by side with people different from himself; the government worker who quietly and efficiently labors to see to it that the programs we depend on are honestly and properly carried out; most of all, a parent who works long years for modest pay and sacrifices so that his or her children can have the education that you have had and the chances you are going to have," said Clinton before he concluded by urging his fellow countrymen thus: "I ask you never to forget that…."

Now as we approach the end of the chapter, here is one important question. It is a question targeting the key quality we have finalized with an ideal that is probably the bearer of the rest i.e. being impactful.

Are there rewards for a selfless and an impactful person anyway? But is this question important? To both questions the answer is YES. There are rewards for a selfless and impactful person all along his path. And yes the question is important because men need reasons before they do or commit themselves to do something. So there are rewards to a selfless impactful person, the true ideal scholar. He will live a really meaningful life. And this is a privilege only to him. Being ideal scholar, being impactful, "makes you an appealing, charismatic person. Students will want to learn from you, bosses to promote you, banks to lend you money and customers to buy your products or services (Bill FitzPatrick, Action Principles). Lao Tse summed it up so beautifully in this version from Dale Carnegie's book How to Win Friends and Influence People thus: "The reason why rivers and seas receive many homage of a hundred mountain streams is that they keep below them. Thus are able to rein over all mountain streams. So the sage (a wise person wishing to be above men putteth himself below them wishing to be before them he putteth himself behind them. Thus though his place be above men they do not feel his weight though his place be above them they don't count it an injury!"

As we end this important chapter, let me underscore one important point. It is not too late to change. Reverend Mtikira (RIP) aptly said in a radio interview in Tanzania recently; it was in 2012 (in Kiswahili): "Katika kutenda mema hakuna kuwahi au kuchelewa mno," he said: "It is never too early or too late to be nice to people." Yet this book, and especially this ideal or quality, is being addressed at the backdrop of the fact that indeed to be born human is a little tricky. We normally think of now. We never think and see beyond our today. That's a problem. When we are obsessed with now, when our obsessions in life don't transcend today, when the morrow isn't in our plans, we are prone to doing evil; to accumulate no matter how we do it. That's why I am concerned that swindlers, rapists, killers, political power thirsty crooks are people who only think small. How indeed man is irrational is truly chillingly sickening! Remember I am talking to a very rare person, the very you! Now that you have read this book, having been instructed into these ideals, what stands tall before us and that ideal state—a state near for instance what the Catholic Church classify as sainthood—is action. We should act—and act now! But the question remains: act upon what? We must act upon ourselves—first and last—because we, in the end, are the ones who influence change, and gain from this transformation—you and me—and our families to the nth generation. That's why now, borrowing a phrase from Bill Clinton, with self-assurance, "I ask you never to forget that...."

41. CAN WE IDENTIFY THE IDEAL SCHOLAR: A REAL HE-MAN?

"What you are stands over you the while and thunders, that I can't hear what you say to the contrary." —Ralph Waldo Emerson

Having read through the foregoing chapters, chapters that endeavored to influence you to seek excellence, knowing that it is to no one's advantages but your own on one hand; and on the other, having guided you through the character or DNA of the ideal scholar or indeed the ideal human, let us now briefly try to analyze if you can, at a glance, identify the ideal scholar or generally the ideal personality as described in this book. Is it, I mean this analysis, important? Yes it is. It is very important analysis if we have to guide and inspire many toward this state—the state of body, mind, and soul we finally establish and identify as the real indicator, or the meaning, of education. It is a very important analysis now that we know engineers, for instance, lawyers, economists, hoteliers, auditors, teachers and politicians as professionals have very little in common apart from the ability to read and write (not the appetite to do so).

So can we really identify, or distinguish the ideal scholar from the herd? Can we identify the ideal scholar? Good news is that yes we can! But before we do that, here is a small question we must answer to: is it important? Is it worth our time and resources? Through this, and the proceeding, chapter on self-examination, you shall be assisted to, in words of Napoleon Hill in his extremely wonderful book, Think and Grow Rich, "measure yourself." He said: "...The analysis," he emphasized, "may lead to discoveries that will give you a new grip on yourself." Now back to the question whether we can identify the ideal scholar, how can we do it? We can do that with the help of vast means. We can do by analyzing for instance how he walks or talks; how he dresses; how successful or blessed, I mean how he brings blessings to others? What is the aura around him viz., how do you personally feel in his company etc? Notice however that though the outward personality tends to reflect the inner person, but it can be deceptive. In the end it is the inner glow that tells more about you or me than the outward person. Let me illustrate.

If you are an adult male reader, you will recall the days when you wanted to impress other people around you—especially the ladies! It is a common habit among the youth even today. Now, whether this is how exactly it ensued or not, I have no way of knowing. But the story goes like this: Wishing to impress a lady, a guy borrowed a car from a friend and off he drove with this lady to a good club. Parking the car at a parking lot some distance from where they chose to sit, he squeezed his wallet and managed a few drinks and snacks. The lady probably had begun having high hopes with her male friend when the true colors of the guy presented themselves to her. How? Because he didn't own a car, and therefore only used to pick public transport, as the sun began falling behind the clouds, after they had had their snacks and drinks, suddenly a public bus stopped by. Hearing the conductor shouting the destination of the bus, and knowing how the traffic got heavy in the evening, he grabbed his lady's hand and dragged her to the bus stage as courtesy or civility. The girl didn't understand it and didn't know what to do until when she had been assisted into the bus. That's when he noticed her lamentation.

"Are you kidding me?" she asked. "Why? It is getting late!" he said. "No!" she lamented. "I mean you, you have a car!" You work on the rest of the plot. They stopped the bus and began retracing the path to the pub, the car keys and the car itself. Though this is simple analogy of the whole exercise, suffice to say here that you truly cannot hide. In fact the author has himself borrowed shoes to impress others during those days. He knows that though such men may put on a big smile, but they agonize deep inside. And everything that happens inside is bound to come out. So if at the beginning of this analysis you were indifferent about the ideal scholar concept or personality, imagining it didn't matter, think again! for it really does. People will spot you no matter how cunning you may be or despite how good you are at camouflage. I know this is true.

Truly you cannot hide forever. Let us recall Mathew 26:69-75. Let's learn from what Mathew wrote when Apostle Peter disowned Jesus (despite warning that he would). Apostle Peter was determined and persistent to remain in the shadow. He didn't want to be associated with Jesus. He feared the consequences that would follow after the Jews had accused Jesus of "treason." In this narrative, Mathew describes how Peter disowned

Jesus, but the people persisted and without doubt told him point blank that he was one of the messiah's men. How did they know? So really you cannot hide. People will know you from how you speak, or how you walk and behave.

Let us see.

"Now Peter was sitting out on the courtyard and a servant girl came to him: "You also were with Jesus of Galilee," she said. But he denied it before them all. "I don't know what you are talking about," he said. Then he went out to the gateway, where another servant girl saw him and said to the people there ,"This fellow was with Jesus of Nazareth." He denied it again with an oath, "I don't know the man!" After a little while those standing there went up to Peter and said, "surely you are one of them; your accent gives you away." Then he began to call down curses and swore to them, "I don't know the man." Immediately the rooster crowed. Then Peter remembered the word Jesus had spoken: Before the rooster crows, you will disown me three times." And he went outside and wept bitterly.

IDENTIFYING THE IDEAL SCHOLAR

Here now comes the same question again. Can we really identify the ideal scholar or graduate? Now how do you identify the ideal man or woman? How do you identify a person who is truly educated and learned? Is it possible to see him from afar and spot him? How do you see him and in spot recognize it? Can we really identify a person's true character? That's a million dollar question. But if we can really crack that one, we can help the nation rise from the dark era of failure of recognizing and rewarding the right people and instead we revere and promote and reward wrong ones as it is often the case today.

If we can crack this puzzle, we can help the administration or government, schools, households and both secular and religious organizations—public and private establishments—to reward and therefore promote the right ideals and character in the society. This chapter or generally this endeavor was important because a nation's character is identified by the ideals it reveres, promotes and rewards. If we want to rise from what Professor Lumumba said in his illustrious speech to the scholars in East Africa—quoting Tony Blair——, he identified this as "a scar in the human conscience," we must begin to identify, promote and reward such ideals. Indeed, to crack this puzzle, was the burden of this chapter.

Now behold a truly learned person—the ideal scholar!"

Can we identify the ideal scholar? Yes we can. Now there are different ways to do that—to distinguish the character of individuals. He or she will be generally identified by his or her character. We can do so by identifying their polar opposite—the failures. That was how we can identify the ideal scholar from his polar opposite. We can as well identify him from his true character. They aren't like failures people who according to Ben Carson who put great efforts into helping others fail. They cajole sneer criticize and argue. But as well they are envious. I mean the failures—those who are not ideal scholars. Alfred Adler did so by the negative things they do. "It is the individual who is not interested in his fellow men," said Alfred Adler in his book *What Life Should Mean to You*, "who has the greatest difficulties in life and provides the greatest injury to others. It is from such individuals that all human failures spring." When in the company of such individuals—which you should avoid with greater gusto—don't listen or heed to what they have to say. They are great demoralizers. They are highly accomplished criticizers. Just keep whatever they say out of your mind knowing that in the near future you are going to be employing them.

The second way and most obvious is about his exterior person. You will identify him from anything about him: how he walks and talks, the fruits of his works, the words coming from his mouth, his blessings, the people he keeps company with etc. A good exemplar is what Mathew 26:69-75 narrates on how Simon Peter denounced Jesus, and his accusers identified him nonetheless. They spotted him as one his disciples from not only how he did speak, but also how he walked and behaved. There is also another way to spot the ideal scholar. We can surely do that by first identifying a failure from winners. People who are truly learned scholars are never losers. They are winners.

How then do you recognize a failure or even a mediocre graduate from a distance? Frankly, majority of our graduates today, fall short of what we can call graduates let alone calling them scholars. Most are people who just attended classes only to complete the academic compulsory term, and then call it quits. Not all of the wrong or non ideal scholars scrape though? Some of them have managed to score the alphas but that's not enough for nonetheless most remain ill-qualified when it comes to meeting day to day challenges of leading decent and meaningful lives let alone leading companies or the people under their charge. They aren't in any way aware of whom they truly are as persons, scholars or graduates. Many don't even know what their responsibilities in life are let alone at their present jobs or even at family level! Such persons can never prosper or enhance value to the company where they work or in the community where they live. They simply don't know why they live. They don't know what education means to life—or to their own persons. They don't know that graduating from a classroom isn't the end of education. They don't possess their own lives. They aren't free. They aren't healthy nor are they wealthy. They aren't any happy therefore and they don't see the meaning of life itself.

Such a loser, a failure, a person who went to school to complete the term and return home, has long since he lost enthusiasm in any meaningful living—with or without a job. He may try to camouflage, but that won't take long before he is unearthed from his hole. He's unshaven and nails protrude. He will often have black patches in the heart and the nails. He may as well have scars from hitting something drunk or scars he picks from fights he picks a night before. He is drunk and smokes a lot. He wakes up when the sun is up! He will wake to agonize at going to work as he fights a hangover and killer headache he cannot cure without another bottle. He often will not feel hungry and may become slim as one sick of HIV or starvation while he spends a lot of money on bad choices. His sexual life is erratic and unpredictable. In his first stage he will—over the longer period of time—turn to beer and bar hookers. But in the next, they will dump him for he will have nothing to offer. He is a rug! Useless! They don't buy beauty or your face. At this stage he takes nothing to bed except a bottle of beer or preferably hard liquor. Reasons? A few glasses of beer quite see you well through the darkest hours! But why dark hours? Instead of beer why not remove the dark moments from your life!

At such a stage, many tell that that's when they started hating women. Why! They were unpredictable—women I mean! But in reality it's because they have nothing to do with a loser! Even them! That they were unpredictable like horses? Beer was better than women as a bad mate for that company of liquor bottle never complained! It kept you warm and never nagged or talked back. It was I want you and here I'm at your service sir! Total submission! This has greater far reaching impact despite the splendid obedient romance of the bottle. He will turn into a wanker if you know what I mean. Self satisfaction sexually isn't all. He tries to run from people. He finds peace in too much of running from public eyes. Quick drinks will be his lunch. He will lunch on a liquid lunch. His sex will be quick ones whenever he has money. Anything in skirt is quite adequate. Barmaids and harlots are a preferred menu.

Ganja and drugs and thievery and going out of law are his next destination. His—if any—is a nagging wife and children complain nonstop before they get used to it and surrender to the streets. His family is a mourning bunch of people. They don't know who they are and have lost their own as well as their father's identity. There's no hope in the family and the father has many of drinking friends. At the height of it all, often his wife tends to follow suit. Luckily females are strong enough and like Mama Julius or Nafro, they will tend to pray and focus on the family. Women—surprisingly—when subjected to this situation, tend to be understanding and provide the best one can. Slowly this act of a good wife may return the wonderer! For after all a wife has got to do her part for inaction will lead to ruination of the whole family. And herself. She afterall had pledged until death do us part! Married myself, I know what I say. I know how this has helped me to become a more refined person. I wrote this piece very sober. I didn't write it for personal gains intending to ask you to vote for me or marry me for I am catholic. But truly, if a damn thing can work in a marriage institution, it can work wonders elsewhere.

And we can spot him or her by how he or she is truly responsible yet loyal to all around him or her. He or she is honest, truthful and trustworthy. He is a man of great impact viz: an impactful person as a leader to the people around him, a teacher to all not by reaching to them but through his way of life. He is also a person who researches and comes out with the problems his people are facing and put on record recommendations from his experiences and lessons for his generation and the next generation. He isn't self cantered. He or she doesn't complain or mend. He never criticizes others but volunteers to bridge the gaps, to heal the wounds. He doesn't look forward to winning favors from others, but instead he expects more from himself and looks upon himself as a tool of service to others. Indeed Wattles were right. "The very best thing you can do for the whole world is to make the most of yourself..." Ben Carson wrote in Think Big thus "the best way to please yourself is to know you have done the best for yourself that you can do. " The ideal person being impactful , he recognizes that he was born for a purpose! Steve Bow was right. "God's gift to you is more talent and ability than you will ever use in one lifetime. Your gift to God is to develop and utilize as much of that talent and ability as you can, in this lifetime."

Recall that we are engaged in identifying the ideal scholar. The ideal scholar—to effectively be impactful—is self reliant. Napoleon Hill in Think and Grow Rich indicates that: "Experience has proven that best educated people are often those known as self made or self educated. It takes more than a college degree to make one a person of education. Any person who is educated is the one who has learned to develop faculties of

his mind that he may acquire excellence in any career or vocation of his choice and improve his life as well as lives of his family and people around him without infringing rights of the others. " In other words, he is a person who brings injury to none while beefing up healing to all. His opposite number's persona is equally evident. He will bring adversities to all, with an increase to none.
But as we approach the climax in this *tete a tete* with the scholars and all worthy people—academics, leaders of men, policy makers, curriculum specialists, parents and the nation as a whole—let respond to some strange readers out there who will be saying, "I have harmed none, even if I have not brought an increase to anyone else, and therefore I am safe I am blameless!" Liar! As Jesus asked his disciples, I am asking you: "What have you done better than the others (the illiterates)?" Let me ask you a small question before we proceed. How do you rank yourself against the proceeding statement? Is it possible? I mean the shorter preceding statement?

Yes it is possible. Innovation for instance. Or invention. If a person can be able to tap wealth from ether as an example of a virgin ground without affecting nature and in doing so create wealth and employment for majority of those now living and million yet unborn, this man is generously educated. How do you use your education? Is it for personal gain or overall benefits? Mwalimu Julius Kambarage Nyerere was right. "Those who receive this privilege of education have a duty to return the sacrifice which others have made. They are like a man who's been given all the food available in a starving village in order that he might have the strength to bring the supplies back from a distant place. If he takes this food and doesn't bring the help to his brothers, he is a (nothing but) traitor!"

Here are more questions you have got to ask yourself in censorship of your life; if you want to know that you lead an ideal living. To start with, how do you define your health? Health is "A state of complete physical, mental, and social well-being, and not merely the absence of disease or infirmity."

How do you endeavor to live your life? Do you plan to put your money in your mouth or between your trousers zipper or in your head and education of your children and welfare of people around you or in some form of income and employment generating property? Notice that you must revise what is education before answering this question. "Those people who only think of themselves" aptly said Dr. Nicholas Murray Butler, longtime president of Columbia University, "are hopelessly uneducated.". In his article on Self-reliance, Emerson defines an educated person through self-reliance. Now compare yourself with what makes you happy in life. Is it personal pleasure, or the difference you may make in lives of others? When I began working as a company representative after my graduation, Pio Bwanakunu once instructed me saying, "If you work hard and have good character, not only job opportunities, but also money (and all good things it can buy), and women will cause stampede, lining up like ants as they scramble to touch the helm of your garment." Please go back and reread read on the impactful person.

A truly educated person is one who adds value to his own life through creative means of making life more and better. But he does so through efficient tools and means that don't harm himself, his family, society and environment around him. Talking to the first ever graduating class, Jesus said: "You are the light of the world." That means as a truly educated person you show the way, i.e., he is a leader and role model. A leader and an educated person must find a way to help improving thinking, working, relating and living. When Jesus said you are the salt of the earth, he meant that you add life to people and environment around you. Remember those days salt was used to lengthen life of fish probably the major source of livelihood those days in the Holy Land. Salt and not coolers kept fish fresh for long, with or without, good catches during low season. I've a couple of brothers who own boats enough to learn this fact. In the end, Sir David King Mason said in a book, The Promise by Professor Maliyamkono and Masson that a *"technically qualified population is needed for sustained development...a technically literate community...capable of producing, identifying (and) capitalizing on local opportunities for growth..."* How do you see your keenness to opportunity?

The ideal scholar is diligent and a man of action. Most of our graduates today can only boast of degree papers and long CVs of workshop they listened to! Education is intended to help you meeting life's situations. To be truly educated is concurring challenges of life and demands of a better new day every other single day. "We know that the wealth of a country depends on the ability and skills to translate the resources into products and services," *aptly* said former Malaysian premier Mahathir Mohammed writing about wealth which we have in plenty but seldom put to use.

"We know that the wealth of a country depends on the ability and skills to translate the resources into products and services that can be marketed. The very rich oil producing countries had oil throughout the centuries of their existence. But," he continued;" they only became rich when this oil was piped from the bowels of the earth and sold...Gold in the ground and wealth under our feet doesn't make us rich. But producing and selling it will. This is elementary." This—I mean a person who can do this—is an educated person.

Emerson or Einstein, Thomas A. Edison or Newton, Ford or Marconi and a couple of other great writers and inventors fall in this class of people whom we call educated. Think of the discovery of fire. It made it possible for man to dwell in many more places even in the cold weather. It as well as made it possible to have more varieties of food and for the first time, he could cook or roast his food and preserve it. Man could, of one of the major advantages, also use fire as a security agent against wild animals. When man began taming, and milking cattle or even when he began taming and riding the hoarse, made life better. He could be certain of milk and meat. He could travel on a hoarse back for short time over long distances. Both discoveries gave man an upper hand over his environment more than before. These discoveries allowed man to do more within a short span of time. With more time at his disposal, man could use time in more productive and innovative works.

Think of how penicilium made life better for all. Besides my mother's burning desire for self-reliance, an attribute he planted in us, but when Julius, my brother, discovered that one can indeed stand on his feet—with or without the support of one's parents no matter one's age—he created a take off stage before we sprung to prosperity we may see in the family today. Rockefeller gave his millions for invention and studies on drugs and prevention of diseases. Paul apostle wrote many epistles on healthier life doctrine. Philosophers write philosophies of better life for majority and sustainable society. Karl Marx and Plato and Julius Nyerere not only wrote or spoke but implemented with great enthusiasm about how a society must be led toward a new way of life. Nelson Mandela gave his lifetime in prison to serve others. Martin Luther King Jr. Kennedy, Lincoln and Jesus and laid down their lives for better lives for others. Truly character is everything. And we can readily identify it one way or the other. Lincoln said: "Character is like a tree and reputation its shadow. The shadow is what we think of it. The tree is the real thing. Character is the root of credibility. Chop off roots and the tree falls...!

And now, warning! You cannot hide your character. Ralph Waldo Emerson said, "what you are stands over you the while and thunders that I can't hear what you say to the contrary." Using other words Emerson said "Say what you may, but you cannot say anything but what you are." Facts don't go away! They don't cease to exist even if you attempted to hide them in the deep, far reaches of your conscience. A wicked man can smile up at you and he can even offer you some generous grants. But either way, and behind all that courtesy, behind the sugarcoated phrases and smiles, you will still notice untrustworthiness, lying, slandering and trickery now slumbering inactive in some shell somewhere awaiting for the right moment to spring up to life. Yes he may try to look cool, but the ulterior motive is still very much alive nonetheless—waiting for right moment! The bible says what you say behind doors shall be proclaimed on the top of the roof! You cannot hide from view. You cannot put who you are out of sight! You truly cannot conceal your character. You can never put out of sight that what you are! You can never hide from view—whether you have good or bad intentions! "We pass for what we are," wrote Emerson in his fine essays of self reliance: "Character teaches above our wills. Men imagine that they communicate their virtue or vice only by overt actions, and do not see that virtue or vice emit a breath every moment!"

CARDINAL RATSINGER'S EXEMPLAR

Before he was ordained as a boss, this seventy plus years old clergyman, Cardinal Ratsinger, was spotted leading a crowd of priests into a meeting to discuss and finalize the matter. The church was plunged in a sad moment losing its beloved leader and almost everyone was reluctant—reluctant? Did I say reluctant? No! I think indifferent is the word, indifferent to do anything even electing a new leader! Mind you he took leadership not because he aspired for leadership of his church himself, but out of force, an internal force. Everybody knows since its establishment by its supreme leader, the Christ, a little over two thousand years ago. It is yes around 2000 years particularly since its naming following splendid works by the greatest writer and orator by the name of apostle Paul at Antioch.

I hope you realize that there's never been a cardinal Festo Michael Kambarangwe! So the author didn't attend this conclave. Though I wasn't there in one of these great basilicas in the Vatican, that is not going to stop me to try and describe the most momentous event. I can't because it illustrates that even though we can learn to be leaders, but the truth is leaders just be! It is there or it isn't! So the events I'll lay out aren't exactly as how exactly they transpired in the headquarters of this church! Now this old cardinal, knowing he was aged; he didn't even have a thought of ever dreaming for a higher office. I was not in his heart—which is another handicap I face in laying out the precedents, for I cannot fit in it—but you and I can see that in every such moments, when one dreams for a high office he will weep and leap for joy on winning the nomination—we in Tanzania have witnessed candidates weep in public after winning political nominations. Abu Bakr didn't even accept to be caliph even after he was nominated—until when he was literally forced to give in. Saul had to hide himself when he was about to be nominated king of Israel. He had to be dragged from among the goods and flocks to be crowned king. So I can rely on what we see publicly. It is to this information that I can substantiate.

So cardinal Ratsinger had no thought at all that he would be nominated. That's why he was even spotted, and somehow unkindly, almost bullying, leading others into the cathedral! He wouldn't do that if he was trading for votes! Number two; we have information that his name didn't enter the race by forces of his own ambition. His name was proposed by the others to which call again he fiercely turned down. What he had done, I mean offering leadership, was simply a gesture of accountability on his part as any ideal person ought to have done now that the leader of that church was gone. But that was all! He had no ulterior motives. Now here is my message and the cream of whole thing: after long deliberations, the concave ended with a unanimous decision, and the crowd of healthy white smoke ascended through the top roof of this Basilica in Rome to announce the ordination of the new Pope Benedict 16.

Can you guess who was it that rose to that high office? Yes you can. No other than the same-same German bully, Cardinal Ratsinger! It is probably because he wasn't that much into the papacy rather power monger that only a little less than eight years on the throne he did the unprecedented when on another eleventh day of February 2013 he announced his resignation before a team of cardinals in the Vatican and in the same month, only on 28th of February 2013, he made his resignation effective. Notice that his decision was unprecedented since Pope Gregory XII resigned in 1415, and the first to do so on his own initiative since Pope Celestine V, in 1294.

You can surely not miss the ideal person because he is responsible. Because he is responsible he has control over his own body soul and intellect, knowing that true victory is to conquer the self. That's why the ideal scholar is a victorious man—a self reliant and an impactful person whom whatever his hand touches prospers. Don't be deceived to take the foregoing statement literally though? The ideal scholar works hard and is—in the end—prosperous not because he read this statement, but because he was obsessed to do achieve it, worked hard. Because of his affluence he will have no debt. Thus he will be free. For as the proverbs say, "The rich rule over the poor, and the borrower is the slave of the lender (Proverbs 22-7)."

With both affluence and influence, he also earns freedom. With freedom, he will be self confident. Like a shining star in the dark clouds, like the Kilimanjaro, he will throw his shoulders behind and walk upright, wearing a cheerful, encouraging smile, "elegantly dominating the hills and fields." He will walk in front of others when it is necessary because he is not afraid to lead and, he is confident. He speaks when necessary, and does a great deal of encouraging others to speak as he remains keen to listening. A bitten man accepts anything thrown at him. Prosperous, he is positive forceful radiant and confident in his ways.

You can clearly identify winners from losers in the penalty shoot-outs during football games. A winner will walk upright and confident reaching for the ball. Unsure of what he wants and unconfident about himself, a loser, on the contrary, will walk slowly, unsteadily and limping. He will appear to be seventy years old, when he is really fifty. Something other than years has been the cause of his aging. His hair and long, full beard will be dirty, and his nails unattended and therefore filthy. His gray, lifeless eyes are sunken. His face is wrinkled. He is tall and thin with drooping shoulders even when he is actually short. That's how I know a score and a miss. Recent European championships have revealed that excellently!

You cannot also miss the ideal scholar because he is self confident, and purposeful. They are thus not after cheap popularity. Yet we know people who are barely informed about something and yet they speak noisily and frequently on the topic almost authoritatively as if they were authorities. People who tend to speak so much know so little about what they say. Watch out for such people. They brag and seek glory. Often if I want to know useless people, I go to a bar or club. People with money or purpose don't speak so much—indeed rarely do they do so. They only do so when necessary. Such individuals think as they drink. They are there to soothe the mind. Losers shout and tell all kinds of stories praising everyone who is handy. Behind all this generosity on their part as far as praising others is concerned, there's an ulterior motive for a free beer.

Now that we have highlighted the qualities, and key indicators, both of which signal the kind of a person one is, let me add that these qualities tend to blend; and as they blend and become a mix, they tend to reveal the power, self-confidence, that surface in form of a cool and humble persona—character that distinguishes him from an average person. Writing about such personalities in his book Think Big, Ben Carson said: "By contrast, we have all met individuals who just seem to know what they are talking about—not because they boast and because they tell how much they know. It is simply apparent by the way they function. This kind of knowledge gives them confidence. When we are in their presence, they exude self-assurance and somehow, that makes us feel more self-confident (ourselves)." Finally, "the competent, self-assured knowledge doesn't show off, behave obnoxiously…cocky—it is just there," aptly observed Ben Carson in Think Big.

These are other signs that will tell you more about yourself—signs whose awareness will help you intensify the desire to transform your life. Here is what we have developed from a book, How Universities Under Develop You! "…You are frustrated and unhappy, your productivity is gone, and your life is miserable ... Your car is a mess with cans of beer and energizers on the chairs, cigarette butts on the floor; you have become dirty and a headache never ends; your house, your living room a living hell; There are constant conflicts in the your marriage; your nails are protruding and you are unshaven and your shoes have not seen the shoe shiner for ages…and you have become a wanker. You are useless and cannot be accepted either as future spouse; neither as son nor daughter in law. He or she cannot manage his own life. He cannot be self-employed and cannot get a job. There's only one thing for him or her. That's death. And he will probably beg for a sadistic tragic death that hits all nations that even the rich can suffer. This is the psychology of a loser!

Such a person has surrendered and that is all. What we think all day out is what our lives become. I was training at St. Ann's and they loved a story I'll repeat briefly here for your reading. I'd visited Mbeya and Tukuyu for school training in the town to inspire students to seek prosperity and thus read hard. Our lives are what we choose. While Tukuyu is too cold and whereas I asked for a blanket and hot shower, yet I still slept in a jacket, I realized the sharp contrast in lives we choose. By our thought and lives you will identify a person who has surrendered upon life. Now as I was served with hot shower, a thick clean blanket and a mosquito net, just outside my window, I could see a watchman of my age, a strong guy who slept—no he sat bolt upright—and had only a poor transparent soft uniform and shoes at least. He didn't ask for a hot shower or a blanket. He didn't take tea or coffee that night. No. He slept outside for a couple of days I was there. That's not a kind of life that can be said to enchanting. A bitten man accepts anything thrown at him. He has no choice whether to clean the sewage, till the land by a hand hoe, or picking coffee bending one's back for ten hours of backbreaking labor under the daylight overhead sun until fingers bred. And what about his earnings? For him money is measured by how much he can buy a drink. Food and shelter aren't of any importance to his poor soul. This is the tragedy of poverty.

This is nothing but a sign of having surrendered upon life. Such a person has laid down his arms: he has given in to defeat. There is more fight left in him. He has given up on life; yielding and admitting defeat. Such a person doesn't see another escape except waiting for his death. He is so sincere about dying but he is so weak that he cannot even take his life. This is what befalls a bitten man. You are bitten when you are like the dog that was sitting on a sharp nail wailing with determination, lamenting about it, but never moving an inch. Do you have to lament constantly, or rise to the occasion and take steps to change the state, or direction, of your life? The choice, to be sure, lies with you. It is you who knows your problem better than anyone else if you take time to meditate about your life. The answers are all in there; in your heart, within you, and in your grasp.

As we come to a close, how do you see your relation with your superiors? Your parents? What is your relation with your Maker? Do you approach Him in fear and trembling or with love and confidence of the brethren? Remember He is the one who made you to be who you are and where you are. Having learned to take advantage of who you are you will not run from yourself or hate who you are—or even your Maker— but leverage on your personality with great enthusiasm striving to make the most of who you are for yourself and others around you and thus becoming impactful to yourself, your family and the society as a whole. The above is an analysis of whether you are an educated person or not. This is the difference between a wealthy person and a pauper. Where do you fall? The choice lies with you!

Now compare yourself against the rest of the ideals or core values or set of character of the ideal scholar or person and merge the whole study of ideal scholars to find where you can make most of yourself. Remember your gifts, talents, skills and education, your career, possessions, and all are but the beginning! Tracing your true desires in relation with your abilities, if you do this, you will then be able to harness your highest potential. That we have possessions is not enough. That we are educated or that we are wealthy or that we hold high career positions today all aren't enough. I've narrated how my dad was wealthy. Yet there are a lot of better things he could have done better in many other ways! We will discuss further the foregoing through the upcoming chapters in this book and its series.

The following additional information has been shared before. But since it was introduced as qualities of the ideal leader, and because the ideal scholar is naturally a leader in his own way, we will therefore reproduce it here. The ideal scholar is not afraid to take low profile. Mandela said it is better to lead from behind and to put others in front especially when you celebrate victory when nice things occur. You take the front line when there is danger. Then the people will appreciate your leadership.

The ideal scholar is a confident leader. Nelson Mandela said: "a leader ...is like a shepherd," said Nelson Mandela in his book *Long Walk for Freedom*. "He stays behind the flock, letting the most nimble go out ahead, whereupon others follow, not realizing that all along they are being directed from behind. The ideal scholar is clean—body and heart. Mandela said: "Appearances matter—and remember to smile." The ideal scholar is confident and knows what he wants and goes for it. He is confident; and therefore respects others irrespective of their age, size, race, wealth or sex. He speaks when necessary and does a great deal of listening; He is not like a bitten man;"A big man," said Mwalimu Nyerere, "A big man doesn't keep shouting that he is big. A clever man doesn't keep shouting that he is clever. It is the small and stupid who constantly reiterate their claims to size and intelligence, hoping to convince themselves if no one else, and of course earning derision in the process."

Finally, the ideal scholar is strong in his heart, loyal, has determination and endurance to do good things but weak to vice. He has vision, character initiative, courage and willpower to organize things. He is calm, self-confident and compassionate. That's why he is habitually called upon to step forward when most gladly have already turned and fled fearing to shoulder their personal and collective responsibilities. You wouldn't wonder therefore to find him on the front line whether they like it or not. That's why he has mustered and mastered skills and is always prepared to serve when others are still struggling. You realize now that the ideal scholar, employee, mother or father, the ideal person and citizen, whatever he or she touches prospers—like a tree planted on the fertile soil on the bank of river. With this book, or program, at your disposal, you are now like that lucky tree planted on these rich river bank—the books and training programs therein!

That's why we are confident whatever the reader touches from now on shall prosper because the book in his hands now, or program thereof, represent both the fertile riverbank and the water from the river that springs with life. What can parents, schools, organizations, employers and the nations pay in return for such a service? Think! A trainee from St. Ann's Secondary school recently in our session suggested a ten Million Dollar value! What do you think? Well, you cannot judge it right until you experience the difference. I believe it is more than that. In Napoleon Hill's words, "There is no fixed price for a sound idea."

WHY AND HOW YOU CAN PROMOTE GOOD VALUES

Now the question is about how we should promote the sense of ideal personality? We award top students and employees in our schools and work places respectively even as I write. I know that. The author has for about ten years of his schooling and through my tenure at work received some top school awards both in the semiannual and annual ceremonies to award ideal students or employees. The author cannot find words to describe how it feels to hear your name being spelt out as top award winning individual. He cannot find words to describe how he felt for first when as a class five student, heard his name being spelt out aloud—and before the multitude of school and teachers—to move forward when he had risen to number two almost from the bottom in the whole class of sixty students. He cannot explain the motivation it fetched for him ever since. It is certainly one of the reasons he desired and vowed to remain there—at the top. And the foregoing testimony is not for the author. It is for you the reader. That's why I am going to add something to such motivation however great that was. It was the same when he received the best employee award of the year etc. etc. etc.

Through the preceding chapters, we introduced to you Mugaywa Magafu, a student who was a true genius in the traditional sense. Through him, we introduced the aspect of bookworms, or even academically genius students who may not necessarily be representative of the ideal scholar. Let us now turn to a Samson Kahwemama paradigm. Mr. Kahwemama was a genius in his own ways. He performed well at the top. But he liked his drink! In fact Michael S.O.J., the author's colleague and classmate, and longtime Samson Kahwemama's classmate suggests that without his drink, un-intoxicated, Mr. Kahwemama would have been a downright failure in school. Without his drink he would seat in a high school examination like a toddler! That's why we brought Balotelli into this discussion. Balotelli can score well. He can as well have wonderful dribbling skills and can give you a winner any time. But the tragedy with Balotelli is that he is unpredictable. He can squander victory any moment. He can hit or kick someone in the rib following a slight misunderstanding. That's how he can squander chances of winning even after he has scored a couple of important goals. That's how he often was red carded. How do we know? Well, that's easy.

Jose Mourinho has been his coach and while he praised his talents and gift he explains how he would spend fifteen minutes during break with no other ten players but one Balotelli. Unless you are a little like the messiah who would leave the 99 flock and embark on returning the 100th sheep such an endeavor is not only uneconomical. It is also unwise. It is also not good for the youngsters who learn from those at the top. We must therefore attach awards with other qualities such as character and participation in extra curricula activities. I have seen and disapprove how we awarded bookworm antisocial students who nonetheless performed extremely well in class, students who sat on the extreme opposite in other areas of social life. Such examples are ubiquitous in every field.

We must identify these core values or ideals in our society family workplace or even in the church, or at work and accordingly vote for and award the ideal student, ideal workmate, ideal youth, ideal husband or wife. I was a young catholic when at Isingiro Parish, when the church began promoting a certain sense of ideal living. That way the church often portrayed Dr. Balthazar's family as the ideal family. Amidst the typical traditional society, men who enjoyed the traditional marriage settings, at the time and space when the real man was a polygamous man like the author's father, the church innovatively promoted o*ne Man One Wife One Smaller Famil*y the kind of Dr. Balthazar. Balthazar was at the time serving in the same establishment and therefore provided the ideal man, and family. He served as medical doctor and had been so faithfully attached to a Christian credo—a one-man-one-church–married-wife, and had had only three children in contrast to Kambarangwe's forty plus children and ten minus a few wives. So the church presented the Balthazars in many creative ways as the ideal leader and ideal spouse, whereas Benja and his siblings as the ideal children. I can close my eyes and see how Benja was admired among his peers. In fact he grew up to be truly an ideal person, graduating from the university as an engineer years later.

During the holy mass, they sat in front seats. They stood in front of the church beside the catholic American and European White Fathers. No wonder they were quite an influence to the whole society. The church rewarded them albeit in nonmonetary terms. And it was very effectively.

The church even rewarded such couples by hiring them and their family members in whatever big or petty jobs that made themselves available. I suppose that's how Almachius was employed at the hospital even though many others met his qualifications but he was Balthazar's nephew. So naturally he held high respect among the church ranks. I was young then but I can assure you it was effective even for a boy who would go on to be an author had himself a dream to raise a family in the model of Balthazar's. It was effective. I know it is because today that boy raises a family bearing the same testimony and influence. Apart from financial rewards, we must, with media association in Tanzania when they promote such ideal and multiply recognition to such deeds and individuals, as recently did media in Tanzania, supported by corporate sponsorships by rewarding the woman of the year, or the entrepreneur of the year etc. Ben Carson was voted by his peers the most ideal student, to be specific, the student most likely to succeed. It is for the same cause that Mo Ibrahim Foundation rewards the best African President of the year, in order to promote good governance during one's time in office.

Finally, let us together bear the responsibility to reassess and reevaluate one profession against another in our society—and across our borders. How ought every profession or professional to conduct oneself? This is important because most of the youngsters are influenced by what the television or media houses say and show. It is the same in our schools or workplaces and in our homes. The youngsters should know that it is indeed to their advantage to seek to be impactful—to be of value to themselves and others—than only being concerned about being financially or materially successful, or conducting themselves well instead of the trending bad boys or gangster image. Whereas a person who conducts himself well wins everything, the patter will attract forces that will conspire to beat you, to put you down.

Probably as if to supplement the quest for fresh re-role-modeling of, and in, our society today, and just as much of a shock—but a delightful one—I am a witness that with commitment and hard work we can change the perception about who really is a true role model. This happened when we were concluding a training program for university students at Crown Hotel in Dodoma—and among them students from Ethiopia, Congo and Somalia and Burundi. As a ritual, before we end the training—it was a training program that bore the book you are now reading—we ask the trainees to cite what transformation they have picked up through the training, probing for what inspiration they can cite from the training program as a means of analyzing where we can improve, and of course to affirm if the training was successful. In fact in the end our training intends to make our trainees more impactful as persons.

Now diverging from businessmen, sports or entertainment personalities—individuals who traditionally are considered as heroes, many trainees chose better options than these traditionally money making vocations. But there was one student whose decision is worth mentioning. Now his name was Ekocho, a student from D.R Congo, one who in fact named himself: *President de L'état*. When his turn came, he stood up and said that he finally had stumbled upon what he wanted to do and be in future. What was that? Referring to the author and our principle trainer, in his words he said: "I want to be like you. I want to train people, to influence them to change their own lives—and the lives of the people around them!!!" Suddenly, "Six thousand lovely," I whispered! I said, "Oh wow" as an arrow of pleasure shot through me. Guiding our youngsters to choose rightly, that is the right role modeling, and having shaped their thought patterns and therefore their future around the more impactful course, I am convinced that such youngsters are going places. That's why I am going to conclude this important chapter by the poem I have paraphrased from the lyrics from a song that was so popular when the author was still young back in Ngara, Tanzania, a community whose tongue, Kishubi, is closely written and spoken like its bordering community Burundi's tongue, where the song actually originates:

A REAL HE-MAN

A real man is judged…by his heart,

A real man is identified by the works of his hands,

A real man has a good name among all the people,

A real man, is never idle,

A real man advances himself, his family, his nation;

A he-man, always tells the truth, no matter what,

Always strives to enhance peace and prosperity wherever he is,

Always strives to enhance peace and prosperity wherever he is;

A real man works to advance cohesion;

A real man is always there for his people,

By his heart you will judge him,

By the works of his hands he will be spotted...UMUGABO W'UKULI

(Lyrics from an famous song in Ngara, Tanzania, a song so close to the author's tongue (Kishubi) originating from neighboring Burundi)

Umugabo w'ukuli, arangwa...n'umutima,

Umugabo w'ukuli, arangwa n'ibikogwa,

Umugabo w'ukuli, yam'avugwa neza mu'bantu bose,

Umugabo w'ukuli, nhiyiligwa yichaye,

Umugabo w'ukuli, alangwa n'ibikogwa,

Vyomutez' imbele, uwe n'igihugu chiwe,

Umugabo nyamugabo, yam'avugu kuli,

Akama agwanila amahoro, ahali hose;

Akama agwanila amahoro, ahali hose;

Umugabo w'ukuli, akund'ubumwe,

Akama ashinzehamwe, n'abagenzi biwe,

Umugabho w'ukuli akund'ubumwe;

Umugabo w'ukuli arangwa n'umutima,

Umugabo w'ukuli, arangwa n'ibikogwa...

PART III

FINALE: THE WISE AND FOOLISH BUILDERS

> *"...Everyone who comes to me and hears my words and puts them into practice...is like a man building a house, who dug down deep and laid the foundation on the rock. When a flood came, the torrent struck that house but could not shake it, because it was well built. But the one who hears my words and does not put them into practice is like a man who built a house on the ground without a foundation. The moment the torrent struck that house, it collapsed and its destruction was complete."*
>
> *—Matthew 7:24-28*

42. SELF-CRITICISM: BEING HONEST TO ONESELF

"One thing I remember my father told me is to always do good things and stop those who don't." —Jackie Chan in a movie Who Am I?

Through the preceding pages you learned that to attain success to your true potential, you require certain ideals or core values. We went through the ideals only in a nutshell because we revisit these ideals through volume two of this very book. Because of the significance of this concept, we chose to expound these ideals, to give further details and provide more clarity about these ideals, through the twin sister title of this very book. You recognize that we learned that households, schools and workplaces as well as nations and individuals cannot—and aptly should not expect to—progress and to attain success to your true potential without these ideals if the progress or development we talk about is sustainable. We know we have to a great extent addressed an individual person. It is in line with what we indicated earlier on, that the national income is the sum total of all individual households put together. Besides exploitation can only be healed if each individual is prepared to do away with it by understanding his rights and responsibilities such as working hard; and that his life is in his own hands.

To transform a society, we need to transform the individuals. Indeed Margaret Thatcher was right: "There is no such a thing as society," so aptly said Margaret Thatcher. "There are individual men, and women, and families." By addressing these individual men and women and families, we transform the whole society. In words of Berner and Phillips, "Ironically, the community idealism so beloved by the new populists is a creation of outsiders. Only outsiders would see homogeneity and harmony where there is complexity and conflict. Bottom-up approaches to development need to start from the recognition that exploitation and marginalization also take place inside the slums." By addressing the individual, we have high hopes that this book will help to transform many of our needy individuals, households, the schools and academic institutions, organizations and private and public departments, the nation and humanity as a whole.

Nonetheless, we recognize that, however great piece of work it could be, it will benefit only those who are committed to personal advancement. Therefore, generally speaking, this work will be beneficial to only those who are worthy individuals—those who will not pay lip service but act. Recognizing that the book targets the youth and the adults or old people who are young at heart, as President Kennedy used to call it, we find that the honesty to oneself deserves further attention. What does that say?

It would do a nation a greater service if we enlightened the reader how responsible they are to their lives. To understand the magnitude of the foregoing statement, we dedicated this chapter to self criticism as a means to one being honesty to oneself. To be effective—to realize a new way of life you are required to make a serious and fearless moral censorship of the one-self if we have to realize personal as well as national advancement. We are normally quick to judge others but we often stay silent about our own faults. If we should reclaim our true potential we have got to fearlessly face up to our weaknesses before we even take pride in our strengths.

However, when we are faced with self inventory of our strengths against weaknesses, however indispensable that process is, if we have to prosper, yet we tend to shrink hiding in our shell. This shell is counter development. It is in the form of self righteousness and shying away from our weaknesses. This by itself is self defeating. In history it is the major cause why even the mighty were vanquished and defeated.

The handicap of most successful people is that they become so self-righteous as to imagine they know every answer to their problems. These people may be intelligent that is why they are self confident in the first place. But they forget no one knows everything. Besides, times and circumstances change. That is why self righteousness never succeeds. In order to face your own weaknesses, start by reviewing your role as a parent, or leader–which is what you are.

What are the roles of the parents? What is the role of leaders? The role of either the parents or leaders is far reaching and wide but I've found better definition than the one I've chosen to consolidate here which is: To prolong successful long happy, meaningful and impactful lives for themselves their children and their constituencies. The author is himself a parent and has a big family whose future I've to protect. The same goes for you. But as owners or members of the management team, wellbeing and better lives for the organization, staff and their families are in your hands too. Are we measuring up? We often tend to please ourselves and are drunk in our own accomplishments such that we become unjustifiably overconfident.

You must have heard of the parable of Biblical wealthy man. Here let me tell it in my own words as narrated by its author Jesus of Nazareth. This man had worked hard over the years. He had through drudgery and determination managed to own a large farm and he had many laborers. He then decided he was going to do one thing that would ensure a breakthrough allowing him to take a break and party for the rest of his life. What was the trick? He would plow and sow various crops in his hefty farm; he would breed and fatten a host of cattle and goats and sheep. Then he would stock up the cereals and all produces in the barn and settle down and enjoy the rest of his whole life. As planned, he gathered enormous wealth. But when he was just about to settle down the Maker called upon him. He left behind all his wealth, the wealth he had ruthlessly amassed.

What do we learn? The moral of the story is the folly of man. You should never be over confident. The Fall of the Roman Empire is an exemplar of folly of men. The Romans believed they had conquered the world. In their naivety, and self gratification, they settled down and indulged in excesses of leisure and pleasure. They did not work anymore vastly depending on taxing and siphoning wealth from other countries. They therefore didn't engage in material production or nurturing the Roman society until when they were defeated and vanquished. Where's the might of the Greeks? The great Hitler or Mussolini, where are they? Where's the influence of the Great Britain in international affairs? All these examples illustrate the folly of self-righteousness. The folly of the Brits had reached its tip when they sang: "Rule Britain rule. Rule Britain rule. Britons shall never be slaves." Whether this was decided upon by sheer instincts or based on credible observation, I have no way of knowing. But one thing I know. And that is: today people question either of the assertions.

Self-righteousness with one's own recent successes is the standard and habitual cause of any business slump. It is behind almost all political and social breakdowns. Equally, it is behind downfall among rulers and kings. What is the solution? Litheness of the heart, vigilance, watchfulness. Probably you have seen how boats, travel to the far distances and come back in one piece albeit a stormy sea. Why not learn from the most stupid and therefore humblest being I mean the heartless and bloodless wood boats. If we sail with waves, our business boats would sail as far as the Antarctic and I'm not exaggerating even one bit. We would rejuvenate and find a new momentum.

What do we on the contrary do? What happens? We break ourselves trying to bend the emerging challenges. We are fools failing to go round but instead attempt to break the structures. It is not atypical to humans. When we are not yet top we tend to go all-out we do the utmost we try hard we make every effort to learn to keep abreast with what it takes to be successful and prosperous. Sadly like children of the rich when we succeed and achieve the highest potential we aspired for we tend to stop working or even thinking indulging in leisure. Power has its drawbacks! We assume power after a hard struggle and then tragedy strikes: we get promoted—and that's when the doom begins. We stop learning. We stop thinking. We stop working.

"Before you became a CEO you prided yourself on visiting every unit in the region, you got to know all employees, you spoke directly with customers —you had your hands on the pulse of the business. Since you became a CEO…You have lost touch and unavoidable gaps in your own expertise loom larger than ever." The foregoing statement isn't the author's. It is a Harvard Business Review. Now the question is: Do we do it deliberately? No! No sane CEO MD or manager or even any typical political leader would dare do that. It all stems from the change within our lifestyle working schedule and priorities as business leaders.

And this habit is not deliberate. No! No business owner, CEO or MD who can consciously do that. They rather are occupied by many of their long and wrong schedule. Self righteousness become far more a folly act when you consider the fact that human society has not yet crossed or even come close to the boundary of knowledge. Besides rapidity of pace of change, the landscape of competition, the rapidity with which we forget all make self righteousness one of our greatest personal foes we must fight. If we have to keep meeting the emerging business challenges and do business or any endeavor in which we are so comfortably and competitively sustainably and profitably as individual persons schools corporations or nations we must subject ourselves to self analysis as we shall see going forward. That's why we have got to allow a room to question our positions. We have got to stay alert if we shouldn't sink. Self criticism is one of the chief characters of a leader, manager or of parent. As leaders we have got to prolong successful long happy, meaningful lives of our children. *Bad Heirs/Children of the Rich, "Corruption, Wealth and Children's Free Spending,"* an article by US Trust survey of affluent Americans, I stumbled upon in a magazine Savor Tanzania, revealed that, that is why wealth never crosses to the third generation. Why?

This is an important matter to ponder about. The children of the rich tend to stop worrying for the future and they are only concerned with the immediate needs such as leisure. As a result soon they run bankrupt even becoming paupers. As directors, managers and stakeholders of education, the wellbeing of the schools, and education as a whole, the students, workforce, staff and their families are in our hands. "For in the long run" said Epictetus "in the long run everyman will pay the penalty of his misdeeds."

The world history is filled with brimming examples of how erroneous is self righteousness. Gorbachev was president of the great USSR when the foregoing precedent was shown to him the hard way. He had quite arrogantly announced the great future plans in which The Soviet Union was about to launch the great future economic and technological breakthrough such that no foe would stand her! According to him the USSR was the greatest cohesive and strong nation for others to emulate. USSR, he said was on its final minutes to become an invincible super power! But the astonishing thing is, even before echoes of his speech were literally over, he was shocked to find that he was no longer president. Why? How? Both are sound questions. By virtue of his function as president of the Soviet Federation, the nation he had just so highly spoken about no longer existed! How? The USSR had disintegrated into Russia, Ukraine, Georgia etc! USSR was then nonexistent! The cunning Americans offered him a chance to work as a lecturer in one of their universities! Think about that fall! From the highest office in the vastest nation on the face of the earth to a lecturer of an average college amongst his former foes! It is in your interest to stay alert. I sincerely fear that to concur with any concession thoughtlessly is likely to set a dangerous precedent–like skating on a dangerous field!

My longtime fears are no longer baseless. The ubiquitous lessons from the recent experiences in the world of business and politics provide conclusive proof. We have seen how big boys are losing out. Old followers—people who are ready to learn and adapt and adopt new ideas and ways have become market leaders in politics, economics and in the market place. Also so beautifully does the world of football illustrate the foregoing assertion. Recently Ivory Coast went to the African cup of nation's finals as unanimous favorites. And there was sound reason for that. The main challengers the big favorites such as Egypt, Cameroon and Nigeria had been ousted earlier on. Suddenly Côte d'Ivoire became a giraffe in the midst of a group of mice. Competing against the underdogs and a nation which never won the championship but Ivoirians were surprised and the world with them when they were whipped by the Zambian underdogs. Indeed Mo Kamilagwa, who is this author's personal associate helped to sum up the moral of the precedent after the recent Woza World Cup in South Africa so illuminatingly when he observed that: "If not well managed, those we call underdogs turn out to be great threats to big players. USA, Brazil, Italy and Spain have all helped to put that into the right context during the 2009 confederation cup."

What had happened? Spain had shocked the world. The big boys such as Brazil, Germany and Italy were stunned. Spain went on to win Euro and World Cup the same semester. Now notice that even though we are verbally mentioning football and sports but Mo wasn't in fact speaking about flowing football or entertainment at all! He was discussing far more serious business. His analogy referred not only to football but also in other areas such as households, business organizations and in politics. Such is the case of rise and fall of the giants in the telecom or banking industry not only in Tanzania but in the whole world today.

At the time when he made this observation, Tigo, the customary underdog, had become literally the market leader whipping the giants of Celtel and Vodacom. Tigo's leadership hadn't come as an effortless chance or luck. It came because they set a strategy and worked focused towards the same goal. They had foreseen the potential of mass market. Amid economic down turn, corporations trimmed down the staff and expenses and among them mobile allowances. By catering for the mass market Tigo were heading for triumph whether unawares or not. Soon Celtel and Vodacom had to revise their business strategies and follow suit. These two giants who traditionally eyed the corporate market failed to be favorites among long time abandoned low income earners. Tigo's market share soared the profits brimmed! Whether they still have managed to maintain their position, or not, that's another thing altogether. How do I know it is true? I worked with Mo Kamilagwa at Celtel a telecom company when at the height of its market dominance to understand what he is saying.

Behind all this mess, is one fundamental fact: "Many business 'managers' are so convinced they know the answers to every situation. Hence they don't want to be bothered with the facts. (Effective Leaders...take the opposite track. They start assuming they don't know .., and keep on asking questions until a clear picture of reality and its implications can be built up, "rightly observed Prof Jim Collins, author of Good to Great. Notice also that I do not deny the fact that experience is a good teacher. But you don't have to suffer in the process before you learn. That's why here we have set examples of how great people accepted criticism. Here you have a choice to make: to emulate them, learn from their successes and failures and how they responded every time they failed and be as great as they were, or else choose to be a little man—who in whose arrogance—never learns, and as a result he will never know more than what he already knows, which is very little!

Probably you have heard of Henry Ford. If you haven't don't worry. I will only tell you briefly because you can read more about self-criticism and how it helped many people in Dale Carnegie's book How to Stop Worrying and Start Living. His book so generously demonstrates importance of self criticism. Here's a long list of people who prospered because of unbiased impartial self criticism. Back to Ford. You don't have to take a flight to the States to learn from his character. You simply can watch over the window from your house or office to see the Ford motor car passing from wherever you may be in America as is in Africa or Europe and Asia. The secret behind such monumental success? Ford Company welcomed employees to criticize the management; and this is not all: these people would win awards and be promoted if they gave strong criticism against the company plans or management style, priorities or even car designs.

One young salesman found that he didn't sell his merchandize even when he believed in the merchandize. Was it the merchandizes? Packaging? What was it? Pricing? He didn't know. He had done his best but every other single time he failed to round the bend after he had successfully taken the prospective buyer through a sales pitch. This guy was pragmatic. He went back and asked the prospect what his mistakes could have been that he failed to sell the magnificent product. Was it his selling skills? What and where he did he wrong. What did he need to do better? When he did this little self criticism with open heart he often found that the prospects offered to buy from him. Not only that. They began to love him. No wonder he rose to become president of largest world soap Maker for which he worked Colgate—Palmolive-Peet soap. His name is E. H Little.

Take Charles Luckman. He was president of Pespsodent. He never looked at the letters praising the operations of his company but those criticizing both himself and the company. Einstein—an undisputed genius admitted he made mistakes 99% times. Thomas Edison conducted 10,000 experiments and did same number of mistakes before he discovered an electric bulb. Roosevelt, president and the greatest thinker of last century admitted that his best performance was at only around 75%. Charles Darwin spent 15 years criticizing his own work, The Origin of Species. No wonder the work transformed sciences and thinking.

And that is not about academics the standard habitual cause among businesses only. Let's take sports. Michael Jordan an all time NBA most successful person said he managed to reach that score because he tried many times and made so many mistakes failing as many times. As a result? He as well did score a good number of points. When Abraham Lincoln was mocked by his own appointee, his secretary of war based on Lincoln's decision to send regiments to a European war what would an average person do. I would fire him. That is standard answer. But Lincoln said is that so? Then I'll step over and hear it myself, because he always makes better judgment on these matters. Then he did step over. And what happened? He withdrew his order to transfer regiments. He knew the criticisms were sincere founded on knowledge and spirit of helpfulness. Thus we ought to say to ourselves that: May be I ought to be 20% mistaken, maybe I deserve these criticisms, maybe I should be thankful and try to benefit from them."

While most of us may be running away from a very little criticism H. P Powell who did criticize himself so often had gone to an extra mile. He had almost seemed to fall in love with self criticism that he set a specific day in the week to criticize himself. Take Ben Franklyn. He didn't wait for a specific day in a week we made mistakes every day and indeed every time of the week. So he would pick a bad habit and put on gloves and when the bell rang he would come out of his corner fighting the bad habit until he knocked it down before going to bed (How to Stop Worrying and Start Living by Dale Carnegie).

Dale Carnegie wrote that, *"The small man flies into a rage over the slightest criticism but the wise man is eager to learn from those who have censured him and reproved him and disputed the passage with him."* Indeed waste no time in heeding self criticism much more criticism from others. Indeed: "The opinion of our enemies, come nearer to the truth about us than do our opinions (about ourselves said the French philosopher Rochefoucauld. Walt Whitman said "Have you learned lessons of those who only admired you, and were tender with you, and stood aside for you? Have you not learned the great lessons from those who rejected you, and braced themselves against you, or disputed the passage with you?"

Dan Brown was right. "In my experience," he wrote, "In my experience men go to too far greater lengths (trying) to avoid what they fear than (trying) to obtain what they desire." Reinhold Niebuhr prayed that "God grant me the serenity to accept the things I cannot change the courage to change the things I can and the wisdom to know the difference!" Fredrick Hegel concluded that "Comprehension without critical evaluation is impossible." But you grumble and say all this stuff is a set of fables and unrealistic guess work. You have a point. Probably these people just said this in an interview to woo votes' goodwill. Probably they made decisions based on conscience and called it self-criticism. Do we have proof of such public acknowledgement of admission of mistakes? Lincoln went to greater trouble to acknowledge he was wrong, and did it as if he was proud of it.

Here's a line from his letter to General Grant his army commander in the war front during the American civil war. Notice that it wasn't a mere opinion tossed down on him by an adversary. It was his own commander and appointee and notice again that he had just defied Lincolns own orders his own president. But Lincoln recognizing how his utopian arm chair war strategy wouldn't work after all because when you are on the ground you act responding to circumstances and that certainly the general didn't have a mobile phone at the time and if so there're actions that need instantaneous and immediate decisions if one had to take advantage of the opportunities that presented themselves. Considering all these facts and the fact that the generals own strategy came out winning a battle for Lincoln and the country, he conceded. Lincoln admits he was wrong with much grace. Did he just call and admit in an untraceable means such as mere conversation? No. Not Lincoln. He put it on record.

"I never had any faith…When you got below, and took Port-Gibson, Grand Gulf, and vicinity, I thought you should go down the river and join Gen.

Banks; and when you turned Northward East of the Big Black, I feared it was a mistake. I now wish to make the acknowledgment that you were right, and I was wrong." Well, probably one question remains. Did he just send a merely handwritten note out of duty? No! Not Lincoln. He went to lengths of signing it. While he even would have had the assistant write and stamp it for the presidential seal, instead here's how he chose to end the letter. "Yours very truly,

A. Lincoln!"

From Lincoln we learn that if we learned to appreciate that we are not infallible, we would redress where we went wrong and find a new momentum. But instead when we succeed what happens? We break ourselves trying to bend the emerging structures. We endeavor to bend the rules. It is typical to humans. When we are not yet top we tend to strive to learn to keep abreast with success. Sadly like children of the rich when we succeed and achieve the highest potential we aspired for we tend to stop working and thinking but instead we indulge in spending and partying. Instead of remaining industrious, clubbing turns out to be our new personal and business culture. Power has both its perks and disadvantages! When we get a new job we work hard. What then follows is that the tragedy strikes when we get promoted—and the doom starts. We stop learning. We start enjoying ourselves. That's how we begin to lose touch.

What is the point? Here it is. We have got to provide for the unexpected. We need to be watchful and vigilant for otherwise we may sink if we only have to make use of our own past ways. This calls for self criticism which is one the major chief qualities of a good leader—at work, or at home. And to do so it is to prolong successful long happy, prosperous meaningful lives for their children. As directors, managers and stakeholders of education, the wellbeing of the schools, and education as a whole, the students, workforce, staff and their families are in your hands. For "In the long run," said Epictetus "everyman will pay the penalty of his misdeeds."

FINAL THOUGHTS ON SELF CRITICISM
To be so successful we need to understand that the first precondition is to be able to manage yourself. You cannot manage yourself without criticizing yourself let alone accepting criticism from others. We will discuss more on the topic later, but for now recognize no man or woman ever progressed without being criticized by himself or others—either way.

An article in Bits and Pieces offers a superb admonition when we face disagreement! Let's learn from this wonderful mind how to react in the situation we are faced with, as adapted from the book How to Win Friends and Influence People by Dale Carnegie:

"Welcome the disagreement...If There's some point you have not thought about, be thankful if it is brought to your attention. Perhaps this disagreement is your opportunity to be corrected before you make a serious mistake. Distrust your first instinctive impression. Our first natural reaction in a disagreeable situation is to be defensive. Be careful. Keep calm and watch out for your reaction. It may be you at your worst, not your best. Control your temper. Remember you can measure the size of a person by what makes him or her angry. Listen first. Give your opponent a chance to talk. Let them finish. Do not resist defend or debate. This only raises barriers. Try to build bridges of understanding. Don't build higher barriers of misunderstanding!

"Look for areas of agreement. When you have heard your opponents out dwell first on points and areas on which you agree. Be honest. Look for areas where you can admit error and say so… Promise (yourself) to think over your opponents' ideas and study them carefully. And mean it. Your opponent may be right. It is a lot easier at this stage to agree to think about their points than to move rapidly ahead and find yourself in a position where your opponents can say" we tried to tell you but you wouldn't listen" Thank your opponents sincerely for their interest. Anyone who takes the time to disagree with you is interested in the things you are! Think of them as people who really want to help you… Postpone action to give both sides time to think through the problem. Suggest that a new meeting be held...when all facts may be brought to bear. In preparation for this meeting ask yourself hard questions (such as) could your opponents be right? Partly right? Is there truth or merit in their position or argument? Is my reaction one that will relieve or will it just relieve any frustration, will my reaction drive my opponents further away or draw them closer to me? Will my reaction elevate the estimation good people have of me?? Will I win or lose? What price will I've to pay if I win? Will the disagreement blow over? Is this difficult situation an opportunity for me?"

Indeed we must remember the universe has principles. You need not fight it. You have learned through the preceding chapters that it is like swimming in waters of the sea. To arrive safe you must learn to go by the waves. We emphasize that you look into why people succeed and others fail. My other books all discuss the differences and parity between winners and failures. This book builds that base for you. Writing the other way round Dale Carnegie narrates how Margaret Fuller the famous New England feminist I suppose after fighting inequality between sexes and gender imbalance against women for ages and probably failed after a great deal of self torture she offered as her credo and declared "I accept the universe!"

Mr. Carnegie in his book "How to Stop Worrying and Start Living writes that "When Thomas Carlyle heard that I mean when he heard that Mrs. Fuller had conceded he snorted "By Gad she had better!" And yes and by Gad you and had better accept the inevitable too! We are printing this little episode because hereafter we bring you a full chapter on why we must accept the universe. Just tack on the next page and sail through. This then assuming we are prepared the inevitable brings us to the obvious inescapable call for transformation. A call for change. And now. Indeed Francois Hollande was right. Le Changement, C'est Maintenent! Change is now!

SELF RIGHTEOUSNESS AND HISTORY OF SELF DEFEAT
Having presented failure in our systems and in particular the education system, I questioned myself if you my reader and any other stakeholder will not take the matter personally. Don't. It is to your benefit. There has always been trouble with the human individual. We all imagine we are right. This is what is called self righteousness.

THE VANITY OF THE BIBLICAL WEALTHY MAN
You must have heard of the parable of Biblical wealthy man. He had a large farm and many laborers. He then decided he was going to plant cereals in the largest part of the farm, and rear lots of livestock, and then reap, and keep the produces in the barn. And then having accumulated wealth, sit back and party for the rest of his days! Why not! He had worked so hard. He had all the money he wanted for the rest of his life. He deserved *ambience* of some kind. Why not? Then he did according to his plans and accumulated wealth and lots of produces. But we learn in this parable that sadly when he was just about to embark on partying for the balance of his life ,tragedy hit! His Maker called upon him. He left all his possessions, and dust to dust down to earth he descended. What then is the moral of this parable?

The moral of the parable is the folly and vanity of human individual. Over confidence is illusive. The Fall of Roman Empire is another best exemplar. The Romans thought they had conquered the world. They settled down and indulged in pleasures of life. They didn't care anymore about production or advancement of the Roman society until when unawares they were vanquished. Where's the might of the Greeks. Hitler and Mussolini? Where's the clout of the Great Britain? Britain became big headed after conquering the world and like Romans they sang in their praises Britain rule Britain rule. Britons shall never ne slaves! Instead of putting tools and systems in place like the one we are advocating in this chapter, they indulged in craziness of spending and luxuries until when their own colony in the states shocked the so called Great Britain.

As it is the song and its essence,"Britons shall never be slaves" is questionable! If you believe the foregoing statement is questionable consult events before and during George Bush invasion of Iraq! No any sane Briton who would not agree with me! Americans now rule Britons! Is the US herself any invincible? No! The unlikely Chinese are the power to reckon with! The recent economic down turn and the crisis in the Euro zone shout out in favor of this argument!

I've brought the proceeding discussion into the mix in order to illustrate the folly of self righteousness.

SELF CRITICISM AND CRITICAL EVALUATION: TOOLS FOR SELF DEVELOPMENT

They say experience is a good teacher, but you don't have to suffer the consequences of your actions before you learn. Here we have that experience for your instant use. Here're few examples of how great people accepted criticism. Now as you approach the actual ways and means they used to criticize themselves in order to be better people as great as they were who or where're you in terms of accomplishment that your achievement is trouble free.

Take Ford. He had established his own company from the scratch and at the time the largest car Maker in the world, Ford Company welcomed employees to criticize the management; and this is not all: these people would be awarded be that financially materially of in terms of promotion if they presented outstanding criticism. A young salesman by the name E. H Little who was nowhere near any significant attention used to go back and ask the prospect about what his mistakes in selling skills were; what he did wrong or what he didn't do better. He rose to be president of the same largest world soap Maker Colgate—Palmolive-Peet soap. Charles Luckman president of Pespsodent never looked at the letters praising the operations but those criticizing it. Einstein admitted he made mistakes 99% of his times. Thomas Edison conducted 10000 experiments and admitted he did same number of mistakes before he discovered an electric bulb. Roosevelt, president and the greatest thinker since the last century admitted that his best performance was at only around 75%. Charles Darwin spent 15 years criticizing his own work, the origin of species before he accepted to publish it. The impact it has contributed to the world of science is inexplicable!

Michael Jordan the all time NBA top scorer said he managed to attain that accomplishment because he tried many times and made so many mistakes. Lincoln happily responded to a mock and scorns from his appointees, and particularly in this case his secretary of war and withdrew his order to transfer regiments. Dale Carnegie whose studies and books reveal a lot on the topic of self criticism records that Lincoln knew the criticisms were sincere founded on knowledge and spirit of helpfulness. Thus Mr. Carnegie admonishes that we ought to say to ourselves that: "May be I ought to be 20% mistaken, maybe I deserve these criticisms, maybe I should be thankful and try to benefit from them."

H. P Powell did criticize himself so often and had set a specific day in the week for self criticism. Probably the fascinating description Dale Carnegie gives is about Ben Franklyn. He didn't wait for a week; he would pick a bad habit and put on gloves and when the bell rang he would come out of his corner fighting the bad habit until he knocked it down before going to bed.

Waste no time in questioning soundness of criticism from people around you. They are more right about you than you are! "The opinion of our enemies, come nearer to the truth about us than do our opinions (about ourselves) as rightly observed the French philosopher Rochefoucauld. Walt Whitman said "Have you learned lessons of those who only admired you, and were tender with you, and stood aside for you? Have you not learned the great lessons from those who rejected you, and braced themselves against you, or disputed the passage with you?" sadly as D. Brown wrote, I've come to a sad conclusion that "In my experience men go to too far greater lengths (trying) to avoid what they fear than (trying) to obtain what they desire." How fool we always play! Reinhold rightly Niebuhr prayed that "God grant me the serenity to accept the things I cannot change; the courage to change the things I can and the wisdom to know the difference!"We cannot expect to grow and prosper if we don't scan our own persons to which Fredrick Hegel said "Comprehension without critical evaluation is impossible."

And these aren't my own feelings. No! You can read it in Dale Carnegie's great book, *How to Stop Worrying and Start Living* page 224. The greatest leader and an honest man should emulate King Saul. Like Saul, I've often realized that "I've played the fool and have erred exceedingly." The greatest leader and an honest man in King David, recognizing the blunder he had done, he shouted in a lamentation saying: "I have erred greatly in what I have done...I have done so foolishly (2 Samuel 24:10). Didn't Lincoln write to his junior man to admit thus: "I now wish to make the personal acknowledgment that you were right, and I was wrong...?" That was typical of Lincoln, typical of every sensible or ideal scholar. He, Lincoln, would have sent a word and that would not go on record. He would have asked his secretary to write the same note. He would have written a note and have it sent without signing it. Instead he chose to finish the letter with "Yours very truly, A. Lincoln!"

Now you must have began to realize the inevitable haunting truth. The truth is that: you can never be prosperous if you can't manage yourself. Yet you cannot manage yourself without criticizing yourself. As a final point you must remember the universe works around certain principles. You need not fight the universe. It is like swimming in waters of the sea. Go by the waves. Try to review why people succeed and others fail. All my other books discuss the differences and parity between winners and failures.

Writing the same thing the other way round, Dale Carnegie narrates how Margaret Fuller the famous New England feminist I suppose after fighting inequality between sexes and gender imbalance against women for ages and failed after a great deal of self torture she offered as her credo declaring that "I accept the universe!"You and I'd better accept the inevitable too! This then brings us to the inevitable need for transformation. And change. The world today demands change than ever before. We have seen that happening almost everywhere. When change swept the Arab nations in what they called Arab spring, the west giggled saying, *we knew it was apt to happen*. Transformation was inevitable in the barbaric Arab society—they said! When the same happened in Africa they said the embezzlers, corrupt African leaders were behind it. Yet we have seen youth demanding change in America and voters went out in line to bring change in the form of Barack Obama. In UK Gordon Brown was ousted. The Frenchmen laid off president Sarkozy, sending him packing from the state house prematurely sending him home to Chic 16th Arrondissement to retirement even after he had ordered the gunning down of the terrorists in the streets of Paris, as the Frenchmen chose Hollande's slogan: Le Changement C'est Mentainent—instead!

43. PERSONAL SELF-CENSORSHIP AND LASTING PROSPERITY

"It is not hard to make decisions when you know what your values are." —Roy Disney

This is a chapter you may have judged that it could be skipped! I tell you it is a critical chapter. It is so because without direction, guidance or courses to aim for, call it anything; you will end up underperforming even with our great gifts and talents resources or superior character we have taught you in this very book. That's the credo of the universe to which Brodi Ashton concluded rightly that: "Heroes are made by paths they choose, not the powers they are graced with!" how true! Indeed it cannot be truer! So here we are. This chapter is like a mirror with which we use to scan ourselves if we have to stay on track, and by doing so, keep our enthusiasm with which we are assured to make the most of whatever we are in.

Now you recall that I have dedicated this book to one person the author judge to be the true ideal scholar and person. But naturally the *Original Thought* is dedicated to my mother and my brother Julius Kambarangwe (watch closely the balance of an N and a W in the names of the two Juliuses in the lines above) for they indeed stand out originally as true role models for the author himself. But being his own mother and brother respectively, little would be its impact to the diversity of my readers if I chose to dwell on only my mother and my own sibling! Not simply for that reason that I've had to wonder about seeking anyone else to rescue the mission though? For though I had so many options to choose from,, yet there was no one who could stand against the person excepting of course one Nicholas. And this is no exaggeration.

It is rather the reflection of the ideal we taught in this very book i.e., to be impactful. That's why I taught that to be impactful is invaluable. It is no fiction that when you live an impactful life, humans tend revere that person so eternally. You must have heard the life story of saint Nicholas—one way or the other. Born in Parata, Lycia and growing up in modern day turkey, Nicholas was born to a very wealthy family and inherited quite a fortune he didn't touch. In a famous story , he threw bags of gold through the windows of three girls who about to be forced into the life of prostitution He distributed it to the needy.

He was very famous that the Emperor Justinian dedicated a church in Constantinople to him. By 900s AD., according to www.christianitytoday.com/ch/news/2004/nick.html, a famous Greek writer wrote, the west as well as the east glorifies him. wherever there are people, his name is revered and churches are built in his honor," he wrote, "all Christians reverence his memory," he continued, "and call upon his protection," He is said to have been presented more frequently by artists than any saint but Mary, and nearly 400 churches were dedicated in his honor in England alone during the late middle ages. The same website reveals.

Indeed you have heard his nick name before. It is Saint Claus—a life giving saint whose life is marked on every December 6 also to mark the beginning of Christmas season, also marking the birth of life giving child Christ, also his other nickname which began with martin Luther's reformation. But probably what is the cream of the whole thing, when you are impactful, people go out of their way to serve you. But for Nichols it was unprecedented. His congregation believed they couldn't manage without him. That's why after his death, a set of his believers organized themselves, and secretly they dug his tomb and reclaimed his bones, bringing Nicholas back into their lives.

Yet I chose him because of not only the impact this man's life has had on the lives of millions of people now living and billions yet unborn, but also because of the impact that cannot be easily equaled, I referred him to Nicholas because I saw him. I lived in the vicinity of his house at one point in time. This makes my story real than if I chose Saint Nicholas. But indeed it is because of his outstanding character —and not his political power or elegance that I didn't have to think twice to decide that this book should be written in memory of his life. I don't write or dedicate the book and chapter to this person only based on what I read or listened to—mind you! My life has been a reflection of his work. And certainly that's not all. The first time I met him in person, I realized he was different. He remains a true ideal human ever as you are about to see. Truly I've read about the ancient and especially the great biblical heroes, people who supremely fall into the category of ideal human person, yet my readers demand and deserve more plausible exemplars. Therefore even if I would just present the old men of the holy bible and successfully seal my message, I chose to do some scratching of the head to get someone you, my reader, can relate to. And after some serious thought, I managed to come up with a person my readers can easily and happily connect with!

Let us talk a little about the great biblical heroes. They remain real great men in all history. Besides, they are almost accepted as fathers of faith among the major three world religions—and their multiplicity of denominations or sects— that form nearly half the world's population. The great among them you and I can recall Moses, Ibrahim, Judah son of Jacob and his young brother Joseph despite the latter's little trifling occasions he brought to himself bragging about yes, his dazzling dreams; but inherently because he was darling to their father. And you cannot blame the old man! To him Joseph was the first born. Remember if not for Labani tricking him, marrying him Leah his elder daughter instead of Rachel, a lady he would have married many years back, but had to marry after many years of back-breaking labor! Read the book of Genesis!

All these people were fiercely serviceful to their people. They were loyal and honest people, humble, diligent, belligerent, listening persistent, pragmatic yet they were fiercely faithful yes to God but equally so to people around them as is humanly possible. Take David for instance. Despite his lust and an affair with Uriah's wife, he was so an honest servant of God. Well before we move farther probably it is high time I reminded you my reader that we are engaged in an undertaking of scanning ourselves. We are attempting to form the character in relation to the people who triumphed, people we can learn from and connect with.

We see almost all great men in history be that the American history, Napoleon's, or even the Hinda triumph in the pre-colonial Southern Uganda and northern Tanzania. They, yes, were vigilant but risk takers. Ibrahim complied with God's commandment almost unquestionably. He obeyed to leave his people and possessions trailing to a new land, the land he knew not yet knowing the tremendous cost he was paying and incredible risk involved. Incredibly still almost like half wits grabbed a machete sharpened it and laid down his only son having lost his other son handcuffed him and straightened his own son's neck ready to it in obedience to the call on loyalty and submission to God. We know that God stopped him short but that doesn't change anything about his loyalty! Take Moses for instance. He was loyal to his people to the extent of abdicated the throne in Egypt choosing instead to serve his people. Notice that he hadn't just abdicated the throne but also had risked his own life siding with people Pharaoh considered enemies.

He had staked his life to save his people. It was a tough task ahead of him that emotionally he wrote a book about it and named it Exodus! Noah heeded the wise counsel and by faith built and entered into the ark, a deed that portrayed nothing but insanity in the eyes of beholders. Floods? The end of an era? A massive wooden structure? Collection of all kinds of animals! That's insanity, they concluded! He entered the crazy structure, and shutting himself and his obedient sons and their families with him alone, away from the magnificent world. Enough! He was insane and needed some high powered machines for mental check up! But such machines never existed at the time, let alone therapy. So they pitied the man. Yet in a couple of days the bright sky gloomed and the dark cloud above slowly but surely shocked the crowds below. Soon his predictions turned out to be true.

Judas risked his own life against his envious brothers when he chose to protect Joseph. The ideals or virtues or the core values we teach are really the compass to a person. Ideals persons tend to have exclusive devotion to their preset virtues and as a result they never falter. Such persons include the biblical Moses, Joseph, David, Daniel, Shadrack, Meshach and Abednego. In captivity they didn't turn away from God. Bribed or amidst the Gods they didn't forsake God. And it pays. Moses was called to be God's prophet. Joseph became prime minister in Egypt a foreign land. David defeated the giant goliath and went on to be king over Israel. Daniel survived the lion in its own den. Shadrack, Meshach and Abednego survived the inferno.

All these people are certainly great ideal persons. Yet to too many people, and they may be humanly right, that is history. I never saw them. I can read and write about these heroes but it is by faith. That brings in my mother and sibling. Yet they are my own flesh and blood. I can be under the influence of bias on one hand and on the other a few of you will justifiably say they would stake their own lives to save one's own brothers son or daughter and you may be right. Besides, the impact and extent of their deeds may even though did cross the family borders still they can be judged regional. That's why I suggest taking you down the memory lane of my own first-hand personal contact with my chosen ideal person. He is different. Yes far different from others who had something to gain materially or morally when supporting others. He didn't do it to gain anything personally. He had all things you would dream of materially and fame or recognition. He didn't do it to claim his voters support on the ballot box. That he was assured of. He didn't give all his life in order to accumulate wealth or a stake on the national wealth which we have in plenty from gold to diamond and huge land enclosures. Instead he banned personal ownership of the land and shut down all mines.

He didn't do it to get for himself a possession of a house. He had one enough for him and didn't even bother to build or buy another. He went to great heights distributing wealth and property among them a high storey building often offered to him. He was in power yet he abandoned power and possessions choosing to serve his people.

The astonishing thing and far more incredible still, is that this person I met down my memory lane, didn't pursue anything whatsoever for personal gain. He quantified his success based on the wellbeing of the others, and of the future generation. That's what puts him in his own league, a league in which he can only be dwarfed by Jesus of Nazareth. This person is a great prophet—a teacher and leader—a selfless individual; a true role model for many praiseworthy people—an individual who gave his all for the others, his people, his nation, the southern African States and all humanity across the globe; one the author regards as true and real ideal scholar —and an ideal human. He remains an ideal person, one of the few ideal humans who ever lived!

He isn't a fictional character, mind you! That is the incredible part of the story. He walked and worked on the face of this very speeding rotating and revolving oval planet some men God-knows-who chose to call the earth. He travelled over the waters and through the air preaching ideals in his own unique way. While many choose to shut up and enjoy the party he chose instead not just wording ideals but as wrote about it. That is all. For if that is what he did the author would probably approaching that privilege! Far from just speech or writing about ideals he lived an ideal life in an incredible way such that it transfused into his own life and body and thought and deeds such that even the air around him danced at it crossed his path that short of vegetation birds and beasts even great men abroad sung halleluiah whenever they were privileged to be in his presence. Today after many years since he departed to the next world, his principles not only they still are true, but indeed they are truer and getting even more attention than during his time that the author finds the works of God above so tantalizing. I cannot stop to imagine that probably God called him so his works could live on and on their own without his patronage so they could blossom even ever more. No protégé ever stood taller in presence of the patron! I've said this because I can see most you almost on the verge of weeping mourning loss of this person you don't even know yet! It is not loss! It happened that we may gain more!

I repeat. He is not a fictitious character crafted by this author. The author being man and not God cannot create life though he can create books. Remember again you are engaged in self evaluation and indeed I'm building this mental picture of the ideal person so you can map your own person and character around him.

I can already almost hear some of you say: it cannot be! He is lying. He is a liar like all fiction writers, "you say. This isn't work of fiction. It isn't a novel! I insist he is authentic and bona fide! Here's my declaration. I, the author was privileged not simply to only hear his speeches, read the books he wrote, or just simply behold his portrait. No. I saw him personally and with a naked eye when the author happily volunteered to serve as a helping hand in his farm in Butiama during this author's one year military national service term at Buhemba and Rwamkoma—in Tanzania. Talk about being responsible, during his entire life, this man would never go home to sleep and let his country go to the dogs! It is because of his hard choices in life that you can read this book, a book written by a poor and less privileged village boy. The author wouldn't have written this book without free universal education system that the he had championed. Indeed, beginning with my own family and my neighborhood, when I see humble contribution you and I can play in transforming others; when I see, read or hear the influence our works and examples have impacted upon others, I'm shocked by how a small and humble part a person plays can make big difference in other people's lives. That's why I'm short of words at the influence of the waves of his influence!

Relinquishing power and choosing to retire back in his home village, wasn't something strange to him. In his campaign trail during the first years of independence and thereupon the union with Zanzibar, after the latter had deposed the Arab ruler popularly known as Sultan) Zanzibaris asked him to stay on permanently but he told them that, that would be unfair to the people; saying that if he stayed on forever, their efforts to depose the Sultan would be meaningless even though the man in power was black. He told them that that wouldn't make any difference for by staying on, he would himself become a sultan and probably he would then demand to be called Sultan Nyerere. When in our neighborhood a president demanded he be addressed as something close to *The Almighty*, Mwalimu chose to be addressed as *comrade*. And this is not the author's own sentiments only because he is his country man, or even because he gained directly from Mwalimu's character, leadership and persona. No! President Robert Mugabe of Zimbabwe has recently called upon his fellow African leaders to honor Mwalimu Julius Kambarage Nyerere.

"I want to say, when all honor has been showered on heroes in Africa, the man who has been humiliated is Mwalimu Julius Nyerere. There we are, liberation movements, there we were— depending on the resources in Tanzania. But there has been nothing said about this man and his country at the OAU. Nkrumah, yes, he had that support ... But Tanzania, to say Nyerere was like any other. I want Zimbabweans, to stand for Nyerere. Africa should be reminded of the responsibility that it thrust on this man, a burden to train all liberation movements. It was a burden that was not only political, but, at the end of the day, there is no one to say Tanzania deserves to be mentioned. At the end of the day, there is no one to say Tanzania deserved to be even mentioned, just mere mentioning as having accomplished that mission, that mission to have us as friends, that mission to make us train our liberation movements in Africa. There is none, none, none, none, none at all who have recognized what Nyerere did. Just look at the nature of the mission he undertook. He never changed at all and we were all there. We of Zimbabwe are not ungrateful, we are not ingrates. We are a grateful nation and we shall undertake to honor this man. We all went in various ways, in various dimensions, to Tanzania to liberate our countries and we have not gone back to Tanzania. Well, I am going to be chair of the AU and I am going to tackle this issue," he said, drawing applause from guests at the function." And well, Mugabe didn't end there. He has just written and launched a book in Mwalimu Nyerere's honor.

A devout Catholic, he often fasted and lived a humble life by not enriching himself at his nation's expense. When Tanzania, which was then called Tanganyika, attained its independence in 1961, President Nyerere strongly believed that his own country's independence would be meaningless if other African countries were not free. He worked tirelessly in support of this goal for Zambia (1964), Malawi (1964), Botswana (1966), Lesotho (1966), Mauritius (1968), Swaziland (1968) and the Seychelles (1976). When the other countries of Southern Africa were forced into wars of liberation to eventually achieve the same end, Tanzania provided political, material and moral support until independence and majority rule was achieved in 1975 (Mozambique, Angola), 1980 (Zimbabwe), 1990 (Namibia) and finally, 1994 (South Africa). President Nyerere pursued the ideals of liberation, democracy and common humanity for the rest of the continent and with the leaders of the other few African countries that were independent in 1963, established the Organization of African Unity (OAU), now the African Union, whose main objective was political liberation for the rest of the continent. He was the first Chairman of the Frontline States, a body that was set up to support liberation movements in Southern Africa…fighting colonialism, racism and… minority rule.

A charismatic leader of sharp intellect and great personal integrity, he welded a country and a national identity from over 120 ethnic groups, united by their language Swahili and by a social harmony constructed on the ideals of peace, justice, unity and personal commitment. His firm support for equality and tolerance ranged across all diversity of race, religion, class and gender. He encouraged Tanzanian women to play a leadership role in society and adopted a parliamentary system that has guaranteed seats for women. His pursuit of an equitable socio-economic society through collective self-reliance was more difficult than he had envisaged, and he once said that "we are very good at sharing the wealth in Tanzania but I only wish we had made more wealth to share."

One very successful campaign drew a voluntary contribution of one shilling each to support Mozambique. Nyerere pursued the ideals of liberation, democracy and common humanity into the rest of the continent. Tanzania has had three presidential transitions since then, first to Ali Hassan Mwinyi for two five-year terms, in 1995; Benjamin Mkapa for two five-year terms; and then in 2005 to the current President, Jakaya Kikwete, (and now JPM). Mwalimu often said that his generation had achieved at least one goal, that of the political liberation of Africa, and that the next generations must take up the next goals. A long memorial verse by his close friend and colleague, Dr Kenneth Kaunda, the former President of Zambia, reminds us all that, "The best way of mourning him is to carry on where he has left."

Born in Butiama near Lake Victoria on 13 April 1922, when he passed away 10 years ago on 14 October 1999, Africans everywhere shared the sense of loss felt by Tanzanians. Reporting events during his mourning, as quoted in Dar es Salaam Guide magazine, Saidi Ibrahim wrote thus: the positive reaction came from millions of Tanzanians who regarded Mwalimu as the Father of the Nation (Baba wa Taifa) a great leader committed to promoting and protecting their equality and welfare. Miss

Joan Wicken, Mwalimu's closest aide…attended the official state funeral in Dar es Salaam and burial in his village Butiama on 23 October 1999. Observing the events, she wrote, "It was sad but also awesome. The people went in the hundreds of thousands more wherever the coffin was. For the most part they stood in quietness. The grief was palpable….millions of Tanzanians were involved because they wanted to be. The police just stood back and let the people go where they wanted to only gently keeping path clear when necessary. Some people were crying but there was none of the formal wailing. For the most part, it was the quietness, the standing in sorrow and slow movements afterwards that made me want to cry," She wrote! "There was no pushing or shoving it was a depth of community mourning in which there was nothing formal or forced. It was individual as well as coming together." Mr. Saidi then, revealing the greatness of this man, reports that upon his death, even crime in Tanzania was temporarily suspended in order to honor his memory. The criminals argued that Mwalimu was a man of peace and therefore his mourning should be peaceful, concluded Saidi Ibrahim.

Though this might not be a reason why the Catholic Church began a process of anointing him saint, nor associating this true and fair analysis as anything near the author's campaign to influence this great church, yet the author recognizes that it is through such rare God's own creation, that today others, people who live today—you and I—may learn to live a life of giving our very own lives for the others—and doubtlessly why in whose name the author's father dedicated his long awaited son, the author's big brother after Julius Kambarage Nyerere. It is for all this that this book is thus written in the memory of none other but Mwalimu Julius Kambarage Nyerere, the first president of the United Republic of Tanzania, and father of the nation; with gratitude, admiration and fondness. May God rest his soul in eternal peace, Amen! Before we launch into actual self-censorship, let us ponder a little about the whole thing. Is self-censorship important? Yes it is. Recall that the right definition of education: To draw out from inside. Therefore true change comes from the inside out. But if this change has to be sustained, it has to be tested often, and tested against the best—whether that best persona is Mwalimu Nyerere's, or that of your own at its best. Indeed self-censorship can best be described in words of Ornstein and Hunkins as *future intelligence*. In their analysis of the same, using words of Toffler, they wrote that it (self-censorship) is "as though a once-dead organism…. (can) suddenly … (check) its own blood pressure, pulse and breathing rate (Ornstein and Hunkins 1998 p.392).

SELF SCANNING FOR INDIVIDUAL SCHOLARS

You business in this world is not to judge others but yourself. In his Action Principles, FitzPatrck says: "No one ever built a stronger self if he relied upon what may be the self-serving false appraisal. Do yourself a favor and be honest with yourself. Ask yourself: Am I doing all I can do? During your quiet time each day, quickly contemplate: Is this the way that I want to be thinking and acting? Make self—reflection a daily habit. Pay close attention to yourself." Stay home. That's where the truth and healing are found. So go on and ask yourself the following questions: Am I ready and able to generate an income on my own, or simply I'm attuned to work for somebody else? Yes I work for somebody else but do I produce value as I ought to? Am I in harmony with myself at this job or endeavor I'm in? What impact do I bring to the job? Do I only do my part according to job description and then relax or I can cross my JD and are willing and able to offer support physically and at thought to my peers and other departments. How do I contribute to output and harmony at work? How do I stand against professor Maliyamkono's KPI in which the performance of graduates should thus judged on criteria that relate to their ability to respond flexibly creatively and competently to work after graduation to national development and to the needs of the employer or the workplace.

How do I see myself vis a vis "…the ability to understand and unravel problems within the society; caused by the ever changing economic, technological, and social environment in which we live."How do you respond to other people's opinion? The solution is to make a thorough study of who you are and learn to accept thyself for otherwise you will always be a slave to people and environment around you! And that's not God's plan for you. God didn't create you and your children that you may slave forever. Never. Don't you ever heed the propaganda of the evil men in some uniforms? To be educated is to be free from others but bound by the indispensable interdependence. How do you stand against a person who has concise information and succinct knowledge that give instant solutions to solve the company problems or add immediate value to the company? Indeed an educated person cannot be identified by the amount of general knowledge one has but how that knowledge can be interpreted into profitable gainful cost effective advantages and commercially beneficial results.

How do you compare with Miriam Chirwa? Miriam Chirwa is a talented young Tanzania girl with sight deficiency. Yet her physical impairment has been outstripped by her credo—a credo she made plain in her singing when she prayed that she be recognized for the work of her hands and her brains and not by mere lip service, a pledge she made in her Kiswahili song: *Unitambulishe*, which may stand for "*Let the people recognize my impact.*" In this song—the song in which she certainly referred to the biblical king David—she teaches us that true impact is often wrapped in uphill struggle. David was just a boy when he rose to eminence because of the work of his hands and his resilience. He worked hard looking after the flock of his father's; he severally did fight predators protecting his flock before he actually fought and defeated the Goliath. And that's the moment he became king even though it took a couple of years before establishing his throne.

How do you see yourself socially? Do you or you never pride yourself on of your achievements? Do you have any, anyway? Small or big, count it, and build on it. (Alongside his fellow MPs from Kagera region, Sebastian Kinyondo, the then cabinet minister in Tanzania, addressing the author and a number of his peers from Kagera who studied at the university of Dar es Salaam, challenged us saying it wasn't a bad thing to remind yourself—not others—about your accomplishments, in order to be motivated by what you have achieved. That's probably how we picked Kinyondo spirit in bringing to surface some of personal accomplishments—to inspire the reader to seek the same and somehow to feel happy about his achievement). Are you humble and down to earth? Are you or not a person who may walk into a crowd of people and no one would even notice your presence? If you don't grasp what I say, go to any shop next door and pick Eddy Murphy's film *Coming to America* and compare yourself with Prince Akim.

With reference to *Coming to America,* are you akin to low profile Akim the prince, or to the showy Semmi? How do people feel in your company? Do you help people get filled with a sense of confidence and harmony or anxiety—and why? Do you encourage or discourage people around you to think and do better? Do you interfere with peoples thoughts impose or influence your opinion or respect other people's views? Do you listen to others or just want to be heard. Are you truthful that you try to find harmonious ways to correct others or simply keep quite fearing to antagonize with them when actually they are going astray. Are you the self appointed main speaker in every occasion; or you endeavor to let others rise to the occasion?

Do you listen and try to learn from others and speak only when necessary? Is this for you important because it builds others? Notice however that even when you must respect other people's views you should be able to suggest an appropriate alternative when necessary. You must however be able to do it in a way that you won't offend another person. You must do so with a twinkle in your eye, always friendly, supportive. Again, are you happy to be seated in the backbenches and always not thinking about your own person or importance but service to others? What does leadership mean to you? Is it to serve and to be there when needed or to occupy places of glory or to be main attraction and attract most attention? How do you rank yourself against producing actual viable deliverable applicable plans down to actual results against theorizing? You will notice this if future tense dominates your conversation when talking about your plans. I'll do this I do that wait and see etc. to an ideal person plans are important to him so as is order but getting results and quality results is far more important. "Education," said Herbert Spenser, "is not knowledge but action."

How do you see yourself in terms of your thoughts—and ideal—in the fast changing world? How do you measure up with your peers? Even when we shouldn't be driven by our peers but casting a blurred eye can help you to judge your own person. Your family or wife and children are they in harmony with you and in line with this questionnaire. What is your reaction when you face temporary defeat? Does this series of questions torment or excite you. Do you expect more from others than you do from yourself? Do you already know what you want in life? Are pursuing it or you are you lack ambition to pursue it. Do you read books and pursue self-advancement in that line. How do I measure up with Mwalimu Nyerere's responsible demand for commitment for your family community and the nation as a whole?" Those who receive this privilege of education have a duty to return the sacrifice which others have made. They are like a man who's been given all the food available in a starving village in order that he might have the strength to bring the supplies back from a distant place. If he takes this food and doesn't bring the help (back) to his brothers (and sisters), he is (nothing but) a traitor!" concluded Mwalimu Julius Kambarage Nyerere

Self scanning—or self censorship, is beneficial to you because you cannot pin down, locate, identify and ascertain your potential, or turn it around without identifying, and addressing or redressing your strength and weaknesses. By accurate analysis you can augment your strength and reduce if not to get rid of your weaknesses altogether. It is mainly through these two aspects that we are assessed—aspect through which we can spot opportunities and use them to grow. The foregoing analysis is very important for without it—without this hindsight—you or I cannot spot the opportunities that are actually silently lying low, waiting for us. How then do you display what you don't know you posses as strength or conceal as weaknesses as you work to *purify* yourself. Probably you are asking yourself if this is really important. It is more than that. For indeed the goal of education is not mastery of subject matter, but of one's person. Really if the education in place cannot afford us to have mastery over our own persons what then is it for?

SELF EVALUATION FOR THE YOUTH: GENERAL CHECKPOINTS

Probably some of my curious readers may already be suggesting that certainly I should have ended this book right here—without further ado. May be not far too long from now that they will realize they were off the mark. So let me take my liberty to go on a little further into this analysis, considering that this and the preceding books seem to have placed lot of blames on the youth, and so it would otherwise be unfair if we didn't show them the path, guidance. We should not only point fingers, but guide them; lead them as to how they may be leading themselves towards becoming their own leaders.

Article 26 of the African youth charter identifies a number of responsibilities of Youth. How do you evaluate yourself against these responsibilities? The Charter can be said to be a declaration of the rights of the youth in their homeland. But we know that right come with responsibilities. So the document also identifies a set of responsibilities of the youth. Notice also that though the charter identifies these as responsibilities of the youth, African youth, but they are responsibilities of every member of every other society regardless of the continent or country one comes from, or his age. Besides, talking about the youth, that he is no longer youthful? It is tricky. Therefore these are responsibilities for all of the readers who are young at heart as president Kennedy used to say.

Every young person—the charter indicates—that he shall have responsibilities towards his family and society, the State, and the international community. Youth, thus, shall have the duty to: a) become the custodians of their own development; b) protect and work for family life and cohesion; c) have full respect for parents and elders and assist them anytime in cases of need in the context of positive African values; d) partake fully in citizenship duties including voting, decision making and governance; e) engage in peer-to-peer education to promote youth development in areas such as literacy, use of information and communication technology, HIV/AIDS prevention, violence prevention and peace building.

Others include: f) to contribute to the promotion of the economic development of state parties and Africa by placing their physical and intellectual abilities at its service; g) espouse an honest work ethic and reject and expose corruption; h) work towards a society free from substance abuse, violence, coercion, crime, degradation, exploitation and intimidation; promote tolerance, understanding, dialogue, consultation and respect for others regardless of age, race, ethnicity, color, gender, ability, religion, status or political affiliation; j) defend democracy, the rule of law and all human rights and fundamental freedoms; k) encourage a culture of voluntarism and human rights protection as well as participation in civil society activities; l) promote patriotism towards and unity and cohesion of Africa; m) promote, preserve and respect African traditions and cultural heritage and pass on this legacy to future generations; n) become the vanguard of re-presenting cultural heritage in language sand in forms to which youth are able to relate; o) protect the environment and conserve nature.

SELF EVALUATION FOR THE WORTHY PARENTS—AND GUARDIANS

Probably you should be interested to know that the author learned to read and write at home. You certainly should be interested to recall that the author turned the marionette he inhabited himself and later with his wife and children for long time as a school for a number of his sibling. It is also worthy to note that with support of my sibling as art of returning help after the sacrifice the family had done and our setting was hailed and upraised even copied throughout all Karagwe and Bukoba and later in Kigoma, Shinyanga and Dar es Salaam the neighborhood we lived. I know that whether directly or indirectly the system we crafted, I mean, myself, my brothers and sisters have impacted lives of many since then—going forward. It was mutual responsibility—and so economical. The boys and girls went on to be exemplary wherever they were in schools or later at workplaces and families they built. These aren't my words. I have received commendations from people like Super Rwamkina—among others. Super is a senior a veterinary officer back in the township where the author grew up. That's why he knows the history of the author's history probably than the back of his hand. So that's why—and how—he called the author all the way from, Kyerwa, Karagwe near Uganda border, after he had watched the author on television launching the last couple of his books. Therefore when I say self analysis as a parent or guardian should carry more weight than any other self analysis I know what I say.

Probably you should consider that the home forms the primary educational institution for everyone. Here're some of the key questions we should be questioning ourselves as parents: Am I helping my child to be an ideal man or woman? As a father or mother how do I help my child to become a keen learner who will be hard working and committed to his endeavor? How do I help to identify and nurture my child's talent and calling? How do I support his or her intuition, instincts and choice of calling? How do I support the school? How do I support his or her career development and the spirit of continued self learning? Do I support or curtail his or her relocation into his own chosen vocation or self employment and entrepreneurship. Finally do I support his or her struggle toward becoming an impactful and a self reliant person? How do ration my time and resources in favor of education and child upbringing.

Do I regularly check her home-work? How do I cooperate with the school and the teachers? How open do I converse with my child? Have I prepared myself to provide for her now and future? Do I simply command, or take part in her learning? How do I set example or my child? How do I compare with Bill Clinton's assessment of an ideal parent? The reader may be compelled to reread about the quality of being impactful. But in short, the ideal parent can be said to be the one who cares for his or her family's happiness than his or hers. How truly do you weigh against with this ideal? It is important to remember that even if we love our children we must allow ourselves to allow them to stand on their feet than letting them lean on us their whole lives. And this must start as early as possible.

As a final point in underscoring the role of parents and guardians, no one should take the responsibility over their children as a sport. They shouldn't take it for granted saying I am upright and if my children aren't, it is upon them to answer. This is not true. In the first book of Samuel, 1 Samuel 2:12-36, we learn that Eli's sons had became scoundrels. But they had been so under their father's watch. Prophet Eli was himself steadfast before the Lord. God didn't punish only his sons nonetheless! He also penalized both Eli's sons along with Eli himself. If God penalized his own prophet for the same thing you are doing, what about you? Isn't your situation worse?

SELF-CENSORSHIP FOR SCHOOLS AND TEACHERS
The schools or colleges as individual entities and probably the most important one in educational agenda ought to ask themselves the following questions at the beginning of every semester to see if they really are ideal schools or institutions. The school admin team should ask itself such

questions such as: What is it that I'm chiefly obliged to offer as my service to my constituency? What is my chief goal in this service? Is it money or service? Am I helping in creating and developing my students to be ideal persons? (Please reread the traits of the Ideal Scholar from the preceding pages and mark off one against your performance.) And if not so, why not? What are the reasons? What is the intent of my teaching? Content? Do I dictate or rightly guide the students and trainees to find it out in their hearts the inspirations that deeply touch them? What is the level of my preparedness? What can I do to improve my teaching methodology?

How do I leverage the potential and opportunities lying idle both physical and intellectual such as talents of my staff and buildings? How are we going (and now) to start taking advantage of this program and the partnership thereof? Do I know my weaknesses? strength? Threats? How do I respond to challenges from my customers and from ICT? You cannot keep business thriving and making money on the backs of poor parents or lowly paid employees (read on other sources of income or even let us know if we can be of help). Is the management aligned and in congruence with the role and goals of schools and education as a whole the students and education itself apart from the owners' equity? How are we treating students with poor or low self- esteem? And failures? Are we helping them or cursing them as fall outs.

How do we treat children from the rich families? Do we envy them or praise them? Do we treat them with impartiality? Or do we ridicule weak students whose parents are relatively less wealthy. How does it affect their learning process, character and their self- esteem? Do we dictate terms or allow teachers to supplement their teaching styles and explore their talents and intuition while allowing students to think and create? By entrusting students with responsibility we give them ability to think out of the box. We allow them to see that the sky is the limit. It is only through this way and none other that we can progress and exceed our expectations as tutors and schools or colleges. Finally what impact are we imparting to the students and staff? Is it positive or negative? Do the students return home the same person or even disillusioned bunch of hopeless people on graduation? What about teachers? Do they prosper as free minds and people who are keen to self-advancement or hopeless people who only wish to end the day and rush to the nearby bottle store? What about their families? The environmental issues: how do we address them?

In words of David Orr: "If education is to be measured against the standard of sustainability, what can be done? I would like to make four proposals.

First, I would like to propose that you engage in a campus-wide dialogue about the way you conduct your business as educators. Does four years here make your graduates better planetary citizens or does it make them, in Wendell Berry's words, "itinerant professional vandals"? Does this college contribute to the development of a sustainable regional economy or, in the name of efficiency, to the processes of destruction? My second suggestion is to examine resource flows…

"Collectively, begin a process of finding ways to shift the buying power of this institution to support better alternatives that do less environmental damage, lower carbon dioxide emissions, reduce use of toxic substances, promote energy efficiency and the use of solar energy, help to build a sustainable regional economy, cut long-term costs, and provide an example to other institutions. The results of these studies should be woven into the curriculum as inter-disciplinary courses, seminars, lectures, and research. No student should graduate without understanding how to analyze resource flows and without the opportunity to participate in the creation of real solutions to real problems. Third, reexamine how your endowment works. Is it invested according to the Valdez principles? Is it invested in companies doing responsible things that the world needs? Can some part of it be invested locally to help leverage energy efficiency and the evolution of a sustainable economy throughout the region?

"…I propose that you set a goal of ecological literacy for all of your students. No student should graduate from this or any other educational institution without a basic comprehension of: the laws of thermodynamics; the basic principles of ecology; carrying capacity; energetic; least-cost, end-use analysis; how to live well in a place; limits of technology; appropriate scale; sustainable agriculture and forestry; steady-state economics and environmental ethics. (You have got to ask yourselves): Do graduates of this college, in Aldo Leopold's words, know that "they are only cogs in an ecological mechanism such that, if they will work with that mechanism, their mental wealth and material wealth can expand indefinitely (and) if they refuse to work with it, it will ultimately grind them to dust." Leopold asked: "If education doesn't teach us these things, then what is education for?"

Finally, how do we define health be it for ourselves, our children, employees or managers, teachers and students? Remember health is, according to World Health Organization: "not merely the absence of disease or infirmity but instead and indeed a state of complete physical, mental, and social well-being!" Besides the foregoing, we ought also to consider spiritual or ethical aspect. A healthy person is therefore a person who is growing, sustainable, is delighted with what he does privately and in public, loves his social and professional engagements in his career or vocation which is itself profitable, elevating and gratifying to all of the parties involved, yet an endeavor that doesn't harm but nourish the environment around him.

WORKPLACE SCRUTINY
Nurturing of the students is mainly believed by many to be done in schools and at home. That is not right. Workplaces have a lot to do with child upbringing. Company politics and the people we associate with tend to flow down the high buildings into our apartment and bungalows at home inside the bedroom and living room. A father or mother who is plunged in the workplace competition for whatever cause is likely to import the sane cause in his, or her, home. Workplaces also ought to recognize that they cannot hire employees from the moon. Like national football teams, the players are produced in the youth teams as are schools and homes in this case. Developing the graduate into future great workers is the responsibility of the workplaces too. Like in athletics the homes and schools have done their part but it upon the workplaces to recognize that they have to identify and develop these traits among employees. Loyal and hardworking employees don't get assembled out of some spare parts or simply get produced out of the blue. They are developed based on certain principles.

The employers ought to recognize that the ideal scholar will be more productive a number of times than the carefree floppy graduate. Besides, it is imperative that you develop principles among your staff because without these ideals, you can hire *great candidates* based on wrong assumptions and may regret at a later stage when you recognize they are useless when it comes to performing real work or getting results. Real work and results are a result of discipline and interpersonal relationships. We may also wonder to find they are academically top performers but without the right character and attitude they may turn out to be mediocre employees in that they aren't flexible and cannot learn to cope with new environment or fail to team up with the rest of the staff toward the core organizational goals. You may wonder to find that instead of being assets they turn out to be great liabilities.

That's why we need to combine technical skills with a right dose of character as the right combination of right skills. The right education and skills development at workplaces ought to help identify and seek and teach a certain specific way of life vis-a-vis "the cunning intellectual discipline of schoolmen." It doesn't represent the actual work and delivery of results. That's why we need to promote the need for, and the habit of desiring to work, and to work hard. This cannot be done without influencing their decision emotionally why they should, and in which direction. If we do so, we will influence change. Go to self-analysis for schools and adopt the self-censorship for the employees and students for employees.

In the final analysis, corporations and schools ought to cooperate in advancing practice. Workplaces should invite students as volunteers. They must as well offer their workplaces as ideal place for continuity and sustainability of these ideals or values through practice, principles and rewards. Managers ought to ask themselves such questions as: how do I personally, or my office, help to instill and develop the ideal values among the novices and fresh graduates. How do I make it the culture of my company? This is important because experience shows that people may often start working with great passion and enthusiasm but soon they become as cold as the Arctic Sea for lack of use, and indeed the denial of their share of voice in the decision making.

Let me give you an example. I was working with Celtel when our marketing team went for regular marketing review meetings with our suppliers and advertising agents. But in the end it was only the directors and senior managers between the organization and the agency who aired their views and soon we would be closing. I saw novices who had so much to say or ask but they were normally railroaded, bullied and made to hide into their shells. I wouldn't let this go on unchecked. I remember advising Yesse Oenga who was my superior as marketing director at the time to let the trainees and novices speak first before the senior personnel wrapped up. This helps to build confidence and indeed to extract inputs from all human resources. You may wonder to find that novices have better ideas since they are still on fire and enthusiastic about the job and their own names unlike the working retired people those who have already reached the apex in their career ladder and thus have no motivation for new thoughts or thinking out of the box.

Furthermore as employers and the organization as a whole we ought to question how you do reward results. How do you endeavor to promote achievers? How do we promote new ideas and leadership? How do we develop roles down to individual employees and departments? How do we help communication bottoms up rather than top down? How do we encourage self development and new skills? How are we involved with our employees self development? How do we link up with schools? How do we support new ideas and reading books and seeking and pursuing new and emerging success factors and business drivers? Do we support actual education such as reading and writing competition as once did BP in Tanzania or we are rather engaged in supporting drinking competitions, arts, and modeling, music and beauty contests? Corporations should remember where they put their money is how their employees in future come from.

GOVERNMENT/MINISTRY AND DEVELOPMENT PARTNERS

The government and development partners too must not stray. They cannot afford to pass the buck. They ought to ask themselves such questions as: how do I support individual initiatives? How do I/we encourage new ideas? How do I / we allocate adequate funds: in sports, family, academics or new ideas. How do I/we allocate time and resources on real education and transformation? How do I / we support family as an institution. How do I or we support the local people in terms of industrial skills as well as personal development namely empowerment of the local people? We cannot import mainstream employees from abroad. How are we involved with self development? How do we link up with schools? How do we support new ideas and reading books and seeking and pursuing new growth drivers? Since education is the main change driver, how do the government and its partners weigh against the United Nations backed youth charter initiative in fostering education and skills development? Here below are a few of areas the governments are required to discharge.

Every young person shall have the right to education of good quality. The value of multiple forms of education, including formal, non-formal, informal, distance learning and life-long learning, to meet the diverse needs of young people shall be embraced. The education of young people shall be directed to: the promotion and holistic development of the young person's cognitive and creative and emotional abilities to their full potential; preparing young people for responsible lives in free societies that promote peace, understanding, tolerance, dialogue, mutual respect and friendship among all nations and across all groupings of people; the preservation and strengthening of positive African morals, traditional values and cultures and the development of national and African identity and pride; the development of respect for the environment and natural resources; the development of life skills to function effectively in society and include issues such as HIV/AIDS, reproductive health, substance abuse prevention and cultural practices that are harmful to the health of young girls and women as part of the education curricula etc... Harness the creativity of youth to promote local cultural values and traditions by representing them in a format acceptable to youth and in a language and in forms to which youth are able to relate; Promote youth entrepreneurship by including entrepreneurship training in the school curricula, providing access to credit, business development skills training, mentorship opportunities and better information on market opportunities etc.

MEDIA AND GENERAL PUBLIC

The media and the general public, together, form one of the top key players in personal, institutional and national transformation program. People in media, and our peers, have thus to ask themselves the following questions concerning their contribution in shaping the society: How is the media transformed—and transforming—for better? How do I/we support individual initiatives? How do I/we encourage new ideas and institutional change? How do I/we allocate our funds: in sports, family, academics or new ideas? How do I/we allocate time and resources in favor of new knowledge, research and transformation? How do I/we support family as an institution? How do I/we support the local folks in the wake of EAC or any regional block such as EU?

THE IDEAL SCHOLAR AND DEATH: THE ULTIMATE METER OF A PERSON'S LIFE

In ending the chapter, let me recall the dialogue the author held with his in-laws the first day he went to get introduced to the family after he had sought their daughter's hand in marriage. Now because he was Christian, his wife's people were worried—and one elder asked the author about his response—he wouldn't honor the Muslim funeral norms when the inevitable comes. I have narrated this before through my previous books, but let here say briefly that he told them that he didn't seek their daughter's hand in marriage to go and die quite in style. Rather he did so to go out there and, with grace of the Lord, help each other to make life better for both of them, their children, their parents and people and environment around them. With enormous soberness, he stated that he didn't think about death when he chose her in a million leaving girls from his own region, tribe or religion, but about life. He was emphasizing that rather it was the life we live that vindicates us; that it is not how we die, or how we get buried that makes a difference, but how we live—the difference we make with our lives!

Now how do you know you have undergone genuine transformation or have become successful? I mean, how do you know you have been transformed, and have lived a successful responsible life? The question is valid. Transformation is very broad. It is also a very complex process. For instance, when a person stops his drinking habit, or smoking, he may assume that it is change worth to brag of. Another person can make money and give the tenth to the poor and believe he has accomplished his part. Lasting transformation or success that's worth praise is all-round. It must also shine all the time until your last day. Changes that shine over time and last soon and forever aren't changes we are talking about.

You can only know if you are transformed if and only if, stretched out during your final moments in that bed you won't need anymore, and knowing it is time for you quit to the next world and that you loved all your children and the whole family and all people who surrounded you not by only sweet lifting words but knowing you contributed to the creation of a better for their better days today and in the future; without mercilessness to animals and vegetation and ecosystem in the general the within and without; knowing you didn't make enemies by getting in their way on your way up and that even at the final hour you can proudly reflect on all you have done and still be able to say, to yourself, *"Oh, wow! Thank God I did my best!"*

And then closing your eyes and for the last time not feeling any anxiety with what your eyes have always desired to see, praying, not appealing for mercy out of fear that you are about to expire, thus asking for a few more years; but rather you somewhat gratefully are thanking God that though you could still do more, but you have served your purpose in life. And when people surrounding your deathbed begin to fret that this could be their final moment to be with you, you can be able to pass on a delightful grateful encouraging smile; and whether they understand it or not, and looking how they are still full of life with the whole world ahead of them, finally as they begin to shed tears realizing it was the end, you can still keep your eyes closed—gracefully nonetheless—whispering: *"Our father in great heaven, I thank Thee Lord, I thank Thee Lord, I thank Thee Lord!"*

Now take a couple of seconds and ponder about a dying person singing halleluiah, praising the Lord that finally he has made it, made it, dying! Think about it! He has accomplished all he had to do in life, and what he couldn't accomplish personally, he passed the leaf on to his next of kin, his children, his family, his sibling and through them, the society as a whole! Indeed that's all that matters in life, the life all worthy religions of the earth teach! That is the ideal graduate! The ideal scholar! That is the ideal person! That is our ideal scholar. That is our ideal leader. So if you think you have done enough, think again!

CONCLUSION

As we wrap up the endeavor to build the ideal scholars that is as well the ideal persons remember this is a maiden attempt to rescue potential of each individual person or organization and community or nation as a whole. And recall this individual can be a person in the form of the student the drop out or youth in the streets the parents the schools and colleges the employers and the corporations but as well the ministries involved with youth education labor and generally the leadership or the government that endeavors to progress its economy and empower its people. The analysis is also directed to grantors and development partners who recognize that we cannot do it alone but as well that we need one another.

These are the worthy people to whom I wrote this book. After all this is what you seek and crave to achieve as individuals or institutions. Importantly for your own evaluation seek to have in place an integrated system which is a DIY approach. Today's education and approach to life with a dependent mind is wrong. We need to help our trainees and students to become multi disciplinary. We must re visit division of labor and specialization for instance. To view this point crisp clearly reconcile with what our economies are doing currently. Think of a team of workers on the farm. One has a duty to dig a hole with a hand hoe another is responsible to plant or sow a seed while the third covers the hole with soil. And they are so specialized and attuned to each ones role religiously such that if one finished his work he is free to leave whether the seed is sown or not. What will happen when one doesn't finish his role? No results.

What is happening today is the same. Yes we can pipe the crude oil from the bowels of the soil. But without refinery at home we have to transport it to the US or UK where we have to re import it only at a higher cost. We grow cotton but have to send it to India for fabrics and later import clothes. We mine iron ore or even Tanzanite but export it to Germany or Switzerland or Japan and in return we import cars and watches and necklaces. That's also reveals the importance of doing own evaluation as an individual or as an institution. We need to look at our competitors as a mirror to our own progress. Sometime and more often we need both. We may be self righteous and or our foes may deliberately discourage our efforts even when that is what we have got to. But remember our rivals have a lot to tell us more about us than we or our friends do endeavor to. At KI we help coordinate this evaluation. We help you to do this as individuals or institutions. We also combine school's inspirational Key Performance Indicators with commercial performance evaluation in order to cover a wide range of indicators which will naturally warrant your success in whatever endeavor you so desire to achieve. (Please refer to What Business Leaders Should Know but They Don't).

At last remember this decision or exercise isn't the kind you do once off and then you pack your bags and go home to sleep. It isn't like the ancient angels who did descend the high heavens and quickly dropped by pass on the message and ascend the stairs of heaven with the next winds. Like churches, believers attend masses at least once a week. Muslims attend the mosques five times a day repeating the same litany of prayers day in day out. Does it matter? Is it crucial? Why? The answer to both first questions is yes. As for why, the rapidity of pace with which we forget is so astonishing. We need to keep records and keep reading the same things every day. Indeed like most authors, I witness the fact that I've had to reread my own books to recall what I've personally written and taught! God knew better when he ordered His Ummah (his people) to pray five times a day. Did you know that even inventors like the greatest Edison at time of his death he had about 2500 notebooks keeping record of the hunches that developed into discoveries, and lessons he learnt for future references. The human mind is made like that by the creator.

You must therefore keep filling the gaps for otherwise you will soon find yourself engaged in quite the opposite of what you ought to be doing. Besides, because of failure to fill the empty space between you and your goals or your knowledge amidst fast changing environment, you may soon wake up to find the skills you revered or products you produce already expired even when they are still in the production line! Human nature works in line with natural law. And according to Aristotle, "Nature abhors vacuum." When we allow vacuum to transcend into our minds, we will soon find awful things and distortions filling the emptiness we didn't fill with positive things. That is why we need to keep in touch with ourselves in almost second to second basis. Mahatma Gandhi couldn't have been more right when he said: "Keep your thoughts positive because your thoughts become your words. Keep your words positive because your words become your behavior. Keep your behavior positive because your behavior becomes your habits. Keep your habits positive because your habits become your values. Keep your values positive because your values become your destiny."

As we come to the end, you must be wondering what the author has to say in few words about the whole book. It all boils down to one word: an ideal, character, principles. "So use all that is called Fortune. Most men gamble with her, and gain all, and lose all, as her wheel rolls. But do thou leave as unlawful these winnings, and deal with Cause and Effect, the chancellors of God. In the Will work and acquire, and thou hast chained the wheel of Chance, and shalt sit hereafter out of fear from her rotations," counseled Ralph Waldo Emerson. "A political victory, a rise of rents, the recovery of your sick, or the return of your absent friend, or some other favorable event, raises your spirits, and you think good days are preparing for you. Do not believe it. Nothing can bring you peace but yourself. Nothing can bring you peace but the triumph of principles!"

As we come to the end, I feel obliged to add one remark. You have read through the fundamentals we have placed before you if you should transform your life, your family, your business and the nation as a whole. We know that this isn't necessarily exhaustive to the east and west, north and south. But by exploring the basis of our downfall, by giving them an idea about where we ought to go, and suggesting alternative path to growth, we inspire the reader and his team to think for themselves how to find what they ought to do to get there. So far we don't intend to put a limit to people's imaginations and accomplishments. We rather inspire them to push the boundaries, to think outside the box, to break the fence, to know that the limit is but the blue sky! We are heartened, therefore, by this accomplishment because we know that when people are inspired to do something and they know why they should do it, and have direction of where to go, they will astonish not only you, but also themselves with what they can do.

Let also the reader recall that we introduced the concept of *Kaizen*, which means the practice, or virtue, of continuous improvement. One of the most notable features of kaizen is that big results come from many small changes accumulated over time. Whereas a person who keeps learning, thereupon, advancing himself, must eventually progress, yet true changes, or transformation, in an organizational team, or society, come when everyone in the team, or society, responds to change; and when such changes or transformation are sustained over a significant (duration of) time and space. As I present this book to the nation, I am presenting the statutes and ordinances that I recommend "that you should do and keep for (that will be) your wisdom and understanding in the sight of peoples, who when they hear all these statutes, they will say, 'surely this great nation is a wise and an understanding people (Deuteronomy 4:5-6).'"

Finally, farewell: and do keep my admonition. Grace be with you. Heed my appeal, agree with one another, live in peace...Whatever is true, whatever is honorable, whatever is just, whatever is pure, whatever is lovely, whatever is gracious, if there is any excellence, if there is anything worthy of praise, think about these things. What you have learned and received and heard and seen in me, do; and God of peace will be with you!"[173]

—Author
Dar es Salaam, Tanzania, EA

November 11, 2015

————To be continued————

---

[173] *Final salutation adapted from traditional farewell notes from epistles of Apostles Peter and Paul*

EPILOGUE: From the Home of Hopelessness to the Land of Opportunity— The Quest for National Renaissance—A Word to the Academics, Policy Makers, Corporations, School Owners, Parents, and Authorities in Charge of the Pedagogy

> *"The kingdom of heaven is like a grain of mustard seed that a man took and sowed in his field. It is the smallest of all seeds, but when it has grown it is larger than all the garden plants and becomes a tree, so that the birds of the air come and make nests in its branches."* —Matthew 13:31–32

When I first began writing the manuscript of this book, well, even after I had wrapped it up, I had no plans to supplement it with the additional epilogue. But after reading the whole manuscript and made reflections about it, I was led to believe that this addition was necessary. Why? This book contains ideas that need your attention—ladies and gentlemen. It, I mean this book, carries a message that is not less than an emergency. I had to include it not only because it is an emergency, but also because no matter how great intentions or ideas we may have presented, success of the whole thing depends on the choices you make—the decisions you are going to make today. That's why I chose to address you personally.

To put emphasis to the foregoing assertion, let me take you back to A SICK NATION AND HOW HEAL IT, a book that precedes the one in hands now, because that book builds the ground for the other titles that supersede it—including the one you are reading now, THE IDEAL SCHOLAR. A SICK NATION AND HOW HEAL IT introduced the fact that as long as there is nothing as a nation but a collection of individual men, women and families, and that, as long as these individuals fall sick, nations too can fall sick. And therefore, to heal such a nation, one needs to go to the basics: He has first to make a diagnosis of the symptoms of the malady that faces that nation or society before he can prescribe the right therapy. That's why through the book we identified the symptoms of the sicknesses—social, political, economic, psychological, cultural, and moral illnesses–that pervade that society. As such, if such maladies aren't healed, and limitations mitigated, that society will continue to wallow in underdevelopment earn the status of a poor and un-developing nation when others prosper.

This then takes us back to why this additional note was necessary. Having suggested that the therapy lies in education, and thus in the curriculum; having highlighted the weaknesses that stifle our education, we come to a realization that these same same weaknesses, weaknesses that choke education, work to choke our personal, institutional and organizational performances, they also choke our social, political, economic, psychological, cultural and moral growth—and the vicious circle sets itself in motion. We included this note particularly to address you, because having laid down the answers to our problems, the wise and prudent decision that lies at our hands is to act, i.e., IMPLEMENTATION. That's indeed where you come in. It is you who have the mandate to save, or sacrifice the nation as an offering. I had to make this additional the note on the fact that all eyes are on you; to emphasize that, with desperate anticipation, the whole world looks up to you, hoping, believing, trusting that you will do the necessary!

I also call upon you to contribute to the initiative because you are aware that education has no end, and upgrading a constant process. Indeed I will be deceiving myself and my readers to say that this work doesn't need upgrading, or customization. With your proficiency, and will, you can make a big difference. Afterall it is the lives of your children, the future of your businesses and the prospects of your nation that are under microscope! We also wrote this addition to encourage you to mold the program to suit your goals and environment without necessarily following the pattern we have chalked out for you. Afterall not every suggestion can fit the same way into all situations. Notice however that, though we know this work cannot be foolproof, we encourage you to introduce the program into your curriculum because we are certain it will do you a world of good. You are aware, aren't you, that most of the ideas we cherish today as priceless all sprang up from the very humble and crudest beginnings. The Wright's brothers' airplane couldn't fly with the speed we experience today; couldn't fly a significant distance away; wasn't anything near the magnificence of the Concorde. The oak began as a mere seedling that you or me could simply uproot by the small finger before it stood out as a forest giant.

Having diagnosed the sicknesses our nation is agonizing from; having prescribed the alternative therapy to these ailments; having chalked out the alternative path, the author believes it is time we took a little break and meditated a little about the way forward if we should fully heal the nation, making her whole, and once more restore her independence (whose health depends on—among others—the extents of the budgetary dependence and the depth of the national debt), hope, prosperity and dignity to our people—our children and families—and the nation as a whole. That's why with the consideration of the challenges we face as individual persons, families, educational and religious institutions, business sector, the government and the general public as a whole, the author is convinced that the suggestions given present us with an opportunity worth of more thought and reflection should we shorten the path to wholeness and sustained growth.

REFLECTIONS
That we have spent far too long stagnating, and our youth ruined in the curse of self neglect, indifference, low ambition, low self-pride, schizophrenia of the self, a curious loath of classrooms, the love for quick fix approaches to wealth such as Hip-hop, corruption, drugs etc., is not a secret anymore. Again, because these weaknesses—grimy weaknesses that have already piled up fearlessly staring at us demanding answers—we believe that, with your good judgment, you won't miss the fact that we, as a nation, need to take action—coordinated comprehensive action—and take it now! We all know that it is impossible—in words of Cathy Williams, to just "snap your fingers and—lo and behold!—your children's untidy lives are changed only because you so decree!" You cannot also miss the fact that an inspirational, transformational program like the one we have placed on your laps, a program that addresses the inner person, will make a big difference. That's why because of the difference the program will make you will welcome the proposal with both hands outstretched.

Though we have highlighted a range of benefits to different stakeholders through Part One of these books, we believe it is, for policy purposes, worthwhile to bring to light the differences the program will make on the big picture level. These differences are between the past and the future: The difference between the past 55 years of unremitting dependence and uncertainty, fetching us instead a new era of hope, confidence and prosperity going forward; the difference between contempt, and the dignity of the nation, its leadership and the people; the difference from begging to working hard; the difference between the people who slave in their own country, to those who take charge of their lives; the difference between limited possibilities in terms of prosperity, to one of possibilities and the belief that the limit is the blue sky; the difference between education and opportunities for the few, to one where we have free and quality education and opportunities for all (in the model of the American Dream); the difference between not only mysterious but also open and out nepotism, to an open-minded but responsible society where honesty and openness are virtues; the difference between the tradition where opportunities are in the hands of few, to one where it is extended to majority according to each one's dreams and efforts; the difference between an environment where the few impose their own dreams on the people, to one where the people decide their own destiny.

The program presents the difference between business as usual, to new thinking; the difference between not only low, but also narrow investment in education in terms of budget and innovativeness, to one where investment in education—in the people—is not only a priority, but also innovative; the difference between an education that attends to the needs of the few, to one that envelops the people's needs, desires and convictions; the difference between the education that places national resources into the hands of the foreigners, to one that empowers the people, the people who contribute to the growth and prosperity nationally and internationally; the difference between education that abuses the environment because of the narrow thought pattern i.e., the old use of charcoal as source of energy, or where others trade in elephant's tusks and rhino's horns, drugs etc., to one which spreads responsibility, love and care for the ecology through alternative discounted sources of fuel, trade and innovation; the difference between education that has sidelined the youth, an education where dropout figures and hopelessness grow by the day, to one that recognizes the youth as the backbone of the nation, etc, etc, etc. And yet, what we have highlighted is just a drop in the sea. Briefly, with the publication of this book, with implantation of this program in your household, your school, at workplace and in the society as a whole, we are convinced that we will prove to you, in words of Horace Mann that: "Education has a market value" with a yield similar to "common bullion." The "aims of Industry…and wealth of the country" would be augmented "in proportion to the diffusion of knowledge," albeit knowledge, or education of a certain kind!

WAY FORWARD
Miracles are no more. Nothing happens out of the blue. Anything that happens has its origin in something else, something that preceded it. Everything is an effect of a certain cause. That's how we find ourselves where we are today—as individual persons, households, school or any other institutions, business corporations and the nation as a whole. It is the decisions we made yesterday that brought us where we are today. Way forward? Dale Carnegie suggests the following antidote through his book How to Stop Worrying and Start Living. As such ask yourself the following questions: 1.what is the problem? 2. What is the cause of the problem, 3. What are the possible solutions to the problem? 4. What solutions do you suggest? Paraphrased from Bob Proctor's magnificent book, You Were Born Rich, we must then analyze the following: 1. How have we been conditioned? 2. Why are we getting the results we are getting? And finally 3. How can we change our way of thinking; or our conditioning? It should by now seem obvious to you that we can do so by changing what and how we teach analyzing what is education, its purposes and roles.

At this point in time, let me say that though we have made a mention about prioritization of our resources if we have to make the most of what we have, but because of the strength of the argument, we are going to recall it here once again. And the point is this: With simile to Tanzania, since independence, our founding fathers identified three major challenges, the challenges we christened national enemies, the nation was facing; the challenges on which the nation was going to focus her attention: poverty, diseases and ignorance. By identifying these focus areas; we had the battle lines drawn. We are all witnesses of the promising outcomes during Mwalimu Nyerere's administration. Yet, because of the scarcity of the resources, we have not managed to effectively battle the three war fronts. That's why in order to triumph over the enemy, we must prioritize what we are going to do with our resources. Where, then, should we focus our efforts? On poverty? Diseases? Ignorance? That's the question—and a challenge at our hands.

Since it is already scientifically substantiated that "all causation was the Mind, and every effect a Mental Phenomenon," we must focus our scarce resources—finances, time and effort—largely on fighting ignorance! Indeed the best war strategy is the battle of the mind. We must therefore focus on ignorance by financing education, and not education education? if you know what I mean! But the education of a certain kind; education that strengthens the mind; education that empowers the people intellectually, culturally, psychologically, morally and spiritually, rather than an education that prepares them to get employed in some factory. And if we do so, if we defeat ignorance, I have good news for you: by defeating ignorance, we will have naturally defeated the other two enemies, namely poverty and diseases. A truly enlightened person, THE IDEAL SCHOLAR, seldom attracts poverty or diseases! The ideal scholar is rarely poverty's or diseases' best bedmate. And what's more, if we vanquish ignorance—moral and intellectual ignorance—by addressing weaknesses in our education and social economic system, we will also have addressed the broken family institution, quick fix, low spirit toward self-reliance and youth unemployment, the other critical factors that conspire with ignorance to choke the nation. And that's where you come in. That's why we had to write this addition. That's why we had to address you personally, yes you the academics, school owners, parents, policy makers and authorities in guard of the pedagogy.

ENLIGHTENMENTATION OF THE NATION: LESSONS FROM THE RENAISSANCE

Now that the ball is in your court, we believe it is your turn to interpret into practice the suggestions presented to you. We are confident you can do it—with or without us. We are confident you have already made your mind that you are going to embrace the suggestions and put them into practice immediately—with or without us. That's why we judged it was imperative that we learn a little more from the success story of the Renaissance. So, what is Renaissance? Edited by the author from: Beginning and Progress of The Renaissance, by R. A. Guisepi, University of California, the term Renaissance literally means: "rebirth" or the "revival of learning." It is defined as the activity, spirit, or time of great revival of art, literature, and learning in Europe beginning in the 14th century and extending to the 17th century.

This change marked the transition from the medieval to the modern world. It is also a renewal of life, vigor, interest, etc rebirth; revival *etc; it is* cultural, mental, psychological, moral and spiritual revival but beginning with Intellectual Renaissance (http://history-world.org/renaissance.htm).

To the scholars and thinkers of the day, however, it was primarily a time of the revival of classical learning and wisdom after a long period of cultural decline and stagnation. Considered to have begun in Italy in the fourteenth century, some date its origin from the reign of Frederick II, 1215-1250; and by this Prince—the most enlightened man of his age—it was at least anticipated. Well versed in languages and science, he was a patron of scholars, whom he gathered about him, from all parts of the world, at his court in Palermo. And as a result, a new ideal was established, whereby man strove to make himself the monarch of the globe on which it is his privilege as well as destiny to live. The Renaissance was the liberation of humanity from a dungeon (a prison cell of mind).

Notice also that this was made possible because at the time, desires and faculties were evenly balanced, and the perceptions were not blunted, nor the senses cloyed, so that the pioneers of renaissance found themselves opening their eyes for the first time on a world of wonder. That's how these pioneers of the Renaissance enjoyed what we may term *The First Transcendent Springtide of the Modern World*. Nothing is more remarkable than the fullness of the life that throbbed in them. Nature's rich in all capacities and endowed with every kind of sensibility. Nor was there any limit to the play of personality in action. That's how, and why, it was made possible the double discovery of the outer and the inner world. Thus what the word Renaissance really means is new birth to liberty—the spirit of mankind recovering consciousness and the power of self-determination, recognizing the beauty of the outer world and of the body through art, liberating the reason in science and the conscience in religion, restoring culture to the intelligence, and establishing the principle of political (and intellectual) freedom.

It was during this momentous period that men toiled laboring by night and day, employing scores of scholars, men of supreme devotion and of mighty brain, to commit to the press, the labors of the men with genius, and enthusiasm that Vergil was printed in 1470, Homer in1488, Aristotle in 1498, Plato in 1512 and they then became the inalienable heritage of mankind. It was during the same time that Nicholas V, founded the Vatican Library in 1453 to promote readership and modern day scholarship; Columbus made known America in 1492; the Portuguese rounded the Cape in 1497; Copernicus explained the solar system in 1507; and Galileo made the proof of the world's mobility in 1610: a titanic accomplishment. To these men, and time, we owe, in a great measure, the freedom of our spirit, our stores of intellectual enjoyment, our command of the past, our certainty of the future of human culture, etc., etc., etc.

AUTHOR'S WORD CONCERNING RENAISSANCE
We have discussed the meaning and purposes or goals or education through this book. I would like to sum all that with a paraphrased mission statement of the Mwananchi Communication (whose original version is available in the introductory part of this book). The basic purpose of education therefore is: "To enrich the lives of the people by enhancing positive mindset and empowering them through the content that sets their minds free." That's the basic fundamental of education since the beginning of life. That's what we learn from Renaissance. That's the spirit we need to revive ourselves, our families, the schools, education, religion and the nation as a whole. Did I say to revive? Well—yes! As such, the spirit of Renaissance was not new in every other aspect. It is rather as old as life itself. When man first began learning, he didn't discriminate between ideas. He didn't know or care about what could be right or wrong, consumed in the intent of discovering the better way to tame nature in man's—and nature's own good (Source: How Universities Under Develop You)!

In their, I must add, fine and well-loaded, book Curriculum Foundations, Principles and Issues, Allan C. Ornstein and Francis P. Hunkins (3rd Ed. page 51), it is thus written: The immediate task before the teaching (profession) is to draw upon this strength and thus to strengthen the control of the schools by, and for, the goal seeking interests of the overwhelming majority of mankind," they observed. Success of this challenge depends on a society's elite's open-mindedness. "John Gardner emphasized that: 'A society like ours has no choice but to seek the development of human capabilities at all levels.'" Why? "'It takes more than educated elite,'" he concluded, "'it takes more than educated elite to run a complex technological society. Every modern…society is learning that hard lesson.'" Thus not only schools but also households and workplaces should become change agents and institutions for reforms.

Furthermore, times have changed. And with this change, growth factors and the equation of success have shifted. This assertion suggests that we have to start afresh—if we have to find lasting solutions to the ailments our society is facing. Indeed, these aren't my own imaginations. Writing after a detailed analysis of the economic depression, times very close to ours today, Napoleon Hill suggested in Think and Grow Rich thus: "The economic crisis has created new perspectives...Out of this experience, will arise new breed of leaders...who will enjoy the greatest following ever known in history of mankind. These leaders," he prophesied, which is my message, "these leaders will come from the rank and file of unknown men and women who now labor in the steel plants, the coal mines, the automobiles factories and in the small towns and cities of America (or Tanzania for that matter)!"

And. Besides, I have good news for you: This could be your opportunity! This assertion then calls both the academics and politicians to, not only encourage those outside their circles to participate as listeners, but also, must find ways to draw any available fine academic resources from without the traditional domain. They must find ways to engage themselves in the dynamics that are taking place outside the formal or traditional circles. That's in fact the ground where potential lies—as the basis, and the true end of education. We know you can't miss that. With the description of how education is run, and how the youth perceive it, to say we need new ideas is understatement. That's why this program presents you with the privileges of unthought-of of. It is wise therefore—and the timing can't be more right—to seize the opportunity with fair grace! And these aren't my words. "Unquestionably," wrote Ornstein and Hunkins Curriculum Foundations, Principles and Issues 3rd Edition, "educational aims and especially school reform must be relevant or meaningful to our times," the emphasized. Why? "If the schools are not adaptable to changing conditions and social forces, how can we expect them to produce people who are?"

CALL FOR ACTION

Having encouraged you to introduce this program into your curriculum, we know with your acumen, you already know where to start. But for the sake of objectivity, here is a starting point as you embark on the implementation stage, as adapted from Ornstein and Hunkins from their magnificent scholarly book: Curriculum Foundations, Principles and Issues 3rd Ed, p. 183.

Blending theory with practice is an old ideal. If we were to make serious progress toward this goal in curriculum, as in other fields, we need to recognize basics steps.

1. *Read the literature: Any attempt to relate theory and practice must be based on knowledge of the literature.*

2. *Identify the major terms: The need is for the curriculum theorists and practitioners to identify and agree on the major constructs, concepts and questions for discussion.*
3. *Check the soundness of the existing theories: The existing theories need to be analyzed in terms of the validity, evidence, accuracy, underlying assumptions, logic of argument, coherence, generalizability, values and biases.*
4. *Avoid fads... (N/B: according to: http://www.urbandictionary.com/define.php?term=fadTop, a fad is defined as "a thing that becomes very popular in a short amount of time, and then is forgotten at about the same speed").*
5. *Align theory with practice: Theory must be considered in context with the real world of classrooms and schools; it must be plausible, applicable and realistic in terms of practice.*
6. *Test theory: If the theory is credible and makes common sense then it must be empirically tested by trying it in practice and measuring the results...*
7. *Interpret theory: The results must be interpreted and implemented in terms of realistic conditions over realistic time periods. The theory must be evaluated in schools for a minimum of one year and ideally over a three-year time period to test for 'fading out."*
8. *Modify theory and reduce complexity: A theory is a generalized construct....Nonetheless, theory must be modified from paper to practice, from the abstract to the concrete world, from complex concepts to lay terms...include many people (and resources) to make it work. Theory must fit with people (not mold people to theory).*

Following the last point, i.e. "Theory must fit with people (not mold people to theory) when moving it from an idea to action," in his work, Developing the Curriculum, 4th Ed, Peter Oliver listed a set of points to consider should the balance in the curriculum be attained. The curriculum should therefore be, or consider:

7. *The child-centered and subject-centered.*
8. *The needs of the individual and those of the society.*
9. *The needs of common education and specialized education.*
10. *Breadth and depth of the curriculum content.*
11. *Traditional content and innovative content.*
12. *The needs of a unique range of pupils regarding their learning styles.*
13. *Different teaching methods and educational experiences.*

14. Work and play.
15. The community and school as educational forces.

CONCLUSION
Beyond doubt, we need practical education, an education that can steer new inspiration among the masses, one that they can easily relate to, and master effortlessly. We need an education which is handy to the average citizen's day to day life. And since typical lecturers and professors can't be in the different spots at the same time, and much as we need typical scholars who specialize in scholarly works, we need men and women who have a store of knowledge developed from the workplace experiences if we have to blend the two for the good of the nation. To execute this program can only help to add value to education and the society as a whole, helping to transform the lives of the masses—which is, indeed, the key performance indicator of success, or failure, of the education system, political leadership, or even, the leader himself.

Concerning the program, though we suggest that what we have presented could be presented as a separate course content which can as well be considered as additional content to related existing courses in our schools, i.e., civics and development studies aside from adult and workplace training programs, we believe that this program has significant implications on other disciplines: sociology, economics, marketing, science, etc. Furthermore, because we believe this program has significant implications on the curriculum, teaching methodologies, and the overall philosophy of the society, we believe the implementation of, and absorption into the separate school programs or in the national curriculum will benefit the student, the parent, the school, the teacher, the school owner, the government and the society as a whole, as you may feel free to review through the chapter on the benefits thereof—the central being to rebuild the intellectual, cultural, psychological, spiritual and moral fiber.

Otherwise, if schools and the curriculum can't help to transform the education of a certain kind, if our children and employees cannot acquire these core values or ideals, ideals that transform them into ideal sons and daughters, productive and innovative employees, responsible citizens and caring parents and future leaders, the hope of transforming the society is trimmed down in the line of the hope finding a needle, possibly a broken one, in a massive sand beach. With this analysis, I needn't paint you a picture of what is in store for our children—and the nation as a whole—if education fails them. To allow this to happen is a mistake of biblical proportions.

In the end, the time is now. With globalization and ICT, growth drivers and success factors have changed a great deal. Old tricks don't work the same way anymore. And now that we are witnesses of how pitiable and downhill school performances are ; and now that partly because of it, the youth have turned their back on education; again, as we realize that fewer are the jobs now created, among which only deplorable ones are available to the local boys and girls with superior jobs set aside for foreign "experts"; now that the rate of unemployment is growing; national and per capita incomes dwindling; dependence ratio on the rise; income gap or inequality among people and nations skyrocketing, and the donor fatigue almost a proverb with economic crisis still looming; and as moral decay—nepotism, corruption, thievery, prostitution, drug abuse and the collapse of the family institution—rises at epidemic proportions, we can't wait to introduce this antidote into our schools or curriculum, if we don't respond, yes with class, but also in urgency, all these shortcomings pile up and without an iota of compassion, are now conspiring to pull our society further down. That's why we urgently need new ideas—new thinking.

And once again, this is not my own exaggeration—and I am not a pessimist! After the great depression, times very close to ours today, Napoleon Hill concluded that: We need new ideas, new literature, new books, new ways of doing things, new leadership, and of course the definiteness of purpose (Paraphrased from Think and Grow Rich). That is certainly why when he was installed president at Harvard, one of the earliest advisors of President Obama, Lawrence Summers, in his acceptance speech concluded that: "In this century that we live, nothing shall matter most like the education of future leaders and development of new ideas." If until now you doubt persuasiveness of my arguments, and recognizing that if education system, the curriculum and how schools and education are organized continue in their present course, we will one day find ourselves on the road from which there would be no turning back. Moreover, if you still think this doesn't affect you because in the present you sit in the driver's seat, recognize still that it wouldn't be far too long before you are "circumvented and left behind!"

LAST WORD
Say what you want to say, but, "You cannot carry out (any) fundamental change," aptly observed Thomas Sankara, "without a certain amount of madness. In this case," he substantiated, "it comes from nonconformity, the courage to turn your back on the old formulas, the courage to invent the future. It took the madmen of yesterday," he continued, "for us to be able

to act with extreme clarity today. I want," he declared, "to be one of those madmen. We must dare to invent the future." If that counsel comes from an army man and therefore less credible in the skeptic's eye, in his book The Promise, Professor Maliyamkono counseled thus: "Education has no boundaries," he said. "Anything can be taught and anything can be learnt. It is a weapon against poverty…a weapon against poor health; and when used wisely, can be a weapon against exclusion and discrimination. It can enable understanding, acceptance and integration." He didn't end there. Suggesting how we should move forward, he said: "The easiest way to achieve this is to use schools to bring together different and disparate sections of young community…under one roof to study can only help understanding."

As we inch to the end, I encourage you to act now. I do so because I am certain that the thought packaged in this book will make a big difference and set apart those who will act now and those who will hesitate. And in fact because of my confidence in the "miracle" this program will make, I feel like standing at the roof of my house and shout at the top of my voice singing *Halleluiah, salvation has come!* Nonetheless, recalling what befell Marconi when he so proudly announced that he had invented a means by which men would communicate without use of wires, (an invention manifest in the wireless communication devices like cell phones and televisions we so proudly use today), his friends seized him and locked him up in a clinic for the lunatics, I will deny myself the pleasure of making noise. It is for this reason that instead I will only make a small whisper—and thus I whisper: "Blessed are those with good hearing and a keen conscience to open the door now that grace calls. Blessed are they for their families and businesses shall prosper and their names last forever!"

Having finally been able to lay before you the path toward success into whatever one may choose to do, I must add that you are privileged. Yes you are because you now have the audacity to pursue your own program without being dissuaded, or influenced by the demands or opinions of the others. You are not going to be influenced by others, for they may be contented with low aims, but you are not. You are also privileged because you and I know many people who are potentially successful, men and women with education, but are still disgracefully struggling against, or already surrendered to the afflictions of lack only because they didn't know the secret you already now know.

Finally, now that the battle lines have already been drawn, and because we are convinced that you can now achieve anything you set out to do with or without us, trusting that you will determine for the best, using the words of Kwame Nkrumah on the independence of Ghana, March 6, 1957, I can now say with confidence that: "At long last, the battle has ended; and thus Tanzania (put the name of your country) shall be free forever;" and because likewise, if we implement the program into our schools your children shall be free forever, and as we bequeath the future of the nation into your capable hands, it is with all this hindsight that: "I call upon heaven and earth to witness against you this day, that I've set before you life and death, blessing and curse: Oh, that you would choose life that you and your children might live (Deuteronomy 30:19)?"

Thank you!

—Author

November 11, 2015[174]
Dar es Salaam, Tanzania, EA

---

[174] Note: in our efforts to stay up-to-date, the events in the book may supersede the date when the book went to the printer.

CONTACT US: CALL US NOW

Immediately after you were privileged to be directed to this book, the New Beginning began unfolding to you, your business, your family and community as a whole. And as Lady Opportunity beckons, right now as grace calls, we would love to hear from you! Really!

As for training, support, cooperation, revision or enquiries about this and other books, or to find more exciting insights into the training opportunities we offer please call us now!

Cell: +255 715 11 11 06
E-mail: author.tanzania@gmail.com

BIBLIOGRAPHY AND RECOMMENDED READING

1. Why Mugabe Urges Africa to Salute "Liberator Nyerere", The Guardian, 26th February 2014 by Daniel Semberya (www.ippmediacom)
2. Allan C. Ornstein and Francis P. Hunkins (1998), Curriculum Foundations, Principles and Issues 3rd edition
3. Dr Lynn Kwaku, Illiterate Graduates, The Citizen p.7, Dar es Salaam, Tanzania February 13, 2010
4. Batista, O.A, (1959), The Power to Influence People
5. McCormack, H. M(1986), What They Can't Teach You at Harvard Business School
6. "Luck" a story by Mark Twain adapted for Special English Program, American Stories, by Harold Berman (http://www.manythings.org/voa/stories/The_Boarded_Window_-_By_Ambrose_Bierce.html (Re-retrieved on February 14, 2014)
7. Maliyamkono and Mason (1982), The Promise
8. http://www.davidworr.com/files/What_is_Education_For.pdf (David Orr's commencement address to the graduating class of 1990 at Arkansas College. Reprinted from Ocean Arks International's excellent quarterly tabloid Annals of Earth, Vol. VIII, No. 2 in Fox, AR, and is currently on the faculty of Oberlin College in Ohio— retrieved on February 14, 2016)
9. Hill, Napoleon, Think and Grow Rich, unabridged edition Embassy Books
10. Kambarangwe, Festo Michael (2015), A Sick Nation and How to Heal It (KI, Dar Es Salaam Tanzania)
11. Kambarangwe, Festo Michael (2007) How Universities Under Develop You! (RosedogBooks, Pittsburgh, Pennsylvania USA)
12. Kambarangwe, Festo Michael (2010),What Makes People Rich and Nations Powerful(RosedogBooks, Pittsburgh, Pennsylvania USA)

13. Kambarangwe, Festo Michael (2008),What Business Leaders Should Know But They Don't (RosedogBooks, Pittsburgh, Pennsylvania USA)
14. Kambarangwe, Festo Michael (2016), Mohammedans: Villains or Victims? (KI, Dar Es Salaam Tanzania)
15. Bob Proctor, You Were Born Rich
16. Carson, Ben, with Murphey, Cecil (1990), Think Big, International Bible Society East Africa
17. Covey, Stephen R. Seven Habits of Highly Effective People by
18. Sarros, James C., How to Lead, How to Manage Executives
19. Carnegie, Dale Rev. Ed., How to Win Friends and Influence People, Pocket Books
20. Carnegie, Dale (1984), How to Stop Worrying and Start Living Revised edition Pocket Books
21. Judy C. Pearson et al. (2003), Human Communication
22. Science of Getting Rich by Wallace D. Wattles
23. The Institute Of Social Science, The Hague, Netherlands (2007), An Exercise in World Making 2007
24. http://researchonline.jcu.edu.au/16985/1/P_Pagliano_Care_ed_4-11.pdf (Care and teacher education for a sustainable future: A critical survey of the literature Paul Pagliano School of Education, James Cook University, Townsville—Retrieved on February 14, 2016)
25. Cosmo Magazine November 2011
26. *http://www.oldandsold.com/articles35/why-be-tired-2.shtml (Re-retrieved on February 14, 2016)*

www.ingramcontent.com/pod-product-compliance
Lightning Source LLC
Chambersburg PA
CBHW071640160426
43195CB00012B/1315